INFRASTRUCTURE ECONOMICS AND POLICY

INTERNATIONAL PERSPECTIVES

EDITED BY

JOSÉ A. GÓMEZ-IBÁÑEZ
AND ZHI LIU

75 YEARS
LINCOLN INSTITUTE
OF LAND POLICY

Library of Congress Cataloging-in-Publishing Data

Names: Gómez-Ibáñez, José A., 1948- editor. | Liu, Zhi, editor.
Title: Infrastructure economics and policy : international perspectives /
    edited by José A. Gómez-Ibáñez and Zhi Liu.
Description: Cambridge, Mass. : Lincoln Institute of Land Policy, 2022. | Includes bibliographical
    references and index. | Summary: "Presents the concepts, theories, international experiences, and
    policy debates in the infrastructure sector and the role of this sector in economic performance,
    funding and financing, demand forecast and project appraisal, and the challenges faced by climate
    change and technological advances"—Provided by publisher.
Identifiers: LCCN 2021034316 (print) | LCCN 2021034317 (ebook) | ISBN 9781558444188
    (paperback) | ISBN 9781558444195 (pdf) | ISBN 9781558444218 (epub)
Subjects: LCSH: Infrastructure (Economics) | Economic policy/
Classification: LCC HC79.C3 .I5164 2022 (print) | LCC HC79.C3 (ebook) | DDC 363.6—dc23
LC record available at https://lccn.loc.gov/2021034316
LC ebook record available at https://lccn.loc.gov/2021034317

Cover designed by Kevin Clarke.
Composed in Adobe Caslon Pro by Westchester Publishing Services in Danbury, Connecticut.
Printed and bound by Books International in Dulles, Virginia.

♻ The paper is FSC certified, acid-free, 30% post-consumer content.

MANUFACTURED IN THE UNITED STATES OF AMERICA

CONTENTS

Foreword

It is hard to exaggerate the importance of infrastructure for sustaining human habitation on this planet. Without it, to quote Thomas Hobbes, "there is no place for Industry; because the fruit thereof is uncertain; and consequently no Culture of the Earth; no Navigation, nor use of the commodities that may be imported by Sea; no commodious Building; no Instruments of moving, and removing such things as require much force . . . And the life of man, solitary, poore, nasty, brutish, and short" (*Leviathan* 1660). Infrastructure is the physical manifestation of a social contract that liberates us from Hobbes's natural state. Whether we arrive at this social contract through an authoritarian government or through democratic processes is an important question, and this volume might provide the answer.

The Lincoln Institute is excited to launch this book. It is one of the very few books about infrastructure published in the last decade. It could not come at a better time. Today, we are on the cusp of historic investments in global infrastructure, and we need this book desperately. The World Bank estimates that we will need more than US$90 trillion in new infrastructure by 2050 to prepare cities for two billion new inhabitants, primarily in sprawling metropolises in low-income countries. This total investment exceeds the current annual gross domestic product of all the countries on the planet by around 20 percent. In order to formulate new sustainability strategies and polices for cities in Asia and Africa with exploding populations and for OECD countries and Latin America where city structures continue to evolve to adjust to innovations in technology and commerce, we need to understand the relationship between urbanization and infrastructure.

The world also faces new challenges associated with the climate crisis, the sharing economy, and the fallout from COVID-19. If we want to protect ourselves from the impacts of the climate crisis, the World Bank suggests we add another US$1 trillion per year to the global investment noted above. If we are to live in a "new normal" shaped by global pandemics, infrastructure design and usage must be modified. It is important to understand the implications of all these challenges and uncertainties, and this volume will help us to do just that.

For most of us in developed countries, infrastructure is invisible and is only noticed in its absence, or failure. We are chagrined when the power goes out or the Internet goes down. More distressingly, infrastructure failures can be catastrophic—when the leaking centuries-old gas pipes destroyed buildings in Manhattan in 2014, or when the Ponte Morandi collapsed into the Polcevera River in Genoa, Italy, or when the levees failed, and floodwater inundated New Orleans for weeks after Hurricane Katrina. But for a large portion of the world's population, infrastructure is both invisible and absent. Most people in low-income countries live with inadequate roads, unreliable power supplies, and a lack of safe drinking water and basic sanitation. They have a diminished quality of life, a reduced life expectancy, and their local and national economies' growth is constrained.

Infrastructure represents humanity at its best. Designing, developing, and financing infrastructure requires formidable technical expertise. But to get the job done, we also need to exercise our best social and political skills and work together to provide durable public goods that solve seemingly intractable social, economic, and environmental challenges. Colossal dams spanning treacherous canyons are a great example: they demand exceptional engineering acumen and provide decades of flood prevention, crop irrigation, drinking water, and electricity. Planning and financing infrastructure demands that we dispose of short-term thinking and make investments with benefits that will span generations.

Infrastructure also represents humanity at its worst. We are at our worst when we allow opaque infrastructure decisions to disadvantage those without the economic or political power to influence them—when new thoroughfares are driven through thriving minority neighborhoods to reduce drive times for suburban commuters, or when sweetheart deals are struck behind closed doors between public officials and beltway bandits. Process is as important as, or sometimes more important than, outcomes. Infrastructure planning must include all stakeholders and account for their needs, aspirations, and rights.

The stakes are high with infrastructure. We commit dizzying sums of money for decades to build and manage projects and systems of unimaginable scale and ambition. The very complexity of all aspects of infrastructure demands paramount integrity—conforming assiduously to engineering specifications, adhering to the rule of law, exercising fiscal discipline, and maintaining absolute transparency and accountability. Decisions to build infrastructure using public funds must be grounded in rigorous cost-benefit analysis. Although such methodologies are well developed in theory, in practice they can be abused with political pressure, intentional bias, or selective myopia. Moreover, public decision processes cannot always be trusted to produce optimal resource allocations. If we can understand the complexity of infrastructure within real-world constraints, we will make better spending decisions.

Despite the obvious need for infrastructure, low-income countries struggle to pay for long-term investments. While these constraints are real, there are many ways to finance infrastructure, even in the most impoverished places. Several involve land value capture mechanisms, which have been used for millennia and which involve recovering the increased value of land associated with infrastructure improvements. For example, betterment levies were used by the Roman Empire to build roads, bridges, tunnels, and viaducts connecting a vast area from Portugal to Constantinople (modern Istanbul). Land readjustment, where land is pooled and improved with new infrastructure that is paid for through the sale of a small share of the land, has been used hundreds of times on multiple continents to build capital cities like Washington, DC, or rebuild towns and cities in countries ravaged by war.

How effectively infrastructure meets economic and social goals depends critically on its management and regulation. Both the public and private sectors are active in infrastructure development and service provision. The infrastructure industry has gone through a cycle of domination by the private sector followed by public takeover and public provision, then to privatization, and to the increasingly popular public-private partnerships. Who gets served, and how they are served, by infrastructure is determined by regulatory structures that protect the public interest and require absolute transparency and accountability of vendors and public officials. There is a lot to be learned from international experiences on the management and regulation of the infrastructure sector.

Some countries and regions develop and implement infrastructure plans and strategies to achieve specific social and economic objectives. The European Union used infrastructure grants and loans to help integrate new members both politically and economically through two rounds of expansion. Chinese policy makers advanced high-speed rail development strategies that supported the formation of several major city clusters (or megalopolises) to drive the growth of the national economy. In contrast, Japan's rail transport policy relied mainly on the private sector to provide vital social services. The lessons learned from such experiences are important for many countries that aspire to not only formulate effective infrastructure plans but also use infrastructure planning to achieve other important goals. This volume will inform such future planning and practice around the world.

At the Lincoln Institute, we have spent the last eight decades addressing social, economic, and environmental challenges using innovative land policies. Among those we have studied and recommended to address global challenges, none is more important than infrastructure. Without the lifeline goods and services delivered by effective and efficient infrastructure, human life would be nastier, more brutish, and shorter. I say with confidence that if we can learn from the authors in this book, life will be nicer, more civilized, and longer for a multitude of people around the world.

—*George W. McCarthy, President and CEO,*
Lincoln Institute of Land Policy

PREFACE

Infrastructure is a perennial topic of policy debate throughout the world. Although infrastructure is widely considered fundamental for economic growth and the quality of life, infrastructure polices vary significantly by country. Many developing countries struggle to overcome significant infrastructure deficits, while others—such as China and India—invest heavily in infrastructure to boost economic growth. The United States, once a global leader in infrastructure development and management, is currently debating a shift to a fix-it-first policy that emphasizes infrastructure repairs as an essential prerequisite for or complement to investment in a new generation of infrastructure. The United Kingdom plans to revitalize its "northern powerhouse" of aging industrial cities through high-speed rail investment. And the infrastructure sector around the world is facing the new changes driven by climate change, artificial intelligence, and the emerging shared economy.

Infrastructure Economics and Policy: International Perspectives strives to inform these policy debates by exposing interested readers to the essential concepts, economic theories, and international experiences in the infrastructure sector. The book contains 20 chapters contributed by leading academics and practitioners around the world in the field of infrastructure economics and policy. The chapters are written to be accessible to a wide range of global audiences, including policy makers, practitioners, business executives, and graduate students in the fields of infrastructure, planning, management, and public policy, as well as the general public interested in infrastructure policy.

Unlike most existing books that focus on individual infrastructure industries (such as transportation, water, energy, and telecommunications) or on the infrastructure issues in individual countries, this volume strives to make comparisons across industries and countries. The book stresses the evolution of the methodological and policy debates and brings the readers up to date on issues in infrastructure development, finance, and management. In addition, the book covers a limited number of issues that we consider timely and critical. A book on a sector as broad and diverse as infrastructure will necessarily leave many important issues aside. It is our hope that *Infrastructure Economics and Policy* will not only inform policy debates on the issues that are covered but also attract more research interests in the issues that are not covered.

1

WHAT MAKES INFRASTRUCTURE SPECIAL?

José A. Gómez-Ibáñez and Zhi Liu

This book was inspired by the observation that the industries traditionally defined as infrastructure—including roads, railways, ports, gas and electric power supply, telecommunications, and water and sanitation—have at least five special characteristics that make the tasks of policy makers, managers, and analysts both more difficult and more interesting. These characteristics are not unique to infrastructure: some are found in other sectors of the economy but rarely to the extent or in the combinations found in traditional infrastructure. For example, our claims apply less to schools, health care, public safety, and sport facilities—sometimes referred to as social infrastructure—or to greenways, permeable pavements, retention ponds, and constructed wetlands—sometimes referred to as green infrastructure. These other industries and infrastructures are important but are not the topic of this book. The five characteristics are essentiality; costly, durable, and immobile facilities; difficulty to store; equity; and externalities.

Essentiality

The word *essential* means basic, indispensable, and necessary and is often applied to infrastructure in a modern economy. The primary reason for considering public infrastructure as essential for growth and quality of life is that infrastructure is an input to virtually every important good and service in the economy and society. Transportation and electricity, for example, are the basic services that the famous development economist Albert Hirschman (1958) defined as social overhead capital, without which primary, secondary, and tertiary productive activities could not function. But Hirschman could have said the same of water, sanitation, and, especially today, telecommunications. Transportation links people with resources and markets and provides interconnectivity between regions and nations, making trade, specialization, productivity gain, and economic growth all possible. Similarly, electricity provides light, heat, and power and is an essential input to the production of almost all manufactured goods. Infrastructure is also considered essential for our quality of life. Clean water and sanitation keep us healthy, for example, while smartphones keep us connected in the globalized world. The essentiality of infrastructure is perhaps most obvious for saving lives and rebuilding in times of natural disaster.

One reflection of infrastructure's essentiality is that the demand for infrastructure is often said to be "derived" in that it is usually desired not for its own sake but instead as a means to something else or an input to the production of final goods. This is particularly obvious in transportation: a few people enjoy driving per se, but most see it as a means to access a job, health care, education for their children, a social visit, or another important activity. Electricity is similar in that there is little demand for electrons per se but much demand for lighting and reading at night. With so many applications embedded in the economy, the performance of the economy must depend importantly on the performance of its infrastructure.

A related concept is the wider economic impact of an infrastructure project. A project directly affects its immediate users in, for example, travel time savings in the case of a new subway line and better health in the case of a water treatment plant. But these direct effects may make possible productivity improvements by firms that are downstream or upstream of those directly affected, especially since the demand for the improved service is often derived.

Whether these wider economic impacts should be included in the evaluation of the improvement is hotly debated. The conventional practice is to consider direct effects only on the grounds that most of the impacts in the wider economic effects are not new or additional and instead merely measure transfers of some direct effects to other parties upstream or downstream. If housing prices appreciate around some of the stations on the new subway line, for example, it is because property owners have captured part of the time savings enjoyed by the subway riders in the form of higher rents; to count both the travel time savings and the property value increases as benefits is to double count. Nevertheless, the prevalence of these wider effects illustrates how deep the relationship is between infrastructure and the rest of the economy.

Another reason for considering infrastructure as essential to growth is its role in reducing the cost of basic services such as water, electricity, and transportation. Infrastructure provides basic inputs throughout the economy, but the unit costs of infrastructure services typically decline. Infrastructure reduces these costs by exploiting technologies that exhibit substantial economies of scale. For example, many electric companies in emerging economies could probably trace their origins to a single diesel generator serving one household or shop. The capital cost of a generator does not increase proportionately with output, which makes it profitable for the proprietor to sell any excess power to neighbors for little more than the cost of the extra fuel. Thus, reduced costs of infrastructure services contribute to the increases of marginal productivity of private capital. This is why a number of countries made sizable investment in infrastructure as a precondition for private investments in productive capacity in the secondary and tertiary sectors.

The history of the World Bank's lending operations reflects an appreciation for the essential role of infrastructure in economic development. The primary focus of the World Bank's lending in the 1950s and 1960s was on large infrastructure projects such as dams, electrical grids, irrigation systems, and roads. Later, the scope of lending was extended to other sectors, such as health, education, social protection, and rural and urban development; however, infrastructure remains the largest sector in the lending portfolio. Infrastructure continues to be a priority in international development business, as demonstrated by the establishment of the Asian Infrastructure Investment Bank in 2016.

Despite the widespread appreciation of infrastructure's essentiality, infrastructure gaps (or deficits) exist in many parts of the world. According to Oxford Economics (2017), the global infrastructure investment needs are US$94 trillion between 2016 and 2040, which is 19 percent higher than is likely to be delivered under current trends. A World Bank report assesses the physical infrastructure gaps in low- and middle-income countries and concludes that new infrastructure could cost these countries 2–8 percent of gross domestic product per year to 2030, depending on the quality and quantity of service targeted and the spending efficiency achieved in reaching this goal (Rozenberg and Fay 2019).

Not surprisingly, infrastructure investment is high on the policy agenda of most countries and regions. It is also a major component in the regional integration initiatives around the world, such as the European Union (EU), the South Asian Association for Regional Cooperation, the Greater Mekong Subregion, the Central Asia Regional Economic Cooperation Program, and the China-led Belt and Road Initiative.

Costly, Durable, and Immobile Facilities

Nature of Investments

Another special characteristic of infrastructure—second only to its essentiality for economic growth—is its reliance on facilities that are costly, durable, and essentially immobile. The term *infrastructure* comes from the Latin for *below* (*infra*) and was first applied to pipes and drains underground and to roads on the ground's surface. Such constructions are typically expensive, last a very long time, and once in place cannot be moved without essentially destroying much of their value.

Not all the activities of infrastructure industries involve such investments, however. For example, small electricity systems that serve communities not connected to national or regional grids often get their power from diesel generators or solar panels with batteries that are costly per kilowatt hour of capacity but are mobile and not particularly long-lived. Telecommunications companies provide a different kind of exception in that they must make investments in cellular phone towers and antennae that are immobile and (if we ignore the speed of technological change) durable. Much of the remaining investment in that industry is made by consumers, however, in the form of phones, tablets, and other portable communications devices needed to access the network. Similarly, expressways require land assembly, basic grading, and civil structures that are often very costly and essentially immobile and have useful lives of 50 or more years. Most of the remaining outlays required to realize expressway service are made by the motorists, however, in the form of vehicles, fuel, and driver time and inconvenience.

Typically, the durable and immobile costs are incurred in building the basic networks over which services are delivered, such as cellular towers and expressway systems. The costs that vary in the short term are more a function of the actual volumes of traffic—voice, data, passenger, freight—delivered over those networks.

Competition

An important problem with extensive, durable, and immobile investments is that they make it harder to maintain competition among infrastructure providers. These types of investments often result in a condition called *natural monopoly* in which the firm enjoys economies of scale so large that they are not exhausted even when one company serves the entire market. Consider the example of a company providing piped water to a residential neighborhood by running a supply pipe down the street to connect to all the households that choose to subscribe. The cost of running the supply pipe is simply the cost of the pipe itself, digging a trench to drop the pipe in, refilling the trench, and repairing the road surface. None of these costs are very sensitive to the diameter of the pipe and thus to its capacity. As a result, the most economical way to provide service to a neighborhood is with a single pipe and company, as running a second supply pipe down the street would be wasteful.

The durability and immobility of investments are arguably even more common, and thus more important, obstacles to competition in infrastructure than a natural monopoly. Suppose the piped water company in our example has made its investment in pipe, trenches, and pavement repairs, but now a second water company is threatening to enter the same market. The fact that the incumbent's investments are durable and immobile makes it rational for the incumbent to treat them as sunk or committed and if necessary to discount or even ignore them entirely in deciding how to respond to the challenger's threatened entry. And the knowledge that the incumbent is almost certainly going to undercut the challenger's prices is likely to deter the challenger from entering.

This analysis ignores possible effects of competition from other products and locations. Piped water, for example, may compete with private wells in some settings and with bottled water in others. But often competition from other products and locations seems insufficient to offset the obstacles to entry posed by natural monopoly or durable and immobile investments. Bottled water is so much more expensive than piped water that customers do not consider them close substitutes in most applications, while private wells can compete with piped water only where the groundwater is relatively clean.

Remedies

How best to protect consumers against the shortage of competition has been a topic of intense debate in infrastructure circles. One possibility, popular in many countries from the 1950s through the 1970s, was to rely on state-owned enterprises (SOEs) to provide infrastructure services. One hope was that SOEs, not motivated primarily by profit, would be less likely to take advantage of limited competition by increasing prices well above costs. Many SOEs seemed to suffer instead from the opposite problem—increasing costs well above prices—and the resulting government deficits and inflation contributed to the economic collapse of a number of countries, particularly in Latin America and Asia in the late 1980s and early 1990s.

The next remedy attempted was to privatize SOEs to encourage efficiency but with government regulation to ensure that the prices charged and the quality of services offered were reasonable. Many different regulatory schemes were tried; the simplest and most popular was to competitively award contracts to provide an infrastructure facility or service for a limited term, often 15–30 years. Advocates argued that where competition "in the market" might be impossible because of natural monopoly or durable and immobile investments, competition "for the market" could be used to make sure prices were fair and up to date. This approach depended on the ability to draft a contract that was relatively complete, however, in that it anticipated all the important eventualities and provided workable contingencies for them. Drafting complete contracts proved hard where a complex network was involved or the technology or the economic or political environment was in flux, and renegotiating an incomplete contract often left the government and the operator vulnerable to charges of corruption.

In the end, no one solution has emerged to the competition problems caused by costly, durable, and immobile investments. Private ownership is common in many developed countries, particularly in certain sectors such as telecommunications and electricity generation. SOEs are very important as well, however, and dominate infrastructure in China and India, the world's most populated countries. A great deal of energy has gone into the design of regulatory schemes to replace the contract; while so far there have been notable advances, particularly with so-called price cap or incentive regulation, every scheme has its limitations.

Investment Evaluation

A second and perhaps more obvious consequence of the expense, durability, and immobility of infrastructure is to greatly increase the importance and challenge of evaluating, funding, and financing investments. International financial institutions such as the World Bank as well as the EU and many national governments rely on social cost-benefit analysis to compare the goods, services, and amenities created by proposed projects or polices with the goods, services, and amenities that would be foregone if the project or policy were undertaken.

Cost-benefit analysis differs from the more familiar financial analysis in that it includes social and economic benefits or costs, such as travel time saved and health damage from added pollution, that might not be fully captured in the project sponsor's income and expense accounts. Cost-benefit analysis is similar to financial analysis, however, in that it seeks to place a monetary value on the social benefits and costs in order to calculate summary measures of a project's desirability, such as the project's net benefits and benefit-cost ratio. Projects with positive net benefits, a benefit-cost ratio greater than one, or an internal rate of return greater than the market rate of interest are presumably worth doing.[1]

A measure of the importance of project evaluation in infrastructure is that—as described in more detail in chapter 6—many of the key methodological issues in applying cost-benefit analysis first arose from and were resolved in infrastructure and only later applied in other sectors of the economy. The basic framework of cost-benefit analysis is generally credited to Jules Dupuit, a 19th-century French engineer interested in cases when user cost savings could justify the construction of a new bridge or other type of infrastructure.

Dupuit's framework was rediscovered, starting in the 1930s, as analysts in the United States and the United Kingdom demonstrated its practicality in dealing with water resource and transportation projects. The U.S. Congress forced the issue in 1935 when it ordered the Army Corps of Engineers to show that the navigation aids, flood control, irrigation, and recreation projects it was building along U.S. waterways were beneficial (Eckstein 1958). In the late 1950s and early 1960s, as the British government was contemplating the choice between investing in motorways or extensions to the London Underground, British transportation economists Michael Beesley and Christopher Foster pioneered methods of estimating consumer willingness to pay for benefits and costs that are not traded directly and thus where market prices cannot be readily observed, such as reductions in time spent traveling thanks to the opening of a new motorway or railway line (Beesley 1965; Foster 2001; Foster and Beesley 1963). And at the end of the 1960s, Thomas Schelling convinced cost-benefit analysis practitioners to abandon the practice of valuing the benefit of lives saved from traffic safety improvements by the years of earnings that would be lost because of the victims' premature deaths, an assumption that valued the lives of retirees and stay-at-home parents at zero. Instead, analysts in medicine, public health, and traffic safety began to use the differences in wage rates in more and less risky occupations to impute the willingness of people to pay to reduce the statistical chance of death (Schelling 1968).

Reduced or Deferred Maintenance

Finally, the durability of infrastructure creates an additional problem: reduced or deferred maintenance. Public officials seem to believe that their constituents are more impressed by the opening of new infrastructure facilities than by the maintenance of existing ones. This bias toward new over old can be particularly costly if it leads to the abandonment of a program of routine preventive maintenance. But the basic problem arises in both developed and developing countries because the infrastructure is durable, so the effect of reduced maintenance spending on the quality of services rendered is not immediate or obvious. Equipment rated for a specified life is usually designed with a margin of safety, for example, so that its performance deteriorates gradually rather than all at once. Thus, when an infrastructure provider or regulator is under financial pressure, the temptation is to cut the maintenance or the scheduled refurbishment of existing facilities first since it will be noticed last.

Indeed, some argue that a vicious cycle often develops that further discourages adequate maintenance (Gómez-Ibáñez and Meyer 1996). The heart of the problem is, again, that the effect of deferred maintenance on service quality is typically poorly understood by the public. Prices for infrastructure services, on the other hand, are very visible and politically sensitive if only because they must be paid every month in the case of most utilities and twice a day for urban public transport. This sensitivity combined with the inability to defer maintenance forever can encourage a vicious cycle in which public dissatisfaction with the quality of service prevents politicians from approving a needed tariff increase, which in turn leads to further declines in the quality of service and in popular support for a tariff increase. To the extent that this cycle applies, tariffs and service quality will tend to be low and to increase only when the firm is in crisis so that the increases tend to be infrequent but large.

In theory, the possibility of deferring maintenance is potentially advantageous in that one can wait until the economy is in recession and needs a stimulus to catch up on the replacement of worn-out assets. A recession is also typically accompanied by low interest rates, which reduce the cost of investment. And the prospect of creating a durable asset makes the stimulus program more acceptable to fiscal conservatives. However, statistical analyses of countercyclical programs, discussed in chapter 2, suggest that in developed economies, infrastructure spending has little stimulus effect in the first several years, after which the economy is likely to have begun growing again anyway. In any event, the timing of the asset replacement seems more often dictated by the failure of key assets than by countercyclical considerations.

Various efforts to strengthen maintenance incentives have been tried over time, among the most notable the creation, with the encouragement of the World Bank, of road funds and road agencies in 27 countries of sub-Saharan Africa (Sub-Saharan Africa Transport Program n.d.). The agencies were governed by boards made up of a mixture of private and public officials and were to be funded by dedicated road-user fees or taxes. But the key was that the agency could be a purchaser but not a provider of road maintenance services. This formula was never adequately tested, however, as the governments often reneged on their funding commitments.

More recently, one of the key motives for public-private partnerships whereby the private companies operate and maintain as well as build infrastructure is to avoid deferred maintenance by encouraging a life-cycle perspective on costs. However, this arrangement requires workable contracts whose duration is as long as the life of the principal assets, which can be difficult to draft. Perhaps partly as a result, the evidence on whether private provision of infrastructure saves money is mixed, as discussed in chapter 11.

Difficulty to Store

The third unusual characteristic of infrastructure is the difficulty of producing and storing services for later consumption. Storage is not impossible. For example, water is often stored in reservoirs for release in dry weather. Similarly, electricity generated by solar panels during the daytime can be stored for nighttime use in batteries, and in the case of a hydroelectric dam, nighttime power can be used to pump water behind the dam for daytime release. However, the reservoirs, dams, batteries, and equivalents in other storage schemes are typically too expensive to make storage a common practice with most types of infrastructure.

Peaking

The loss of storage as an option means that infrastructure providers must try to produce when and where their customers want while keeping the costs of doing so under control. A particular challenge is that the demand for different types of infrastructure peaks in both time and space. With most urban rail transit and urban highway systems, for example, demand peaks inbound to major employment centers during weekday mornings and outbound during weekday afternoons. Storage is an impractical solution to this peaking, as it would require some workers to spend the night in an employment center to be ready to report for work at that center the next day without commuting. But accommodating this peaking means that these expressways and rail lines have a great deal of excess capacity outbound during the morning, inbound during the afternoon, and in both directions in the early morning, at midday, and in the evening.

Where the excess capacity is modest, a profit-maximizing service provider may simply ignore the problem and provide the same service and charge the same price in both peak and off-peak times. Ignoring the excess capacity is harder in infrastructure than in other industries, since costly capacity is practically the defining characteristic of the sector. An obvious alternative response is to reduce the burden of excess capacity by charging more or providing a lower quality of service in peak time. The most attractive strategy, however, is to identify where possible some complementary use for the same type of capacity but with the opposite temporal and spatial pattern of demand.

Complementary Uses

The development of complementary uses has been critical to the success of many infrastructure industries. Classic examples are the electricity and street railway industries in the United States in the late 19th century (Gómez-Ibáñez 2003). In the mid-19th century, electric companies were small, providing only nighttime lighting for local streets, private homes, and businesses, while streetcars were powered by horses. After the demonstration of the first practical electric-powered streetcar in 1888, the horses were quickly retired, a process encouraged in some cities by far-sighted electricity companies that offered deep price reductions to the railway companies and to manufacturers who needed daytime rather than nighttime power.

Similarly, the shortage of complementary uses is at least partially responsible for the difficulties that modern U.S. mass transit rail systems have in competing with the highway system. Because rail transit lines enjoy strong economies of traffic density, they are usually designed to serve the corridors with the densest traffic flows, typically those radiating out from the central business district. Highways do not exhibit such strong economies of traffic density, so their network can be more extensive and thus serve more diverse types of traffic—including freight, nonwork, and commuting to secondary business districts—that peak at different times and places and in different directions. In short, highways have more potentially complementary traffic, while most U.S. rail transit systems are mainly used for commuting purposes. Only the dense rail transit networks developed in high-density megacities such as Beijing, Hong Kong, London, New York City, Singapore, and Tokyo serve many different travel purposes.

The search for complementary uses is important to the success of individual firms as well as industries. For example, an airline that has only north–south routes that peak in the winter will be less profitable than an airline that also has some east–west routes that peak in the summer. And most airlines as well as many firms in other infrastructure industries have a special office high in the organizational chart responsible for scheduling. This special regard for scheduling reflects the importance and challenge of providing a product when and where consumers need it.

Cost Allocation in Multiproduct Firms

One drawback to relying on complementary uses is that this often results in confusion about how costs should be allocated among the various services being provided with the same facilities. The economist's answer is to allocate the cost of the basic facility that is jointly used to serve several different types of customers to the type who would be willing to pay the most for an extra increment of that facility's capacity. The reasoning is that their willingness to pay for incremental capacity will determine how large that facility should be.

Equity

Another distinctive characteristic of infrastructure is that equity considerations loom large and focus on not just how widely available and affordable infrastructure services should be but also whether infrastructure facilities are sited and operated in a manner that places disproportionate burdens on minorities, indigenous peoples, and other disadvantaged groups.

Universal, Affordable Service

As noted, infrastructure is regarded by many people as essential for everyday life as well as for economic development. It is difficult to imagine modern life without electricity, clean water, paved roads, and some form of telecommunications, including access to the Internet. But adequate infrastructure is also taken for granted in many countries, which makes infrastructure most important in its absence, meaning that service interruptions are intolerable and lead to pressures to make reliable infrastructure universally available and affordable.

There is no consensus as to just how available and affordable infrastructure should be or who should foot the bill. However, the studies reviewed in chapter 3 generally support the widely held view that access to infrastructure is particularly important for economic development in rural areas. The construction of all-weather access roads is thought to be critical for expanding markets for rural products, while electricity allows refrigeration and light machinery as well as extended hours when reading is possible. Infrastructure subsidies are also more easily targeted toward the poor in rural areas because the rural poor tend to live in self-contained communities (Gannon and Liu 1997). In contrast, the urban poor are often scattered among the middle- and upper-class neighborhoods, which means that subsidies to urban infrastructure for helping the poor often leak to unintended beneficiaries.

Cross Subsidies Versus Direct

Overall, infrastructure subsidies that are targeted directly to the poor are relatively rare, especially in urban environments. To the extent that subsidies are required to keep infrastructure available and affordable, traditionally the most politically palatable approach has been to embed the subsidies in the schedule of prices charged to customers for various services. The idea is to cross-subsidize losses from catering to customers who have modest means or are located in places unusually costly to serve with profits earned by catering to well-off or easily served customers. Compared with direct subsidies, cross subsidies are less visible and also politically contentious, presumably because of the difficulties of allocating costs and revenues among different services and customers in multiproduct firms.

Such progressive cross-subsidy schemes cannot be sustained, however, in the face of competition. For example, gas and electric utilities throughout the world almost always charge their commercial and industrial customers much less per cubic foot or kilowatt hour than their residential customers simply because the former can credibly threaten to switch fuels. Similarly, during most of the 20th century, U.S. regulators encouraged the American Telephone and Telegraph (AT&T) monopoly to cross subsidize its losses on local calls and rural subscribers with profits on long-distance calls and urban subscribers. Competition in telecommunications exploded in the 1980s—with the appearance of domestic and international private long-distance lines, the breakup of AT&T, and eventually the coming of the Internet—making the old strategy of cross subsidies unworkable and forcing the United States to switch in 1996 to an explicit surcharge on telephone bills, the Universal Facility Charge, used to subsidize service in schools and libraries.

Siting Controversies

Infrastructure facilities such as highways, dams, and power plants are often poor neighbors because they require lots of land and can pollute local air and water. Moreover, in the past these facilities have often been situated in or near poor, minority, or indigenous neighborhoods—where land is often cheaper and the residents are less politically influential—and thus those communities are thought to bear a disproportionate share of the local social costs of infrastructure.

Particularly controversial are projects that involve the involuntary resettlement of large numbers of people. Among developing countries in the 1960s and 1970s, dam developers had a reputation for forcing out large numbers of farmers and other people to make way for their projects. During those same decades in the United States, the culprits were typically highway departments laying out modern urban expressway systems and redevelopment authorities wanting to upgrade neighborhoods considered to be slums.

Social and Environmental Impact Studies and Safeguards

The taking of land helped provoke reforms, first in the United States and soon after at the World Bank and other international organizations. In 1969, the United States passed a law requiring that federal agencies prepare an environmental impact statement to assess the environmental, social, and human effects of significant programs before making decisions. In the 1990s, the World Bank adopted a qualitative but binding set of "safeguard" standards with which the organization's staff and borrowers had to comply. For instance, World Bank staff had to consult with local communities; carefully assess and minimize the economic, environmental, and social risks; avoid displacement of people; ensure that displaced persons would improve or at least maintain their standard of living; and respect the rights and vulnerabilities of indigenous peoples. Critics argued that the safeguards were not always carefully applied, however, so that resettlement often amounted to the "forcible impoverishment of displaced communities" (Clark 2002, 206; see also Bugalski and Pred 2013).

The requirements for social and environmental impact studies have been gradually strengthened and expanded over time. A few U.S. states copied the federal idea, requiring state agencies to produce environmental impact statements of their major decisions, while local governments often created other provisions to review large development proposals. In 2018, the World Bank expanded its safeguards to cover, among other issues, climate change and labor protection. Many other international aid agencies, including the Asian Development Bank and the United Nations, have established similar safeguard polices.

The expansion has stimulated a debate over whether the requirements for social and environmental impact analyses have gone too far (Altshuler and Luberoff 2004). Proponents of the requirements argue that, without them, we risk a return to the environmental damage and mistreatment of vulnerable groups of the past. Opponents to further requirements argue that they add to the already high cost and long delays experienced by infrastructure proposals at a time when many countries are suffering from infrastructure deficits. They also label the opposition as the "not in my backyard" movement, or NIMBY for short, implying selfishness in the face of regional needs. It is hoped that some balance among these different positions will emerge with study and experience.

Externalities

A fifth and final characteristic of infrastructure that distinguishes it from other sectors is the importance of various kinds of externalities. Externalities occur when a transaction between a willing buyer and seller affects a third party through a mechanism other than price. If the third party is adversely affected, there will be more transactions than are socially desirable. If the third party is favorably affected, there will be too few transactions. The excesses and shortfalls occur because the buyer and seller do not consider the effects on the third or "external" party.

Global Warming

Infrastructure is both cause and remedy of the most consequential externality of our time: global warming. Global warming is caused by negative externalities in that the producers and users of fossil fuels do not consider the consequences of their carbon emissions on others. Infrastructure is also a potential cure for global warming in that, as explained in chapter 18, a promising but still very difficult and costly method of reducing greenhouse gas emissions is to replace much of our current energy infrastructure with a new system that relies on electricity generated by renewable sources such as solar, wind, and hydroelectric power.

Agglomeration and Congestion

Agglomeration and congestion are a pair of externalities crucial to understanding the need for urban infrastructure. Agglomeration economies are the result of the increase in productivity that occurs when firms and households locate close to one another. These economies are the reason that cities and central business districts within cities exist; they are thought to arise for a variety of reasons, discussed in more detail in chapter 5, including the opportunity to support more specialized suppliers, provide a larger labor pool that allows better matching of firms with employees, and learn from nearby firms and industries that are pursuing different strategies.

A key feature of agglomeration economies is that they are in part external to the firms and households that create them. In other words, if an additional firm or household moves into a city, it does not capture all the benefits of the move for itself. Some of the benefits are captured by the households and firms already located in the city inasmuch as the arrival of the new firm or household increases the productivity of all firms and households.

If there are benefits to agglomeration, there are also costs, particularly in the form of added congestion and pollution as well as higher rents caused by having so many people live and work in the same location. The congestion costs are largely external as well inasmuch as the new firm or household does not suffer from all the added congestion, pollution, and other costs it generates. Since both benefits and costs are external, there are no assurances that market forces alone will generate the right size of agglomeration.

Indeed, one ambitious conception of the role of city governments in economic development—implied by the authors of chapter 5—is to manage the forces of agglomeration. City governments might do so by recruiting firms in industries with relatively high agglomeration benefits while building the infrastructure to reduce the congestion and pollution they create; they might then charge fees for private transport and public transit use that reflect the remaining net externalities of those modes.

Land Value Increase

The fact that the benefits and costs of infrastructure are typically location-specific has at least one advantage in that it makes levying taxes to fund urban infrastructure easier. Since land is in fixed supply and the infrastructure on it is often immobile, all or part of the value of the benefits created by an infrastructure improvement is typically capitalized into the value of the land it serves. In such cases, government often can, as chapter 10 explains, fund the improvements by imposing property taxes, selling development permissions, or utilizing similar measures to capture all or part of the uplift in land value that the improvements create. Such measures are often seen as fair, since the parties who benefit from the improvement projects pay.

Local Siting Externalities

A final type of externality important to infrastructure is the negative effects of an infrastructure facility on its surrounding neighbors, such as pollution, noise, smells, nighttime lights, the obstruction of views, and the destruction of local parks, playgrounds, and other amenities. We sometimes treat this category as an equity issue, especially if disadvantaged groups end up in these locations. But it also is an externality inasmuch as the parties creating the noise, obstructing the views, or causing other problems do not consider the costs they impose on others. The negative impacts of infrastructure construction and operation can be mitigated through better planning, engineering design, and construction management and more generous compensation to those groups adversely affected by the project, all measures that make infrastructure construction more expensive and time-consuming. Finding an acceptable and equitable balance among the interests involved is often a major challenge for infrastructure development.

Structure of the Book

The rest of the book contains 19 chapters organized around seven topics. The remainder of this chapter briefly introduces the other chapters to give the reader a sense of the overall scope of the book as well as the specific issues covered. A summary of the key points raised is presented at the end of each chapter.

Issue 1: Infrastructure, Growth, and Poverty

Chapters 2 and 3 examine the evidence on two basic issues in infrastructure policy: the degree to which infrastructure investments and policy interventions can stimulate economic growth and alleviate poverty. In chapter 2, Gregory K. Ingram and Zhi Liu note that until 1989, most economists took it for granted that infrastructure investments made an important contribution to economic development. That year, David Aschauer published an article with the provocative title "Is Public Expenditure Productive?" in which he estimated extraordinarily high economic returns to spending on public infrastructure in the United States from 1949 to 1985.

Aschauer's (1989) article stimulated an avalanche of empirical studies of the relationship between economic growth and infrastructure using ever more sophisticated statistical techniques to control for endogeneity or reverse causality, a variety of different ways of measuring infrastructure inputs, and data from different countries, time periods, and infrastructure sectors. Ingram and Liu review these studies carefully—and include a statistical analysis of their own—and conclude that returns as high as Aschauer (1989) initially reported are highly unlikely, but they vary considerably, being generally higher in developing countries than in developed countries and in electricity and telecommunications than in transport. One of the most interesting results is that the returns are higher if the infrastructure inputs are measured by their physical quality or quantity rather than their cost, a finding that suggests that improvements in the quality of the infrastructure might have high returns.

In chapter 3, Sameh Wahba, Somik Lall, and Hyunji Lee from the World Bank argue that the poor suffer most from a lack of access to infrastructure networks since they must spend a disproportionate share of their income securing basic services such as water and electricity from costly tankers, bottles, and batteries rather than from networks. Among developing countries, access increased in all sectors between 2005 and 2017, with the biggest gains in mobile communications, the least in basic sanitation, and electricity and basic drinking water between the two. (Measures of transportation access were not available.) Access was typically higher in urban areas, although many of the urban areas were struggling to keep up with the infrastructure demands of rapid urbanization.

The effectiveness of programs targeted on the infrastructure problems of the poor depends greatly on the details of their design, the authors argue. It helps if an improvement to physical infrastructure is coupled with complementary social policies such as combining slum upgrading with reforms to dysfunctional land markets, pairing isolated rural electricity systems with the expansion of local educational or business opportunities, or matching basic sanitation facilities with public health or basic water programs. Similarly, when a new infrastructure facility or service is established, it is also important that it includes a realistic plan for funding ongoing operating and maintenance.

Issue 2: Infrastructure and Cities

Given that much of infrastructure is durable and immobile, infrastructure decisions often have strong and long-lasting implications for the built environment. Chapters 4 and 5 explore the relationships between infrastructure, urban form, and productivity. Edward Glaeser discusses how infrastructure technology shapes the economic role and physical form of cities, while Daniel Graham, Daniel Hörcher, and Roger Vickerman adopt the opposite perspective and examine how a city's physical form determines its productivity.

In chapter 4, Glaeser observes that the density and form of a city reflect the transportation technology prevailing at the time when it was growing most rapidly. The full effects of technological change develop in three steps; however, that development can take many decades. The first step is the invention and refinement of a new vehicle type such as the wheeled wagon, the horse-drawn and then electric streetcar, the subway, the elevator, or the automobile. The second step is the construction of a network over which those vehicles operate; the third is the rebuilding of the cities around that network.

The automobile, for example, was invented in the late 19th century but was not very reliable, comfortable, or affordable until the first decades of the 20th century. The United States responded at first by paving farm-to-market roads but soon embarked on building a national high-performance, limited-access expressway system. That system, in turn, stimulated the restructuring of urban areas in the United States in the second half of the 20th century by moving housing and workplaces within metropolitan areas from the central cities to the suburbs and across metropolitan areas from the older Frostbelt to the newer Sunbelt cities.

Glaeser notes that our ability to shape cities around their important highway, subway, and other transportation networks is limited by the value and durability of the existing stock of houses and workplaces. A big change in transportation costs would be needed to make worthwhile tearing down the building stock and rebuilding it to a different density. Durability slows change for cities as well as for infrastructure; by the time we appreciate the full costs and benefits of the environment we are creating, it may be too late to stop it.

In chapter 5, Graham, Hörcher, and Vickerman, unlike Glaeser, assume that residential and workplace locations are fixed and that infrastructure affects only the productivity of city workers and the levels of congestion and pollution caused by its transportation system. Their main propositions are that urban agglomerations generate both positive and negative externalities simultaneously and that the failure to consider them together may lead to poor investment and pricing decisions. The positive externalities stem primarily from the increases in productivity as the agglomeration grows, while the negative externalities stem from increases in traffic congestion, pollution, and safety risks.

Graham, Hörcher, and Vickerman describe the considerable methodological challenges of empirically estimating the relevant externalities (in a brief section that might be skimmed by readers with less interest or background in statistics). They go on to report their own estimates of the elasticities of productivity with respect to agglomeration size (estimates that have been endorsed by the U.K. government for use in required cost-benefit analyses). Their findings are of important policy implications to congestion pricing on the road. In the presence of positive agglomeration externalities, congestion pricing on vehicles traveling into the city center should be substantially lower than the standard Pigouvian externality tax.

Issue 3: Investment Appraisal, Biases, and Politics

Given the high cost of infrastructure investments, picking the right projects is important. This part of the book consists of three chapters (6, 7, and 8) on project appraisal and decision making.

In chapter 6, Don Pickrell describes the evolution of cost-benefit analysis from the initial efforts of Jules Dupuit in the 19th century to the highly detailed manuals on benefit and cost estimation issued today by finance or infrastructure ministries and international financial institutions. Much of the chapter describes the development of methods used to estimate the value that infrastructure users place on the benefits they receive, especially when many benefits, such as travel time saved and fatalities avoided, are not traded directly in a market so that there are no prices to observe.

At least as interesting and important are choices made about what constitutes a benefit or a cost and, in particular, whether to focus on only the direct effects of a project or to include the wider economic impacts. Dupuit and Alfred Marshall both focused on direct effects. Dupuit first estimated the benefits that new infrastructure would provide to users of raw materials and products that were transported over the new facilities. Marshall later demonstrated that these could be captured by measuring benefits to operators of transportation services who carried people and goods via the new routes. Nevertheless, proponents of the wider impact approach argue that the direct benefits may allow downstream firms to implement further productivity improvements, which if ignored will understate the benefits of the project.

The gap between the traditional approach to valuing infrastructure's benefits and what Pickrell calls the macroeconomic approach narrowed at some point when proponents of the traditional approach conceded that they should also count certain benefits and costs of improved infrastructure experienced by nonusers, such as environmental and other external costs and benefits, along with user benefits. But fundamental differences remain, in that one approach focuses on the benefits of a particular project to its users and others directly affected, while the other approach essentially considers the impact on gross domestic product or some measure of the economy as a whole.

The arbiters of this kind of dispute in the United Kingdom are Her Majesty's Treasury and the Department of Transport, operating through the department's Transport Analysis Group. Line agencies can petition the Transport Analysis Group for permission to include novel benefits, but the group generally denies petitions unless reliable quantifiable measures of the benefit exist and the benefit is based on the correction of a downstream market failure. As a result, agglomeration economies are among the only supplemental benefits that have been routinely approved in recent years.

Advocates of using cost-benefit analysis to select infrastructure projects typically assume that the benefits and costs can be forecast reasonably accurately. A careful analysis by Bent Flyvbjerg and Dirk Bester in chapter 7 reveals overwhelming statistical evidence that the actual project costs tend to be strongly underestimated, while the actual usage or traffic attracted (which the authors use as a proxy for the project's benefits) is strongly overestimated. Their amazing data set includes 2,062 infrastructure projects in 6 investment types in 104 developed and developing countries, which were put in service between 1927 and 2011.

Critics often blame forecasting errors such as these on scope changes, complexity, higher than expected inflation, lower than expected competition, and various similar factors. But Flyvbjerg and Bester argue that the root causes of the errors are well-known behavioral limitations, especially optimism bias and overconfidence bias. This observation suggests that improving forecasting will be difficult because the problems are so deeply engrained in human nature. Flyvbjerg and Bester make specific recommendations for reforming cost-benefit analysis.

Chapter 8 is an exploration by John Donahue of the political forces that lead to excesses or shortfalls of infrastructure spending. The approach adopted is that of public choice economics, the theoreticians of which assume that individuals rationally pursue their self-interest in a democratic society governed by voting rules of various kinds. One famous public choice scholar, Anthony Downs, argues that spending will be less than optimal mostly because voters tend to underestimate benefits more than they underestimate costs. Another scholar, Mancur Olson, argues that we may not underspend on classic public goods, despite the incentives to free ride, if the latent group of supporters is small or can devise selective incentives to offer others who join them. Finally, Gordon Tullock demonstrates how majority voting to determine whether to fund similar projects would lead to overspending because the proponents of each project have incentives to exchange support with the proponents of the other projects.

Issue 4: Infrastructure Finance

The discussion of investment evaluation is followed by two chapters on infrastructure finance. In chapter 9, Akash Deep provides a basic primer on the subject, explaining that finance is a key challenge in infrastructure development because the costs of infrastructure assets are typically front-loaded, while the benefits are spread thinly over their long economic life. This difference between the timing of costs and benefits is bridged essentially by the owner of the future benefit stream borrowing against it by issuing some combination of the two basic financing instruments: debt and equity. Note that financing differs from funding. The funder is the entity that ultimately bears the cost of the infrastructure, which is either the general public (in the form of taxes) or the direct users of infrastructure (in the form of user charges). The borrowers and lenders who reconcile the timing of the benefits and costs can be public or private. Deep continues describing the role of the capital structure in reflecting the riskiness and the cost of financing and thereby the financial value of infrastructure. Furthermore, he explains how proper structuring and risk allocation can make infrastructure more efficient and less risky.

Deep then illustrates the potential for innovation in financing infrastructure by recounting efforts to tap the huge and growing savings in insurance and pension funds for public and private financing of infrastructure. Such funds prefer the combination of modest but stable long-term returns that infrastructure offers but are often required to maintain their debt portfolio at investment grade or higher. One solution developed by the European Investment Bank is to enhance the credit rating of the senior debt by underwriting a modest tranche of subordinated debt or providing a contingent line of credit. A more widely imitated innovation is infrastructure funds modeled after the funds pioneered by Australia's Macquarie Group in 1996. The Macquarie Group introduced features such as active asset management, financial engineering, listing on capital markets, leverage at the fund level, and a flexible investment horizon. Infrastructure funds have attracted both institutional and retail investors, thereby significantly expanding the pool of equity available for infrastructure investment beyond just industrial sponsors.

Chapter 10, by José Gómez-Ibáñez, Yu-Hung Hong, and Du Huynh, examines the practices of financing infrastructure improvement by capturing all or part of the uplift in land prices that usually results. As explained earlier, land value capture (LVC) seems fair because landowners who typically benefit from the improvement pay for at least part of the costs. LVC schemes are particularly popular among developing countries, which have enormous infrastructure needs but fewer alternative funding sources. LVCs come in many different types. The property tax is an LVC, for example, as are betterment levies, special assessments, charges for building rights, exactions, and land readjustment.

Chapter 10 focuses on the experiences of Brazil and Vietnam with one of the most important types of LVC: the sale of development rights, such as the right to convert land from rural to urban uses or to add to the density of existing or proposed urban developments. The two cases confirm that sales of development rights can generate substantial proceeds, often more than enough to pay for the extra infrastructure needed by the change in rights. But the examples also caution that successful implementation requires a clear and widely accepted delineation of property rights. Also important is a system of registries and impartial courts to record and protect those rights, a realistic and reasonably detailed land use master plan, and politically sensitive sponsors.

Issue 5: Regulation, Privatization, and State-Owned Enterprises

As noted earlier, policy makers have tried a variety of measures to counter infrastructure's tendency toward natural monopoly and support the popular desire for affordable access to such essential services. This fifth part of the book consists of four chapters on different kinds of enterprises that have served as the vehicles for government involvement.

The part begins with chapter 11, a summary by Antonio Estache of the experiences in privatizing SOEs over the last several decades. Privatization was viewed as a radical reform when it was initiated in the United Kingdom and Chile in the early 1980s. In fact, however, privatization could be viewed as a throwback to an earlier time in that all modern forms of infrastructure—canals, railroads, steamships, electric power, streetcars and subways, telegraph and telephone, and local water supplies—originated as private companies in the 19th century and were nationalized or municipalized only after the turn of the century and often not until the 1960s and 1970s in those developing countries that declared their independence around that time. Estache gives special attention to the results of privatizations beginning in the early 2010s in the hope that they captured some learning from earlier efforts.

Estache estimates that private finance accounts for only 17 percent of the total finance for a typical public-private partnership project, with the bulk of the remainder raised through government bonds or loans and as grants or loans from international financial institutions. By sector, privatization is much more common in ports and electricity generation than in electricity distribution, roads, water, and sanitation.

Particularly interesting are Estache's interpretations of the results of research on the effects of ownership on performance. Ownership alone does not appear to have much effect on social dimensions of performance, particularly the lack of much improvement in access and affordability for the poor. Ownership may have an effect on costs, however, although the influence may weaken once the "easy" measures to increase labor force productivity have been exploited, and further gains require adoption of improved technology. Instead, Estache blames the disappointing performance on the failure to address major governance issues including corruption, lack of technical skills, lack of commitment to allocate the resources needed to get the regulatory job done, and lack of accountability for failing on any or all of the previous issues.

Concern over monopoly contributed to the nationalization of private infrastructure companies in the first half of the 20th century, so it was only prudent to adopt some scheme to regulate the prices that the firms being reprivatized at the turn of the century could charge. In chapter 12, Sock-Yong Phang uses three case studies—the telecom and utilities sectors in the United Kingdom, the electricity sector in California, and the public transport sector in Singapore—to examine the choice between cost of service and price caps, the two most popular strategies for regulating the prices charged by large investor-owned utilities.

Phang argues that the evaluation of the two approaches depends on the priority and clarity of the objectives of the regulatory scheme. She lists four possible objectives: (1) the financial health of the regulated firm, particularly its ability to raise capital; (2) the firm's technical efficiency; (3) access and affordability for the poor; and (4) allocative efficiency, particularly protection against monopoly markups.

The use of price caps reflects concern primarily with technical efficiency, while the use of cost of service reflects concern with financial health. However, no regulatory scheme can afford to pursue one goal single-mindedly (as illustrated by the California case); further, to the extent that a scheme has additional concerns, these can compromise the achievement of its primary goal (as illustrated by the Singapore case).

In chapter 13, Sir Ian Byatt, the highly regarded regulator of the United Kingdom's water industry in its first decade after privatization, describes the challenges faced and the lessons learned during his tenure. Two themes emerge: (1) the importance of being politically sensitive and proactive; and (2) the critical decisions a regulator must face in addition to periodically setting the price cap and

X (the maximum allowable rate of price increase between reviews). These other decisions include the treatment of ancillary activities and revenue and the extent of ring-fencing, quality regulation, introducing competition in procurement for major projects, supervision of nonprofits, capital structure, regulation of dividends and equity funds, among others. Indeed, the combined lessons of Phang's cases and Byatt's tenure would seem to be the pressures for, but potential pitfalls of, regulatory mission creep.

In chapter 14, O. P. Agarwal and Rohit Chandra examine the changing roles of SOEs in providing infrastructure. SOEs were considered key to economic growth by many developing countries in the immediate postcolonial period of the 1950s and 1960s. The private sector often consisted of small traders and workshops without the resources or appetite for heavy investment thought needed at the time for development. The attraction of SOEs faded in the face of disappointing performance, leading to various reform efforts in the 1970s and 1980s and ultimately to the privatization of many SOEs in the 1990s. However, SOEs remain significant players in the infrastructure sectors. This is especially true in China and India.

Agarwal and Chandra map the global landscape of SOEs in the infrastructure sectors and present the rationales that are often used to justify the existence of SOEs. They also present a host of studies on the performance of SOEs versus the private sector. Despite their less efficient performance, SOEs have valid reasons to exist, among which is the inability of the market to supply classic public goods such as local road networks. Most importantly, Agarwal and Chandra recognize the emerging role of SOEs over the last decade. As they observe, infrastructure SOEs have become more versatile through innovations in organizational form, financial management, public-private partnerships, and private contracting.

Issue 6: Infrastructure Plans and Regional Integration

Infrastructure is often used to try to integrate economically or socially lagging regions or to bridge urban-rural divides. This part examines the efforts of the EU, Japan, and China in developing and implementing national infrastructure plans to promote growth and regional development.

As José Manuel Vassallo explains in chapter 15, the members of the EU should have a strong interest in promoting integration, since many have relatively small populations and thus would benefit from the opportunities that integration offers, at least in theory, to develop their competitive advantages or exploit economies of scale. Toward those ends, in 1992 EU members agreed to designate a trans-European network of priority transport (TEN-T) projects, which was subsequently divided into a core TEN-T network and a larger comprehensive

TEN-T network. At that same time, trans-European networks for energy and communications were also established.

A major drawback, however, is that the TEN-T facilities are owned and operated by the member states where they are located rather than by the EU, and the states do not always share EU priorities. This has meant that the EU has had to motivate the states to improve TEN-T facilities by offering special matching grants and other financial support available only for TEN-T improvements. The need for these grants effectively increased the cost of TEN-T projects to the EU and made it even less likely that the core will be finished by its 2030 announced deadline.

As Fumitoshi Mizutani and Miwa Matsuo explain in chapter 16, Japan's intercity passenger railroads are among the few systems that are both privately owned and vertically integrated in that the railroad that owns the track also operates almost all the trains that run over it. The railroad companies are admired for their enterprise in developing ancillary activities, such as shopping malls in stations, that reduce their dependence on passenger revenues but at the same time attract more passengers.

Japan is also among the few countries that have used high-speed passenger railroads as a tool to shape regional development. The proposal for the first Shinkansen (bullet train) line, originally planned in 1939, was revived after World War II to promote the economic development of the country's Tokyo–Osaka–Nagoya core corridor (with a western extension from Nagoya to Fukuoka a few years later). The success of the original line stimulated pressure from less-developed regions for their own lines, and the central government responded in 1970 with a national Shinkansen plan that includes five new Shinkansen lines plus a new magnetic levitation (maglev) line.

Unlike the EU, the Japanese government will build and own the new Shinkansen high-speed lines and simply lease them to operators, with the lease fees based on the expected operating profits from each line. The new maglev line is scheduled to open in 2027, with a branch to Osaka by 2037. Japan Railways Central, the railroad company that currently operates Shinkansen service between Tokyo and Nagoya, offered to pay the entire cost of the line's construction if the maglev service direct to Nagoya can open before the rival service to Osaka. Japan could make credible commitments to the duration and magnitude of the maglev program in part because of the political stability attributable to rule by one party, the Liberal Democrats, from 1955 to 1993.

China is similar to Japan in its reliance on high-speed rail as an important tool for shaping its national development and on the political stability of one-party rule. The two countries differ, however, in that 92 percent of Japan's population lives in urban areas, while urbanization in China is catching up, having risen rapidly from under 20 percent in 1980 to 64 percent in 2020 and projected to reach 70 percent by 2030. Meanwhile, the Chinese government has recognized urbanization as a key source of income growth for the country, thereby effectively committing itself to absorbing large numbers of rural migrants in entry-level factory jobs while more productive and experienced workers move up to better-paid and more productive employment.

China's city cluster strategy—described in more detail in chapter 17 by Zheng Chang—involves the creation of 19 enormous city clusters, or megalopolises, each with several major cities linked by high-speed rails. This strategy can be seen as an effort to create a variety of opportunities to absorb rural migrants and improve urban worker productivity by encouraging various forms of agglomeration economies. If the rail service is sufficiently fast and convenient to encourage commuting among the cluster's cities, it will increase the effective size of the labor pool and the quality of worker matches with employers. If, in addition, each major city in the cluster is large enough to support a high degree of specialization (e.g., in trade, high-tech manufacturing, tourism, or finance), it can support specialized suppliers as well. Whether the productivity gains will be enough to justify the costs of the high-speed rail system remains to be seen.

Issue 7: Coping with Radical Uncertainties

Climate change, automation, and the emerging sharing economy are three of the major sources of radical uncertainties that are affecting the performance of infrastructure and may also shape the future of the infrastructure sectors. The three chapters in this part of the book assess the (likely) positive and negative impacts of these radical uncertainties and discuss how public policies should be made to respond to the challenges.

Severe weather conditions and natural disasters due to climate change can seriously disrupt infrastructure services and damage or destroy infrastructure facilities. In chapter 18, Henry Lee focuses on ways that jurisdictions may adapt their infrastructure to the growing threats of climate change. Because the impacts of climate change vary by location, Lee argues that effective policies will emerge mainly at lower levels of government in a bottom-up process. He predicts that the magnitude of investments in climate-resilient infrastructure will be unprecedented. He then discusses the characters of these investments and the enormous scope of the transitions that will be required, particularly in electricity but also in the water and transportation sectors. After identifying the governance challenges that underlie climate mitigation and adaptation options, Lee proposes changes in governance to enable more effective planning, delivery, and management of infrastructure.

New technologies have emerged quickly in the infrastructure sector in recent years, thanks to the rapid advancement in information technologies such as cloud computing, the Internet of Things, and artificial intelligence. Are these new technologies going to revolutionize the infrastructure sector? This is the central question examined in chapter 19 by Shashi Verma, a senior executive on the front line of London's public transport services. Taking the history of transport technological changes as an example, he stresses that fundamental change in the world of infrastructure came only very slowly. But automated vehicles (AVs) seem to be an exception. He discusses the economics of AVs, their likely impacts on other modes and consumer behavior, and the institutional challenges that AVs face before their widespread acceptance. He argues that the advent of AVs presents a prospect for disruptive change larger than anything seen in our lifetime. It is important for policy makers to take actions to prepare for the arrival of the technology, including in particular licensing, allocation of road space, economic support to public transport, and control over pricing structure.

The sharing economy is an economic model of activities acquiring, providing, or sharing access to goods and services on the basis of online platforms. What impacts might the sharing economy have on infrastructure services and assets? In the final chapter, Andrew Salzberg and O. P. Agarwal look into this question with a case study on the urban transport sector. Over the last decade, new methods of sharing motor vehicles (e.g., Zipcar, car2go, Uber, Lyft, Didi, Ola) as well as smaller motorized electric vehicles (e.g., Bird, Lime, Gojek) have grown at rapid rates around the globe. Salzberg and Agarwal discuss the potential benefits, costs, and risks of shared vehicles and argue that the sharing economy model has the potential to enable better utilization of fixed assets and thereby allow wider access to services. However, the current experience of shared vehicles in U.S. markets indicates that the market penetration remains tiny, as most people still prefer individualized mobility services. Therefore, it remains to be seen if the service will grow to a significant size. The authors predict that new regulations will emerge to address the disruptive impact of this model on traditional businesses. More importantly, public policies in road and parking pricing and congestion charging will be crucial for the future of the sharing economy in the urban transportation sector.

Future Research Directions

Infrastructure Economics and Policy: International Perspectives covers a broad range of infrastructure issues and experiences that we consider important. The book leaves out some important topics, however, due to a desire to keep it at a reasonable length and the limitations of our understanding of the rich variety of experiences and issues that might be covered. A few significant topics that are left out or not discussed in depth include maintenance, green infrastructure, integrated infrastructure planning, and the role of infrastructure in climate resilience. Nature-based solutions, an important emerging topic, is not covered here; the reader is directed to another Lincoln Institute publication, *Design with Nature Now* (Steiner et al. 2019). We hope this book will trigger more attention to and interest in the research of these issues and others.

Note

1. Where the choice is among mutually exclusive projects, only the highest net present value gives the correct results, while the benefit-cost ratio or internal rate of return can recommend projects that are too small.

References

Altshuler, Alan, and David Luberoff. 2004. *Mega-Projects: The Changing Politics of Urban Public Investment*. Washington, DC: Brookings Institution Press.

Aschauer, David A. 1989. "Is Public Expenditure Productive?" *Journal of Monetary Economics* 23(2): 177–200.

Beesley, Michael E. 1965. "The Value of Time Spent in Travelling: Some New Evidence." *Economica* (n.s.) 32(126): 174–185.

Bugalski, Natalie, and David Pred. 2013. "Reforming the World Bank Policy on Involuntary Resettlement: Submission to the World Bank's Safeguards Review." Washington, DC: Inclusive Development International, the International Accountability Project, Bank Information Center, and the Habitat International Coalition.

Clark, Dana. 2002. "The World Bank and Human Rights: The Need for Greater Accountability." *Harvard Human Rights Journal* 15: 205–226.

Eckstein, Otto. 1958. *Water and Resource Development*. Cambridge, MA: Harvard University Press.

Foster, Christopher D. 2001. "Michael Beesley and Cost Benefit Analysis." *Journal of Transport Economics and Policy* 35(1): 2–31.

Foster, Christopher D., and Michael E. Beesley. 1963. "Estimating the Social Benefit of Constructing an Underground Railway in London." *Journal of the Royal Statistical Society* (ser. A) 126(1): 46–93.

Gannon, Colin, and Zhi Liu. 1997. "Poverty and Transport." World Bank working paper No. TWU-30. Washington, DC: World Bank.

Global Infrastructure Hub. 2019. "Private Infrastructure Investment by Country Income Group." https://www.gihub.org/infrastructure-monitor/insights/private-infrastructure -investment-by-country-income-group-2019/.

Gómez-Ibáñez, José A. 2003. *Regulating Infrastructure: Monopoly, Contracts, and Discretion*. Cambridge, MA: Harvard University Press.

Gómez-Ibáñez, José A., and John R. Meyer. 1996. *Going Private: The International Experience with Transport Privatization*. Washington, DC: Brookings Institution.

Hirschman, Albert O. 1958. *The Strategy of Economic Development*. New Haven, CT: Yale University Press.

Oxford Economics. 2017. *Global Infrastructure Outlook: Infrastructure Investment Needs, 50 Countries, 7 Sectors to 2040*. Oxford, UK: Global Infrastructure Hub. https://cdn.gihub.org /outlook/live/methodology/Global+Infrastructure+Outlook+-+July+2017.pdf.

Rozenberg, Julie, and Marianne Fay. 2019. "Beyond the Gap: How Countries Can Afford the Infrastructure They Need While Protecting the Planet." Washington, DC: World Bank. https://openknowledge.worldbank.org/handle/10986/31291.

Schelling, Thomas C. 1968. "The Life You Save May Be Your Own." In *Problems in Public Expenditure Analysis: Studies of Government Finance*. ed. Samuel B. Chase, 127–162. Washington, DC: Brookings Institution.

Steiner, Frederick R., Richard Weller, Karen M'Closkey, and Billy Fleming, eds. 2019. *Design with Nature Now*. Cambridge, MA: Lincoln Institute of Land Policy.

Sub-Saharan Africa Transport Program. n.d. "Second Generation Road Funds." Newsletter. https//www.ssatp.org/en/page/road-funds, accessed August 5, 2021.

INFRASTRUCTURE, GROWTH, AND POVERTY

2

INFRASTRUCTURE STOCKS AND MACROECONOMIC PERFORMANCE ACROSS COUNTRIES

Gregory K. Ingram and Zhi Liu

What are the impacts of infrastructure on the form, quality, and rate of economic growth of industrial and developing countries? The decades-old answer to this question was that the impacts were obvious and large, so relatively little careful research was done to confirm the linkages. This view began to change about 50 years ago when economists started to address the question both analytically and empirically. The results have followed an arc, with early findings of modest effects followed by some findings of profoundly large effects and then a prolonged period of ever more sophisticated empirical work showing normal or reasonable returns in many countries and for many types of infrastructure. However, the results vary depending on country conditions, variable definitions, time period, data quality, and underlying analytical frameworks and assumptions. Accompanying this economic research has been an evolution in the provision of infrastructure, with private provision dominating a century ago followed by mainly public or governmental provision in the mid-20th century and then the reemergence of private investment and management in some infrastructure sectors over the past 30 years. This chapter first summarizes the past few decades of empirical work on infrastructure's macroeconomic effects, presents the results of recent empirical work on the short-term impact of infrastructure investment, and concludes with new empirical work using recent data.

Challenges Faced in Measuring the Economic Impact of Infrastructure

In this chapter, the scope of infrastructure follows the usual definitions (World Bank 1994) and includes public utilities, public works, and other transport facilities. Public utilities' main sectors comprise electric power, telecom, piped water, sanitation, and sewerage; public works comprise roads and major dams and canals for irrigation and drainage; other transport includes urban and interurban railways, urban transport, ports and waterways, and airports. Often called *economic infrastructure*, these sectors share technical features such as economies of scale, network effects, and immobility and economic features such as externalities (spillovers from users to nonusers). And many sectoral characteristics vary across sectors. Some sectoral services are rival and excludable—essentially private goods—such as telephone, urban transit, electricity, rail, airport, and port and airport services, though they may have significant externalities. Other services are nonrival and nonexcludable—essentially public goods—such as rural roads. Some sectors where exclusion is difficult, such as urban roads, are subject to congestion and are club goods. Some infrastructure sectors that have attributes of private goods also often have scale economies that lead to their production by the public sector or by private firms subject to government regulation. Thus, while *infrastructure* is a useful aggregate term, its elements are quite heterogeneous, and this feature accounts for some of the different results across empirical studies of infrastructure's economic impact.

Another challenge in measuring the economic impact of infrastructure is that the impacts vary, and benefits can take several forms. Direct benefits to consumers may take the form of time savings from improved transport or better health from piped water and sanitation as well as lower costs of goods and services. Indirect benefits arise when infrastructure services are intermediate goods in production—such as faster transport and reliable electric power—that are of joint and cross-industry use and can affect interregional and international trade (Arrow and Kurz 1970). Infrastructure can also produce structural changes in the economy by opening up new areas for commercial agriculture, diversifying the economies of rural areas, enlarging markets and making them more efficient through improved communication, and fostering diffusion of new technology (Kessides 1993). Many but not all of these impacts will show up in the usual measures of gross domestic product (GDP).

In studies of its economic impact, infrastructure's economic input is typically represented by its stock of capital, and this is often measured as invested capital (cumulative expenditures adjusted for depreciation) or in physical terms (e.g., generating capacity). Across countries, some infrastructure sectors grow more rapidly than income and some do not. Typical estimates of the income elasticity of infrastructure stocks by sector across countries are electric generation and distribution capacity, 1.17; phone lines, 1.10; paved roads, 0.97; mobile phone subscriptions, 0.58; access to sanitation, 0.38; and access to water, 0.12 (Ingram, Liu, and Brandt 2013). Accordingly, the sectoral composition of infrastructure

FIGURE 2.1 Sectoral mix of infrastructure as it relates to country income.

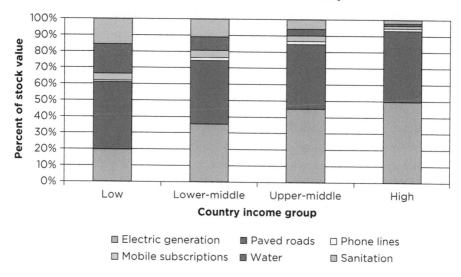

Sources: Based on data from ITU (2010); World Bank (2011).

varies systematically with country income (figure 2.1). It is noteworthy that the value of electric generation and distribution capital stock exceeds that of paved roads in high-income countries, as shown in figure 2.1. Telecom capital stock is relatively small because the capital costs per user are much less than for electric power and roads. Mobile phone service has particularly low capital costs per user, and mobile penetration in poor countries has been driven primarily by reductions in cost (Sridhar and Sridhar 2007) and not by income growth, hence its low-income elasticity. Across countries, infrastructure stocks are virtually independent of the percent of the population that is urban. This seems to reflect two offsetting forces: higher urban incomes increase the demand for infrastructure, while much higher urban population densities reduce the per capita cost of infrastructure services (Ingram, Liu, and Brandt 2013). The patterns in figure 2.1 are useful to keep in mind when reviewing studies that use only one sector (e.g., telecom) as a proxy measure for all infrastructure.

Econometric efforts to determine the contribution of infrastructure normally involve using GDP as a dependent variable and measures of labor, private capital stocks, and infrastructure as independent variables. When the measure of infrastructure is based on a perpetual inventory of cumulative annual investments adjusted for depreciation, sometimes infrastructure investment is accumulated alone, and sometimes it is represented by all public investment even though infrastructure typically comprises about half of public capital. A difficulty with investment-based measures is that the actual value or quantity of infrastructure may bear little relation to its investment cost because of government inefficiencies in producing or operating infrastructure capital stocks. On average in developing countries, the value of public capital is likely to be about half its investment cost (Pritchett 1996). In the United States, the cost of interstate highways constructed from 1971 to 1993 varied by location substantially more than other government expenditures (e.g., Medicare), and this spatial variation is independent of the spatial variation in residential construction costs (Brooks and Liscow 2019). Across industrial countries, some infrastructure costs vary surprisingly: urban rail projects in the United States cost from two to seven times more than their European counterparts (Levy 2018). To quantify infrastructure, an alternative that avoids many valuation issues is to use measures of the physical stock—such as miles of paved road or installed generating capacity—that also are more widely available in developing countries than investment data. Many studies use such physical measures. However, very few studies address the efficiency with which the stocks are used.

In addition to measurement, several other aspects of the impact of infrastructure make comparisons across studies more challenging. These issues include seven factors:

1. *Aggregate infrastructure versus sector-by-sector impact.* The latter often use physical stocks.
2. *Geographical coverage: United States, Organisation for Economic Co-operation and Development (OECD), or many countries.* Early studies focused on single countries.
3. *Short-term impact versus long-term effect.* The former use annual time series, the latter periodic changes.
4. *Differences in time periods covered.* Vary greatly, with more recent studies covering longer periods.
5. *Reverse causation/endogeneity.* Typically addressed with more complex models and econometrics.
6. *Anticipatory effects, delays.* Typically addressed with lagged variables and program data.
7. *Operational efficiency.* Rarely addressed, varies widely, and not highly correlated with infrastructure stocks.

The review of analytical and empirical work assessing the relation between infrastructure and economic activity is organized here into three sections by time period and objective. The first section addresses work done before 1989. The second section addresses work done in 1989 and later that examines the relation between infrastructure and economic growth. The third section addresses work done after 1989 that addresses the short- and long-run fiscal multiplier of infrastructure investment. The use of 1989 as a milepost reflects the impact of work published by Aschauer (1989a, 1989b) that stimulated much empirical work on infrastructure and economic growth that continued over the following two decades. The flow of studies on this topic narrowed after 2010, and numerous recent studies have focused on infrastructure's fiscal multiplier. The review presented here is selective and illustrative rather than comprehensive.

Pre-1989 Studies on the Economic Impact of Infrastructure

In the first half of the 20th century, a strong impact of infrastructure on economic growth and development was viewed as obvious and unquestionable. Perhaps as a result, little analysis of this interaction was undertaken until the 1960s, when concerns about government failure began to grow (Yergin and Stanislaw 1998). Although infrastructure provision undertaken by governments is not market-driven, Hirschman (1958, 26) argued that public infrastructure is provided in a framework of "induced decision-making" responsive to economic needs in the context of unbalanced growth with its process of overbuilding and shortfalls. In a pathbreaking analysis of the impact of transportation on the economic development of the United States, Fogel (1964) documented the developmental effects of canals and railroads on the western United States, arguing that canals, with modest extensions, would have produced the large development impact normally attributed to railroads. On the analytic side, Arrow and Kurz (1970) set forth a formal theoretical treatment of the effects of public capital on output and welfare. Their framework formulates an economy-wide aggregate production function that explicitly includes public capital as an input along with private capital and labor. This approach underpins much of the empirical work undertaken on the relation between infrastructure and economic growth.

One of the first efforts to use production functions to measure the economic impact of infrastructure predated Arrow and Kurz (1970) and was carried out using data for Japan (Mera 1967). Mera divided Japan into five regions and used data from 1954 to 1963 (a period of intense reconstruction) to analyze the effect that transport and communication public infrastructure had on the output of manufacturing and services. He estimated that output elasticities were 0.35 for manufacturing and 0.40 for services, foreshadowing the magnitudes obtained in later work. A very different approach to analyzing the relation between transport and economic development was a systems analysis model of Colombia that combined a regionally disaggregated model of the Colombian economy with detailed network representations of Colombia's road, rail, river-based, and port systems (Kresge and Roberts 1971). This was a product of the Brookings Institution's Transport Research Project, directed by John R. Meyer, that addressed the role of transport in economic development and was undertaken from 1963 to 1971. Policy simulations with this model produced reasonably normal rates of return for transport improvements, revealed important network effects as transport improvements shifted imports and exports among ports, and demonstrated that many nontransport policy changes or investments were necessary for transport improvements to be effective.

1989 and Subsequent Work Addressing Infrastructure and Economic Growth

Empirical work on this topic increased rapidly following a paper by Aschauer (1989a) using a production function framework that found very large returns—rates of return of 100 percent or more—from U.S. public capital, a variable that included all nonmilitary public investment in the period 1949–1985. In the United States, the public capital stock is about half as big as the private capital stock, and 80 percent of the public capital stock is nonmilitary, of which about half is infrastructure (Munnell 1992). Productivity declined during 1949–1985, as did public investment (partly because of the completion of the interstate highway system). A replication of Aschauer's national-level results using data from 1948 through 1987 produced somewhat smaller output elasticities; similar regressions using state-level data produced output elasticities half as large, hypothesized as reflecting the excluded spillovers of infrastructure across state lines (Munnell 1992). Critics pointed to problems of spurious correlation, reverse causation, and omitted variables. An analysis using state-level data for 1969 through 1996 that included fixed effects at the state level found no impact of public sector capital on productivity, and this result also held for regressions at the regional level, thereby not supporting the existence of state-level spillovers (Holtz-Eakin 1994). Another study that applied a growth accounting framework at the state level (implicitly including state fixed effects) from 1951 through 1986 found that the residual of economic growth not accounted for by private inputs was not explained by public investment (Hulten and Schwab 1991).

Additional work during this period moved beyond a focus on the United States and examined the economic impacts of public investment in infrastructure (or specific infrastructure sectors) across groupings of countries. In an analysis of G-7 countries relating annual change in GDP to lagged annual private and public nonmilitary investment from 1966 through 1985, Aschauer (1989b) found a strong positive relation between public investment and productivity. Increasing public investment by 1 percent of GDP raised the labor productivity growth rate by between 0.37 and 0.73 percent while adjusting for reverse causation. Turning to public investment in only the component sectors of infrastructure, a study of fiscal policy and growth covering about 100 countries from 1970 to 1988 found that among sectors, only the share of annual investment in transport and communication was highly correlated with economic growth. This share was also a significant variable in growth regressions, often with high coefficients—somewhat reminiscent of Aschauer's earlier results for the United States (Easterly and Rebelo 1993). In this work, tests with instrumental variables suggested that reverse causation was not an issue. Studies also began to focus on individual sectors and combine investment data with physical measures of infrastructure service levels. One study analyzed the impact of the telecom sector on economic growth using annual data from 21 OECD countries from 1970 to 1990 (Röller and Waverman 2001). The authors specify a four-equation model that makes telecom services endogenous, includes fixed effects at the country level and a measure to account for network effects, and uses variables for investment and a physical measure (telephone lines per 1,000 persons). With this approach, they found a rather large and nonlinear effect of telecom service on economic growth—an effect that increases with country income levels. For example, their results imply that if Germany had the same telephone penetration rate as the United States (a rise from 32 percent to 40 percent), its economic output would increase by 6.36 percent, a remarkably high impact.

Meanwhile, other studies continued to examine the impact of infrastructure on economic growth across a sample of OECD and developing countries using physical measures of infrastructure stocks, such as the length of paved roads, number of telephone land lines, and installed generating capacity. A series of papers using a large database of physical infrastructure measures underpinned this work (Canning 1998). The first study examined the impact of transport (road and rail) facilities on economic growth using a sample of 96 countries from 1960 through 1985, with data averaged over five-year intervals (Canning and Fay 1993). Based on a production function approach and including measures of human capital and construction costs and allowing for country fixed effects, the return to transport varies across countries, being normal for developed countries, high for industrializing countries, and moderate for underdeveloped countries. An increase in transport infrastructure has a modest short-term impact but yields higher output in the long run. Overall, doubling a country's stock of roads increases GDP growth by about 1 percent per year. Another study using physical measures of infrastructure for all sectors included 57 countries and covered 1960 through 1990 (Canning 1999). Based on a production function approach and using cointegration methods, this study found returns to electric-generating capacity and transportation similar to those for capital as a whole but relatively high returns for telephone networks. The high returns for telephone networks are present for both developed and developing countries when the sample is subdivided. A related study using physical measures of infrastructure for 42–67 countries from 1950 through 1990 in a sophisticated cointegration framework found on average normal returns and long-run growth impacts for infrastructure but with much variation across countries, with some countries undersupplied and some oversupplied (Canning and Pedroni 2008).

The measures of infrastructure capital (whether cumulated investment or physical stocks) used in most studies are taken at face value and not adjusted for differences in their effectiveness of use, which varies widely across countries. For example, electricity losses range from 2 to 70 percent, faults per 100 phone lines vary from 1 to 70, and unpaved roads range from 0 to 96 percent of all roads. Moreover, infrastructure effectiveness varies widely across sectors within countries, and sectoral effectiveness has a much lower correlation with per capita income than sectoral stocks (Ingram, Liu, and Brandt 2013). However, only a few studies have attempted to adjust for effectiveness, and the impacts are important. Perhaps the first study to adjust the impact of infrastructure stocks for their effectiveness used data from 42 to 46 developing countries over the period 1970–1990 (Hulten 1996). Hulten found that a 1 percent increase in the effectiveness of existing infrastructure stocks had an effect on growth seven times larger than a 1 percent increase in annual investment in infrastructure, and that differences in effectiveness accounted for up to 40 percent of the difference in growth rates between low- and high-growth economies. Another study, which covered 136 countries from 1960 to 2005 using nonoverlapping five-year averages, employed indices of physical infrastructure quantity and quality to explain economic growth (Calderón and Servén 2010). Results indicated that about one-third of the total impact of infrastructure on growth was due to quality and two-thirds were due to quantity. Whereas low-quality infrastructure is usually attributed to poor management or weak institutions, some argue that the regulatory incentives faced by infrastructure providers encourage low-quality provision (McRae 2009). Infrastructure effectiveness continues to be an important omitted variable in many studies of infrastructure's impacts and was highlighted in a recent literature review (Timilsina, Hochman, and Song 2020).

Because of the availability of data, the size of the investment, and the debate about its impacts, many studies have focused on the economic impacts of the U.S. interstate highway system. Rather than examine aggregate impacts of the system, an innovative study looked carefully at its impact on vehicle-intensive industries, comparing their performance with other industries (Fernald 1999). The study found that changes in the growth of roads (particularly the interstate highway system) are associated with larger changes in productivity growth in industries that are more vehicle-intensive. As a result, road growth contributed about 1 percentage point more to total factor productivity growth before 1973 than after (when construction of the interstate highway system was substantially completed) and that subsequent road growth has not produced an abnormal rate of return. The study concluded that while the interstate highway system produced large returns, an additional interstate highway system in the United States likely would not. Another study focused on the impact of the interstate highway system in nonmetropolitan counties (Chandra and Thompson 2000). Counties directly benefiting from construction enjoyed a cumulative growth premium of 6–8 percent 24 years after opening, but their adjacent neighboring counties saw earnings fall by 1–3 percent. Estimates based on a seemingly unrelated fixed-effects model found the net effect of a new interstate on regional growth to be essentially zero. Testing whether interstate highways in conjunction with other state roads produce spillovers across state lines, Holt-Eakin and Schwartz (1995) used a production function–based model with state fixed effects. Their data for 48 states were organized in overlapping annual five-year intervals from 1969 through 1986. They measured spillovers to neighboring states by entering the stock of state highways in neighboring states in a production function framework and found no evidence of such spillovers or of own-state impacts on output and productivity.

Addressing a transportation project as monumental as the interstate highway system, a remarkably broad and ambitious study analyzed the economic impact of the construction of the 67,247 km Indian railway system, focusing on the period of its construction, 1870–1930 (Donaldson 2018). After digitizing a database covering 235 districts in which 98 percent of the railway length was built, the author employed a general equilibrium trade model with a detailed representation of the rail network to estimate the economic effects of the rail system. (This granular approach is reminiscent of the Colombia model described above.) These effects are driven by the railway's performance advantage over waterways and roads. At that time, rail freight costs were one-eighth to one-quarter of road freight costs; daily rail travel distances, 600 km, were 20 times greater than daily road travel distances, 30 km. The author found that railroads reduced trade costs, which in turn increased trade volumes and reduced interregional price differences, enabling previously almost autarkic districts to enjoy gains from trade. On average, when the rail network was extended to a new district, its real agricultural income rose by approximately 16 percent.

A similar technique using a general equilibrium trade model was subsequently applied to evaluate the economic impact of railways in the United States (Donaldson and Hornbeck 2013). This work, which revisits analyses by Fogel (1964) and Fishlow (1965), used counties as the basic spatial unit and built a network to calculate county-to-county transport costs, which were used to calculate the variation in market access at the county level. Relative to the case with the historic rail network, two scenarios were analyzed: a world without the rail network and a world without the rail network but with Fogel's (1964) hypothetical expanded canal network. The first scenario produces a 63.5 percent reduction in the value of agricultural land and an annual economic loss of 3.4 percent of gross national product, and the second would have offset only 13 percent of the loss from eliminating railroads. This analysis, and the trade models on which it is based, gives pride of place to the role that transport plays in integrating markets to promote economic development. It is important to note that the applications in both India and the United States are based on the production and trade of agricultural goods that are land extensive in production. Although infrastructure often reduces production or consumption costs, it is not obvious how this trade-based approach might be applied to networked infrastructure other than transport.

China also has a large rail system that in January 2019 included 108,000 km of conventional rail network for passengers and freight and 31,000 km of high-speed rail network for passengers only (Lee 2019). (High-speed rail has speeds of more than 200 kph and up to 350 kph, while the maximum speed for conventional rail is 125 kph.) China's high-speed rail and its conventional intercity rail networks each carried about one billion passengers in 2017. Its high-speed rail system, the construction of which began in 2004, aims to connect 550 cities, including all cities with populations of more than 100,000. The goal is to have 38,000 km of high-speed rail by 2025, with much of the additional length to be built in China's western region, where distances between cities are greater and population densities are much lower than in the east (Zou, Chen, and Xiong 2018). In 2017, the high-speed rail system included about 25,000 km, mostly in eastern regions, and additional investment needed from 2017 to 2025 was then estimated to be US$1.04 trillion (Wang, Xia, and Zhang 2016). Using average construction costs, the investment in China's high-speed rail up to 2017 was in the range of US$450 billion, so the total investment cost of the completed high-speed rail network is likely to be around US$1.5 trillion.

Even though China's high-speed rail system is a work in progress, many attempts have been made to evaluate the economic and social returns of completed portions. To anticipate the findings, early studies of newly opened lines were skeptical of the economic returns of high-speed rail investments. Over time, passenger volumes have grown on the early lines in eastern regions, and their economic returns have become more favorable. However, as the system has expanded from eastern regions, where cities are relatively close together, population densities are high, and land is flat to more western areas, where intercity distances are higher, cities are smaller, and the geography raises construction costs, analysts have questioned the economic logic of further system growth. In addition, many have questioned the use of conventional approaches to the economic evaluation of such massive investments and argue that assessments should include additional benefits from agglomeration and labor market efficiencies.

The initial financial and economic performance of high-speed rail lines was poorer than expected, as actual construction costs were often 30–50 percent above feasibility stage estimates while traffic volumes were below forecasts (Wu 2013). Most of the early lines were in the most developed part of China and have benefited from traffic growth so that early projects became more successful over time, whereas later projects sometimes have very high costs (Hayashi, Seetha Ram, and Bharule 2020). The ShiZheng project, a 355 km section on the Beijing-Guangzhou high-speed corridor that opened on budget (its cost per kilometer averaged a low US$14.7 million) and on time in December 2012, was subject to a detailed appraisal in 2018. It carried 50.4 million passengers that year at an average speed of about 300 kph with a travel time of 81 minutes compared with 197–261 minutes on a conventional train. Its economic rate of return was estimated at 15 percent, lower than the 20 percent forecast at appraisal (World Bank 2018). However, the World Bank's appraisal noted that its return would be much higher if agglomeration benefits were taken into account. Such benefits take the form of increased business productivity and are estimated to range from 0.5 to 1 percent of GDP in second- and third-tier cities (World Bank 2014). Several attempts have been made to estimate aggregate effects of the existing high-speed rail system. Using a data set covering 268 cities from 2009 through 2016, a recent study estimated that the increased connectivity of cities increased the urban economic growth by 0.11, mainly from local effects rather than spillovers (Chong, Chen, and Qin 2019). Some small cities were negatively impacted because of regional competition. Another study using a market access measure across 110 main prefecture cities from 2006 through 2015 (in a general equilibrium trade modeling context inspired by Donaldson's approach) found that a 1 percent increase in market access increased a city's real income by 0.123 percent and that if all high-speed rail was removed in 2015, aggregate real income would decline by up to 9.4 percent (Zou, Chen, and Xiong 2018). Analysts who believe that continued expansion of the high-speed rail network into western regions will be uneconomical have focused on passenger airlines as an alternative (Wang, Xia, and Zhang 2016).

In addition to examining the impact of infrastructure on economic growth, many studies—particularly those on developing countries—have examined infrastructure's impact on income inequality. Infrastructure is hypothesized to raise the value of the assets of the poor (e.g., land, human capital); improve their access to education, health services, and markets by lowering transport costs; and reduce the cost of infrastructure services that are necessities, such as water supply, that take up a larger share of their incomes than is the case for better-off households. The rehabilitation of rural roads improves local community and market development (Calderón and Servén 2010). Public infrastructure also benefits the poor because they have less access to private substitutes. Two approaches have been used to relate infrastructure provision to inequality. The first examines the impact of infrastructure provision on macromeasures of income inequality such as Gini coefficients; the second is micro and examines the effects on the poor of specific interventions. The macro approach typically finds that infrastructure provision reduces income inequality (Calderón and Servén 2014; Timilsina, Hochman, and Song 2020). Microstudies have shown that (1) better and safer transport and roads raise school attendance (Brenneman and Kerf 2002); (2) better access to electricity allows more time for study (Leipziger et al. 2003); and (3) expansion of mobile phone networks improves the ability to conduct business, access financial services, and track current market prices of goods and agricultural commodities. One source of simultaneity in this area is that inequality might impede the provision of infrastructure services because societies with more unequal income distributions spend fewer resources on public goods, including infrastructure.

In summarizing the empirical work on the relation between infrastructure and economic growth, we note several results. The majority of empirical studies find that infrastructure is supportive of economic growth. One survey found that 32 of 39 studies of OECD countries found positive effects, as did 9 of 12 studies that include developing countries (Romp and De Haan 2007). Findings do display a wide variety in terms of the magnitude of the effect. Studies that use investment data find fewer positive effects than those using physical indicators, likely because the indicators data more accurately reflect the actual situation (Straub 2011; Timilsina, Hochman, and Song 2020). Specifications that define the dependent variable as a level are more likely to find positive effects than those defining it as a change over time, such as growth in output or productivity. Infrastructure's economic impacts also tend to be larger in lower-income than higher-income countries, and this is true for both production function and growth accounting frameworks (Estache and Fay 2009; Timilsina, Hochman, and Song 2020). In terms of the elasticity of output with respect to aggregate infrastructure, there has been some convergence in results to a magnitude around 0.10, much lower than initial estimates in the literature (Calderón and Severn 2014). Studies of individual sectors find the strongest results for roads and telecom, particularly for longer-run effects. Little progress has been made in defining optimal sizes of infrastructure stocks, and the concept has little meaning when additions to infrastructure are location-specific and may address the relief of bottlenecks. A country may have the right quantity of infrastructure but has the sectoral or geographic distribution wrong. Country-level studies are the appropriate tool for determining the return of particular projects, whereas aggregate-level studies might inform cross-sectoral investment allocations. While a few studies have included measures of the effectiveness of infrastructure stocks, virtually none have included institutional or incentive measures such as the quality of regulation, the extent of competition, and institutional factors such as the enforcement of contracts (Straub 2011).

Work Addressing the Fiscal Impacts of Infrastructure

Much recent research on the economic impacts of infrastructure investment has focused on its short-term versus long term fiscal impacts. This focus results from the 2008 financial crisis and recession that stimulated interest in the design of fiscal stimulus packages. At the time, there was much discussion of identifying shovel-ready infrastructure projects whose expenditures would stimulate demand and economic recovery, but the policy discussion revealed that there was little consensus on the magnitude of the investment multipliers for different types of government spending (Ramey 2013). Expenditure of funds for road building—even for shovel-ready projects—occurs with a delay of many months. From the date that the federal government distributes grants to the states, the states have four years to write contracts with builders. As work completes, bills go via the states to the federal government that then pays the bills. Thus, while the American Recovery and Reinvestment Act was passed in February 2009, by the end of 2010 just over half its funds were spent—and nearly all not until the end of 2012. Moreover, road construction is so capital-intensive in the United States that only about 8 percent of its costs are for labor. Even when infrastructure investment is productive in the long run, the size of its short-term fiscal multiplier has been uncertain. Recent empirical work has sought to reduce the uncertainty about the size of infrastructure's fiscal multipliers.

A recent paper estimated short-term multipliers from government investment and consumption shocks using quarterly data from OECD countries from 2003 through 2016 (Boehm 2020). Boehm demonstrated that a large class of macroeconomic models will predict smaller short-term multipliers for government investment shocks than for government consumption shocks. Using the OECD panel data, Boehm tested this result by estimating the short-run multiplier of government investment shocks and found it to be zero and that of government consumption shocks to be 0.8. He then investigated the cause of this difference and found evidence that increases in government investment, but not government consumption, are offset by declines in private investment. Private investment declines by 57 cents per dollar of government investment after four quarters and by 75 cents after eight quarters. Neither government investment nor consumption shocks increase or decrease private consumption. The productivity of government investment plays little or no role in these outcomes. Accordingly, government investment may be less effective at stimulating aggregate demand than government consumption, even when such investment produces long-run benefits.

Might this result apply particularly to road building? Studying the fiscal effect of road construction raises a number of conceptual and econometric challenges. First, stimulus spending is not independent of economic conditions, so there is a simultaneity problem. Second, decisions to spend road funds are decentralized to the states. Third, long lags occur between decisions to spend and the disbursement of funds, as noted above. Fourth, decisions to spend are discussed publicly and produce anticipatory behavior. One attempt to define expenditure shocks and to address these issues is based on a data set of highway funding, highway spending, and numerous economic outcomes from 1993 through 2010 (LeDuc and Wilson 2013). The analysis found modest to no short-run multiplier in expansionary economic times but a distinct short-run multiplier during recessions. Longer-term multipliers, six to eight years out when the projects are completed, are larger and do not differ between contemporaneous expansionary or recession economic conditions. At about 10 years out, the long-run multiplier is about two. A more recent study of the multiplier effects of the interstate highway system used data from 1957 through 1991 to estimate the long-run relative multiplier of spending on the interstate highway system (Yaffe 2019). Taking steps to account for endogeneity and anticipatory behavior, Yaffe estimated a long-run 15-year relative multiplier of 1.7, including insignificant spillover effects. This long-run multiplier is similar to that obtained by LeDuc and Wilson (2013).

Empirical estimates of the short-run multiplier of government investment are converging on zero or very modest numbers that are much less than the multipliers for government consumption. This finding is true even when the benefits of the investment are substantial in the long run. The small multipliers are due in part to the substantial time required to undertake and complete construction and in part to the crowding out of private investment by government investment. With respect to public investment in infrastructure, transport investment provides very modest short-term impacts, even for investments with attractive long-term returns (Gallen and Winston 2018). Analyses of the American Recovery and Reinvestment Act stimulus investments—undertaken when interest rates were low, unemployment was high, and the economy had slack—found that their effects on construction employment were small and perhaps negative (Ramey 2020). Recent studies indicate that public investment, including infrastructure investment, produces a very weak short-term stimulus effect.

New Evidence of the Relationships Between Infrastructure and Economic Growth Across Countries

Most of the cross-country empirical studies reviewed above were conducted using data from before 2000. Over the last two decades, however, the global landscape of infrastructure has changed significantly in terms of technology, demand, and supply. Mobile telephony has witnessed dramatic increases in access and usage and large declines in costs. Middle-income countries have increased the percentage of roads paved and the access to water, sanitation, electricity, and mobile phone and Internet services. However, the lowest-income countries (mostly sub-Saharan countries) still largely lag behind in access to infrastructure services. These trends are illustrated by charts in figure 2.2.

The charts are generated from a cross-country data set for two years: 2006 and 2015. The data sources include the World Bank Development Indicators (World Bank 2020), the International Road Federation's *World Road Statistics* (IRF 2020), and the International Telecommunications Union's statistics (ITU 2020). The year 2006 is the earliest year over the last two decades for which we could obtain usable road statistics for a large sample of countries, and the year 2015 is the latest year with a similar large usable sample. Each line in the figures represents a country in the sample. One end of the line shows the levels of per capita GDP and an infrastructure indicator in 2006; the other end indicates the levels in 2015. The 2015 GDP per capita point is always above the 2006 GDP per capita point in these figures because countries that experienced a decline in real per capita income are

FIGURE 2.2 Per capita GDP and infrastructure service or access, 2006 and 2015.

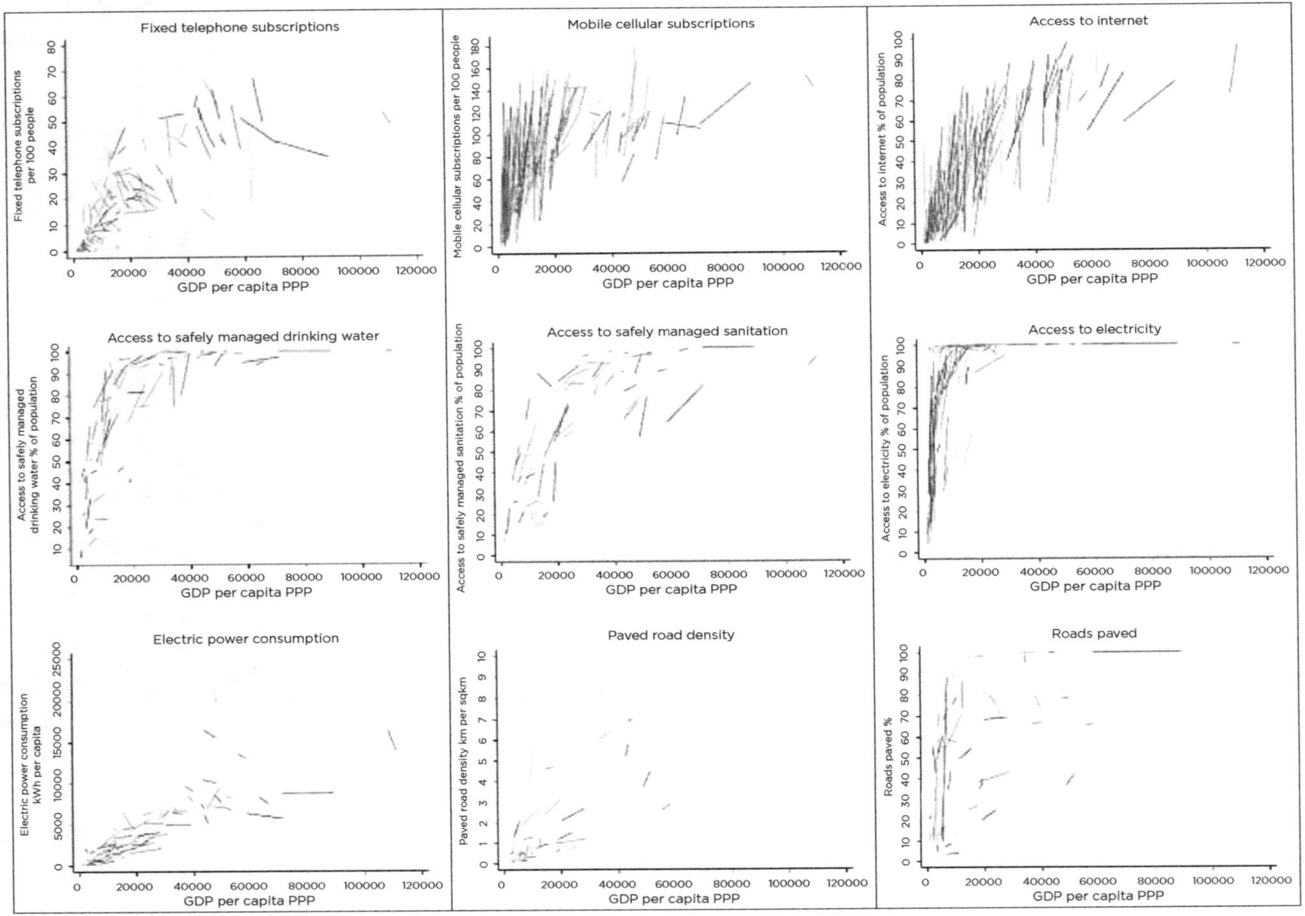

Based on data from IRF (2020); World Bank (2020).

not included. When the lines are nearly vertical and very similar across countries (e.g., Internet access), the increases in infrastructure indicators are associated with modest GDP growth, indicating that other factors common across countries (large cost reductions in these cases) are likely associated with service growth, and cross-section and time series relations between infrastructure and income are likely to differ greatly. When the individual country lines fall in a similar path (e.g., access to sanitation), time series and cross-section associations of infrastructure with income growth are likely to be similar in magnitude.

Regression models are estimated using the cross-country data for 2006 and 2015 (the same data used in figure 2.2) to obtain the income elasticities of infrastructure usage or access. Demand is measured as the amount of infrastructure services used such as mobile phone subscriptions per 100 people and electricity consumption in kWh per person. Access is measured by the percentage of the population with access to a certain infrastructure service. The general specification of the regression models is

$$Q = c_0 + c_{1\,Y} + \sum c_i X_i + \mu,$$

where Q is either infrastructure usage or access; Y is per capita income; X_i ($i = 2$, 3, . . .) are control variables; c_0, c_1, and c_i are the estimated coefficients; and μ is the error term. The control variables include country population density and urban population as a percent of total population.

Three sets of regression models are estimated: 2006, 2015, and the first difference between 2006 and 2015 (with variables defined as annual percent change). The ordinary least square method is used for the single-year regressions where the dependent variables are the measures of usage. Except for the control variable of urbanization level, which is measured as percent of total population living in urban areas, all other variables are transformed to the natural logarithm so that the estimated coefficients can be conveniently interpreted as elasticities at the mean values. The ordinary least square method is also used for all first-difference regressions. Tobit models are used for the single-year regressions where the dependent variables are defined as percent of population with access to a given infrastructure service. In the Tobit models, the level of access in the initial year is added as another independent variable, as the initial level of access could be one of the determinants of the access level in the end year. The estimated coefficient for per capita income from each Tobit regression model is used to calculate the income elasticity at the mean value. The estimated elasticities are given in table 2.1.

A few observations are suggested by the elasticity estimates. First, compared with the income elasticities estimated by Ingram, Liu, and Brandt (2013), the estimates here for fixed phone subscriptions, mobile phone subscriptions, paved roads,

TABLE 2.1 Estimated Income Elasticities of Infrastructure Usage or Access

	2006 Data		2015 Data		Annual % Change in 2006–2015		Estimates from Ingram, Liu, and Brandt (2013), 2006 Data
	All-Income Countries	Middle- and Low-Income Countries	All-Income Countries	Middle- and Low-Income Countries	All-Income Countries	Middle- and Low-Income Countries	All-Income Countries
Fixed telephone subscriptions per 100 people	1.00*** (174)	1.16*** (116)	1.23*** (182)	1.43*** (122)	0.83** (146)	0.87* (107)	1.10*** (83)
Mobile cellular subscriptions per 100 people	0.68*** (180)	0.76*** (122)	0.21*** (186)	0.25*** (127)	0.92** (150)	0.85* (111)	0.58*** (83)
Electric power consumption (kWh) per person	1.19*** (130)	1.33*** (82)	1.22*** (130)	1.32*** (82)	0.45*** (112)	0.36* (78)	1.17*** (83)
Paved road km per km² of arable land	1.28*** (97)	1.31*** (78)	1.14*** (69)	1.06*** (48)	0.89** (41)	1.01* (31)	0.97*** (83)
% population with access to the Internet	0.63*** (177)	0.69*** (120)	0.36*** (182)	0.47*** (126)	1.73*** (147)	1.99*** (109)	
% population with access to safely managed drinking water services	0.22*** (95)	0.45*** (52)	0.22*** (95)	0.39*** (52)	0.03 (80)	0.14 (49)	0.12*** (83)
% population with access to safely managed sanitation services	0.33*** (85)	0.38* (40)	0.38*** (86)	0.40*** (41)	0.24* (69)	0.41 (36)	0.38*** (83)
% population with access to electricity	0.57*** (178)	0.38*** (119)	0.53*** (188)	0.36*** (127)	0.06 (148)	0.07 (102)	
% roads paved	0.41*** (113)	0.48*** (81)	0.33*** (85)	0.43*** (50)	0.85** (51)	0.79 (32)	

access to sanitation, and access to water are broadly similar; these elasticities remain stable between 2006 and 2015. Second, income elasticities of access for 2015 are mostly smaller than 2006 (except for sanitation in the all-income country sample), implying that the gaps in access to infrastructure services narrowed as low-income countries continued to improve access. Third, elasticities obtained from the developing country sample are mostly greater than those from the all-income country sample, implying that the percent increase in infrastructure usage or access in response to a 1 percent increase in per capita income in a developing country would be greater than that in a high-income country. Fourth, income elasticities for fixed telephone subscriptions, electricity consumption, and paved road density are greater than 1.00 using cross-section data for both 2006 and 2015 but become smaller using first-difference estimates. This finding implies that the usage differentials are generally bigger than the income differentials at a fixed point in time, but the rate of change in usage becomes smaller than the rate of change in income over a long period of time. Finally, for mobile phone and Internet service, the first difference elasticities differ greatly from the cross-section elasticities, consistent with figure 2.2.

We also examine the effect of infrastructure quality on economic output by using two infrastructure quality indicators: (1) electric power transmission and distribution losses (percent of output), as a proxy of power service quality; and (2) percent of roads paved, as a proxy of road service quality. Infrastructure service quality varies sector by sector (Ingram, Liu, and Brandt 2013). These two indicators represent the quality of the two most important infrastructure sectors. We consider them good indicators to approximate the overall infrastructure quality of a country. We expect that poor electricity service would constrain the growth of economic output and that better roads would enhance the growth of economic output.

Based on the classic economic growth model originated by Solow (1956) and extended by Mankiw, Romer, and Weil (1992) and Hulten (1996), we hypothesize that the change in per capita GDP in a country over a period of time is a function of changes in the key inputs to the economy. We construct an aggregate production function where all variables are measured as the percent change between the starting and ending years:

$$\frac{Y_j - Y_i}{Y_i} = c_0 + c_1 \frac{PK_j - PK_i}{PK_i} + c_2 \frac{HK_j - HK_i}{HK_i} + c_3 \frac{EC_j - EC_i}{EC_i}$$
$$+ c_4 \frac{EL_j - EL_i}{EL_i} + c_5 \frac{RD_j - RD_i}{RD_i} + c_6 \frac{PV_j - PV_i}{PV_i} + \mu,$$

where i and j denote the starting year and ending year; Y_i and Y_j denote GDP per capita (in purchasing power parity constant 2017 international dollar) in the starting year and ending year, respectively; PK_i and PK_j denote per capita gross private fixed capital over the starting and ending years, respectively; HK_i and HK_j denote the ratio of children of official school age who are enrolled in school to the population of the corresponding official school age in the starting and ending years, respectively; EC_i and EC_j denote electricity generating capacity per capita in the starting and ending years, respectively; EL_i and EL_j denote electricity distribution losses in the starting and ending years, respectively; RD_i and RD_j denote total road length per area of arable land in the starting and ending years, respectively; PV_i and PV_j denote the percentage of road paved in the starting and ending years, respectively; and μ denotes the error term.

Data on per capita GDP, private capital, and human capital were collected from the World Development Indicators database. The electricity data are from the U.S. Energy Information Administration. Data on road length and percentage of road paved were gathered from *World Road Statistics* compiled by the International Road Federation (IRF 2020). Our samples were selected from available data between 2000 and 2017. Because the data on our defined variables are not available for each year in the time period, we selected the earliest year with available data on all variables as the starting year and the latest year with available data on all variables as the ending year. We estimated three regressions, with results shown in table 2.2. The countries in our samples are listed in tables A1, A2, and A3 in the appendix to this chapter.

All coefficient estimates have the expected signs, although some of them are statistically insignificant. As the variables are specified in percent change, the coefficients can be interpreted as elasticities. The elasticities of EL and PV indicate that improvements in electricity system performance and road paving have a positive impact on GDP. Because the elasticities of EC and EL are similar in size and opposite in sign in regression 1, limiting electricity losses is a good substitute for adding capacity. Improving road quality through paving can make road capacity use more productive but also save resources to build more road capacity. Due to the small samples for regressions 2 and 3, the estimates are much less significant statistically. It would be worthwhile for future research to expand the size of the samples.

Conclusions

This review makes clear that infrastructure is heterogeneous across sectors in its types of economic effects; in its manifestations of private, club, or public good

TABLE 2.2   Regression Results for Cross-Country Production Functions

	Regression 1	Regression 2	Regression 3
EC	0.2092*** (3.9436)		0.3584* (1.9689)
EL	−0.1885*** (−3.5978)		−0.1128 (−1.6704)
RD		0.1342 (1.5522)	0.1079 (1.3998)
PV		0.0368 (1.5961)	0.0389* (1.9227)
PK	0.1748*** (3.5839)	0.3375*** (3.4972)	0.2769*** (3.3289)
HK	0.1472* (1.9082)	0.0294 (0.2148)	0.1026 (0.7397)
Constant	0.1732*** (4.1265)	0.0507 (1.0691)	0.0139 (0.3005)
Observations	72	23	22
Adjusted R-squared	0.3394	0.5280	0.5861

Note: The t-statistics are in parentheses; * $p < 0.1$, ** $p < 0.05$, *** $p < 0.01$.

aspects; and in its scale economies and other externalities. Accordingly, it is difficult to aggregate infrastructure across sectors in a useful way. Moreover, infrastructure is generally locationally specific, so local bottlenecks (or shortages) and excessive capacity can coexist at different locations simultaneously. Accordingly, empirical work using aggregate measures of infrastructure (usually based on cumulative investment) produces weaker measures of infrastructure's economic impacts than do sector-specific measures based on physical capacity, where positive economic impacts are more routinely found. Empirical work on the economic impacts of infrastructure are subject to several econometric challenges—including reverse causation, fixed effects, anticipatory actions, endogeneity, and omitted variables—but when these are addressed, positive economic impacts of infrastructure typically endure.

Recent studies that have revisited historical experiences with large infrastructure projects (mainly rail and highway systems) have produced fairly compelling evidence of the positive economic impacts of these projects, while ongoing studies of China's high-speed rail expansion have yet to lead to a final verdict. The recent empirical analyses of the short-run multiplier effects of infrastructure investment have led to a near consensus that such investment has little to no short-term economic impact even when the long-term economic impacts are clear. While much analysis has been done on the economic impacts of infrastructure stocks, relatively few studies have included measures of infrastructure performance or efficiency of use. The few studies that have been done—including the new estimates noted above—indicate that performance is likely to be a very important determinant of infrastructure's economic impacts. Given the heterogeneity of the relation between various infrastructure sectors and economic output (illustrated well in figure 2.2) and the locational specificity of most infrastructure, the analysis of new infrastructure investments needs to be done at the project level and not from a macro or even sectoral level.

Summary

- Economists have made numerous efforts to measure the economic impacts of infrastructure. While the empirical results vary significantly, they are generally positive.
- The empirical analyses of the short-run multiplier effects of infrastructure investment find little to no short-term economic impact, however, even when the long-term economic impacts are clearly positive.
- Available studies indicate that infrastructure performance or efficiency of use is likely to be a very important determinant of infrastructure's economic impacts.

References

Arrow, Kenneth, and Mordecai Kurz. 1970. *Public Investment, the Rate of Return, and Optimal Fiscal Policy*. Baltimore: Johns Hopkins Press for Resources for the Future.

Aschauer, David A. 1989a. "Is Public Expenditure Productive?" *Journal of Monetary Economics* 23(2): 177–200.

———. 1989b. "Public Investment and Productivity Growth in the Group of Seven." *Economic Perspectives* 13(5): 17–25.

Boehm, Christoph. 2020. "Government Consumption and Investment: Does the Composition of Purchases Affect the Multiplier?" *Journal of Monetary Economics* 115: 80–93.

Brenneman, Adam, and Michel Kerf. 2002. "Infrastructure & Poverty Linkages: A Literature Review." Washington, DC: World Bank.

Brooks, Leah, and Zachary Liscow. 2019. "Is Infrastructure Spending Like Other Spending?" Paper presented at NBER Conference "Economics of Infrastructure Investment," Cambridge, MA (November 15–16).

Calderón, César, and Luis Servén. 2010. "Infrastructure and Economic Development in Sub-Saharan Africa." *Journal of African Economies* 19: i13–i87. https://doi.org/10.1093/jae/ejp022.

———. 2014. "Infrastructure, Growth, and Inequality: An Overview." Working paper No. 7034. Washington, DC: World Bank.

Canning, David. 1998. "A Database of World Infrastructure Stocks, 1950–1995." *World Bank Economic Review* 12: 529–547.

———. 1999. "The Contribution of Infrastructure to Aggregate Output." Working paper No. 2246. Washington, DC: World Bank.

Canning, David, and Marianne Fay. 1993. "The Effect of Transportation Networks on Economic Growth." Discussion paper. Columbia University: Department of Economics.

Canning, David, and Peter Pedroni. 2008. "Infrastructure, Long-Run Economic Growth and Causality Tests for Cointegrated Panels." *Manchester School* 76 (5): 504–527.

Chandra, Amitabh, and Eric Thompson. 2000. "Does Public Infrastructure Affect Economic Activity? Evidence from the Rural Interstate Highway System." *Regional Science and Urban Economics* 30: 457–490.

Chong, Zhaohui, Zhenhua Chen, and Chenglin Qin. 2019. "Estimating the Economic Benefits of High-Speed Rail in China: A New Perspective from the Connectivity Improvement." *Journal of Transport and Land Use* 12(1): 287–302.

Donaldson, David. 2018. "Railroads of the Raj: Estimating the Impact of Transportation Infrastructure." *American Economic Review* 108 (4–5): 899–934.

Donaldson, David, and Richard Hornbeck. 2013. "Railroads and American Economic Growth: A 'Market Access' Approach." Working paper No. 19213. Cambridge, MA: NBER.

Easterly, William, and Sergio Rebelo. 1993. "Fiscal Policy and Economic Growth: An Empirical Investigation." *Journal of Monetary Economics* 32: 417–458.

Estache, Antonio, and Marianne Fay. 2009. "Current Debates on Infrastructure Policy." Working paper No. 49. Washington, DC: World Bank.

Fernald, John G. 1999. "Roads to Prosperity? Assessing the Link Between Public Capital and Productivity." *American Economic Review* 89(3): 619–638.

Fishlow, Albert. 1965. *American Railroads and the Transformation of the Antebellum Economy.* Cambridge, MA: Harvard University Press.

Fogel, Robert. 1964. *Railroads and American Economic Growth: Essays in Econometric History.* Baltimore: Johns Hopkins University Press.

Gallen, Trevor, and Clifford Winston. 2018. "Transportation Capital and Its Effects on the U.S. Economy: A General Equilibrium Approach." University of Purdue, Krannert School of Business.

Hayashi, Yoshitsugu, K. E. Seetha Ram, and Shreyas Bharule, eds. 2020. *Handbook on High-Speed Rail and Quality of Life.* Tokyo: Asian Development Bank Institute.

Hirschman, Albert O. 1958. *The Strategy of Economic Development.* Yale Studies in Economics 10. New Haven, CT: Yale University Press.

Holtz-Eakin, Douglas. 1994. "Public-Sector Capital and the Productivity Puzzle." *Review of Economics and Statistics* 76(1): 12–21.

Holtz-Eakin, Douglas, and Amy Ellen Schwartz. 1995. "Spatial Productivity Spillovers: Evidence from Highways." Working paper No. 5004. Cambridge, MA: NBER.

Hulten, Charles. 1996. "Infrastructure Capital and Economic Growth: How Well You Use It May Be More Important Than How Much You Have." Working paper No. 5847. Cambridge, MA: NBER.

Hulten, Charles R., and Robert Schwab. 1991. "Public Capital Formation and the Growth of Regional Manufacturing Industries." *National Tax Journal* 44(4): 121–134.

Ingram, Gregory, Zhi Liu, and Karen Brandt. 2013. "Metropolitan Infrastructure and Capital Finance." In *Financing Metropolitan Governments in Developing Countries*, ed. Roy Bahl, Johannes Linn, and Deborah Wetzel, 339–365. Cambridge, MA: Lincoln Institute of Land Policy.

IRF (International Road Federation). 2020. "World Road Statistics." Washington, DC: International Road Federation.

ITU (International Telecommunications Union). 2010. *World Telecommunications Development Report*. Geneva: International Telecommunications Union.

Kessides, Christine. 1993. "The Contributions of Infrastructure to Economic Development: A Review of Experience and Policy Implications." Discussion paper No. 213. Washington, DC: World Bank.

Kresge, David T., and Paul O. Roberts. 1971. "Systems Analysis and Simulation Models." In *Techniques of Transport Planning*, vol. 2, ed. John R. Meyer. Washington, DC: Brookings Institution.

Leduc, Sylvain, and Daniel Wilson. 2013. "Roads to Prosperity or Bridges to Nowhere? Theory and Evidence on the Impact of Public Infrastructure Investment." In *NBER Macroeconomics Annual 2012*, No. 27, ed. Daron Acemoglu, Jonathan Parker, and Michael Woodford, 89–142. Chicago: University of Chicago Press.

Lee, Michael. 2019. "Passenger Rail Development." *High-Speed Intercity Passenger Speedlines* 26 (September): 7–12.

Leipziger, Danny, Marianne Fay, Quentin Wodon, and Tito Yepes. 2003. "Achieving the Millennium Development Goals: The Role of Infrastructure." Working paper No. 3163. Washington, DC: World Bank.

Levy, Alon. 2018. "Why It's So Expensive to Build Urban Rail in the U.S." *Bloomberg CITY-LAB*, 2018.

McRae, Shaun. 2009. "Infrastructure Quality and the Subsidy Trap." Discussion paper No. 09-017. Palo Alto, CA: Stanford Institute for Economic Policy Research, Stanford University.

Mankiw, N. Gregory, David Romer, and David N. Weil. 1992. "A Contribution to the Empirics of Economic Growth." *Quarterly Journal of Economics* 107: 407–437.

Mera, Koichi. 1967. "Tradeoff Between Aggregate Efficiency and Interregional Equity: A Static Analysis." *Quarterly Journal of Economics* 81(4): 658–674.

Munnell, Alicia H. 1992. "Policy Watch: Infrastructure Investment and Economic Growth." *Journal of Economic Perspectives* 6(4): 189–198.

Pritchett, Lant. 1996. "Mind Your Ps and Qs: The Cost of Public Investment Is Not the Value of Public Capital." Working paper No. 1660. Washington, DC: World Bank.

Ramey, Valerie. 2013. "Comment on 'Roads to Prosperity or Bridges to Nowhere? Theory and Evidence on the Impact of Public Infrastructure Investment.'" In *NBER Macroeconomics Annual 2012, No. 27*, ed. Daron Acemoglu, Jonathan Parker, and Michael Woodford, 147–153. Chicago: University of Chicago Press.

———. 2020. "The Macroeconomic Consequences of Infrastructure Investment." Working paper No. 27625. Cambridge, MA: NBER.

Röller, Lars-Hendrik, and Leonard Waverman. 2001. "Telecommunications Infrastructure and Economic Development: A Simultaneous Approach." *American Economic Review* 91(4): 909–923.

Romp, Ward, and Jakob De Haan. 2007. "Public Capital and Economic Growth: A Critical Survey." *Perspektiven der Wirtschaftspolitik* 8(5): 6–52.

Solow, Robert M. 1956. "A Contribution to the Theory of Economic Growth." *Quarterly Journal of Economics* 70: 65–94.

Sridhar, Kala Seetharam, and Varadharajan Sridhar. 2007. "Telecommunications Infrastructure and Economic Growth: Evidence from Developing Countries." *Applied Econometrics and International Development* 7(2): 37–56.

Straub, Steven. 2011. "Infrastructure and Development: A Critical Appraisal of the Macro Level Literature." *Journal of Development Studies* 47(5): 683–708.

Timilsina, Govinda, Gal Hochman, and Ze Song. 2020. "Infrastructure, Economic Growth, and Poverty: A Review." Working paper No. 9258. Washington, DC: World Bank.

Wang, Kun, Wenyi Xia, and Anming Zhang. 2016. "Benefits Assessment of Large-Scale High-Speed Rail Network in China: The Effect on Low-Cost Carriers." University of British Columbia. https://ssrn.com/abstract=2888274.

World Bank. 1994. *World Development Report: Infrastructure for Development*. Washington, DC: World Bank.

———. 2011. "World Development Indicators." Washington, DC: World Bank.

———. 2014. *Regional Economic Impact Analysis of High-Speed Rail in China: Main Report*. Washington, DC: World Bank.

———. 2018. *China: ShiZheng Railway Project*. Independent Evaluation Group, Project Performance Assessment Report No. 129933. Washington, DC: World Bank.

———. 2020. "World Development Indicators." Washington, DC: World Bank. https://datacatalog.worldbank.org/dataset/world-development-indicators.

Wu, Jianhong. 2013. "The Financial and Economic Assessment of China's High-Speed Rail Investments: A Preliminary Analysis." Discussion paper No. 2013-28. Paris: OECD.

Yaffe, Daniel Leff. 2019. "The Interstate Multiplier." Paper presented at the NBER Conference on Economics of Infrastructure, Cambridge, MA, March 1.

Yergin, Daniel, and Joseph Stanislaw. 1998. *The Commanding Heights: The Battle for the World Economy*. New York: Free Press.

Zou, Wei, Liangheng Chen, and Junke Xiong. 2018. "High-Speed Railway, Market Access, and Economic Growth." Working paper No. 852. Tokyo: Asian Development Bank.

Appendix

TABLE A1 List of Sample Countries for Regression 1

Country Name	Starting Year	Ending Year	Country Name	Starting Year	Ending Year
Angola	2008	2010	Guinea	2001	2005
Australia	2015	2017	Guyana	2009	2012
Bahrain	2000	2017	Honduras	2013	2017
Bangladesh	2000	2017	Iran, Islamic Rep. of	2009	2017
Belarus	2010	2013	Jamaica	2011	2017
Belize	2010	2017	Jordan	2000	2017
Benin	2000	2015	Kazakhstan	2000	2006
Bhutan	2000	2017	Kenya	2000	2005
Bolivia	2000	2017	Korea, Rep. of	2000	2017
Botswana	2000	2003	Liberia	2014	2015
Burkina Faso	2001	2017	Malawi	2000	2016
Burundi	2009	2017	Malaysia	2000	2017
Cabo Verde	2007	2014	Mali	2008	2017
Cambodia	2000	2008	Mauritania	2001	2017
Cameroon	2012	2016	Mauritius	2000	2017
Chad	2001	2016	Mexico	2000	2017
Comoros	2013	2017	Moldova	2000	2005
Cote d'Ivoire	2014	2017	Mongolia	2000	2006
Croatia	2001	2017	Namibia	2005	2007
Dominican Republic	2007	2017	Nepal	2007	2017
Ecuador	2000	2017	Nicaragua	2006	2010
Egypt, Arab Rep. of	2014	2017	Niger	2001	2017
El Salvador	2000	2017	Oman	2000	2001
Eswatini	2000	2015	Pakistan	2006	2017
Ethiopia	2014	2015	Panama	2000	2017
Georgia	2000	2009	Peru	2000	2017
Ghana	2000	2005	Philippines	2001	2015
Guatemala	2000	2017	Poland	2000	2017

(continued)

TABLE A1 *continued*

Country Name	Starting Year	Ending Year	Country Name	Starting Year	Ending Year
Romania	2014	2017	Thailand	2006	2015
Senegal	2006	2017	Togo	2000	2017
Serbia	2008	2017	Uganda	2002	2008
Seychelles	2000	2010	Ukraine	2000	2009
Sierra Leone	2013	2017	United States	2010	2013
South Africa	2000	2017	Uruguay	2007	2017
Suriname	2009	2010	Uzbekistan	2010	2017
Tanzania	2016	2017	Zimbabwe	2000	2013

TABLE A2 List of Sample Countries for Regression 2

Country Name	Starting Year	Ending Year	Country Name	Starting Year	Ending Year
Bahrain	2006	2015	Malaysia	2006	2010
Bangladesh	2006	2015	Mauritania	2006	2012
Belize	2010	2014	Mexico	2006	2015
Bhutan	2006	2015	Nicaragua	2006	2010
Bolivia	2006	2015	Niger	2010	2015
Burundi	2010	2015	Pakistan	2006	2015
Croatia	2010	2015	Panama	2010	2015
El Salvador	2006	2011	Peru	2010	2015
Guatemala	2010	2015	Philippines	2006	2015
Korea, Rep. of	2006	2015	Poland	2006	2015
Lao PDR	2006	2015	Serbia	2010	2015
Malawi	2006	2010			

TABLE A3 List of Sample Countries for Regression 3

Country Name	Starting Year	Ending Year	Country Name	Starting Year	Ending Year
Bahrain	2006	2015	Malaysia	2006	2010
Bangladesh	2006	2015	Mauritania	2006	2012
Belize	2010	2014	Mexico	2006	2015
Bhutan	2006	2015	Nicaragua	2006	2010
Bolivia	2006	2015	Niger	2010	2015
Burundi	2010	2015	Pakistan	2006	2015
Croatia	2010	2015	Panama	2010	2015
El Salvador	2006	2011	Peru	2010	2015
Guatemala	2010	2015	Philippines	2006	2015
Korea, Rep. of	2006	2015	Poland	2006	2015
Malawi	2006	2010	Serbia	2010	2015

3

INFRASTRUCTURE AND THE POOR

Sameh Wahba, Somik Lall, and Hyunji Lee

Over the past few decades, many researchers have attempted to answer a simple yet challenging question: does infrastructure boost economic growth and poverty alleviation? A review of the literature and global experience suggests a positive answer; however, to realize the heterogenous impacts of improved infrastructure coverage, the question deserves a closer fresh look at how the delivery and impact of infrastructure have evolved across countries, cities, and communities.

Improvement to infrastructure coverage has not been straightforward. Developing countries may have achieved dramatic increases in infrastructure coverage, but stark spatial and territorial inequities remain in many countries between urban and rural areas and between leading and lagging regions. By contrast, developed countries have mostly achieved universal access to infrastructure, but several countries face challenges in maintaining service levels and sustaining infrastructure quality.

Globally, cities tend to have higher levels of infrastructure access than rural areas in the same countries, but they often struggle to meet massive financing needs estimated at more than US$4.1–4.5 trillion per annum, with additional costs of US$0.5–1.1 trillion associated with climate mitigation and adaptation scenarios (CCLFA 2015). Notably, an important share of the estimated infrastructure financing needs in cities is likely to be concentrated in developing countries, where rapid urbanization is still ongoing and infrastructure deficits are most pronounced (White and Wahba 2019).

Moreover, lack of access to infrastructure and service delivery disproportionately affects the urban poor—especially those at the bottom of the income distribution or living in slums and informal settlements. They typically spend a large share of their household budget on accessing basic services such as water and electricity due to lack of access to infrastructure networks (Straub 2008). For instance, owing to the lack of connection to the municipal water systems, the urban poor often end up buying water from vendors at unit rates that are five times higher than the cost of water in the municipal systems to which richer households have access (Klein 2012). More recently, the COVID-19 pandemic has demonstrated how a combination of infrastructure shortages alongside affordability challenges can exacerbate exposure and community contagion risk across underprivileged neighborhoods in cities.

The extent to which infrastructure can contribute to poverty alleviation and welfare gains for the poor will be dependent on the way infrastructure investments are prioritized and designed as well as on the quality of infrastructure, the cost of connection and of the recurrent service itself, the effectiveness of targeting of the poor, and the complementarity between infrastructure and other related investments such as land and housing. In fact, the identification, design, and targeting of infrastructure investments face many constraints, including political economy considerations emerging from weak governance; these considerations include elite capture and an inclination by many policy makers for gray over green infrastructure and for brick-and-mortar solutions over nonstructural interventions such as nature-based solutions and building codes. Similarly, infrastructure projects often are overdimensioned, and their design does not follow cost-benefit analysis or cost-effectiveness considerations.

In this context, this chapter discusses two important aspects relating to infrastructure and the poor. First, it provides an overview of infrastructure coverage across the globe, focusing on the extent to which infrastructure reaches out to poor communities, especially in developing countries, as well as the contribution of infrastructure access toward reducing inequalities. It then discusses global experience in designing and implementing policies that aim to promote economic growth and alleviate poverty through improving infrastructure access. To enable infrastructure to achieve the objectives of economic growth and poverty alleviation, complementary constraints, such as land market dysfunctions, design of effective tariffs and subsidy and targeting policies and expanding private sector participation in infrastructure, must be tackled. These considerations notwithstanding, the extent of infrastructure's impact on economic growth will also depend on other existing binding constraints to growth, such as unstable macroeconomic conditions, insecure land and property rights, weak governance, and the rule of law, among other things.

Infrastructure, Inequalities, and the Poor

While it would be ideal to make careful distinctions between issues of infrastructure access and quality, the primary focus of this section is on access by drawing on a review of the evidence and literature. This focus is due to the challenges in consistently measuring quality across countries at different stages of development.

How Has Access to Infrastructure Evolved over the Past 20 Years?

Across Countries

The levels of access to infrastructure services are strongly correlated with a country's average income. Table 3.1 shows that upper-middle-income countries are the closest to universal access; low-income countries lag behind, particularly in access to electricity and sanitation. Across world regions, South Asia has the largest share of population with a consistently lowest access to sanitation followed by sub-Saharan Africa, where access seems to have worsened.

It must be noted that access levels have improved across all income levels over the past decade. Mobile cellular access has improved the most and sanitation access the most slowly, related to policy and market structure challenges discussed later in the chapter.

Within Countries

Considerable heterogeneity also exists in access to infrastructure within countries, notably between rural and urban areas. Typically, comparing rural-urban differences across countries is difficult because national definitions of urban and rural areas differ significantly from one country to another. Consider Denmark, which defines thresholds of 200 inhabitants to identify urban areas, and China, which uses a threshold of 100,000 inhabitants. In some countries, urban areas are designated by administrative decision or the sectoral composition of employment. To facilitate international comparisons, a coalition of six international organizations developed new global definitions of a city, a town and a semidense area, and a rural area. The United Nations Statistical Commission has endorsed the "Degree of Urbanisation" as a recommended method for international comparisons.

This new approach is simple and transparent, relying on the combination of population size and density applied to a population grid instead of a multitude of criteria or complex and lengthy calculations.[1] Using this method, Henderson et al. (2020) found that many sectoral measures of infrastructure access follow a density gradient whereby overall access increases and rural urban gaps decrease with rising levels of development. Figure 3.1 shows that levels of access to safely managed drinking water are higher in cities, second highest in towns and semidense areas, and lowest in rural areas in almost all the countries covered by the survey. Similar patterns are seen in access to electricity.

While cities may appear to have higher levels of infrastructure access, they often struggle to maintain service levels. This struggle is driven by rapid population growth alongside weak finance and management systems. In Ghana, for example,

TABLE 3.1 Access to Utility Services by Sector in 2005 and 2017

Country Income Level	Access to Electricity (% of Population)		Fixed Telephone Subscriptions (per 100 People)		Mobile Cellular Subscriptions (per 100 People)		People Using at Least Basic Drinking Water Services (% of Population)		People Using at Least Basic Sanitation Services (% of Population)	
	2005	2017	2005	2017	2005	2017	2005	2017	2005	2017
Low income	24.00	39.63	1.62	1.36	5.25	63.88	50.14	60.74	26.39	32.63
Lower-middle income	57.41	77.40	5.04	4.90	15.34	94.82	73.00	80.88	48.41	59.33
Upper-middle income	90.52	95.86	16.12	15.19	40.41	111.63	90.80	94.77	80.57	87.60
Developing	63.97	76.94	8.90	8.41	23.57	95.14	75.47	82.32	57.03	65.32

Sources: Estache and Fay (2009); World Bank (2020c).

FIGURE 3.1 Access to services as classified by the United Nations Statistical Commission's Degree of Urbanisation: *top*, safely managed drinking water (2010–2016); *bottom*, electricity (2016).

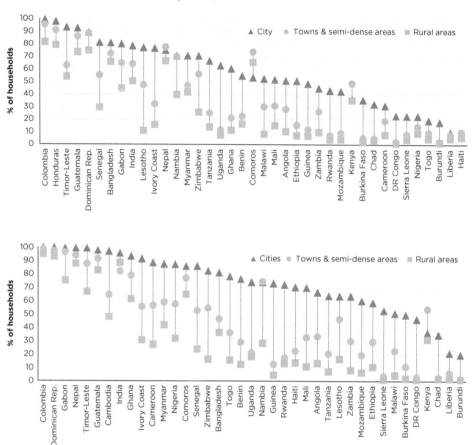

Source: Based on data from Henderson et al. (2020).

rapid urbanization has resulted in growing demand due to population growth far outpacing service supply, leading in turn to a declining share of the urban population with access to piped water, sanitation, and toilet facilities (figure 3.2). Similar patterns can be seen across rapidly urbanizing low-income countries.

Across Income Groups

An important question relates to the extent to which infrastructure services reach the poor. Estache and Fay (2009) highlighted that infrastructure shortfalls hurt the poor the most, driven by policy failures that do not extend services to

FIGURE 3.2 Change in access to piped water and toilets in Ghana, 2000–2010.

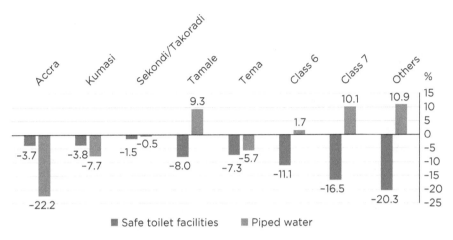

■ Safe toilet facilities ■ Piped water

Source: Based on data from World Bank (2015).

places where people are concentrated and tariff designs are inconsistent with the poor's cash flows and ability to pay.

Consistent and comparable data on access to infrastructure by various income groups are not readily available. We carefully analyzed data from household surveys from across the world, relying on a unique database of more than 6.3 million individuals from harmonized surveys, representing 54 countries with a combined population of 3,340 million people. These data cover the period 2015–2017.

For each country, we calculated the share of people with access to electricity, improved water, improved sanitation, and a cellular phone. Improved water is, by nature of its construction or through active intervention, protected from outside contamination, in particular from contamination with fecal matter. For some countries, mostly in Latin America and the Caribbean, the variable for water access did not provide specific information about whether it was improved.

Improved sanitation is defined by the World Health Organization as sanitation with sewer connections, septic system connections, pour-flush latrines, ventilated improved pit latrines, or pit latrines with a slab or covered pit. For countries in Latin America and the Caribbean, the improved sanitation variable was not available. Instead, we had "access to toilet" and "access to sewer connection." It is important to note that these estimates are likely to be upward-biased, particularly among low-income countries. The least developed countries are likely to have both low access to services and low capacity to collect data, meaning that the worst-performing countries are likely to be excluded from this analysis.

TABLE 3.2 Access to Infrastructure Services by Richest and Poorest 20 Percent of Population

Country Grouping According to Income Level	Electricity		Improved Water		Improved Sanitation		Cellular Phone	
	Poorest 20%	Richest 20%	Poorest 20%	Richest 20%	Poorest 20%	Richest 20%	Poorest 20%	Richest 20%
Low income	11.5	47.2	76.1	83.7	8.9	43.9	17.5	65.8
Lower-middle income	65.2	95.2	51.2	57.7	59.9	89.2	77.3	95.6
Upper-middle income	95.8	99.6	84.6	98.2	37.0	78.9	86.4	96.8
High income: non-OECD	99.5	100.0	94.0	97.0	38.8	79.7	88.1	92.3
High income: OECD	99.3	99.9					97.8	

Sources: Global Monitoring Database; World Bank Team for Statistical Development, using the Datalibweb Stata Package, latest survey available for 2005-2017.

Table 3.2 clearly shows that access challenges are most severe for poor households in low-income countries, particularly access to electricity and sanitation. While improvements in economic development levels tend to be systematically associated with improvements in access for the poor, sanitation remains a challenge well into upper-middle incomes. Access to cellular phones shows the fastest convergence, as countries move from low to low-middle incomes.

Measures of access to infrastructure need to be complemented by a nuanced understanding of affordability. While no empirically derived benchmarks suggest what families should be spending on infrastructure, practitioners have come up with a variety of rules of thumb. Estache and Fay (2009) highlight the prevalence of an informal rule suggesting that poor households should not have to spend more than 15 percent of their income on infrastructure services.

The affordability problem is likely to be particularly severe in low-income economies. On average, households in low-income countries spend 47 percent of their total budget on food, middle-income countries spend 29 percent, and high-income countries spend just 13 percent (Regmi et al. 2001). Similarly, income elasticities for food shrink as incomes grow, suggesting that lower-income countries make larger expenditure adjustments on food in response to changes in income (Regmi et al. 2001). Both of these findings suggest that lower-income economies and lower-income households in these economies allocate larger amounts of their budgets to subsistence goods. With competing demands for basic housing and community, allocating 15 percent of budgets to infrastructure services is quite challenging.

COVID-19, Infrastructure Shortages, and the Poor

Recently, infrastructure shortages alongside affordability challenges have exacerbated exposure and community contagion risk from COVID-19 across neighborhoods in cities. In fact, the coronavirus pandemic has cast a light on social and spatial disparities within cities as never before. A major concern is a city's economic geography: the interplay between its economic and physical setting.

A large share of city residents in Africa and Asia live in slums and informal settlements, where cramped living conditions and inadequate public services, especially water and sanitation, can exacerbate contagion. In Dar es Salaam, Tanzania, 28 percent of residents live at least three to a room; 50 percent of Abidjan, Côte d'Ivoire, is overcrowded. Residents lack open space and suffer from inadequate infrastructure, sharing taps and latrines often with 200 people per communal facility. In South Africa, only 44 percent of people have access to water inside their house, and only 61 percent have access to a flush toilet.

To respond to the emerging crisis in developing cities, the World Bank has developed a methodology that can help city leaders direct medical and other critical resources to potential hot spots, the places with highest exposure and contagion risk. The methodology is based on three globally sourced data sets that reveal population density, available floor area, and access to basic services such as taps and toilets (Lall and Wahba 2020).[2]

In Mumbai, India, for example, the slums of Dharavi face a triple challenge of extremely high population density, very limited floor space, and a scarcity of infrastructure, public space, and amenities. It is mind-boggling to think of the contagion risk presented by 68,400 people packed together on 1 km² of land without taps or toilets at home. Our hot spots methodology predicts that 5.2 million people in Mumbai are at risk of infection, even with lockdown measures in place. Figure 3.3 shows Mumbai's containment zones[3] as of May 9, 2020, as overlaid with predicted hot spots. More than 30 percent of the current zones are located in the predicted hot spots, with considerable coincidence in Dharavi's crowded settlements. It is likely that a higher prevalence of testing in many developing

FIGURE 3.3 Mumbai's COVID-19 infections in crowded and underserviced neighborhoods.

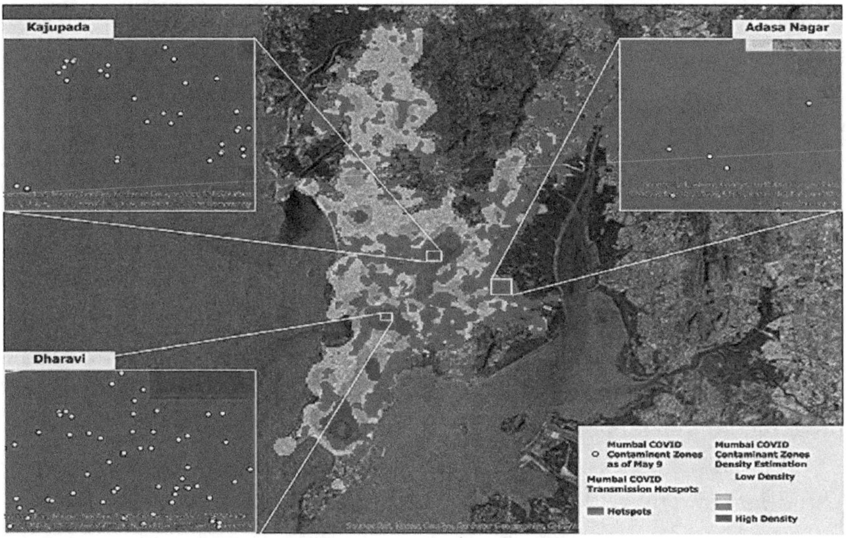

Source: Lall and Wahba (2020).

cities, especially in underprivileged neighborhoods, would improve match rates and more accurately predict infection. Hot spots have been identified in 15 developing cities to support city-led efforts to manage contagion and protect the vulnerable, with a plan to extend this identification to another 30 cities.

What We Know About Infrastructure's Contribution to Reducing Inequalities

A modest body of empirical evidence examines the contribution of infrastructure and services to reduce inequalities. In general, there appears to be consensus that physical infrastructure can help reduce income inequality. However, the economic dividends are contingent on complementary investments in other infrastructure (complementarities between water and sanitation) as well as noninfrastructure (infrastructure, housing, and health) sectors. In other words, infrastructure is a necessary but not sufficient condition for reducing inequalities. The evidence also suggests that gains from infrastructure expansion often accrue disproportionately to nonpoor households and nonpoor regions. Finally, subsidies may exacerbate inequality. Universal subsidies that apply across all consumption levels are essentially regressive, and thus the nonpoor, who use more electricity and water, get more subsidies than the poor, who use less.[4]

Infrastructure and Inequality

A recent meta-analysis of infrastructure's contribution to development shows that the lack of roads, electricity, and other basic infrastructure severely constrains economic development and poverty reduction, although the magnitude of such impact and the relevance of other factors is subject to debate (Timilsina, Hochman, and Song 2020) (table 3.3). The stage of economic development of a country impacts the nature of returns to infrastructure investments. Studies on Latin America (Sanchez-Robles 1998) sub-Saharan Africa (Estache, Speciale, and Veredas 2005), South Asia (Sahoo and Dash 2012), and a panel of 75 countries around the world (Esfahani and Ramirez-Giraldo 2003) found that returns from investment in infrastructure are positive and significant. In less-developed economies, where lack of infrastructure is a bottleneck for economic development, investment in infrastructure can propel growth (Kodongo and Ojah 2016).

Inequalities are exacerbated in the absence of basic physical infrastructure. A study of more than 100 countries reveals that a higher infrastructure stock—telecommunications, energy, roads, and railways—lowers income inequality (Calderón and Chong 2004). The study also finds that increasing infrastructure stocks reduces the income inequality measured by the Gini coefficient by 2 points in the five-year period and 11 points over a 35-year period. The impact is higher for developing countries. A similar analysis in sub-Saharan Africa found that improving access and the quality and quantity of infrastructure decreased the Gini coefficient (Calderón and Servén 2010).

Equality in access to physical infrastructure reduces income and spatial inequalities in the most lagging, forgotten, and unequal areas. Investment in highways was more effective in U.S. states at the bottom 40 percent of income distribution (Hooper, Peters, and Pintus 2018). Faced with limited resources, countries confront a crucial question on prioritization. A meta-analysis compares studies across regions employing different econometric tools and raises important questions on the type, quality, level of access, and magnitude of investment in infrastructure (Timilsina, Hochman, and Song 2020). Most studies have found that physical infrastructure helps reduce inequality and boost economic growth, a relationship more prominent in low-income countries.

However, in the absence of proper housing and health infrastructure, physical infrastructure has little marginal impact. How we define the quality of infrastructure matters when analyzing the impacts of infrastructure investments on inequality and economic growth. The marginal effect of infrastructure investment in poor areas with poor housing conditions, lack of basic health, and little education access is low (Chakamera and Alagidede 2018; Kodongo and Ojah 2016).

TABLE 3.3 Examples of Studies Analyzing Relationships Between Infrastructure Investments, Income Inequality, and Poverty Reduction

Study	Methodology	Findings
Calderón and Chong (2004)	GMM on dynamic panel data set for 101 economies for 1960–1997	Infrastructure stock is negatively linked with inequality; relationship is more prominent in low-income countries; estimated elasticity: –1.3830
Calderón and Servén (2004)	GMM on dynamic panel data set for 1960–2000 from 121 countries	Infrastructure investment played a larger role to lower income inequality in East and South Asia and played only a modest role in sub-Saharan Africa; estimated elasticity: –0.0464
Calderón and Serven (2010)	Panel data analysis of 87 countries for 1960–2005 focusing on sub-Saharan Africa; GMM technique for the econometric analysis; two scenarios for infrastructure shocks	Income inequality, measured in terms of Gini coefficient, is strongly negatively correlated with synthetic indices used as measures of infrastructure quantity and quality; correlation values range from –0.47 to –0.56
Chatterjee and Turnovsky (2012)	General equilibrium model of a closed economy	Public spending on infrastructure reduces income inequality in short run and increases it in long run
Sasmal and Sasmal (2016)	Panel data analysis for Indian states	The larger the public expenditures on infrastructure development, the higher per capita income and lower poverty headcount
Chotia and Rao (2017a)	ARDL bound testing approach	Infrastructure development reduces poverty in India
Chotia and Rao (2017b)	Pedroni's panel co-integration test and PDOLS method	Infrastructure development and economic growth lead to reduced poverty and urban-rural inequality in BRICS
Hooper, Peters, and Pintus (2018)	U.S. state-level panel data for 1950–2010	Infrastructure investment reduces income inequality; relationship is stronger in bottom 40% (by income) of population

Source: Timilsina, Hochman, and Song (2020).

ARDL = auto-regressive distributed lag; BRICS = Brazil, Russia, India, China, South Africa; GMM = generalized method of moments; PDOLS = panel dynamic ordinary least squares.

In Lusaka, Zambia, for instance, 6,542 cases of cholera and 187 deaths were reported between November 2003 and June 2004. Mapping the cases using a geographic information system (GIS) and a matched case-control method revealed a high concentration of the outbreak in regions lacking latrine and drainage systems (Sasaki et al. 2008). The insufficient facilities increased the risk of defecation in households. The study used a multivariate analysis to analyze the association of the outbreak between family members, income levels, latrines, drainage, and drinking water facilities. Results showed that households without latrines and who retrieve drinking water from shallow wells observed high cholera incidents. Complementary investment can indeed boost the protective power of infrastructure.

A broader point is that complementary investments are needed to magnify the impacts of infrastructure investments. Bennett (2012, 147) makes the point that "neighborhoods with the most piped water in the Philippines tend to exhibit the worst sanitation," and the welfare improvement from infrastructure hinges on the quality and complementarity of the investments. The study in the Philippines highlights the importance of clean water and sanitation investments as complements (Bennett 2012).

An important issue here is that the time frame for measuring the benefits of infrastructure is important. For example, sanitation has a health benefit that is generally paid off over a longer time frame (such as longer life expectancy). A research project examined the longer-term benefits of sites and services projects that the World Bank used in the 1970s and 1980s to lay down infrastructure ahead of the growth of urban settlements. Many of these projects were undertaken with the idea of preventing slum formation or setting up durable foundations for slum upgrading into formal neighborhoods. World Bank projects covered tens of thousands of households in more than 20 neighborhoods in cities in Brazil, El Salvador, Jamaica, Peru, Senegal, Tanzania, Thailand, and Zambia. Both types of sites and services projects—building on unpopulated lands (known as *de novo construction*) and upgrading squatter settlements—included infrastructure investment in roads, electricity, water, and public buildings (e.g., schools, clinics, community centers). The projects were discontinued during the late 1980s because their costs were high, despite anecdotal evidence that they had beneficial long-term impacts.

Researchers have recently evaluated the long-run outcomes of both types of projects on neighborhoods, including the costs and benefits of each program. Benefits included whether infrastructure investments increased the value of certain areas and whether and how each type of project shaped the urban landscape. In the long run, the sites and services programs are expected to increase land values, which translates into a potential tax base. Slum areas have low land value and require recurrent investments in upgrading.

In Dar es Salaam, sites with de novo development projects have higher land values than land in other parts of the city, including rich neighborhoods, partly because the sites and services areas have a higher building-footprint-to-plot area ratio (figure 3.4).

The research also shows that plots are bigger where investment was made ahead of settlement; these projects have higher land value per square meter than projects in upgraded areas, where roads are disorganized, plots are small and irregular, and the

FIGURE 3.4 Land values of de novo development projects compared with other neighborhoods (including rich ones) in Dar es Salaam, Tanzania.

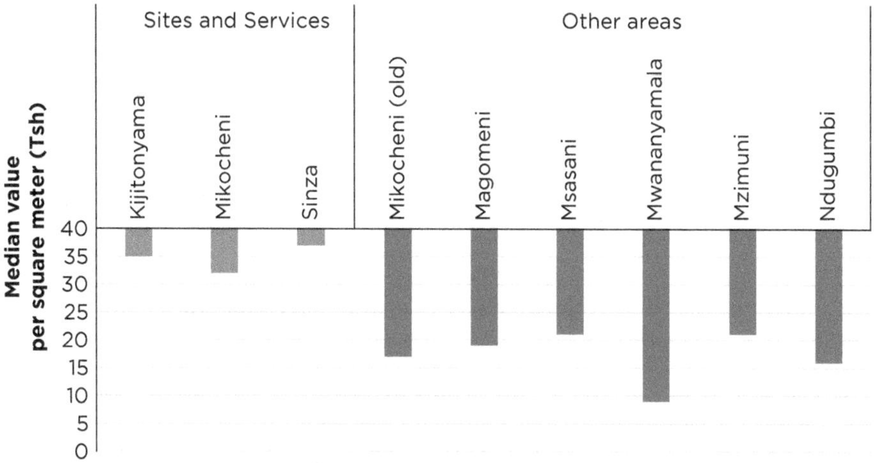

Source: Based on Regan et al. (2016).

benefit-cost ratio of valuing for tax collections would be prohibitive. The sites and services plans drawn in the 1970s closely match the shape of today's road network, showing that investment in infrastructure is enduring, shapes urban landscapes, and leads to higher land values, which are taxable and can finance future investments.

Interestingly, limited and poor infrastructure in poor areas has a behavioral impact on households. When Cebu, Philippines, improved piped water access, the households that invested in it evaded sanitation investment and responsibilities. An increase of one standard deviation in uptake of piped water increased diarrhea by 8 percent due to declining sanitation. There is a negative correlation between diarrhea and piped water for households but a positive correlation between diarrhea and piped water prevalence in the community, suggesting that clean water and sanitation are weak substitutes and neighbors' sanitation choices are strong complements (Bennett 2012).

Infrastructure is critical for poverty alleviation through its role in improving human capital and the resulting returns to improved health and educational outcomes over the long term. In particular, rural and urban roads enable households to access schools and health centers, while water supply, sanitation, and hygiene infrastructure reduce disease incidence. Similar to the nexus with growth, infrastructure is necessary but insufficient for poverty alleviation. The quality of education, cultural norms regarding school enrollment (especially for girls), and affordability of health and education services are all equally important for realizing the returns to human capital from the introduction of access roads.

Finally, investments in disaster risk reduction, especially flood protection infrastructure, are also important to avoid damages to infrastructure and assets and economic losses to firms and households, which in turn reduce the likelihood of falling into poverty. According to a World Bank study (Hallegatte, Rentschler, and Rozenberg 2019), global damages to transport and power generation infrastructure due to natural hazards reach an estimated US\$30 billion per annum, causing estimated economic losses to households and firms in the range of US\$391–647 billion. An estimated 84 percent of global exposure of transport infrastructure—mainly roads and rail systems—is due to surface, river, or coastal flooding (Hallegatte, Rentschler, and Rozenberg 2019). These estimates highlight the importance of flood protection infrastructure that could prevent exacerbating inequalities and putting more vulnerable people at risk of impoverishment due to disasters.

Spatial Efficiency and Equity Trade-Offs

While expanding infrastructure services such as water, sanitation, electricity, and telecom to the poorest communities and regions has merit in terms of enhanced welfare, there may be efficiency-equity trade-offs in expanding network infrastructure in equal amounts to all parts of a country. Spatial development policies and debates are often politically charged, with advocacy making a case for spreading infrastructure everywhere. The new economic geography literature (Lall and Lebrand 2019; World Bank 2009) suggests that infrastructure interacts with economic and physical characteristics to affect the comparative advantage and welfare of a region.

Such equity concerns need to be examined for network infrastructure—particularly transport, which is seen as critical in efforts to stimulate economic opportunities in poor and disadvantaged regions. In choosing where to prioritize spatially connective interventions, policy makers will need to assess trade-offs between the goals of spatial equity and aggregate economic efficiency.

Duhaut and Lall (2017) examined the impacts of enhancing transport connectivity among three types of areas in Nigeria: (1) remote rural areas that focus on subsistence agriculture and eventually trade their surplus with connected rural areas; (2) connected rural areas that are active in agribusiness and trade outputs with the nearby city; and (3) urban areas that produce tradable manufactured goods and trade with the connected rural areas, which in turn trade them with the remote rural areas. A simulation exercise showed that a 10 percent reduction in transport cost between remote and connected rural areas has a bigger welfare impact than a similar reduction in transport cost between cities and connected rural areas (13 percent versus 8 percent) (table 3.4). This

TABLE 3.4 Projected Welfare Gains from Reducing Transport Costs in Two Types of Areas in Nigeria

	Agricultural Share of GDP (Changes in %)		Agricultural Share of Labor Force (Changes in %)		Difference in Welfare (%)
Benchmark	0.47		0.45		
Reduction of 10% in transport costs in remote rural areas	0.45	(–4.3)	0.42	(–6.7)	13.4
Reduction of 10% in transport cost in connected rural areas	0.46	(–2.1)	0.44	(–2.2)	8.0

Source: Duhaut and Lall (2017).

difference suggests that local welfare gains are clearly higher for investments supporting rural connectivity.

However, for aggregate economic efficiency, higher gains come from focusing on the development of interregional corridors, linking the major urban centers. Upgrading road quality along these corridors can boost overall economic efficiency. In fact, the elasticity of local increase in the gross domestic product to transport investments is higher for the southern zones. This increase is largely because the marginal productivity of infrastructure investment would be larger in places where the network has been well established.

Analytic work of the type reported above is important for policy makers, as the implications of alternative choices in the spatial allocation of public investment will be known only once such work is done. Managing these trade-offs is challenging but not insurmountable. An important issue here is that resource allocation of durable infrastructure should follow principles of enhancing aggregate efficiency. As shown in table 3.4 above, transport connectivity supports structural transformation in remote rural areas, but complementary investments beyond transport would be needed to stimulate broader economic transformation. Policies that enhance welfare directly, such as improving health and education, would also be needed for local economic development.

Infrastructure, Binding Constraints, and Policies

As discussed, most studies have documented a positive causal relationship but with an impact of wide-ranging magnitude; in one metastudy, the elasticities of outputs to infrastructure were found to range between –0.06 and 0.52 (Rozenberg and Fay 2019). This range occurs because infrastructure is not the only constraint to growth; other binding constraints include unstable macroeconomic conditions, insecure land and property rights, and weak governance and rule of law. Infrastructure also needs to be delivered efficiently and cost-effectively in a way that is responsive to demand from firms and households. Equally important is the maintenance of such infrastructure, which is often neglected in developing and emerging markets.

In this regard, while infrastructure is a necessary enabler of growth, it is insufficient to bring about growth in the absence of tackling other binding constraints that affect the identification and design of infrastructure investment and their impacts on the poor. This section discusses some of the key binding constraints and policy designs, drawing on representative cases in cities across developing countries.

Dysfunctional Land Markets Hindering Infrastructure Planning and Delivery

In cities in most developing countries, dysfunctional land markets mean that the poor typically face a trade-off between livability and opportunity. The poor are often forced to make a choice between, on the one hand, settling in substandard housing and poor living conditions in slums and informal settlements in areas at risk of flooding or landslides to enjoy proximity to economic opportunities or, on the other hand, accessing formal land and housing at affordable prices in remote locations at the periphery but at the cost of lost productivity of four to six hours per day in commuting back and forth to jobs (World Bank 2020a). This trade-off is caused by the prevalence of weak and insecure property rights, lack of up-to-date spatial plans, and ineffective management of public land assets.

In fact, Tuck and Zakout (2019) estimated that globally only 30 percent of land and property titles are legally registered, which not only causes conflicts but also significantly delays infrastructure investments due to the inability to assemble the needed land and deterrent of private investment. In India, for example, land acquisition for private investment and infrastructure projects commonly takes around 10 years owing to litigation (Wahba 2019). In Egypt, only 5–10 percent of urban land and property is registered, and while about 80 percent of rural land and property has undergone a systematic first registration, more than 75 percent of these titles are outdated owing to inheritance, transfers, and mutations (World Bank 2006). In Romania, weak land and property rights (only 15 percent of land titles were registered in 2014) limit the absorptive capacity of regional development funds and delay the implementation of infrastructure investments (Wahba 2019). In all, lack of access to lands and insecure land tenure prevent the poor from finding livable conditions and accessing feasible infrastructure solutions.

The result is the proliferation of slums and informal settlements, which house nearly one billion people today. The delivery of urban infrastructure postoccupancy through slum upgrading or urban regeneration projects tends to come at a considerable additional cost, often far higher than servicing greenfield development, especially in locations with complex topography and limited preservation of public rights-of-way. For instance, Metrovivienda—a city agency for land developments in low-income neighborhoods in Bogotá, Colombia—quantified that the provision of basic infrastructure networks in slums costs three times more than new developments (Ferguson and Navarrete 2003).

Thus, investing in GIS is critical to underpinning spatial planning efforts, while the expansion of land and property registration and the reform of public land management are critical to enabling the delivery of needed urban infrastructure. In Tanzania, for example, a new urban management tool (the Local Government Revenue Collection Information System) that uses a GIS platform has been developed in seven Tanzanian cities as part of the World Bank's Tanzania Strategic Cities Project. The platform supports local governments' overall revenue collection, operations and maintenance (O&M) of infrastructure, tax reporting, and land management systems. As a result, the country saw a 30 percent increase on average in municipal own-source revenues along with transparent and up-to-date data on land systems, which allowed the country to be better prepared for future infrastructure planning and investments.

Infrastructure Design, Pricing, and (Lack of) Availability Penalizing the Poor

The urban poor, especially those living in slums and informal settlements, have limited access to network public infrastructure and thus end up paying for informal or privately owned infrastructure and services at higher unit prices than the rich. For instance, the urban poor often buy a battery to power basic electronic appliances, which is one of the most expensive ways to get electricity (Klein 2012).

In terms of mobility, the urban poor are also at a great disadvantage when it comes to access to jobs because inadequate public transport infrastructure fails to connect low-income neighborhoods with places of work in a timely and affordable way. In Nairobi, Kenya, the average commuting time is one of the longest in cities in the developing world (Lall, Henderson, and Venables 2017). Because of a lack of sufficient road space and the city's deficient public transport infrastructure, together with prevailing poverty, 70 percent of Nairobi's residents commute to work either by walking (42 percent) or by taking informal, privately owned minibuses called *matatus* (28 percent). Those unable to afford transportation walk to work; within one hour of the commute they can only reach on average 11 percent of the job opportunities in the city (Avner and Lall 2016). In Kampala, Uganda, the share of those who cannot afford transportation and thus walk to work is 70 percent (World Bank 2013a). With such limited affordability impacting the number of users of infrastructure services, operators' ability to reach a critical scale—especially in networked services—might be challenging, and the extension of infrastructure services to poorer neighborhoods might not prove economical.

It is against such backgrounds that subsidies are typically introduced. Subsidies are given on the supply side either to service providers and operators to cover gaps in investment expenditures that tariffs and fares and other related service revenues may be unable to recover (capital expenditure subsidies) or to cover shortfalls in operating expenditures due to losses from subsidized tariffs and fares (operating expense subsidies, which are linked per unit of service provided). Alternatively, subsidies are given on the demand side to consumers either as an allowance (e.g., for public transport use or water consumption) or per unit of consumed service (e.g., per public transport trip or unit of water consumption). Such demand-side subsidies serve as a form of income transfer for the poor or to plug the gap between the cost of the service and willingness to pay to enable the achievement of government's policy objectives (e.g., subsidizing the poor or incentivizing the use of public transportation systems to reduce congestion and emissions).

The challenge exists when subsidies are applied universally or without effective targeting, therefore leading to important leakage from the original intended beneficiaries—the poor. When the cost of subsidized tariffs is insufficient to cover capital expenditures as well as the cost of O&M of infrastructure systems, the systems therefore operate at a loss; such subsidized pricing hinders the ability to attract private investment and will require a constant outlay of subsidies to plug the deficit. This problem is often the case in water and sanitation as well as in mass transit.

In Brazil, for example, the government launched the National Sanitation Plan in 1971, which aimed to supply piped water in all urban areas. While in theory the policy aimed to achieve a pareto outcome by cross-subsidizing the high- and low-income users through tariffs, the plan prioritized water services over sewerage in fast-growing areas (Gamper-Rabindran, Khan, and Timmins 2010). The allocation of water has been politically motivated where policies have favored prosperous urban counties, while the poorer areas of northeastern and northern Brazil continue to see poor piped water coverage. The ineffective, mistargeted policy resulted in worsening welfare in these regions: a low allotment of water coverage (31 percent), even by 2000, and a high infant mortality rate (15 percent of total infant mortality across the country).

Another example of inefficient pricing design can be found in Uganda, where there is still limited access to basic services. In 2017, 20 years after the water reform in 1998, only 49 percent had access to basic drinking water services, which is far below the average for all developing countries (82 percent, calculated using recent World Development Indicators). This poor access mainly exists because Uganda's reform has not promoted cost recovery through a well-designed user fee structure. A uniform fee was charged across all cities and customer categories, causing a shortfall in cost recovery across served areas (World Bank 2013b).

By contrast, well-targeted subsidies for the poor—especially if embedded within a price discrimination system that can enable cross subsidization between the rich and poor—are a more efficient way to enable access to infrastructure services without compromising the ability to ensure cost recovery. One example is the use of block tariffs for water supply and electricity wherein consumption is divided into brackets with differential unit pricing. The first bracket—serving to meet basic water and electricity consumption needs—is priced at an affordable level and is cross-subsidized by the tariff rate for subsequent higher brackets, which reflect the consumption patterns of middle- and upper-income groups, including swimming pools and a larger volume of electrical appliances. This approach enables the poor to enjoy affordable access to a minimum level of service reflecting their needs. Similarly, in the transport sector, cross subsidies can occur between modes of travel such as by charging drivers of private cars for the externalities they impose in terms of congestion, pollution, and greenhouse gas emissions and using the proceeds to subsidize public transportation systems.

In terms of infrastructure design, prepaid metering is another approach that reduces the perceived risk to infrastructure service providers from extending service to the urban poor while also being helpful for the households themselves, as it allows them to prepurchase the amount of water and electricity that meets their needs and monitor consumption and use closely. Finally, differentiating the quality of the service, such as installing communal water standpipes—or condominial sewerage systems as is commonly used in some Brazilian cities—versus individual water connections, is another way of lowering costs and enhancing affordability for the poor and limited-income groups.

Ultimately, the government can also use the general budget to provide subsidies to the poor to address affordability issues. However, governmental subsidies often yield a critical issue in that they do not contribute to expanding access and benefit only those who already have connections (Klein 2012).

In this context, governments should regularly measure the welfare increase associated with infrastructure services provided and ensure that pro-poor infrastructure policies are carefully designed in an effective, efficient, and equitable

FIGURE 3.5 Access to basic services by city size in Colombia, 1964–2005.

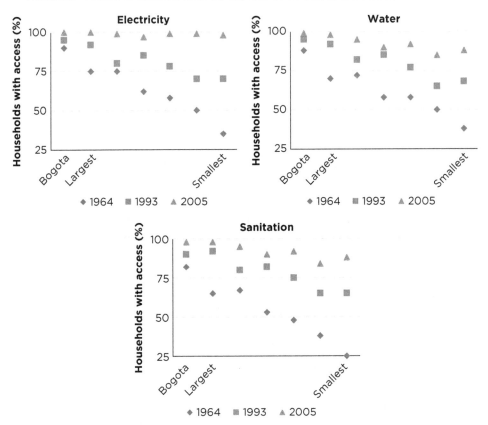

Source: Based on World Bank (2013b).

way. In Colombia, for example, basic services coverage has become nearly universal across all sizes of cities. This coverage is a significant improvement over the last 40 years, given that in 1964 only some residents in Bogotá and other large cities had access to electricity, water, and sanitation; the coverage was even lower in smaller cities (figure 3.5). The main enabler of this successful expansion was policy reforms that allowed competitive user fees and cross subsidies to cover service costs. The residential water fees more than doubled on average between 1990 and 2001, but the government's price discrimination policy kept water service affordable. As a result, poor households spent on average less than 5 percent of their income on utility services (World Bank 2004).

Expanding the Poor's Access to Infrastructure Services Through Targeted Subsidies

To better serve poor households that are excluded from infrastructure and service delivery, the Global Partnership for Results Based Approaches (GPRBA), formerly the Global Partnership for Outputs Based Aid (GPOBA), a multidonor trust fund administered by the World Bank, was established to fund, design, demonstrate, and document results-based approaches to improve delivery of basic infrastructure and social services to the poor in developing countries. As of June 2020, the GPRBA had built a portfolio of 55 pilot projects with US$274 million in subsidy funding that had reached more than 11 million beneficiaries across 34 countries, including 11 projects in fragile and conflict-affected situations. The results include last-mile connections to basic infrastructure provided to the poor in developing countries: around 20,000 houses with piped water connections in Indonesia, more than 12,000 network-connected toilets built in Morocco, and more than 27,000 biogas plans in low-income households in Nepal, to name a few of the investment projects' results (GPOBA 2017).

By definition, GPRBA subsidies are provided to private service providers at a previously agreed subsidy rate against the achievement of results. There is also an emphasis on shifting subsidies away from outputs toward outcomes—for example, going beyond subsidizing water and sanitation connections to expand poor people's access in slums to include dimensions of sustainability of service delivery (reduction in nonrevenue water) or improved health outcomes. Results are verified through independent third-party monitoring before payment is made. GPRBA schemes thus emphasize accountability by transferring the performance risk to the service provider. There is also emphasis on innovation in finding solutions to improve quality, accessibility, and affordability of services to the poor and spin-off effects of strengthening local markets related to service delivery. In Kenya, for example, every US$1 spent on community water connections realized around US$3–6 of economic benefits, including the unexpected benefit of promoting small-scale local enterprises (GPOBA 2017).

The rationale for the subsidies varies based on the difference between affordability/willingness to pay and the cost of the service, which in turn varies depending on the service in question. For instance, in urban transport systems, affordability for poor households is typically measured as a range of between 6 and 15 percent of monthly income (GPOBA 2016). The difference between the cost of the service provided by a private sector operator and the affordability of the household would be contributed through the subsidy.

Securing Financing Needed for O&M of Infrastructure Systems

Limited investment in O&M often results in the rapid degradation of existing infrastructure and increases overall replacement costs. Not surprisingly, maintaining infrastructure and operating expenses often requires more funds than capital expenditure. According to a recent study by the World Bank, average annual O&M costs for the water and sanitation sector include more than 50 percent of the total annual expenditure for service delivery, exceeding actual capital investment costs (Rozenberg and Fay 2019).

However, it is difficult for cities to recoup these tremendous O&M costs in general. In fact, 40 percent of utilities in low- and middle-income countries cannot fully cover O&M costs through user fees. For example, Vietnam has successfully increased electricity coverage from only 14 percent in the early 1990s to almost universal coverage today. A public enterprise established in 1995 kept prices well below cost and leveraged fiscal transfers for the rapid service expansion. However, the success in quantity increase did not come with the desired quality; the service was inefficient and spotty with frequent outages (World Bank 2007, 2013b). Moreover, the strain on the budget and low revenues from electricity services led the Vietnam Electricity Corporation to focus on profitable ancillary businesses rather than on improving services in the long term. As such, the failure to meet the minimum requirements for maintenance results in a significant inefficiency and reduction in the lifetime of infrastructure and in turn increases replacement costs by around 60 percent (Rozenberg and Fay 2019).

Therefore, securing enough funding resources for O&M in infrastructure investment plans from the outset is a prerequisite for successful provision of infrastructure and services for all. Setting up appropriate tariffs that cover O&M costs and improving the efficiency of service delivery (e.g., through tackling nonrevenue water due to systems leakages or illegal connections while at the same time expanding coverage) are critical steps for ensuring sustainable service delivery.

Private Participation in Infrastructure

In 2019, the amount of private investment commitments in infrastructure in low- and middle-income countries reached US$96.7 billion across 62 countries, some 3 percent below the 2018 levels (World Bank 2020b). Such private investment commitments were made in 409 projects covering energy, transport, the information and communication technology backbone, and the water and municipal solid waste infrastructure. Transport was the dominant sector in attracting private investment, with 50 percent of total global commitments, followed by energy, with 40 percent of total commitments. East Asia and the Pacific—on account of China—was the dominant geography, with nearly two-fifths of all investment commitments. Interestingly, 40 percent of the projects attracted international sponsors for a majority of their equity. With regard to financing, 62 percent came from the private sector, with 25 percent from international finance institutions and export credit agencies and 13 percent from the public sector levels (World Bank 2020b).

The overall trend of private investment in infrastructure is of a gradual decline, reaching 7 percent less than the five-year average of US$103.5 billion and nearly a 45 percent drop relative to the highest recorded level of private investment in infrastructure in 2012 (World Bank 2020b). Reasons for the low levels of private investment in infrastructure include a weak regulatory environment regarding public-private partnerships (PPPs), low own-source revenues and city creditworthiness with a perception of risk of nonrepayment, and unclear land and property rights, among other things (see chapter 15 for more details on private participation in infrastructure by sector).

The reality is that a small improvement in the efficiency of public spending in infrastructure—say a 20 percent improvement in efficiency of public spending of the US$420 billion that gets spent on infrastructure in 2017 in emerging and developing economies—could surpass the impact of all private investment in infrastructure (US$80 billion) in those countries (World Bank 2019). To achieve such efficiency improvements requires among other things better prioritization of infrastructure projects within capital investment plans through the application of cost-benefit analysis or other project assessment methodologies that evaluate beneficiaries and impacts versus costs.

Similarly, introducing outcomes-based financing and procurement approaches that allow infrastructure operators and service providers the flexibility to identify the optimal project design and technologies—through design-build-operate or relational contracting—could improve the efficiency of delivery of the services and minimize O&M costs throughout the life cycle of capital infrastructure. For example, instead of prescribing a specific sewage treatment technology, specifying the desired outcomes in terms of treatment quality and service coverage and leaving operators to design the relevant treatment technology could result in cost savings. Obviously, such outcome-oriented procurement requires stronger governmental capacity to prepare robust bidding documents and effectively and transparently evaluate different bids.

In short, private participation in infrastructure can succeed only if public sector capacity is strong, with appropriate legal and sector frameworks, transparent and competitive procurement, robust monitoring systems, and flexibility for adapting to unpredictable events, among others methods. As Estache points out in chapter 15, private ownership is not a key determinant of successful infrastructure performance; adequate local institutional capacity and institutional systems matter more. South Africa is known for successful infrastructure financing through PPPs. In 1999, the South African government enacted a law that defines a PPP process, specifies the necessary requirements and approvals, and spells out the institutional responsibilities of all entities involved (World Bank 2013b). While each step throughout the process for creating a PPP is clearly stated as an independent module, the regulation is flexible and adaptable by allowing updates as appropriate. Specifically, the National Treasury is responsible for approvals and reviews and conducts feasibility analyses; the auditor general oversees the entire PPP process, including annual contracting audits.

Conclusions

A comprehensive overview of the global evidence and literature distills three key issues. First, while there has been significant progress in expanding infrastructure across developing countries over the past two decades, the lowest-income countries are still far from meeting the needs of universal access, particularly to electricity and sanitation. In addition, considerable gaps exist in access across income groups and subnational regions, with these differences being particularly pronounced in low-income countries.

Second, investments and policies that promote equality in access to physical infrastructure tend to reduce income and spatial inequalities. Calderón and Chong (2004) and Calderón and Servén (2010) found that increased access to infrastructure services can decrease income inequality (measured in terms of the Gini coefficient), with the relationship being stronger in low-income economies.

Third, the contribution of infrastructure in reducing inequalities is strongly contingent on complementary investments across and beyond infrastructure as well as a household's ability to pay for infrastructure and complementary services. Overall, the poor are heavily reliant on basic infrastructure and essential services; lack of access to networked services results in a greater financial burden on the poor than on the rich because the poor must procure services from private providers at much higher unit rates.

Tackling the lack of physical infrastructure access is a necessary but not sufficient condition for economic growth and welfare gains for the poor. To realize the potential benefits of infrastructure investments, it is critical to put in place an integrated set of policies that aims to address other binding constraints, including distorted land and housing markets, the pricing system, and inefficient implementation of infrastructure. The absence of credible records on land and property titles not only causes conflicts but also hinders welfare gains to households and livability enhancement because infrastructure investments would be significantly delayed due to the inability to assemble the needed land and deter private investment. Thus, investment in a GIS platform has been considered an efficient and effective measure for rapidly expanding land and property registration while underpinning spatial planning and reform of public land management to enable the delivery of needed infrastructure in a timely manner. It is equally important to note that infrastructure can lead to economic growth only if the investment climate, such as labor, tax, and anticorruption regulations, is adequately reformed.

The public sector has also planned and implemented various policy options to optimize user fees and subsidies. A common lesson from global cases is that a well-targeted price discrimination system can be an efficient way to enable access to infrastructure services without compromising the ability to ensure cost recovery. However, caution is warranted to avoid failure: the designed policies must follow clear and coherent rules of thumb that value effectiveness, efficiency, and equity, building on a consensus among stakeholders.

To help countries and cities better serve poor households that are excluded from infrastructure and service delivery, the World Bank has invested US$274 million in subsidy funding that has reached more than 11 million beneficiaries through the GPRBA, a multidonor trust fund established to fund, design, demonstrate, and document results-based approaches. Such investments are expected to further expand, acknowledging the importance of last-mile connectivity with local communities for both alleviating poverty and improving welfare.

Inadequate O&M also increases the burden of infrastructure costs for municipalities, households, and especially the poor because of the rapid degradation of existing infrastructure and the increase in overall replacement costs. Experiences around the world suggest that setting up appropriate tariffs that cover O&M costs and improving the efficiency of service delivery are critical steps for ensuring sustainable service delivery.

Finally, it should be noted that private investments in infrastructure are not a silver bullet that can address all the infrastructure financing challenges. Global examples suggest that private participation can succeed only if public financial management and policy frameworks are put in place correctly. A small improvement in the public financial management of infrastructure could surpass the impact of all private investment in infrastructure in emerging and developing economies at large. Similarly, introducing outcomes-based financing and procurement approaches would provide infrastructure operators and service providers with the flexibility to identify the optimal project design and technologies, to improve the efficiency of delivery of the services, and to minimize O&M costs.

Summary

- While there has been significant progress in expanding infrastructure across developing countries over the past two decades, the lowest-income countries are still far from meeting the needs of universal access, particularly to electricity and sanitation.
- Considerable gaps exist in access to infrastructure services across income groups and subnational regions, with these differences being particularly pronounced in low-income countries.
- Investments and policies that promote equality in access to physical infrastructure tend to reduce income and spatial inequalities.
- The contribution of infrastructure to reducing inequalities is strongly contingent on complementary investments across and beyond infrastructure as well as a household's ability to pay for infrastructure and complementary services.

Notes

1. The United Nations Statistical Commission's classification of Degree of Urbanisation identifies three types of settlements: (1) cities, which have a population of at least 50,000 inhabitants in contiguous dense grid cells (> 1,500 inhabitants per km²); (2) towns and semidense areas, which have a population of at least 5,000 inhabitants in contiguous grid cells with a density of at least 300 inhabitants per km²; and (3) rural areas, which consist mostly of low-density grid cells.

2. Data on where people live come from WorldPop and Facebook; data on key services are accessed through Open Street Map. The density and floor space data are available for 100 × 100 m grids, giving us fine-grained information at the subneighborhood level. We also partnered with the German Aerospace Center to access its innovative World Settlement Footprint 3-D product (WSF-3D), which provides information on the height of buildings, making it possible to estimate floor area available in a given building.

3. Containment zones are identified based on the number of active cases where stringent measures are taken to prevent contagion.

4. Reforming subsidies is hard, as these lead to rent seeking and are the currency of political patronage.

References

Avner, Paolo, and Somik Lall. 2016. "Matchmaking in Nairobi: The Role of Land Use." Working paper No. 7904. Washington, DC: World Bank.

Bennett, Daniel. 2012. "Does Clean Water Make You Dirty? Water Supply and Sanitation in the Philippines." *Journal of Human Resources* 47(1): 146–173.

Calderón, César, and Alberto Chong. 2004. "Volume and Quality of Infrastructure and the Distribution of Income: An Empirical Investigation." *Review of Income and Wealth* 50(1): 87–106.

Calderón, César, and Luis Servén. 2004. "The Effects of Infrastructure Development on Growth and Income Distribution." World Bank Policy Research Working Paper No. 3400. Washington, DC: World Bank.

Calderón, César, and Luis Servén. 2010. "Infrastructure and Economic Development in Sub-Saharan Africa." *Journal of African Economies* 19: i13–i87.

CCLFA. 2015. "The State of City Climate Finance." New York: City Climate Finance Leadership Alliance.

Chakamera, Chengete, and Paul Alagidede. 2018. "Electricity Crisis and the Effect of CO2 Emissions on Infrastructure-Growth Nexus in Sub Saharan Africa." *Renewable and Sustainable Energy Reviews* 94 (October): 945–958.

Chatterjee, Santanu, and Stephen J. Turnovsky. 2012. "Infrastructure and Inequality." *European Economic Review* 56: 1730–1745.

Chotia, Varun, and N. V. M. Rao. 2017a. "An Empirical Investigation of the Link Between Infrastructure Development and Poverty Reduction: The Case of India." *International Journal of Social Economics* 44(12): 1906–1918.

———. 2017b. "Investigating the Interlinkages Between Infrastructure Development, Poverty and Rural-Urban Income Inequality: Evidence from BRICS Nations." *Studies in Economics and Finance* 34(4): 466–484.

Duhaut, Alice, and Lall Somik. 2017. "Spatial Equity Efficiency Tradeoffs in Infrastructure Investments: Application to Nigeria." Mimeo.

Esfahani, Hadi, and Maria Ramirez-Giraldo. 2003. "Institutions, Infrastructure, and Economic Growth." *Journal of Development Economics* 70(2): 443–477.

Estache, Antonio, and Marianne Fay. 2009. "Current Debates on Infrastructure Policy: Commission on Growth and Development." Working paper. Washington, DC: World Bank.

Estache, Antonio, Biagio Speciale, and David Veredas. 2005. "How Much Does Infrastructure Matter to Growth in Sub-Saharan Africa?" European Center for Advanced Research in Economics working paper. Universite Libre de Bruxelles, Belgium. Washington, DC: World Bank.

Ferguson, Bruce, and Jesus Navarrete. 2003. "A Financial Framework for Reducing Slums: Lessons from Experience in Latin America." *Environment and Urbanization* 15(2): 201–215.

Gamper-Rabindran, Shanti, Shakeeb Khan, and Christopher Timmins. 2010. "The Impact of Piped Water Provision on Infant Mortality in Brazil: A Quantile Panel Data Approach." *Journal of Development Economics* 92(2): 188–200.

GPOBA (Global Partnership for Output-Based Aid). 2016. *Analyzing the Use of Output-Based Aid (OBA) in Urban Transport.* Washington, DC: Global Partnership on Output-Based Aid.

———. 2017. *Basic Infrastructure for the Poor: Results of DFID Support for Results-Based Financing through GPOBA.* Washington, DC: World Bank.

Hallegatte, Stephane, Jun Rentschler, and Julie Rozenberg. 2019. *Lifelines: The Resilient Infrastructure Opportunity.* Washington, DC: World Bank.

Henderson, J. Vernon, Vivian Liu, Cong Peng, and Adam Storeygard. 2020. *Demographic and Health Outcomes by Degree of Urbanisation: Perspective from a New Classification of Urban Areas.* Luxembourg: Publications Office of the European Union.

Hooper, Emma, Sanjay Peters, and Patrick A. Pintus. 2018. "To What Extent Can Long-term Investments in Infrastructure Reduce Inequality?" *Journal of Infrastructure, Policy and Development* 2(2): 858.

Klein, Michael. 2012. "Infrastructure Policy: Basic Design Options." Working paper No. 6274. Washington, DC: World Bank.

Kodongo, Odongo, and Kalu Ojah. 2016. "Does Infrastructure Really Explain Economic Growth in Sub-Saharan Africa?" *Review of Development Finance* 6(2): 105–125.

Lall, Somik V., Vernon Henderson, and Anthony J. Venables. 2017. *Africa's Cities: Opening Doors to the World.* Washington, DC: World Bank.

Lall, Somik V., and Mathilde Lebrand. 2019. "Who Wins, Who Loses? Understanding the Spatially Differentiated Effects." Working paper No. 8806. Washington, DC: World Bank.

Lall, Somik V., and Sameh Wahba. 2020. "No Urban Myth: Building Inclusive and Sustainable Cities in the Pandemic Recovery." World Bank, June 18. https://www.worldbank.org/en /news/immersive-story/2020/06/18/no-urban-myth-building-inclusive-and-sustainable -cities-in-the-pandemic-recovery.

Regan, Tanner, Dzhamilya Nigmatulina, Neeraj Baruah, Ferdinand Rauch, and Guy Michaels. 2016. "Sites and Services and Slum Upgrading in Tanzania." Annual Bank Conference on Africa: Managing the Challenges and Opportunities of Urbanization in Africa, Oxford, UK, July 13, 2016.

Regmi, Anits, M. S. Deepak, James L. Seale Jr., and Jason Bernstein. 2001. "Cross-Country Analysis of Food Consumption Patterns." In *Changing Structure of Global Food Consumption and Trade,* ed. Anita Regmi. International Agriculture and Trade Outlook No. WRS-01-1. Washington, DC: U.S. Department of Agriculture.

Rozenberg, Julie, and Marianne Fay. 2019. *Beyond the Gap: How Countries Can Afford the Infrastructure They Need While Protecting the Plane.* Washington, DC: World Bank.

Sahoo, Pravakar, and Ranjan Kumar Dash. 2012. "Economic Growth in South Asia: Role of Infrastructure." *Journal of International Trade & Economic Development* 21(2): 217–252.

Sanchez-Robles, Blanca. 1998. "Infrastructure Investment and Growth: Some Empirical Evidence." *Contemporary Economic Policy* 16(1): 98–108.

Sasaki, Satoshi, Hiroshi Suzuki, Kumiko Igarashi, Bushimbwa Tambatamba, and Philip Muleng. 2008. "Spatial Analysis of Risk Factor of Cholera Outbreak for 2003–2004 in a Peri-Urban Area of Lusaka, Zambia." *American Journal of Tropical Medicine and Hygiene* 79(3): 414–421.

Sasmal, Ritwik, and Joydeb Sasmal. 2016. "Public Expenditure, Economic Growth and Poverty Alleviation." *International Journal of Social Economics* 43(6): 604–618.

Straub, Stephane. 2008. "Infrastructure and Growth in Developing Countries: Recent Advances and Research Challenges." Working paper No. 4460. Washington, DC: World Bank.

Timilsina, Govinda, Gal Hochman, and Ze Song. 2020. "Infrastructure, Economic Growth, and Poverty." Working paper No. 9258. Washington, DC: World Bank.

Tuck, Laura, and Wael Zakout. 2019. "7 Reasons for Land and Property Rights to Be at the Top of the Global Agenda." https://blogs.worldbank.org/voices/7-reasons-land-and -property-rights-be-top-global-agenda.

Wahba, Sameh. 2019. "Land Administration and Geospatial Infrastructure (Presentation)." Washington, DC: World Bank.

White, Roland, and Sameh Wahba. 2019. "Addressing Constraints to Private Financing of Urban (Climate) Infrastructure in Developing Countries." *International Journal of Urban Sustainable Development* 11(3): 1–12.

World Bank. 2004. *Colombia Recent Economic Developments in Infrastructure (REDI): Balancing Social and Productive Needs for Infrastructure.* Washington, DC: World Bank.

———. 2006. *Egypt Public Land Management Strategy*, vol. 1, *Policy Note.* Washington, DC: World Bank.

———. 2007. *Vietnam Rural Energy Project, Implementation Completion and Results Report.* Report No. ICR485. Washington, DC: World Bank.

———. 2009. *World Development Report 2009: Reshaping Economic Geography.* Washington, DC: World Bank.

———. 2013a. *Harnessing Urbanization to End Poverty and Boost Prosperity in Africa.* Washington, DC: World Bank.

———. 2013b. *Planning, Connecting, and Financing Cities Now: Priorities for City Leaders.* Washington, DC: World Bank.

———. 2015. *Rising Through Cities in Ghana: Ghana Urbanization Review Overview Report.* Washington, DC: World Bank.

———. 2019. *Who Sponsors Infrastructure Projects? Disentangling Public and Private Contributions.* Washington, DC: World Bank.

———. 2020a. *Convergence: Five Critical Steps Toward Integrating Lagging and Leading Areas in the Middle East and North Africa.* Washington, DC: World Bank.

———. 2020b. *Private Participation in Infrastructure (PPI): 2019 Annual Report.* Washington, DC: World Bank.

———. 2020c. "World Development Indicators." Washington, DC: World Bank. https:// datacatalog.worldbank.org/search/dataset/0037712.

INFRASTRUCTURE AND CITIES

4

INFRASTRUCTURE AND URBAN FORM

Edward L. Glaeser

Cities are defined by their density, which enables the movement of goods and the connection of people. Transportation infrastructure is also meant to speed the flow of goods and people over space. Urban form reflects the interplay between the demand for space and the demand for proximity, and the demand for physical proximity is shaped by transportation technology. In this chapter, I review how past transportation innovations have influenced the location and form of cities and discuss both future trends and five policy questions related to cities and infrastructure.

Within metropolitan areas, the dominant effect of transportation technology has been to enable the expansion of cities and increase the amount of living space consumed by households. Horse-drawn omnibuses and subways enabled the spread of 19th-century cities. Elevators enabled vertical mobility, which further expanded the supply of space. Highways and cars expanded the reach of a 40-minute commute more dramatically. The car had a particularly dramatic impact on density and living space, because unlike older communal forms of transit, the car required no outside walking at any point along the journey.

Transportation innovations have also shifted populations across metropolitan areas as well as within metropolitan areas. The advantages of waterborne mobility drove the location of most premodern cities, from medieval Venice to Minneapolis. Only rarely did the location of roads have so much power before the age of the car, but access to rail seems to have boosted the urban population during the mid-19th century (Atack et al. 2010).

During the 20th century, the spread of highways was a great spatial equalizer. Transportation costs for goods fell dramatically, which allowed people and firms to move from areas where firms had a productive advantage because of access to rail, water, and natural resources to places where people like to live, such as the temperate locations along the Pacific Ocean. Consumer amenities are powerful predictors of urban growth in the wealthy world (Glaeser, Kolko, and Saiz 2001) but not in the poorer parts of the planet (Chauvin et al. 2017).

The impact of transportation technology on urban form takes decades and proceeds in three distinct steps. The first step is the vehicular innovation, such as the creation of the steam engine locomotive, the horse-drawn omnibus, and the car. The second step is to build a transportation network to accommodate the new form of mobility. The third step is to build or rebuild our urban spaces around the new technology and its network. Arguably, much of the world is still in the process of rebuilding its urban spaces around the automobile.

The connection between urban form and transportation infrastructure raises difficulties for the evaluation of transportation infrastructure. The simplest and often safest form of cost-benefit analysis simply asks whether the benefits to the users of a new road or highway can justify the costs of that highway. A more complicated task is to consider the entire transportation network and evaluate the overall improvement in mobility created by the new investment, holding location constant, as in Allen and Arkolakis (2019).

But a complete cost-benefit analysis would evaluate value created by infrastructure when the entire system, including housing and businesses, has rebuilt itself around the new roads or subway lines. This task is difficult because there is no such thing as an optimal urban form. This complete welfare impact of infrastructure can be evaluated within the context of a specific general equilibrium model, such as in Heblich, Redding, and Sturm (2018). Unfortunately, we are far from having models that we fully trust as a basis for future infrastructure investments. The Henry George theorem (Arnott and Stiglitz 1979) suggests that it is enough to know the impact of infrastructure on land values to capture the overall social benefit of new investment, but the ex post impact on land values is also unknown at the time of investment decisions and practically unknowable for land that is sufficiently distant from the infrastructure.

This chapter is largely historical and does not try to develop the general equilibrium tools needed for incorporating the impact of urban form on transportation evaluation. I illustrate that transportation investments have shaped cities over time, which suggests the value of embedding the malleable nature of the built environment into transportation analysis.

I start with a conceptual discussion of three core concepts that shape this chapter. First, as noted, transportation innovation always comes in three steps. Second, cities are nodes of a large transportation network and hubs of a local transportation network. Third, the impact of new transportation is mediated by the elasticity of the supply of local structures.

I then provide three historical discussions that suggest the enormous power that transportation infrastructure has had to shape cities over history. I have chosen to focus on transportation, but other forms of infrastructure, such as sewers, may be at least as important in developing world cities. Just as the urban ripples of transportation investment should be incorporated into transportation evaluation, the city-building effects of sewers and water pipes should enter into analyses of those investments.

Three Concepts

The first idea emphasizes a three-step process through which transportation innovation shapes cities. The second idea is that most cities are both the hub of a local transportation network and a node in a larger network that connects across cities and countries. The third idea is that both housing technology and regulation often limit the ability of infrastructure to change the built environment.

Three Steps of Transportation Innovation and Urban Change

In 1885, Karl Benz built his Patent Motorwagen, arguably the first true car. Henry Ford produced his first Model T 23 years later. By that time, the basic technology of the car had been established, but no country had yet adapted its transportation network or its cities to the car.

Cars first traveled along the dirt roads that were meant to accommodate foot traffic, carts, and bicycles, but smooth paving is more important for a car than for a horse or a pedestrian. Bumps and extra entrants coming onto a road have more impact when vehicles are moving more quickly. The U.S. government spent at least 60 years building a new transportation network for the car after Ford's first Model T. The construction of the Dwight D. Eisenhower National System of Interstate and Defense Highways may be the most famous episode in this network-building odyssey, but the building of limited access highways began in greater New York in 1907.

The final step of the process occurs when urban form reshapes itself around the technology and the network. After World War II, car-oriented suburbs were mass-produced, even within well-established metropolitan areas, to take advantage of the fast commutes made possible by highways. New metropolitan areas such as Las Vegas, which lacked access to the older forms of transportation, became accessible and grew thanks to the car and its network.

This three-part pattern repeated the earlier path followed by steam-powered trains, which depended even more heavily on the network of rails and also reshaped cities. In the case of waterborne transportation, major innovations (such as steamboats) and major network construction (canal systems) complemented one another.

The Erie Canal became more valuable because technology enhanced New York's value as a port. But the new technologies mostly used the old network of oceans, and the new network of canals typically relied on traditional barges. Nonetheless, those innovations also reshaped cities. Future transportation innovations, such as autonomous vehicles, are likely to follow a similar course.

Cities Are Nodes in the Large Network and Hubs in the Local Network

A map of the London Underground shows a central oval, which is the path taken by the ancient Circle line, connected to lines that lead off to far-flung parts of the metropolis. That central oval is the hub of the local transportation network. The other lines and aboveground roads are the spokes that connect to that hub. The hub is less compact than in smaller cities, for London's center includes both the financial square mile of the old city and the political capital in Westminster. That center city has seven rail stations with more than 10 tracks. Nonetheless, the basic structure of the metropolitan area's internal transport lines is clearly a center linked to periphery.

Almost all precar cities take this hub-and-spoke form, and often the central hub is a rail station. Transport hubs can be at the center of a city because they were placed there to begin with or because transportation is so important that the hub became the new city center. New York City's Grand Central Station was originally placed at the edge of the developed city; the city then re-formed itself around the station, which anchors the midtown financial district.

The hub of a metropolitan area is less obvious in the polycentric car-oriented cities that have grown up during the age of the car. In Phoenix, a rectangle made by Highway 10 and Highway 17 bounds the central city. Five different highway rays shoot off to the suburbs.

Cities are also part of an external transport network that links them to other cities close and near. Phoenix's airport lies right outside that rectangle formed by Highways 10 and 17. Los Angeles's Union Station, which is still at the center of the city, was once the western terminus of intercontinental rail trips. The Thames River was once London's connector to the North Sea and the world.

The internal transport network shapes the city; the external network explains the location of the city itself. Waterways significantly determined the location of most premodern cities. The rise of the train and the automobile has reduced the power of natural geography and made the accidents of road and rail location far more important. Some also argue that airports have come to play an outsized role in the growth of particularly metropolitan areas (Kasarda and Lindsay 2011).

Central nodes become more important when there are larger returns to scale in transportation. In the colonial era of 300-ton ships, there was a rough equality among Boston, New York, Philadelphia, Baltimore, and Charleston. As ships grew during the early 19th century, New York became the dominant node on the intercity Atlantic network in the United States. The large economies of scale in rail also abetted the dominance of particular cities such as Chicago and New York. Truck transport has leveled the playing field. The links between the within-city network and the across-city network are strong when the same mode travels within and between cities, as with rail and cars, and weaker when the modes are distinct, as with water and oxcarts.

Elasticity of Building Stock Determines Impact of Transportation on Urban Form

If all structures were malleable clay, they could react swiftly to changes in any external conditions. If a new freeway was built along a particular route to the central city, houses would immediately spring up near the freeway entrance, and the buildings at the city center would stretch a little higher to the sky. But structures are durable and cannot be easily relocated. Land use regulations and historic preservation commissions further limit streetscapes' ability to change. Natural geography also constrains the reshaping of cities. As Harrison and Kain (1974) emphasize, the many limitations on change meant that obsolete transportation systems have left sizable imprints on most older cities and that the impact of new transportation innovations may be limited. They also note that postwar building in metropolitan Boston was actually lower density than postwar building in greater Los Angeles. Boston was denser than Los Angeles because it was built before widespread automobile ownership.

The older cities of Europe were built when mobility was overwhelmingly pedestrian. Humans on foot and on donkeys are nimble and have little need for wide or even straight streets. Consequently, we still find dense mazes of narrow, winding streets in central Rome, Barcelona's Barri Gotic, and even Boston's North End. These neighborhoods still function superbly as pedestrian spaces, attracting thousands of tourists who just want to walk, but can be practically impassable to automobiles.

Cars are particularly demanding of street space, yet the durability of urban structures meant that many older cities could never really adapt well to the car. Indeed, one reason why Americans left their older eastern cities and moved to newer Sunbelt metropolises is that those new cities, such as Phoenix and Los Angeles, were built to enable the easy use of automobiles.

The elasticity of housing is restricted in green fields by regulation, which also mediates the impact of transportation on urban form. If a new train line into Paris runs through a leafy townlet at a distance of 50 km, the value of space in that townlet will soar, and the natural impulse will be to build more housing near the train station. However, if land use regulations block the supply of new housing, those regulations may also limit the benefits of building the train line.

Large Network and Urban Form Before the Car

Before the automobile, the world was spanned by three important transportation networks made of water, road, and rail. The water network was typically the most important for long-distance trade and, since it is mostly natural, persisted even during periods of political chaos. In places with high state capacity, most notably China, canal building extended the water network. The Romans built a road network that still influences the shape of urban Europe today. During the 19th century, the rail network made swift land travel possible and had a particularly large impact on urban growth in areas with productive land and initially low population densities, such as the noncoastal region in the United States.

Water and Urban Growth

Throughout most of human history, the connection between water and urban growth has been enormous. Water provided mobility but also safety, drinking water, and energy. If anything, the importance of water to urban locations is even more visible in the United States than in Europe and Asia. All of the 20 largest U.S. cities were on waterways in 1900.

The power of water in U.S. urban locations is so clear both because transportation costs were such an important part of early U.S. history and because the other factors that influenced European and Asian urban development mattered less. In the 19th century, the United States was a country of great agricultural abundance and enormous distances. Cities such as Buffalo, Detroit, and St. Louis all grew at major nodes of a transportation network that facilitated the flow of agricultural wealth toward the eastern United States. Waterways dominated that network until 1850.

Population was dispersed throughout Europe by the 13th century, probably in rough proportion to the ability of the land to feed its own residents. Luxury goods such as high-quality wool were shipped, and cities such as Bruges and Florence were important centers for the trade in cloth. But regions typically had limited food surpluses. Consequently, European cities did not grow up around the production and shipping of basic foodstuffs, as Cincinnati did as the U.S. "Porkopolis."

Christaller's (1933) central place theory emphasizes the link between modest local shipping and urban growth that seems to fit many parts of western Europe. In Christaller's view, small towns served local agricultural communities by providing commonly needed services such as blacksmithing and brewing. Larger towns provided rarer and less standard commodities. In this view, the point of cities is not to link to each other but instead to link to the surrounding countryside. Waterways still mattered for these small local towns, but they matter less than when cities exist primarily to facilitate the flow of grain or beef to the Atlantic and beyond.

Political and ecclesiastical factors were more important in the growth of European cities than they were for U.S. cities. Historically, cities were defined by the presence of a bishop, who could be a major temporal as well as spiritual force. Premodern Europe had an abundance of petty potentates, each of which supported a court and often a small city. The cultural flowering of urban Weimar in the 18th century, for example, came out of the interests of Duke Karl August of Saxe-Weimar and his mother.

Nonetheless, almost all of the large historic European cities are on waterways. As all cities need to import food to survive, the rivers often served as a nutritional lifeline and usually as a means of exporting manufacturing commodities as well. Cities often emerge at points where goods move from water to another transportation mode. Bleakley and Lin (2012) found that U.S. cities remain disproportionately located on the fall lines of major rivers, where goods need to be loaded on or off boats.

Exports were less important for imperial cities, such as Rome, that acquired their wealth through political and military power rather than through trade. For some of the most famous political cities, water seemed to have originally served for protection rather than transportation. The original settlement of Paris on the Ile de La Cite seems to have served primarily to protect the residents from raids. Similarly, the Tiber seems to have played a defensive role for the early Romans even after they built the Pons Sublicius that spanned the river. Horatius allegedly was able to defend the narrow bridge against the Etruscan onslaught practically single-handed. Water similarly served to defend Venice against land-based aggression.

Access to water was also important to provide drinking water and, during the early days of the Industrial Revolution, power. The capital of Massachusetts, for example, was relocated from Charlestown to the south side of the Charles River to provide better access to a good spring. Larger cities, however, tend to pollute or overtax their local water sources and must either purify or import water from lower-density locales through aqueducts.

Aqueducts represent another form of transportation infrastructure that has played an outsized role in enabling city growth. Waterborne pandemics, such as cholera, can be particularly fearful scourges on urban life. Other forms of water-related infrastructure, such as purification plants and Singapore's remarkable water-recycling system, can be vital for urban health, but they do not shape the forms of cities in the same way as transportation infrastructure. Similarly, power-related infrastructure is also vital for urban survival; however, since the coming of the steam engine, sources of power can also generally be relocated, and power can be moved along the electric grid.

Before those steam engines existed, waterways also served as a source of power and helped determine the location of early industrial cities. In 1769, Richard Arkwright patented his water frame that used water power to spin thread; two years later, he located his mill at Cromford, England, on the Derwent River. Industrial towns then expanded along the Derwent Valley. Some of these early factories were then visited by Americans such as Samuel Slater and Francis Cabot Lowell, who brought the technology to the United States and also located factories along rivers, such as the Blackstone River of Rhode Island and the Charles and Merrimack Rivers in Massachusetts. The textile mills on the Merrimack then produced the large factory towns of Lowell and Lawrence.

Steam power eventually made water less important as both a source of power and a means of transportation because steam trains could replace canals. But the Industrial Revolution also made transportation more important, since there was so much more to move; for a while, waterways became even more important.

The importance of waterways led to increased investment in artificial waterways to supplement rivers, lakes, and ocean. The Bridgewater Canal connected Manchester with the port of Liverpool in 1776. Liverpool's access to the waterways of the world would carry raw cotton to Manchester and Manchester's cotton fabric to the world. Between 1811 and 1831 as the cotton industry boomed, Liverpool's population rose from 106,000 to 195,000. Matthew Boulton, protoindustrialist and maker of Boulton and Watt steam engines, was one of the early supporters of the Birmingham Main Line Canal, which would eventually connect the other birthplace of the Industrial Revolution to the Staffordshire and Worcestershire Canal, which provided access to some of England's greatest waterways.

In the mature urban systems of 19th-century England and Europe, canals typically connected well-established urban areas. Cities and towns had emerged over centuries into any area with fertile soil, and canals made it easier for those places to connect with each other. Over a millennium earlier, China's Grand Canal had been built to connect the even more ancient urban areas of that civilization. In the 19th century, when the United States was sparsely populated, canals provided access to the natural wealth of the U.S. interior.

Chicago's real estate boom of the 1830s was precipitated by the news that the Illinois and Michigan Canal would make that city a major node on a transportation network that extended from New York to New Orleans. Cleveland's initial growth owed much to its location as the spot where the Ohio and Erie Canal brought commerce from the Cuyahoga and Ohio Rivers into Lake Erie. Buffalo was the western terminus of the Erie Canal. While later rail and road networks were built to accommodate new forms of transportation technologies, canal boats were an ancient form of transport. The innovations came from creating the locks and the organizations that built them.

Roads Before Cars

Just as canal boats are ancient, wheeled vehicles pulled by animals have also traversed our planet for millennia. For just as long, it has been known that some form of planking or paving facilitates the speedy rotation of those wheels. When terrain is rough, goods must be carried directly by animals, as they were on the Silk Road that connected Europe with China and the Incan roads that spread out from Cusco. Both Bukhara and Samarkand were great cities along that unpaved thoroughfare, although their existence long predated regular trade between Europe and Asia. Transport overland becomes much cheaper if animals can pull wagons.

The first and greatest of Roman roads was the Appian Way, built to enable the passage of both troops and military supplies through the malaria-filled Pontine marshes during the Samnite Wars. By the time of the emperor Hadrian, legionaries could march along Roman roads from Gesoscribate (Brest) to Byzantium, passing through Lugdunum (Lyon) and Mediolanum (Milan) along the way. It is hard to assess today the exact contribution that road access made to urban growth during the Roman era, since we lack clear data on population growth and on the other factors that might explain growth (Hitchner 2012). Nonetheless, Milan could not have emerged as the capital of the western Roman Empire had it not been situated in the middle of the Roman road network.

There is a robust literature that investigates the impact of the Roman road network on cities todays. Dalgaard et al. (2018) show a correlation between Roman road density with both population density in 500 C.E. and the density of economic activity today. Interestingly, Roman roads did not predict modern urban agglomerations in those parts of Europe that abandoned wheeled transport during the medieval period. Wahl (2017) finds that even today the parts of Germany that were in the Roman Empire are more developed, at least as measured by night lights, than the parts of Germany that were non-Roman. Percoco (2016) shows that the location of Roman roads in Italy predicts economic activity there today.

Roman roads also helped mold the internal shape of cities by contributing to the internal network that supplements the extent network. Garcia-López (2012) shows that suburbanization in Barcelona followed the path of old Roman roads that formed the basis for subsequent highways. Garcia-López, Holl, and Viladecans-Marsal (2015) show that Roman roads helped shape the highways of the Bourbons, and the presence of those roads predicts the level of population decentralization within Spanish cities today.

The fundamental problem of assessing the impact that interurban roads had on urban growth during the premodern era is the endogeneity of road locations. Roads and cities grew side by side. While the course of the Thames River was in place before the Tower of London was built, every road that led out of London owed its existence to the presence of the city.

The United States did build several large-scale roads to the west that clearly preceded the existence of the cities and towns that would spring up along their routes. The Philadelphia and Lancaster Turnpike connected Philadelphia with central Pennsylvania after 1795. That paved road reached the Susquehanna River and Columbia. While it was an impressive piece of engineering, none of the cities along its path exploded in population during the road's brief heyday. The National Road or Cumberland Pike was an even more impressive stretch of macadamized road running from the Potomac River to the Ohio River and then farther west. Towns such as Unionville, Pennsylvania, and Zanesvillle, Ohio, gained population due to their position along the road; however, these early roads were far less important pieces of infrastructure than either the waterways that preceded them or the highways that followed them.

The Train and the City

The train is our first full example of the three steps in technological innovation, vehicle invention, network-building, and urban transformation, which includes both the reshaping of older cities such as London and New York and the emergence of newer cities such as Los Angeles whose growth was enabled by rail.

The steam-powered vehicle itself required several distinct breakthroughs. James Watt first had to create his separate condenser steam engines, which required him to connect with and learn from a top scientist (Joseph Black at the University of Glasgow), a superb ironmaker (John Wilkinson in Birmingham), and a brilliant entrepreneur (Matthew Boulton). Converting reciprocating motion into the rotary motion that would turn a wheel required the sun-and-planet gear devised by Boulton and Watt employee William Murdoch. With that gear and his engine, Watt could produce the first working model of a locomotive and a steam-powered paddle-wheeler. Even so, it took 17 more years before Richard Trevithick built a steam locomotive that carried passengers up a hill. Cugnot's earlier steam wagon had little obvious impact on the later development of transportation technology.

While steam-powered cars can travel on streets, the early engines were both heavy and fragile. Trevithick's own engine appears to have lasted only three days before it was grounded by an accident in a rough road. Locomotives were better matched with rails that could reduce friction and avoid the chance of becoming bogged down in soft earth. Luckily, short stretches of rail already existed in the late 18th century. The Middleton Railway started hauling coal in 1758 by horse.

Building the world's rail network is one of the greatest industrial sagas of the 19th century. George Stephenson was an early locomotive builder, but he was an even more important railway developer. He was not the first railway builder, of course. Jessop engineered the Kilmamook and Troon in 1812; I have already mentioned earlier railways built for horse-drawn carriages. Stephenson's first railways, such as the Hetton Colliery Railways and the Stockton and Darlington Railway, carried coal. He added passengers to the Stockton and Darlington after 1833. Stephenson then built the Liverpool and Manchester Railway, which was the first railway to carry passengers between two major population centers.

The vast scale of railway building in North America required both engineering and organization innovation, which has typically been true for large-scale infrastructure investment. U.S. cities in the 19th century were able to invest in sewers and water mains because bond markets were increasingly willing to trust those cities with financing (Cutler et al. 2006). The creation of railroads was associated with the growth of stock markets and the development of the modern corporation (Chandler 1993; Jenks 1944). Railroads such as the Union Pacific were also subsidized with vast federal land grants.

The third step of the innovation process occurred when railroads transformed cities. The literature on the economic impact of railroads is dominated by the enormous contributions of both Fogel (1964) and Fishlow (1965). Fogel famously concluded that railroads contributed little to economic transformation in the United States because canals could have done the work. Fishlow estimated that railroads had a larger impact because he compared railroads with the canals that did exist in 1840, not the canals that would have been built if railroads had not existed.

Even if Fogel is right, the coming of the railroads still shaped the locational choices of people and firms. Los Angeles's population would not have reached 320,000 in 1910—four years before the opening of the Panama Canal—without railroads. Los Angeles's own boosters fought hard to bring the Southern Pacific Railroad to the city.

Atack et al. (2010) compare midwestern counties that received rail stations between 1850 and 1860 with comparable control counties that did not have a rail connection. In 1840, neither the counties that were treated by rail nor the control counties had an average urbanization rate of more than 3 percent. By 1860, the treated counties had an urbanization rate of 14.3 percent, while the control counties had an urbanization rate of 2.5 percent. Berger and Enflo (2017) perform a similar analysis on railroads and urban growth in 19th-century Sweden and draw similar conclusions about the last impact of railroad access on population growth.

Donaldson and Hornbeck (2016) advance the methodology of 19th-century railroad analysis by using the market access measures that come from international trade. Their work recognizes the general equilibrium nature of a rail network, which means that a new railroad in Ohio can increase the value of agricultural land in California. Their focus is on agriculture rather than on urban growth, but they conclude that removing access to all railroads in 1890 would have reduced the value of U.S. agricultural land by 60 percent. Donaldson (2018) similarly finds large impacts of railroad on the 19th-century economy of India.

Nagy (2017) also uses a formal general equilibrium model with specialization and innovation to assess the impact of railroads on U.S. urbanization in the 19th century. He estimates that railroads were responsible for 27 percent of U.S. growth before the Civil War, and that much of their impact occurred because they enabled urbanization. Fajgelbaum and Redding (2018) use similar methods and draw similar conclusions about the Argentine rail network.

This general equilibrium approach raises the even larger question of whether overall U.S. urbanization would have been significantly lower in 1890 without access to the rail network because eastern cities needed to import food from midwestern farms. Perhaps that transportation could have been done by canal, but Donaldson and Hornbeck (2016) seem to suggest not. Developing country cities today can import their food by water, which perhaps explains why urbanization in the developing world can proceed despite low levels of income (Glaeser 2014).

Local Network and Urban Form Before the Car

While the larger network shapes where cities locate within a country or a continent, the local network determines the shape of the city itself, most obviously in the premodern commercial cities such as Venice, Bruges, and Amsterdam that relied on canals for local movement. Almost all cities bear the imprint of the transportation technology that was dominant during the epoch in which that city came of age.

Walking, Wagons, and the Rise of the Grid

Amsterdam and Venice were exceptions. Movement within most older cities depended on walking, animals, and vehicles drawn by animals. Few cities predate the wheel or domesticated animals, so these modes of transportation have been almost universally available in urban history. (While the Incas had one of the few great civilizations without the wheel, even their greatest cities, such as Cusco, seem to have had fewer than 50,000 people.)

Pedestrians and animals can easily walk narrow, curved streets. Consequently, many of our oldest urban spaces have densely packed dwellings separated by semi-lightless alleys. Short blocks aid pedestrian maneuverability; in weak legal environments, defending road space against encroachment is difficult. A clear system of roads is a boon for strangers, but what strangers would be wandering around a modestly sized 11th-century town? Consequently, traveling through a medieval quarter can be dank and disorienting.

Wagons, which require less human labor per pound carried, benefit from wider, straighter streets. Urban thoroughfares that could accommodate the cart had the added advantage of providing fine marching space for triumphs and other displays of the power of potentates. The Romans built relatively wide paved roads even in lesser cities such as Pompeii, presumably to accommodate both wagons and the legions. Julius Caesar was sufficiently interested in the problem of street congestion that he banned wheeled vehicles from Rome for much of the day (Laurence 2013).

Street-widening is a simple accommodation of wheeled vehicles. A grid is a more complete restructuring of urban space to accommodate movement. Nowhere is that fact more obvious that in Barcelona, which provides pedestrians with a dramatic shift from the medieval alleyways of the Barri Gothic Quarter to Cerda's unique design for the Eixample district.

Grid plans are ancient. Mohenjo-daro in Pakistan appears to have been built on a grid 4,500 years ago. Yet, urban spaces have gone back and forth in their use of rectilinear grids, depending on the state of both transportation technology and political order. Grids also need to be defended against encroachment by abutters, who may put a structure in the middle of thoroughfares and convert public spaces into private space.

Bertaud (2018) provides a compelling argument for laying down grids even in areas that will not be occupied for decades. Certainly, grid users often express considerable satisfaction with the clarity of their street plan (Ballon 2012). Yet, we have relatively little hard evidence on the longer-term benefits of different road structures. We know only that these structures, such as Haussman's Parisian boulevards or the dense warren of streets in old Jerusalem, shape our experience of a city.

Streetcars and Omnibuses

New York adopted its grid in 1811, 16 years before Abraham Brower's horse-drawn omnibus provided the city's first public transportation. Horse-drawn buses and streetcars were a relatively simple technology relative to the steam engine loco-motive, but cities still went through the three stages with omnibuses. The basic technology was just a long carriage pulled by a horse, such as Trevithick's steam carriage, that could travel on existing streets. However, also like steam engines, horse-drawn omnibuses work better with rails that reduce friction. Rails were embedded into existing city streets to enable buses to move more quickly.

Finally, as streetcars made it far easier to commute longer distances, the city began to sprawl outward. New York's Greenwich Village was an early example of a leafy suburb that became connected to the city through a streetcar. Warner (1978) describes the growth of streetcar suburbs outside Boston that were con-nected to the city through streetcar lines.

The streetcars reshaped the city mostly by expanding its size, but there were more subtle changes as well. The streetcar was the mode of the prosperous; feet were the mode of the poor. Since the mode of the poor was so much slower, the poor started to live closer to the city center after the coming of the streetcar. Gin and Sonstelie (1992) document how this pattern of centralized poverty emerged in 19th-century Philadelphia. The poor could afford proximity to the city center only because they crammed into less-than-hygienic tenements. The rich, who paid for streetcars, gained access to cheaper land that enabled them to build more comfortable homes, such as brownstones in Greenwich Village and detached cot-tages in Brookline.

The streetcar, like the elevated railway that followed it, did not completely alleviate the need for walking. Travelers typically walked from their streetcar stop to their home. This meant that while streetcars could expand the city, buildings still needed to be close enough to a streetcar line to be reached on foot. The two modes of streetcar and walking enabled sprawl but still required density.

Subways and Elevators

In the first half of the 19th century, urban public transit innovation made animal power more efficient. In the late 19th century, transit innovations replaced living sources of energy with steam and electricity. Intraurban rail provided a faster alternative to the horse. Overhead electrification and traction provided mobility with less burning of coal. Vertical mobility increased with Elisha Otis's safety elevators, which were powered first by steam and then after 1880 by electricity.

Cities built new networks for their intraurban railways both to save space and to reduce the smoke created by the steam trains. London put its trains belowground. New York initially ran them aboveground. At their most basic, these urban trains were just like omnibuses on steroids. The city could expand farther. The rich were more likely to take the train than the poor, and the greater mobility of the prosperous continued to abet the decentralization of the wealth. Still, people had to walk to their train stops, so the basic pattern of walking densities persisted.

The revolution in vertical transportation may have had the most visible impact on urban form. Powered safe elevators were as crucial to the success of skyscrapers as the steel frames that define them. Before the elevator, residential buildings almost never reached above six stories, which still defines the upper limit of many older European cities. These two revolutions in urban mobility—urban rail and the elevator—shaped the city of 1910. The new towers rising in Chicago's Loop and on Wall Street reflected the ability to build up, thanks to the elevator; the apartment buildings on the Upper West Side of Manhattan reflected the ability to build out.

Heblich, Redding, and Sturm (2018) provide a quantitative assessment of the impact of the London Underground on the development of that metropolis between 1801 and 1930. They document that its introduction was associated with the spatial segregation of residences from workplaces and with the overall growth of the city. The authors provide a counterfactual of removing trains from London that suggests that "removing the entire railway network reduces the population and the value of land and buildings in London by up to 51.5 and 53.3 percent, respectively, and decreases net commuting into the historical center of London by more than 300,000 workers" (Heblich, Redding, and Sturm 2018, 3).

The Automobile and 20th-Century Restructuring of Urban Areas

While the 19th century's transportation innovations produced tall downtown buildings and immense public transit systems, the 20th century's dominant transportation innovation was the mass-produced, inexpensive internal combustion engine–powered vehicle.

Cars and Suburbanization

German engineers, including Nikolaus Otto, Gottfried Daimler, and Karl Benz, developed the internal combustion engine and the first cars. U.S. entrepreneurs, including Henry Ford, Billy Durant, and Ransom E. Olds, developed the mass-production techniques that made cars affordable. A new network was then built up around cars that included paved roads and limited-access highways. The federal government became a large-scale highway funder during the New Deal and especially after the Federal Highway Aid Act of 1956.

The rebuilding of urban space around the car began before World War II, with car-based suburbs such as Palos Verdes Estates outside Los Angeles. After World War II, the process expanded dramatically with help from the highway system and an expansion of federal support for home lending. The view that cars enabled the growth of suburbs seemed obvious even before economists had solid empirical tools for estimating the impact of highways on suburbanization. How could the vast number of U.S. suburbs without any public transportation have grown without the car?

Baum-Snow (2007) uses the 1947 Highway Plan, which designated routes between metropolitan areas based largely on military rather than economic benefits, to identify the causal impact of highways on suburbanization. He found that each new highway that runs through a city increases suburban population, relative to central city population, by 18 percent. He also documents that new developments clustered around the highway routes that provided fast access into the central city. In one way, the highways were just like 19th-century streetcars and subways in that they allowed the central city to sprawl.

But highways were also quite different from these older forms of mobility because cars are generally used from start to finish of a trip and require almost no walking at all. Indeed, that fixed time cost is responsible for most of the gap in average commute times between cars and public transit (Glaeser, Kahn, and Rappaport 2008). Office buildings clustered around stops on Chicago's El and New York City's Grand Central Station, but cars allowed dispersed low-rise offices and housing, enabling the consumption of vast amounts of land relative to all previous transportation modes. The ease of driving led many businesses to relocate away from dense urban centers to suburban office parks, where the space was cheap and there was plenty of parking. Garreau (1992) called these sprawling areas "edge cities," which captures the reality that both jobs and homes moved away from older urban cores.

Glaeser and Kahn (2004) discuss the decentralization of employment across U.S. cities and argue that few modern urban areas fit the monocentric structure of the Alonso-Muth-Mills mode.

People might commute as long as they always have, but the most common commute is now from one noncentral location to another, often at relatively high speeds. Space-intensive industries such as manufacturing were particularly prone to decentralization after the coming of the car.

Cars and the Rise of the Sunbelt

Cars and highways moved people across metropolitan areas for three distinct reasons. Some areas received more highways than others, and those areas with more highways grew more (Duranton and Turner 2012). It was easier to add car-oriented infrastructure into newer cities; consequently, there was a shift away from old metropolitan areas to new metropolitan areas. Highways eliminated most of the remaining transportation cost–related advantages of the country's northern and midwestern cities. Firms and people could move to areas that had other advantages, including a car-based infrastructure and a warm climate. That combination of rising populations and declining prices in the U.S. Sunbelt is best understood as reflecting a highly elastic supply of housing that was created by the combination of abundant highways, simple topography, and few restrictions on local land use.

The coming of the highway decreased the cost of moving goods over space. The real cost of moving a ton over a mile of rail has declined by more than 90 percent since the late 19th century (Glaeser and Kohlhase 2004). In the 19th century, cities grew because of access to waterways or coal mines, even in climates that were less than hospitable. In the 21st century, low transportation costs mean that few locations offer any natural production advantages because of proximity to either inputs or outputs.

When traded goods are easy to ship, it makes sense to build cities around amenities that are valued by consumers. The rise of Los Angeles in the late 19th and early 20th centuries provides an early example of a city whose appeal was tied to its Mediterranean climate. Throughout the 20th century, January temperature has regularly been the strongest predictor of metropolitan area population growth.

Retrofitting Older Cities for the Automobile

The final shift in urban form occurred within older cities that tried to fit cars into older urban infrastructure. In some cases, older neighborhoods were leveled to create space for highways. In other cases, highways were elevated to add extra road space and leave existing arrangements intact. As cities became more concerned about the local disamenities of elevated highways and neighborhood destruction, tunneling became more appealing despite its high cost.

Many of the most spectacular infrastructure projects of the past 75 years can be interpreted as attempts to retrofit older cities for the car. While many of Manhattan's bridges predate the automobile, the George Washington and Triboro Bridges were built to enable more driving, as were the major tunnels under the Hudson and East Rivers.

Caro (1974) argues that Robert Moses's attempts to allow cars into New York City were misguided failures, but there are no compelling economic studies analyzing the counterfactual. Older cities, such as New York City, were competing against cities such as Los Angeles that were overwhelming car-based. New York City suffered in the 1970s, but it is hard to know if that suffering was exacerbated or alleviated by Moses's infrastructure.

Current Innovations and Urban Change

In the speculative section, I consider two innovations that have the potential to shift urban form in the future: autonomous vehicles and telecommuting. These discussions are brief because these topics are more fully addressed in chapter 19 on automation and chapter 20 on the sharing economy.

Autonomous Vehicles

Autonomous vehicles can, in principle, eliminate the need for human labor to direct the path of a moving vehicle, which effectively reduces the time cost of driving. The first-order impact of autonomous vehicles will presumably be an increase in the number of vehicle miles traveled. Lower costs of driving should increase the willingness to drive long distances, which would normally lead to even more decentralized cities.

Autonomous vehicles are easy to fit with real-time pricing mechanisms that are toll based on the route traveled. Limiting congestion pricing to autonomous vehicles might also reduce the political backlash to congestion pricing. If autonomous vehicles led to a wider embrace of congestion pricing or automobile sharing, autonomous vehicles might do less to decentralize urban arears. If the congestion charge is applied following the standard Pigouvian formulas, it would only offset the lower cost of driving on crowded highways and in the urban core. On lower-density roads away from the city center, autonomous vehicles would work to lower the cost of driving and generate even more development on the exurban fringe.

Autonomous vehicles create particular advantages for the mobility of the young and the elderly. With autonomous vehicles, older people with weak eyesight could remain in homes that are accessible only by car. Autonomous vehicles might also reduce time spent by suburban parents ferrying teenage children to far-flung activities. These possibilities increase the centrifugal power of driverless cars.

Autonomous vehicles have a particular advantage in ride-sharing because they can travel around the city on their own. Improved bus or ride-sharing services will be more valuable in moderately dense environments. The ability to design dedicated neighborhoods for autonomous vehicles, such as the ones that Sidewalk

Labs designed in Toronto, enhances the natural complementarity between autonomous driving and urban density. An autonomous vehicle on a dedicated highway may be able to drive safely at 150 miles per hour, thereby eliminating much of the speed advantage currently enjoyed by interurban rail. The more that autonomous vehicles are shared vehicles, the more they are likely to increase the demand for urban proximity.

Telecommuting

For decades, pundits have predicted that the ability to connect electronically would make face-to-face interactions and the cities that enable those interactions obsolete. For decades, those seers have largely been wrong, perhaps because electronic interactions and face-to-face interactions have been complements rather than substitutes or perhaps because other forces made cities more attractive in the late 20th century (Gaspar and Glaeser 1998).

Yet, the COVID-19 pandemic has made working from home the new normal for vast swaths of the global economy. Bureau of Labor Statistics data show that about 50 million Americans switched to remote work in May 2020. The education gap associated with telecommuting was enormous. Almost 70 percent of Americans with advanced degrees but only 5 percent of American high school dropouts were working remotely. The knowledge workers in the large cluster known as professional and business services were able to keep working online, but the 32 million Americans working in retail trade, leisure, and hospitality had a more difficult time.

Many businesses have already declared that they are sticking with remote working after the pandemic ends. Bartik et al. (2020) report that more than 40 percent of firms in their sample of small businesses say that 40 percent or more of their workers who switched to remote work will continue to work remotely. Some firms have discovered that working remotely is less painful than they expected and have now paid the fixed costs of learning the new technology. Nonetheless, a switch to telecommuting could easily reduce the demand for big-city office space going forward. Even a modest switch to telecommuting, involving a few days a week or 10 percent of the population, could have a significant impact on urban traffic congestion and commuting costs.

A postpandemic increase in telecommuting will have more of an immediate effect on urban rents than on urban form. In the world's more expensive cities, the gap between current commercial rents and the rents that can cover maintenance costs are sufficiently large that the offices will remain occupied even after rents fall. In the medium term, lower commercial prices mean that fewer downtown high-rises will get built. Some office buildings in low-cost metropolitan areas may actually go vacant. Others will convert to residential uses.

A switch to remote working could lead to a shift away from commercial districts within metropolitan areas and across metropolitan areas. If remote work is concentrated in highly educated, better-paid workers, some of those workers will choose to move to metropolitan areas with robust consumption amenities. Vacation destinations and college towns seem most likely to attract more footloose knowledge workers.

The rise in remote working may not mean an urban exodus. Many of our cities have succeeded over the past 40 years as places of consumption as well as production (Glaeser, Kolko, and Saiz 2001). The young in particular are likely to continue to demand the pleasures of city life even if they do their jobs from their apartments. As cities switch from production to consumption, intraurban trips will be increasingly motivated by leisure rather than by work.

Policy Choices About Infrastructure and Urban Form

The five policy decisions discussed below impact infrastructure and urban form and are examples of the integration of urban form considerations into transportation policy analysis.

Policy Decision 1: Subsidizing Infrastructure and Its Use

Governments have subsidized infrastructure and its usage for centuries. The connection between infrastructure and urban form should enter into any evaluation of transport subsidies. Subsidizing highways implicitly subsidizes the move from cities to suburbs. Do those spatial consequences cause the optimal highway subsidy to rise or fall?

The Whig Party advocated so-called internal improvements, including canals and railroads, as nation-building investments that would create common markets and a common national identity. Transportation links, including the railroads that enabled speedy German mobilization in 1914 and the Eisenhower Interstate Highway System, were also understood to have national security value. If roads and rails carry sizable fixed costs and low marginal costs, subsidizing construction enables more efficient use, although economists have long questioned the existence of a large gap between marginal and average costs. Finally, subsidizing public transportation is also seen as a tool for reducing traffic congestion and enabling the poor to access the labor market.

Americans have used general tax revenues to fill the highway trust fund for almost 15 years. Europeans significantly subsidize passenger rail. Few if any public transit systems cover their full costs. In every canonical urban model, subsidizing the cost of mobility will induce people to live farther away from the city center. Glaeser and Kahn (2004) find that countries with higher gas taxes have higher levels of urban density.

We also subsidize public transportation, which should induce consumers to live near existing public transit stops and encourage more building near those stops. Baum-Snow, Kahn, and Voith (2005) suggest that demand has been limited for new U.S. metro systems built since the coming of the car, which seems likely to limit their impact on urban form. Yet, many older cities in the United States have inelastic housing supply either because prices are below construction costs (Glaeser and Gyourko 2005) or because new construction is highly regulated. The more elastic supply of housing in the exurbs than in the urban core suggests that new highways will have a larger impact on urban form than new mass transit stops.

Policy Decision 2: Urban Land Use Regulations and Infrastructure Usage

In the United States, a plan to build a new rail line would emanate typically from a state secretary of transportation, usually with support from a state governor and probably with some additional funding from the U.S. Department of Transportation. Yet, the social value of that speedy rail line depends on the number of people who will take it each morning to get into the city. The number of people who will board the train depends on the amount of new housing that is built around the new rail stations; those decisions are made at the hyperlocal level by the dispersed townships that maintain iron-fisted control over the ability to build any new housing. The possibility that only a small amount of new housing will be built radically reduces any benefits that might come from this new construction.

Coordinating land use decisions and infrastructure decisions is an old problem because infrastructure itself requires land. In the days of corrupt urban machines, overcompensation for land purchases produced rents for privileged insiders. As George Washington Plunkitt of Tammany Hall explained: "Or supposin' it's a new bridge they're goin' to build. I get tipped off and I buy as much property as I can that has to be taken for approaches. I sell at my own price later on and drop some more money in the bank" (Riordon 1995, 1). Infrastructure projects of the 20th century, such as those run by Robert Moses, were more honest but also more likely to meet with neighborhood opposition to the use of eminent domain. The strength of local community opposition to rail lines has bedeviled attempts to straighten the Acela route in New England and to build the California high-speed rail.

As Altshuler and Luberoff (2004) demonstrate, community power to block new projects expanded steadily from the 1950s to the 1970s, which led to the emergence of more sensitive and more expensive projects, such as the Big Dig. Communities have also become more empowered in their ability to block new buildings, and this creates an indirect challenge for infrastructure spending. When rails were laid down along the course of Manhattan, developers could easily erect high-rises to take advantage of the speedy access to the city's business districts. When the Eisenhower Interstate Highway System connected cities with the open space surrounding them, developers similarly enjoyed a free hand in building suburban tract housing. Today, however, communities are far more likely to block the new construction that would increase the value of the infrastructure (Glaeser, Gyourko, and Saks 2005).

If infrastructure planners are hoping to deliver more value to their users, then the regulatory environment matters. If place A is likely to build 1,000 new homes in response to a new rail stop, and place B is likely to build only 10 new homes in response to a rail stop, then a planner who desires to deliver more value may want to build in place A rather than in place B, even if place B is better from an engineering perspective. The number of people who will actually move in response to new infrastructure is presumably significant for any cost-benefit analysis.

A second implication is that there may be gains from integrating land use planning with infrastructure provision. At the small scale, this integration occurs already. Towns control local roads and new building. But the transportation agencies that oversee large-scale projects rarely have control over new building. It is at least legally possible, if politically difficult, for a state government to impose a new zoning code along with new infrastructure.

Policy Decision 3: Durability Versus Flexibility, Rail Versus Bus

Economists have been skeptical about intraurban rail transit since, as Meyer, Kain, and Wohl (1965) point out, a bus on a dedicated lane could achieve almost all the speed of rail at a fraction of the cost. From the perspective of city spaces, the most obvious distinction between bus and rail is permanence. Bus routes can change quickly. Even designated bus tunnels can be repurposed. Train routes can be even more durable than housing. Routes designed for 19th-century needs still shape the 21st-century city.

Most train systems use rails that allowed Stephenson's steam engines to glide over the British countryside, rails that are not compatible with any other transit mode. Some light rail systems share road infrastructure with cars; others do not. Gómez-Ibáñez (1985) discusses many of the ways in which light rail systems are not so different from heavy rail systems. Buses can be rerouted over the existing road network or removed altogether. The flexibility of the bus would seem to be a major advantage in an uncertain world.

Yet, that flexibility has sometimes been seen as a downside of buses. The durability of trains is seen as a way of resolving uncertainty and coordination problems. For example, a real estate investor who is considering building a new project on the edge of a high-poverty neighborhood may have confidence in the fact that a new rail line is much less likely to be rerouted. A new bus route carries no security.

In a sense, the decision to invest in fixed local infrastructure can be understood as a game between the public sector and private investors, a game in which all actors want someone else to bear the risk. The permanence of rail loads the risk onto the public sector and makes the private sector less vulnerable. But in many cases, the public sector will benefit from keeping its options open.

Policy Decision 4: Public Health and Public Transportation

Cities are defined by the absence of physical space between individuals, but that urban proximity becomes a threat during a pandemic. The density of travelers on an urban bus or rail car can seem life-threating in a time of plague. In a Suffolk University PRC/WGBH/*Boston Globe* poll of Massachusetts residents taken from April 29 to May 2, 2020, 79.2 percent of respondents indicated that they would not be "comfortable riding buses, subways and commuter trains when it is allowed." Even if there was treatment (but no vaccine), 56.6 percent responded that they would not be "comfortable taking public transit" (Massachusetts Department of Transportation 2020).

If the threat recedes quickly, then the simple steps that are being taken now should help bring riders back onto public transportation. Regular disinfection and a norm of wearing masks should help a bit. Plastic barriers can reduce the risk of infection for drivers; autonomous vehicles would pose even less of a risk. Riders are already receiving real-time information about the level of crowding, but lowering the density level in buses and trains is a two-edged sword. If public transit runs at 25 percent of capacity for the foreseeable future, it will be even further away from covering its costs.

If the threat of pandemic persists and all shared public transit is shunned, cities will have to fall back on three older technologies—walking, cars, and bicycles—and hope that new technologies can help fill the gaps. Autonomous cars and buses with airtight barriers between passengers might provide a feasible form of ride-sharing. Walking and riding are easiest at high densities, where there is proximity between workplace and home. Cars and lower-density ride-sharing will work better in more suburban densities.

To allow more space for bicycles and walking, the inner city could in principle ban cars and have parking structures around its periphery. Health concerns can further limit high densities if elevators or shared air systems are also seen as dangerous. In that case, we may see an even larger move away from high-density metropolitan areas, especially in the United States. In that case, cars rather than walking or bicycling seem likely to be the dominant transportation mode in a world with recurring pandemics, just as cars are the dominant mode in U.S. lower-density areas today.

Policy Decision 5: Infrastructure and Natural Disasters

Before COVID-19, urban leaders were far more worried about the threat of global warming than the threat of a pandemic. Climate change is addressed more in chapter 7. Here, I briefly discuss responding to the possible impacts of global warming rather than reducing the extent of global warming. But these issues are handled more completely by chapters later in this volume. Those impacts include rising sea levels and temperatures and the increased threat of natural disasters, especially hurricanes. The potential responses include relocation, shields, and more resilient infrastructure.

Many cities are near the water and close to sea level precisely because waterways were the critical interurban transportation network in the premodern period. Access to those waterways is less valuable today, and urban populations can potentially be moved out of the range of water-related risk. If urban infrastructure were mobile, relocation would provide a relatively easy solution to floods. Indeed, a crucial issue is the speed of climate change relative to infrastructure depreciation. If change is sufficiently slow, perhaps we can gradually move population centers away from high-risk areas. Yet, it seems unlikely that we will ever abandon the enormous investments that have been made in cities such as New York, Boston, and San Francisco. Cities of the developing world have less infrastructure to lose, which might make the case for relocation stronger in poorer places. Yet, the political capacity to move large populations will be limited in poor countries.

If cities remain vulnerable to the sea, shields such as seawalls become a plausible solution to climate risk. In principle, such barriers can protect against both storm surges and the relentless rise of the seas, but the costs can easily be enormous. The political norm in which protection from natural disasters is the job of the federal government seems to reward risky behavior. If the owners of the sea-front property pay for their seawalls, there are stronger incentives against building in more vulnerable settings.

A third response is to make structures and infrastructure more resilient to flooding. Resilience is unlikely to solve the problem if the city is going to be under a foot of water, but public transit systems and power grids can be protected against the threat of flooding. Again, this protection increases costs and helps make the case for building in less vulnerable areas in the future.

I chose not to dwell on the goal of reducing carbon emissions, but that goal will remain and shape both urban form and infrastructure. Looking forward, this goal will create a conflict between the post-COVID-19 desire to segregate oneself in a car and the pre-COVID-19 desire to reduce carbon usage.

Conclusions

Infrastructure has shaped cities for thousands of years since ancient walls provided protection against marauders and paved roads made it easier for the passage of wheeled vehicles. This chapter has focused primarily on the transportation infrastructure that has played a primary role in shaping the cities of the wealthy world today and that seem most likely to influence the future of those cities. Water, sewers, and power generation have played much less of a role in this chapter, and yet these are particularly central to life in cities of the developing world today.

Manila is a metropolitan area with more than 12 million inhabitants, yet only a small fraction of that population has access to sewers. Septic tanks are far more common, even in extremely dense parts of the region. In many cities in India and sub-Saharan Africa, pit latrines are far more common than sewers or septic tanks. The cities of the West became healthy only by spending vast sums on their sewers. Will the cities of the developing world continue to grow without spending on public health–related infrastructure?

The current residential electricity demands of much of the developing world are relatively limited because populations are too poor to expect their homes to be artificially air-conditioned throughout much of the year. As these populations become richer, their desire for electricity at home seems likely to increase enormously. That demand for electricity will require more power-generating infrastructure or will lead to prices that are so high that they are sure to engender discontent.

Infrastructure is at the center of our urban world. The connection between transportation and urban density is particularly tight, since the ultimate purpose of density is to reduce transportation costs between people and firms. That is also the purpose of transportation infrastructure. The need for serious cost-benefit analysis to bring intellectual rigor to future infrastructure investments is one of the great policy-planning tasks of the 21st century.

Summary

- A city's density and form reflect the urban transportation technology prevailing at the time when the city was growing most rapidly.
- The full effects of technological change develop in three steps, each of which can take decades: the invention and refinement of a new vehicle type, the construction of a network over which those vehicles operate, and the rebuilding of the cities around that network.
- This third step of rebuilding the cities is slowed by the value and durability of the housing stock, which means that a significant change in transportation costs is needed to make rebuilding economical.
- Because durability slows change for both cities and infrastructure, by the time we appreciate the full costs and benefits of the environment we are creating, it may be too late to stop it.

References

Allen, Treb, and Costas Arkolakis. 2019. "The Welfare Effects of Transportation Infrastructure Improvements." Working paper No. 25487. Cambridge, MA: National Bureau of Economic Research.

Altshuler, Alan A., and David E. Luberoff. 2004. *Mega-Projects: The Changing Politics of Urban Public Investment*. Washington, DC: Brookings Institution Press.

Arnott, Richard J., and Joseph E. Stiglitz. 1979. "Aggregate Land Rents, Expenditure on Public Goods, and Optimal City Size." *Quarterly Journal of Economics* 93(4): 471–500.

Atack, Jeremy, Fred Bateman, Michael Haines, and Robert A. Margo. 2010. "Did Railroads Induce or Follow Economic Growth? Urbanization and Population Growth in the American Midwest, 1850–1860." *Social Science History* 34(2): 171–197.

Ballon, Hilary, ed. 2012. *The Greatest Grid: The Master Plan of Manhattan, 1811–2011*. New York: Columbia University Press.

Bartik, Alexander W., Zoe B. Cullen, Edward L. Glaeser, Michael Luca, and Christopher T. Stanton. 2020. "What Jobs Are Being Done at Home During the COVID-19 Crisis? Evidence from Firm-Level Surveys." Working paper No. 27422. Cambridge, MA: National Bureau of Economic Research.

Baum-Snow, Nathaniel. 2007. "Did Highways Cause Suburbanization?" *Quarterly Journal of Economics* 122(2): 775–805.

Baum-Snow, Nathaniel, Matthew E. Kahn, and Richard Voith. 2005. "Effects of Urban Rail Transit Expansions: Evidence from Sixteen Cities, 1970–2000 [with Comment]." *Brookings-Wharton Papers on Urban Affairs* (2005): 147–206.

Berger, Thor, and Kerstin Enflo. 2017. "Locomotives of Local Growth: The Short- and Long-Term Impact of Railroads in Sweden." *Journal of Urban Economic* 98: 124–138.

Bertaud, Alain. 2018. *Order Without Design: How Markets Shape Cities*. Cambridge, MA: MIT Press.

Bleakley, Hoyt, and Jeffrey Lin. 2012. "Portage and Path Dependence." *Quarterly Journal of Economics* 127(2): 587–644.

Caro, Robert A. 1974. *The Power Broker: Robert Moses and the Fall of New York*. New York: Knopf.

Chandler, Alfred D., Jr. 1993. *The Visible Hand*. Cambridge, MA: Harvard University Press.

Chauvin, Juan Pablo, Edward Glaeser, Yueran Ma, and Kristina Tobio. 2017. "What Is Different About Urbanization in Rich and Poor Countries? Cities in Brazil, China, India and the United States." *Journal of Urban Economics* 98: 17–49.

Christaller, Walter. 1933. *Die zentralen Orte in Süddeutschland (The Central Places in Southern Germany)*. Jena, Germany: Gustav Fischer.

Cutler, David, Grant Miller, Edward Glaeser, and Claudia Goldin. 2006. "Water, Water, Everywhere: Municipal Finance and Water Supply in American Cities." In *Corruption and Reform: Lessons from America's Economic History*, ed. Edward Glaeser and Claudia Goldin, 153–183. Chicago: University of Chicago Press.

Dalgaard, Carl-Johan, Nicolai Kaarsen, Ola Olsson, and Pablo Selaya. 2018. "Roman Roads to Prosperity: Persistence and Non-persistence of Public Goods Provision." CEPR discussion paper No. DP12745. https://ssrn.com/abstract=3130184.

Donaldson, Dave. 2018. "Railroads of the Raj: Estimating the Impact of Transportation Infrastructure." *American Economic Review* 108 (4–5): 899–934.

Donaldson, Dave, and Richard Hornbeck. 2016. "Railroads and American Economic Growth: A 'Market Access' Approach." *Quarterly Journal of Economics* 131(2): 799–858.

Duranton, Gilles, and Matthew A. Turner. 2012. "Urban Growth and Transportation." *Review of Economic Studies* 79(4): 1407–1440.

Fajgelbaum, Pablo, and Stephen Redding. 2018. "Trade, Structural Transformation and Development: Evidence from Argentina 1869–1914." Working paper No. 20217. Cambridge, MA: National Bureau of Economic Research.

Fishlow, Albert. 1965. *American Railroads and the Transformation of the Ante-bellum Economy*, vol. 127. Cambridge, MA: Harvard University Press.

Fogel, Robert William. 1964. *Railroads and American Economic Growth*. Baltimore, MD: Johns Hopkins University Press.

Garcia-López, Miquel-Àngel. 2012. "Urban Spatial Structure, Suburbanization and Transportation in Barcelona." *Journal of Urban Economics* 72(2–3): 176–190.

Garcia-López, Miquel-Àngel, Adelheid Holl, and Elisabet Viladecans-Marsal. 2015. "Suburbanization and Highways in Spain When the Romans and the Bourbons Still Shape Its Cities." *Journal of Urban Economics* 85: 52–67.

Garreau, Joel. 1992. *Edge City: Life on the New Frontier*. New York: Anchor.

Gaspar, Jess, and Edward Glaeser. 1998. "Information Technology and the Future of Cities." *Journal of Urban Economics* 43(1): 136–156.

Gin, Alan, and Jon Sonstelie. 1992. "The Streetcar and Residential Location in Nineteenth Century Philadelphia." *Journal of Urban Economics* 32(1): 92–107.

Glaeser, Edward L. 2014. "A World of Cities: The Causes and Consequences of Urbanization in Poorer Countries." *Journal of the European Economic Association* 12(5): 1154–1199.

Glaeser, Edward L., and Joseph Gyourko. 2005. "Urban Decline and Durable Housing." *Journal of Political Economy* 113(2): 345–375.

Glaeser, Edward L., Joseph Gyourko, and Raven Saks. 2005. "Why is Manhattan so Expensive? Regulation and the Rise in Housing Prices." *Journal of Law and Economics* 48: 331–369.

Glaeser, Edward L., and Matthew E. Kahn. 2004. "Sprawl and Urban Growth." In *Handbook of Regional and Urban Economics*, vol. 4, ed. J. Vernon Henderson and Jacques-François Thisse, 2481–2527. Amsterdam: Elsevier.

Glaeser, Edward L., Matthew E. Kahn, and Jordan Rappaport. 2008. "Why Do the Poor Live in Cities? The Role of Public Transportation." *Journal of Urban Economics* 63(1): 1–24.

Glaeser, Edward L., and Janet E. Kohlhase. 2004. "Cities, Regions and the Decline of Transport Costs." In *Fifty Years of Regional Science*, ed. Raymond Florax and David A. Plane, 197–228. Berlin: Springer.

Glaeser, Edward L., Jed Kolko, and Albert Saiz. 2001. "Consumer City." *Journal of Economic Geography* 1(1): 27–50.

Gómez-Ibáñez, José A. 1985. "A Dark Side to Light Rail? The Experience of Three New Transit Systems." *Journal of the American Planning Association* 51(3): 337–351.

Harrison, David, Jr., and John F. Kain. 1974. "Cumulative Urban Growth and Urban Density Functions." *Journal of Urban Economics* 1(1): 61–98.

Heblich, Stephan, Stephen J. Redding, and Daniel M. Sturm. 2018. "The Making of the Modern Metropolis: Evidence from London." Working paper No. 25047. Cambridge, MA: National Bureau of Economic Research.

Hitchner, R. Bruce. 2012. *Roads, Integration, Connectivity, and Economic Performance in the Roman Empire*, vol. 5. Chichester, UK: Wiley.

Jenks, Leland H. 1944. "Railroads as an Economic Force in American Development." *Journal of Economic History* 4(1): 1–20.

Kasarda, John D., and Greg Lindsay. 2011. *Aerotropolis: The Way We'll Live Next*. New York: Farrar, Straus and Giroux.

Laurence, Ray. 2013. "14: Traffic and Land Transportation In and Near Rome." In *The Cambridge Companion to Ancient Rome*, ed. P. Erdkamp, 246–261. Cambridge, UK: Cambridge University Press.

Massachusetts Department of Transportation 2020. "Secretary Stephanie Pollack's Report to the MassDOT Board, May 11, 2020." https://www.mass.gov/doc/secretaryceo-report -presented-to-the-board-on-05112020/download.

Meyer, John Robert, John F. Kain, and Martin Wohl. 1965. *The Urban Transportation Problem*. Cambridge, MA: Harvard University Press.

Nagy, Dávid Krisztián. 2017. "City Location and Economic Development." Princeton, NJ: Princeton University. https://www.crei.cat/wp-content/uploads/2017/02/jmp _citylocation_nagy-2-1.pdf.

Percoco, Marco. 2016. "Highways, Local Economic Structure and Urban Development." *Journal of Economic Geography* 16(5): 1035–1054.

Riordon, William L. 1995. *Plunkitt of Tammany Hall: A Series of Very Plain Talks on Very Practical Politics*. New York: Penguin.

Wahl, Fabian. 2017. "Does European Development Have Roman Roots? Evidence from the German Limes." *Journal of Economic Growth* 22(3): 313–349.

Warner, Sam Bass. 1978. *Streetcar Suburbs*. Cambridge, MA: Harvard University Press.

5

INFRASTRUCTURE AND THE COMPETITIVENESS OF CITIES

Daniel J. Graham, Daniel Hörcher,
and Roger Vickerman

Urbanization is the root cause of the majority of challenges that transport policy aims to resolve, including the fight against congestion and local pollution. Urbanization is characterized by the spatial clustering of economic activities, which results in a geographical concentration of traffic-generating and traffic-attracting locations in areas where land is scarce and a large population of urban residents is active. Typical outcomes are congested urban road and public transport networks and intensification of the transport sector's detrimental effects on the quality of life.

Why are cities still growing if, at least from the viewpoint of transport policy, spatial concentration induces a range of negative consequences for urban residents? The economist's answer to this question is enshrined in the theory of agglomeration economies, which states that urban concentration provides tangible benefits to both workers and firms. For workers, cities are attractive because of the wide spectrum of employment opportunities and the higher wages offered than in lower-density locations. For firms, the flip side of the same process is that cities provide benefits that manifest themselves in higher productivity (e.g., of labor and other inputs as reflected in wages) and ultimately in greater productive efficiency. The existence of agglomeration economies thus implies that spatial concentration brings increasing returns.

In this chapter, we argue that a policy focus on the transport sector in isolation will fail to deliver effective solutions for managing congestion and urban pollution without a deeper understanding of agglomeration economies, the mechanisms that often work against traffic management efforts. In that sense, a key challenge in urban transport policy is to achieve a balance between the productivity benefits and the congestion costs of agglomeration. A failure to appreciate the significance of these offsetting effects can lead to inefficient or even ineffective policies.

Agglomeration benefits and traffic-related costs are both in part externalities. Their externality nature means that the activities of the agents directly involved in production and consumption generate benefits and costs that have wider societal consequences. For example, one employee's contribution to work may affect the productivity of another employee, and one driver's travel decision can cause delay for another driver sharing the road. Economic theory suggests that optimal outcomes will arise when workers and consumers receive a financial incentive to internalize the external effect. For example, a wage subsidy should be provided in the presence of positive agglomeration externalities, and transport taxes should be levied to make the user aware of negative traffic externalities. In theory, without such financial incentives, the city will not reach an optimal configuration of economic activity and associated traffic volumes. Governments typically do not implement this strictly optimal system of financial incentives, often because it is politically or technically infeasible to do so or otherwise practically undesirable. However, the underlying principle that users' valuation of their own costs and benefits does not cover their total impact on society should remain an important fundamental consideration in devising and evaluating urban policy.

The main proposition of this chapter is that agglomeration generates positive as well as negative externalities simultaneously, and consequently cities require a fine-tuned portfolio of tailor-made policies to tackle market failures without neutralizing the benefits of spatial concentration. In the specific case of the transport sector, this proposition implies that congestion and the well-known distortions it causes should be mitigated by carefully considering the productivity benefits that accessibility and affordable mobility generate for urban industries and households. Our aim here is to synthesize existing knowledge on agglomeration economies and transport externalities and to highlight their relevance for infrastructure policy.

The forthcoming discussion is closely linked to two other chapters of this book. Chapter 4 discusses in detail how infrastructure can affect urban spatial form. We recognize the importance of such dynamic effects but do not duplicate discussion of them here, as they do not materially change the key arguments we present. The relevance of agglomeration to infrastructure project appraisal is discussed, but we do not include comprehensive coverage of cost-benefit analysis methods and related theories, which appears in chapter 5.

Theoretical Foundations: Benefits and Disbenefits from Agglomeration

One needs to review two relatively isolated branches in the literature to explore the benefits and disbenefits of agglomeration comprehensively (Vickerman 2008). On the "benefit" side of physical proximity, the urban economics literature describes productivity advantages stemming from various forms of scale economies. The "disbenefits," or costs, of agglomeration are consequences of various individual activities and frictions between members of society. Most of our discussion here is concerned with personal interactions in the urban environment that require physical displacement in geographic space because this is where transport infrastructure plays a key role.

Understanding why cities exist and economic activity clusters in specific locations has been a central subject in the economics literature since the contributions of Alfred Weber, Alfred Marshall, and Joseph Schumpeter. The consensus understanding developed over the last century and more revolves around the existence of agglomeration economies: positive externalities that arise through the spatial concentration of economic activity.

Agglomeration economies describe the productive advantages that firms and workers derive by locating in close proximity; the existence of these benefits, it is argued, can explain the formation and growth of cities and industrial locations. The key sources of agglomeration externalities arise from improved opportunities for labor market pooling, knowledge interactions, specialization, and the sharing of inputs and outputs, as well as from the existence of public goods.

Following Duranton and Puga (2004), the recent literature classifies the sources of agglomeration economies into three mechanisms: sharing, matching, and learning. Duranton and Puga (2004, 2065) argue that "the micro-foundations of urban agglomeration economies interact with other building blocks of urban models in ways that we cannot recognize unless they are explicitly stated." Following their observation, we review these mechanisms by paying detailed attention to how the availability, quality, and price of transport infrastructure contribute to the functioning of the building blocks.

Microfoundation 1: Sharing

Cities enable firms and households to share primary or intermediate inputs, indivisible facilities, and local public goods and services. In the production process of individual firms, sharing leads to scale economies in input procurement, while for households the city might be the only place where amenities that require an expensive and indivisible facility are available. Traditionally, organizing large marketplaces to facilitate market exchange also has required a shared physical infrastructure. Keeping indivisible shared facilities accessible for the urban population is one of the main challenges of transport policy, as these facilities constitute major generators of travel demand. The challenge further intensifies when the travel demand associated with shared facilities is concentrated both spatially and temporally. Mass events, densely built office blocks, and shopping malls are typical sources of congestion and crowding where the welfare loss caused by negative externalities also depends on (1) investment in infrastructure; and (2) the quality of regulation (e.g., pricing) in the transport market. Thus, transport policy is a crucial determinant of the city's ability to extract benefits from the scale of shared inputs and facilities. Congestion-related costs can be mitigated easily by restricting access to the shared facility, but in this case the returns from sharing would remain unexploited.

Microfoundation 2: Matching

Matching benefits arise when economic transactions require contact between agents with heterogeneous characteristics and geographical locations: if the number of "potential" agents involved in a particular economic transaction increases, then the quality of matching improves because it becomes more likely that an agent with ideal characteristics will be selected. This definition can be generalized to a variety of urban interactions, but the literature assigns increased attention to matching in the labor market. Specialized firms offer a range of jobs that require specific skills: the larger the labor pool they have access to, the more likely that they will find a worker with the ideal set of skills. The consequence of successful matching is once again an improvement in productivity, the benefit of which might be partly external to the actual employer-employee pair directly involved in the transaction. From a transport point of view, connectivity between major employment centers and residential areas is the most relevant criterion of improved labor market interactions. Traditionally, the population or total employment of cities was used as a proxy for the size of the available labor pool. However, with advanced transport technologies used for commuting, the administrative boundary of a city is no longer definitive as a measure of the labor market catchment area. The population or employment densities weighted by distance, travel time, or generalized travel cost (including monetary, time, and inconvenience factors) turn out to be more reliable for representing the potential for matching in the labor market; a detailed discussion is provided below.

Microfoundation 3: Learning

The third major mechanism behind agglomeration is learning, which captures knowledge spillovers between firms or between the employees of firms. We can consider learning processes on three levels. First, individuals learn from each other and from the environments in which they live and work. The transfer of knowledge requires communication between people; without an existing network of acquaintances, physical proximity to experienced and skilled individuals is necessary to establish learning channels (Jovanovic and Rob 1989). In this sense, learning can be viewed as a specific transaction with matching, whereby the parties involved are individuals with varying skill levels (Glaeser 1999). Second, on the level of firms, Duranton and Puga (2001) suggest that newly established start-ups take advantage of diversified cities where process innovation (i.e., trialing various production technologies to find the optimum for a new product) can be executed without costly relocations. The authors explain the existence of diverse cities with a range of industries via the need for new firms to innovate. In contrast, specialized cities cater to mature firms with a sufficiently developed production process, for which scale economies in mass production are more important than learning from a diverse range of innovative firms. Third, on the level of industries, some studies assume that firms generate information as a localized by-product of their primary output, which then improves productivity for other firms depending on how far apart their production facilities are located (Fujita and Ogawa 1982; Helsley 1990). This typology leads us to the distinction between localization (intraindustry) and urbanization (interindustry) agglomeration, whereby the former is driven by scale economies in input sharing by mature firms in the same industry while the latter is motivated by new firms' intention to learn and benefit from information spillovers across sectors.

The general lesson from learning mechanisms is that home-to-workplace accessibility matters for the competitiveness of cities, as does the connectivity between workplaces and toward places where social interactions are usual. Workplace-to-workplace connectivity may seem easy to realize when firms are clustered together in a central business district. However, with insufficient attention paid to the quality of public spaces and travel possibilities for short distances, transport policies focusing exclusively on the daily commuting problem may lose some of the benefits of local knowledge spillovers.

A key point of the literature reviewed above on the sources of agglomeration economies is that it is not traveling per se that leads to productive advantages and scale economies in cities but instead other transactions and activities that agents perform in physical proximity to each other. This point implies that purposeless trip generation does not necessarily improve productivity. A key underlying hypothesis of the literature is that productivity-enhancing transactions and activities require some form of displacement; otherwise, workers and consumers cannot meet and interact. This assumption seems plausible, given the diversity of the preferred geographical locations of our daily activities. From this point of view, the main benefit of cities is that travel costs can be reduced, and thus many firms and urban residents have the chance to interact with relatively low transport costs.

The recognition that urban interactions require travel is at the heart of the concept of economic density and a range of closely related quantitative metrics frequently used to express the degree of agglomeration. The spatial density of economic activity or access to economic mass (ATEM) are measures of the potential at a given point in space to interact with others. Productivity is often explained by a particular ATEM metric, the mean effective density of a geographical location that takes the following general form for location i:

$$\rho_i = (1/n)\sum_n m_j f(d_{ij}),$$

where n is the number of spatial units $\{j\}$ in reasonable distance to i; m_j is the mass of spatial unit j, which may represent the population or employment of the spatial unit; d_{ij} is a measure of transport costs between i and j; and $f(d_{ij})$ is an impedance function derived from d_{ij} (for an in-depth discussion, see Mackie et al. [2011] and Graham and Gibbons [2019]). The empirical evidence reviewed here indicates a positive causal relationship between ρ_i and the productivity of firms located in point i or the wages earned there. The role of local mass as a determinant of urban interactions is straightforward, but how transport costs affect productivity is less obvious. The most likely explanation behind this result is that traveling and sharing, matching, and learning-related activities are at least partial complements; therefore, improved travel conditions intensify the frequency of such interactions, which eventually leads to productivity gains. Complementarity between travel demand and productivity-enhancing activities such as labor supply implies that transport policies can regulate the volume of the latter as well.

Transport policy becomes particularly relevant in the presence of inefficiencies in the urban economy. Increasing returns and externalities are typical examples of market imperfections. Thus, the critical question that attracts considerable attention in the literature is whether the benefits of agglomeration are accrued to the parties directly involved in productivity-enhancing activities only or a part of the benefits spill over to other firms or households in the local economy. Based on the intuitive description of the microfoundations above, it seems that some of the agglomeration benefits must be external to the firms or households directly involved in sharing, matching, and learning processes. Households rely on shared facilities in the city, thus reducing the average cost of the service for other users, but the individual household neglects this external benefit. Similarly, when someone moves to a more suitable job and thus becomes more productive, this move may affect the output of other coworkers as well, which is not taken into account in the individual's job search. Knowledge spillovers are evident externalities. Economic theory suggests that in the presence of positive externalities, productivity-enhancing activities should be supported by wage subsidies or similar positive monetary incentives. In the absence of adequate wage and other transaction subsidies, transport policy may come into play as a second-best tool to trigger interactions through improved mobility.

At the same time, externalities and associated potential distortions are present in the transport market. Understanding capacity scarcity and congestion-related externalities has been high on the transport economics research agenda for decades. In a static representation of road transport, the negative externality emerges because the average travel time cost of drivers increases with traffic volume, and thus the marginal road user imposes a delay cost on fellow users as well. In a time-varying model in which queues form temporarily in front of infrastructure bottlenecks, external costs may also be generated because some commuters are forced to travel earlier or later than their desired schedule. Despite the simplicity of the static modeling approach, there is increasing consensus about the importance of dynamic (time-varying) congestion modeling in the urban environment. A third modeling approach builds on the observation of regularities in traffic characteristics on the macroscopic level of urban neighborhoods with a homogeneous road network. In this case, the fundamental relationship between traffic density and aggregate inflows/outflows at the boundary of homogeneous zones shows similar properties to those of a homogeneous road section (Daganzo and Geroliminis 2008).

A common feature of all three congestion-modeling approaches is the existence of a gap between user behavior and what is "socially desirable," that is, what minimizes resources, primarily travel time and schedule delay, on the aggregate level of all travelers. The resulting distortions call for regulatory interventions in the form of demand incentives. In the absence of government intervention, travel often takes more than the necessary time required. The optimal set of incentives affects the total number of trips undertaken as well as the transport mode, route, and timing of trips. Environmental costs, health risks, and accident risks are also substantial external costs of road use, especially in sensitive urban areas with high population density. Without suitable demand for management mechanisms, the dominance of negative externalities in this mode gives rise to the threat of overconsumption.

Mass transit and other transport modes based on vehicle sharing might also be prone to capacity scarcity. Congestion in public transport leads to crowding inside vehicles, on platforms, and at bus stops; a growing body of literature indicates that the inconvenience felt by passengers can double the perceived value of travel time (Hörcher, Graham, and Anderson 2017; Li and Hensher 2011; Wardman and Whelan 2011). In taxi, car-sharing, and ride-hailing services, high-capacity use leads to excess waiting time. Naturally, these are negative external effects of the marginal trip when capacity is fixed. However, in shared transport modes, the literature documents other types of scale effects as well when capacity (i.e., service frequency or shared fleet size) is responsive to the level of demand. A pioneering contribution by Mohring (1972) reveals that the user cost of waiting time decreases with patronage when service frequency in public transport is adjusted to the actual level of demand, thus generating inherent density economies in this mode. Equivalent phenomena can be observed in the access cost of car sharing and ride hailing as well. On top of that, recent empirical research by Anupriya et al. (2020) identifies the presence of strong operational cost economies with respect to both service frequency and network size in the urban rail industry specifically. Scale economies in any of these forms imply that the average social cost of service usage decreases with demand, and therefore the marginal user generates additional benefits besides net personal gain from traveling.

From the discussion above, we conclude that what microeconomic theory calls the marginal social cost, or net welfare effect, of traveling in an urban area may vary across a wide range depending on the transport mode considered and the level of demand relative to the available capacity. When travel and the collective activities that induce external productivity benefits in the urban economy are complements, the marginal trip can be linked to further positive externalities. The net welfare effect of urban mobility becomes a rather complex and context-dependent quantity. (Positive) agglomeration economies, (positive) scale economies in transport technology, and (negative) costs of capacity scarcity have opposite signs and thus may lead to offsetting patterns of externalities. The sign of the net welfare effect of urban traveling might lead to qualitatively different policy recommendations in both optimal pricing and the welfare-maximizing level of capacity investment, which is discussed below.

Measurement of Agglomeration Economies: A Review of Empirical Evidence

Can we measure the impact of the spatial concentration of economic activity on productivity? This empirical question has gained a lot of attention in the last two decades, primarily owing to its increased policy relevance. Combes and Gobillon (2015) and Graham and Gibbons (2019) provide in-depth reviews of the evolution of the literature. Therefore, we focus only on the main results.

The key parameter of interest in empirical studies is the elasticity of productivity (ω) with respect to ATEM (ρ):

$$\delta = (\partial \omega / \omega)/(\partial \rho / \rho).$$

The measure of ρ used is typically a zone-level ATEM index constructed using data on the scale of economic activity and on zone-to-zone geographic distances, as described above. To represent productivity, two broad approaches have been adopted. First, via estimation of a firm-level production function, $Y = g(Z, \rho) f(X)$, studies seek to determine whether ATEM affects the efficiency of producing output Y using input vector X (e.g., total factor productivity), given other determinants of productivity Z. Second, via an approach that estimates the effect of ATEM on labor productivity, as captured by workers' wages, $W = g(\rho) f(U)$, where U includes relevant determinants of the variance of wages beside the agglomeration metric ρ.

The literature is split between these approaches; however, it is important to emphasize that resulting estimates do not tend to exhibit substantial differences (Melo, Graham, and Noland 2009). The main challenges in empirical work involve addressing potential sources of endogeneity bias, which can arise from a number of sources including unmeasured influences of productivity, selection bias from the sorting of workers and firms, spatial heterogeneity in prices, reverse causality, and other sources of confounding. Combes and Gobillon (2015) and Graham and Gibbons (2019) describe in detail these challenges and the econometric methods that are commonly used to address them.

The number of new estimates of the agglomeration elasticity has been growing rapidly over past decades. Naturally, the estimates vary by continent, country, city type, and industrial sector; the meta-analysis of Melo, Graham, and Noland (2009) also reveals systematic variations due to the type and quality of data as well as estimation methods. Graham and Gibbons (2019) review 47 international empirical studies and find an unweighted mean agglomeration elasticity of 0.046 and a median value of 0.043.

The United Kingdom had been among the first countries to introduce agglomeration externalities in its official transport appraisal methodology, the Department for Transport's Transport Analysis Guidance. This guidance is based on the estimates of Graham, Gibbons, and Martin (2009). The agglomeration elasticities are estimated by using a total factor productivity approach and a Euclidean distance-based effective density measure:

$$\rho_i = (1/n) \sum_{j=1}^{n} m_j d_{ij}^{-\alpha},$$

where distance decay parameter α is calibrated together with other production function parameters. Separate elasticities are estimated for the manufacturing, construction, consumer services, and business service sectors. The recommended elasticities and distance decay parameters are provided in table 5.1. The point estimate for the U.K. economy as a whole is almost the same as the global average of

TABLE 5.1 Agglomeration Elasticity (δ) with 95% Confidence Intervals (CI) and Distance Decay (α) Estimates Currently Recommended in the U.K. Transport Analysis Guidance

Industry	δ	Lower CI (δ)	Upper CI (δ)	α
Manufacturing	0.024	0.020	0.028	1.122
Construction	0.034	0.028	0.040	1.562
Consumer services	0.024	0.018	0.030	1.818
Business services	0.083	0.069	0.097	1.746
Economy-wide weighted average	0.044			1.659

Source: Graham, Gibbons, and Martin (2009).

4.6 percent cited above. This average is far exceeded by the sensitivity of productivity in the business services sector, where the point estimate is δ = 0.083, while the manufacturing, construction, and consumer services industries have lower elasticities. In contrast, the distance decay estimates suggest that the impact of agglomeration fades more quickly with distance in the case of the services sector.

Despite the growing interest in adopting agglomeration elasticities in various areas of policy making, there is certainly room to improve empirical identification methods further. That said, the overwhelming consensus in the literature is that agglomeration economies do exist and induce higher productivity for firms and workers. Furthermore, the empirical evidence is reasonably consistent in terms of the order of magnitude of this positive effect.

Applications in Decision Support for Transport Policy

The tension between the benefits and costs of geographical proximity affects several aspects of transport policy (Vickerman 2008). In the following discussion, we focus on investment appraisal (i.e., the economic assessment of infrastructure development and other public investment decisions) and discuss infrastructure pricing, where the key observation is that transport pricing can offer a sophisticated tool for regulating travel demand and thus the magnitude of economic activity and the level of agglomeration in urban areas.

Investment Appraisal

Infrastructure construction, expansion, and renewals require one-off decisions by policy makers, while the social, economic, and financial impact of such decisions may last for several decades. To improve the quality of policies linked to infrastructure development, public authorities rely on cost-benefit analysis to evaluate investment decisions on an objective basis. The most straightforward consequence of infrastructure investments is the substantial financial cost of construction, whereby engineering estimates are normally available for a range of alternative implementation scenarios. The key challenge of ex ante cost-benefit analysis is to quantify on a comparable basis the following: (1) the direct benefits of the investment for future users, including firms and households; and (2) any external economic and financial effects that arise as a result of the new infrastructure.

The measurement of direct benefits has an established literature in surplus theory. Consumer surplus is usually derived from the individual traveler's willingness to pay for infrastructure use, while aggregate consumer surplus on a well-defined transport market can be inferred from three ingredients: (1) the observed level of demand; (2) the assumed shape of the demand function; and (3) the predicted change in demand as a result of the investment. In a simple case, the second and third inputs may boil down to the assumption of linear aggregate demand and demand prediction based on an empirical estimate of the elasticity of demand. The benefit estimation may also be performed using a full-blown urban traffic model in which functional forms as well as demand sensitivities are determined by the underlying mode choice and assignment algorithms. If the traffic model is based on a random utility maximizing discrete choice model, consumer surplus may also be calculated from the *logsum* formula of expected utility in the choice situation (Small and Rosen 1981).

It is reasonable to assume that people's willingness to pay for traveling in an urban environment is partly driven by potential benefits of agglomeration: they travel to access shared facilities, reach an attractive employment location, or meet others for business or leisure reasons. In other words, transport improvements affect consumer surplus through the range and duration of activities that residents undertake and the locations where these activities take place. However, as discussed earlier, investment costs and consumer surplus do not measure the entire welfare effect of an intervention in the presence of market failures. Through their decisions based on personal benefits and costs, individuals affect (1) the degree of scale economies in shared facilities and production; (2) various positive and negative externalities from the transport process itself and physical proximity; and (3) tax revenues not taken into account by the individual, to name only the most influential welfare effects beside investment costs and consumer surplus. The literature groups these additional consequences of transport improvement under the term *wider economic impacts* (WEIs); see Graham (2007). Figure 5.1 depicts one potential channel through which transport improvements might lead to WEIs

FIGURE 5.1 Infrastructure improvement and the channel through which it leads to wider economic impacts, in this case benefits.

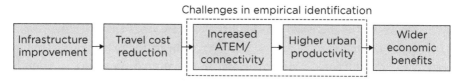

and indicates the critical relationship from a statistical point of view. The goal of a growing literature at the boundary between urban and transport economics is to expand the scope of the traditional appraisal methodology with the WEIs of transport improvements.

Venables (2007) illustrates the gap between the direct and wider economic benefits of transport improvements in a simple theoretical model of the monocentric city. City size is endogenously driven by the after-tax wage gap between the city and its hinterland. Venables (2007) adds agglomeration economies to the model by expressing urban productivity as a function of city size, which implies, under perfect competition, a wage gap curve that depends on city size. Equilibrium city size is determined by the tension between urban net wages and the cost of commuting. The model reveals that a commuting cost reduction (i.e., transport cost reduction) has four benefits:

1. The net wage of incumbent residents increases.
2. The city expands, and thus new commuters join the local labor market who retain consumer surplus from the changing wage gap.
3. The wage rate increases with city size due to improved productivity. This wage hike pushes the city limits even further, and both the incumbent commuters and the new ones joining the labor market experience an increase in their net earnings, this time as a result of the rising urban wage rate (holding transport costs constant).
4. Induced urban output generates tax revenues for the government.

Thus, after adopting a number of simplifying assumptions, the model clearly illustrates the presence of benefits beyond the pure travel cost savings (effect 1) and induced demands (effect 2) if the urban wage rate reacts positively to the thickness of the labor market (leading to effects 3 and 4, which are WEIs).

Recent improvements in cost-benefit analysis methodology incorporate the basic idea outlined by Venables (2007). The calculation involves two main steps:

(1) compute the impact of the project on the level of agglomeration (or ATEM);
(2) derive the incremental urban output using the estimated agglomeration elasticity and the corresponding extra tax revenue.

The distinction between personal travel time savings and wage increase is transparent in the Venables model. However, some of the model's assumptions may have left additional economic effects undiscovered. Working location is fixed in the original model; that is, transport improvement has no impact on the trip destination of residents who were already present in the city before the intervention. Lower transport costs might in fact enable urban residents to visit shared facilities, where services are cheaper and increasing utilization generates external benefits for service providers and other consumers. Improved accessibility may induce a reshuffle in the labor market, so some employees may switch to better-paying jobs. This benefit is partly enjoyed by the commuters themselves and might be a factor in people's travel time valuation; however, employers and other workers also receive a dividend from the productivity effects of matching.

These theoretical models of investment appraisal provide very few insights into how congestion affects urban agglomeration. Naturally, city size is not a suitable measure of agglomeration when it is very difficult to move around in the city. On the other hand, connectivity improvements are likely to accelerate interactions even if city size remains constant. The empirical literature reviewed above relies on economic density measures of agglomeration, whereby the economic mass around a point in space is accounted for with a distance or generalized cost-dependent decay factor. There is no theoretical justification behind this measure of agglomeration; the intuition that the attractiveness of a geographical location to economic interactions decreases with the generalized cost of traveling is convincing, partly based on the lessons learned from gravity models of transport demand. Note, however, the caveat that the generalized travel cost actually increases with the number of movements between two points in space, holding infrastructure supply constant. If a noninfrastructure-related policy intervention intensifies interactions between points A and B, the mean economic density metric decreases due to congestion, which predicts a reduction in the degree of agglomeration in points A and B. It is clear that mean effective density was developed to quantify the agglomeration effect of capacity expansions, but it is unable to measure the agglomeration effects of travel demand variations that are unrelated to changes in capacity supply.

Transport improvements may generate a range of additional welfare effects besides productivity benefits. Despite the availability of advanced land use/transport interaction models (Wegener 2011), the majority of practical investment appraisal exercises neglect the long-run effect of transport supply on urban spatial form. Relocation effects, discussed in more depth in chapter 3, can lead to a reduction in productivity in distant locations from where productive firms move closer to the new investment, thus leaving an agglomeration shadow behind (Redding and Turner 2015). In a recent numerical experiment, Eliasson, Savemark, and Franklin (2020) show that even though the welfare effect of relocation can be substantial in magnitude, it is normally proportional to other social benefits, including the traditional consumer surplus. Therefore, the simplified (and more widely used) cost-benefit analysis framework does not induce serious bias in the ranking and selection of transport projects.

Inherent scale economies in transport technology offer another source of additional benefits. In public transport and other modes, where the operational cost of service provision and infrastructure supply depend on the scale of operations, investment appraisal should consider the system-level benefits of service expansion. The empirical evidence reviewed above identifies returns to scale with respect to network size in the metro industry. This implies that the appraisal exercise of a metro expansion should include the network-level reduction of operational costs as a benefit of the project. Anupriya et al. (2020) show that the degree of returns to scale depends on metro size itself. For relatively small systems, returns to scale may exceed 1.5, meaning that the network size elasticity of operational costs is less than 60 percent, while very large metros feature constant returns to network scale. That is, taking account of system-level operational cost savings is especially important for urban rail networks in their early stages of development.

Infrastructure Pricing and Subsidies

Transport pricing has multiple roles in the urban economy. The best-known role is that taxes, tolls, and fares contribute to the financial balance of infrastructure provision. Pricing policies are also suitable for achieving certain redistributional goals by the differentiation of tariffs frequently used by specific groups in society. From an economic point of view, pricing is the tool with which demand can be regulated to ensure an efficient allocation of resources: in the present case, the available road space, public transport capacity, shared vehicle fleets, and resources required to run these services. In essence, microeconomic theory suggests that the pricing system provides the right incentives if the price that each user pays is equivalent to the marginal welfare effect that the trip generates for the rest of society. Thus, the main objective of pricing research is to understand and quantify the welfare implications of urban travel, potentially on a disaggregate basis.

From a methodological point of view, the derivation of optimal pricing in a transport market is very different from the investment appraisal exercise; therefore, these topics are relatively isolated in the literature and sometimes also in policy debates. This practice is unfortunate because the pricing policies implemented on new infrastructure can be a major determinant of a range of social benefit and cost components in investment appraisal. Put differently, low infrastructure charges might lead to a fundamentally different level of consumer surplus and further welfare effects in investment appraisal compared with high infrastructure charges, not to mention a series of other attributes of a complex transport tariff system. Pricing may cause huge variations in the expected benefit-cost ratio of a planned project, and this aspect is often overlooked in policy debates relying on only a single distinguished benefit-cost ratio estimate. The most usual practice in cost-benefit analysis is that the present tax, toll, and fare levels are assumed to prevail in the long run, perhaps with an adjustment to inflation and other macroeconomic factors. However, this assumption is very uncertain in a changing political climate or when the industrial organization of service provision is foreseen to change.

Focusing more closely on the optimization of infrastructure pricing, the mainstream literature is concerned with the integration of (1) capacity-scarcity–related external costs such as the congestion externality; and (2) environmental- and public health–related social costs into pricing policy. Road congestion pricing policy in particular is an intensively analyzed subject, which is indeed justified by the empirical evidence on very substantial marginal external congestion delay costs in dense traffic on the one hand and the public interest in finding a solution to the congestion problem in large cities on the other hand. Despite the availability of a large body of theoretical knowledge, most cities around the world are still reluctant to implement congestion pricing policies, and the breakthrough in this area that the research community has expected for a while is yet to be realized. In the meantime, the predominant means of road capacity allocation as a scarce urban resource will happen in the form of queueing, which is undoubtedly a major obstacle for the competitiveness of cities.

Public transport is also prone to capacity shortages. Crowding occurs inside vehicles as well as in rail stations and at bus stops when demand approaches the available capacity. The user cost of inconvenience in crowded environments can be measured with statistical tools. Thus, empirical evidence is available on the external crowding cost of traveling whereby the externality stems from the inconvenience that the marginal user imposes on fellow travelers. Public transport is often considered an "uncongestible" alternative of urban car use. This assumption is false, at least in the short run, when technology or regulatory restrictions constrain public transport capacity. The magnitude of the crowding externality varies widely with the occupancy rate of public transport vehicles. We observe temporal, spatial, and directional imbalances in travel demand, while it is practically impossible to adjust the level of supply to instantaneous changes in demand. The presence of demand imbalances makes the reappearance of crowding inevitable in large networks, which raises the importance of scarcity-dependent pricing. The efficiency of dynamic pricing is proven in the taxi and ride-sourcing markets, where the competitive advantage of firms with a differentiated pricing policy is apparent.

In the medium to long run, however, public transport capacity is much more flexible than road supply. Increasing the density of supply (i.e., the number of shared vehicles running on a fixed network) is feasible without costly investments in infrastructure. The literature provides evidence of increasing returns to the density of public transport services in terms of both operational and user costs. Assuming responsive capacity, marginal travelers may generate an external benefit for fellow users because, for example, they have to wait less as service frequency increases or have to walk less when stop and route density are also endogenous. User benefits are coupled with density economies in operational costs simply because of the technology of vehicle sharing. These inherent scale economies in public transport push the welfare effect of the marginal trip in a positive direction, which implies a negative shift in the optimal price of this mode. The tension between negative crowding externalities and positive scale effects requires increased attention in the design of optimal fare policies. At the same time, we see that simple solutions in public transport pricing rarely produce the right set of incentives for the efficient use of the service as an urban resource, especially when the magnitudes of partially offsetting externalities vary over a wide range. Hörcher and Graham (2020) reach this conclusion in a quantitative analysis of unlimited-use travel passes versus usage-dependent pricing.

Thus far, we have limited our discussion of pricing policies to the narrowly defined transport market, while above we concluded that transport may be complementary to other activities with WEIs. Such benefits are increasingly considered in investment appraisal but should also play a role in the determination of individual travel incentives. There is surprisingly little attention in the literature to the combination of (negative) congestion and (positive) agglomeration externalities in the context of transport pricing. Arnott (2007) is the first exception, with a simple commuting model in which the representative workers' wages increase with total labor supply, but intensive commuting generates congestion externalities as well on a fixed road infrastructure. He finds that in a plausible range of agglomeration elasticities and congestion parameters, the agglomeration benefit of commuting might be comparable in magnitude with the well-known congestion externality. However, the signs of the two externalities are the opposite; therefore, the optimal road toll should be significantly lower than the standard Pigouvian externality tax. Hörcher et al. (2020) adapt Arnott's modeling approach to public transport provision under agglomeration economies, showing that the productivity benefits of commuting might indeed reduce the optimal cost recovery ratio (fare revenues relative to operational costs) of public transport as well.

The opposite sign and offsetting effect of capacity scarcity and agglomeration externalities may be both an alarming result for the proponents of congestion pricing on the road and peak-load pricing in public transport and a reassurance for those who oppose these ideas (so far quite effectively). The threat of this alarming result might explain the scarcity of pricing analyses in the literature considering both congestion and agglomeration economies. Our position is that the conclusion above would be misleading, however. Agglomeration benefits do offset part of the negative externalities of congestion when one computes these metrics for the representative consumer, as Arnott (2007) and Hörcher et al. (2020) do. There is substantial heterogeneity in all types of externalities considered in this chapter among urban travelers. The contribution of a driver or passenger to agglomeration depends heavily on the purpose of the trip, especially whether it is work-related; the type of industry if a commuting trip is considered; and various characteristics of the surrounding economy, such as the effective economic density of the trip destination. Similarly, the congestion or crowding externality depends on the origin-destination pair, mode, route, and departure time chosen. Thus, the net welfare effect of urban trips can be extremely heterogeneous, and consequently the averaging bias can also be very substantial. For this reason, the representative traveler model cannot be fully informative for practice-ready policy recommendations (i.e., enormous efficiency potential exists in the disaggregation of pricing incentives). We believe that the main challenge of transport science will be to mobilize the increasingly available disaggregate data sources and computing power to disaggregate its policy recommendations as well.

Conclusions

For several decades, research on socially optimal transport policies has been dominated by the appropriate modeling and measurement of personal travel benefits versus various investment, operational, user, and environmental costs. The presence of externalities became apparent at an early stage of the evolution of our field, primarily in the form of externalities due to the scarcity of capacity amid fluctuating demand (i.e., congestion on the road and crowding in public transport) and the environmental impacts of transport. As a consequence, the majority of current transport appraisal methodologies are dominated by the cost-reduction benefits of infrastructure development combined with the consumer surplus of induced demand, and the main purpose of existing transport pricing models is to internalize congestion and environmental externalities.

This paradigm is gradually changing as we learn more about the external benefits of transport infrastructure and service provision. A growing body of empirical evidence indicates that good transport services improve the connectivity of spatial markets and that these shifts in agglomeration in turn raise the productivity of firms and workers who benefit from enhanced proximity. Agglomeration economies have a long history in urban economics theory dating back to Marshall (1890), but the adaptation of the related external benefits in transport policy has been delayed by practical challenges on the side of empirical identification. With the availability of large-scale firm- and worker-level panel data sets, advanced causal inference econometric methods open new avenues for measuring the contribution of transport infrastructure to urban productivity. This external benefit can be coupled with new findings on scale economies in specific transport modes, such as public transport provision.

The simultaneous presence of negative and positive transport externalities in the urban environment calls for extra care in policy development. Tackling the negative externalities of congestion and pollution should remain high on the agenda, but transport policy must also recognize that seemingly straightforward solutions to such problems might have severe impacts on productivity and scale economies in cities. On the other hand, broad-brush modeling of average externalities could (falsely) imply that negative and positive externalities neutralize each other, eliminating the need for major government intervention in transport markets. This chapter argues that such aggregate approaches are also misleading because of the heterogeneity of the externalities reviewed, and thus disaggregate modeling and policy development are required to ensure the efficient functioning of cities.

Summary

- Urban agglomerations generate both positive and negative externalities simultaneously.
- The positive externalities stem primarily from the increases in labor productivity as the agglomeration grows but also from scale economies in public transit. The negative externalities stem from increases in road traffic congestion, pollution, and safety risks.
- The net benefits of an agglomeration can be enhanced by a combination of efficient investment in the transportation sector and efficient pricing and subsidies to compensate for the remaining externalities.

References

Anupriya, Anupriya, Daniel J. Graham, Jose M. Carbo, Richard J. Anderson, and Prateek Bansal. 2020. "Understanding the Costs of Urban Rail Transport Operations." *Transportation Research Part B: Methodological* 138: 292–316.

Arnott, Richard. 2007. "Congestion Tolling with Agglomeration Externalities." *Journal of Urban Economics* 2(62): 187–203.

Combes, Pierre-Philippe, and Laurent Gobillon. 2015. "The Empirics of Agglomeration Economies." In *Handbook of Regional and Urban Economics*, vol. 5, ed. Gilles Duranton, J. Vernon Henderson, and William C. Strange, 247–348. Amsterdam: North Holland.

Daganzo, Carlos F., and Nikolas Geroliminis. 2008. "An Analytical Approximation for the Macroscopic Fundamental Diagram of Urban Traffic." *Transportation Research Part B: Methodological* 42(9), 771–781.

Duranton, Giles, and Diego Puga. 2001. "Nursery Cities: Urban Diversity, Process Innovation, and the Life Cycle of Products." *American Economic Review* 91(5): 1454–1477.

———. 2004. Micro-foundations of Urban Agglomeration Economies." In *Handbook of Regional and Urban Economics*, vol. 4, ed. J. Vernon Henderson and Jacques-François Thisse, 2063–2117. Amsterdam: North Holland.

Eliasson, Jonas, Christian Savemark, and Joel Franklin. 2020. "The Impact of Land Use Effects in Infrastructure Appraisal." *Transportation Research Part A: Policy and Practice* 141: 262–276.

Fujita, Masahisa, and Hideaki Ogawa. 1982. "Multiple Equilibria and Structural Transition of Non-monocentric Urban Configurations." *Regional Science and Urban Economics* 12(2): 161–196.

Glaeser, Edward L. 1999. "Learning in Cities." *Journal of Urban Economics* 46(2): 254–277.

Graham, Daniel J. 2007. "Agglomeration, Productivity and Transport Investment" *Journal of Transport Economics and Policy* 41(3): 317–343.

Graham, Daniel J., and S. Gibbons. 2019. "Quantifying Wider Economic Impacts of Agglomeration for Transport Appraisal: Existing Evidence and Future Directions." *Economics of Transportation* 19. https://doi.org/10.1016/j.ecotra.2019.100121.

Graham, Daniel J., Stephen Gibbons, and Ralf Martin. 2009. "The Spatial Decay of Agglomeration Economies: Estimates for Use in Transport Appraisal." Final Report. London: United Kingdom Department for Transport.

Helsley, Robert W. 1990. "Knowledge and Production in the CBD." *Journal of Urban Economics* 28(3): 391–403.

Hörcher, Daniel, Bruno De Borger, Woubit Seifu, and Daniel J. Graham. 2020. "Public Transport Provision Under Agglomeration Economies." *Regional Science and Urban Economics* 81. https://doi.org/10.1016/j.regsciurbeco.2019.103503.

Hörcher, Daniel, and Daniel J. Graham. 2020. "MaaS Economics: Should We Fight Car Ownership with Subscriptions to Alternative Modes?" *Economics of Transportation* 22. https://doi.org/10.1016/j.ecotra.2020.100167.

Hörcher, Daniel, Daniel J. Graham, and Richard J. Anderson. 2017. "Crowding Cost Estimation with Large Scale Smart Card and Vehicle Location Data." *Transportation Research Part B: Methodological* 95: 105–125.

Jovanovic, Boyan, and Rafael Rob. 1989. "The Growth and Diffusion of Knowledge." *Review of Economic Studies* 56(4): 569–582.

Li, Zheng, and David A. Hensher. 2011. "Crowding and Public Transport: A Review of Willingness to Pay Evidence and Its Relevance in Project Appraisal." *Transport Policy* 18(6): 880–887.

Mackie, Peter, Daniel Graham, and James Laird. 2011. "The Direct and Wider Impacts of Transport Projects: A Review." In *A Handbook of Transport Economics*, ed. André de Palma, Robin Lindsey, Emile Quinet, and Roger Vickerman, 501–526. Cheltenham, UK: Edward Elgar Publishing.

Marshall, Alfred. 1890. *Principles of Economics*. London: McMillan.

Melo, Patricia C., Daniel J. Graham, and Robert B. Noland. 2009. "A Meta-analysis of Estimates of Urban Agglomeration Economies." *Regional Science and Urban Economics* 39(3): 332–342.

Mohring, Herbert. 1972. "Optimization and Scale Economies in Urban Bus Transportation." *American Economic Review* 62(4): 591–604.

Redding, Stephen J., and Matthew A. Turner. 2015. "Transportation Costs and the Spatial Organization of Economic Activity." In *Handbook of Regional and Urban Economics*, vol. 5, ed. Gilles Duranton, J. Vernon Henderson, and William C. Strange, 1339–1398. Amsterdam: North Holland.

Small, Kenneth A., and Harvey S. Rosen. 1981. "Applied Welfare Economics with Discrete Choice Models." *Econometrica: Journal of the Econometric Society* 49(1): 105–130.

Venables, Anthony J. 2007. "Evaluating Urban Transport Improvements: Cost-Benefit Analysis in the Presence of Agglomeration and Income Taxation." *Journal of Transport Economics and Policy* 41(2): 173–188.

Vickerman, Roger. 2008. "Transit Investment and Economic Development." *Research in Transportation Economics* 23(1): 107–115.

Wardman, Mark, and Gerard Whelan. 2011. "Twenty Years of Rail Crowding Valuation Studies: Evidence and Lessons from British Experience." *Transport Reviews* 31(3): 379–398.

Wegener, Michael. 2011. "Transport in Spatial Models of Economic Development." In *A Handbook of Transport Economics*, ed. André de Palma, Robin Lindsey, Emile Quinet, and Roger Vickerman, 46–66. Cheltenham, UK: Edward Elgar Publishing.

INVESTMENT APPRAISAL, BIASES, AND POLITICS

6

THE DEVELOPMENT OF EVALUATION METHODS FOR INFRASTRUCTURE PROJECTS

Don H. Pickrell

Evaluating proposed investments in infrastructure is a vital exercise because they typically require large capital outlays and promise a wide range of economic benefits. Moreover, the organizations contemplating them inevitably face limited capital budgets and competing demands for other infrastructure services. There is also much for analysts, investors, and the public to learn about the effective design, location, and timing of potential investments from carefully evaluating the performance of past and current projects. For these reasons, large businesses, central government budget agencies in most developed countries, and international funding agencies promoting economic development now almost universally require detailed economic evaluations of proposed investments in infrastructure.

Typically, this evaluation takes the form of a detailed analysis of the likely economic benefits and costs of investments designed to increase the capacity or improve the performance of infrastructure; this is followed by careful comparison of the anticipated economic outcomes from competing options before choosing among them. This process is by now so ubiquitous and institutionalized that many national governments and virtually all international agencies that fund infrastructure publish detailed guidance for assessing the likely costs and benefits of proposed investments, summarizing and comparing projects' anticipated outcomes, and identifying the most promising candidates. Although the influence of economic evaluation on their ultimate choices among competing investment proposals varies widely among nations and funding agencies, it has become a nearly universal element of their processes for planning infrastructure investments.

Of course, the economic easements conducted by governments and funding agencies differ from the typical financial analyses of proposed capital investments done by private firms. Most conspicuously, private firms focus on the financial effects of the projects—including the changes in revenues, operating expenses, and capital outlays—while governments and international aid agencies focus primarily on social benefits such as improved health or convenience.

Although still less prevalent than comparative economic evaluation of proposed investments in new or expanded infrastructure, ex post assessment of recent infrastructure projects has recently become more widespread. In some cases, analysts make detailed efforts to verify projects' actual investment outlays and to reconstruct the economic benefits they actually deliver to users and others. More commonly, however, analysts approximate the relationship between projects' confirmed and originally anticipated benefits by comparing actual to predicted usage of the new or improved infrastructure—for example, passengers carried by a new transportation service or the increased volume of water that expanded distribution facilities actually deliver. How extensively such backward-looking evaluation influences the design or choice of subsequent infrastructure projects is rarely clear and probably varies widely among funding agencies, but it certainly offers the potential to improve decision making.

Origins of Economic Evaluation

The practice of evaluating infrastructure investments is a relatively recent development; however, like much of modern economic analysis, it has distant intellectual roots. The French civil engineer and economist Jules Dupuit introduced the idea of evaluating proposed capital investments in public infrastructure in the mid-19th century, including facilities as diverse as roadways, bridges, railroads, canals, and water supply systems. He was particularly concerned with measuring the value of investments that seemed likely to foster major increases in traffic. Dupuit even seems to have originated the technique of developing alternative project designs or locations that could serve the same intended purpose and assessing them in comparison to one another (Nash 1979; Vatin, Simonin, and Marco 2016). His approach to project design also recognized the trade-off between initial capital investments to construct new infrastructure and the recurring costs to operate and maintain it.[1]

Intellectual Roots

Most important, Dupuit outlined a method to measure the increased "relative utility" that new or expanded infrastructure provided to suppliers and users of materials or goods whose production and distribution it facilitated (Ekelund and Hebert 1985). His measure not only captured the savings in costs to produce and deliver existing outputs that new infrastructure could provide but also imputed the value of increased supply and use of products that investments could spur by reducing their delivered prices. Somewhat later, Alfred Marshall developed the closely analogous "consumer surplus" measure of benefits from lower product prices and increased consumption (Ekelund and Hebert 1997). Marshall's measure differed critically from Dupuit's because it focused on benefits to users of new or expanded facilities—passenger and freight carriers who used them to provide transportation services—rather than to the ultimate consumers of goods whose production and distribution depended on transportation infrastructure (Ekelund and Hebert 1997; Rothengatter 2017).[2]

Development of Modern Evaluation Practice

Despite its early theoretical origins, the modern practice of economic evaluation evolved only considerably later, in the early 20th century, as a means of resolving political and bureaucratic conflicts over the selection of appropriate investments to improve the navigability of U.S. rivers and harbors. The process originated with the U.S. Army Corps of Engineers, which initially established a board of engineers under the Rivers and Harbors Act of 1902. The board was charged with overseeing the selection of investment projects by certifying those that were beneficial, as demonstrated by their favorable benefit-cost ratios. As evidence of its impact, the board rejected more than half of the proposed projects that came before it for certification, usually on the basis that they were not viable economically.

By the 1920s, the Army Corps of Engineers' practice had evolved to require that projects it recommended promised to generate economic benefits exceeding their costs. This important restriction was codified in amendments to the earlier Rivers and Harbors Act adopted in 1920 and reinforced in the 1936 Flood Control Act, which authorized the U.S. Congress to fund only projects the corps had previously approved (Hammond 1966). Not surprisingly, the corps' exercise of its discretionary authority bred controversy among the barge operators who benefited directly, the railroads with whom they competed, and the increasingly powerful public utilities on whose interests the corps encroached. The corps' exercise also prompted challenges from rival federal agencies with water projects under their own separate jurisdictions, whose practices for assessing their benefits and costs differed from the corps' own (Chicago Chapter of the American Statistical Association 2011).

Disputes over the correct methods for measuring benefits and costs ultimately threatened the legitimacy of rival agencies' evaluations, so they agreed to establish the Federal Inter-Agency River Basin Committee and appointed the Subcommittee on Benefits and Costs to standardize practices (Banzhaf 2010). The subcommittee issued its landmark *Proposed Practices for Economic Analysis of River*

Basin Projects in 1950 (known as the Green Book), which carefully enumerated the services that investing in water infrastructure could deliver (irrigation, flood control, land conservation, river navigation, hydroelectric power, outdoor recreation, and species protection) and spelled out detailed procedures for measuring the benefits each service offered and estimating the costs of providing it.

Shortly thereafter, the U.S. Bureau of the Budget published circular A-47, offering still more detailed guidance to refine and standardize government agencies' methods for estimating benefits and systematically comparing them with projects' costs (USBOB 1952). These government-led efforts to standardize procedures for cost-benefit analysis and ground them in accepted economic principles widened the appeal of the practice to analysts as well as political officials while forging agreement on appropriate methods also set the stage for extending economic evaluation to other forms of infrastructure (Banzhaf 2010; Chicago Chapter of the American Statistical Association 2011; Pearce 1983). Thus, over several decades the cost-benefit approach to evaluating proposed infrastructure investments evolved from its origins as a conflict-resolution process to a systematic practice based on clearly articulated principles of basic economics.

Theory Catches Up to Practice

Curiously, the intellectual underpinnings of cost-benefit analysis developed largely independently of its rapidly evolving practice, and the two converged only after the latter had become firmly entrenched within U.S. government agencies (Pearce 1983). Again, there were distant intellectual roots, principally Dupuit's framework for measuring the utility gains that infrastructure provided to shippers and Marshall's consumer surplus measure of benefits consumers derived when the price of a transportation service declined and its usage increased. These critical antecedents had fallen into disrepute after a century of intellectual objections from prominent economists. In the 1940s, however, the prominent British economist John Hicks developed formal measures of individuals' welfare gains and losses resulting from price changes and showed that these could be translated into monetary measures of benefits and costs.

By demonstrating how his two measures bracketed Marshall's consumer surplus, Hicks lent new legitimacy to its original logic, although Hicks's measures in principle applied strictly to individuals and summing them required assumptions that he (among many others) seemed reluctant to make. But combining them with Kaldor's proposal that a project could improve overall economic welfare if the dollar measure of its collective benefits to affected individuals exceeded the combined monetary value of welfare losses it inflicted on others—regardless of whether the former actually compensated the latter—offered a convenient synthesis. Although controversial, this resolution solidified the intellectual foundation for cost-benefit analysis as it was already being practiced (Chicago Chapter of the American Statistical Association 2011).

Practical Measures of Infrastructure Benefits

Although Hicks's measures of individual benefits could not be empirically observed, analysts could calculate Marshall's aggregate consumer surplus measure using market data on prices and consumption, provided they were willing to ignore the long-standing objection that the measure treated changes in income as equally valuable to everyone (most were). For the cases where infrastructure's services were not sold in markets and no prices existed to value them, Harold Hotelling outlined a method for using the costs people incurred in traveling to and using them—his example was recreational use of reservoirs—to infer the benefits they apparently derived.

Using their expenses for traveling to a recreation site as a proxy for the prices its users were willing to pay to swim, boat, and fish there, Hotelling demonstrated how the relationship of the price to the number of people who came from varying distances could be interpreted as a demand curve and used to calculate users' aggregate consumer surplus (Banzhaf 2010; Hotelling 1947). Later studies firmly established the idea that benefits from investing in infrastructure included welfare gains from cost savings not just for its current users but also for new users it attracted and demonstrated how monetary valuation of those latter gains was possible (Banzhaf 2010; Clawson and Knetsch 1966; Knetsch 1963, 1964).

Alternative Approaches

As cost-benefit analysis was inheriting firmer theoretical foundations, and as its practice spread, other prominent scholars were experimenting with alternative methods to evaluate infrastructure investments. Tinbergen (1957) outlined a framework for measuring the effects of highway investment on a nation's aggregate economic output and income; his model accounted for the effects of resulting changes in production, the delivered prices of goods shipped by highway on demand, and the geographic patterns of their supply and distribution. He demonstrated that these responses generated additional benefits in the form of increased economic output and income, including in geographic regions well outside those where investments were made.

Tinbergen's approach seemed to demonstrate that by relying on cost savings to highway users as its primary measure of benefits, cost-benefit analysis would overlook predictable responses to lower transportation costs that could be sources of much larger benefits. A later application of his method verified this result, suggesting that measuring benefits from infrastructure investment from an economy-wide perspective would produce systematically larger values than those calculated in conventional cost-benefit analysis (Bos and Koyck 1961).

Why Did Cost-Benefit Analysis Prevail?

Despite the obvious appeal to proponents of infrastructure investment that its systematically higher estimates of benefits offered, the macroeconomic approach to evaluating proposed investments did not attract widespread use. However, applications of cost-benefit analysis continued to expand. One explanation was the greater mathematical complexity and much larger number of parameter values that needed to be estimated (or, more likely, assumed) to calculate the changes in economic output and income resulting from infrastructure improvements. These demands made the macroeconomic approach more suitable for occasional evaluations of large investment programs than for routine application to individual projects.

In contrast, cost-benefit analysis originated primarily as a means for assessing the value of localized improvements to infrastructure, required only limited information about their costs and usage to implement, and employed mostly transparent, reproducible calculations. Therefore, it offered obvious practical advantages. At the same time, its natural focus on individual projects rather than on ongoing investment programs or overarching government policies toward infrastructure helped insulate cost-benefit analysis against concerns over the distributional impacts of decisions it underpinned (Krutilla 1981). In the end, cost-benefit evaluation prevailed simply because it offered a more tractable approach to guiding the complex investment decisions that regularly confronted government agencies with responsibility for managing infrastructure budgets (Pearce 1983).

Globalization and Formalization of Economic Evaluation

Cost-benefit analysis as pioneered for assessing investments in water supply and distribution infrastructure was initially exported from the United States to the United Kingdom, where academic researchers had become interested in its theoretical foundations, and government agencies, most notably the Treasury, were seeking defensible methods to evaluate the desirability of capital investments in public enterprises. Having authorized construction of a London–Birmingham motorway without conducting such an evaluation, the Treasury was eager to demonstrate that the project promised a satisfactory economic return and subsequently commissioned a cost-benefit evaluation modeled on U.S. assessments of water resource projects (Foster 2001).

Crossing the Atlantic

This pioneering effort was followed closely by a study of the proposed Victoria line of the London Underground. This study highlighted the contrast between conventional financial analysis, which had shown the project's likely adverse effect on Transport for London's profitability and made the Treasury hesitant to fund it, and cost-benefit evaluation by imputing the estimated economic value of nonmonetary benefits to riders and highlighting its accompanying financial effects on Transport for London's bus services. (For the record, the Victoria line study persuaded the Treasury to change its mind and fund the substantial investment it required.)

Subsequent applications of cost-benefit analysis in the United Kingdom included several proposed port development projects, further extensions of the London Underground, electrification of British Rail commuter lines, a controversial master land use plan for the London metropolitan area, and the proposed Channel Tunnel connecting England and France. The Ministry of Transport began to develop formal methods for conducting cost-benefit analysis of proposed road projects in the early 1960s, although these were not officially adopted until somewhat later (Price 1999).

Not all of these early showcase applications of cost-benefit analysis were successes, however. The Roskill Commission was established to choose the site for a third airport serving London, but the commission's ultimate decision disregarded some key findings from its staff's analysis of benefits and costs for alternative locations (Dasgupta and Pearce 1972). Together with the implausibility to many interested observers of some of its staff's benefits estimates, the commission's decision to overrule the findings of its own economic evaluation of competing sites seemed to discredit the usefulness of the practice, at least temporarily.

In 1967, however, a U.K. government white paper recognized that in some situations the social benefits or costs of an investment could differ from the purely financial measures of its consequences and directed that in such cases cost-benefit analysis could be an appropriate supplement to the usual purely financial analysis of its prospective returns (Pearce 1983).[3] Over time, the scope of infrastructure investments requiring cost-benefit evaluation was gradually extended, and government agencies issued increasingly detailed guidelines for evaluation. Echoing developments in the United States, the government's guidance accorded progressively greater emphasis to valuing adverse environmental and social impacts and deducting these from user benefits, particularly for road projects (Price 1999).

Spread of Evaluation to International Development Agencies

Starting in the late 1960s, the application of cost-benefit analysis spread to developing nations—where it was first used to assess investments in irrigation, hydroelectric power, and transportation facilities—via its embrace by international aid agencies that guided or funded infrastructure investments intended to promote economic development. The foundational effort was the *Manual of Industrial Project Analysis*, prepared for the Organisation for Economic Co-operation and Development (OECD) by prominent British academics who had been deeply involved in (and at times skeptical of) developing and formalizing the practice (Little and Mirrlees 1969). The guidance that the manual presented was sufficiently widely accepted that it was revised and expanded within a few years (Little and Mirrlees 1974).

In the meantime, the United Nations Industrial Development Organization, established a decade earlier to promote industrialization in countries emerging from colonial rule, issued its own guidelines, again the work of academic experts who had made major contributions to the evolution of cost-benefit analysis (Dasgupta and Pearce 1972).[4] Within a few years, the World Bank weighed in with guidelines for its analysts conducting cost-benefit analysis of infrastructure investments in developing nations. These guidelines also relied extensively on Little and Mirrlees's (1969) report to the OECD (Squire and van der Tak 1975). The World Bank's evaluation guidelines were periodically expanded and updated, even as its use of cost-benefit analysis to evaluate projects was declining gradually from the time its earliest guidance was issued (World Bank 2010).

More recent guidance from international development agencies includes that issued by the U.S.-based Millennium Challenge Corporation (MCC 2017). The European Commission also offers guidelines for member nations conducting cost-benefit analysis of infrastructure projects, including transportation, water supply and wastewater treatment, energy supply, and broadband services. These require both financial and cost-benefit evaluation of proposed investments as well as an examination of the financial and economic risks confronting proposed projects (European Union 2014). Many nations around the globe also offer sector-specific guidance for conducting cost-benefit analysis of proposed investment projects, most commonly for transportation infrastructure but often extending to water supply, wastewater management, and energy supply.[5]

Extending the Scope of Infrastructure's Benefits and Costs

The global spread of cost-benefit evaluation was accompanied by continuing expansion of the range of economic benefits it attempted to address and improved theory and methods for measuring them in the practical setting of major infrastructure projects. The first critical step was expanding the range of benefits to infrastructure users themselves beyond the savings in recurring future costs that had been the mainstay of navigation, water supply, and flood control benefits from the water projects that were the first subjects of a benefit analysis. A second major step was to recognize the potential for infrastructure investments to generate companion benefits (and in some cases costs) that extended beyond their immediate users via their indirect impacts on markets for related goods, residents of surrounding communities, and perhaps even regional or national economies.

Beyond User Cost Savings

The U.S. government's Green Book had endorsed measuring water projects' benefits primarily from the cost reductions they offered to users, such as reducing operating expenses for barge and ship operators, providing lower-cost water supplies to farmers and municipalities, reducing expenses for controlling periodic flooding and redressing the damage it caused, sustaining the fertility of farmland, and generating lower-cost hydroelectric power (Subcommittee on Benefits and Costs 1950). The Green Book went on to describe secondary benefits that could arise where these savings reduced production costs and selling prices for what was termed *downstream products*, such as for food processed from crops grown on better-irrigated or more fertile land or manufactured goods produced from raw materials shipped at lower costs, thus prompting increases in their output and consumption. But the Green Book's guidance limited these secondary benefits to producers' cost savings; in the interest of avoiding double counting, it stopped short of including additional benefits to consumers when infrastructure projects reduced prices and prompted higher output (Subcommittee on Benefits and Costs 1950).

Value of Faster Travel

Recognizing the potentially pivotal role of benefits to infrastructure users over and above savings in businesses' operating expenses and costs that households paid out of pocket, new applications of the practice cast their net more widely, first by imputing an economic value to savings in users' time enabled by faster travel. The pioneering cost-benefit analysis of England's M1 motorway expanded the catalog of user benefits beyond savings in fuel use and other costs of operating cars and trucks by using workers' wage rates to impute an economic value of the time drivers and passengers would save by traveling at the faster speeds and over the more direct route that the new facility would permit (Coburn, Beesley, and Reynolds 1960). In the process, its authors also highlight the importance of comparing benefits for alternative project designs and explored the effect of uncertainty over their future use on the ideal timing of long-lived infrastructure investments (Foster 2001).

The subsequent cost-benefit evaluation of the London Underground's planned Victoria line expanded the range of nonmonetary benefits to include the value of the time that riders would save in transit, using typical hourly wages to value savings in working time but valuing time spent traveling for other purposes at only a fraction of wages. The analysis also imputed the value of improving the likelihood that riders would be seated throughout their trips by observing the additional time passengers were willing to wait to avoid full trains until one offering empty seats arrived (Foster and Beesley 1963). Its authors also took a pioneering step in the direction of including benefits that the investment would generate beyond those to underground passengers by valuing cost and time savings for London drivers and cost savings to Transport for London from operating its buses on less congested streets (Foster 2001).

The central role that the value of time savings played in these studies' estimates of benefits prompted an outpouring of empirical studies of the value of travel time, which persisted for three decades. The broad consensus of theory and empirical research on travel time to date is that its hourly value must bear some relationship to individuals' earnings rates (or to the value of leisure time for nonworking people), but that travel time also includes a component measuring the inconvenience of spending time in the circumstances traveling requires, whether in the controlled environment of private automobiles, in crowded public transit vehicles, or even on public sidewalks.

The most widespread current practice seems to be to value savings in working time using travelers' wage rates—often including an allowance for fringe benefits and taxes, since these are part of employers' costs for dispatching employees on trips during working hours—while valuing time savings during travel for other purposes at half or more of typical wage rates. Whether the hourly value of saving time should depend on the duration of time saved, either in absolute terms or in relation to trips' overall duration, remains in dispute; while researchers frequently express doubts about using the same hourly value for savings ranging from seconds to hours per trip and independently of trip length, using that same value remains the most widespread practice for the moment.

Benefits from More Reliable Travel

Over the past two decades, much of researchers' attention has turned to measuring the reliability of travel time—how much it varies for repeated daily trips departing at the usual hour and headed for the same destination, usually via the same route—and estimating the economic value of reductions in different measures of variability. No clear consensus about this value has yet emerged for three key reasons. Suitable measures of repeated trip times have only recently become available, many alternative (but mathematically and empirically related) measures of variability have been proposed, and finding situations where travelers or shippers choose among alternatives whose expected trip times and day-to-day differences vary independently from each other is difficult.

Empirical research on the value of reliability can be difficult to interpret, but overall it clearly suggests that improving the reliability of travel times has some distinct value over and above that of reducing trips' average or expected duration. Empirical estimates of the value of improving the same measure of reliability drawn from different studies even differ widely in response to their geographic settings, the travel modes they examine, the nature and source of their data, and estimation procedures. While some suggest that the hourly economic value of reducing variability is higher than that of reducing mean travel time, perhaps significantly so, this result is extremely sensitive to the specific measure of reliability that individual studies employ. Probably for these reasons, most nations' official guidance on valuing travel time do not yet recommend including any value for reducing variability in travel times in cost-benefit evaluations of proposed investments in transportation infrastructure, although they often do allow analysts to report anticipated improvements and discuss their likely utility (U.K. Department for Transport 2019; U.S. Department of Transportation 2016, 2020).

Valuing Unpriced Infrastructure Services: The Example of Recreation

Another early extension of the range of benefits to infrastructure users that might be practical to measure was to recreational use of water facilities such as reservoirs, even where these were primarily built to serve other purposes (power generation, flood control, domestic water supply, or navigability for shipping) where benefits could be measured as cost savings. The earliest analyses measured travel costs incurred by users residing at different distances from recreation destinations, often assigning monetary values to travel time in addition to expenses for driving, lodging, and meals.

Interpreting travel costs from different distances as prices and the frequency of visits by users traveling each distance as a measure of demand, as Hotelling

(1947) had proposed, analysts constructed demand curves that allowed them to infer the aggregate value that newly built or improved facilities provided to users. As long as the number of visitors traveling from different distances could be projected reasonably reliably for a new more proximate or desirable recreation facility, this process could be repeated to estimate the recreation benefits that building the facility would provide. Over time, studies of recreational use became more complex and provided more reliable measures of its value, including estimates of the value users attached to specific attributes such as cleaner water for swimming, abundance of fish, and even distinctive or unique scenic attractions (Phaneuf and Smith 2005).

Value of Safety

In contrast to other nonmarketed commodities such as travel time and recreational opportunities, the economic valuation of changes in public health and safety resulting from infrastructure investments has a shorter and less well-documented history. Until the early 1970s, reductions in the risks of accidental injury and death arising from the use of infrastructure (mainly motor vehicle travel on public roads and highways) were estimated by compiling historical data on injury-producing incidents and using engineering methods to estimate the reduction in their frequency likely to result from design features of new or expanded facilities.

Reductions in fatalities were initially assigned economic values by calculating the discounted value of typical victims' expected future contributions to economic output, usually measured by the income they were expected to earn over the remainder of their working lives (sometimes net of the value of their future consumption). The value of labor provided by those not formally employed outside the home was typically imputed from wages earned for similar work done on a paid basis. Other direct economic costs associated with accidental injury or death such as medical care expenses, emergency response services (e.g., police and fire), and incidental property damage were sometimes included as well (Jones-Lee 1985).

Later, several prominent analysts simultaneously concluded that this approach bore only accidental resemblance to the conceptually sounder measures of individuals' willingness to pay to reduce the safety risks they faced or the compensation they would demand to tolerate higher risks. In addition, the analysts noted, the foregone earnings measure had objectionable implications for valuing the safety of nonworking and retired persons (Jones-Lee 1969; Mishan 1970; Schelling 1968). To develop initial empirical estimates of these preferred measures of the value of reducing safety risks, researchers used statistical analyses of the higher wages workers earned in riskier occupations or of their responses to surveys asking how much they would pay or require as compensation for changes in the risks they regularly faced (Acton 1976; Jones-Lee 1976; Smith 1973; Thaler and Rosen 1976). Early dollar-denominated estimates using the former approach varied by an order of magnitude while those derived from surveys differed by more than two orders, so their practical value was limited (Jones-Lee 1985).

Fueled by improved occupational data, more rigorous survey methods, and advances in econometric analysis, estimates of individuals' collective willingness to pay to reduce the risks of accidental death they face have since proliferated. Many of these more recent analyses employ the original wage-risk approach, while others examine trade-offs involving time or convenience for risk (e.g., use of automobile safety belts). Still others rely on survey respondents' stated willingness to pay or a statistical analysis of their choices among hypothetical alternatives that entail different combinations of cost or income and safety risk. Cost-benefit evaluations of proposed investments in transportation infrastructure now routinely include estimates of benefits from users' reduced risks of being fatally injured, although their use in evaluating other forms of public infrastructure appears to be less common.

Improving the "Resilience" of Infrastructure

Recently, the looming prospect of climate change has drawn attention to the value of protecting infrastructure assets against potential weather-related reductions in their capacity, interruptions of the services they provide, and even structural damage, although methods for estimating benefits from improving resiliency are still in their early stages. Measuring costs to public agencies for restoring the functionality and capacity of assets on an emergency basis is straightforward, but anticipating the impact of alternative infrastructure designs on the likelihood or frequency of damage and repairs is not. Further, the protection afforded by alternative facility designs or locations is likely to be specific to individual investment projects.

Other benefits from fortifying infrastructure against extreme weather events include less widespread or shorter disruptions to services. However, these advantages often require detailed models of supply to calculate reliably, and valuing them is complex and data-intensive. Another challenge is estimating how economic benefits from avoiding disruptions to infrastructure services will change in the future, as their use is typically expected to grow over time, while the frequency, scale, and severity of extreme climate-related events—all highly uncertain and with wide distributions—seem likely to do the same.

Beyond User Benefits: Accounting for External Benefits and Costs

Another realization spawned by the increasing global reach of cost-benefit evaluation was that by extending the availability of and reducing costs for the services it provided, investing in new infrastructure often generates benefits (and perhaps costs as well) beyond those it offered to its users. One obvious way these supplemental benefits or costs might arise was through the impacts of new or expanded infrastructure on demand and prices for substitute services, such as when constructing a new subway line drew travelers out of automobiles or when building a new dam and reservoir to expand water supply and generate power drew recreational users away from less attractive sites. Another avenue for benefits from building new facilities to extend beyond their immediate users is by reducing economic or environmental spillovers, such as where hydroelectric power generation replaces fossil fuel plants or improving local roads makes pedestrians safer and reduces noise for surrounding residents.

There is widespread consensus that when the use of infrastructure generates economic or environmental externalities, infrastructure investments that reduce these harmful spillovers generate supplemental benefits that should be included when assessing proposed improvements. This principle for recognizing supplemental benefits applies to reductions in externalities from the use of improved or expanded infrastructure as well as from reduced use of competing facilities from which it draws new users.[6] Symmetrically, where the construction or subsequent use of new infrastructure aggravates any of these externalities, the resulting increase in economic damages represents an additional cost of investing in it (Boardman et al. 2017).

Current Issues and Challenges

Job-Creation Argument

Rigorous use of cost-benefit analysis is often challenged by its rivalry and confusion with the deceptively similar practice of economic impact analysis, which applies the measurement conventions of cost-benefit analysis within a geographically circumscribed area without accounting fully for its economic linkages to the region or nation within which it is embedded. One consequence is that local analysts and officials often focus on a project's job-creation potential, usually measured by wage payments to local workers employed during its construction phase without accounting for the fact that projects are funded largely or entirely by taxpayers living elsewhere. While a broader geographic perspective would value workers' labor services as the opportunity cost of sacrificing their output in alternative jobs from which the project draws labor and treat their wage payments as a transfer, delimiting the area encompassed by the evaluation makes their income appear as a local benefit with no offsetting cost.[7]

The job-creation argument for investing in infrastructure can also arise even when proposed projects are evaluated from a national perspective. Constructing public infrastructure facilities normally employs workers who would otherwise have been employed in private construction, in which case the value of their labor in activities that are sacrificed when a government agency hires them away represents a cost of the public project. But if the workers it hires were previously unemployed, that cost is limited to the opportunity value of their leisure time; political officials implicitly assume that the latter situation prevails when they claim that projects they advocate will create jobs.

The main difficulty with this argument is verifying that workers would otherwise have been unemployed by the time a planned project gets underway. Even if unemployment is unusually high when a project is in its formative stages, the period that elapses until its construction begins is often measured in years, by which time the economy may have recovered to essentially full employment. In addition, major infrastructure projects often require skilled construction labor that remains in high demand throughout all but extreme economic cycles. Thus, the assertion that skilled workers would be unemployed if a project does not go forward is often empirically unpersuasive.[8] While it seems wise for analysts to be skeptical of claims that infrastructure projects will actually create jobs and to place the burden of proof on advocates making such claims, this skepticism can bring them into predictably unproductive conflicts with powerful political interests.

Continuing Controversies over Discounting

While no serious analyst disputes the importance of discounting benefits and costs anticipated to occur during future years to comparable present values, the proper rates for doing so remain controversial, and practices differ widely around the globe. One reason is that there are two different rationales for discounting future benefits or costs. The first holds that if capital investments earn positive economic returns elsewhere in the economy, future benefits from infrastructure should be discounted using the rate of return on alternative private or public investments from which they divert capital (often termed the *social opportunity cost of capital*). In contrast, a consumption-based discount rate reflects the trade-off a society is collectively willing to make between current and future consumption, measured as the annual rate at which the latter must grow for people to regard it as equivalent to (and thus for them to be willing to defer) current consumption (usually called the *social rate of time preference*).

If markets for financial intermediation worked seamlessly and were unaffected by taxes or other interventions, the rate of return on savings and investment would equal this consumption discount rate, but this is rarely the case. Hence, it is nearly always necessary for analysts to choose between the two measures. One strategy under these circumstances is to calculate a weighted average of the two rates using the proportions of infrastructure funding believed to be drawn from deferred consumption and private investment as weights. A more practical alternative is to repeat the analysis by using estimates of both rates to test whether the choice between them has a pivotal effect on its outcome.

Other rationales sometimes offered for discounting include accounting for inflation and risk, but the general consensus is that these are better dealt with separately and directly than by attempting to incorporate them in discount rates. Inflation can be accounted for in one of two ways. One approach is to denominate future costs and benefits promised by an investment in real or constant dollar terms and discount them at a rate that excludes any inflation component. The other approach expresses future values in nominal or current dollar terms and discounts them at a rate that incorporates expectations about future price inflation. For their part, risk and uncertainty are better recognized explicitly and treated using one of the approaches discussed below than accounted for by incorporating a risk premium into the discount rate. Of course, interest rates observed in financial markets incorporate inflation expectations and a range of risk premiums, so both of these need to be estimated and subtracted out to convert the rates to risk-free real interest rates.

Measuring Discount Rates

Although interest rates on investment are usually easy to measure, the discount rate that society applies to future consumption cannot be observed, leaving analysts to construct it from first principles or approximate it using market interest rates on low-risk investments such as government bonds. Deriving the social discount rate on future consumption requires knowing people's inherent preference for current versus future consumption (usually called the *pure rate of time preference*), how fast the economy will grow over the future, and the effect of increasing consumption levels on the incremental value of consuming still more. Each of these components is extremely difficult to estimate.

The choice between using investment returns or consumption-based discount rates ultimately boils down to a philosophical choice, pitting the view that the discount rate should be anchored in observed market behavior against the perspective that the importance of according the future is an ethical choice that should be a matter of public policy. Many economists take the appealingly simple position that because investing in infrastructure is intended to enhance future consumption opportunities, a consumption-based rate is appropriate for discounting them to their present values.[9] In contrast, many governments and most international agencies continue to recommend discounting future benefits from infrastructure investments at market rates of interest.[10]

Discounting the Distant Future

Infrastructure facilities can produce benefits that extend for decades into the future; over such a long period, discount rates are inherently uncertain regardless of whether they are based on investment returns or consumption behavior. In theory, such uncertainty supports using discount rates that decline over time, at least for the longest-lived forms of investment (e.g., dams, rail lines, tunnels), and some research finds that people even appear to use declining discount rates in their own decision making (Pearce, Atkinson, and Mourato 2006). One complication is that declining discount rates imply seemingly irrational behavior over the future, in which individuals will initially be willing to defer current consumption to make long-term investments yet consistently make the opposite decision once future years arrive. A proposed resolution for evaluating long-lived infrastructure investments is to use a constant investment-based discount rate but reduce it slightly from the value suggested by financial market interest rates to compensate for uncertainty about its correct value (Cropper and Laibson 1998).[11]

What Do Analysts Actually Do?

Table 6.1 summarizes discounting practices for various types of infrastructure investments recommended by national governments and international funding agencies. The wide range of recommended discount rates it reports mainly reflects governments' and funding agencies' differing choices between consumption- and investment-based measures. These choices presumably reveal their contrasting views of how investing in public infrastructure is likely to affect domestic consumption, private investment, and in some cases foreign borrowing, which are apparently viewed as having sharply differing opportunity costs. The wide range of rates that governments and agencies endorse may also reflect efforts to incorporate other considerations such as intergenerational distribution of economic opportunity, risks that projects' benefits may not be fully realized, and the perceived merits of wider public benefits versus enhanced private consumption.

TABLE 6.1 Recommended Discount Rates for Infrastructure Investments

Source	Application	Recommended Rate(s)	Rationale
European Commission	Transportation, water supply and wastewater management, energy production and distribution, broadband service	4%	Consumption discount rate
Australia	Transportation, housing, energy	7%	Government borrowing rate plus significant risk premium
	Schools, hospitals, civic buildings	4%	Government borrowing rate plus minimal risk premium
Canada	All infrastructure	10%	Opportunity cost of capital
China	All infrastructure	8% but lower for long-term projects	Weighted average of opportunity cost of capital and consumption discount rate
France	All infrastructure	4%	Consumption discount rate
Germany	All infrastructure	3%	Government borrowing rate
India	All infrastructure	12%	Opportunity cost of capital
New Zealand	Infrastructure, except telecommunications and information technology	8%	Opportunity cost of capital
Norway	Transportation projects	4%, declining with project life	Government borrowing rate
Philippines	All infrastructure	15%	Opportunity cost of capital
United Kingdom	Transportation, water supply and treatment, energy supply	3.5% but lower for long-term projects	Consumption discount rate
United States	Federally funded infrastructure	3%, 7%	Consumption discount rate, opportunity cost of capital
Sweden	Transportation projects	3.5%	Consumption discount rate
World Bank, African Development Bank, and Asian Development Bank	All infrastructure	10–12%	Weighted average of opportunity cost of capital and consumption discount rate

(continued)

TABLE 6.1 *continued*

Source	Application	Recommended Rate(s)	Rationale
Inter-American Development Bank	All infrastructure	12%	Opportunity cost of capital
European Bank for Reconstruction and Development	All infrastructure	10%	Opportunity cost of capital
Millennium Challenge Corporation	All infrastructure	10%	"Required" rate of return on public funds

Sources: Asian Development Bank (2013); European Union (2014); Grimes (2010); Infrastructure Australia (2018); MCC (2017); Swedish Transport Administration (2020).

Coping with Uncertainty in Future Costs and Benefits

Most of the parameters, forecasts, and assumptions necessary for conducting cost-benefit analysis are inherently uncertain; this uncertainty can be particularly significant over the extended lifetime of many forms of infrastructure.[12] Accounting explicitly for uncertainty provides one means for examining the robustness of investment decisions and identifying proposed projects that are particularly risky for planning and funding agencies. Cost-benefit analysts have developed progressively more complex methods for incorporating uncertainty in estimates of proposed investments' costs and benefits, although analysts seem to rarely employ even the simplest of these, perhaps because it is often inconvenient for the public officials they serve to acknowledge the fragility of favored investment choices.

Sensitivity Testing and Probabilistic Methods

The simplest method for examining uncertainty about an investment's outcome is to test the effect of plausible departures from the estimated or assumed values of specific parameters or other inputs on which its cost-benefit evaluation relies. This straightforward approach offers an effective way to identify the specific inputs on which the desirability of a proposed investment rests. Where plausible variation in any of them changes the economic case for a project, this variation provides an obvious signal that additional efforts to resolve critical uncertainties are worthwhile.

Sensitivity testing can also be used to examine the consequences of simultaneous departures of multiple inputs from their assumed or most likely values; this process is often referred to as *scenario analysis*. Possible combinations of multiple uncertain inputs proliferate quickly, so this method is best reserved for cases where the possibilities can be restricted by anticipating how multiple inputs are likely to vary jointly for some common underlying reason, such as in response to alternative economic growth rates.

Probability-Based Approaches

More formal methods for incorporating uncertainty in estimates of infrastructure projects' future outcomes involve specifying the probabilities associated with alternative values of key parameters or other inputs and using them to calculate probabilistic expected values of benefits and costs. A still more demanding approach, known colorfully as the Monte Carlo analysis, specifies complete (although often greatly simplified) probability distributions for each critical parameter or other input used in a cost-benefit analysis. Each trial draws randomly from those distributions to produce a complete combination of inputs, and this process is repeated a number of times to trace the resulting probability distributions of benefits and costs.

Because assessing the exact probabilities of alternative input values can be analytically demanding, these approaches are often invoked after sensitivity analysis has identified those (hopefully few) uncertain inputs where alternative values would have the largest impact on a project's anticipated benefits and costs, leaving the other parameters to be held at their central values. Advances in computing power and data management capabilities have removed the original objection that this method was too demanding computationally for regular use. However, the challenge of specifying even simplified probability distributions for each critical parameter remains daunting, so this method is still not widely used.

Dealing with Extreme Uncertainty

Most recently, advances in data analytics and computing power have enabled the development of methods for incorporating extreme forms of uncertainty in investment decisions that arise where the probabilities associated with alternative possible values of critical parameters affecting projects' future benefits are not just uncertain but also unknowable. Their general approach is to specify a wide range of plausible alternative combinations of future conditions without assigning probabilities to each one and to assess the performance of different decisions (here, the design and selection of infrastructure projects) under alternative versions of the future (Groves and Lempert 2007; Kalra et al. 2014; Lempert and Groves 2010). Visualization techniques or statistical analyses can then be applied to the extensive database of results to identify choices that perform well under a wide range of possible future conditions.

Many different decision rules exist for selecting the best-performing alternative, such as picking the choice that produces the least undesirable worst outcome under any future conditions or whose outcome compares most favorably to the decision one would make if the future were certain. However, this approach generally favors choices that yield maximum benefits under the widest range of possible future states. So far, most applications of this approach to proposed infrastructure investments have involved designing water supply or treatment systems and evaluating alternative measures to improve the resilience of flood control and transportation infrastructure (e.g., Dessai and Hulme 2007; Fischbach et al. 2015; Ghile 2014; Groves et al. 2013; Lempert and Groves 2010; Zeff et al. 2014).

Alternative Measures of User Benefit in Transportation

Accessibility-Based Benefit Measures

Alternatives to travel time savings include gravity-type measures that weight travelers' access to alternative destinations such as employment or shopping opportunities by the inverse of the time required to travel to each one, so destinations that can be reached more quickly are valued more highly. Simpler versions of this same idea count the number of such opportunities that travelers can reach within some travel time threshold, and these appear to be more commonly used (Boisjoly and El-Geneid 2017; Venter 2016). Changes in either of these measures resulting from proposed investments in new or expanded transportation facilities would measure the improved accessibility to desirable destinations they offer, which proponents argue offers a more meaningful index of project benefits.

The challenge with such measures is converting them to monetary values to make them conformable with other measures of proposed investments' benefits and costs. One obvious way to do so would be to apply some economic value to the shorter trip time required to reach each alternative destination, presumably weighted in some way by the likelihood that each destination would be chosen. However, this approach would generate benefit measures exactly analogous to aggregate travel time savings, even if their measurement scale differed systematically from the traditional metric. Perhaps anticipating this outcome, most analysts seem to recommend using accessibility measures to supplement rather than replace conventional estimates of the economic value of travel time savings.

Logsum Measures

An alternative measure that seems capable of incorporating the effect of changes in travel time on the trip destinations people choose is the utility improvement that can be calculated using multilevel (or nested) statistical models of travel choices.

These choices can include the frequency, timing, and destinations of trips as well as the modes and routes that travelers select. Changes in travel speeds on routes or services that are improved by new investments will alter the values of these measures—commonly referred to as *logsums* because of the mathematical formula used to calculate them—to reflect their influence on the entire hierarchy of travelers' potential choices that models recognize. By using the estimated weights that travelers attach to the dollar costs of travel as a numeraire, these logsum measures can then be translated from utility changes to equivalent dollar values.

Again, however, these measures reduce mathematically to conventional consumer surplus calculations and under plausible conditions will duplicate the usual monetary measures of benefits from faster or more direct travel.[13] (Specifically, they reduce to Hicks's original measures of changes in welfare for which consumer surplus usually offers a close approximation.) Thus, while these measures offer a convenient and internally consistent method for estimating user benefits from improved travel conditions within demand modeling frameworks that represent a hierarchy of travelers' choices, they do not provide broader or more inclusive measures of user benefits than traditional methods (Eliasson 2019; Pozdena 2015). While it may be easier to extend logsum-based benefit measures to evaluate simultaneous improvements in attributes of travel beyond faster speeds, constructing models that generate these measures requires exactly the same information about these other features' influence on travelers' choices as is necessary to impute their respective dollar values and include them in the conventional consumer surplus measures of user benefits (Eliasson 2019).

Land Value Increases

Some analysts propose measuring the value of accessibility improvements by calculating increases in aggregate land value within the area served by new infrastructure investments (e.g., Cervero 2011). One complication is the difficulty of isolating any contribution of improved transportation access to a site from the myriad other factors that influence land values there, particularly in rapidly growing urban areas. Another is that the value of travel time savings that are the original source of any accessibility improvement are likely to have been measured separately and already included in the economic evaluation of proposed investments, raising the possibility that they will be counted twice. Where measuring direct benefits to travelers is too difficult, however, relying on land value increases may offer an attractive alternative, provided that property transactions or appraisals are sufficiently frequent and historical records are reliable enough to enable isolating the contribution of improved infrastructure.

Are There Wider Economic Benefits from Investing in Infrastructure?

An increasingly frequent assertion is that the measures of user and external benefits normally employed to evaluate investments in infrastructure—particularly new or expanded transportation facilities—can omit important economic adaptations that occur in response and, by doing so, underestimate projects' benefits.[14] The current consensus is that additional benefits beyond those measured in a conventional economic analysis of proposed investments can arise via three channels: denser clustering of economic activity that investments in high-capacity transportation facilities support, changes in the value or geographic pattern of private capital invested at and around sites where new infrastructure improves access, and improvements in competition in local markets for delivered products (Laird and Venables 2017).

Even in these cases, however, wider benefits are likely to arise only when the effects of new infrastructure are transmitted through the broader economy via markets that are inadequately competitive, incompletely developed, or performing inefficiently as a consequence of externalities, taxes, or other distortions. Some analysts argue that firms' reorganization of their production processes or logistics and distribution systems to take advantage of improved accessibility to specific sites can be another source of wider benefits, but the resulting cost savings are most likely to be internal to those firms and are thus more accurately viewed as user benefits (Laird and Venables 2017; Mohring and Williamson 1969).

Agglomeration Effects and Productivity

Expanding the scale or capacity of transportation infrastructure increases the effective proximity of households and firms to one another by shortening travel times among them and may also prompt some to relocate to sites that improved infrastructure makes more advantageous or desirable. Both of these responses increase the effective density of economic activity and thus facilitate closer interactions among firms and their workers, which can contribute to improved productivity by enabling firms and their workers to specialize and synergistic clusters of service suppliers and users to form.

Larger agglomerations of firms and workers also spur productivity by increasing opportunities to more closely match firms' demands for specialized skills with those that workers offer. At the same time, closer interactions within dense clusters of economic activity can spur more rapid development and diffusion of innovations in technology, products or services, and production processes as knowledge and innovation spill over from one firm or its employees to neighboring firms. Finally, reducing the barriers of travel time and shipping costs can make local labor and product markets more competitive, thus eroding price markups and other economic inefficiencies that can arise where competition is less than robust.

Public Infrastructure and Private Investment

The improved accessibility of particular sites or land parcels that infrastructure investment provides can also reduce production costs or raise economic returns to private capital investment there, thus altering the geographic pattern of private investment and conceivably even leading to an overall increase in investment. Normally, this process will not generate benefits beyond those experienced directly by users of the improved infrastructure. If real estate or product markets in some locations served by new facilities are not fully competitive, the resulting expansion of supply can provide supplemental benefits beyond those experienced directly by infrastructure users.

If investment at sites where new infrastructure improves access expands the range or variety of employment, shopping, or entertainment opportunities there, additional benefits beyond time savings to travelers destined there can also arise. To some extent, however, these benefits are likely to overlap with the agglomeration effects described above. Finally, consolidation of property ownership into limited hands, interdependencies among competing developers' investment decisions, and government land use controls sometimes inhibit development at otherwise opportune sites. If by making such sites more accessible new or expanded infrastructure helps overcome these barriers and spur more intense development, new investments in infrastructure can again generate benefits beyond the savings to travelers themselves on which the evaluation of proposed investments normally focuses.

Conclusions

Now that nearly a century of intensive effort has so thoroughly revamped evaluation methods, and extensive resources are routinely lavished on assessing proposed infrastructure investments, it is only natural to ask how much influence evaluation actually has on selecting those projects that are ultimately funded. One early U.S. study found that California's highway department appeared to base its investment choices mainly on how competing projects' anticipated benefits compared with their likely costs (McFadden 1976). In contrast, a subsequent study found that the results of cost-benefit analysis had only a very limited effect on the central government's choices among alternative investments in transportation facilities in Sweden (Nilsson 1991). Other early analyses reached similar conclusions about investment decisions in Norway (Fridström and Elvik 1997; Nyborg 1998; Odeck 1996).

A detailed study of road and highway investment decisions in the United Kingdom concluded that while the summary numerical results of competing projects' cost-benefit evaluations did not appear to influence government agencies' choices among them, certain detailed components of projects' benefits (improving the reliability of travel, reducing highway noise, promoting redevelopment, historic preservation, and protecting the natural landscape) did seem to affect funding decisions (Nellthorp and Mackie 2000). A similar analysis of road and highway investments in the Netherlands showed that proposed projects whose benefits appeared likely to fall short of their costs tended to be postponed for later reconsideration, and their scope and cost were often pared back to improve their chances of being selected later (Annema, Koopmans, and Van Wee 2007).

Nevertheless, there is some limited evidence that the numerical results of cost-benefit evaluations for proposed investment projects directly affect funding prospects. Eliasson and Lundberg (2012) note that projects' likelihood of being selected for the Swedish Long-Term Transport Investment Plan depended partly on their ratings from cost-benefit evaluation, and their finding was echoed in a more recent study of the next Swedish plan (Bondemark et al. 2020). Most emphatically, a study of decisions to fund public infrastructure investments in Chile showed that projected benefits exceeding a project's anticipated cost were almost always necessary for it to be selected (Gómez-Lobo 2012).

In short, most evidence about whether economic evaluation directly affects infrastructure funding decisions comes from the transportation sector and tells a decidedly mixed story. Circumstances where favorable numerical results from cost-benefit analysis directly affect projects' chances of being selected for funding certainly seem to be limited. However, government agencies and elected political officials often seem to rely on specific aspects of economic evaluation when they choose projects to promote and ultimately fund. In some cases, cost-benefit evaluation seems to make it more awkward for advocates to promote their favored investments publicly when those do not appear promising on the basis of economic evaluation, or at least pressure the advocates to reveal their motivations for favoring projects. By doing so, economic evaluation probably helps forestall some truly unwise investments even if it cannot ensure that the most promising projects will always proceed.

Summary

- Cost-benefit analysis is almost universally used by governments and international financial institutions to evaluate major public infrastructure projects.

- The practice has become increasingly sophisticated, mainly in the development of methods used to estimate the value that infrastructure users place on the benefits they receive.

- One controversy is whether to continue to exclude wider economic impacts from cost-benefit analyses on the grounds that they typically do not reflect separate and additional costs or benefits but instead reflect transfers of costs and benefits from those directly impacted to other parties.

- The little available evidence suggests that decision makers rarely adopt the alternative ranked most highly in cost-benefit terms, but the rankings may discourage the adoption of one of the worst options.

Notes

1. Dupuit even appeared to recognize how the performance of capital facilities could deteriorate as a consequence of continued use under conventional maintenance practices and recognized such depreciation as a cost whose correct measure could differ from the periodic outlays for labor and materials used to maintain facilities (Vatin, Simonin, and Marco 2016, 9597).

2. Like Dupuit, Marshall recognized that expanding infrastructure could provide important economic benefits to both previous users of the improved facilities and additional users who were newly attracted by its improvement. In many ways, the contrast between Dupuit's focus on the consumers of transported products and Marshall's focus on the providers of transportation services who used public infrastructure presaged the current debate over whether infrastructure provides benefits beyond those to its users that need to be accounted for separately when evaluating proposed investments.

3. This cautious approach and the supplemental role of cost-benefit analysis seems to persist even in the most recent U.K. government guidance on evaluating investments in some forms of infrastructure: transportation capital investments require an evaluation of financial impacts on private operators (as well as on the central government budget) in addition to the usual comparison of user and social benefits to project costs.

4. These were later updated to incorporate selected principles from Little and Mirrlees's project evaluation guidelines for the OECD (UNIDO 1986).

5. One particularly detailed and prescriptive example is the guidelines for evaluating proposed investments in transportation infrastructure maintained by the U.K. Department for Transport (2019). An extreme case is the United States, where several different federal agencies offer separate guidance for cost-benefit evaluation; within the U.S. Department of Transportation alone, agencies offer separate—and occasionally conflicting—guidance for evaluating proposed investments in highways, freight and passenger rail service, public transit, airports, and air traffic control facilities.

6. While it might seem counterintuitive that expanding infrastructure can increase its use but reduce the externalities it generates, this phenomenon can occur where expanding road capacity reduces traffic congestion and the resulting delays that vehicles cause to one another. Other examples arise where improvements to the design of major facilities reduce safety

risks for their users, visual or noise impacts on surrounding residents, or emissions of air pollutants and climate-altering greenhouse gases.

7. Correctly recognizing the opportunity cost of labor that would otherwise be employed in an alternative use should help remedy this problem, but that recognition seems rare even where the skilled construction labor that infrastructure projects generally use is already in high demand and fully employed.

8. The research reported in chapter 2 of this volume, which finds that stimulus packages have very little impact on gross domestic product or employment within their first two years, generally supports this view.

9. For example, early project evaluation guidelines from the United Nations International Development Organization (UNIDO) unequivocally endorse consumption discount rates: "The discount rate depends on the numeraire; for example, the numeraire in the UNIDO method is consumption, so the discount rate is the consumption rate of interest" (UNIDO 1986, 123).

10. Cost-benefit guidance issued by the U.S. government provides estimates of both rates and delineates the circumstances whereby each should apply but encourages analysts to discount proposed projects' future benefits and costs using both rates and to compare the results to test whether the choice between them is pivotal. Strictly speaking, this guidance is intended for cost-benefit analysis as applied to proposed government regulations rather than investments, but it is often applied to the latter (U.S. Office of Management and Budget 2003).

11. This approach differs from adjusting market interest rates to reflect risk that future returns may not fully materialize.

12. Something of a cottage industry has arisen to document departures of projects' actual performance from the forecasts of their costs and usage on which decisions to fund them originally depended. It is not yet clear whether documenting large errors for past projects has tempered planners' enthusiasm for risky future investments. For more on this issue, see chapter 12 of this volume.

13. Specifically, they reduce to Hicks's original measures of changes in welfare, for which consumer surplus usually offers a close approximation.

14. Some analysts trace the possibility for omitted benefits back as far as Marshall's focus on measuring benefits from investing in transportation infrastructure using price and activity changes within transportation markets themselves in contrast to Dupuit's earlier focus on measuring benefits from changes in prices and quantities of raw materials and finished products that are transported. The latter perspective introduces the possibility that investments can generate benefits that arise outside the markets for transportation services and that focusing exclusively on changes in transportation costs and activity when evaluating proposed investments might ignore those benefits (e.g., Rothengatter 2017).

References

Acton, Jan Paul. 1976. "Measuring the Monetary Value of Lifesaving Programs." *Law and Contemporary Problems* 40(4): 46–72.

Annema, Jan Anne, Carl Koopmans, and Bert Van Wee. 2007. "Evaluating Transport Infrastructure Investments: The Dutch Experience with a Standardized Approach." *Transport Reviews* 27(2): 125–150.

Asian Development Bank. 2013. *Cost-Benefit Analysis for Development: A Practical Guide.* Mandaluyong City, Philippines: Asian Development Bank.

Banzhaf, H. Spencer. 2010. "Consumer Surplus with Apology: A Historical Perspective on Non-market Valuation and Recreation Demand." *Annual Review of Resource Economics* 2: 183–207.

Boardman, Anthony, David Greenberg, Aidan Vining, and David Weimer. 2017. *Cost-Benefit Analysis: Concepts and Practice.* Cambridge, MA: Cambridge University Press.

Boisjoly, Genevieve, and Ahmed El-Geneid. 2017. *Measuring Performance: Accessibility Metrics in Metropolitan Regions Around the World.* Washington, DC: Brookings Institution.

Bondemark, Anders, Pia Sundbergh, Patrik Tornberg, and Karin Brundell-Freij. 2020. "Do Impact Assessments Influence Transport Plans? The Case of Sweden." *Transportation Research Part A: Policy and Practice* 134: 52–64.

Bos, Hendricus C., and Leendert M. Koyck. 1961. "The Appraisal of Road Construction Projects: A Practical Example." *Review of Economics and Statistics* 43: 13–20.

Cervero, Robert. 2011. *Going Beyond Travel Time Savings.* Washington, DC: International Bank for Reconstruction and Development and World Bank.

Chicago Chapter of the American Statistical Association. 2011. "History of Cost Benefit Analysis." https://community.amstat.org/zthechicagochapterold/calendar/pastevents/20052006 /may52006conference/downloadpresentationshistoryofcostbenefitanalysis.

Clawson, Marion, and Jack Knetsch. 1966. *Economics of Outdoor Recreation.* Washington, DC: Resources for the Future.

Coburn, Thomas, Michael Beesley, and D. J. Reynolds. 1960. "The London-Birmingham Motorway: Traffic and Economics." Technical paper No. 46. Road Research Laboratory. London: HMSO.

Cropper, Maureen, and David Laibson. 1998. "The Implications of Hyperbolic Discounting for Project Evaluation." Policy Research working paper No. 1943. Washington, DC: World Bank Economic Development Group. https://www.econ.umd.edu/sites/www.econ.umd .edu/files/pubs/jc41.pdf.

Dasgupta, Ajit, and David Pearce. 1972. *Cost-Benefit Analysis: Theory and Practice.* London: Macmillan.

Dessai, Suraje, and Mike Hulme. 2007. "Assessing the Robustness of Adaptation Decisions to Climate Change Uncertainties: A Case Study on Water Resources Management in the East of England." *Global Environmental Change* 17(1): 59–72.

Ekelund, Robert, Jr., and Robert Hebert. 1985. "Consumer Surplus: The First Hundred Years." *History of Political Economy* 17(3): 419–454.

———. 1997. *A History of Economic Theory and Method.* Long Grove, IL: Waveland.

Eliasson, Jonas. 2019. "Reconciling Accessibility Benefits with User Benefits." Discussion paper No. 182. International Transport Forum. https://www.itf-oecd.org/sites/default/files/docs /reconciling-accessibility-user-benefits.pdf.

Eliasson, Jonas, and Mattias Lundberg. 2012. "Do Cost-Benefit Analyses Influence Transport Investment Decisions? Experiences from the Swedish Transport Investment Plan 2010–21." *Transport Reviews* 1: 29–48.

European Union. 2014. *Guide to Cost-Benefit Analysis of Investment Projects: Economic Appraisal Tool for Cohesion Policy 2014–2020.* Brussels: European Commission Directorate General for Regional and Urban Policy.

Fischbach, Jordan, Robert Lempert, Edmundo Molina-Perez, Abdul Tariq, Melissa Finu-
cane, and Frauke Hoss. 2015. "Managing Water Quality in the Face of Uncertainty:
A Robust Decision-Making Demonstration for EPA's National Water Program." Report
PR-1148-EPA. Santa Monica, CA: RAND Corporation.

Foster, C. D., and Michael Beesley. 1963. "Estimating the Social Benefit of Constructing an
Underground Railway in London." *Journal of the Royal Statistical Society, Series A* 126(1): 46–93.

Foster, Christopher. 2001. "Michael Beesley and Cost Benefit Analysis." *Journal of Transport
Economics and Policy* 35(1): 3–30.

Fridström, Lasse, and Rune Elvik. 1997. "The Barely Revealed Preference Behind Road Investment Priorities." *Public Choice* 92(1–2): 145–168.

Ghile, Yonas, Mehmet Tanner, Casey Brown, Johan Grijsen, and Amal Talbi. 2014. "Bottom-
Up Climate Risk Assessment of Infrastructure Investment in the Niger River Basin."
Climatic Change 122 (1–2): 97–110.

Gómez-Lobo, Andres. 2012. "Institutional Safeguards for Cost Benefit Analysis: Lessons
from the Chilean National Investment System." *Journal of Benefit-Cost Analysis* 3(1): 1–28.

Grimes, Arthur. 2010. "The Economics of Infrastructure Investment: Beyond Simple Cost
Benefit Analysis." Working paper 10-05. Wellington, New Zealand: Motu Economic
and Public Policy Research.

Groves, David, Jordan Fischbach, Erika Bloom, Debra Knopman, and Ryan Keefe. 2013.
"Adapting to a Changing Colorado River: Making Future Water Deliveries More Reli-
able Through Robust Management Strategies." Report No. 242-BOR. Santa Monica, CA:
RAND Corporation.

Groves, David, and Robert Lempert. 2007. "A New Analytic Method for Finding Policy-
Relevant Scenarios." *Global Environmental Change* 17(1): 73–85.

Hammond, Richard J. 1966. "Convention and Limitation in Benefit-Cost Analysis." *Natural
Resources Journal* 6(2): 195–222.

Hotelling, Harold. 1947. "Letter to the National Park Service." Reprinted in National Park
Service, Recreational Planning Division, *An Economic Study of the Monetary Evaluation of
Recreation in the National Parks*. Washington, DC: U.S. Department of the Interior, 1949.

Infrastructure Australia. 2018. "Assessment Framework." Australian Government Department
of Infrastructure, Transport, Regional Development, and Communications. Canberra,
Australia.

Jones-Lee, Michael W. 1969. "Valuation of Reduction in Probability of Death by Road Accident." *Journal of Transport Economics and Policy* 3(1): 37–47.

———. 1976. *The Value of Life: An Economic Analysis*. London: Martin Robertson.

———. 1985. "The Value of Life and Safety: A Survey of Recent Developments." *The Geneva
Papers on Risk and Insurance* 10(36): 141–173.

Kalra, Nidhi, Stephane Hallegatte, Robert Lempert, Casey Brown, Adrian Fozzard, Stuart Gill,
and Ankur Shah. 2014. "Agreeing on Robust Decisions: A New Process of Decision Making Under Deep Uncertainty." Working paper No. 6906. Washington, DC: World Bank.

Knetsch, Jack. 1963. "Outdoor Recreation Demands and Benefits." *Land Economics* 39(4):
387–396.

———. 1964. "Economics of Including Recreation as a Purpose of Eastern Water Projects."
Journal of Farm Economics 46(5): 1148–1157.

Krutilla, John V. 1981. "Reflections of an Applied Welfare Economist." *Journal of Environmental Economics and Management* 8(1): 1–10.

Laird, James, and Anthony Venables. 2017. "Transport Investment and Economic Performance: A Framework for Project Appraisal." *Transport Policy* 56: 1–11.

Lempert, Robert, and David Groves. 2010. "Identifying and Evaluating Robust Adaptive Policy Responses to Climate Change for Water Management Agencies in the American West." *Technological Forecasting and Social Change* 77(6): 960–974.

Little, Ian M. D., and James Mirrlees. 1969. *Manual of Industrial Project Analysis*, vol. 11. Paris: OECD Development Centre.

———. 1974. *Project Appraisal and Planning*. London: Heinemann.

MCC (Millennium Challenge Corporation). 2017. "Compact Development Guidance: Guidelines for Economic and Beneficiary Analysis." https://www.mcc.gov/resources/story/story-cdg-guidelines-for-economic-and-beneficiary-analysis.

McFadden, Daniel. 1976. "The Revealed Preference of a Government Bureaucracy: Empirical Evidence." *Bell Journal of Economics* 7(1): 55–72.

Mishan, Ezra. 1970. "Evaluation of Life and Limb: A Theoretical Approach." *Journal of Political Economy* 79(4): 687–705.

Mohring, Herbert, and Harold Williamson. 1969. "Scale and Industrial Reorganization Economies of Transport Improvements." *Journal of Transport Economics and Policy* 3: 251–271.

Nash, Christopher. 1979. "The Use of Economic Appraisal in Transportation Analysis." *International Journal of Management Science* 7(5): 441–450.

Nellthorp, James, and Peter Mackie. 2000. "The UK Roads Review: A Hedonic Model of Decision Making." *Transport Policy* 7(2): 127–138.

Nilsson, Jan-Eric. 1991. "Investment Decisions in a Public Bureaucracy: A Case Study of Swedish Road Planning Practices." *Journal of Transport Economics and Policy* 25(2): 163–175.

Nyborg, Karine. 1998. "Some Norwegian Politicians' Use of Cost-Benefit Analysis." *Public Choice* 95(3–4): 381–401.

Odeck, James. 1996. "Ranking of Regional Road Investment in Norway." *Transportation* 23(2): 123–140.

Pearce, David. 1983. *Cost-Benefit Analysis*. London: Palgrave Macmillan.

Pearce, David, Giles Atkinson, and Susana Mourato. 2006. *Cost-Benefit Analysis and the Environment: Recent Developments*. Paris: OECD.

Phaneuf, Daniel, and V. Kerry Smith. 2005. "Recreation Demand Models." In *Handbook of Environmental Economics*, vol. 2, ed. Karl-Gran Mler and Jeffrey R. Vincent, 671–761. Amsterdam: North Holland.

Pozdena, Randall. 2015. "Evaluating Alternative Benefit-Cost Analysis Computational Methods." Technical memo. Portland, OR: ECONorthwest.

Price, Andrew. 1999. "The New Approach to the Appraisal of Road Projects in England." *Journal of Transport Economics and Policy* 33(2): 221–226.

Rothengatter, Werner. 2017. "Wider Economic Impacts of Transport Infrastructure Investments: Relevant or Negligible?" *Transport Policy* 59: 124–133.

Schelling, Thomas. 1968. "The Life You Save May Be Your Own." In *Problems in Public Expenditure Analysis: Studies of Government Finance*, ed. Samuel Chase, 127–162. Washington, DC: Brookings Institution.

Smith, Robert. 1973. "Compensating Wage Differentials and Hazardous Work." Technical Analysis paper No. 5, Office of Evaluation. Washington, DC: U.S. Department of Labor.

Squire, Lyn, and Herman van der Tak. 1975. *Economic Analysis of Projects*. Washington, DC: World Bank.

Subcommittee on Benefits and Costs. 1950. "Proposed Practices for Economic Analysis of River Basin Projects: Report to Federal Inter-Agency River Basin Committee." Washington, DC: U.S. Army Corps of Engineers.

Swedish Transport Administration. 2020. "Analysmetod och samhällsekonomiska kalkylvärden för transportsektorn: ASEK 7.0." Kapitel 19 English summary of ASEK Guidelines.

Thaler, Richard, and Sherwin Rosen. 1976. "The Value of Saving a Life: Evidence from the Labor Market." In *Household Production and Consumption*, ed. Nestor Terleckyj, 265–302. Cambridge, MA: National Bureau of Economic Research.

Tinbergen, Jan. 1957. "The Appraisal of Road Construction: Two Calculation Schemes." *Review of Economics and Statistics* 39(3): 241–249.

U.K. Department for Transport. 2019. "Wider Economic Impacts Appraisal." Transport Analysis Guidance Unit A2.1. London: Department for Transport. https://assets.publishing.service.gov.uk/government/uploads/system/uploads/attachment_data/file/933466/tag-a2-1-wider-economic-impacts-appraisal.pdf.

UNIDO (United Nations Industrial Development Organization). 1986. *Guide to Practical Project Appraisal: Social Benefit-Cost Analysis in Developing Countries*. Project Formulation and Evaluation Series No. 3. Vienna: United Nations Industrial Development Organization.

USBOB (U.S. Bureau of the Budget). 1952. "Reports and Budget Estimates Relating to Federal Programs and Projects for Conservation, Development, or Use of Water and Related Land Resources." Washington, DC: Executive Office of the President.

U.S. Department of Transportation. 2016. "The Value of Travel Time Savings: Departmental Guidance for Conducting Economic Evaluations, Revision 2 (2016 Update)." Washington, DC: Office of the Secretary of Transportation.

———. 2020. "Benefit-Cost Analysis Guidance for Discretionary Grant Programs." Washington, DC: Office of the Secretary of Transportation.

U.S. Office of Management and Budget. 2003. "Circular A-4: Regulatory Analysis." Washington, DC: Executive Office of the President.

Vatin, Francois, Jean-Pascal Simonin, and Luc Marco. 2016. "The Works of Jules Dupuit: Engineer and Economist of the French XIXth Century." HAL Archives-Ouvertes.Fr, https://hal.archives-ouvertes.fr/hal-01335642/document.

Venter, Christo. 2016. "Developing a Common Narrative on Urban Accessibility: A Transportation Perspective." Washington, DC: Brookings Institution.

World Bank. 2010. "Cost-Benefit Analysis in World Bank Projects." Washington, DC: World Bank.

Zeff, Harrison, Joseph Kasprzyk, Jonathan Herman, Patrick Reed, and Gregory W. Characklis. 2014. "Navigating Financial and Supply Reliability Tradeoffs in Regional Drought Management Portfolios." *Water Resources Research* 50(6): 4906–4923.

7

HOW (IN)ACCURATE IS COST-BENEFIT ANALYSIS?

DATA, EXPLANATIONS, AND SUGGESTIONS FOR REFORM

Bent Flyvbjerg and Dirk W. Bester

Most cost-benefit analyses assume that the estimates of costs and benefits are more or less accurate and unbiased. But if in reality estimates of costs and benefits are highly inaccurate and biased, the assumption that cost-benefit analysis is a rational way to improve resource allocation would be a fallacy. Using the largest data set of its kind, we test the assumption that cost and benefit estimates of infrastructure capital investments are accurate and unbiased. We find this is not the case with overwhelming statistical significance. We document the extent of cost overruns, demand shortfalls, and forecasting bias in infrastructure investments. We further assess whether such forecasting inaccuracies seriously distort effective resource allocation, which is found to be the case. We explain our findings in behavioral terms and explore their implications for infrastructure economics and policy. Finally, we conclude that cost-benefit analysis stands in need of reform, and we outline four steps to such reform.

Data and Methodology

For testing the thesis that cost and benefit estimates are accurate and unbiased,[1] we collected a sample of 2,062 infrastructure investments with data on cost overrun and benefit shortfall. The sample includes 8 investment types: bridges, buildings, bus rapid transit, dams, power plants, rail, roads, and tunnels. Geographically, the sample incorporates investments in 104 countries on 6 continents covering both developed and developing nations. Historically, the data cover almost a century, from 1927 to 2013. Older investments were included to enable analyses of historical trends. For each investment in the data set, the accuracy of cost estimates was measured by cost overrun (actual cost divided by estimated cost), while the accuracy of benefit estimates was measured by benefit overrun (actual benefits divided by estimated benefits).

Data on estimated and actual costs and benefits of infrastructure investments are difficult to obtain. No statistical agency or other data service exists from which valid and reliable data may be secured. The data therefore have to be mined item by item from the source, which is time-consuming. All investments that we know of for which data on estimation accuracy were obtainable were considered for inclusion. Data were collected from a variety of sources, including annual accounts, cost and procurement accounts, revenue accounts, auditors' data, questionnaires, interviews, and other studies. Only data that could be supported by reliable documentary evidence were included in order to avoid the well-known problems with recalled data and interviewee biases. In sum, all investments for which data were considered valid and reliable were included in the sample.

Preferably, costs and benefits would be measured over the full life cycle of an investment. However, such data are rarely if ever available. The convention is therefore to measure the costs of an infrastructure investment by the proxy of construction or capital costs and benefits by the proxy of first-year benefits. This convention is followed here. Estimated costs and benefits are the estimates made at the time of decision to build (sometimes called the *final investment decision*, based on the final business case), which is the baseline in time from which cost and benefit overruns are measured. Actual costs are measured as recorded outturn costs, and actual benefits are measured as first-year benefits or a later value as close to this as possible if available and if first-year benefits were not available. Estimated and actual benefits are recorded in the unit of measurement that the planners of the investment decided to use for measuring benefits. Pros and cons of measuring benefits by first-year benefits and the issue of wider benefits are discussed in this chapter's appendix.

Ideally, data would be available for both cost and benefit overruns for each investment in the data set. However, data availability is far from ideal in the measurement of estimated and actual costs and benefits of infrastructure investments. Data were available for both cost overrun and benefit overrun for only 327 investments out of the 2,062 in the sample. Using this ideal criterion would therefore result in scrapping large amounts of useful information for the 1,735 other investments in the sample, which would clearly be unacceptable. We therefore decided to run the statistical tests twice, first for the full sample of 2,062 investments and second for the subsample of 327 investments, with data available for both cost overrun and benefit overrun for each investment. This gave us the advantage of being able to test whether results were robust across different samples, which proved to be the case.

Investments were included in the sample based on data availability, as mentioned. Using this criterion means that the results of the statistical analyses presented below are probably conservative; that is, cost overruns in the investment population are most likely larger than in the sample, and benefit overruns are most likely smaller. These departures occur because the availability of data often indicates better than average investment management and because data from badly performing investments are often not released and are therefore likely to be underrepresented in the sample. This bias must be kept in mind when interpreting results.

How Accurate Is Cost-Benefit Analysis?

Table 7.1 summarizes the results from testing the thesis that cost and benefit estimates are accurate and unbiased. Taking rail as an example, the average cost overrun is listed in the table as 1.40, which means that for rail investments, actual costs turned out to be 40 percent higher than estimated costs on average and in real terms, indicating substantial inaccuracy in cost estimates for rail. The average benefit overrun for rail is listed in the table as 0.66, which is evidence of a benefit shortfall of 34 percent, meaning that on average, 34 percent of the estimated passengers never showed up on the actual trains, again indicating substantial inaccuracy.

If cost estimates were largely accurate and unbiased, cost overruns would be narrowly and more or less symmetrically distributed around one. Table 7.1 clearly shows this thesis to be false, which is verified by statistical tests that reject the thesis at an overwhelmingly high level of statistical significance ($p < 0.001$, Wilcoxon test).[2] Cost overruns are highly inaccurate and biased for infrastructure investments, ranging from an average cost overrun for roads of 24 percent to dams at 85 percent, in real terms.[3] The Wilcoxon test was supplemented by tests of skewness (D'Agostino test) and kurtosis (Anscombe test). The cost overrun data have a skewness of 23.2, and the D'Agostino test confirmed that this is significantly different from 0 ($p < 0.0001$). The cost overrun data furthermore have a kurtosis of 724.1, and the Anscombe-Glynn kurtosis test found that this is significantly different from 3 ($p < 0.0001$), which is the kurtosis of a normal distribution, from which we conclude that the data have tails much fatter than the normal distribution. This finding is crucial, because whereas errors cancel out, biases compound. Biases—and especially biases with fat tails, as here—are therefore much worse news than errors in infrastructure investing.

Table 7.1 further shows that benefit estimates are also inaccurate, though less so than cost estimates. Bus rapid transit and rail investments have significant benefit shortfalls, on average 58 percent and 34 percent, respectively. In contrast, for

TABLE 7.1 Cost Overrun and Benefit Overrun for Eight Infrastructure Investment Types

Investment Type	Cost Overrun (A/E)			Benefit Overrun (A/E)			p^a
	N	Average	p^b	N	Average	p^b	
Dams	243	1.96	<0.0001	84	0.89	<0.0001	<0.0001
Bus rapid transit	6	1.41	0.031	4	0.42	0.12	0.007
Rail	264	1.40	<0.0001	74	0.66	<0.0001	<0.0001
Tunnels	48	1.36	<0.0001	23	0.81	0.03	0.015
Power plants	100	1.36	0.0076	23	0.94	0.11	0.0003
Buildings	24	1.36	0.00087	20	0.99	0.77	0.01
Bridges	49	1.32	0.00012	26	0.96	0.099	<0.0001
Roads	869	1.24	<0.0001	532	0.96	<0.0001	<0.0001
Total	1603	1.39/1.43[c]	<0.0001	786	0.94/0.83[c]	<0.0001	<0.0001

Source: Flyvbjerg database.

A/E = actual cost (or benefit) divided by estimated cost (or benefit).

[a]The p-value of the Mann-Whitney test with null hypothesis that cost overrun is balanced by benefit overrun.

[b]The p-value of the Wilcoxon test with null hypothesis that the distribution is symmetrically centered around 1. The Wilcoxon test was supplemented by tests of skewness (D'Agostino test) and kurtosis (Anscombe test), which confirmed at an overwhelmingly high level of significance ($p < 0.0001$ for both tests) that the data are skewed and heavy tailed for both cost and benefit overruns.

[c]Weighted and unweighted average, respectively.

bridges, buildings, power plants, and roads, benefit estimates are fairly accurate on average. If benefit estimates were generally accurate, benefit overruns would be narrowly and more or less symmetrically distributed around 1. Statistical tests reject this thesis at an overwhelmingly high level of statistical significance ($p < 0.001$, Wilcoxon test). Like cost estimates, benefit estimates are inaccurate and biased. Again, the Wilcoxon test was supplemented by tests of skewness and kurtosis, and again these tests confirmed that the data on benefit overrun are skewed and heavy tailed. The benefit overrun data have a skewness of 1.1, and the D'Agostino test confirmed that this significantly differs from 0 ($p < 0.0001$). The benefit overrun data furthermore have a kurtosis of 6.5, and the Anscombe-Glynn kurtosis test found that this number significantly differs from that of a normal distribution ($p < 0.0001$). We see that the kurtosis for cost overrun (724) is much larger than for benefit overrun (6.5), meaning that although both types of overrun are significantly fatter-tailed than the normal distribution, the data on cost overrun have a more extreme tail than the data on benefit overrun.

Considering cost and benefit overruns together, we see that the detected biases work in such a manner that cost overruns are not compensated by benefit overruns; on average, quite the opposite is true. This finding is important because errors do not cancel out for costs and benefits viewed separately, as documented above, and inaccuracy is accelerated by the fact that the combination of cost overrun and benefit shortfall hampers the average investment, undermining investment viability on two fronts, that is, for both costs and benefits. Table 7.1 includes a statistical test of the thesis that cost overrun is balanced by benefit overrun, that is, that errors of cost underestimation are compensated by similar errors of benefit underestimation (the p-values for this test are shown in the far right column of table 7.1). We see that the thesis is rejected with overwhelming statistical significance ($p < 0.0001$, Mann-Whitney test).[4]

Finally, we tested whether error and bias in cost-benefit estimates have improved over time and found that this is not the case. In sum, the data show that the main problem with cost-benefit analysis is not error but rather bias. This finding is bad news because where errors tend to cancel out each other because of their randomness, biases are systematic and therefore compound, leading to results of cost-benefit analysis that are highly misleading.

It is noteworthy that for not a single of the eight investment types in table 7.1 did forecasters overestimate cost, and for not a single investment type did they underestimate benefits on average. That fact shows how strong and consistent the biases are. Theories such as Hirschman's (2014) hiding hand theory and similar just-start-digging theories, which predict that cost underestimates will be offset by benefit underestimates of similar or larger magnitude and therefore that resource allocation will be okay despite initial errors in cost-benefit estimates, are not supported by the data; they are rejected, again at an overwhelmingly high level of statistical significance ($p < 0.0001$) (Flyvbjerg 2016).

We see that the average investment is impaired by a combination of substantial cost underestimates compounded by significant benefit overestimates. Such a systematic and significant bias in cost-benefit analysis is likely to lead to resource misallocation, including initiating investments that ultimately turn out to have negative net benefits and should never have been started, as argued by Ansar et al. (2014) and the World Bank (2010).[5] If investments are large enough and the economies where they are built are fragile, then just one major misallocation of resources in this manner for a single investment can negatively affect the national economy for decades, as Brazil and Pakistan learned with their large-dam investments (Ansar et al. 2014) and Greece did with the 2004 Olympic Games (Flyvbjerg and Stewart 2012).

We emphasize that the finding above—that investments are on average undermined by a combination of cost underestimates, leading to cost overruns and benefit overestimates resulting in benefit shortfalls—does not mean that no investments exist for which cost underestimates were fortuitously outweighed by similar or larger benefit underestimates. For instance, the German Karlsruhe–Bretten light rail line, which is in the data set, had a cost overrun in real terms of 78 percent but an even larger benefit overrun of 158 percent. Similarly, the Danish Great Belt toll road bridge—the longest suspension bridge in the world at the time of completion—had a cost overrun of 45 percent combined with a benefit overrun of 90 percent, making the investment profitable. Such investments, however, are in the minority. For the vast majority of investments (80 percent), cost overrun is not compensated by benefit overrun according to our data.

One might speculate of course that conceivably the one-fifth of investments where benefit overrun compensated cost overrun may have generated more benefits in the aggregate than the four-fifths that did not. We tested this thesis and found at an overwhelmingly high level of statistical significance that this is not the case; the opposite is true, since the net effect of the situation where cost overrun is not compensated by benefit overrun (80 percent of investments) is larger than the net effect of the situation where benefit overrun compensated cost overrun ($p = 0.001$, two-sided Mann-Whitney test).

Table 7.1 shows that a typical ex ante benefit-cost ratio produced by conventional methods is overestimated by between approximately 50 and 200 percent, depending on investment type. Again, this is a statistically significant bias showing that standard cost-benefit analysis consistently overestimates the net benefits of investments by a large margin and therefore may not be trusted.

To conclude, the data show that cost and benefit estimates for infrastructure investments are highly inaccurate and biased. Cost underestimates and benefit overestimates are much more common than cost overestimates and benefit underestimates at an overwhelmingly high level of statistical significance ($p < 0.0001$). The average investment is impaired by a double whammy of substantial cost underestimates compounded by significant benefit overestimates. As a consequence, benefit-cost ratios are overestimated by between 50 and 200 percent, depending on investment type. The data show ex ante cost-benefit analysis to be so misleading as to be worse than worthless because decision makers might think they are being informed by such analysis when in fact they are being significantly misinformed about the return on planned investments. As a consequence, decision makers may give the green light to investments that should never have been started, leading to misallocation of resources, whereas the whole purpose of cost-benefit analysis is the opposite: improved resource allocation. Such false green-lighting points to a central problem for welfare economics and for any type of economics or policy that relies on cost-benefit analysis: ex ante estimates of costs and benefits are so erroneous and biased that instead of being the powerful tool for effective resource allocation and improved welfare depicted by theory, in practice cost-benefit analysis is a poor and highly misleading guide for policy. Biases creep in and derail the logic and good intentions of theory. To disregard such biases, as is common, is a fallacy. We call it the *cost–benefit fallacy* and add it to the list of other fallacies and biases in human decision making identified by behavioral science in recent years.

Cost-Benefit Fallacy

We define the cost-benefit fallacy as the situation whereby individuals behave as if cost-benefit estimates are more or less accurate and unbiased when in fact they are highly inaccurate and biased. Two questions arise. First, how does one explain the cost-benefit fallacy in more depth? Second, how does one eliminate or overcome the fallacy?

The data presented above show with overwhelming statistical significance that it is not the fact that cost-benefit forecasts are in error that needs to be explained, as is the common view for cost-benefit analysis if the question of accuracy comes up at all (which it mostly does not). The fact that needs to be explained is that the majority of cost-benefit forecasts are systematically biased, with underestimation for cost and overestimation for benefits. Our data go back 86 years, and for this period the bias in cost-benefit forecasts has been constant. Cost-benefit forecasters are "predictably irrational" regarding bias, in the words of Ariely (2010, iii). To begin to understand why, consider the following example.

Recently, the CEO of one of the biggest and most successful infrastructure providers in the world explained why the cost forecast for one of its multibillion-dollar investments—a high-speed rail line—had proven to be too low, resulting in a significant cost overrun. The CEO noted three causes of the underestimate and overrun. First, construction had taken longer than scheduled. Second, the investment, which involved extensive tunneling, had run into unexpected geological conditions, resulting in unplanned costs. Third, price inflation for both labor and materials had been higher than expected. This is a typical and plausible way to account for cost overrun, which most people would accept. Delays, geology, and price inflation are commonly stated causes of cost overrun in construction investments, as are, for example, project complexity and scope changes. This is the industry standard in terms of explanation.

We analyzed the evidence for the specific investment and assured the CEO that he was right. On the surface, it appeared that delays, geology, and price inflation caused the cost overrun. However, he would neither truly understand nor solve the problem as long as he saw it like this, or so we argued. To really understand what happened to his company's investment, he would need to think in terms of root causes. And at the level of root causes, the explanation of the overrun is much simpler, with a single source: optimism. First, his company was optimistic about the schedule in assuming it could deliver the rail line several years faster than is usual for this type of investment without having good reasons for this assumption. Second, the company was optimistic about the geological conditions without having investigated them sufficiently. Third, the company was optimistic about price variations, assuming that variations would be small when in fact history shows they are large. This is optimism, pure and simple, unless the company deliberately misrepresented the schedule, geology, and prices, in which case it would be strategic misrepresentation, we further argued.[6] In either case, the problem is a behavioral one, related to the company's own conduct. To understand and solve the problem, the company would need behavioral science, not a better understanding of geology or market prices or better Gantt charts.

Behavioral scientists would agree that schedules, geology, market prices, scope changes, and complexity are relevant to understanding what goes on in infrastructure investment projects but do not see them as root causes of inaccuracy and bias in cost-benefit forecasts. The root cause of cost underestimates and overruns, according to behavioral science, is the well-documented fact that planners and managers keep underestimating the importance of schedules, geology, market prices, scope changes, and complexity. From the point of view of behavioral science, the mechanisms of scope changes, complex interfaces, geology, bad weather, business cycles, and so forth are not unknown to planners of infrastructure investments, just as planners know that such mechanisms may be mitigated. However, planners often underestimate these mechanisms and overestimate the effectiveness of mitigation measures because of well-known behavioral phenomena such as overconfidence bias, the planning fallacy, and strategic misrepresentation.

In behavioral terms, scope changes and so on are manifestations of such misjudgment on the part of planners, and in this sense, planners' behavior is the root cause of inaccuracy and bias in cost-benefit forecasts. But because scope changes and so on are more visible than the underlying root causes, they are often mistaken for the cause of inaccuracy and bias. In behavioral terms, with scope changes as an example, the causal chain starts with human bias (deliberate or not), which leads to underestimation of scope during planning, which leads to unaccounted-for scope changes during delivery, which leads to cost overrun. Scope changes are an intermediate stage in this causal chain through which the root causes manifest themselves. Similar reasoning applies for complexity, geology, and other so-called causes. With behavioral science, we say to infrastructure planners and managers, "your biggest risk is you." It is how planners and managers misconceive and underestimate through overconfidence bias, the planning fallacy, and strategic misrepresentation. Behavioral science brings this profound and proven insight to cost-benefit forecasting and infrastructure investment planning but, unfortunately, it is not always readily acknowledged and integrated in cost-benefit scholarship and practice (Flyvbjerg et al. 2018).

Behavioral science entails a change of perspective. The problem with cost-benefit forecasts is not error but rather bias; as long as we try to understand and solve the problem as something it is not (error), we will not solve it. Forecasts, policies, and decisions need to be de-biased, which is fundamentally different from eliminating error (Flyvbjerg 2008, 2013; Kahneman 2011). The main problem is also not cost overrun, even if overrun is what hurts, is visible, and therefore gets the attention. The main problem is cost underestimation. Overrun is a consequence of underestimation, with the latter happening upstream from overrun, often years before overruns manifest. Again, if one tries to understand and solve the problem as something it is not (cost overrun), one will fail. We need to solve the problem of cost underestimation to solve the problem of cost overrun.[7] Until we understand these basic insights from behavioral science, we are unlikely to overcome the cost-benefit fallacy and get cost-benefit forecasting and resource allocation right.

Four Steps to Cost-Benefit Reform

Cost-benefit analysis may no doubt be a helpful tool in infrastructure economics and policy. However, cost-benefit analysis as practiced today is less than useful because it is highly biased, as documented above. Cost-benefit theory and practice were developed long before behavioral science and have yet to adapt to its findings about the nature and causes of bias. This lack of adaption needs to change. We saw above that for infrastructure investments, the biases are so substantial that the average cost-benefit analysis results in resource misallocation instead of contributing to the effective use of scarce assets, which is the whole point of cost-benefit analysis.[8] For cost-benefit analysis to become useful in infrastructure economics and policy, the following need to happen:

- Systematic and effective de-biasing of cost-benefit forecasts.
- Introduction of skin in the game for cost-benefit forecasters.

- Independent audits of cost-benefit forecasts.
- Adaption of cost-benefit forecasting to the messy, nonexpert character of democratic decision making.

First and most important, behavioral science predicts that any forecast—including cost-benefit estimates—is prone to bias. If forecasts are biased, they must be de-biased before they can be reliably used in policy making and investment decisions, or policies and decisions will be biased, too. Nudges will not suffice. Deliberate and precise de-biasing will be needed. Taking our clue from Kahneman and Tversky (1979) and using Kahneman's (2011, 245) "outside view," we developed methods for such de-biasing for infrastructure investments. We use the distributional information about actual estimation errors in previous investments (established via ex post studies) to precisely assess by how much the cost-benefit estimates for a planned venture must be adjusted before they may be considered effectively de-biased (Flyvbjerg 2006; Flyvbjerg, Glenting, and Rønnest 2004). In his book *Thinking, Fast and Slow*, Daniel Kahneman reviews this work, especially our advice to use empirical distributional information for de-biasing and concludes:

> This may be considered the single most important piece of advice regarding how to increase accuracy in forecasting [of costs and benefits] through improved methods. Using such distributional information from other ventures similar to that being forecasted is called taking an "outside view" and is the cure to the planning fallacy [and thus to bias]. . . . The outside view is implemented by using a large database, which provides information on both plans and outcomes for hundreds [now thousands] of projects all over the world, and can be used to provide statistical information about the likely overruns of cost and time, and about the likely underperformance of projects of different types. (Kahneman 2011, 251–252)

The method for systematically (mathematically and statistically) taking the outside view is called *reference class forecasting* and is today used at scale in infrastructure investing around the world, including in countries where the method has been made mandatory, such as the United Kingdom and Denmark (Danish Ministry for Transport and Energy 2006, 2008; U.K. Department for Transport 2006). Independent evaluations of the method confirm its value and accuracy (Awojobi and Jenkins 2016; Batselier 2016; Batselier and Vanhoucke 2017; Bordley 2014; Chang et al. 2016; Kim and Reinschmidt 2011; Liu and Napier 2010; Liu, Wehbe, and Sisovic 2010).[9] Only with such de-biasing will cost-benefit forecasts be accurate and help allocate resources effectively.

Second, better incentives for accuracy in cost-benefit forecasts should be introduced. Better methods alone will not solve the problem. Akerlof and Shiller (2009, 146) suggest "firing the forecaster" when forecasts are very wrong and the consequences are severe. Flyvbjerg (2013, 771–772) goes one step further in proposing "suing the forecaster" in cases of gross neglect and gross deliberate manipulation of forecasts and investors. The first court cases in infrastructure investing were decided in 2015, for Sydney's Lane Cove toll tunnel, which went bankrupt when more than half the forecasted cars never appeared in the tunnel, and for Brisbane's Clem 7 tunnel and airport link, which had comparable problems (Rubin 2017; Saulwick 2014; Worthington 2012). More litigation quickly followed in the United States, treating traffic forecasters as criminals (Dezember and Glazer 2013; Evans 2010; Hals 2013; Miller 2013; Singh 2017; Wright 2014). Recently, those responsible for the Muskrat Falls dam inquiry in Canada decided to report executives to the police for possible criminal charges related to cost underestimation for the dam (LeBlanc 2020; Roberts 2020). Criminalizing planners and cost-benefit analysts this way has sent shock waves through the global forecasting and cost-benefit community, contributing to much-needed discipline and accountability. Here we suggest, as a more general and more moderate heuristic, that often it would make sense to consider giving cost-benefit forecasters skin in the game. Lawmakers and policy makers should develop institutional setups that reward forecasters who get their estimates right and punish those who do not. We should not be surprised that cost-benefit estimates are wrong if forecasters have no incentive to get them right. True, forecasters are supposed to be neutral and unbiased. But to confuse such normativity with reality is naive for policy makers and scholars alike.

Third, independent audits are needed to ensure that points one and two above—better methods and better incentives for more accurate forecasts—work according to intention and to adjust them when they do not. Auditing must be effectively separated from political motivations to avoid the type of political distortion of cost-benefit forecasts described in detail by the Flyvbjerg, Glenting, and Rønnest (2004); Flyvbjerg, Holm, and Buhl (2002); Harrington (2006); Harrington, Morgenstern, and Nelson (2000); Wachs (1986, 1989, 1990, 2013); and the World Bank (2010). If this separation does not happen, audits will not and cannot serve their purpose. Audits should allow for transparency and external scrutiny, including scrutiny by independent experts, the public, and media.

Finally, and perhaps most important, for cost-benefit analysis to be accepted and have impact, it must be understood and practiced not in the top-down technocratic fashion that is common but instead in ways that fit with the messy, nonexpert character of present-day democratic decision making. Here, cost-benefit analysis is just one of many inputs that are amalgamated in the overall decision-making process. Top-down technocratic approaches are anachronistic and will not work in this context. Kahneman (2011) contrasts cost-benefit technocrats with cost-benefit democrats, exemplifying technocrats with the Harvard law professor Cass Sunstein and democrats with the University of Oregon psychology professor Paul Slovic. Kahneman writes about Sunstein, who is a self-declared cost-benefit technocrat and whose work Kahneman otherwise holds in high regard:

> He [Sunstein] starts from the position that risk regulation and government inter-vention to reduce risks should be guided by rational weighting of costs and benefits. . . . [He] has faith in the objectivity that may be achieved by science, expertise, and careful deliberation. . . . Cass Sunstein would seek mechanisms [such as the cost-benefit principle] that insulate decision makers from public pressures, letting the allocation of resources be determined by impartial experts who have a broad view of all risks and of the resources available to reduce them. (Kahneman 2011, 141–12)

Kahneman (2011) here captures the key beliefs and a priori assumptions of cost-benefit technocrats, including (1) the view that cost-benefit analysis is a force for good in deciding policies; (2) faith in the objectivity of science as a basis for cost-benefit calculations; and (3) belief in impartial experts for making better decisions. He juxtaposes this position with that of Slovic (2000) and other cost-benefit democrats and notes that Slovic "trusts the experts much less and the public somewhat more than Sunstein does" (Kahneman 2011, 145). Kahneman approv-ingly cites Slovic (2000) for arguing that expert-based decision making, like that supported by cost-benefit technocrats, produces policies that the public will reject, which he considers an untenable situation in a democracy. "Slovic rightly stresses the resistance of the public to the idea of decisions being made by unelected and unaccountable experts," concludes Kahneman (2011, 144).

Kahneman (2011, 144) considers both Sunstein and Slovic "eminently sen-sible" and explicitly states "I agree with both." We agree with Kahneman. Nobody in their right mind would argue that expert input, science, and cost-benefit analysis are undesirable in deciding which policies and investments to pursue in a society, including for infrastructure. But similarly, no one in their right mind would depend on only experts in making such decisions, especially when we know that experts are subject to the cost-benefit fallacy and produce, over and over, the kind of biased cost-benefit analyses documented above. Sunstein and other cost-benefit technocrats overemphasize the importance of experts and place too much trust in them. By supplementing Sunstein with Slovic—technocracy with democracy—Kahneman (2011, 144–145) develops a more balanced position, from which he argues that democracy "is inevitably messy" and emphasizes that the public's concerns, "even if they are unreasonable, should not be ignored by policy makers." Experts, science, and cost-benefit analyses are not enough to arrive at high-quality policy decisions, argues Kahneman. The messy process of democracy is called for to merge all concerns, including unreasonable ones, because only in this manner will policy be able to muster the support necessary to be successful.

The four measures for better cost-benefit analysis outlined above are not ivory tower theory. They have recently been implemented in innovative, full-scale experiments around the world with encouraging results, as documented by the Danish Ministry for Transport and Energy (2006, 2008); Flyvbjerg et al. (2018); Flyvbjerg, Hon, and Fok (2016); Her Majesty's Treasury (2003); Kahneman (2011); the Swiss Association of Road and Transportation Experts (2006); the U.K. Department for Transport (2006); and the U.K. Department of Transport and Oxford Global Projects (2020). More such work is in the pipeline, finally bringing the findings of behavioral science to welfare economics and cost-benefit forecasting, resulting in more realistic and more useful forecasts.

Conclusions

In this chapter, we set out to test the accuracy of cost-benefit forecasts in capital infrastructure investments. We found a fallacy at the heart of conventional cost-benefit analysis. Forecasters, policy makers, and scholars tend to assume that cost-benefit forecasts are more or less accurate when in fact they are highly inaccurate and biased at an overwhelmingly high level of statistical significance. In infrastructure investing, the fallacy results in average overestimates in ex ante benefit-cost ratios of 50 to 200 percent, depending on investment type. Individual estimates of benefit-cost ratios are routinely off by much more than these averages.

Cost-benefit analysis can undoubtedly be a useful tool in infrastructure economics and policy but only after the cost-benefit fallacy has been acknowledged and corrected. For this to happen, the following must become part and parcel of cost-benefit practice: (1) new methods for effective de-biasing of ex ante cost-benefit estimates, based on behavioral science; (2) incentives for using these methods, including skin in the game; (3) independent audits to check that the methods and incentives work according to intention; and (4) integration of results in messy real-life democratic decision-making processes, which consider concerns other than the results of cost-benefit analyses. The good news is that the theoretical and methodological rationale for this type of behaviorally based cost-benefit analysis has already been developed and is finding use in policy and practice. The bad news is that the cost-benefit fallacy seems to be as ingrained in human behavior as the many other biases and fallacies identified by behavioral science and will therefore be as difficult to root out as these. That obstacle should not keep us from trying, needless to say, which is what we have done with the research reported in the present chapter.

Summary

- Advocates of using cost-benefit analysis to select infrastructure projects typically assume that the benefits and costs can be forecasted reasonably accurately, but behavioral science predicts that any forecast from cost-benefit analysis is prone to bias.

- A careful analysis of 2,062 infrastructure projects reveals a new behavioral fallacy, called the cost-benefit fallacy: project costs tend to be greatly underestimated, while the actual usage of infrastructures (a proxy for project benefits) is strongly overestimated.

- The root causes of the errors are well-known behavioral limitations, especially optimism bias, overconfidence bias, and power bias (strategic misrepresentation), which although deeply engrained in human nature might be reduced by measures such as de-biasing, holding forecasters legally accountable, using independent audits, and integrating cost-benefit analysis with democratic decision making.

Notes

1. Here and throughout the chapter, we use the term *bias* in the sense it is used in behavioral science, including behavioral economics. This should not be confused with the way the term is used in statistics in the frequentist-estimator sense, especially for the statistical tests reported in the main text and in the appendix.

2. Significance is here defined in the conventional manner, with $p \leq 0.05$ being significant, $p \leq 0.01$ very significant, and $p \leq 0.001$ overwhelmingly significant. In addition to standard statistical tests using p-values, we also tested results for the influence of investment type, geography, and time period using Bayesian modeling. Finally, we ran the tests using different samples. We found that the results reported in the main text proved highly robust across investment type, geography, and time period. Results were also robust across both conventional and Bayesian testing and across different samples (see the appendix).

3. These findings correspond to other findings based on smaller samples, which we take to attest to the robustness of results (see, e.g., Albalate and Bel 2014; Altshuler and Luberoff 2003; Ansar et al. 2014; Bain 2009; Bain and Wilkins 2002; Cantarelli,

Flyvbjerg, and Buhl 2012; Dantata, Touran, and Schneck 2006; Federal Transit Administration 2003, 2008, 2013; Flyvbjerg, Glenting, and Rønnest 2004; Flyvbjerg, Holm, and Buhl 2002, 2005; Fouracre, Allport, and Thomson 1990; Gao and Touran 2020; Huo et al. 2018; Leavitt, Ennis, and McGovern 1993; Lee 2008; National Audit Office 1992; Nijkamp and Ubbels 1999; Pickrell 1990, 1992; Riksrevisionen 2011; Riksrevisionsverket 1994; Walmsley and Pickett 1992; World Bank 1994).

4. We ran the same tests with similar results for a subsample of 327 investments for which data were available for both cost overrun and benefit overrun for each investment (see the appendix).

5. Negative impact on gross domestic product is not limited to public infrastructure investments. Misallocation of resources similarly happens in the private sector with similar consequences. For private-sector examples, see Flyvbjerg and Budzier (2011).

6. Strategic misrepresentation is deliberate, while optimism is nondeliberate; see more in Flyvbjerg (2007).

7. Cost overrun may also originate with subpar delivery, needless to say. However, if the original cost estimate for an investment is truly optimistic, as is common, then no matter how good the delivery team is they will not be able to deliver to the estimate (Flyvbjerg 2016).

8. For an in-depth case study of how cost-benefit analysis may lead to resource misallocation even in an organization with deep experience with and extensive use of the method, see the World Bank (2010) and Ward (2019).

9. A typical assessment of reference class forecasting (RCF) concludes that "the conducted evaluation is entirely based on real-life project data and shows that RCF indeed performs best, for both cost and time forecasting, and therefore supports the practical relevance of the technique" (Batselier and Vanhoucke 2017, 36).

References

Akerlof, George A., and Robert J. Shiller. 2009. *Animal Spirits: How Human Psychology Drives the Economy, and Why It Matters for Global Capitalism.* Princeton, NJ: Princeton University Press.

Albalate, Daniel, and Germa Bel. 2014. *The Economics and Politics of High-Speed Rail.* New York: Lexington Books.

Altshuler, Alan, and David Luberoff. 2003. *Mega-Projects: The Changing Politics of Urban Public Investment.* Washington, DC: Brookings Institution Press.

Ansar, Atif, Bent Flyvbjerg, Alexander Budzier, and Daniel Lunn. 2014. "Should We Build More Large Dams? The Actual Costs of Hydropower Megaproject Development." *Energy Policy* 69 (March): 43–56.

Ariely, Dan. 2010. *Predictably Irrational: The Hidden Forces That Shape Our Decisions.* New York: HarperCollins.

Awojobi, Omotola, and Glenn P. Jenkins. 2016. "Managing the Cost Overrun Risks of Hydroelectric Dams: An Application of Reference Class Forecasting Techniques." *Renewable and Sustainable Energy Reviews* 63: 19–32.

Bain, Robert. 2009. *Toll Road Traffic and Revenue Forecasts: An Interpreter's Guide.* Self-published.

Bain, Robert, and Michael Wilkins. 2002. *Traffic Risk in Start-up Toll Facilities*. London: Standard and Poor'.

Batselier, Jordy. 2016. "Empirical Evaluation of Existing and Novel Approaches for Project Forecasting and Control." Ph.D. dissertation, University of Ghent.

Batselier, Jordy, and Mario Vanhoucke. 2017. "Improving Project Forecast Accuracy by Integrating Earned Value Management with Exponential Smoothing and Reference Class Forecasting." *International Journal of Project Management* 35(1): 8–43.

Bordley, Robert F. 2014. "Reference Class Forecasting: Resolving Its Challenge to Statistical Modeling." *American Statistician* 68(4): 221–229.

Cantarelli, Chantal C., Bent Flyvbjerg, and Søren L. Buhl. 2012. "Geographical Variation in Project Cost Performance: The Netherlands Versus Worldwide." *Journal of Transport Geography* 24: 324–331.

Chang, Welton, Eva Chen, Barbara Mellera, and Philip Tetlock. 2016. "Developing Expert Political Judgment: The Impact of Training and Practice on Judgmental Accuracy in Geopolitical Forecasting Tournaments." *Judgment and Decision Making* 11(5): 509–526.

Danish Ministry for Transport and Energy. 2006. "Aktstykke om nye budgetteringsprincipper" [Act on New Principles for Budgeting]. Document No. 16, Finance Committee, Folketinget, Copenhagen, October 24.

———. 2008. "Ny anlægsbudgettering på Transportministeriets område, herunder om økonomistyrings–model og risikohåndtering for anlægsprojekter" [New Principles for Budgeting under the Ministry of Transport, Including Cost Control and Risk Assessment for Infrastructure Projects]. Report from the Ministry, Copenhagen, November 18.

Dantata, Nasiru A., Ali Touran, and Donald C. Schneck. 2006. "Trends in US Rail Transit Project Cost Overrun." Paper presented at the Transportation Research Board Annual Meeting, Washington, DC.

Dezember, Ryan, and Emily Glazer. 2013. "Drop in Traffic Takes Toll on Investors in Private Roads." *Wall Street Journal*, November 20. https://www.wsj.com/articles/SB1000142405 2702303482504579177890461812588.

Evans, Anthony G. 2010. "Declaration of Anthony G. Evans, Chief Financial Officer of South Bay Expressway, L.P., in Support of the Debtors's Chapter 11 Petitions and First Day Motions." Case 10-04516-LA11 filed March 22, 2010, United States Bankruptcy Court, Southern District of California.

Federal Transit Administration. 2003. *Predicted and Actual Impacts of New Starts Projects: Capital Cost, Operating Cost and Ridership Data*. Office of Planning and Environment with support from SG Associates, Inc. Washington, DC: Federal Transit Administration.

———. 2008. *Before and After Studies of New Starts Projects*. Report to Congress. Washington, DC: Federal Transit Administration.

———. 2013. *Before and After Studies of New Starts Projects*. Report to Congress. Washington, DC: Federal Transit Administration.

Flyvbjerg, Bent. 2005. "Measuring Inaccuracy in Travel Demand Forecasting: Methodological Considerations Regarding Ramp Up and Sampling." *Transportation Research A* 39(6): 522–530.

———. 2006. "From Nobel Prize to Project Management: Getting Risks Right." *Project Management Journal* 37(3): 5–15.

———. 2007. "How Optimism Bias and Strategic Misrepresentation in Early Project Development Undermine Implementation." In *Beslutninger på svakt informasjonsgrunnlag: Tilnærminger og utfordringer i projekters tidlige fase* [Decisions Based on Weak Information: Approaches and Challenges in the Early Phase of Projects], ed. Kjell J. Sunnevåg, 41–55. Trondheim, Norway: Concept Program, Norwegian University of Science and Technology.

———. 2008. "Curbing Optimism Bias and Strategic Misrepresentation in Planning: Reference Class Forecasting in Practice." *European Planning Studies* 16(1): 3–21.

———. 2013. "Quality Control and Due Diligence in Project Management: Getting Decisions Right by Taking the Outside View." *International Journal of Project Management* 31(5): 760–774.

———. 2016. "The Fallacy of Beneficial Ignorance: A Test of Hirschman's Hiding Hand." *World Development* 84 (May): 176–189.

Flyvbjerg, Bent, Atif Ansar, Alexander Budzier, Søren Buhl, Chantal Cantarelli, Massimo Garbuio, Carsten Glenting, Mette Skamris Holm, Dan Lovallo, Daniel Lunn, Eric Molin, Arne Rønnest, Allison Stewart, and Bert Van Wee. 2018. "Five Things You Should Know About Cost Overrun." *Transportation Research Part A: Policy and Practice* 118 (December): 174–190.

———. 2019. "On De-bunking 'Fake News' in the Post-Truth Era: How to Reduce Statistical Error in Research." *Transportation Research Part A: Policy and Practice* 126 (August): 409–411.

Flyvbjerg, Bent, and Alexander Budzier. 2011. "Why Your IT Project May Be Riskier Than You Think." *Harvard Business Review* (September): 601–603.

Flyvbjerg, Bent, Carsten Glenting, and Arne Rønnest. 2004. *Procedures for Dealing with Optimism Bias in Transport Planning: Guidance Document.* London: U.K. Department for Transport.

Flyvbjerg, Bent, Mette K. Skamris Holm, and Søren L. Buhl. 2002. "Underestimating Costs in Public Works Projects: Error or Lie?" *Journal of the American Planning Association* 68 (3): 279–295.

———. 2005. "How (In)accurate Are Demand Forecasts in Public Works Projects? The Case of Transportation." *Journal of the American Planning Association* 71(2): 131–146.

Flyvbjerg, Bent, Chi-keung Hon, and Wing Huen Fok. 2016. "Reference Class Forecasting for Hong Kong's Major Roadworks Projects." *Proceedings of the Institution of Civil Engineers* 169 (November CE6): 17–24.

Flyvbjerg, Bent, and Allison Stewart. 2012. "Olympic Proportions: Cost and Cost Overrun at the Olympics 1960–2012." Working paper. Saïd Business School, University of Oxford.

Fouracre, P. R., R. J. Allport, and J. M. Thomson. 1990. *The Performance and Impact of Rail Mass Transit in Developing Countries*, Research Report No. 278. Crowthorne, UK: Transport and Road Research Laboratory.

Gao, Nan, and Ali Touran. 2020. "Cost Overruns and Formal Risk Assessment Program in US Rail Transit Projects." *Journal of Construction Engineering and Management* 146(5): 1–11.

Hals, Tom. 2013. "Detroit Windsor Tunnel Operator Files for Bankruptcy." *Reuters*, July 25.

Harrington, Winston. 2006. "Grading Estimates of the Benefits and Costs of Federal Regulation." Discussion paper No. RFF DP 06-39. Washington, DC: Resources for the Future.

Harrington, Winston, Richard D. Morgenstern, and Peter Nelson. 2000. "On the Accuracy of Regulatory Cost Estimates." *Journal of Policy Analysis and Management* 19(2): 297–322.

Hirschman, Albert O. 2014. "The Principle of the Hiding Hand." In *Megaproject Planning and Management: Essential Readings*, vol. 1, ed. Bent Flyvbjerg, 149–162. Cheltenham, UK: Edward Elgar. Originally published in *Public Interest* (Winter 1967): 10–23.

Her Majesty's Treasury. 2003. *The Green Book: Appraisal and Evaluation in Central Government*. Treasury Guidance. London: TSO.

Huo, Tengfei, Hong Ren, Weiguang Cai, Geoffrey Qiping Shen, Bingsheng Liu, Minglei Zhu, and Hengqin Wu. 2018. "Measurement and Dependence Analysis of Cost Overruns in Megatransport Infrastructure Projects: Case Study in Hong Kong." *Journal of Construction Engineering and Management* 144(3): 1–10.

Kahneman, Daniel. 2011. *Thinking, Fast and Slow*. New York: Farrar, Straus and Giroux.

Kahneman, Daniel, and Amos Tversky. 1979. "Intuitive Prediction: Biases and Corrective Procedures." In *Studies in the Management Sciences: Forecasting*, vol. 12, ed. S. Makridakis and S. C. Wheelwright, 313–327. Amsterdam: North Holland.

Kim, Byung-Cheol, and Kenneth F. Reinschmidt. 2011. "Combination of Project Cost Forecasts in Earned Value Management." *Journal of Construction Engineering and Management* 137 (11): 958–966.

Leavitt, Dan, Sean Ennis, and Pat McGovern. 1993. "The Cost Escalation of Rail Projects: Using Previous Experience to Re-evaluate the CalSpeed Estimates." Working paper No. 567. Berkeley, CA: Institute of Urban and Regional Development, University of California.

LeBlanc, Richard D. 2020. *Muskrat Falls: A Misguided Project*, vols. 1–6. Province of Newfoundland and Labrador, Canada: Commission of Inquiry Respecting the Muskrat Falls Project.

Lee, Jin-Kyung. 2008. "Cost Overrun and Cause in Korean Social Overhead Capital Projects: Roads, Rails, Airports, and Ports." *Journal of Urban Planning and Development* 134 (June): 59–62.

Liu, Li, and Zigrid Napier. 2010. "The Accuracy of Risk-Based Cost Estimation for Water Infrastructure Projects: Preliminary Evidence from Australian Projects." *Construction Management and Economics* 28(1): 89–100.

Liu, Li, George Wehbe, and Jonathan Sisovic. 2010. "The Accuracy of Hybrid Estimating Approaches: A Case Study of an Australian State Road and Traffic Authority." *Engineering Economist* 55: 225–245.

Miller, Eric. 2013. "American Roads LLC Files for Bankruptcy." *Transport Topics*, August 5. https://www.ttnews.com/articles/american-roads-llc-files-bankruptcy-0.

National Audit Office. 1992. *Department of Transport: Contracting for Roads*. London: National Audit Office.

Nijkamp, Peter, and Barry Ubbels. 1999. "How Reliable Are Estimates of Infrastructure Costs? A Comparative Analysis." *International Journal of Transport Economics* 26(1): 23–53.

Pickrell, Don. 1990. *Urban Rail Transit Projects: Forecast Versus Actual Ridership and Cost*. Washington, DC: U.S. Department of Transportation.

———. 1992. "A Desire Named Streetcar: Fantasy and Fact in Rail Transit Planning." *Journal of the American Planning Association* 58(2): 158–176.

Plummer, Martyn. 2003. "JAGS: A Program for Analysis of Bayesian Graphical Models Using Gibbs Sampling." In *Proceedings of the 3rd International Workshop on Distributed Statistical Computing*. https://www.r-project.org/conferences/DSC-2003/Proceedings/Plummer.pdf.

———. 2012. "Rjags: Bayesian Graphical Models Using MCMC." R package version 3–7.

R Core Team. 2012. *R: A Language and Environment for Statistical Computing.* Vienna R Foundation for Statistical Computing.

Riksrevisionen. 2011. "Kostnadskontroll i stora järnvägsinvesteringar?" [Cost Control in Large-Scale Rail Investments]. Swedish National Audit Bureau Report No. RiR 6. Stockholm: Riksrevisionen.

Riksrevisionsverket. 1994. "Infrastrukturinvesteringar: En kostnadsjämförelse mellan plan och utfall i 15 större projekt inom Vägverket och Banverket" [Infrastructure Investments: A Cost Comparison of Plan and Outcome in 15 Large Projects with the Highways Agency and Railroad Agency]. Report No. RRV23. Stockholm: Riksrevisionsverket.

Roberts, Terry. 2020. "Scathing Muskrat Falls Inquiry Report Lays Blame on Fired Executives." *CBC News*, March 10. https://www.cbc.ca/news/canada/newfoundland-labrador/muskrat-falls-inquiry-misguided-project-1.5492169?__vfz=medium%3Dsharebar.

Rubin, Debra K. 2017. "Suit over Failed Brisbane P3 Focuses on Traffic Projections." *Engineering News-Record*, October 18.

Saulwick, Jacob. 2014. "Trial to Start on $144 Million Lane Cove Tunnel Debacle." *Sydney Morning Herald*, August 10.

Singh, Anil C. 2017. *Syncora Guar. Inc. v. Alinda Capital Partners LLC*, 2017 NY Slip Op 30288(U), Supreme Court, New York County, Docket No. 651258/2012.

Slovic, Paul. 2000. *The Perception of Risk.* Sterling, VA: EarthScan.

Swiss Association of Road and Transportation Experts. 2006. *Kosten-Nutzen-Analysen im Strassenverkehr.* Grundnorm 641820, valid from August 1. Zürich: Swiss Association of Road and Transportation Experts.

U.K. Department for Transport. 2006. "The Estimation and Treatment of Scheme Costs." Transport Analysis Guidance, Unit 3.5.9. London: Department for Transport.

U.K. Department for Transport and Oxford Global Projects. 2020. "Updating the Evidence Behind the Optimism Bias Uplifts for Transport Appraisals: 2020 Data Update to the 2004 Guidance Document 'Procedures for Dealing with Optimism Bias in Transport Planning.'" London: Department for Transport.

Vickerman, Roger. 2017. "Wider Impacts of Megaprojects: Curse or Cure?" In *The Oxford Handbook of Megaproject Management*, ed. Bent Flyvbjerg, 389–405, Oxford, UK: Oxford University Press.

Wachs, Martin. 1986. "Technique vs. Advocacy in Forecasting: A Study of Rail Rapid Transit." *Urban Resources* 4(1): 23–30.

———. 1989. "When Planners Lie with Numbers." *Journal of the American Planning Association* 55(4): 476–479.

———. 1990. "Ethics and Advocacy in Forecasting for Public Policy." *Business and Professional Ethics Journal* 9(1–2): 141–157.

———. 2013. "The Past, Present, and Future of Professional Ethics in Planning." In *Policy, Planning, and People: Promoting Justice in Urban Development*, ed. Naomi Carmon and Susan S. Fainstein, 101–119. Philadelphia: University of Pennsylvania Press.

Walmsley, D. A., and M. W. Pickett. 1992. *The Cost and Patronage of Rapid Transit Systems Compared with Forecasts.* Research Report No. 352. Crowthorne, UK: Transport Research Laboratory.

Ward, William A. 2019. "Cost-Benefit Analysis: Theory versus Practice at the World Bank 1960 to 2015." *Journal of Benefit-Cost Analysis* 10(1): 124–144.

World Bank. 1994. *World Development Report 1994: Infrastructure for Development.* Oxford, UK: Oxford University Press.

———. 2010. *Cost-Benefit Analysis in World Bank Projects.* Washington, DC: World Bank.

Worthington, Elise. 2012. "Clem7 Tunnel Investors Launch $150m Class Action." *ABC News,* June 1.

Wright, Robert. 2014. "US Infrastructure Crisis Drives Toll Road Bankruptcy." *Financial Times,* September 21. https://www.ft.com/content/7991d488-40da-11e4-9ce5-00144feabdc0.

Appendix

The sample for testing accuracy and bias in cost-benefit analysis includes 2,062 infrastructure investment projects across 8 investment types: bridges, buildings, bus rapid transit, dams, power plants, rail, roads, and tunnels. Geographically, the investments are located in 104 countries on 6 continents, including both developed and developing nations. Historically, the data cover the period from 1927 to 2013. Older investments were included to enable analyses of historical trends. For each investment in the data set, the accuracy of cost estimates was measured by cost overrun (actual divided by estimated cost, in real terms), while the accuracy of benefit estimates was measured by benefit overrun (actual divided by estimated benefits).

Data on estimated and actual costs and benefits of infrastructure investments are difficult to obtain. No statistical agency or other data service exists from which valid and reliable data may be secured. The data therefore have to be mined item by item from the source, which is extremely time-consuming. Data collection for the present study systematically followed international standards. Investments were included in the sample on the basis of data availability. We considered for inclusion all investments that we knew for which data on estimation accuracy were obtainable. Data were collected from a variety of sources, including annual accounts, cost and procurement accounts, revenue accounts, auditors' data, questionnaires, interviews, and other studies. Only data that could be supported by reliable documentary evidence were included to avoid the well-known problems with recalled data and interviewee biases. Even so, substantial amounts of data had to be rejected because of insufficient data quality, approximately 25 percent of cost data and 50 percent of benefit data.

Recently, we and colleagues discovered that some ex post studies of cost forecasting have been contaminated by significant statistical errors, such as in pooling data with incompatible baselines and excluding outliers that should have been included (Flyvbjerg et al. 2018, 2019). Such studies cannot be trusted. The same holds for meta-analysis studies that included these studies without being aware of their shortcomings. This unhappy situation—which signifies the arrival of junk science in infrastructure scholarship—is accounted for in Flyvbjerg et al. (2018, 2019) together with recommendations on how to avoid the problem going forward. The importance of rooting out studies with faulty data and statistics from the body of work in infrastructure scholarship cannot be overemphasized if the field wants to enjoy continued credence in academia and policy making and with the general public. Data from studies that proved contaminated are not included in the present research, needless to say.

In sum, we included in our sample all investments for which data were considered valid and reliable. Data collection and the data set are described in more detail in Flyvbjerg, Holm, and Buhl (2002, 2005) and Flyvbjerg (2016).

Preferably, costs and benefits would be measured over the full life cycle of an investment. However, such data are rarely if ever available. Therefore, the conventional method is to measure the costs of an infrastructure investment by the proxy of construction or capital costs and to measure benefits by the proxy of first-year benefits. This convention is followed here. Estimated costs and benefits are the estimates made at the time of decision to build (the final investment decision, based on the final business case), which is the baseline in time from which cost and benefit overrun are measured. Actual costs are measured as recorded outturn costs; actual benefits are measured as first-year benefits or a later value as close to this as possible if available and if first-year benefits were not available. Estimated and actual benefits are recorded in the unit of measurement that the planners of the investment decided to use for measuring benefits.

First-year benefits may seem a narrow proxy to use for benefits and has been criticized as such. In fact, however, first-year benefits have proven to be a reliable proxy for overall benefits, which is fortunate because the existence of benefits data for later years is so rare that benefit measurement would be rendered impossible for large samples if one had to rely on later-year data. For investments for which data are available on estimated and actual benefits covering more than one year after operations began, it turns out that investments with lower than estimated benefits during the first year of operations also tend to have lower than estimated benefits in later years (Flyvbjerg 2013, 766–767). Using the first year as the basis for measuring benefits therefore rarely appears to result in the error of identifying investments as underperforming in terms of benefits that would not be identified as such if a different time period were used as the basis for comparison. Actual benefits do not seem to quickly catch up with estimated benefits for investments with overestimated first-year benefits, and mostly they never do. Ramp-up of benefits is commonly assumed but often does not happen or occurs only partly. To take a typical example, for the Channel tunnel between the United Kingdom and France, more than five years after opening to the public train passengers numbered only 45 percent of those forecasted for the opening year, rail freight traffic was 40 percent of the forecast, and actual numbers had not caught up with the forecasts after 20 years and never have. In conclusion, we would prefer to measure benefits for all years, but data for this are generally unavailable. Given the lack of such data, the good news is that first-year benefits appear to be a fair proxy, with data more readily available than for later years.

Using first-year benefits has also been criticized for not considering wider development effects, such as increased real estate values following from improved transport services. Such effects undoubtedly exist. However, if transport infrastructure has wider benefits, these must be expected to be roughly proportional to traffic so that if traffic has been overestimated, the development benefits must also have been, which means that the case for proceeding with the investment was exaggerated. The difference between estimated and actual traffic, including first-year patronage, would therefore be a good proxy for assessing the extent of the problem. The same applies to other types of infrastructure. For the full argument and for further documentation regarding wider benefits, see Vickerman (2017) and Flyvbjerg (2005, 2013).

Ideally, data would be available for both cost and benefit overruns for each investment in the data set. However, data availability is far from ideal in the measurement of estimated and actual costs and benefits of infrastructure investments. Data were available for both cost and benefit overrun for only 327 investments out of the 2,062 in the sample. Using this ideal criterion would therefore result in scrapping large amounts of useful information for the 1,735 other investments in the sample, which would clearly be unacceptable. We therefore decided to run the statistical tests twice, first for the full sample of 2,062 investments and second for the subsample of 327 investments with data available for both the cost overrun and the benefit overrun for each investment. This approach gave us the advantage of being able to test whether results were robust across different samples, which proved to be the case.

Investments were included in the sample based on data availability, as mentioned. This means that the results of statistical analyses presented in the main text are probably conservative; that is, cost overruns in the investment population are most likely larger than in the sample, and benefit overruns are most likely smaller. One explanation of conservatism bias is that availability of data often indicates better than average investment management. Another is that data from badly performing investments are often not released and are therefore likely to be underrepresented in the sample. The existence of such conservatism must be kept in mind when interpreting results (Flyvbjerg 2005, 2016; Flyvbjerg, Holm, and Buhl 2002, 2005).

Standard statistical tests are described in the main text. In addition to these, we tested results for the influence of investment type, geography, and time using Bayesian modeling.[1] We found only a few significant differences across investment type, geography, and time; none of them ran counter to the main conclusion that cost and benefit estimates are inaccurate and biased and compound each other. This finding is unsurprising, given the overwhelmingly high level of statistical support for the main conclusion. In sum, results from the statistical tests proved robust across both conventional and Bayesian testing and across different samples.

Note

1. Parameters for the Bayesian models were estimated using MCMC. The language JAGS was used for this, through the rjags interface to R (Plummer 2003, 2012; R Core Team 2012). Statistical significance for the Bayesian tests was measured by the Bayes Factor (BF) instead of by p-values, where $12 < BF \leq 150$ indicates a statistically significant result, and $BF > 150$ indicates a highly significant result.

8

INFRASTRUCTURE'S NARROW PASSAGE

BETWEEN PERVERSE EXCESS AND PERVERSE DEFICIT

John D. Donahue

Scholars and citizens alike lament chronic failures to spend the right amount, at the right time, on the right kinds of infrastructure. No single explanation accounts for error-prone spending. But two of infrastructure's signature characteristics bedevil investment decisions. First, infrastructure tends to take years to design and construct and, once it is built, to last for a long time. Second, its gains and losses are rarely in perfect alignment, whether as a classic public good or because of idiosyncratic causes of disjuncture between costs and benefits. Either feature on its own would pose special impediments to fair, efficient, well-targeted infrastructure projects. Combined, they can create such a dysfunctional tangle of information and incentives that it is remarkable we ever get infrastructure spending right.

Before we map the pathologies, consider what it means to make smart decisions about infrastructure investments. The standard economic test is to undertake those projects—and only those projects—for which the present value of aggregate benefits exceeds the present value of aggregate costs. This test is easy to state but often hard to meet, for multiple reasons. One category of reasons is quite important in practice but is not our central focus, though it does show up as an aggravating factor: uncertainty (about the scale of future or indirect benefits and costs, the appropriate discount rate, or alternative ways to meet the project's goals or alternative uses of the resources it requires) can undermine any confident tally of net benefits.

Our concern here is less with information deficits per se than with cases where self-seeking private interests conflict with and prevail over the broad public good. Such cases come in two major forms. What might be called *perverse excess* occurs when infrastructure spending goes forward, despite costs outweighing benefits, because influential constituencies are able to push costs onto others, claim disproportionate benefits, or both. Perverse deficit occurs when narrow interests block spending that they see as disadvantageous to themselves despite its broadly favorable balance of gains and losses. Like sailors in Greek mythology braving the straits between Scylla and Charybdis, infrastructure decision makers must navigate the narrow political passage between too much and too little. I make no categorical claims about the relative prevalence of the two classes of error, but I do assert that both are common enough to squander a consequential quotient of otherwise achievable welfare gains.

Hypothetical Illustration

For a concrete illustration, let us choose an infrastructure example that is sufficiently new and unsettled to permit freewheeling speculation without trampling unduly on the known facts: hyperloop transport. This nascent technology involves pressurized vehicles that travel via electrical propulsion through sealed tubes that are so nearly emptied of air that friction is drastically reduced, permitting extremely fast and energy-efficient travel. Several companies are experimenting with hyperloop technology and have taken prototypes and test tracks to the point where we know that hyperloop works in a narrow technical sense. But is it a good idea to build a full-scale hyperloop network to replace a significant share of travel by car, train, and air by midcentury? Nobody knows yet.

But stipulate, for argument's sake, that a major shift toward hyperloop would be a boon on balance. The costs, of course, would be staggering. Even in a single country—and for simplicity let us focus on the United States—veining the nation with sealed tubes 3 m in diameter and installing the equipment to suck out most of the air, pressurize the passenger pods, and power the rails would make the interstate highway system's construction budget look like spare change. Let us indulge our imaginations, however, in a hypothetical future where the benefits amply repay the investment. Speeds in excess of 1,000 km per hour make jetliners obsolete for most overland routes. Hyperloop pods do not need runways, so passengers can go directly from city center to city center with no wasted time or energy climbing and descending. While we are at it, assume that by the time hyperloop technology is mature, all electricity is generated sustainably. So, channeling that clean energy into a fully electric transport mode would radically reduce the damage we inflict on the climate as we get from here to there.

Yet, narrow interests could easily spoil this happy scenario by suppressing hyperloop investment. The forces of perverse deficit could take several forms. Those with stakes in air, road, and rail transport could deploy legal and political stratagems to defeat, delay, or diminish any hyperloop network. Hyperloop tubes are unlovely things, and aesthetic objections could block construction or deform routes in ways that drain away many of the benefits. (Burying the tubes would improve the view but make the expense yet more ruinous.) Both of these forms of perverse deficit are caused by the disjoint costs and benefits characteristic of infrastructure.

Another likely spoiler flows from the extended time frame that hyperloop, like most infrastructure investment, would feature. Colossal construction costs would be incurred for many years before the first passenger pod was ready to ride. Governmental investment in hyperloop might founder on elected officials' reluctance to ask today's voters to pay for future benefits. There are potential fixes for this, of course. Debt financing can narrow or even eliminate the temporal gap between costs and benefits. A wholly private hyperloop system could in principle put investment decisions in the hands of those whose business it is to make smart trade-offs between big costs now and bigger payoffs later. But it is all too easy to imagine these fixes failing to generate hyperloop investments extensive enough or fast enough to harvest the full benefits.

Now consider an alternative state of the world where a hyperloop network is a truly terrible idea. People could turn out to hate zipping through tubes in windowless pods, carbon-sparing convenience be damned. Real or perceived safety hazards could scare off riders. The persistence of unsustainable electricity generation could undermine hyperloop's environmental edge over other transport modes, or the gargantuan carbon cost of building the network would swamp any imaginable environmental advantage of operating it. Perhaps high-quality telepresence, luxury airships, or some as yet unimagined technological or cultural developments could make fast surface transport superfluous. How might the forces of perverse excess burden us with a hyperloop network that, reckoned rightly, we should leave unbuilt?

Amid myriad specific scenarios three big categories stand out. The first involves information gaps or distortions that present a misleading picture of net benefits. Government might subsidize construction, for example, so that true costs are disguised. (To be precise, subsidies can promote the right investments when they correct flawed market prices; they invite perverse excess only when they lack such justification.) Or the decision to build the hyperloop network could ignore the aesthetic and environmental damage that, if taken into account, would discourage the investment. A second category arises when beneficiaries are especially well organized or otherwise politically powerful. If city dwellers who benefit disproportionately from hyperloop transport form an especially effective constituency, they may be able to force through investments that are a bad deal for suburban and rural taxpayers. A similar situation occurs when providers of capital, technology, management, and labor anticipate premium earnings from hyperloop investment and have the political clout to bend public spending to their interests.

Nobody can yet have a well-founded prediction of what is in store for hyperloop—overinvestment, underinvestment, or the elusive Goldilocks scenario of precisely the right level. The data are just not in. Segueing from our hypothetical example, what can be said about the greater risk—perverse excess or perverse deficit—for infrastructure in general? Each of us no doubt has a stockpile of anecdotes from which we are tempted to construct a general rule. Some of us may even have a considered opinion that is anchored in evidence. I am neither equipped for nor inclined to propound some general assertion that the world makes its mistakes in one direction or the other. But in the hope of clarifying the generic impediments to wise infrastructure investment, I invoke three seminal mid-20th-century theoretical texts.

Tullock on Majority Voting

Gordon Tullock formed half of the intellectual duo, along with Nobel Laureate James Buchanan, who essentially invented public choice economics. A few years before the pair produced their landmark book *The Calculus of Consent*, Tullock (1959) on his own published a short but influential piece titled "Problems of Majority Voting." Tullock organizes his theory around a simple story about infrastructure—a parable about 100 farmers' dependence on public roads to bring their crops to market. The farmers are similar in their skill at coaxing food from the soil but sharply different in their attitudes toward public spending.

Some of the farmers, whom Tullock terms *maximizers*, are rustic whizzes at calculating their self-interest and wholly undeterred by scruple, shame, or public spirit in advancing it. Other farmers are (or at least start out as) *Kantians*, who ask for themselves only the caliber of public roads they are prepared to support for everyone. The roads are maintained (or not) on the basis of direct voting, project by project. Only if a majority of farmers approve of the legislative proposal providing for a particular road's maintenance is that road kept in good order.

At the start of Tullock's parable, the amoral maximizers constitute a narrow majority of the 100 farmers. Exploiting their political leverage, they form a cabal to vote for the maintenance of their roads and against any spending on the Kantians, who nonetheless must pay their share of the costs for each enacted maintenance-funding bill. Since they expect to be subsidized by the Kantian minority, the maximizers demand ritzier standards of road maintenance than they would want if they had to pay the costs themselves.

This situation is unstable, however. The formerly fair-minded Kantians, once awakened to the harsh ways of the world, get to work organizing their own legislative cabals. But as farmers each scramble to strike deals to get their own roads repaired, aiming for a new and different bare majority to exploit the hapless minority, they find that everybody else is playing the same game. The good news for each farmer is that his road does get maintained, lavishly so. The bad news is that when tax time comes, he finds that he is also paying for other farmers' roads—and at the same gold-plated standard. Roads are "maintained at a level considerably higher and at greater expense than is rational from the standpoint of the farmers living along it" (Tullock 1959, 572). Perverse excess prevails. And Tullock (1959, 578) predicts that this sorry outcome will be quite general for any category of public investment—not only but especially infrastructure—that everybody pays for but where some benefit more than others: "if a given sum of money is to be spent on two different types of governmental activity, one of which is of general benefit and one of which benefits a series of special groups, too much will be spent on the latter. Defense, for example, will be slighted in favor of river and harbor work" (Tullock 1959, 579).[1]

Downs on *Under*spending

Less than a year after Tullock's piece appeared, the economist Anthony Downs (1960) published his own article, whose title tells the story: "Why the Government Budget Is Too Small in a Democracy." Downs, like Tullock, is considered a member of the public choice school but a somewhat heterodox one, intellectually eclectic and hard to pigeonhole ideologically. Given the article's thrust, it is important to note that Downs's story rests on no rosier view of politics or human nature than Tullock's. For example, Downs (1960, 542) writes that "political parties are primarily motivated by the desire to enjoy the income, prestige, and power of being in office. Each party regards government policies as means to these ends."

To establish the hypothetical benchmark of the right level and pattern of public spending—in contrast to what politics actually produces—Downs (1960, 545) eschews social utility functions or other sophisticated constructs and simply declares that the correct budget is "the one which would emerge from the democratic process if both citizens and parties had perfect information about both actual and potential government policies." But they do not. Most people, quite rationally, have only a foggy and partial notion of the governmental budget and its consequences or alternatives. And not even the most obsessive political junkies are fully informed about all of the imaginable options and the likely outcomes of each option for every potential public spending agenda.

There is no logical necessity for ignorance to result in too little rather than too much government spending. But Downs (1960) plausibly argues that citizens are less likely to undervalue the private benefits they can acquire with money left in their pockets than they are to lowball the perceived worth of tax-financed public goods and services. He adduces two main reasons. First, the costs of private goods tend to be much more closely associated—temporally and otherwise—with their benefits than is the case for public goods. Second, while people mostly choose whether to acquire a good or service for themselves, for public goods—even in the textbook ideal of a representative democracy—few citizens have much engagement with spending deliberation or decisions. For private but not public goods and services, some individual reflection on the balance of costs and benefits and a considered judgment that the benefits predominate will precede the decision to spend. So, the typical citizen will be much more confident about the value produced by her or his own budget choices than by those of the government.

This sets up the crux of Downs's logic: "If society is at all complex, the government's gigantic policy mix is bound to contain at least one act which any given voter opposes. It is either positively repugnant to him (i.e., it produces negative utility apart from its resource cost), or else he knows of better uses to which the resources it absorbs could be put. As long as only one such act exists for him, he is out of equilibrium with government" (Downs 1960, 549). Even if our hypothetical citizen favors a long list of new public initiatives and would be comfortable with a Scandinavian-scale public sector, there will be budget items that the citizen wants to cut. Since every taxpayer believes they could be made better off by some reduction in public spending, politicians are always on the lookout for ways to reduce aggregate spending that do not provoke any potent constituencies. So, government will retain in the budget "only those expenditures which produce benefits that voters are aware of, for hidden benefits cannot influence votes" (Downs 1960, 552). Downs argues that people are myopic about both the benefits and the costs of collective undertakings but tend to undervalue benefits more than costs.

Downs (1960, 556) notes an important refinement: a citizen will be "much more aware of government policies that affect him as an income-earner than he is of policies that affect him as a consumer." So, governments will be motivated to spend in ways that generate identifiable benefits to producers as long as the costs of the spending do not lose more votes than the focused producer benefits wins. This factor will tend to make aggregate public spending too large as will any ability to hide costs, as with indirect taxation or inflation. The net effect, as Downs notes multiple times, can go either way. But he predicts that the forces suppressing spending will predominate mostly because tools to hide the costs of public spending are relatively weak and because there are incentives for rival politicians and others to unmask attempts at such concealment. According to Downs (1960, 560), "The forces which tend to enlarge budgets beyond the 'correct' level are inherently limited, whereas those which tend to shrink it are not."

Olson on Collective Failure

People come together to advance common goals. If four of us are on a road trip and our car skids into a ditch, will we not all get out and push to get ourselves back on the highway? We would be fools not to, and for most of us it is just common sense to expect shared effort for shared benefit. Alexis de Tocqueville viewed Americans in particular as masters of collective self-help, but he saw the instinct toward mutually beneficial collective action as entirely general. Unless iniquitous authority prevents it, people "end up seeing in association the universal and, so to speak, unique means that men can use to attain the various ends that they propose" (de Tocqueville 2010, 912). If a community stands to benefit from a road, an airport, or even a hyperloop network, it seems natural to anticipate that the community will organize to make it happen. The notion that people will seize opportunities to do themselves some shared good is so self-evidently "right" that even after half a century Mancur Olson's account of why it is all wrong seems fresh and surprising.

The Logic of Collective Action (Olson 1965) starts with basic public goods reasoning but goes on to both deepen and broaden it. We have long known that you cannot count on people to chip in voluntarily to provide for national defense, to take a classic example. Even if I am perfectly aware that I benefit from the military's protection, I will reason that withholding my minuscule share of the cost will make no discernible difference in the resources available. So, I will simply free-ride and let others pay. As everybody else makes the same calculation, the defense budget dwindles to a pittance. To forestall this outcome, we fund defense with tax revenues to which everybody is obliged to contribute. In a paradox that has become so familiar it does not seem odd, coercion to limit our choices makes us better off.

So far there is nothing that would surprise a first-semester economics student. But Olson's genius was to recognize that the same logic that threatens the scale of appropriations for the military budget also imperils, at the limit, the existence of a defense capacity at all. Suppose I believe that an army is a regrettable necessity in this wicked world and want the U.S. Congress to devote appropriately big sums to it—and I accept that my tax bill, like everybody else's, will go up to cover the costs. The rub is that Congress is unlikely to fund national defense unless it knows that the public thinks it is a good idea. And they are only going to know that the public thinks it is a good idea if the public tells them so. Now, it is not all that costly to inform Congress that I support having an army—a few minutes of my time, maybe the price of an envelope, a sheet of paper, and a stamp. But if I am confident that many millions of other citizens share my opinion that we ought to have a national defense, why should I incur even the trivial cost of indicating "my" support? If everybody makes the same calculation—and why should they not?—the neglect of defense spending would be nearly total. And, likewise, we would spend little or nothing on medical research, K–12 education, space exploration, diplomacy, fire protection, and infrastructure.

This is not what we see in practice, of course. But we have summarized just the first round of Olson's reasoning. He is not simply echoing Downs's prediction of chronic underspending on collective missions. Nor, unfortunately, does Olson project the middle ground of "just right" to counter both Downs's generalization of "too little" and Tullock's of "too much." Whether a group will get its act together to accomplish latent common goals depends on a range of nonobvious considerations. Group size matters, for one. To loop back to the homely example at the start of this section, four fellow travelers probably would manage to get their car back on the road. It will be pretty obvious that it is in everybody's interest and that it will only happen if everybody helps and even more obvious if one of the four stays in the warm car while the other three get out to push.

Beyond scale, however, what matters most for a latent group's ability to organize for collective purposes is whether it can create compelling private motives to join and support the group. Olson starts with the puzzle that in his mid-1960s America, some economic interests (such as skilled industrial works, doctors, and farmers) were quite effective at pressing government for spending and other policies they wanted, while others (such as agricultural laborers, most white-collar workers, and consumers) were not. What overarching factor could explain the ability or inability to come together around common interests?

Olson deduced that it was whether the latent group could devise "selective incentives" that it could deliver to members who pitched in for the shared agenda and withhold from those who shirked. Such private motives push or pull individuals into collective endeavors they would otherwise shun. "The only organizations that have the selective incentives available are those that (1) have the authority and capacity to be coercive; or (2) have a source of positive inducements that they can offer the individuals in a latent group" (Olson 1965, 133). Labor unions—at the time, less so now—could require all employees at a worksite to pay dues. The American Medical Association could offer members professional connections, continuing education, and other perks, with the collective good of lobbying against "socialized medicine" as a side benefit. The Farm Bureau could provide dues-paying members with private goods such as tailored lending and insurance plans as well as public benefits such as lobbying for federal price supports.

Other groups with latent common interests might try to improvise such special incentives—at the time Olson was writing there were efforts afoot to organize farm laborers, retirees, and consumers—but the ability to succeed in such efforts was uneven and idiosyncratic. Some species of insects, dinosaurs, and small mammals were able over millennia to evolve the capacity for flight, but most were not. Both the starting place and accidents of trajectory mattered. In a similar way, some latent groups will prove able to cobble together a package of threats and inducements that motivate organizing around a shared agenda, and others will not.

In Search of Generalizations

What, if anything, can we make of this brief tour of some highlights of the collective-choice literature? Would a careful survey of the evidence show that Tullock has it right about overspending? Or that Downs has it right on underspending on infrastructure (and other shared goals)? Does Olson's more complex logic invite us to anticipate any particular result with respect to perverse excess or perverse deficit? It is, perhaps obviously, silly to look for solid conclusions from three texts and basically no data. But I fear it would be ill-advised to expect clean generalizations to emerge even from a far more sweeping inquiry.

To a significant extent, this ambiguity is simply the curse of social science. Its objects are almost always too heterogeneous and imprecisely defined to permit firm, final conclusions. Even economists—whose domain is far more tractable than, say, sociology—look with envy on the physical sciences. Once somebody discovered that helium has two protons and two electrons, we had a characteristic of helium we could count on. We could be confident that helium would behave the same way in labs in Istanbul and in Indianapolis and that its properties a century hence would be the same as they are today. Likewise, after the first person to pay attention while dissecting a standard cottontail rabbit realized that its left lung had two lobes while its right lung had four, we knew something about cottontail rabbits in general (Autifi, El-Banna, and El-Sayed Ebaid 2015).

Of course, there are anomalies, misidentifications, and taxonomic ambiguities even in the hardest of hard sciences.[2] But they tend to be far graver in the social sciences. Do charter schools deliver student learning more effectively than conventional public schools? There are so many different kinds of charter schools, such a diversity of students, so many legitimate metrics for student learning, and so many valid definitions of effectiveness that one can invoke studies to support both a resounding "yes!" and a thunderous "no!" without any egregious lapse in intellectual honesty (Donahue and Zeckhauser 2011). The most honest answer, though, is, "it depends"—as the preface to an arduous and likely incomplete exploration of the factors on which it depends.

So it is with infrastructure. In the United States, public spending on transportation—by far the biggest category of infrastructure—has wandered within a narrow range of a little less than 1 percent of the gross domestic product since the 1980s, down just slightly from a little more than 1 percent during the postwar surge of road building (Congressional Budget Office 2019). Within this range are countless examples of wasteful spending, and beyond it there are plenty of valid needs that remain unmet. Altshuler and Luberoff (2003) relate example after example. In a telling footnote about one of his stints in public service as Massachusetts's secretary of transportation, Altshuler relates his inability to achieve a sensible compromise between the powerful political forces advocating both excessive and inadequate highway construction in Boston (Altshuler and Luberhoff 2003, 87). Any observer who cannot point to both "roads to nowhere" and glaringly neglected needs is just not trying.

At the risk of opening up a topic to which a brief treatment can in no way do justice, let me suggest just a few factors on which the hazards of infrastructure investment depend.

Consider first the features of the technology itself—or of the political and institutional context—that establish a risk of perverse excess in infrastructure spending:

- *Concentrated benefits and diffuse costs.* Tullock's tale of farmers and their roads offers perhaps the purest case of this scenario. His parable features excess even by the standards of the self-serving beneficiaries, but even without that twist, the real world displays plenty of wasteful infrastructure spending triggered by this scenario. Some would point to the Big Dig project that figures prominently in *Mega-Projects* (Altshuler and Luberoff 2003), with the gains clustered in and around Boston and the fiscal burden shared with the entire country, as a classic case.

- *Disproportionately visible benefits.* While Downs argues that the more common situation is that costs are visible and gains are obscured, there are certainly cases where the benefits are far more vivid. Consider the obvious advantages of a new bridge arcing between two highly developed urban regions. Even if the costs cannot be offloaded to the nation as a whole, they may be less obvious if the project is bundled into a broad investment package or if subtle environmental damage forms any large share of the total costs. Or the perceived benefits of the bridge may loom misleadingly large if older and less visible crossings had already delivered some large fraction of the new bridge's benefits. Glaeser and Ponzetto (2017) address precisely this issue of differentially visible costs and benefits in an article that seeks to account for the historical trajectory of U.S. transportation investment that Altshuler and Luberoff (2003) relate. Their logic predicts that the forces conducing to overspending will tend to dominate in sparsely populated areas, and they summon data suggesting that this is precisely what occurs. Glaeser and Ponzetto (2017) also show how, in principle, judicious blends of financing models can curb tendencies to excess and deficit but that, in practice, getting the incentives right tends to be quite difficult.

- *Disproportionately influential beneficiaries.* One variant of the speculative hyperloop example raised early in this chapter suggests that wasteful investment could result if politically influential urbanites stood the most to gain. Perverse excess is a pervasive risk if groups with political clout—whether because of their wealth, partisan affiliation, ethnicity, or status—have an outsized interest in seeing an infrastructure asset built.

A particularly potent contributor to perverse excess, which can embrace aspects of all of these factors, is rent-seeking by producers. If suppliers of capital, labor, or technology see a potential infrastructure project as especially lucrative, they may make it their business to ensure that the project goes forward—whatever its net benefits to the community at large.

The factors conducive to perverse deficit, in turn, include the inverse of all the above: if benefits are diffuse and costs are concentrated, if costs are obvious and benefits are submerged, or if beneficiaries lack political power, the odds of neglecting a potentially valuable investment escalate. Some additional—or perhaps special-case factors—include the following:

- *Imperiled rents.* Rents—a surplus beyond what the market would otherwise offer to producers—can flow from existing assets, not just potential new investments. Those whose rents would be imperiled by new infrastructure can form a focused and highly motivated constituency to oppose it even if the net benefits would be enormous. Examples might include ferry operators fighting a bridge proposal or (in some imaginable future states of the world) the air travel industry seeking to snuff out hyperloop investment.
- *True public goods.* The standard definition of a public good hinges on two rather inelegant terms: *nonrival* (one person's consumption does not come at the expense of anybody else) and *nonexcludable* (it is not possible to deny benefits to those who do not pay). Few goods or services, in infrastructure as elsewhere, align completely with that definition. A bridge, for example, is semiprivate—it is entirely feasible to charge users; if there is any congestion at all, additional users diminish others' benefits. But pure cases certainly exist. Some experts foresee geoengineering—typically either terrestrial or atmospheric reflective material—to combat climate change.

If this turned out to be a good idea and to be very costly (it may not be either), it would approach a pure public good. And, as such, it would be at risk of underprovision.

Conclusions

Much of this chapter's discussion has implicitly or explicitly assumed a democratic political system as the context for infrastructure decision making. This is not the only way communities organize themselves for collective choice. Details of political institutions, norms, and procedures will, of course, make a difference in how infrastructure policy plays out, including the relative risk of errors of omission or commission. Differences across political structures, however, may be less fundamental than they first appear. The forces unleashed by interests, information, and incentives will flow down somewhat different channels to somewhat different effect depending on the institutional and political lay of the land. But there probably never has been or ever will be a polity in which they are entirely absent.

We have mostly discussed the diverse pathologies that attend infrastructure investment with a heavily governmental role. Might extensive, even dominant, private roles offer a broad-spectrum remedy? Infrastructure privatization and partnerships form a rich, complex topic all their own, and this is not the place to attempt a summary. But the private sector has always been heavily involved in infrastructure, so the key questions must concern the nature rather than the scale of private engagement. The right private roles can clarify costs and benefits, help overcome truncated time horizons, and boost incentives for efficiency and innovation. Wrongheaded privatization, conversely, can turbocharge pathological politics with high-powered incentives, and there is certainly no assurance that the right kinds of private engagement will prevail. Sometimes plenty of privateness makes things better; sometimes it makes things worse. Once again, it depends.

Much of the political-economy logic pointing to potential improvements via privatization applies as well to public sector measures that incorporate market-style approaches to clarify both costs and benefits and better align the two. User fees, for example, can bring home to beneficiaries the true investment burden and discourage perverse excess (Olson 1965). Even Tullock's selfish maximizer farmers, after all, would think twice about maneuvering for gold-plated roads if they knew their own toll payments, not just tax levies on everyone, would have to cover some of the costs. Situating more responsibility for making and financing investment decisions at the state or local rather than federal level can combat excess in two related ways. Most obviously, state- and local-level investment decision making and financing diminishes somewhat the ability to foist burdens onto those who fail to benefit, in principle improving both fairness and efficiency. Less obviously, shifting the fiscal debate into a smaller, simpler arena may disperse the clouds of empirical complexity that can lead even fair-minded people to escalate their infrastructure demands unduly. Yet, it is always worth remembering that these remedies against perverse excess can themselves provoke perverse deficit if they undermine efforts to recognize and act on infrastructure's broad benefits.

Neither market models nor any other single, simple fix can banish the inherent hazards of infrastructure investment. It is the job of scholars to eschew dogma, anchor on the evidence, and be clear and candid about the assumptions upon which their predictions rest. It is the job of practitioners to be eclectic and skeptical whenever they seek guidance from theory—and abundantly cautious as they steer their own perilous passages between perverse deficit and perverse excess for infrastructure.

Summary

- Some of the political forces that lead to excesses or shortfalls of infrastructure spending can be understood using public choice economics, the theoreticians of which assume that individuals rationally pursue their self-interest in a democratic society governed by voting rules of various kinds.
- Their predictions vary from more to less spending than would be socially optimal.
- Overspending is likely if, for example, voters tend to overestimate benefits more than they overestimate costs, project benefits are concentrated but costs are diffused, or majority voting is used to select among similar projects.
- Underspending is likely if voters tend to overestimate costs more than benefits or if costs are visible but gains are obscured. The tendency to underspend on public goods because of the free-rider problem can be overcome if the latent group of supporters is small or can devise selective incentives to offer to others who join them.

Notes

1. Total public spending on highways had risen sharply from 1902 to 1959, as Tullock was writing, but over the same period, military spending grew nearly five times as much (U.S. Census Bureau 1973). There was a reasonably compelling public-interest rationale for defense spending to soar over that period, but Tullock's whole point is that such reasons should lack political potency.

2. An article in *Evolution* about the range of unrelated creatures sharing the basic features and behaviors we associate with that standard cottontail has perhaps the most plaintive title in all of biology: "What, If Anything, Is a Rabbit?" (Wood 1957).

References

Altshuler, Alan, and David Luberoff. 2003. *Mega-Projects: The Changing Politics of Urban Public Investment*. Washington, DC: Brookings Institution Press.

Autifi, Mohamed Abdul Haye, Ahmed Kamal El-Banna, and Ashraf El-Sayed Ebaid. 2015. "Morphological Study of Rabbit Lung." *Al Azhar Assium Medical Journal* 13(3): 41–51.

Buchanan, James M., and Gordon Tullock. 1962. *The Calculus of Consent: Logical Foundations of Constitutional Democracy*. Indianapolis: Liberty Fund.

Congressional Budget Office. 2019. *Federal Investment: 1962 to 2018*. Washington, DC: Congress of the United States.

de Tocqueville, Alexis. 2010. *Democracy in America: Historical-Critical Edition of De la démocratie en Amérique*, ed. Eduardo Nolla, trans. James T. Schleifer. Book 2, section 2. Indianapolis: Liberty Fund.

Donahue, John D., and Richard J. Zeckhauser. 2011. *Collaborative Governance: Private Roles for Public Goals*. Princeton, NJ: Princeton University Press.

Downs, Anthony. 1960. "Why the Government Budget Is Too Small in a Democracy." *World Politics* 12(4): 541–563.

Glaeser, Edward L., and Giacomo A. M. Ponzetto. 2017. "Fundamental Errors in the Voting Booth." Working paper No. 23683. Washington, DC: National Bureau of Economic Research. https://ssrn.com/abstract=3023078.

Olson, Mancur. 1965. *The Logic of Collective Action: Public Goods and the Theory of Groups*. Cambridge, MA: Harvard University Press.

Tullock, Gordon. 1959. "Problems of Majority Voting," *Journal of Political Economy* 67(6): 571–579.

U.S. Census Bureau. 1973. "Series Y 533–566: Federal, State, and Local Expenditures, by Function, 1902 to 1970." In *Historical Statistics of the United States: Colonial Times to 1970*. Washington, DC: U.S. Government Printing Office.

Wood, Albert E. 1957. "What, If Anything, Is a Rabbit?" *Evolution* 11(4): 417–425.

INFRASTRUCTURE FINANCE

9

INFRASTRUCTURE FINANCE

Akash Deep

When we think about infrastructure, two features stand out in most people's minds: the high magnitude of investment costs and the up-front concentrated nature of its incurrence versus the low per-user benefits with a usage pattern that is spread over the long economic life of infrastructure assets. Thus, the challenge of infrastructure financing may be described as that of creating mechanisms for cumulating and capitalizing the lifetime benefits from infrastructure assets to mobilize and justify its large up-front costs.

A result of the large temporal and spatial dispersion between benefits and costs of infrastructure is the emergence of risks. Larger investments with broader impacts and longer horizons are more uncertain. Given the specific economic features of most infrastructure—regulated natural monopoly, low-demand elasticity, need for affordability, among others—the risks and opportunities of infrastructure emanate from not only its financial peculiarities but also its political exposure. Therefore, risk management is an exercise in managing both financial and nonfinancial risks.

Many studies have documented the large gap between the need for infrastructure and the stock of existing infrastructure. The estimate of annual infrastructure needs across the globe has varied depending on sectors covered and assumptions made, but they are uniformly massive (OECD 2017a, table 3): US$3.3 trillion (Woetzel et al. 2016), US$6.3 trillion (OECD 2017b), US$6.4 trillion (NCE 2014), and US$7.9 trillion (Bhattacharya et al. 2016). This gap has often been interpreted as a result of insufficient availability of funds for financing infrastructure. Therefore, mobilizing adequate finance is an important goal for infrastructure development.

The mainstay of infrastructure investment has always been the public exchequer. It has been a long-standing practice for governments to create additional fiscal space through borrowing (Heller 2005) to finance infrastructure projects. However, the growing stockpile of public debt is stymieing investment choices: 40 percent of low-income developing countries face debt-related challenges (IMF

213

2018b), while the debt of advanced economies stands at 105 percent of the gross domestic product (IMF 2018a), the highest it has been since World War II (Baum, Mogues, and Verdier 2020).

In most countries, part of the financing gap for infrastructure has been met by tapping into private resources. Private participation in infrastructure has also been thought to engender efficiency and spawn innovation. Most important, however, the search for private financing solutions has provided us with insights into the nature of infrastructure—its structuring, valuation, and risk management—that are essential to all forms of infrastructure finance: public, private, or public-private partnerships (PPPs). The discussion in this chapter focuses on private finance primarily because of ease of exposition: the broad impact (public) of infrastructure is better distinguished from its narrower financing (private) modality. The most salient considerations and challenges of infrastructure development remain essentially similar across public and private financing mechanisms. Indeed, the solution to a specific infrastructure financing problem should ideally be explored in the multidimensional continuum between private and public financing instruments and institutions rather than as a purely public or purely private solution.

Another challenge closely related to financing is that of translating the benefits from infrastructure, which accrue to both its direct users and those farther removed from it in the form of positive externalities, into monetary proceeds. This decision is referred to as the infrastructure funding question, namely who pays for infrastructure: users or taxpayers, immediate beneficiaries or those who benefit from the spillovers, the current generation or the future one, and so on. The answer to these questions is important for a variety of fiscal and political reasons but typically does not rule in or out any specific financing method. The main focus of this chapter is the infrastructure financing problem, not the infrastructure funding question.

This chapter is split into two parts. The first part is a primer on infrastructure finance and begins with a description of the main sources of infrastructure financing. Project finance is defined and distinguished from balance sheet finance, and the cash flow waterfall feature is used to highlight the role of the two broad components of capital structure: equity and debt. The management of risk over time and across the different stakeholders involved in infrastructure is then examined, as is the role of government in mitigating risk for infrastructure projects. The valuation of infrastructure using the core principles of finance to determine the risk-adjusted discount rate and the cost of capital is also discussed.

The second part of the chapter describes two significant innovations in infrastructure financing using examples. The first innovation relates to credit enhancement as an innovation in debt financing using the example of the European Investment Bank's (EIB) Project Bond Credit Enhancement (PBCE) facility.

The second focuses on infrastructure funds as an innovation in equity financing, tracing the history of the infrastructure fund structure pioneered by Australia's Macquarie Bank.

Financing Sources and Structures

Where does the financing for infrastructure come from? The majority is provided by national, state, and local governments as direct allocations from the public budget. The most prominent example of public budgeting for infrastructure is China, which was estimated to have spent 13.5 percent of the gross domestic product on urban infrastructure alone (Chong and Poole 2013). Governments raise budgetary resources through user fees and various types of taxes. To meet the large up-front outlay required for infrastructure capital investments, governments also issue long-term debt that is typically paid back gradually over many years.

Public investments into infrastructure are usually allocated through the ministry of finance but implemented through a portfolio of government ministries that are typically organized based on different infrastructure sectors such as transport, power, energy, water and sanitation, and communications. In many developing countries, aid from bilateral and multilateral agencies may play a substantial role in bolstering the public budgetary capacity for infrastructure investments.

Another widely used conduit for government funding of infrastructure projects is infrastructure-focused, state-owned enterprises. Governments around the world own, in whole or in part, firms that build, operate, and finance infrastructure assets. (Chapter 14 discusses state-owned enterprises in this sector further.) A wide spectrum of state-owned enterprises and public agencies has been designed to provide varying levels of control to the state over infrastructure resources. These firms raise financing through budgetary allocations as well as financial instruments such as debt and equity issued with or without the financial backing of the state. Indeed, state-owned entities are the largest builder, owner, and manager of infrastructure assets. A recent study estimated that 83 percent of the infrastructure project investment commitments in 2017 in emerging markets and developing economies came from public investment mechanisms (Bhatia et al. 2020). Two-thirds of all public investments were channeled through state-owned enterprises.

While public financing has always been and continues to be the dominant source of infrastructure finance, the search for sufficient and suitable financing has been one of the catalysts for seeking private financing sources. For example, the United Kingdom estimated that 50 percent of its infrastructure pipeline would be provided by the private sector (Infrastructure and Projects Authority 2018). Owing to the specialized nature of infrastructure, private investments are protected and circumscribed by regulatory mechanisms to a greater extent than other noninfrastructure-related activities.

Private firms have mobilized financing for infrastructure on their own balance sheet or through off–balance sheet mechanisms. This financing may support one or more subactivities in the infrastructure life cycle such as building or operating an infrastructure asset or owning and managing the infrastructure asset and therefore being entitled to its proceeds.

Finally, a variety of arrangements seek to pool public and private resources—financial and others—for the financing of infrastructure. These can take the form of privatization, joint ventures and capitalized state-owned enterprises, and PPPs.

Corporate and Project Finance

Financial managers can choose to finance infrastructure in a variety of ways. The first decision they face is whether to finance the infrastructure asset on the balance sheet of an existing public or private entity or by creating a new entity using a mechanism called project finance. On-balance-sheet finance involves financing raised by an existing private firm or public entity against all the assets that it owns or are backed by a guarantee of the state.

An alternative form of financing is project finance using dedicated financial structures called *special-purpose vehicles*. Project finance involves creating a separate legal and economic entity with the primary role of setting up an organizational structure and obtaining the necessary financial resources in the form of debt and equity to develop and manage an infrastructure project. The functions of this entity are clearly defined and devoted to a single objective, that of building, operating, financing, and managing the identified project.

A typical project finance structure would consist of the following main agreements: a design-and-build contract with a group of construction firms; an operating and management agreement covering a significant part of the life of the asset; debt and equity contracts with lenders and shareholders, respectively; and an authorizing contract with the state or a public agency granting the special-purpose vehicle special protections and responsibilities. In some cases, an offtake contract—such as a power purchase agreement in the case of a power project—might also be present (Yescombe 2014).

A number of private firms and even public entities may come together to create a consortium that underlies the special-purpose vehicle, whose major shareholders are referred to as sponsors. The main and crucial distinction from conventional corporate or public financial structures is that in project finance, repayment to debt and equity providers depends solely on the capacity of the project to generate cash flows, with typically no recourse to the balance sheets of the sponsors or the resources of the government. Hence, project finance has also been described as nonrecourse financing or off-balance-sheet financing.

Project finance entails the creation of a new entity for a specific purpose, which it seeks to achieve through a bundle of real and financial contracts. Not surprisingly, establishing these contracts involves significant time and transaction costs that may be justifiable only in the case of larger infrastructure deals. However, the ring-fenced structure of project finance allows for effective risk allocation, while its single-purpose nature allows for greater transparency and easier restructuring. The combination of a detailed cash flow waterfall and high leverage, along with a strict allocation of risks, makes project financing not only a financing structure but also a corporate governance mechanism (Brealey, Cooper, and Habib 1996).

Financing Instruments

Financing for infrastructure can be raised using a variety of financial instruments, of which the two broad categories are debt and equity. Debt and equity can also be seen as the two broad mechanisms through which investors can make investments in infrastructure. Public or private firms and project-financed entities can borrow money from investors as debt. Alternatively, they can sell a share of ownership of the firm or project to investors in the form of equity, thus also sharing the firm's control and future profits.

Lenders and borrowers agree on the terms of debt servicing such as the rate of interest and maturity at the time of debt issuance. Inability to service debt in the manner agreed upon typically results in bankruptcy. Debt most commonly takes the form of bank loans, which are lending instruments held by banks on their balance sheets. The large size and substantial leverage of infrastructure projects often require more debt than can be financed by one entity. In such situations, a syndicated loan or a club deal might be used to pool the lending capacity of multiple banks.

An alternative form of debt financing for infrastructure is through bonds, which may be issued by private or public firms (corporate bonds), a project (project bonds), or a government entity (e.g., sovereign bonds and municipal bonds). Bonds are traded; that is, they can be bought and sold after issuance—in retail markets or only among qualified institutional buyers—and are therefore a more liquid form of debt financing than bank loans.

Equity in a firm or a project represents a share of ownership, signifying control and a share of profits. For firms and projects, this may take the form of public equity, which is listed on an exchange, or private equity, which is held closely by some investors or financial institutions. State-owned entities may offer some of their shares to private investors but typically retain the controlling share.

A range of hybrid instruments that combine the characteristics of debt and equity have also been used as additional instruments for financing infrastructure. These instruments include subordinated debt, convertible debt, and mezzanine finance.

Cash Flow Waterfall

When revenue in excess of operating costs is generated by a public or private firm or a project-financed entity, the flow of that net revenue is clearly delineated, creating a pecking order that places debt above equity. After the firm's current obligations such as costs and taxes as well as debt servicing have been met, any remaining funds are distributed to its equity holders in the form of dividends. For public and private firms, these revenues and costs may arise from the full range of activities that the firm might be engaged in. Therefore, debt and equity investors gauge and monitor the prospects of their investments using financial flows for the entire firm. Lending to such firms is often collateralized or secured using other assets on its balance sheet.

However, the single-purpose nature of a project-financed deal limits revenues, costs, and obligations to the specific activity that it is engaged in. Revenue earned by a project-financed entity is traced through a cash flow waterfall that delineates the different costs that must be met before payments to debt providers can be made. Any remaining revenue is typically used to make dividend payments to equity holders.

In financial planning for project finance, the adequacy of cash flows to debt providers is commonly gauged through the debt service coverage ratio (DSCR), which is the ratio of cash expected to be available in a particular period for debt servicing and the debt service obligation for that period. Thus, a minimum DSCR of 1.2 (over all periods) means that at least US\$1.20 is expected to be available to cover every US\$1.00 of debt service obligations. Debt with a higher DSCR is considered safer and therefore rated higher by credit rating agencies. If the same cash flow supports more debt, the coverage ratios would be lower and the debt riskier. Similarly, the dividends that equity investors can expect to earn on their investment in a project or firm may be expressed as the internal rate of return (IRR). For a given stream of expected dividend flows, the IRR can be enhanced by issuing less equity and more debt.

The cash flow waterfall of a project-financed transaction is particularly specific about the rights and protections of debt providers. This specificity is necessary not only to provide comfort to debt providers whose investments are tied to a large undiversified infrastructure project but also one where the collateral value is low and not portable. The goal is to build an early warning system to provide debt holders enough time to make changes necessary to avert or at least prepare for any impending financial distress or failure of the project. Common project-financed debt covenants include prefunding for expected major maintenance during the life of the debt contract, a debt servicing reserve fund to set aside funds for the following few debt servicing payments, forward-looking DSCRs to ensure current and future adequacy of cash flows to fulfill debt servicing requirements, and well-defined procedures in case of termination or restructuring of the project.

Not suprisingly, these features have been found to make project-financed debt attractive to debt providers. Empirically, project-financed infrastructure debt has been found to be more highly leveraged and yet less prone to loss than comparable corporate debt. This holds in spite of the fact that project-financed debt is often raised before the project has even commenced major construction, is dependent on a more narrowly defined set of cash flows, and has much higher structuring cost and political exposure.

The nature of the cash flow waterfall makes equity not only a financing instrument but also a powerful mechanism for risk management. As residual claimants of the cash flow, equity holders possess strong incentives. Sourcing equity from investors that have the skills and experience to build, operate, and manage infrastructure projects creates a strong governance structure for the project.

Capital Structure

The capital structure represents the combination of financing instruments—primarily debt and equity—used to finance a firm or project. The ratio of debt to equity is called the *financial leverage ratio*. In project-financed transactions, capital structure decisions cannot be made independently of cash flows: the ability to implement a certain debt-equity financing mix has to be supported by a cash flow waterfall that will fulfill the debt-related obligations and equity-generated expectations that arise from the proposed capital structure. Furthermore, for the issuer, the capital structure represents not only a financing decision but also a risk management decision.

As a financing decision, the capital structure has significant cost implications. A longer discussion of risk and return appears later, but the relative seniority and certainty of debt payments compared with equity makes debt a cheaper financing source than equity. Hence, debt is often desired as a means to lower the overall cost of financing. However, it is important to note that the cost at which investors offer debt and equity financing changes as leverage changes in a manner that offsets some of the benefit of replacing more expensive equity with cheaper debt. This concept follows from the seminal work of Modigliani and Miller (1958). Public and private firms that own long-term infrastructure assets can use these assets as collateral to raise a significant proportion of their financing in the form of debt. Interestingly, even though project-financed entities do not own physical assets that they can collateralize, they can reach significantly higher leverage ratios as a result of their single-purpose nature, dedicated future cash flows, and strong debt covenants.

The capital structure decision also determines the degree of financing risk. The schedule of debt servicing payments is committed to when the debt is issued. Failure to fulfill these terms requires costly financial distress measures to be undertaken and can result in bankruptcy of the firm or project. In contrast, payments to equity holders are not committed to in advance and are made only if residual cash flow is available. Thus, in terms of repayment risk, equity is a less rigid form of financing than debt.

This balance between cost and risk is the main trade-off between debt and equity. In the case of project finance, this trade-off can also be represented as that between the IRR and the DSCR. Higher leverage results in a higher IRR (and thus returns) for equity holders but a lower DSCR (and hence higher credit risk) for debt providers. Capital structure is a major determinant of the riskiness of the financing structure. Therefore, capital structure is also one of the first dimensions of risk management in infrastructure finance.

Risk Management

The concept of risk is central to all of finance. It is widely understood that economic agents, investors, and firms are risk averse and that they take on risk only if they are induced to do so by being offered a commensurate reward, which is called the risk premium. Different agents may differ in their ability to tolerate or manage risks and thereby be willing to accept risks for a different risk premium. Furthermore, not all risks are the result of the vicissitudes of nature. Risks can also arise because of the actions of specific entities or the outcomes of specific types of contingent financial structures that are devised to accentuate or attenuate the impact of risks on different parties.

Every infrastructure asset represents a bundle of many different types of risk. For successful infrastructure project development and execution, devising a project structure that aligns the incentives of the different parties involved in the infrastructure project in a manner that is congruent with the success of the project is imperative. And the mechanism that shapes incentives is proper risk allocation.

Risk Allocation

A major argument in favor of using a project finance structure for financing infrastructure is that this isolates individual projects from the diversified set of assets that inhabit the balance sheets of public and private infrastructure firms. This isolation makes the risks that impinge upon the project more palpable so they can be allocated in a manner that enhances the likelihood of success of the project. Beidleman, Fletcher, and Vesbosky (1990) describe risk allocation as the essence of project finance.

Optimal risk allocation requires that risks be borne by the party that can manage those risks most effectively and at the least cost. It also means that such parties have the ability and willingness to take on those risks. The willingness to take on risk must be generated by offering commensurate return, in the form of rewards and penalties, coupled with allowing sufficient control so that the party on which the risk is incident can act to enhance the likelihood of salutary impacts and reduce that of adverse impacts. Miller and Lessard (2001) argue that risk allocation can mitigate specific and controllable risk. If aligned correctly, the actions that the risk bearer will take for its own benefit also benefit the infrastructure project as a whole.

The first step in putting together a risk allocation plan is to enumerate all the different risks that might be incident on the project over its entire life. Thereafter, each risk needs to be examined in terms of its likelihood, potential impact, cost of transfer, and the extent of control that each of the different parties can exercise on it. While the risks that can affect an infrastructure project are numerous and varied and can change over different stages of a single project, the major ones can be classified into seven categories.

1. *Development and construction.* Development and construction risks range from the suitability of design of the project and availability of required government permits to raising adequate and timely financing for construction. Other related risks involve technology, the likelihood of cost overruns and delays, and the successful transfer of the project from the contractor to the operator. Such risks are particularly suitable for transfer to the parties that control them (which may further parcel them out to the construction company through strong completion guarantees and turnkey contracts).

2. *Operation and maintenance.* The assessment of risks over the second major phase in the life of an infrastructure project—operation and maintenance—is fundamental because these risks affect its long-term viability. Such risks primarily encompass the technological and economic aspects of the project: the failure to achieve adequate performance, the risk of technological obsolescence, the risk of inadequate demand, the possible entrance of new competitors, and the cost and availability of material and labor. In the case of many infrastructure projects, the bundling of construction with operations and maintenance, and payment that is linked to the achievement of specific performance criteria constitute a crucial risk allocation measure.

3. *Demand.* One of the primary risks that an infrastructure project faces is related to demand: will it generate sufficient usage? This risk is most apparent when the revenue generated from the project is centered on usage-based charges and is the primary form of compensation for the private party. Demand risk borne by the lenders can be one of the most significant sources of credit risk. Demand risk often tends to be tied closely to broad macro-economic conditions and growth.

4. *Financing structure.* Risks can also arise from the financial structure adopted for the project. A highly leveraged capital structure for a project may make it more likely to default in case of insufficiency of cash flows to meet debt obligations. The exposure of cash flows themselves to the risks of exchange rate volatility and convertibility, inflation uncertainty, and interest rate fluctuations need to be managed. Such variables are generally outside the control of the main stakeholders and are best addressed via financial instruments. In many countries, financial risks can be hedged through standard derivative instruments such as swaps, futures, and options. Those risks that cannot be hedged are often passed through to users (such as inflation), private parties (exchange rate volatility), or the government (convertibility).

5. *Legal and political.* In assessing legal and political risks, a clear understanding of the political context of infrastructure is fundamental. These risks can include political instability; issues of sovereignty, corruption, and regulatory changes such as the introduction of tariffs and quotas; deregulation; and expropriation. Given the long life of infrastructure projects, they also include the risk of continued support for the underlying contracts across successive government regimes.

6. *Environmental.* Environmental risks include exposure to climate change that might result in stranded assets or unexpected costs and to environmental impact such as pollution and reduced biodiversity.

7. *Force majeure*. Finally, force majeure risks generated by events such as floods, fire, and wars must be taken into account. None of the partners can exercise much control over these risks, and partners are usually insured by purchasing insurance from third-party agencies.

In project finance, the risk allocation scheme is often summarized in the form of a risk matrix that shows the main risk categories along one dimension of the matrix and the main stakeholders across whom the risk would be allocated along the other dimension. The Global Infrastructure Hub (2016) provides a set of annotated risk allocation matrices for PPP transactions in a variety of sectors. While the main principles of risk allocation need to be kept in mind, infrastructure programs in different settings and across different sectors may adopt a risk allocation structure that is based on the needs of the project and the capacity of private parties as well as the political and institutional context.

Role of Government in Risk Sharing

The use of subsidies and transfers is well known in economics as a mechanism to allow private agents to provide infrastructure that is financially feasible for them while also ensuring affordability for end users. In infrastructure finance, governments have offered viability gap funding to ensure financial feasibility for private investors, even as they have instituted revenue or profit sharing to absorb excess profits. Owing to the risk-return trade-off, governments can also lower the cost of infrastructure provision if they are willing to take on a larger share of the risks that are embedded in infrastructure investments.

Infrastructure projects with revenue based on availability payments protect the concessionaire from demand risk. Intermediate arrangements such as long-term procurement and off-take contracts that stabilize the volume of the output or minimum revenue guarantees that can provide a lower bound to the revenues generated from an infrastructure project have been used to share demand risk between public and private partners. Another innovative risk-sharing mechanism has been the creation of flexible maturity contracts: if usage volumes are low, the maturity of the contract is automatically lengthened; if volumes are higher than expected, the maturity is shortened.

Valuation

The large and lumpy investment cost of infrastructure can only be reasonably justified by the expectation that it will generate significant value in the future. For most infrastructure assets, this value tends to be generated over a long period and across a widely dispersed set of direct users and indirect beneficiaries in the form of externalities. Whether the aggregate value generated is sufficient to justify the large up-front financial costs is the broad question that valuation exercises seek to address. The techniques of valuation are used for many different purposes related to infrastructure finance such as estimation of financing costs, regulation, subsidization, project selection, and even arbitration and dispute resolution.

The most common method used for infrastructure valuation is the discounted cash flow approach, which estimates the value of an asset as the sum of the present values of the expected cash flows (revenues and costs) over the life of the asset, discounted at a rate that represents the cost of capital required to finance the asset under existing market conditions. The value of the asset is the capitalized worth of these cash flows. This worth is measured by the opportunity cost of financing the asset in the prevailing market.

The value of the asset as a whole is determined by the cash flows that accrue to all of the owners of the asset. The part of the total value of the asset that belongs to a particular set of investors may be estimated as the present value of the expected cash flows that would accrue to those investors based on their seniority in the cash flow waterfall. For example, the value of debt in the firm may be estimated as the present value of the stream of interest and principal payments that the firm's projected cash flows are expected to generate. Similarly, the value of equity may be estimated as the present value of the dividend stream that the firm would generate after current debt obligations have been fulfilled and any debt covenants satisfied.

Discount Rate and the Cost of Capital

The discounting of cash flows seeks to reflect the opportunity cost of money by incorporating the two defining features of finance: time and uncertainty. While the discounting of cash flows is important for numerous applications in economics and finance, its significance for infrastructure finance is fundamental and substantial. Consider the long gap between the date when infrastructure capital investments are made and when some of its benefits are recouped. The present value of these further-out benefits is significantly attenuated, thereby requiring a larger quantum of later benefits to offset costs incurred early in the life of the infrastructure asset. At a 20 percent discount rate, a dollar of benefits next year would offset 83 cents of today's investment costs. If received 3 years later it would offset 58 cents of up-front costs, but if received 13 years later it would offset less than 10 cents.

Many infrastructure assets have long useful lives running into many decades. This longevity is helpful, as it allows the capital costs to be dispersed over a long period of time and across many users. But the benefit per user declines dramatically over time. Taking the 20 percent discount rate mentioned in the example above, the same benefit generated by 1 user in year 3 requires more than 6 such users by year 13 and 38 users by year 23. Furthermore, the long life of infrastructure causes small differences in the discount rate to have a big impact, making the determination of the correct discount rate most critical and often contentious. For example, at a 20 percent discount rate, a dollar of benefits received 13 years later would offset only 10 cents of up-front costs; at 25 percent, it would offset only about half as much.

Using the present value concept for valuing cash flows also requires that the cash flows and the discount rate be comparable to each other. If the cash flows are denominated in nominal local currency, the discount rate should also reflect the local currency cost of capital in nominal terms. Given the inflation indexation of many financial parameters related to infrastructure (regulated tariffs, debt servicing costs, etc.) in many cases, infrastructure cash flows are projected in real (rather than nominal) terms and therefore have to be discounted using a real discount rate.

However, the most important factor that underlies the determination of the discount rate is the level of risk involved in the infrastructure investment. The choice of discount rate used to calculate the present value of a stream of cash flows depends on the cost of capital that matches the nature and riskiness of cash flows that are being discounted.

Principal and interest payments constitute the cash flows due to debt holders, and the worth of these cash flows represents the present value of debt in the firm or project. The cost of debt represents that interest cost at which lenders are willing to lend to the firm. To reflect the fact that the interest portion of debt servicing costs is considered a business expense and hence not subject to corporate taxes (in most tax jurisdictions), it is the after-tax cost of debt that reflects the cost of debt capital to the borrower. In practice, the cost of debt may be estimated from the market price of debt for the asset being valued or that of firms with similar credit ratings, usually in the same industry and country.

The cost of equity represents the rate of return that equity providers expect to earn from their investment. Unlike debt investments, which provide a promised rate of return (unless there is a default), equity holders' return is based on the residual cash flow that is left over after all other obligations have been met. The cost of equity is calculated based on its estimated risk.

One of the most widely used models to estimate the cost of equity capital is the capital asset pricing model, which states that the expected return on equity in excess of the risk-free rate is given by the sensitivity of the equity returns to excess market returns (measured by a parameter referred to as the beta of the equity) multiplied by the market risk premium. The market risk premium represents the consensus expected return on the aggregate market (usually measured using some broad-based proxy such as the MSCI index for a specific country or region or the world) in excess of that of the risk-free asset.

Mathematically, the capital asset pricing model may be written as

$$R_E = R_f + \beta_E \times MRP,$$

in which R_f is the risk-free rate, that is, the rate of return of an asset theoretically associated with no risk; β_E represents the systematic risk of equity and is calculated as the sensitivity of the equity returns to excess market returns; and MRP is the market risk premium, the difference between the expected return of the market portfolio and the rate of return of the risk-free asset, R_f.

The value of the systematic risk of equity is related to three parameters: (1) β_{Asset}, the systematic risk of the asset in which the equity is held, calculated as the sensitivity of the asset returns to excess market returns (the beta reflects the riskiness of a particular firm that is estimated empirically from similar firms that might be based on the same industry sector or offer close substitutes, are subject to similar regulatory treatment, and share similar future prospects); (2) B/E, the ratio of debt to equity, or the leverage ratio; and (3) T_C, the corporate tax rate.

Together, these parameters determine the systematic risk of equity as follows:

$$\beta_E = \beta_{Asset} \times \left(1 + (1 - T_C) \times \frac{B}{E} \right).$$

If debt in the firm or project has significant market risk, this should also be reflected in the leverage adjustment of the equity beta.

This leverage adjustment of beta reflects the fact that the equity holders view their position in a firm that has issued debt as riskier than that in a firm with no debt. The issuance of debt relegates equity holders to a junior position relative to debt providers, who now have first claim on the cash flow generated by the firm. Equity holders are only the residual claimants of the cash flow. Leverage adjustment is particularly important for infrastructure valuation, as the impact of leverage on beta is substantial. For example, consider a sector that is estimated to have an asset beta of 0.6 based on its industry. This value of beta means that if there were no debt, the level of systematic risk faced by equity holders would be equivalent to a beta of 0.6. However, levered 70:30 (debt/equity), an equity investment would be subject to systematic risk equivalent to a beta value of 1.5 assuming a corporate tax rate of 35 percent.

The discounting of cash flows for public firms or projects financed by government debt represents a particular challenge. The choices vary among a risk-free rate, the government borrowing rate, the social discount rate, and a risk-adjusted discount rate that reflects the riskiness to the government (Park 2012). The choice of the discount rate used in government-funded projects is discussed in more detail in chapter 6 of this volume.

Valuation Methods

The discounted cash flow approach can be implemented using various valuation methods that are distinguished from each other by their focus on the different types of investors, or groups of investors, and the cash flows that they are entitled to. Different valuation methods make different assumptions that work better in certain cases than in others. If more than one valuation method is expected to be suitable for a particular valuation case, the valuation methods can serve as an additional check on the validity of the valuation exercise.

The starting point of cash flow analysis is the excess of revenue earned by the infrastructure asset over its operating and capital expenses, tax payments, and any other changes in working capital. The result is known as the free cash flow of the asset. Free cash flow represents cash that is available for distribution to all the investors in the firm, the two broad classes of such investors being debt investors (or lenders to the firm) and equity investors (or owners of the firm). However, the seniority of payments to these two classes of investors is not the same. Debt payments in the form of principal and interest payments are paid first. Payments to equity in the form of dividends (or retained earnings) are made only if any funds remain after the debt obligations of that period have been fulfilled.

Since the free cash flow belongs jointly to all the investors in the firm—debt and equity providers—the present value of free cash flow represents the value of the firm as a whole. Furthermore, free cash flow must be discounted at a cost of capital that represents the blended cost of raising capital in the form of debt and equity, referred to as the weighted average cost of capital.

The weighted average cost of capital is estimated using the following formula:

$$R_{WACC} = \text{cost of debt} \times \text{fraction of firm financed by debt}$$
$$+ \ cost\ of\ equity \times fraction\ of\ firm\ financed\ by\ equity, \text{ or}$$

$$R_{WACC} = R_B \times (1 - T_C) \times \frac{B}{V} + R_E \times \frac{E}{V},$$

in which $V \equiv B + E$, is the value of the firm as a whole, B is the market value of debt, E is the market value of equity, R_B is the cost of debt and R_E the cost of equity, and T_C represents the corporate tax rate.

The free cash flow approach is widely used for determining the market value of long-lived firms when the leverage ratio is largely fixed. One of the most significant implications of these assumptions is that a constant weighted average cost of capital is used to discount cash flows across the entire time horizon over which valuation is to be performed. However, many infrastructure projects are owned and valued over a finite period (since they are backed by a concession contract with finite maturity) whose leverage changes continuously, typically reaching zero leverage before the end of the concession contract.

The adjusted present value method (Myers 1974) is an alternative and distinct valuation method in which the value of a firm can be arrived at by augmenting (or adjusting) the present value of a hypothetical unlevered firm (i.e., a firm financed only by equity, with no debt) with the additional net value created by including debt in the capital structure. Thus, the adjusted present value method conducts valuation in two steps:

$$V_{unlevered} + NPV_{Debt},$$

where $V_{Unlevered}$ represents the value of the unlevered firm, and NPV_{Debt} represents the net benefit of including debt in the capital structure of the firm.

Since an unlevered firm is assumed to have no debt obligations, all of the free cash flow of such a firm would go directly to its equity holders. The value of the unlevered firm is therefore the net present value of these cash flows at a discount rate equal to the cost of equity of an unlevered firm. The appropriate discount rate to be used to arrive at the value of the unlevered firm is the cost of unlevered equity. This cost of equity can be estimated using the capital asset pricing model but assuming leverage to be zero.

The net benefit of including debt in the capital structure of the firm arises from two main sources: the present value of tax shield, which measures the saving of corporate taxes due to the tax deductibility of interest payments, and the expected cost of financial distress, which represents the ex ante direct expected cost of bankruptcy as well as the indirect cost incurred to deal with the possibility of bankruptcy.

A third valuation method, called the free cash flow to equity method, is used to determine the market value of equity. In this method, the first step is the estimation of the net cash flows that represent the claim of the equity providers only. The market value of equity may then be calculated by discounting these equity cash flows at the cost of equity. The market value of the entire firm or project can be estimated by adding the market value of debt to the market value of equity.

To implement the free cash flow to equity approach, the free cash flow may be decomposed into the cash flow to debt providers and the (residual) cash flow to equity providers. The cash flow to debt providers consists of payments that represent the principal payment, which reduces the volume of total debt outstanding and the interest payment payable on the current amount of debt outstanding. However, owing to the provision that interest payments on debt are deductible, the cash flow value of the tax shield benefit may be added as additional flow to equity providers. Hence, the following relation holds:

net debt cash flow = principal payment + interest payment – debt tax shield.

Different valuation methods might be theoretically equivalent, but they rarely produce identical values in practice because of the different assumptions they make both explicitly and implicitly.

Innovations in Infrastructure Financing

As mentioned earlier, the infrastructure gap is often thought of as a result of the lack of adequate funding. This situation is particularly ironic, since recent years have seen some of the largest accumulation of private savings and some of the lowest interest rates in over half a century (Del Negro et al. 2019). Driven by an aging demographic profile in most parts of the developed world, the largest pool of such private savings exists in the form of pension funds and insurance funds under the management of institutional investors (Lipshitz and Walter 2019).

In recent years, many innovations in infrastructure finance seek to tap into a large and growing pool of private funds. Many are driven by greater cognizance of the preferences and constraints of institutional investors. Two major innovations in debt and equity financing for infrastructure are discussed below.

Innovation in Debt Finance: Credit Enhancement

The ideal type of infrastructure debt finance needs to have long maturity, be relatively illiquid, and have a fixed cost of funding that might be indexed to inflation (since many infrastructure investments generate revenue that is linked to inflation). Infrastructure debt also needs to be able to tolerate some degree of commercial, operational, and political risk.

The bulk of project-financed infrastructure debt outstanding today originated on the balance sheets of banks. Traditionally, banks have been instrumental in putting together the kind of complex financial structure that infrastructure finance requires. Yet, the ability of banks to take on infrastructure debt in the large amount that is required is limited and even shrinking. It is not difficult to see that deposit-based bank finance provides few of the features that infrastructure debt requires. Bank loans have relatively short maturity and are backed by highly liquid short-term deposits with little risk-taking capacity. Banks' funding cost is variable and is linked to the nominal and volatile short-term interest rate. Furthermore, since the global financial crisis in 2008, bank capital requirements have grown significantly, and additional bank capital requirements have been put in place for the types of long-term and illiquid debt that are typical of infrastructure investments (Ma 2016).

In contrast, pension funds consist of a large and illiquid funding base that seeks investments with long maturity and a predictable long-term rate of return. Since many pension fund liabilities are indexed to inflation, pension fund investors are favorably inclined toward investments that can fetch inflation-indexed returns. All of these characteristics make infrastructure debt investment a better match for pension fund investors than deposit-funded banks. However, there are some significant mismatches as well.

The most significant mismatch arises from the moderate to low appetite for risk that pension funds might have relative to the higher commercial and political risk that might be embedded in infrastructure investments. Many institutional investors are required to hold investment grade (rated BBB or higher) project bonds, and many prefer a higher minimum credit rating of A. On the other hand, the majority of infrastructure debt issues are rated BBB or lower (Aberasturi 2018).

As a result, one of the innovations in debt finance for infrastructure is the need for credit enhancement—the idea that the debt issued by infrastructure investments or projects be made safe enough to be a suitable investment for pension funds. Such credit enhancements have taken various forms, which might include direct credit enhancement through the provision of subordinated debt, credit guarantees, partial or full insurance, and the securitization of infrastructure debt.

An early type of credit enhancement took the form of insurance provided by monoline insurance companies that provided unconditional and irrevocable guarantees of timely payment of principal and interest to project debt holders. The monolines maintained a sufficient capital base against those guarantees to achieve their high—usually AAA—credit ratings. The debt issuer would benefit from the high credit rating of the insurance provider rather than its own, thereby obtaining funds at lower cost. This saving would be paid for in the form of a fee to the monolines for issuing the guarantee. This business model was heavily dependent on the monolines' ability to maintain a high credit rating.

Guarantees provided by the monolines—referred to as *wrapping the bond*—enhanced the credit quality of typically subinvestment grade (rated lower than BBB on the S&P 500 Index rating scale) project bonds, making them attractive to private investors with limited risk tolerance. Monoline insurance companies emerged in the 1970s to insure bonds issued by U.S. state and local issuers and later expanded their operations globally. Over time, they also extended guarantees to financial derivative products such as collateralized debt obligations and starting writing credit default swaps. However, during the 2008 financial crisis, defaults on subprime housing loans and other risky debt that were components of such derivatives forced monoline companies to bear staggering losses on these instruments. As a result, monoline companies lost the high credit ratings that were essential to their business model. When the monolines disappeared, project debt came to be regarded as too risky by institutional investors who withdrew from the infrastructure debt market (EPEC 2010).

Fully insuring infrastructure debt is not only expensive but also dulls the incentive of debt investors to monitor the financial viability of infrastructure investments. A cheaper and more incentive-compatible alternative is partial credit enhancement, which seeks to lower the credit risk of infrastructure debt only to the extent necessary to meet the investors' tolerance for risk. For example, partial credit enhancement might only seek to raise the credit rating from subinvestment grade to a BB or single A rating rather than AAA. A credit enhancement mechanism must not provide an artificial lifeline to projects that are not financially viable.

Partial credit enhancement can take a variety of forms, such as mechanisms to provide temporary liquidity support or limiting the loss suffered in the event of default. A notable example of credit enhancement was the PBCE program, launched in 2012. A precursor to the PBCE was the EIB's Loan Guarantee Instrument for Trans-European Transport Network Projects of 2008, which was designed as a guarantee to commercial banks providing standby liquidity facilities that could be drawn down by project sponsors during the first five to seven years of operation if the revenue generated by the project through tolls or other user charges was insufficient to ensure repayment of senior project debt. If the Loan Guarantee Instrument for Trans-European Networks for Transport Projects was called upon, the EIB would pay out the commercial banks and become a subordinated lender to the project.

Under the PBCE scheme, the EIB would provide a subordinated instrument—either a loan or a contingent debt facility—to enhance the credit quality of the senior infrastructure project bonds. The tranche, or debt facility, could help the project absorb several years of revenue shortfalls without impeding the repayment capacity to senior debt, thereby enhancing its credit quality and attractiveness to certain investors. The PBCE targeted an upgrade of project debt credit rating to the A to AA range rather than the AAA level. The subordinated tranche would be repaid only after senior debt. Thus, the PBCE sought to widen access to funding sources and to lower funding costs.

The mechanism for improving the credit standing of projects relied on the separation of project debt into senior and subordinated tranches. The EIB would provide a subordinated tranche to enhance the credit quality of the senior bonds and therefore increase their credit rating. This could be implemented in two different ways: In a funded PBCE, a loan would be given to the project company from the outset. In an unfunded PBCE, a contingent credit line would be available to be drawn if the cash flow generated by the project was insufficient to ensure senior bond debt service or to cover construction costs overruns.

The funded PBCE was similar to typical infrastructure mezzanine finance. The funded PBCE would rank below the senior bonds but ahead of the remaining risk capital of the project. If the project's cash flow fell short in the operations phase, the mezzanine lenders would not be paid until the senior lenders had been paid. This role of subordinated debt would improve the credit quality of the senior debt. The funded PBCE was expected to reduce the probability of default on senior debt during the operating phase of the project.

The unfunded PBCE would be provided in the form of an irrevocable and revolving letter of credit that could be drawn on occurrence of a permitted event that included cash shortfall during construction, debt service shortfall after completion of construction, or any shortfall in amounts payable due on acceleration of the senior debt. For the unfunded PBCE, the EIB would act as a direct standby lender to the project company rather than a guarantor to a third party who would then provide the liquidity. The unfunded PBCE would be available until scheduled final repayment of the senior bonds. As a revolving facility, any amounts drawn and subsequently repaid on the letter of credit would be available for redrawing. The unfunded PBCE would act as a first loss piece; just like a funded PBCE, it would mitigate loss given default of the senior bond. The unfunded PBCE also represented an additional source of financing to fund project costs, even as it would also reduce the probability of default during the construction phase. Once the unfunded PBCE was drawn, the EIB would become a direct subordinated lender to the project.

By July 2015, a total of seven transactions across Belgium, France, Germany, Spain, and the United Kingdom had been supported by the PBCE mechanism. An aggregate credit enhancement amount of €612 million (backed by €230 million from the European Union budget) mobilized €3.7 billion in bonds (European Commission 2016).

Innovation in Equity Finance: Infrastructure Funds

Most infrastructure projects require equity investment. Typically, such investments were provided by industrial sponsors—entities that played a significant role in the provision of equipment, construction, and operation of the project—either directly on their balance sheet or as one of the sponsors of the consortium in a project-financed structure. The result was a governance structure in which the three different responsibilities—provision of engineering and technical expertise, source of equity funding, and management of the infrastructure asset—were bundled together and collectively provided by the industrial sponsors. However, the advent of long-term contracts for the construction and operation of infrastructure assets, as is typical in PPPs, has created the need for a large amount of long-term sponsor equity far exceeding the financial capacity of industrial sponsors.

Infrastructure funds marked the emergence of outside (i.e., nonindustrial) equity investors in infrastructure investments to the point where so-called financial sponsors assumed a central role in consortia that structured, built, owned, operated, and managed infrastructure projects.

Infrastructure funds were initially organized in a manner that was similar to private equity funds with a definite life span, though the rapidly growing asset class has evolved some unique characteristics. A private equity fund would be set up as a limited partnership and managed by a general partner that would raise capital from a number of limited partners, primarily consisting of institutional investors, such as pension funds and insurance companies. The general partner would also serve as fund manager and receive a share of profits from the investments. Management fees payable to the general partner would typically be based on the amount of capital invested, while a share of the investment profits was paid as a performance incentive after a minimum performance threshold had been met. The fund manager enjoyed significant discretion to make investments and control decisions related to the fund subject to some broad guidelines.

The first private equity fund dedicated purely to infrastructure was set up in 1994. The US$1.08 billion AIG Asian Infrastructure Fund was established by Emerging Markets Partnership, a global private equity fund set up by two former World Bank officials, Moeen Qureshi and Donald Roth, along with AIG, the international insurance company. The fund made 24 investments in a variety of sectors, including fixed line and mobile telecommunications, toll roads, container terminals, and electric power and water in China, India, Korea, the Philippines, Taiwan, and Thailand (Blustein 1995). The same year, another private equity firm, Hastings Funds Management Limited, set up in Australia as a specialist manager of infrastructure assets. But it was a couple of years later when a small private trading bank that had listed its shares on the Australian Stock Exchange only in 1996 revolutionized infrastructure investing with a series of bold innovations.

In the mid-1990s, a new law required all Australians to put a part of their salaries in savings for retirement. Around the same time, cash-strapped Australian states were looking to sell some of their public infrastructure assets to private companies in the form of outright privatization or PPPs. Macquarie Bank saw the opportunity to bring pension savings to such infrastructure assets. The argument was that the steady stream of revenues from a stable infrastructure asset such as a toll road provided an ideal investment to pension fund investors over the long term. Often the revenues from such investments would also grow with inflation.

The bank's first infrastructure fund, which became known as the Macquarie Infrastructure Group Fund, was launched in 1996 as a wholly owned subsidiary of the bank, with an initial offering of AUS$300 million. At launch, the official name was Infrastructure Trust of Australia Group. The name Macquarie Infrastructure Group was adopted in 1999 and changed in May 2010 to Intoll Group. The fund was launched with four seed assets, all of which were segments of tolled roads structured as PPP projects. Like traditional private equity funds, infrastructure funds attempted to add value to assets that they acquired through active management at the asset level.

Infrastructure funds sought to unlock value not only from improvements in the physical engineering but also from financial engineering. Existing project debt would often be replaced with new debt that had a longer maturity profile, was indexed to inflation, and could even be cheaper. In some cases, this replacement was possible simply because the existing debt had been arranged before construction: with construction over, the lower risk of the project allowed the opportunity for cheaper and longer-term debt that matched the revenue profile of the project more closely. Furthermore, the refinancing could be structured to produce earlier cash flows for equity investors than was envisaged in the original financing plan.

Perhaps the most significant innovation that Macquarie introduced was the listing of infrastructure funds. Legally, the Macquarie Infrastructure Group was organized in the form of a trust and therefore under Australian law was eligible to be listed on the Australian Stock Exchange. The structure was similar to real estate investment trusts, a common model for real estate investments in Australia and the United States. Exchange-listed funds provided liquidity to investors, allowing them to exit the investment by selling their shares in the stock market. Thus, the listing of funds expanded the pool of infrastructure investors from large institutional investors to retail investors, bringing liquidity to an investment class that had traditionally been considered highly illiquid.

Exchange-listed infrastructure funds also differed from unlisted private equity funds in the investment life span. Longer-maturity funds not only were a natural fit for infrastructure assets but, according to one survey (Probitas Partners 2007), also were preferred by experienced investors. Since exchange-listed funds did not have a limited life span, they could continuously buy and sell assets and also choose to hold on to them almost indefinitely.

Another innovation was the deployment of leverage at the fund level, which allowed further gearing to enhance equity returns. Traditional private equity funds would raise debt only at the asset level even if there was substantial leveraging, as in the case of leveraged buyouts.

The management of the fund was contracted out to an external manager, though typically this was a fully owned subsidiary of the sponsoring bank or financial institution. The fund would also engage the manager's institution for additional investment banking work such as providing or underwriting debt, arranging equity financing, and providing advisory services.

Thus, the new model for infrastructure funds gave rise to a project governance structure in which the three different responsibilities—provision of technical expertise, source of funding, and management of the infrastructure asset—were segregated across three different parties. The crucial difference from the private equity model was that infrastructure fund managers (i.e., the sponsoring financial institution) would manage but not own the infrastructure assets.

Macquarie's lead found many followers, even as Macquarie itself replicated its model both in Australia and around the world. By mid-2007, the bank controlled 35 funds managing more than US$220 billion worth of assets, including Macquarie Airports, Macquarie Media Group, Macquarie Capital Alliance Group, and Macquarie Communications Infrastructure Group, with listings in Singapore, Korea, Toronto, London, and New York along with several unlisted funds focused on assets in Europe and North America.

While listed and unlisted equity funds provided investors with an indirect means of investing in infrastructure projects, some large institutional investors had also started taking direct stakes in infrastructure projects. The trend was particularly notable in some pension funds in Australia and Canada. The Ontario Municipal Employees Retirement System has made direct investments in infrastructure assets since 1998 through an investment arm called Borealis Infrastructure. Similarly, the Ontario Teachers' Pension Plan invested up to 9 percent of its funds directly in infrastructure assets. Even the largest public pension fund in the United States, CalPERS, revised its investment policy in 2008 to invest up to 3 percent of its assets in infrastructure assets.

The success of the Macquarie model was evident from the number of imitators it had spawned and the volume of financing that infrastructure funds had raised. Even as forecasts grew exponentially about the need for infrastructure investments in developed and developing countries, commitments to private infrastructure funds kept growing. The rapid growth of infrastructure funds has not been without controversy. Concerns have been raised about aggressive leveraging, optimistic valuation, high distributions, excessive fees, and convoluted governance structures (Lawrence and Stapledon 2008).

By 2019, Macquarie Infrastructure and Real Assets had raised more than US$60 billion, leading other major infrastructure funds such as Global Infrastructure Partners (US$57 billion) and Brookfield Asset Management (US$39 billion). Together, the top 50 infrastructure fund firms had raised close to half a trillion dollars (Infrastructure Investor 2020).

Conclusions

Mobilizing financing is one of the most significant and substantial challenges of infrastructure development. The large quantum and long duration of that investment may be the most visible dimensions of that problem but are not the only ones.

This chapter has argued that infrastructure finance has many other facets: the multitude of sources and instruments; the different types of underlying public, corporate, and legal structures; the manner in which the many inherent risks are allocated; and the different approaches to measuring the value of infrastructure. All of these require careful design and planning to maximize not only the financial viability of the investment but also the real efficiency of infrastructure.

This chapter has also shown that structures can be conceived that blur the line between markets and financial institutions, private and public entities, and equity and debt in an attempt to devise the most effective instrument of not only financing infrastructure but also managing its risk and governance.

Summary

- Infrastructure finance is challenging because the costs of the assets are typically front-loaded, while the benefits are spread thinly over their long economic life.
- This difference in timing is bridged by the owner of the future benefit stream borrowing against it by issuing some combination of debt and equity.
- Financing differs from funding in that the funder is the entity that ultimately bears the cost of the infrastructure, which is either the general public (in taxes) or the direct users of infrastructure (in user charges).

- Proper structuring and risk allocation can make infrastructure financing more efficient and less risky.

- Infrastructure finance can be enhanced by financial innovations, as illustrated by the success of infrastructure investment funds in tapping the huge and growing savings, insurance, and pension funds for infrastructure finance.

References

Aberasturi, Kyle, Evan M. Gunter, Sundaram Iyer, and Nick W. Kraemer. 2018. *Default, Transition, and Recovery: Inaugural Infrastructure Default Study and Rating Transitions.* New York: Standard & Poor.

Baum, Anja, Tewodaj Mogues, and Geneviève Verdier. 2020. "Getting the Most from Public Investment." In *Well Spent: How Strong Infrastructure Governance Can End Waste in Public Investment*, ed. Gerd Schwartz, Manal Fouad, Torben Hansen, and Geneviève Verdier, 30–49. Washington, DC: International Monetary Fund.

Beidleman, Carl R., Donald Fletcher, and David Vesbosky. 1990. "On Allocating Risk: The Essence of Project Finance." *MIT Sloan Management Review* 31(3): 47–55.

Bhatia, Harman, Apala Bhattacharya, Schuyler House, Teshura Nair, Deblina Saha, Sovannaroth Tey, and Iuliia Zemlytska. 2020. "Who Sponsors Infrastructure Projects: Disentangling Public and Private Contributions." Washington, DC: World Bank. https://ppi .worldbank.org/content/dam/PPI/documents/SPIReport_2017_small_interactive.pdf.

Bhattacharya, Amar, Joshua P. Meltzer, Jeremy Oppenheim, Zia Qureshi, and Nicholas Stern. 2016. *Delivering on Sustainable Infrastructure for Better Development and Better Climate.* Washington, DC: Brookings Institution.

Blustein, Paul. 1995. "Moeen Qureshi Follows Road to Riches." *Washington Post*, December 25.

Brealey, Richard A., Ian A. Cooper, and Michael A. Habib. 1996. "Using Project Finance to Fund Infrastructure Investments." *Journal of Applied Corporate Finance* 9(3): 25–39.

Chong, Sophia, and Emily Poole. 2013. "Financing Infrastructure: A Spectrum of Country Approaches." *Reserve Bank of Australia Bulletin* (September): 65–76.

Del Negro, Marco, Domenico Giannone, Marc P. Giannoni, and Andrea Tambalotti. 2019. "Global Trends in Interest Rates." *Journal of International Economics* 118: 248–262.

EPEC (European PPP Expertise Centre). 2010. "Capital Markets in PPP Financing: Where We Were and Where are We Going?" Luxembourg: EPEC (March). https://www.eib .org/attachments/epec/epec_capital_markets_en.pdf.

European Commission. 2016. "Ad-hoc Audit of the Pilot Phase of the Europe 2020." Brussels: European Commission (March).

Global Infrastructure Hub. 2016. *Allocating Risk in Public–Private Partnership Contracts.* Sydney, Australia: GI Hub. https://cdn.gihub.org/umbraco/media/2528/gihub-allocating-risks-in -ppp-contracts-2016-edition.pdf.

Heller, Peter. 2005. "Back to Basics—Fiscal Space: What It Is and How to Get It." *Finance and Development* 42(2). https://www.imf.org/external/pubs/ft/fandd/2005/06/basics .htm.

IMF (International Monetary Fund). 2018a. "Fiscal Monitor: Capitalizing on Good Times." Washington, DC.

———. 2018b. "Macroeconomic Developments and Prospects in Low-Income Developing Countries: 2018." Washington, DC.

Infrastructure Investor. 2002. "Infrastructure Investor 50: The Big Get Bigger." https://www.infrastructureinvestor.com/infrastructure-investor-50/.

Infrastructure and Projects Authority. 2018. "Analysis of the National Infrastructure and Construction Pipeline." U.K. Government, November 26, https://assets.publishing.service.gov.uk/government/uploads/system/uploads/attachment_data/file/759222/CCS207_CCS1118987248-001_National_Infrastructure_and_Construction_Pipeline_2018_Accessible.pdf.

Lawrence, Martin, and Geofrey P. Stapledon. 2008. "Infrastructure Funds: Creative Use of Corporate Structure and Law—But in Whose Interests?" University of Melbourne Legal Studies research paper No. 314 (February). http://dx.doi.org/10.2139/ssrn.1092689.

Lipshitz, Clive, and Ingo Walter. 2019. "Bridging Public Pension Funds and Infrastructure Investing." January 20. https://ssrn.com/abstract=3319497.

Ma, Tianze. 2016. "Basel III and the Future of Project Finance Funding." *Michigan Business & Entrepreneurial Law Review* 6(1): 109–126. https://repository.law.umich.edu/mbelr/vol6/iss1/5.

Miller, Roger, and Donald R. Lessard. 2001. "Understanding and Managing Risks in Large Engineering Projects." *International Journal of Project Management* 19(8): 437–443.

Modigliani, Franco, and Merton H. Miller. 1958. "The Cost of Capital, Corporation Finance and the Theory of Investment." *American Economic Review* 48(3): 261–297.

Myers, Stewart. 1974. "Interactions of Corporate Financing and Investment Decisions: Implications for Capital Budgeting." *Journal of Finance* 29(1): 1–25.

NCE (New Climate Economy). 2014. "Better Growth, Better Climate: The 2014 New Climate Economy Report." http://newclimateeconomy.report/2014/.

OECD (Organisation for Economic Co-operation and Development). 2017a. "Technical Note on Estimates of Infrastructure Investment Needs: Background Note to the Report Investing in Climate, Investing in Growth." Paris: OECD. https://www.oecd.org/env/cc/g20-climate/Technical-note-estimates-of-infrastructure-investment-needs.pdf.

———. 2017b. "Investing in Climate, Investing in Growth: A Synthesis." Paris: OECD. https://www.oecd.org/environment/cc/g20-climate/synthesis-investing-in-climate-investing-in-growth.pdf.

Park, Sangkyun. 2012. "Optimal Discount Rates for Government Projects." *ISRN Economics* 12: 1–13.

Probitas Partners. 2007. "Investing in Infrastructure Funds." https://probitaspartners.com/pdfs/infrastructure.pdf.

Woetzel, Jonathan, Nicklas Garemo, Jan Mischke, Martin Hjerpe, and Robert Palter. 2016. "Bridging Global Infrastructure Gaps." McKinsey Global Institute, June. https://www.mckinsey.com/~/media/McKinsey/Industries/Capital%20Projects%20and%20Infrastructure/Our%20Insights/Bridging%20global%20infrastructure%20gaps/Bridging-Global-Infrastructure-Gaps-Full-report-June-2016.pdf.

Yescombe, E. R. 2014. *Principles of Project Finance*, 2nd ed. Waltham, MA: Academic Press.

10

INFRASTRUCTURE FINANCE THROUGH LAND VALUE CAPTURE

José A. Gómez-Ibáñez, Yu-Hung Hong,
and Du Huynh

One attractive possibility for financing public infrastructure improvements is to capture part or all of the uplift in land prices that usually accompanies them. This uplift occurs because of the improved accessibility or amenities to the private land served by the infrastructure improvements and not because of the effort of the private landowners themselves. Thus, the 19th-century political economists John Stuart Mill and Henry George advocated the return of the uplift to the public (George 1912 [1879]; Mill 1848). This practice, known as land value capture (LVC), is popular in part because it seems only fair to make the landowners who benefit from the infrastructure improvements pay at least part of their costs.

The practice of LVC is especially attractive in developing countries because they have greater capital needs and fewer sources of finance. Developing countries need capital not just to invest in industry but also to accommodate the urbanization and urban redevelopment that generally accompanies economic growth. The conversion of farmland to urban districts, for example, requires massive investments in roads, water and sewer lines, electricity distribution systems, and affordable housing within both the urban areas and the surrounding region.

While the capital needs of developing countries are enormous, their access to capital is typically very limited. Often they are eligible to receive grants or loans at concessional interest rates from international financial institutions such as the World Bank and the foreign aid programs of wealthy nations. But foreign aid always falls far short of perceived investment needs. Meanwhile, the domestic capital market is typically far too weak to make up the difference, in part because the people are too poor to save enough to finance the desired investments.

This capital shortfall encourages developing countries to be on the lookout for innovative financing techniques. The interest in public-private partnerships discussed in chapter 9 is a product of such searches. Many build-operate-transfer projects can be seen essentially as thinly disguised loans from the investors in the concessions to the government. Similarly, a value capture program can be seen as a means for the government to borrow from the landowners.

While value capture may seem an attractive means of financing needed capital investments, it is hard to implement. If privately owned land is taken, for example, determining the compensation, if any, to the former owners is bound to be controversial. Similarly, if publicly owned lands are sold, the question is often whether the value captured was worth the price.

This chapter examines two programs for capturing land value for financing public infrastructure: an established and financially successful but complex scheme used in Brazil and a simpler and struggling but promising program being developed by Vietnam. These experiences suggest that even the less elaborate schemes may require administrative and regulatory capacities that challenge those found in many developing countries.

Three Options for LVC

There are at least three basic approaches to LVC. Two of the approaches—real property taxation and land pooling/readjustment—are discussed only briefly here. Interested readers can refer to the publications listed in the references for additional information. The third approach—the sale of development rights—is illustrated in two case studies that are the heart of this chapter. We focus on the sale of development rights because it is the approach most often used in large-scale LVC schemes to support rapid urbanization in developing countries.

Taxation of Land and Property

Public officials can tax private land and buildings using, for example, an ad valorem property tax, land tax, capital gains tax, special assessment, infrastructure improvement (or betterment) levy, and tax increment financing. An ad valorem property tax (simply referred to as the property tax) is a biannual or annual levy imposed on owners or occupants of the land and buildings for holding or using the real assets. In the United States, for instance, the tax base of this levy is the assessed market value of the real estate, and the tax rate is determined by the annual fiscal needs of the municipality or county in charge of the tax collection (Netzer 1998). It is often called the *benefit tax* because the payment is perceived as the price that the property owners pay for enjoying a bundle of public goods provided by a local jurisdiction.

In some developing countries where the technique of property assessment for tax purposes is not well developed, the property tax base is simply the area of the premises. If the tax rate does not change, the area-based tax will not recoup any land value increments because its base does not reflect the increases in property value over time. This drawback notwithstanding, the land-based property tax is easier to implement than a value-based tax (Bahl and Martinez-Vazquez 2007; Walters 2013).

Many scholars, such as George (1912 [1879]), Bourassa (1987), Netzer (1998), and Dye and England (2009), advocated a split-rate property tax or land tax that taxes land more heavily than improvements to encourage high-density development. Oates and Schwab (2009) also argue that these taxes do not distort economic decisions or delay land development because the supply of land is fixed. Yet, the empirical evidence of their practicality and effectiveness in recouping public land value is mixed (Dye and England 2009).

The capital gains tax is a onetime payment levied at the instance of a property transaction. The tax enables the government to share with the owner the financial benefit from capital appreciation.

Other tax-based LVC instruments include special assessments (Misczynski 2012) and tax increment financing (Merriman 2012) in the United States, the infrastructure improvement levy in the United Kingdom (Booth 2012), and betterment levies in Colombia (Peterson 2008). In general, these charges are structured as a surtax (or an extra fee) on the taxable properties situated within a defined neighborhood where infrastructure upgrading is taking place. Additional tax collections are for funding a specific infrastructure project or improvement program from which the taxpayers benefit directly. The key advantage of these taxes over the property tax is their explicit linkage between payments and benefits, which can enhance the willingness of service receivers to pay for the public investment.

Land Readjustment or Pooling

Through land readjustment or pooling, a group of private landowners in a designated development area, in collaboration with a public agency, work together to assemble their lands for urban regeneration or rural-to-urban development. These undertakings that require rezoning and infrastructure upgrading will increase land values. Thus, landowners who are the major beneficiaries will be required to contribute to the endeavor by giving up a portion of their land to the project. Reducing the size of the land plot held by each owner makes space available for building infrastructure. This, in turn, minimizes the requirement for government expropriation of private land for the construction of public works. Surplus lands could also be sold to raise funds for covering the project costs. Although landowners will end up owning a smaller piece of land than before, the value of the land will be considerably higher than before because of infrastructure improvements. Otherwise, there would not be sufficient incentives for the landowners to participate in the process.

Land readjustment was instrumental in facilitating urbanization in developed countries such as Germany, Japan, South Korea, and Taiwan during the 1970s and 1980s (Doebele 1982; Hong and Needham 2007; Larsson 1997; Sorensen 1999). Some developing countries, such as Angola, Bhutan, Ethiopia, India, and Thailand, also experimented with this approach mostly on a small scale (Mittal 2014; UN-Habitat 2018). Although these trials have generated promising results, more evidence is needed to prove the effectiveness of this LVC approach for financing public infrastructure in the context of less industrialized economies.

Sale of Development Rights

In Brazil and some countries where private land ownership does not imply the possession of everything beneath and above the land, the government may take control over the development rights caused by up-zoning or land use modification. It can then sell these rights to developers to collect revenue to finance public infrastructure. The rationale behind this method is that existing landowners own only the land rights allowed by the law and do not own any new development potential made available because of regulatory changes.

This approach has been adopted in Brazil, where public functions of land are recognized by its constitution and social norms (Fernandes 2006). Two LVC instruments based on this reasoning are the Outorga Onerosa (Onerous Grant) of the Right to Build (Smolka 2013, 37–41) and the Certificate of Additional Construction Potential (CEPAC). Because CEPACs have gained much international attention, we focus on this approach here.

The situation is more complicated in countries where land is publicly owned, but the land users have the perception of owning most of the land rights. For example, in Vietnam, where all land belongs to the people but is managed on their behalf by the state, the development rights being sold are usually for the conversion of permitted land uses from rural to urban. The government uses the proceeds to fund public works or to incentivize the public-private partnerships in urban development and infrastructure. The Vietnamese call this approach "land for infrastructure" (Nguyen et al. 2018).

We have chosen to compare Brazil and Vietnam because they represent a broad range of circumstances and experiences. Brazil's per capita income is roughly three times that of Vietnam and has a longer, deeper, and unbroken exposure to markets and capitalism. It is no surprise that the Brazilian LVC programs are more elaborate and market-oriented. Moreover, Brazil is highly urbanized, with more than 85 percent of the population living in cities. In contrast, with an urbanization rate at 36.6 percent, Vietnam is quickly urbanizing, requiring more rural land conversion for urban development.

Brazil: CEPACs

Brazil is the largest and most populous country in South America and is also one of the world's strongest emerging economies. The 1988 Constitution of the Federative Republic of Brazil encouraged, among other things, the development of urban planning and management processes. This constitutional modernization also led to the legislation of the 2001 city statute that operationalized many land policy initiatives guided by the constitution and provided the necessary regulatory framework for their implementation (Fernandes 2006).

In Brazil, when an urban neighborhood is ripe for redevelopment, the municipality will designate the area as an urban operation (UO). Public authorities will rezone the UO and improve its infrastructure to support the expected increase in commercial and residential activities. To finance the project, the government will issue a number of CEPACs based on the new development potential of the UO. The development potential along with a preapproved list of required infrastructure investments will be incorporated into the city planning and become an integral part of the city's overall master plan.

In general, a CEPAC is equivalent to 1 m² (or about 10 ft.²) of building rights, adjustable according to location differences. The government will then auction off these CEPACs to developers in small offerings over time or in a single sale. A CEPAC holder can redeem the certificate when the development rights are needed to construct the project. According to the law, the number of CEPACs sold for the UO must be consistent with the city's master plan. The municipality must also keep the sale revenue in a separate account designed for infrastructure investment within the UO where the CEPACs originated (Sandroni 2010; Smolka 2013).

An important aspect of the CEPAC is that it is issued before the actual development project occurs. The preemptive retainment of the future land value increments allows additional public works to be financed and constructed on time to accommodate new private investments. The up-front capture also enables the city to fund public improvements without increasing debts or fiscal deficits (Kim 2018).

The CEPACs are issued through public electronic auctions. Three agencies oversee the process of assigning them. Within the issuing city, the Empresa

Municipal de Urbanização of São Paulo, for example, is responsible for the administration, including setting the investment priorities, establishing the conditions for favorable auction returns, and compiling information and data associated with the auctions. The Empresa Municipal de Urbanização also monitors the real estate market to determine the timing and quantity of releasing CEPACs to allow the city to yield the best prices (Sandroni 2010).

At the central level, two federal banks—Banco do Brasil and Caixa Economica Federal—play critical roles in executing the public auctions for the issuing city. In addition, the Comissão de Valores Mobiliários, which is the Brazilian equivalent of the U.S. Securities and Exchange Commission, regulates the auctions in the stock market. The Comissão de Valores Mobiliários requires the issuing city to publicly disclose information such as past auction outcomes, the latest property valuation of all premises in the UO, environmental impact assessments, and master-plan modifications, all of which could affect the price of CEPACs.

Once a CEPAC is issued, it can be traded on São Paulo's stock exchange. This availability creates another financial vehicle for institutional investors to participate in real estate investment. Developers can buy these certificates in the stock market when they need them and thus will not tie up their capital in land acquisition for future undertakings. Financial regulations require significant transparency in the auctions and public access to information related to CEPACs (Sandroni 2011; Smolka 2013).

São Paulo has been periodically auctioning off CEPACs since 2004. In fact, in 1995 it was the first city in Brazil that experimented with the early concept of this LVC approach to facilitate the redevelopment of the Faria Lima UO. After the enactment of the city statute in 2001 and several refinements of the program, São Paulo finally held the first two CEPAC auctions in 2004. The earliest auction was considered a failure, attracting very little interest from developers. It is partly because developers were able to obtain development rights from the program of the Onerous Grant of the Right to Build. More important, the property market was in a downturn at that time.

Since then, CEPACs have been sold to private investors through a series of public auctions, with their prices increasing gradually over the face value. For example, the average price increase of a CEPAC for the Faria Lima UO from 2004 to 2009 was about 35 percent. The same-period increase for the Agua Espraida UO was almost 80 percent (Kim 2018).

As of 2017, there were 14 approved UOs in São Paulo of which only 3 were funded by CEPAC revenues. The reason for using them less often than they could have been was to ensure market stability. A total of 44 auctions, primarily for the Faria Lima UO and Agua Espraida UO, have occurred. Most of the CEPACs assigned to these UOs have been used up, with a small amount remaining for funding projects in less desirable locations (Kim 2018).

From 2004 to 2015, CEPAC sales for the Faria Lima UO and Agua Espraida UO generated more than US$2.8 billion (in 2018 value) in revenue. Sales accounted for almost 15 percent of all public investments in São Paulo during that period (Kim 2018). Given that the two UOs represent less than 0.1 percent of the city's total developable area, the revenue potential of CEPACs could be huge when other future UOs are taken into consideration.

Other Brazilian cities have also issued CEPACs (Smolka 2013). For instance, the Fundo de Garantia do Tempo de Serviço—a state-run pension fund—bought 6.4 million of them in 2011 for the Porto Maravilha revitalization project in Rio de Janeiro. These certificates encompassed about four million square meters of building rights. The municipality raised an up-front capital of US$1.9 billion (in 2019 value) for financing 85 percent of the planned urban regeneration activities. The pension fund that controlled all the CEPACs was in charge of negotiating the transfers of building rights to private companies for real estate development. As of 2019, participating developers built 10 properties with a total area of more than half a million square meters in the redevelopment area (World Bank 2019).

Despite the encouraging outcomes of adopting CEPACs in Brazil, the implementation of the various programs in different cities was not problem-free. Later in the chapter, we discuss the governance and institutional issues that Brazil faced when they first attempted to put this LVC idea into practice.

Vietnam: Land for Infrastructure

Vietnam is representative in many respects of the rapidly developing countries that are candidates for LVC. The decade after the end of Vietnam War in 1975 saw much fixing up of war-damaged housing but little planning for urban development. In 1986, however, the government adopted the Doi Moi (Renovation) economic reforms, which proved successful by the early 1990s. Vietnam continued to grow during the mid-2000s, benefiting from becoming the 150th member of the World Trade Organization and the popularity of the "China plus one" strategy among global manufacturers.

With economic growth came demands for infrastructure of every type, including mass transit rail systems. The government of Ho Chi Minh City (HCMC) secured financing for two mass transit lines from Japan and European countries. With most of its foreign aid committed to rail, HCMC had to turn to LVC to help finance other urban public works. This section focuses on two such projects that represent the types of infrastructure well suited for LVC. As the first LVC projects developed by HCMC, they also illustrate the early implementation challenges.

Saigon South Urban Development

The pioneer LVC project in HCMC was a joint venture between the Industrial Promotion Corporation—a government-owned development corporation—and the Central Trading and Development Corporation of Taiwan to develop 2,600 ha of land in South Saigon. The project included the following parts:

- A 10-lane road of 17.8 km that connects South Saigon with the national highway 1A.
- A 300 ha export processing zone (EPZ).
- 600 ha of developable land for the joint venture.
- An additional 2,000 ha of land for the HCMC government to develop.

The Taiwanese partner owned 70 percent of the venture in return for contributions of cash and equipment. The HCMC government contributed the land and in return owned the remaining 30 percent. The total investment was valued at US$331 million.

The joint venture was initially very successful. The EPZ and the road were built on time and under budget. The first 400 ha, called Phu My Hung, was built to high standards and became one of HCMC's most prestigious residential neighborhoods (Huynh 2015).

Complaints about inadequate compensation for lost farmlands and relocation expenses were not long in coming, however, despite the fact the government having had no legal obligation to provide compensation. In 1987, a year after the Doi Moi reforms were announced and two years before the joint venture, the government took a tentative step toward encouraging the development of a land market by passing the First Land Law. This legislation recognized the right of individuals to use a plot of land for particular purposes but made no mention of markets and prices.

In 1993, however, as the South Saigon project got under way, the government sought to clarify its primacy in the emerging land market by passing the Second Land Law, which allowed households and individuals to buy and sell land but reserved for the government the right to change land uses or to expropriate land. The law also required local governments to post publicly the Land Pricing Framework that listed the compensation due for changes in use or expropriation.

The prices were to be based on, but not necessarily equal to, market prices. Critics argued that this loophole in the law opened the door for corruption and resulted in compensations that were typically a fraction of market prices (Hansen 2013). However, local governments and private developers regarded the gap between compensation and market prices as badly needed revenue to fund infrastructure. Tensions were particularly high on the periphery of Vietnam's larger cities and after demonstrations against the government were made legal in 2006. The controversy was such that in a survey, the Vietnamese ranked land administration as the second most corrupt governmental function, behind only the traffic police (World Bank 2011).

The EPZ in South Saigon may have set the early precedent for generous compensation by offering affected residents VND110–130 million (US$12,000–14,000) per hectare of land, which was more than twice its agricultural value at that time (Nguyen, Phan, and Ton 2006). There were only a few complaints about compensation at the EPZ initially because only about 500 poor households were involved, and they happily returned their old compensation for the new. The 1993 law seemed to trigger a wave of real estate speculation, however, with market prices increasing rapidly. As a result, compensation increased by sixfold from 1993 to 1996 (Huynh and Ngo 2010).

The development of Saigon South slowed after completion of the EPZ and Phy Mu Hung residential areas. The HCMC government created the Project Management Unit to develop the extra 2,000 ha contemplated in the original scheme. Some of the hectares were wetland or otherwise not suitable for development. The Project Management Unit leased the remaining land slowly, reportedly in small lots suitable for small developers rather than the joint venture. In 2019, HCMC's third most powerful government official (the standing vice secretary of the city's party) and some other senior politicians were accused of corruption involving the Industrial Promotion Corporation, thereby further delaying the progress of the project (Linh-An 2019).

Thu Thiem Peninsula

The Saigon South project encouraged HCMC to adopt a more ambitious LVC scheme to help build a new downtown on the Thu Thiem Peninsula, which is located on the opposite shore of the Saigon River from the existing downtown. The project was inspired by Shanghai's effort to preserve its historic riverfront by building a modern downtown on the opposite shore at Pudong. At that time, HCMC's downtown had only a few 40-story high-rise buildings scattered among

TABLE 10.1 Preliminary Cost Estimation of the Thu Thiem Project by
September 2018

	Trillion VND	Million US$
Infrastructure cost[a]	34,153	1,466
Tunnel[b]	9,863	423
Bridge 1[c]	1,099	47
Bridge 2[a]	4,260	183
Four road[a]	12,182	523
Residential area in the north of Thu Thiem[d]	2,641	113
Compensation and relocation[a]	38,679	1,660
Total actual cost[a]	72,832	3,126
Estimated interest charge[a]	10,503	451
Total estimated cost by 09/2018	83,336	3,577
Total estimated revenue by 09/2018[a]	74,601	3,202

Note: The cost figures in million US$ are undiscounted and converted at an exchange rate of VND23,300 per US$.
[a]Government Inspectorate of Vietnam (2019).
[b]Thanh Nien Online News (2011).
[c]Smart Realtors (n.d.).
[d]Ho Chi Minh City Infrastructure Investment Joint Stock Company (n.d.).

handsome colonial-era mansions that architects and historians agreed merited protection. In 1993, the new downtown appeared on the city's master plan with specific plans released later in 1996 and 1998. Implementation began in 2001 under a new Project Management Unit that organized an international competition to design the Thu Thiem district in 2003, which was won by a distinguished foreign urban design and planning firm.

The city's ambitions were reflected in Thu Thiem's projected expenses, which by 2018 had reached US$3.6 billion (table 10.1). Roughly half was required to build a tunnel and two bridges connecting the two downtowns and four major internal roads. The other half was to pay compensation and relocation expenses for those in 15,000 households who lived on the peninsula. Unlike the Saigon South project, Thu Thiem did not benefit from an injection of foreign capital, equipment, and expertise.

Compensation had been projected at US$350 million in 2002. But the residents—perhaps emboldened by the experience of Saigon South and the significance of the Thu Thiem project for the city—organized a series of demonstrations that gradually forced the city government to raise the number of households qualified for compensation and the rates. Between 2002 and 2009, estimates of compensation quadrupled, and the city government had to borrow US$1.4 billion from a commercial bank to fund the payments (Huynh and Ngo 2010).

The high construction and compensation costs in Thu Thiem meant that HCMC had to give up on the basic strategy of financing the infrastructure with the resulting uplift in land value. That uplift depended on the gap between the market value of the infrastructure improvements the city received and the compensation payments it had to make. With compensation payments so high, however, the gap would be small or maybe nonexistent. And because the costs of the bridges and tunnel were also high, an enormous gap was needed to make the project financially viable. As a result, the project was essentially being supported by other municipal revenue sources and was occurring only because HCMC believed that preserving its heritage made subsidizing the infrastructure worthwhile.

The development of the new downtown in Thu Thiem has been slow. An audit by the national government reported that as of 2018, many of the new serviced lots remained vacant despite a decade-long real estate boom on the other side of the river. The tallest buildings in the city increased from 33 stories in 2008 to 68 stories in 2010 and 81 stories in 2018. The new buildings kept residential, office, hotel, and commercial rents down in the central area; they also strained greatly the downtown traffic, drainage, and electricity grid systems and were destroying the charm of the historic neighborhoods. HCMC planners were being pressed by developers to allow them to purchase rights to add floors or extend the land leases for proposed high rises. The city's land use plan, however, was not detailed enough to provide guidance for public officials to determine the merits of the developers' proposals in terms of traffic congestion, electicity supply, green space, or other public concerns. In 2013, HCMC attempted to correct the situation by publishing a detailed urban design plan for a 930 ha area centered on the old downtown (Nguyen et al. 2017). The planners did not include a formal LVC scheme to finance the infrastructure required, but their negotiations with developers for public amenities in exchange for added floors was de facto a sale of development rights for public benefit.

Meanwhile, Thu Thiem became involved in a corruption scandal similar to that in South Saigon. An investigation by the central government estimated that the city had lost tens of trillion in VND in the Thu Thiem project (Government Inspectorate of Vietnam 2019). Consequently, the city's two former top leaders, the party secretary (also a member of the country's powerful politburo) and the chairman (also the mayor), were disciplined. Several vice chairmen and other senior officials have been prosecuted, and many other officials and businessmen were likely to be charged because of land corruption (Brown 2020).

Good Governance in LVC

The experiences of Brazil and Vietnam in selling development rights strongly suggest that LVC is a policy with great potential for financing infrastructure in developing countries but one that also requires exceptional care in the design of regulations and institutions for its implementation. The following observations are so fundamental that they are not only relevant to the sale of development rights, as illustrated by the two cases, but are also applicable to most other LVC approaches.

Clear Delineation of Property Rights

The first and most basic ingredient is a clear delineation of public and private property rights of land. In essence, LVC involves the redistribution of land development benefits between private individuals and the government. Thus, an adequate understanding of what land rights belong to the owners (or occupants) and what rights belong to the public is essential. The viability of LVC depends on the stakeholders' property expectations shaped by the laws, customary rules, and social norms.

Without this clear definition, government action to repossess building rights generated by rezoning is likely to face legal and popular opposition. For example, the U.S. Constitution allows the use of eminent domain by public authorities to seize private property but only for public purposes and with just compensation and due process. For countries where similar legal protection of private property exists, the question is whether a "taking" would occur if a municipality does not pay any compensation to a landowner when confiscating the building rights beyond zoning and selling them to other private entities for profitable undertakings. As far as we know, there is no existing court case to answer this question.[1] Perhaps the concern that private landowners may engage in prolonged legal battles with the government to fight for their property rights is enough to deter some countries from experimenting with the idea.

It may seem obvious, but having a clear delineation of property rights without agreement on those rights is difficult. And in this regard, there is a fundamental difference between Brazil and Vietnam in that the former has a clear position on the social functions of property, while the latter does not. The CEPAC approach's position is that the government should receive all uplifts in property values caused by public improvements. Moreover, this position is enforced by the CEPAC requirement that development rights must be assigned through open and competitive bidding. In contrast, in Vietnam the ownership of the uplift is unsettled, resulting in considerable controversy and tension. Under Vietnamese law, the land belongs to the people, and the state manages it on the people's behalf. There was no requirement for compensation until the Second Land Law of 1993, and even then the state was given a fair amount of latitude in setting the suggested charges.

The contrast between Brazil and Vietnam suggests, moreover, that adopting some form of LVC is as much a political decision as a legal decision, especially in countries that are urbanizing rapidly. It seems unlikely that the Vietnamese government could have held compensation at a low level for much longer, given the widening and seemingly unfair gap that was emerging in the prices for agricultural versus urban lands. A similar legal and political situation in China led to the adoption of a wider distribution of the value uplift in that country.

Besides the legal and political conditions, other institutions and legislation are needed to delineate and protect property rights of public and private entities involved in land development. For example, nurturing a good understanding of and reasonable expectations for all concerned parties requires an up-to-date and publicly accessible land registry that records public and private land ownership and related transactions. At least as important, the registered land rights should be protected by an impartial and credible judicial system that interprets the constitution and laws and resolves land disputes based on these legal rules. In addition, standardized techniques practiced by certified professionals are needed to calculate the compensation to the parties whose property rights have been infringed upon when implementing an LVC scheme.

Finally and extremely important are efforts to limit corruption in infrastructure procurement and financing. Some countries and sectors have more of a reputation for corruption than others. But at least as measured by Transparency International's Corruption Perception Index in 2019, Vietnam (ranked 96th out of 180 countries) performs about as well as Brazil (106th out of 180). In our small sample of LVC programs, however, Vietnam appears to be doing worse than Brazil, with 92 Vietnamese central government officials disciplined for accepting bribes and violations of the regulation since 2016 (Le-Hiep 2020) versus no mentions of bribes in published accounts of CEPACs. However, Brazil was recently home to a worldwide corruption scandal orchestrated by its huge international infrastructure construction company, Odebrecht; the scandal might have somehow involved Brazil's premier business city, São Paulo. Yet as far as we know, there has been no convicted corruption case related to the CEPAC since its inception. It would be interesting to find out how the CEPAC is insulated from corruption, even though the Odebrecht case suggests that crorruption is rampant in the Brazilian construction industry. It may be that the clearer commitment to public ownership of the uplift noted earlier, matched with public electronic auctions, makes the CEPAC more transparent.

Corruption is an important problem because it is a direct threat to the clear delineation of property rights, which is so critical to LVC. And LVC is an inviting target for corruption simply because infrastructure construction contracts are typically large and lucrative. The rapid appreciation in land prices from urbanization offers additional attraction. Although they are not foolproof, moreover, there are measures one can take to discourage corruption such as the requirement of open and competitive disposition of development rights—a policy long applied in Brazil and being recently promoted in Vietnam.

Master Plan

A second essential ingredient is a master plan that provides guidance on what types of infrastructure will be needed, where, and when. Mapping infrastructure deficits and updating the public land inventory with proper appraisals for each urban jurisdiction are crucial for LVC. This information can guide local officials to plan for infrastructure investments in strategic areas and to use public land to entice the private sector to invest in needed public facilities. Without knowing what types of public works the jurisdiction needs, the infrastructure that private developers are obligated to build may not be relevant for the affected communities.

One hallmark of a good master plan is the recognition that the amount of revenue generated by LVC depends on the supply and demand of the development rights. Thus, for example, the timing of offering plots or issuing CEPACs will affect the financial outcome of the program. In the Brazilian case, city officials need to have a good understanding of the real estate cycles in order to release the right number of CEPACs into the market at the appropriate time. Issuing plenty of CEPACs during an economic downturn will not help finance public infrastructure. Limiting the availability of CEPACs during a property market boom can inflate land prices, rendering housing unaffordable for the urban poor.

The balancing act can be hard to handle for public officials in some developing countries. HCMC seems to have done a reasonably good job in Saigon South, with the land released gradually so that it was mostly developed and serviced, although perhaps more could have been awarded to the joint venture. But in Thu Thiem, officials appeared to have prepared many more sites than the market had demand for, even at prices that, judging from the budget, must have been heavily subsidized. Part of the problem was that they misjudged the property demand in the existing downtown, a problem made worse by the fact that the city's own planners were, at least for a time, allowing higher buildings without insisting on funding for the needed public infrastructure that the extra floors might require (Nguyen et al. 2017).

A good master plan must also be spatially and temporally detailed because the problems it is trying to correct typically vary so much. In Brazil, for example, a unit of CEPAC is usually good for one extra square meter of development but may be worth more than a square meter if applied in a location or manner that the government wants to encourage or less if applied in a less desirable manner. The HCMC's planners are essentially in the business of comparing the infrastructure requirements of different types of land uses in its new downtown, in its old downtown, and on the peripery. Such detailed planning is costly and time-consuming, so the estimates of the extra infrastructure required in exchange for the added development rights are not always accurate.

Public agencies should also have the capacity to negotiate land contracts openly and engage in joint ventures with private investors as long as it does not increase the risk or perception of corruption. Land use regulations and plans at different levels of government must be coherent and linked. To achieve this objective, central and local planning agencies must collaborate to ensure the sharing of information and data.

Patience and Politics

Depending on when one starts and stops the clock, establishing the regulatory institutions and legal procedures needed to facilitate the sale of development rights can take decades. It took Brazil 15 years (1988–2004) to formulate the master-planning and environmental-clearance processes to implement the first auction of CEPACs (Kim 2018; Sandroni 2010). And it took São Paulo another 5 years and 20 auctions before all the participating parties gained enough confidence to manage the program (Sandroni 2010). In addition, if the country wanted the building rights to be tradable like securities, as in Brazil, it would also need the kind of well-developed stock market that is rare in developing countries. In short, CEPACs are complex financial instruments that require a steep learning curve for property owners, developers, investors, financial intermediaries, and other stakeholders.

Implementing LVC has taken even longer in Vietnam than in Brazil. Vietnam is still a work in progress, while Brazil arguably is not. In fairness, however, Vietnam did not start its LVC efforts until the early 1990s and without Brazil's benefit of long exposure to markets of many types. Nevertheless, Vietnam has passed several important milestones, including recognizing in 2003 that compensation is due (although not agreeing on the amount) and encouraging in 2013 open auctions to allocate developable plots to increase transparency. Nevertheless, Vietnam is still struggling to find the effective LVC approaches.

Public understanding and support for LVC is unlikely to emerge spontaneously or automatically. Both central and subnational governments will have to develop outreach programs to explain the benefits that the LVC programs can bring to society. Governments also need to assure the general public that the distribution of the financial gains will be inclusive, equitable, and transparent. Toward that end, for example, the government might create a separate account in its budget to ensure that land revenues will be invested in public infrastructure in localities where the incomes are originated.

These actions are long-term efforts that require patience from all stakeholders and substantial government commitment to the allocation of adequate financial and human resources to design and execute the LVC initiative. It is important to prioritize reform efforts so that the government will not be overwhelmed by new tasks and challenges. Interim results that are achievable in the near term can be presented to stakeholders to maintain their long-term commitment to the program.

Conclusions

The experiences of Brazil and Vietnam with LVC illustrate both the promise and the peril of this method of infrastructure finance. The most obvious attraction is the amount of money that can be raised and the infrastructure that can be built. The numbers from Brazil are particularly impressive. As noted earlier, US\$2.8 billion was raised over 10 years from two of São Paulo's UO districts that together accounted for less than 0.1 percent of the city's developable area. Comparable figures from Vietnam are not readily available, but the fact that HCMC could take out a US\$1.4 billion loan from a commercial bank based on expected LVC payments is suggestive.

Just because substantial sums can be raised does not mean they would be used wisely. In fact, the opposite is sometimes alleged. But the experiences of Brazil and Vietnam suggest that success depends on three key factors.

The first of these is a clear decision about who should capture the uplift in value generated. In the case of urbanization, the possibilities include the farmer, the urban property developers, and the taxpayers; in the case of the installation or upgrading of public infrastructure, however, the possibilities include the providers, the users, and the taxpayers. Some might argue for the sharing of the uplift captured so that all parties have a stake in the success of the scheme. The Vietnamese experience suggests, however, that ambiguity about how the uplift should be shared leads to social conflict and is an invitation to corruption. Considerations of fairness and precedent favor the taxpayer or perhaps the farmer; whoever is chosen, the decision ought to be clear.

A second important determinant of success is a realistic assessment of the market for the types of infrastructure in question. Thu Thiem offers the most obvious cautionary example. Decades from now, HCMC's citizens are likely to be glad and proud that their predecessors decided to preserve a part of the historic downtown. But they might have chosen to implement the protections more gradually and selectively. Based on the initial investment costs, for example, in theory one might have been able to build 10 Saigon South residential communities (at US$331 million each) for the price of those in Thu Thiem (US$3.6 billion so far). Moreover, the timing or pacing of the Thu Thiem investment is just one of dozens of trade-offs that should be considered if the funds raised by value capture are to be used wisely. Brazil appears to delegate decisions to the city that is generating the funds, which may encourage fiscal responsibility but at the expense of overlooking cross-jurisdictional options. On the other hand, HCMC is willing to consider unsolicited proposals by real estate developers, which may encourage innovative ideas but potentially diverts the city's scare planning resources to the study of options of interest to developers at the expense of issues of interest to the general public.

The third key determinant of success is the attention given to the governance of the land development in general and the LVC scheme in particular. By governance, we mean to include the agencies and regulations that determine who gets the uplift and which investments are considered and funded. But particularly if the scheme is based on the sale of development rights, as seems likely, the reliability and integrity of the entire system of registries to record property rights and transactions and of courts to adjudicate commercial disputes also become critical.

In sum, although the sale of development rights has potential for capturing land value to finance public infrastructure, policy makers should never underestimate the difficulties associated with implementation. The challenges are not only about the technical design of the LVC instruments but are also related to broader governmental functions such as the delineation and protection of property rights, master planning, and public education about LVC. Neglect of any of these issues could undermine LVC efforts, as illustrated in our two case studies.

Summary

- Infrastructure improvements usually increase the value of the land they serve, and various LVC schemes attempt to capture part or all of the price uplift to finance the improvements.
- LVC schemes are particularly popular among developing countries, which have enormous infrastructure needs, often created by urbanization, but few alternative funding sources.

- The sale or auction of development rights is an oft-used form of LVC. The rights for sale are typically either for increased density in an existing or proposed urban renewal project (as illustrated by a successful market-oriented program in São Paulo, Brazil) or for the right to convert land from rural to urban uses (as illustrated by a more controversial program in HCMC).

- In either case, successful implementation requires a clear and widely accepted delineation of property rights and a supportive legal system.

Note

1. The scenario is similar to the legal disputes over government exactions in the United States. When a developer asks for a change in land use or an increase in the development density above the zoning limit, public officials could demand a cash payment or an in-kind contribution from the developer for granting the permission so long as the levy does not constitute a taking of private property. The justification for the charges is that new development will impose added burdens on existing public infrastructure; thus, the developer must pay for the new public works to mediate the problem. In the United States, the developer who owns the land (or is in partnership with the landowner) initiates the transaction. In contrast, the CEPAC is a preemptive approach of capturing the increased land value due to changes in zoning regulations. The government initiates the land use change regardless of whether the affected landowners have any intention to redevelop their properties, making the CEPAC more likely to be challenged in court (Kim 2018). That said, private developers so far have not filed any lawsuit against CEPACs in Brazil.

References

Bahl, Roy W., and Jorge Martinez-Vazquez. 2007. *The Property Tax in Developing Countries: Current Practice and Prospects.* Cambridge, MA: Lincoln Institute of Land Policy.

Booth, Philip. A. 2012. "The Unearned Increment: Property and the Capture of Betterment Value in Britain and France." In *Value Capture and Land Policies*, ed. Gregory K. Ingram and Yu-Hung Hong, 74–93. Cambridge, MA: Lincoln Institute of Land Policy.

Bourassa, Steven C. 1987. "Land Value Taxation and New Housing Development in Pittsburgh." *Growth and Change* 18(4): 44–56.

Brown, David. 2020. "Ho Chi Minh City Seeks to Make Up for 20 Wasted Years." *Asia Sentinel,* June 9.

Doebele, William A., ed. 1982. *Land Readjustment: A Different Approach to Financing Urbanization.* Lexington, MA: Lexington Books.

Dye, Richard F., and Richard W. England, eds. 2009. *Land Value Taxation: Theory, Evidence, and Practice.* Cambridge, MA: Lincoln Institute of Land Policy.

Fernandes, Edesio. 2006. "Main Aspects of the Regulatory Framework Governing Urban Land Development Processes." In *Brazil Inputs for a Strategy for Cities: A Contribution with a Focus on Cities and Municipalities*, vol. 2, *Background Papers*, 137–167. Report No. 35749-BR. Washington, DC: World Bank.

George, Henry. 1912 (1879). *Progress and Poverty: An Inquiry into the Cause of Industrial Depressions and of Increase of Want with Increase of Wealth.* Garden City, NY: Doubleday.

Government Inspectorate of Vietnam. 2019. Inspection Announcement of Thu Thiem No. 1041/ TC-TCPP. June 26. https://thanhtra.gov.vn/xem-chi-tiet-tin-tuc/-/asset_publisher/Content /thong-bao-ket-luan-thanh-tra-ve-cong-tac-quan-ly-nha-nuoc-va-thuc-hien-phap-luat -trong-quy-hoach-quan-ly-xay-dung-at-ai-tai-khu-o-thi-moi-thu-thiem-th?5979766.

Hansen, Kaitlin. 2013. "Land Law, Land Rights, and Land Reform in Vietnam: A Deeper Look into 'Land Grabbing' for Public and Private Development." Independent Study Project Collection No. 1722. https://digitalcollections.sit.edu/isp_collection/1722.

Ho Chi Minh City Infrastructure Investment Joint Stock Company. n.d. "Project on Northern Residential Area Infrastructure Investment and Completion of North-South Axial In Thu Thiem New Urban Area." https://bit.ly/3ci8eR4.

Hong, Yu-Hung, and Barrie Needham, eds. 2007. *Analyzing Land Readjustment: Economics, Law, and Collective Action.* Cambridge, MA: Lincoln Institute of Land Policy.

Huynh, Du. 2015. "Phu My Hung New Urban Development in Ho Chi Minh City: Only a Partial Success of a Broader Landscape." *International Journal of Sustainable Built Environment* 4(1): 125–135. https://doi.org/10.1016/j.ijsbe.2015.03.005.

Huynh, Du., and Alex Ngo. 2010. "Urban Development through Infrastructure Land-Based Financing: Cases in Ho Chi Minh City." Unpublished report for the Fulbright Economics Teaching Program.

Kim, Julie. 2018. *CePACs and Their Value Capture Viability in the US for Infrastructure Funding.* Cambridge, MA: Lincoln Institute of Land Policy.

Larsson, Gerhard. 1997. "Land Readjustment: A Tool for Urban Development." *Habitat International* 21(2): 141–152.

Le-Hiep. 2020. "Đã kỷ luật 92 cán bộ diện T.U quản lý từ đầu nhiệm kỳ XII" [92 Senior Officials Administered by the Central Government Were Disciplined]. *Thanh Nien Newspaper,* January 11.

Linh-An. 2019. "Ông Tất Thành Cang và những sai phạm nghiêm trọng tại công ty Tân Thuận" [Mr. Tat Thanh Cang and Serious Violations in Tan Thuan Corporation]. *Vietnamnet,* May 15.

Merriman, David F. 2012. "Does TIF Make It More Difficult to Manage Municipal Budgets? A Simulation Model and Directions for Future Research." In *Municipal Revenues and Land Policies,* ed. Gregory K. Ingram and Yu-Hung Hong, 306–333. Cambridge, MA: Lincoln Institute of Land Policy.

Mill, John Stuart. 1848. "On the General Principles of Taxation." In *Principles of Political Economy with Some of Their Applications to Social Philosophy,* Book V, chap. 2. London: Longmans, Green and Co.

Misczynski, Dean J. 2012. "Special Assessments in California: 35 Years of Expansion and Restriction." In *Value Capture and Land Policies,* ed. Gregory K. Ingram and Yu-Hung Hong, 97–115. Cambridge, MA: Lincoln Institute of Land Policy.

Mittal, Jay. 2014. "Self-Financing Land and Urban Development via Land Readjustment and Value Capture." *Habitat International* 44: 314–323.

Netzer, Dick, ed. 1998. *Land Value Taxation: Can It and Will It Work Today?* Cambridge, MA: Lincoln Institute of Land Policy.

Nguyen, Thanh Bao, Erwin van der Krabben, John H. Spencer, and Kien T. Truong. 2017. "Collaborative Development: Capturing the Public Value in Private Real Estate Development Projects in Ho Chi Minh City, Vietnam." *Cities* 68: 104–118.

Nguyen, Thanh Bao, Erwin Van der Krabben, Clément Musil, and Đức Anh Lê. 2018. "'Land For Infrastructure' in Ho Chi Minh City: Land-Based Financing of Transportation Improvement." *International Planning Studies* 23(3): 310–326.

Nguyen, Kich V., Duong Phan, and Kinh Ton. 2006. *Nha Be Re-habitation from Industry: Tan Thuan Export Processing Zone: A Breakthrough.* [In Vietnamese.] Ho Chi Minh City: General Publisher.

Oates, Wallace E., and Robert M. Schwab. 2009. "The Simple Analytics of Land Value Taxation." In *Land Value Taxation: Theory, Evidence, and Practice,* ed. Richard F. Dye and Richard W. England, 51–72. Cambridge, MA: Lincoln Institute of Land Policy.

Peterson, George E. 2008. *Unlocking Land Values to Finance Urban Infrastructure.* Washington, DC: World Bank.

Sandroni, Paulo. 2010. "A New Financial Instrument of Value Capture in São Paulo: Certificates of Additional Construction Potential." In *Municipal Revenues and Land Policies,* ed. Gregory K. Ingram and Yu-Hung Hong, 218–236. Cambridge, MA: Lincoln Institute of Land Policy.

———. 2011. "Recent Experience with Land Value Capture in São Paulo, Brazil." *Land Lines* 23(3): 14–19.

Smart Realtors. n.d. "Where Is Thu Thiem #1 Bridge Located?" [In Vietnamese.] https://bit .ly/3cenMVM.

Smolka, Martim Oscar. 2013. *Implementing Value Capture in Latin America: Policies and Tools for Urban Development.* Cambridge, MA: Lincoln Institute of Land Policy.

Sorensen, Andre. 1999. "Land Readjustment, Urban Planning and Urban Sprawl in the Tokyo Metropolitan Area." *Urban Studies* 36 (13): 2333–2360.

Thanh Nien Online News. 2011. "Notable Milestones about Thu Thiem Tunnel." [In Vietnamese.] November 20. https://bit.ly/3qMIAro.

UN-Habitat. 2018. *Global Experiences in Land Readjustment: Urban Legal Case Studies.* Nairobi: UN-Habitat.

Walters, Lawrence C. 2013. "Land Value Capture in Policy and Practice." *Journal of Property Tax Assessment and Administration* 10(2): 5–21.

World Bank. 2011. *Recognizing and Reducing Corruption Risks in Land Management in Vietnam.* Washington, DC: World Bank.

———. 2019. *Porto Maravilha: Case Study, Urban Regeneration KSB.* Washington, DC: World Bank.

REGULATION, PRIVATIZATION, AND STATE-OWNED ENTERPRISES

11

INFRASTRUCTURE "PRIVATIZATION"

WHEN IDEOLOGY MEETS EVIDENCE

Antonio Estache

It seems that as soon as the possibility of giving up on the public provision of an infrastructure service is considered, a debate between supporters and opponents starts and never dies. This tendency may explain why one of the characteristics of the economic literature on the effects of privatization is the extent to which its interpretation is so often ideological rather than analytical.[1] When ideology drives a debate, rhetoric (often cheap talk) tends to dominate hard evidence on all sides. And this domination can often bias the way the outcomes of a policy such as privatization are presented.

It is reasonable to predict that conservative analysts will support the idea of infrastructure privatization (defined broadly to include partial or temporary privatization) and focus on the efficiency payoffs that private skills can contribute. And this focus comes in addition to highlighting the potential private contribution to the financing needs of the sector. In contrast, at the other extreme of the political spectrum, progressive analysts are more likely to raise concerns with the risks of exclusions of the poorest populations—that is, cream-skimming by investors looking for high returns and low risks. Some will add a discussion of the fiscal costs of cream-skimming, since pick-and-choose strategies tend to leave the projects most likely to underperform in the hands of the public sector, often at a higher total net fiscal cost as the margin to cross-subsidize disappears.[2] Others will also highlight the risks of confusion between public and private interests by the managers of privatized companies, resulting, for instance, in the excessive distribution of dividends by firms underinvesting in a much-needed capacity.[3]

These ideological biases are not systematic, of course. They are often only implicit but can be observed in the way data are used in ex post assessments of privatization. For instance, if the emphasis is on demonstrating the efficiency payoffs, the raw data on labor are likely to be turned into a partial productivity indicator. If instead equity is the main concern, the evolution of jobs numbers (and staff reductions) will dominate the assessment. Similarly, if the focus is on improvements in investment in the case of utilities, the increase in the number of connections will be emphasized. But critics will argue that this increase is not the same as improvements in access rates if the connection growth rate lags behind the population growth rate.

Omitting these biases can easily lead to a misinterpretation of outcomes in terms of any of the traditional policy criteria (i.e., efficiency, equity, fiscal viability). A policy that looks good in the short run may indeed be counterproductive in the long run. Ignoring the fact that trade-offs are part of the ownership choice can be quite risky for a policy with multidimensional outcomes. Yet, this risk is the product of the too-common decision to rely on statistically weak, biased, or incomplete evidence, with debates being reduced to cheap talk when this policy, like any other, deserves a more encompassing assessment of hard evidence. The main purpose of this chapter is to offer an analytically balanced view of the record on infrastructure privatization, addressing the concerns of both sides of the ideological spectrum with an emphasis on efficiency and equity.[4]

The chapter focuses on the research published since the early 2010s, unless somewhat older sources are useful to set up an historical benchmark. The bulk of large-scale "modern times" privatizations took place over a period of 10–12 years that started in the mid-1990s and then significantly slowed down since the 2008 economic crisis. This period should be a long enough track record to allow the most recent literature to provide reasonably up-to-date credible information on the long-term effects of the policy. In practice, we will see that this is not so simple because the assessment is constrained by three other types of biases (besides the ideological one) that can be used to fuel cheap talk and distort evaluations in any direction.

First, the robust quantitative evidence based on the recent evolution of privatized infrastructure firms is quite modest. Most recent global evaluations are based on narrative overviews (similar to this one) rather than econometric treatments of the data available through techniques such as meta-analysis. Moreover, many of the econometric results quoted in recent surveys still rely on information collected at best in the late 2000s, when only the short-term effects of the changes could be measured. This information gap on recent developments occurs because since the early 2010s, the policy has enjoyed much less academic enthusiasm among empiricists (with a few exceptions discussed later). Yet in most countries, the governance of the sector, the global financial and political context, and the degree of collective knowledge on what works and what does not have evolved.

Second, the diagnostics can be influenced by the choice of analytical tools used to assess the effects of the ownership choice. For instance, financial analysts are interested in the financial rate of return, while economists are expected to concentrate on the social or economic rate of return to account explicitly for a wide range of externalities and sometimes for distributional concerns. More complex assessments will rely on computable general equilibrium models to account for the multiple secondary spillover effects of privatization.

Third, differences in the degree of hands-on experience often lead to different perspectives as well. Authors with operational experience are likely to emphasize transaction costs, administrative constraints, and implementation difficulties in their diagnostics. Those with a largely theoretical background are likely to ignore (assume away) these difficulties, even when these could be handled through control variables in the empirical tests of their theoretical models. These variables are better dealt with in detailed case studies, but these types of studies are less effective at producing generalized results.[5]

Basic Data on Infrastructure "Privatizations"

To put the evaluation in perspective, it may be useful to start with evidence on the relative importance of privatized companies in infrastructure activities. There is actually no "public good" data on the ownership of infrastructure providers around the globe. The following should thus be seen as an imperfect picture. But it is reliable enough to get a quantitative sense of the size of private operations in each subsector at the world level.

How Much Private Participation Is There in Infrastructure?

Table 11.1 summarizes the information from various sources. Sample sizes vary across subsectors but are all large enough to be statistically significant. They are also all recent enough to provide a reasonably current perspective on the extent of infrastructure privatization.

For electricity, privatization has mostly impacted generation thanks to the popularity of independent power producers (IPPs). In a 2018 snapshot of the number of IPPs in the world covering 94 countries, Bertomeu-Sanchez and Estache (2019b) find that 40 percent have signed at least one IPP. For distribution companies, in a sample of 175 countries and 7,621 firms analyzed for 2018, Küfeoğlu, Pollitt, and Anaya (2018) find that only 7 percent of the countries have a fully private operator (6 percent in the 125 developing economies sample and 12 percent in developed economies). About 63 percent have purely public distribution operators (76 percent for the developing countries sample and 30 percent in developed countries).[6] Countries with a combination of public and private ownership (i.e., mixed ownership)

TABLE 11.1 Indications of Global Infrastructure Total or Partial Privatization per Subsector

Sector	Shares of Countries with Private Providers (2015–2018 Data)
Electricity	
Generation (IPPs)	40% (94 countries sample, 2018)
Distribution	7% purely private, 30% mixed (175 countries sample, 2018)
Transport	
Airports	3% (world sample, 2016)
Ports	78% (world sample, 2015)
Rail	5% purely private, 29% mixed (133 countries sample, 2019)
Roads	25% (world sample, 2019)
Water and sanitation	
PPPs with investments commitments	22% (174 countries sample, 2018)

IPPs = independent power producers; PPPs = public-private partnerships.

add up to 30 percent of the total sample (18 percent in developing countries versus 58 percent in developed countries).

Küfeoğlu, Pollitt, and Anaya (2018) also show that monopolies still dominate the distribution activity, since 55 percent of the countries have a single distribution operator. When a distribution operator is public, it is also very likely to function with some degree of vertical integration (in more than 90 percent of the cases in both developed and developing economies). The proportion drops to 61 percent and 29 percent, respectively, when a distribution operator is mixed or private. This finding is a solid first indication of the diversity of contexts to consider in the comparison of state-owned enterprises (SOEs) and private firms.

For water and sanitation (W&S), providing a snapshot is more complex because of the extreme heterogeneity of its governance options. The traditional choice between large public and private firms to ensure the delivery of W&S continues to be common, in particular in medium- and high-income countries. But the drivers of the choices have evolved since the early 1990s, as decisions now focus also on the management of the service rather than mostly the financing of the necessary investment. The main evolution is toward decentralized and community-based solutions, cooperatives, and other forms of autonomous local operations (which can include smaller public-private partnerships [PPPs] to address the needs of those often left out by the larger firms, whether public or private).

This greater diversity of governance options has reduced the importance of the debates on the relative importance of private financing. In their survey of 174 countries of the world in 2018, Bertomeu-Sanchez and Estache (2019b) find that 90 percent of the countries have adopted some PPP approach, including sometimes only for specific small contracts. But out of these, no more than 22 percent managed to get private investment financing. This number is consistent with the data for the 1990–2002 period reported by Gassner, Popov, and Pushak (2009). Their large developing countries sample counts only 15 percent of non-SOE providers. In sum, in most countries, most of W&S investment is publicly financed.

The role of privatization in transport has to cover subsectors as diverse as airports, ports, railways, roads, and urban transport without coherent source information across them. The only strictly comparable (free) source is the World Bank PPI database covering 132 countries. Between 1990 and 2019, 51 deals were signed for airports, 70 for ports, 44 for railways, and 35 for roads. These data mean that in each subsector, less than 40 percent of the countries have experienced some privatization (less than 25 percent for roads). Other sources provide additional insights on each subsector.

For airports, according to Steer Davies Gleave (2016), less than 3 percent are private (about 500, at least partially, out of 17,678), with large differences across regions. Asia, Europe, and Latin and Central America have been more actively moving toward privatization (Airport Council International 2016). In North America, the Middle East, and Africa, however, the majority of airports are still owned and controlled by the public sector.

In 2015 in the port sector, 65 percent of global throughput was handled by terminals owned in full or in part by global and international terminal operators (UNCTAD 2016). Smaller private operators handled 18 percent, and the public operators handled 19 percent. This outcome is the product of the fact that about 85–90 percent of the ports now follow the landlord port model operating 65–70 percent of global container port traffic.[7]

In the case of railways, according to International Union of Railways (2020), for a sample of 133 of the main countries with at least some railways transport capacity, only 5 percent of the countries have a system fully operated by the private sector, with 29 percent by a mixed ownership structure. Essentially two-thirds of the countries still rely on a public provider. The private and mixed approaches are mostly observed in North America, parts of Latin and Central America, and Western Europe. In contrast, most Eastern European, Commonwealth of Independent States, and Asian countries (with the notable exception of Japan) retain government ownership and operation, combined with partial PPPs. There is also heterogeneity in the degree of unbundling, ranging from full integration (common in Africa and Asia) to full unbundling with private operation of both the infrastructure and train services (in Japan). Hybrids are also common, with the public sector owning or operating the infrastructure and private companies paying to use the tracks (in continental Europe). The United States and Australia have developed their own hybrid type, with rail networks dominated by private freight operators and long-distance services operated by the state, or a combination of public and private operators for commuter rail in the case of Australia.

For roads, the role of the private sector is approximated by the importance of private toll roads. According to the International Bridge, Tunnel and Turnpike Association database, 50 countries count at least one toll road, and most are developed or Latin and Central American countries. This represents roughly 25 percent of the world and includes a growing number of poor countries without the ability to finance the development on their own road network.

How (Dis)Similar Are the Contractual Arrangements with the Private Providers?

The evidence suggests that pure private provision of infrastructure is not common. Since the mid-1990s, however, PPP contracts have allowed partial or more targeted approaches to privatization.[8] These approaches have often also been eased by the horizontal and vertical unbundling of the supply chain in industries noted earlier, since this allowed pick-and-choose decisions among various forms of PPPs.

Oddly enough, there is no standard formal or legal definition of a PPP. We rely here on the World Bank approach. The World Bank (n.d.) defines a PPP as "a mechanism for government to procure and implement public infrastructure and/or services using the resources and expertise of the private sector" and identifies four main types:

1. *Divestitures contracts.* These contracts lead to the total or partial sale of public assets to the private partner.
2. *Brownfield contracts.* These contracts cover a wide range of contracts in which the state agrees with the private sector to use or upgrade existing assets, or both, but retains the ownership of assets. The most common are rehabilitate-operate-transfer, rehabilitate-lease/rent-transfer, and build-rehabilitate-operate-transfer. In all these cases, the private partner has to rehabilitate an existing facility and then operate and maintain it at its own risk for a long concession duration period (usually for more than 15 years and regularly up to 30 years). These various types of brownfield contracts differ according to

the cost of the access to the assets during the contract period and the extent of new investments needed.

3. *Greenfield contracts.* These contracts take various forms. They can get a private operator to build a new facility largely at its own risk and operate it for a while before the asset is transferred to the government. They can also get the private operator to lease a public facility and operate it at its own risk. In this second option, the firm can become the owner at the end of the contract period or transfer it back to the government. These contracts include build-lease-transfer, build-operate-transfer, build-operate-own, merchant contracts, and rental contracts.

4. *Management contracts.* These contracts allow the state to retain asset ownership but also the obligation to finance investments while transferring operation and maintenance to a private operator, who bears some of the operating risks but none on asset conditions. These contracts usually last three to five years. The operator is paid a fixed fee by the state. Leases and affermage contracts are peculiar management contracts allowing the operator to charge an operator fee to users to cover its costs. For a lease, the fee revenue is shared with the state as owner of the assets. For an affermage, the fee can include part of the investment costs otherwise paid by the state.

Table 11.2 illustrates the relative importance of PPPs in developing economies for the period 1990–2019. Greenfield projects dominate. In energy, this reflects the development of the generation capacity of countries through IPPs. In W&S, this dominance hides the evolution of the contractual approaches toward management and lease contracts in a sector that is politically sensitive and in which renegotiation rates have been quite high (more than 90 percent in Latin America and Caribbean according to Guasch et al. 2014).[9]

Table 11.2 also illustrates the significant differences across subsectors. East Asia and Latin America and the Caribbean dominate the PPP market. Sub-Saharan Africa and the Middle East continue to be modest actors. The market is actually much more targeted than the regional data suggest. Argentina (until the mid-2010s), Brazil, China, India, Mexico, and Turkey are the main hosts to a large share of the investment commitments made through PPPs.

As a share of the gross domestic product, infrastructure investments for PPPs now stand at 0.9–1.1 percent, about the same level as their peak in 1997. It took until 2002 to get full recovery from the 1997 Asia crisis, but the developing world has so far not surpassed that peak. The public sector continues to be the main source for financing the needs of the private sector (World Bank 2019). According to this study, the private sector share of the financing commitments made through

TABLE 11.2 Types of Contracts in Developing Countries, 1990–2019

Contract	Electricity and Gas	Water and Sanitation	Transport
Brownfield	182	399	206
Divestiture	377	23	28
Greenfield	3185	492	208
Management and lease	49	161	29
Total	3793	1075	471
Basic Statistics			
Number of contracts per year	130.8	37.1	16.2
Number of countries with at least 1 PPP	110	65	70*
Region with the largest share of PPP contracts	Latin America and Caribbean	East Asia	Latin America and Caribbean

Source: World Bank PPI database.

*The transport market is heterogeneous: 50 countries have an airport public-private partnership (PPP), 70 have a port PPP, 43 have a rail PPP, and 35 have a road PPP.

PPPs in 2017 was only 17 percent, for a total of US$0.5 trillion of infrastructure project investment commitments in that year (and only 15 percent of the projects). In sub-Saharan Africa, the private sector share was about 5 percent; in Asia, the Middle East, and transition economies, the share was 25 percent; and in Latin America and the Caribbean, the share was about 40 percent. Private money financed only 16 percent of all infrastructure projects.[10] That study also shows that public financing sources, including public banks and equity, accounted for 25 percent of all PPI projects, while development finance institutions accounted for about 30 percent. Commercial banks and private equity delivered thus accounted for only about 45 percent of the financing associated with PPPs.

The financing of the sector continues to evolve, however, with China playing a growing role around the world. Moreover, in a growing number of countries there is a financialization of sponsors with a growing role for hedge funds and infrastructure funds. This tendency is impacting the sector, including through slower investments.[11]

How Effective Has Privatization Been?

This part of the chapter assesses the ownership choice impacts on two factors: (1) efficiency and equity; and (2) trade-offs between these two policy goals. Looking for reliable and statistically robust evidence is challenging, as few studies rely on counterfactuals. Most studies rely on the econometric or nonparametric treatments of cross-country data sets with heterogeneous ownerships characteristics, but these differ in the extent to which control variables have been properly accounted for. Ignoring the interactions between ownership and other reform dimensions may be one of the most common omissions observed about this research and the insights produced by recent meta-analysis and surveys. We rely extensively on these meta-analyses because they cover both country-specific and cross-country studies and complement their conclusions.

Efficiency

The efficiency assessments follow multiple approaches. The oldest relies on econometric evaluations of partial performance indicators such as the number of connections per worker and system losses. These evaluations help identify the drivers of differences accounting for ownership, regulation, other reforms, and context. They are useful for identifying the interactions between ownership and the other variables but are biased if they ignore the multi-output and multi-input dimensions. This gap is best handled by the latest frontier analysis techniques (Cherchye et al. 2018); however, since these techniques are demanding technically, they are less popular in the field literature.

For electricity, Jamasb, Nepal, and Tilmisina (2017), Bacon (2018), Lee and Usman (2018), and Bensch (2019) have recently synthesized the academic evidence produced until the mid-2010s.[12] They conclude that the privatization of electricity can commonly be associated with improvements in quality and efficiency, including higher quality, lower transmission and distribution losses, and higher labor productivity. However, they add two important limitations. First, the positive impacts of privatization were short- or medium-lived. Second, the outcomes were influenced more by the regulatory and institutional quality than by ownership.

The latest research adds limitations. Imam, Jamasb, and Llorca (2019), for instance, find that privatization has had a positive effect on the generation capacity of countries in sub-Saharan Africa but a negative effect on the access rates, although not always a statistically significant one. Similarly for Asia, Sen, Nepal, and Jamasb (2018) found no correlation of privatization on technical quality. As for Latin America and the Caribbean, De Halleux, Estache, and Serebrisky (2020) find that privatization shows no statistically robust correlation with access or quality indicators.[13] Those three studies, however, validate the importance of regulation and associated institutions for any of the outcomes.

For developed economies, the conclusions are similar. While evidence on the impact of ownership is dominated by the U.S. experience from the 1960s to the 1990s, there is some for Europe, such as that found by Borghi, Del Bo, and Florio

(2014), who emphasize the quality of the institutional framework. This quality seems to define which type of ownership leads to a superior productivity level. Gugler, Rammerstorfer, and Schmitt (2013) add that there is a trade-off between static and dynamic efficiency and between vertical integration and competition in electricity for 16 European countries for the period 1998–2008.

For the W&S sector, Herrera (2019) and Bel (2020) survey an impressive volume of literature. The first study focuses on the growing roles of decentralization and of alternative small-scale operators in the sector. The second discusses the growing importance of remunicipalization of W&S services. Both provide long-term perspectives on privatization and highlight that early studies were more positive on the scope of achieved efficiency gains and cost savings. They also confirm detailed evidence of a lack of systematic long-term improvement (Stutsman, Tzoumis, and Bennett 2016; Worthington 2014). Frontier Economics (2019) confirms this lack with a long-term perspective on the U.K. experience, the poster country of privatization. Private operators initially improved performance, but these improvements eventually reached a ceiling and in some cases were eventually partially reversed.

Bel (2020) notes also that SOEs do much better than private enterprises in developed countries than in developing countries.[14] Amaral, Chong, and Saussier (2018), Suárez-Varela et al. (2017), and Chong et al. (2006) are less categorical, arguing that the ranking can depend on differences in legal and institutional constraints or on the size of the cities. Baker and Ritts (2018) add that improvements in developing countries occurred mostly in middle-income countries, often in cities with middle- and high-income residents. Once again, this finding points to the need to control for multiple dimension in the ownership impact assessments.

For the transport sector, Button (2016), Chen, Daito, and Gifford (2016), and Valila (2019), who summarize empirical work on transport PPPs, show that the literature is largely dominated by case studies and counts very few systematic quantitative diagnostics.

In ports, private sector involvement is associated with better financial performance (Choi and Lim 2018; Lee and Lam 2017; Wang, Knox, and Lee 2013). Yet for investment, Xiao et al. (2012) and Balliauw, Kort, and Zhang (2019) argue that SOEs do better. According to Choi and Lim (2018), a privatized port focuses more on profit than on trade volume. Overall, Panayides, Parola, and Lam (2015) settle all disagreements by showing that regulatory quality, market openness, ease to start a business, and contract enforcement are important institutional determinants of a port's PPP success.

For rail, ownership has not really been on the agenda of academic researchers working on OECD economies for some time. And this gap exists in spite of the de facto renationalization of Railtrack in the United Kingdom, for instance, and similar decisions in Australia and New Zealand (Abbott and Cohen 2016). A notable exception is the review by Nash et al. (2016) of the European experience. They find cost reductions of 20–30 percent as one of the main achievements of rail franchising in Europe.[15] The main exception is in the United Kingdom, where sharp cost increases have been observed. Mizutani (2019) adds that public ownership is associated with higher passenger use of the railways.

In many ways, similar observations are made for developing countries. Private capital has tended to prefer freight business to passenger business in Africa and Latin and Central America. Moreover, globally, PPPs have not really been very effective at stimulating investment. For instance, for Brazil, Sampaio, Regina and Daychoum (2017) show that privatization led to decreased accident rates and improved freight capacity but had no impact on network expansion.

For toll roads, the conclusions are somewhat more negative. Guasch, Laffont, and Straub (2002) for Latin America and the Caribbean, as well as Bajari, Houghton, and Tadelis (2014) for the United States and Albalate (2014) for Europe, have documented the importance of renegotiations (and the frequency of renationalizations of these roads). These renegotiations led to changes in tolls and contract duration but seldom in performance obligations. Albalate (2014) links the failures to poor design and financing strategies. Albalate and Rosell (2019) add that in Spain the multiple ownership switches since 1984 made no difference to efficiency.

In sum, this brief overview of the efficiency achievements of privatization policy through various forms of PPP illustrates the great heterogeneity of experiences. This heterogeneity cannot, however, be turned into a simple ownership narrative. There is some evidence that when SOEs are found to be the less efficient ones in a given study, the results of a number of predictable control variables account for a wide range of relevant structural characteristics. Some are linked to the social, regulatory, institutional, financial, or economic context. Others reflect the results of a restructuring process that allowed cream-skimming, as discussed earlier.

Equity and Distributional Concerns

The statistically robust academic coverage of social concern is modest and focuses on access rates, affordability, and welfare measures of the incidence of reforms across income groups or types of users.[16] Each of these measures carries its share of difficulties. Access rates can be measured in two main ways, and these do not necessarily lead to the same conclusions. The first is in terms of the number of connections produced by a public or private operator; the second is in terms of share of the population with access, with hardly any correction for the quality of the service. For affordability, no real agreement exists on how to define energy, water, or transport poverty (Bagnoli et al. 2020). The only rough agreement is that each quality should be measured as a share of income to be allocated to these services, but there are many disagreements on the acceptable level and on the extent to which this level needs to be normalized to account for contextual dimensions.

With respect to distributional effects, computable general equilibrium models offer the most encompassing tool. They account for, among other things, indirect effects of privatization such as changes in product and labor markets (i.e., which final product prices change because the infrastructure prices change and which type of workers gain and lose from the changes).[17] Chisari, Estache, and Romero (1999) for Argentina, Solaymani, Kari, and Zakaria (2014) for Malaysia for all utilities, Estache and Grifell-Tatje (2013) for water privatization in Mali, and Boccanfuso, Estache, and Savard (2009) for electricity reform in Senegal all illustrate the necessity of accounting for multiple secondary interactions across sectors and factor markets to assess the social impact of ownership choices and to show that although ownership may matter, it does so less than regulation of the service. They all show how regulation can be designed to share any efficiency gains associated with ownership decisions across stakeholders.

The sector-specific details are also useful. For electricity, Foster and Witte (2020) argue that only one-third of countries manage to keep average electricity bills within 5 percent of household income. They find that this ability is related to the need to improve cost recovery, as the correlation coefficient between the affordability indicator and limited capital cost recovery is 0.8. For developing countries, Jasmab, Nepal, and Tilmisina (2017), Bacon (2018), Bensch (2019), and Lee and Usman (2018) show no significant difference on the achievement of social goals according to ownership. Differences in effectiveness in delivering access are largely driven by the rationality of the match of the ownership choice with local needs and constraints and, in particular, the adoption and implementation of complementary reforms (regulation, institutions, subsidies, and pricing structure). As for affordability, Gugler, Rammerstorfer, and Schmitt (2013) argue that ownership matters less than regulation and the design of tariffs.[18] For developed economies, privatization often resulted in positive outcomes, but these were often smaller and more uncertain than expected when the reforms were implemented. For instance, Gugler, Rammerstorfer, and Schmitt (2013), Fiorio and Florio (2013), and Hyland (2016) all find that privatizations do not necessarily impact investment or prices, even if this conclusion may be influenced by the sample (countries and period) and the estimation procedure. More important, from a policy perspective, as explained by Fiorio and Florio (2013), the overall institutional details mattered much more in Europe than the ownership choices.

For W&S, the analysis of the social impact of privatization has usually focused on developing countries where access rates are still often well below 100 percent. The surveys by Annamalai, Mahalingam, and Deep (2016) and Bakker and Ritts (2018) find no or mildly negative social consequences in developing countries. Bel (2020) concludes the same for developed economies. All agree that ownership matters less than governance, regulation, and tariff design if the targeting of access improvement is to be more effective. This latest negative perspective on privatization in W&S is a reversal of conclusions from the first generation of publications, such as Kosec (2014) for sub-Saharan Africa, and Clarke, Kosec, and Wallsten (2009) for Latin America and the Caribbean.

For transport, the debates are again more complex, but the multiplicity of the dimensions of mobility to account for give a good sense of the social implications of the ownership choice.[19] For now, these debates are more conceptual than empirical. One of the debate topics is the definition of transport poverty or equity in the design of transport policy (Gómez-Lobo 2011; Pereira, Schwanen, and Banister 2017; Serebrisky et al. 2009; Venter 2011). Should the design of policy treat all populations equally irrespective of their geographical location, that is, dealing with a key aspect of horizontal equity? Should it focus on specific vulnerable groups (low-income classes, minorities, etc.), that is, use a vertical perspective on equity? Or should it deliver a combination of both but if so in what proportion? This broad uncertainty impedes a robust view on the relevance of ownership choice for any or all of the social goals.

Despite these limitations, the literature makes three contributions. First, it provides evidence of the social importance of the sector. For instance, for Latin America and the Caribbean, Gandelman, Serebrisky, and Suárez-Alemán (2019) show that the share spent by the bottom income quintile of the population on public transport (whether they are publicly or privately operated) is more than twice the share spent by the top quintile (6.2 percent versus 2.5 percent). Second, in general, public provision is more correlated with affordability than private provision, as illustrated by Currie, Truong, and De Gruyter (2018) in the case of urban transport for a sample of 88 world cities.[20] Third, general provision offers a case for the management of the social concerns by regulators (i.e., the targeting of subsidies) and fiscal authorities (i.e., the level of subsidies) rather than through the choice of ownership.[21] These contributions have their own policy limitations stemming from their focus on affordability rather than on access.[22] Yet, in many countries, the main issue is access to transport.

In many contexts, it is more rational to subsidize investment to increase access than use (i.e., the social rate of return will be the highest to subsidize capital expenditure rather than operating expense). And this is where access to private financing can make a difference. From a political perspective, it is a risky strategy. Affordability continues to be perceived as a sensitive issue. In many countries, a fair share of the poorest tend to live outside cities centers or at least far from where they have their jobs. It should thus be no surprise that increasing urban transport fares is still a source of social conflict. In sum, the ability to rely on private funding and management skills in the sector is quite sensitive to the social context and the credibility of the fiscal commitments made by governments to a specific transport mode if fares are to be controlled. In this context, again, cream-skimming is an issue because new developments are unlikely to attract private funding if they are not associated with matching user fees and revenue guarantees.

But cream-skimming and mistargeted regulation have much broader effects. Consider transport again. If the poorest cannot afford to get to where the jobs are, they will face much more general poverty risks rather than just transport poverty. This is nicely illustrated by Currie, Truong, and De Gruyter (2018), who find that on average public operations had normalized scores for average users' trip distances significantly better than the average for nonpublic cities. This finding has additional distributional impacts across different income groups and sometimes across consumer types (i.e., rural versus urban).

Conclusions on the Effectiveness of Privatization

Overall, this (selective) review of the latest evidence on the efficiency and equity effects of infrastructure privatization provides good reasons to make the case for more encompassing and more analytically robust assessments. Partial assessments can be misleading and reinforce the uncertainty linked to data quality, differences in methods, and biases in perspectives. Despite the limitations of the current state of knowledge, research has delivered two strong useful messages.

First, the evidence shows that ownership is not the main performance driver in any of the sectors. The control variables (i.e., the redesign of a market structure, the degree of competition, or the regulatory capacity) matter more to outcomes. This fact implies that matching the overall reform package with local institutional capacity makes a difference.[23]

Second, ownership decisions come with trade-offs. For instance, static efficiency (cost efficiency) may be achieved at the cost of dynamic efficiency (i.e., underinvestment), and access may be achieved faster at the cost of lower quality or lower affordability. But this speed is also much more correlated with the control variables than with ownership. The difficulty is that these factors often influence the trade-offs only slowly over time. This effect implies that first impressions can be misleading.

On the Evolution of Evaluations

In many countries, privatization is often attractive because of the fiscal inability to finance investments needed to meet a fast-growing demand. From the 1990s to the mid-2000s, privatization did bring fresh capital in some countries; in most cases, the initial fiscal payoffs were positive. Also, privatization often came with initial efficiency payoffs. However, the most recent evidence highlights that neither the fiscal nor efficiency gains could always be sustained.

In many cases, the disappointing outcomes resulted from poor contract design, reflected in the large number of contract renegotiations. These outcomes also explain the increased longer-run fiscal burden, as governments were asked to compensate for the inability of the private operators to control costs or to increase revenue as initially committed (Reyes-Tagle 2018). In developing countries, the financing gaps continue to be about as large as they were in the 1990s and 2000s despite the efforts of international organizations to bridge financing needs. As for OECD countries, since the 2008 crisis, political speeches abound with commitments to scale up infrastructure investments in close collaboration with private partners, but there is little evidence that they made much difference in real terms.

The disappointing lack of sustainability of efficiency gains is explained by the poor improvement margin imposed by the initial composition of costs. Early on, the main cost savings came from job cuts. Once cuts have taken place, it becomes harder to gain from other costs components. The alternative is to change technology. This was relatively easier in electricity, port, and telecoms than in roads, rail, and W&S. This difference in the scope to implement costs savings also explains the differences in renegotiation rates across sectors. The subtle point is that part of the renegotiations was to include new fiscal transfers but also switch from pure incentive-based regimes to hybrid ones, in which a fair share of costs enjoyed an automatic pass-through to users or taxpayers.

These fiscal and efficiency disappointments were actually less politically sensitive than the evolutions in the social effects of privatization. The slow progress made in improving access rates in poor countries and, for all country groups, the slow progress made in finding the funding to implement the energy and mobility transitions became political issues. And these issues were exacerbated by the reduction in affordability that took place over time, fueling for some countries the wave of remunicipalization discussed earlier.

So, Why Did Privatization Not Deliver as Much as Expected?

The first explanation for underperformance in both rich and poor countries is that the associated reforms did not seriously address governance issues (corruption, poor technical skills, the inability to commit resources, and a lack of accountability).[24] A majority of countries focused on creating autonomous regulatory agencies to ensure the enforcement of contractual commitments by all parties. The agencies did not do much to address historical governance issues. Political interference with regulation continues to be an issue in all country groups even if some initially enjoyed some success. In addition, the bargaining power of regulators has so far often been insufficient to offset the capacity of some private actors to influence regulatory processes.[25]

The underestimation of the relevance of processes in the design of reforms is the second explanation. According to the International Monetary Fund's Public Investment Management Assessment approach, designed to help identify weaknesses in the implementation of infrastructure policies and tested in a sample of 30 countries, the main weaknesses start as early as the allocation and implementation stages (project appraisal, selection, procurement, and management as well as asset monitoring).[26] These weaknesses led to imperfect competition for the markets. Unbundling the sectors to allow entry of new private players was not enough or did not work out as well as expected. And unbundling was not supported by a more encompassing adjustment to processes inherited from the past approaches to management of the sector. Similar conclusions were reached by the European Court of Auditors (2018) in its review of the European Union's experience with PPPs.

Finally, the efficiency-equity trade-offs were too often underestimated by the reform teams. This can be seen in the mistargeting of tariff designs adopted by regulators discussed earlier. But just as important, underestimation is also the result of the failure to recognize the actual importance of cream-skimming as a way of getting private deals done. The omission of the social consequences of designing packages to maximize the odds of getting some private financing often explains the eventual rejection of the policy. Private investors do not want high-risk, low-returns deals, as seen in W&S (e.g., Marson and Savin 2015) and urban transport sectors (Currie et al. 2018).

So, Where Do We Go from Here?

It is likely that PPPs will stay on the policy agenda for many countries. But their design, implementation, regulation, and enforcement should do a much better job at internalizing the lessons from the mistakes of the last 30 years. And this improvement should probably start with much better diagnostics of the scope to improve governance and the efforts to match the PPP decisions with the various institutional limitations that the countries and the sectors face.

Ultimately, the needs are such that partnering with the private sector (not just to manage but also to finance the large investment and operational costs) must be part of the policy tool kit. This partnering is even more necessary when fiscal constraints are increasingly binding. But it cannot be based on fake news about the risks and the challenges these partnerships imply, in particular the brutal social risks. Such partnering is bound to be counterproductive socially and politically.

It would also be unrealistic to expect that all forms of PPPs will be successful in all country types. The poorest countries are still seen as high risks by investors. In these countries, the risks of renegotiations and of cream-skimming and their social consequences are higher than in richer countries. It is also unrealistic to expect that PPPs will be equally successful across sectors, as illustrated by the wave of W&S and toll roads that remunicipalization and renationalization show.

Some more realism and a lot less ideology will go a long way in allowing PPPs to deliver better and more infrastructure for all. Without a real change rather than simply a narrative change in that direction and as long as politicians and their advisers continue to bet on tools with consequences they do not really fully understand or prefer to ignore, the doubts about the various forms of infrastructure PPPs will continue to prevail. These doubts will often lead to the wrong policy decisions with negative social, efficiency, and fiscal consequences. The pity is that, collectively, we know better with the benefit of more than 30 years of experience.

Summary

- Pure private infrastructure is rare; most privatizations in emerging economies over the last several decades have involved some form of PPP, often a concession contract.
- Privatization is more common in ports and electricity generation than in electricity distribution, roads, water, and sanitation.
- Ownership alone does not appear to have had much effect on access and affordability for the poor and may have had only a temporary effect on costs.
- The disappointing performance is often blamed on insufficient attention to governance issues, including regulation and corruption.

Notes

1. The debate 30 years ago was very similar to those that politicians and their advisers are having today. For early discussions, see Goodman and Loveman (1991) and Clifton, Comín, and Diaz Fuentes (2006).

2. For a detailed assessment of the short-term versus long-term fiscal implications of PPPs, see Reyez-Tagle (2018).

3. For a discussion of the U.K. experience, see Helm (2018).

4. The chapter focuses on electricity, water and sanitation, and transport. It leaves out information and communications technology, where the privatization experience is largely correlated with the fast-evolving technological options in the sector.

5. Gómez-Ibáñez (2006, 2007) offers one of the best illustrations of the policy payoffs to rely on case studies to integrate and highlight the relevance of the historical, institutional, and economic characteristics apparently unrelated to the ownership choice in the diagnosis of the effects of an ownership change in various infrastructure sectors.

6. Purely public distribution system operators are defined as those having more than 50 percent ownership by state or other public entities.

7. In a landlord port, the state owns and manages the port land and infrastructure but enters into PPP agreements for a series of individual terminals.

8. The first PPPs started in the early 17th century in France and expanded fast in the rest of Europe and the United States in the 18th and 19th centuries (Grimsey and Lewis 2004).

9. For a broader perspective, see Saussier and de Brux (2018).

10. This is somewhat influenced by the large commitments made to 12 mega public enterprise projects in seven countries, including four projects in China.

11. For an early discussion, see Helm (2018).

12. Bensch (2019) provides the most technical survey. His quantitative assessment covers 27 publications from 2002 to 2018 (12 cross regions, 8 on Latin America, and 7 on Asia).

13. This finding contradicts Balza, Jimenez, and Mercado (2013), who find, with older data and a different method, that privatization had been robustly associated with improvements in quality and efficiency but not with better access.

14. Clifton et al. (2019) provide a useful more general overview of the debate.

15. Mizutani (2019) adds that public ownership is associated with higher passenger use of the railways.

16. Bayer et al. (2019) find only 31 statistically robust studies out of 7,247 interested in energy access published since 2000, and only 7 draw on a randomized experiment designed for causal inference. Bagnoli, Bertumeu-Sanchez, and Estache (2020) review the evidence on the social effects of ownership choices in detail.

17. For a detailed discussion of the potential use of general equilibrium models in the context of regulatory evaluations, see Chisari, Lambardi, and Romero (2007).

18. For an update on the way regulation impacts outcomes in public services, see Auriol, Crampes, and Estache (2021).

19. For a view on the complex relevance of governance to urban mobility in sub-Saharan Africa, see Poku-Boansi and Marsden (2018).

20. They measure affordability as the cost of fares as a ratio of gross domestic product percent per capita per trip.

21. In a review of the East Asian experience with PPPs for urban rail transit, Chang and Phang (2017) argue that Singapore's experience illustrates that vertically unbundled PPPs reduced the scope to rely on cross subsidization, increased coordination issues, and gave up on economies of scale and scope, ultimately leading to underinvestment and maintenance issues. They argue for vertically integrated publicly owned and driven systems, with some margin to enter into selective PPPs with clearly defined risk sharing.

22. For a recent illustration in the case of Bolivia, see Guzman and Oviedo (2018). For a more encompassing discussion of reform policy and social failures, see Gómez-Lobo (2020).

23. For the relevance of institutional characteristics in the effectiveness of infrastructure policies, see Estache (2019).

24. For water, see Herrera (2019). For electricity, see Imam, Jamasb, and Llorca (2019) and Cummins and Gillanders (2020).

25. The growing role of nonsector-specific actors has accelerated the confusion between public and private interests by the managers of privatized companies, and this acceleration is illustrated by the excessive distribution of dividends by firms underinvesting. For a review, see Bertomeu-Sanchez and Estache (2019a).

26. International Monetary Fund (2018).

References

Abbott, Malcolm, and Bruce Cohen. 2016. "The Privatization and De-privatization of Rail Industry Assets in Australia and New Zealand." *Utilities Policy* 41: 48–56.

Airports Council International. 2016. "The Ownership of European Airports." https://www.aeroport.fr/public/page/the-ownership-of-europe-s-airports-mars-2016-114.

Albalate, Daniel. 2014. *The Privatisation and Nationalisation of European Roads: Success and Failure in Public-Private Partnerships*. Northampton, MA: Edward Elgar Publishing.

Albalate, Daniel, and Jordi Rosell. 2019. "On the Efficiency of Toll Motorway Companies in Spain." *Research in Transportation Economics* 76. https://doi.org/10.1016/j.retrec.2019.100747.

Amaral, Miguel, Eshien Chong, and Stéphane Saussier. 2018. "Comparative Performances of Delivery Options: Empirical Lessons." In *The Economics of Public-Private Partnerships*, ed. Stéphane Saussier and Julie de Brux, 163–201. Cham, Switzerland: Springer. https://doi.org/10.1007/978-3-319-68050-7_7.

Annamalai, Thillai Rajan, Ashwin Mahalingam, and Akash Deep. 2016. "Impact of Private-Sector Involvement on Access and Quality of Service in Electricity, Telecom, and Water Supply Sectors: A Systematic Review of the Evidence in Developing Countries." London: EPPI-Centre, Social Science Research Unit, Institute of Education, University of London.

Auriol, Emmanuelle, Claude Crampes, and Antonio Estache. 2021. *Regulating Public Services: Bridging the Gap Between Theory and Practice*. Cambridge, UK: Cambridge University Press.

Bacon, Robert. 2018. "Taking Stock of the Impact of Power Utility Reform in Developing Countries: A Literature Review." Working paper No. 8460. Washington, DC: World Bank.

Bagnoli, Lisa, Salvador Bertomeu-Sanchez, and Antonio Estache. 2020. "How Does the Ownership of Electricity Distribution Relate to Energy Poverty in Latin America and the Caribbean?" Working paper No. 2020-37. Université Libre de Bruxelles.

Bagnoli, Lisa, Salvador Bertomeu-Sanchez, Antonio Estache, and Maria Vagliasindi. 2020. "Are the Poor Better Off with Public or Private Utilities? A Survey of the Academic Evidence on Developing Economies." Working paper No. 2020-24. Université Libre de Bruxelles.

Bajari, Patrick, Stephanie Houghton, and Steven Tadelis. 2014. "Bidding for Incomplete Contracts: An Empirical Analysis of Adaptation Costs." *American Economic Review* 104(4): 1288–1319.

Bakker, Karen, and Max Ritts. 2018. "Smart Earth: A Meta-review and Implications for Environmental Governance." *Global Environmental Change* 52: 201–211.

Balza, Lenin, Raul Jimenez, and Jorge Mercado. 2013. "Privatization, Institutional Reform, and Performance in the Latin American Electricity Sector." Technical note No. TN-599. Washington, DC: Inter-American Development Bank.

Balliauw, Matteo, Peter M. Kort, and Anming Zhang. 2019. "Capacity Investment Decisions of Two Competing Ports Under Uncertainty: A Strategic Real Options Approach." *Transportation Research Part B: Methodological* 122: 249–264.

Bayer, Patrick, Ryan Kennedy, Joonseok Yang, and Johannes Urpelainen. 2019. "The Need for Impact Evaluation in Electricity Access Research." *Energy Policy* 137. https://doi.org/10.1016/j.enpol.2019.111099.

Bel, Germà. 2020. "Public Versus Private Water Delivery, Remunicipalization and Water Tariffs." *Utilities Policy* 62. https://doi.org/10.1016/j.jup.2019.100982.

Bensch, Gunther. 2019. "The Effects of Market-based Reforms on Access to Electricity in Developing Countries: A Systematic Review." *Journal of Development Effectiveness* 11(2): 165–188.

Bertomeu-Sanchez, Salvador, and Antonio Estache. 2019a. "Should Infrastructure Regulators Regulate Dividends? Hints from a Literature Survey." Working paper No. 2019-18. Université Libre de Bruxelles.

———. 2019b. "A Dataset on the Relative Importance of Public and Private Operators in the Utilities Sector." Mimeo, ECARES, Université libre de Bruxelles.

Boccanfuso, Dorothée, Antonio Estache, and Luc Savard. 2009. "A Macro–Micro Analysis of the Effects of Electricity Reform in Senegal on Poverty and Distribution." *Journal of Development Studies* 45(3): 351–368.

Borghi, Elisa, Chiara Del Bo, and Massimo Florio. 2014. "Institutions and Firms' Productivity: Evidence from Electricity Distribution in the EU." *Oxford Bulletin of Economics and Statistics* 78(2): 170–196. https://doi.org/10.1111/obes.12087.

Button, Kenneth. 2016. "Public-Private Partnerships: A Review of Economic Considerations with Particular Reference to Transportation Projects." *Transportation Planning and Technology* 39(2): 136–161.

Chang, Zheng, and Sock-Yong Phang. 2017. "Urban Rail Transit PPPs: Lessons from East Asian Cities." *Transportation Research Part A: Policy and Practice* 105: 106–122.

Cherchye, Laurens, Bram De Rock, Antonio Estache, and Marijn Verschelde. 2018. "Efficiency Measures in Regulated Industries: History, Outstanding Challenges and Emerging Solutions." In *Handbook of Productivity and Efficiency Measures*, ed. Emili Grifell-Tatjé, C. A. Knox Lovell, and Robin C. Sickles, 493–522. Oxford, UK: Oxford University Press.

Chen, Zhenhua, Nobuhiko Daito, and Jonathan Gifford. 2016. "Data Review of Transportation Infrastructure Public-Private Partnership: A Meta-analysis." *Transport Review* 36(2): 228–250.

Chisari, Omar, Antonio Estache, and Carlos Romero. 1999. "Winners and Losers from the Privatization and Regulation of Utilities: Lessons from a General Equilibrium Model of Argentina." *World Bank Economic Review* 13(2): 357–378.

Chisari, Omar, Germán Lambardi, and Carlos Romero. 2007. "Choosing the Extent of Private Participation in Public Services: A Computable General Equilibrium Perspective." MPRA Paper No. 15358. University Library of Munich, Germany.

Choi, Kangsik, and Seonyoung Lim. 2018. "Tariff Protection and Port Privatization: An Import-Competing Approach." *Maritime Economics & Logistics* 20(2): 228–252.

Chong Eshien, Freddy Huet, Stephane Saussier, and Faye Steiner. 2006. "Public-Private Partnerships and Prices: Evidence from Water Distribution in France." *Review of Industrial Organization* 29(1–2): 149–169.

Clarke, George, Katrina Kosec, and Scott Wallsten. 2009. "Has Private Participation in Water and Sewerage Improved Coverage? Empirical Evidence from Latin America." *Journal of International Development* 21(3): 327–361.

Clifton, Judith, Francisco Comín, and Daniel Diaz Fuentes. 2006. "Privatizing Public Enterprises in the European Union 1960–2002: Ideological, Pragmatic, Inevitable?" *Journal of European Public Policy* 13(5): 736–756.

Clifton, Judith, Mildred E. Warner, Raymond Gradus, and Germà Bel. 2019. "Remunicipalization of Public Services: Trend or Hype?" *Journal of Economic Policy Reform* 24(3). https://doi.org/10.1080/17487870.2019.1691344.

Cummins, Mark, and Robert Gillanders. 2020. "Greasing the Turbines? Corruption and Access to Electricity in Africa," *Energy Policy* 137(C). https://doi.org/10.1016/j.enpol.2019.111188.

Currie, Graham, Long Truong, and Chris De Gruyter. 2018. "Regulatory Structures and Their Impact on the Sustainability Performance of Public Transport in World Cities." *Research in Transportation Economics* 69: 494–500.

De Halleux, Morgane, Antonio Estache, and Tomas Serebrisky. 2020. "Governance Choices and Policy Outcomes in the Latin American and Caribbean Electricity Sector." *Utilities Policy* 67. https://doi.org/10.1016/j.jup.2020.101105.

Estache, Antonio. 2019. "Institutions for Infrastructure in Developing Countries: What We Know and the Lot We Still Need to Know." In *The Handbook of Economic Development and Institutions*, ed. Jean-Marie Baland, François Bourguignon, Jean-Philippe Platteau, and Thierry Verdier, 634–688. Princeton, NJ: Princeton University Press.

Estache, Antonio, and Emili Grifell-Tatjé. 2013. "How (Un)even Was the Distribution of the Impacts of Mali's Water Privatization Across Stakeholders?" *Journal of Development Studies* 49(4): 483–499.

European Court of Auditors. 2018. "Public Private Partnerships in the EU: Widespread Short-comings and Limited Benefits." Special Report 09/2018.

———. 2013. "Electricity Prices and Public Ownership: Evidence from the EU15 over Thirty Years." *Energy Economics* 39: 222–232.

Florio, Massimo. 2014. "Energy Reforms and Consumer Prices in the EU over Twenty Years." *Economics of Energy & Environmental Policy* 3(1): 37–52.

Foster, Vivien, and Samantha Helen Witte. 2020. "Falling Short: A Global Survey of Electricity Tariff Design." Policy research working paper No. 9174. Washington, DC: World Bank.

Frontier Economics. 2017. "Productivity Improvement in the Water and Sewerage Industry in England since Privatisation." Final Report for Water UK, September.

Gandelman, Néstor, Tomás Serebrisky, and Ancor Suárez-Alemán. 2019. "Household Spending on Transport in Latin America and the Caribbean: A Dimension of Transport Affordability in the Region." *Journal of Transport Geography* 79. https://www.sciencedirect.com/science/article/abs/pii/S096669231830142X.

Gassner, Katharina, Alexander Popov, and Nataliya Pushak. 2009. *Does Private Sector Participation Improve Performance in Electricity and Water Distribution?* Washington, DC: World Bank.

Gómez-Ibáñez, José. 2006. *Regulating Infrastructure: Monopoly, Contracts, and Discretion.* Cambridge, MA: Harvard University Press.

———. 2007. "Alternatives to Infrastructure Privatization Revisited: Public Enterprise Reform from the 1960s to the 1980s." Policy research working paper No. 4391. Washington, DC: World Bank.

Gómez-Lobo, Andrés. 2011. "Affordability of Public Transport: A Methodological Clarification." *Journal of Transport Economics and Policy* 45(3): 437–456.

———. 2020. "Transit Reforms in Intermediate Cities of Colombia: An Ex-post Evaluation." *Transportation Research Part A: Policy and Practice* 132(C): 349–364.

Goodman, John B., and Gary W. Loveman. 1991. "Does Privatization Serve the Public Interest?" *Harvard Business Review* 69(6): 26–28.

Grimsey, Darrin, and Mervyn Lewis. 2004. *Public Private Partnerships: The Worldwide Revolution in Infrastructure Provision and Project Finance.* Cheltenham, UK: Edward Elgar Publishing.

Guasch, J. Luis, Jean-Jacques Laffont, and Stephane Straub. 2002. "Renegotiation of Concession Contracts in Latin America." USC Law School, Olin research paper No. 02-7; USC CLEO research paper No. C02-22.

Guasch, José Luis, Daniel Benitez, Irene Portabales, and Lincoln Flor. 2014. "The Renegotiation of PPP Contracts: An Overview of Its Recent Evolution in Latin America." International Transport Forum discussion paper No. 2014-18.

Gugler, Klaus, Margarethe Rammerstorfer, and Stephan Schmitt. 2013. "Ownership Unbundling and Investment in Electricity Markets: A Cross Country Study." *Energy Economics* 40: 702–713.

Guzman, Luis A., and Daniel Oviedo. 2018. "Accessibility, Affordability and Equity: Assessing 'Pro-Poor' Public Transport Subsidies in Bogotá." *Transport Policy* 68(C): 37–51.

Helm, Dieter. 2018. "The Dividend Puzzle: What Should Utilities Pay Out?" http://www.dieterhelm.co.uk/regulation/regulation/the-dividend-puzzle-what-should-utilities-pay-out/.

Herrera, Veronica. 2019. "Reconciling Global Aspirations and Local Realities: Challenges Facing the Sustainable Development Goals for Water and Sanitation." *World Development* 118: 106–117.

Hyland, Marie. 2016. "Restructuring European Electricity Markets: A Panel Data Analysis." *Utilities Policy* 38: 33–42.

Imam, Mahmud I., Tooraj Jamasb, and Manuel Llorca. 2019. "Sector Reforms and Institutional Corruption: Evidence from Electricity Industry in Sub-Saharan Africa." *Energy Policy* 129: 532–545.

International Monetary Fund. 2018. "Public Investment Management Assessment: Review and Update." Washington, DC.

International Bridge, Tunnel, & Turnpike Association database (TollMiner). https://www.ibtta.org/ibtta-tollminer%E2%84%A2.

International Union of Railways (2020). "Railway Statistics Synopsis: 2020 Edition." Paris.

Jamasb, Tooraj, Rabindra Nepal, and Govinda R. Tilmisina. 2017. "A Quarter Century Effort yet to Come of Age: A Survey of Electricity Sector Reforms in Developing Countries." *Energy Journal* 38(3): 195–234.

Kosec, Katrina. 2014. "The Child Health Implications of Privatizing Africa's Urban Water Supply." *Journal of Health Economics* 35: 1–19.

Küfeoğlu, Sinan, Michael Pollitt, and Karim Anaya. 2018. "Electric Power Distribution in the World: Today and Tomorrow." EPRG working paper No. 1826.

Lee, Alan David, and Zainab Usman. 2018. "Taking Stock of the Political Economy of Power Sector Reforms in Developing Countries: A Literature Review." Policy research working paper No. 8518. Washington, DC: World Bank.

Lee, Paul, and Jasmine Siu Lee Lam. 2017. "A Review of Port Devolution and Governance Models with Compound Eyes Approach." *Transport Reviews* 37 (4): 507–520.

Marson, Marta, and Ivan Savin. 2015. "Ensuring Sustainable Access to Drinking Water in Sub Saharan Africa: Conflict Between Financial and Social Objectives." *World Development* 76: 26–39.

Mizutani, Fumitoshi. 2019. "The Impact of Structural Reforms and Regulations on the Demand Side in the Railway Industry." *Review of Network Economics* 18(1): 1–33.

Nash, Chris A., Yves Crozet, Heike Link, Jan-Eric Nilsson, and Andrew Smith. 2016. *Liberalisation of Passenger Rail Services: Project Report*. Brussels: Centre on Regulation in Europe.

Panayides, Photis M., Francesco Parola, and Jasmine Siu Lee Lam. 2015. "The Effect of Institutional Factors on Public–private Partnership Success in Ports." *Transportation Research Part A: Policy and Practice* 71(C): 110–127.

Pereira, Rafael H. M., Tim Schwanen, and David Banister. 2017. "Distributive Justice and Equity in Transportation." *Transport Reviews* 37(2): 170–191.

Pinheiro, Sampaio, Patrícia Regina, and Mariam Tchepurnaya Daychoum. 2017. "Two Decades of Rail Regulatory Reform in Brazil (1996–2016)." *Utilities Policy* 49: 93–103.

Poku-Boansi, Michael, and Greg Marsden. 2018. "Bus Rapid Transit Systems as a Governance Reform Project." *Journal of Transport Geography* 70: 193–202.

Reyes-Tagle, Gerardo, ed. 2018. *Bringing PPPs into the Sunlight: Synergies Now and Pitfalls Later?* Washington, DC: Inter-American Development Bank.

Saussier, Stéphane, and Julie de Brux, eds. 2018. *The Economics of Public-Private Partnerships: Theoretical and Empirical Developments.* Cham, Switzerland: Springer.

Sen, Anupama, Rabindra Nepal, and Tooraj Jamasb. 2018. "Have Model, Will Reform: Assessing the Outcomes of Electricity Reforms in Non-OECD Asia." *Energy Journal* 39(4): 181–210.

Serebrisky, Tomás, Andrés Gómez-Lobo, Nicolás Estupiñán, and Ramón Muñoz-Raskin. 2009. "Affordability and Subsidies in Public Urban Transport: What Do We Mean, What Can Be Done?" *Transport Reviews* 29(6): 715–739.

Solaymani, Saeed, Fatimah Kari, and Roza Hazly Zakaria. 2014. "Evaluating the Role of Subsidy Reform in Addressing Poverty Levels in Malaysia: A CGE Poverty Framework." *Journal of Development Studies* 50(4): 556–569. https://doi.org/10.1080/00220388.2013.841888.

Steer, Davies Gleave. 2016. *Study on Airport Ownership and Management and the Ground Handling Market in Selected Non-EU Countries.* London: European Union. https://ec.europa.eu/transport/sites/transport/files/modes/air/studies/doc/2016-06-airports-and-gh.pdf.

Stutsman, Chadd, Kelly Tzoumis, and Susan Bennett. 2016. "Evaluating the Competing Claims on the Role of Ownership Regime Models on International Drinking Water Coverage." *Environment and Natural Resources Research* 6(2): 145–155.

Suárez-Varela, Marta, María de los Ángeles García-Valiñas, Francisco González-Gómez, and Andrés J Picazo-Tadeo. 2017. "Ownership and Performance in Water Services Revisited: Does Private Management Really Outperform Public?" *Water Resources Management* 31(8): 2355–2373. https://doi.org/10.1007/s11269-016-1495-3.

UNCTAD. 2016. *Review of Maritime Transport.* Geneva: United Nations Conference on Trade and Development.

Valila, Timo. 2020. "An Overview of Economic Theory and Evidence of Public-Private Partnerships in the Procurement of (Transport) Infrastructure." *Utilities Policy* 62(C). https://doi.org/10.1016/j.jup.2019.100995.

Venter, Christo. 2011. "Transport Expenditure and Affordability: The Cost of Being Mobile." *Development Southern Africa* 28(1): 121–140.

Wang, Grace Wenyao, Kris Joseph Knox, and Paul Tae-Woo W. Lee. 2013. "A Study of Relative Efficiency Between Privatized and Publicly Operated US Ports." *Maritime Policy & Management* 40(4): 351–366.

World Bank. n.d. "About Public-Private Partnerships." https://ppp.worldbank.org/public-private-partnership/about-public-private-partnerships.

———. 2019. *Who Sponsors Infrastructure Projects? Disentangling Public and Private Contributions.* Washington, DC.

Worthington, Andrew. 2014. "A Review of Frontier Approaches to Efficiency and Productivity Measurement in Urban Water Utilities." *Urban Water Journal* 11(1): 55–73.

Xiao, Yibin, Adolf K. Y. Ng, Hangjun Yang, and Xiaowen Fu. 2012. "An Analysis of the Dynamics of Ownership, Capacity Investments and Pricing Structure of Ports." *Transport Reviews* 32(5): 629–652.

12

PRICE CAP REGULATION
OF INFRASTRUCTURE

Sock-Yong Phang

Infrastructure has specific features that distinguish it from most other industries: heavy specialized investments, significant economies of scale and scope, and production of essential services (Gómez-Ibáñez 2003). As discussed in chapter 11, the restructuring and privatization of infrastructure sectors have involved numerous policy trade-offs that affect firms' behavior and industry performance. Estache argues that rather than ownership, the quality of regulation and associated institutions seems to matter more for industry performance and success in the longer term. This chapter focuses on price regulation, specifically on the choice between the two most popular forms of price regulation for infrastructure services: rate-of-return (ROR) regulation and price cap regulation (PCR).

When investor-owned infrastructure companies have a high degree of market power, an important mandate of the regulatory authority is to pursue the public interest by ensuring that prices are just and reasonable. Since prices and quality of services can be set in numerous ways, such a broadly defined objective lends itself to various interpretations. The evaluation of outcomes of price regulation will depend on the clarity of objectives and priority accorded to different objectives. There are at least four potentially conflicting objectives in price regulation of infrastructure: financial sustainability of the regulated firm, allocative efficiency, productive efficiency, and social equity (access and affordability).[1] No regulatory scheme can afford to pursue one goal single-mindedly; to the extent the regulatory authority has additional concerns, these can compromise the achievement of its primary goal.

The United States has traditionally used ROR regulation to promote firms' financial viability and an industry's ability to raise funds to finance future investments. In the 1980s, the United Kingdom privatized its state-owned utilities (as well as numerous other state-owned enterprises) and pioneered the use of PCR as a simpler, less restrictive solution that would simultaneously provide incentives for efficiency.

PCR has turned out to be by far the most important regulatory innovation in the past four decades. Since its first major implementation in 1984, when the U.K. government privatized British Telecom, it has profoundly transformed the infrastructure regulatory landscape. This chapter begins with a brief intellectual history of PCR, its advantages over traditional ROR regulation, and its pervasive adoption globally. (While regulation via a contractual approach is an alternative to ROR and PCR, the focus here is on regulation of prices and quality of large investor-owned infrastructure companies with long expected lives, sunk costs, and complex networks. In such a context, the contractual approach for public-private partnerships as discussed in chapter 11 is unworkable.[2])

We then seek to answer the following question: if PCR is superior to ROR regulation, why is there a continued preference for ROR regulation in some sectors and jurisdictions; that is, why has ROR regulation not been replaced completely? It turns out that a number of challenges can arise when regulators need to be concerned with objectives other than efficiency. We use three case studies of PCR to illustrate the challenges: the U.K. utilities sector, the California electricity crisis, and the public transport sector in Singapore. The PCR of U.K. utilities was a success, as big opportunities for efficiency gains of various sorts were realized in telecoms, electricity, gas, and water. However, the biased distribution of those gains in favor of investors became a source of major contention. California's electricity crisis taught us that regulators could not pursue efficiency almost exclusively and ignore financial viability without putting the government at risk of a US$40 billion bailout of the industry. Singapore's public transport PCR shows what happened when important social and political objectives were added to PCR's responsibilities. The chapter concludes with a discussion of more recent developments that attempt to incorporate more flexible efficiency incentives and options.

PCR: A Brief History

The United States, which has a long history of privatized utilities, has traditionally used ROR regulation to ensure that the tariffs charged allow regulated firms to remain financially viable and that the industry can attract funds to finance future investments. Under ROR, the regulator determines the revenue required to allow the firm to recover its aggregate costs. The revenue requirement translates into a set of regulated prices (the rate structure) and quantities such that

$$\text{revenue} = \text{variable expenses} + \text{allowed rate of return} \times \text{rate base},$$

where the rate base (RB) is a measure of the firm's investments for which the allowed ROR is permitted. Only "efficiently incurred" costs are allowed by the regulatory agency to be included in the RB, and "inefficiently incurred" costs can be excluded.[3]

By the 1970s, ROR regulation had come under criticism in the United States for several reasons. As costs would be covered under this form of cost-plus regulation, firms would not be incentivized to minimize costs; this lack of incentive could result in high prices under ROR regulation. Moreover, Averch and Johnson (1962) hypothesize that if the allowed rate of return for the RB is higher than the cost of capital, firms would choose too much capital. This potential excessive infrastructure investment came to be known as the *A-J effect*.

For a multiproduct firm, the rate structure permits the regulator to vary prices and may require the firm to cross-subsidize across consumer groups or product types. Such cross subsidization often results in inefficiencies. The burden of regulation is high and often costly, as ROR regulation requires time-consuming rate hearings, administrative oversight of compliance, measurement of RB and regulated earnings, and knowledge of firms' costs and consumers' demands. There are also additional problems such as the risk of regulatory capture, firms' shifting of costs from unregulated to regulated operations, financial inefficiencies, and other sources of firm inefficiencies associated with ROR regulation (Liston 1993; Sappington and Weisman 2016b).

When the U.K. government under Prime Minister Margaret Thatcher privatized British Telecom in 1984, regulators adopted PCR over ROR regulation following the recommendations of the 1983 Littlechild Report commissioned by the U.K. government (Littlechild 1983). This report can be considered the landmark document that transformed utility regulation from that point. It recommended that the regulator should simply decree that the average weighted price for a basket of regulated services can increase by not more than RPI minus X each year, where RPI refers to the Retail Price Index. The X-factor partly reflects the divergence of the industry's expected productivity growth and input price changes from those of the general economy. Rather than reviewing prices or allowed ROR annually or as required, the regulator would specify X and the length of time for which the X-factor would operate before it is reviewed (usually four or five years).

By delinking prices the firm can charge from its cost and earnings, PCR provides strong incentives for a firm to operate efficiently and to invest in innovations as it retains the profits generated. The A-J effect disappears, and the regulatory burden and administrative costs are smaller than under ROR regulation. Littlechild (1983) also envisaged PCR to be temporary while monopoly power existed in the industry, as the intent was for privatization and deregulation to incentivize competitive entry of new firms. As he states: "Regulation is essentially a means of preventing the worst excesses of monopoly; it is not a substitute for competition. It is a means of 'holding the fort until the competition arrives'" (Littlechild 1983, 7). Competition, however, is not feasible in several infrastructure sectors; regulatory institutions have evolved alongside privatized infrastructure.

Following the adoption of PCR for British Telecom, the U.K. government used PCR for price regulation of all subsequent privatized utilities, such as gas, electricity, water, railways, and airports. The RPI-X limit was applied to average prices or total revenues, where X is the specified level of real decrease or increase (if it is negative). The U.K.'s privatization was considered a tremendous success, with dramatic gains for the industry, customers, citizen shareholders, and the government as well as the U.K. economy (U.S. Department of Energy 1997; Vickers and Yarrow 1991). PCR, which had been associated with the U.K. privatization success story, became a policy alternative to ROR regulation that had to be considered in reform of the utilities sector anywhere in the world.

PCR rapidly displaced ROR regulation as the method for regulating local telephone exchanges in several U.S. states, Australia, Europe, and South America (Sappington and Weisman 2010; Weisman 2002). A mid-2003 survey of regulators of network utilities from 36 developing and transition countries found that PCR was employed in 24 of them (Parker, Kirkpatrick, and Zhang 2005). By the mid-2000s, PCR adoption declined, as competition in retail telecommunications services in most countries had developed to the extent that services were largely deregulated. In contrast, PCR adoption in the transmission and distribution components of the U.S. electricity sector was relatively limited (Sappington and Weisman 2010, 2016b). A 2019 survey of 25 European electricity transmission systems found that 19 countries used incentive methods (mix of price and revenue caps), while ROR regulation was implemented in 7 countries (Council of European Energy Regulators 2020, 121). A recent World Bank study, however, suggests that ROR regulation may be better suited to developing country environments, where providing predictable returns to support large capital investment programs is the priority (Rodriguez-Pardina and Schiro 2018).

Challenges of PCR in Practice

What is apparent from surveys of price regulatory regimes is the prevalence of both PCR and ROR regulation as well as variants of incentive regulation. This part of the chapter discusses some of the challenges of PCR implementation since 1984. The three cases selected span different infrastructure sectors, continents, and time periods: the utility sectors in the United Kingdom in the 1990s, the electricity sector in California at the turn of the 20th century, and the urban rail sector in Singapore in the past decade.

The U.K. case demonstrates the powerful built-in incentive effect of PCR as well as the regulator's information gap on potential efficiencies. The California debacle highlights the importance of market design for complex electricity networks and the need to build in flexibility within a PCR framework to deal with the financial impact of various exogenous unanticipated events. The Singapore Mass Rapid Transit (SMRT) case shows the limitations of using PCR to deal with complex and frequently changing concerns (equity, popular acceptance, and other public policy objectives) as well as the need for clear service quality standards and adequate regulatory oversight.

PCR of U.K. Utilities in the 1990s

The experience in the 1990s of the United Kingdom, the pioneer of PCR, offered several lessons for regulators. The immediate and critical task for the regulator is to set X in the price cap formula. In 1984, for British Telecom, X was set at 3 percent with a scheduled review in 1988. Under this plan, British Telecom generated substantial financial returns that increased steadily from 9.7 percent return on capital in 1983 to 22.1 percent in 1988. In response, the regulator increased X to 4.5 percent for the period 1989–1992 and required British Telecom to provide a low user pricing plan. X was further increased to 6.25 percent in 1991 as an interim correction before the scheduled review for 1992. For 1993–1997, X was set at 7.5 percent. These increases in X together with increasing industry competition reduced British Telecom's earnings, and the regulator reduced X to 4.5 percent for the period 1997–2002. For 2002–2006, X was set equal to the RPI. In 2006, the regulator determined that competition had reached the point where extensive PCR was no longer necessary (Hauge and Sappington 2010).

Setting X and the subsequent reviews of X proved to be controversial in the electricity sector in England and Wales (Guasch and Spiller 1999). In April 1990, the historically integrated electricity industry was vertically disintegrated and privatized. Several simultaneous changes took effect: power generation was separated from transmission and distribution, horizontal competition was introduced into generation, and a power pool was established for wholesale transactions (Joskow 2008b). Following privatization, sharp increases occurred in share prices of the 12 regional electricity distribution companies (RECs), which generated intense public debate over their high profits.

The price caps for the RECs for the first period (X ranging from zero to –2.5 percent depending on the company) were allowed to run their course (U.S. Department of Energy 1997). However, following the first price review in 1994 and after the electricity regulator Stephen Littlechild had proposed onetime double-digit rate reductions and set X at 2 percent for the next period, there was an immediate sharp increase in the share prices of the RECs. Clearly, the regulator had underestimated the magnitude of the profits that could be achieved even with the price reductions. A takeover attempt of an REC (Northern Electric) and the REC's fending off of the takeover via borrowing to finance a stock buyback made transparent the value and financial strength of the RECs. In response to public outcry, the regulator launched a rereview in March 1995 and reset the price cap. The Water Services Regulation Authority, or Ofwat, had similarly intervened ex post and had also persuaded companies to voluntarily share profits after 1995 at the threat of more explicit intervention (Helm 2010).

After Labour won the elections in 1995, Prime Minister Tony Blair imposed a one-off windfall tax on the "excess profits" of the privatized utilities. Helm (2010, 310) describes this ex post intervention by the government as "a very serious setback" into ex ante PCR. Nevertheless, despite this evidence of the regulators' and the government's lack of commitment, the PCR framework survived under the Labour government, even as some of the excessive profits had been clawed back.

The U.K. experience with PCR in the 1990s illustrates that initial price and the Xs are hard for the regulator to estimate, especially in a context when productivity gains are uncertain as industries are privatized and liberalized. When implementing PCR, the regulator will need to determine the regulatory asset base,[4] project the expected demand, and forecast the costs of the businesses including the cost of capital, operating and capital expenditures, and depreciation so that expected profits would be limited. Price regulation would also require the regulator to specify performance standards and associated penalties and rewards for failing to deliver on quality of service. Although the above information requirements and regulation of quality may appear to be daunting, they are forward-looking in nature and could be considered less onerous than the historical accounting costs information required under ROR regulation. In a context where the regulatory information base is weak and the regulator has to decide between ROR and PCR, Laffont (2005) concludes that PCR may be the only option.

In comparison to PCR, ROR regulation has no built-in incentives for efficiency gains. But a key difference is that if the price is set too high or too low, the regulator does not have to wait until the end of the review period to correct it. With PCR, if the initial price or the X is set too high or too low, that mistake cannot be corrected until the beginning of the next control period. The choice for the regulator is between stronger efficiency incentives with PCR versus the possibility of correcting mistakes more rapidly under ROR regulation.

Moreover, if efficiency gains achieved by regulated firms during a control period translate into a higher X-factor in the next review, this occurrence may limit the firms' incentive to be cost-efficient. The efficiency incentives under PCR then become limited to investments, which have a payback period shorter than the length of the review period, usually five years. The five-year limitation is a major disadvantage in capital-intensive industries with long-lived capital such as utility distribution networks and might lead to inadequate commitments by regulated firms to invest in new capacity. Lengthening the review period would presumably increase the power of the incentive mechanism but would also increase the difficulty of getting the prices right and worsen the political and economic consequences of getting them wrong.

The ex post intervention by regulators and the government to claw back the unexpected onetime gains from privatization also shows politics to be as important as economics. However, despite the problems in implementation, PCR was a major step forward in offering an alternative to ROR regulation. Joskow (2008b) describes electricity sector reform in England and Wales as the gold standard. The magnitude of efficiency gains and innovations that were realized in the utility sectors under PCR in the United Kingdom would not have been achieved under ROR regulation. The U.K. experience also showed the rest of the world how PCR as a regulatory institution could be cheaper to administer and more transparent than ROR regulation, how debate and ex post intervention might work during the review period, and also how mechanisms could be set up to allow dissatisfied regulated companies to appeal the decisions of the regulator. (Chapter 13 demonstrates that while setting X is the regulator's most visible task under PCR, more must be done for success.)

PCR in California's Energy Crisis

Following the success of the U.K.'s electricity sector reforms, California was among the first U.S. states to restructure its then vertically integrated electricity sector and permit competition in 1998. However, the crisis that soon followed in 2000–2001 has become "the textbook case of deregulation gone bad" (Joskow 2008b, 18) and provides useful lessons for regulatory policy as well as market design and PCR.

As the California state legislature had expected competition to lead to lower prices, it placed a cap on retail price of electricity at 90 percent of the regulated retail rate in 1996. During a four-year transition period, consumers could buy electricity from their existing utility distribution company (UDC) at this capped rate (US$65 per mwh) or from a nonutility electric service provider. The three UDCs were required to be the default supplier and had to meet all demand for electricity not met by the electric service providers. To promote competition in the generating sector, UDCs had been required to sell their fossil fuel–generating capacity and also to purchase all their electricity from the wholesale market at uncapped prices; that is, they could not enter into long-term supply contracts with electricity producers to hedge their retail supply obligations.

This incomplete deregulation and the restrictions placed on the UDCs exposed them to untenable financial risks when wholesale electricity prices spiked in 2000. For almost a year, prices rose to more than US$150 per mwh and often exceeded US$350 per mwh. With retail prices capped at US$65 per mwh, UDCs were losing up to US$50 million per day and became unable to pay for the electricity they purchased. In 2001, the state government declared a state of emergency and proceeded to issue multiple rolling blackouts, freeze retail competition, and intervene to buy wholesale power, with costly long-term supply contracts negotiated by the state. In all, the crisis cost the state an estimated US$40 billion (Weare 2003).

There have been investigations and numerous studies on the causes of the price hikes that led to California's energy crisis in 2001 (Borenstein, Bushnell, and Wolak 2002; Joskow 2008b; Weare 2003; Wolak 2003). Flawed market design that facilitated market manipulators' withholding or diverting of electricity supplies to drive up prices was a key factor. The regulated retail price caps that coexisted with a deregulated wholesale market was another. (Other states had either deregulated or regulated both producer and retail prices.) This part of the chapter does not delve into the widespread fallout of the California energy crisis other than its implications for PCR.

Arising from the crisis, PCR perhaps became perceived as a higher-risk regime of price regulation than ROR regulation. However, the regulatory risk of PCR is dependent on regulatory policy design. PCR is a flexible regime and can be designed to deal with cost increases, regulatory demands, and unanticipated events. A more flexible formula that would reduce regulatory risk of PCR would be

$$\text{price cap} = \text{RPI} - X + Z,$$

where Z represents the rate of price increase needed to offset the financial implications of other factors impacting the industry. For the water industry in the United Kingdom, Z has been used to allow for improvements in the quality of water and the environment (Byatt 2017). In Singapore's public transport PCR, wage index, energy price index, and network capacity factors were subsequently incorporated (see below). Sappington and Weisman (2010) describe the use of Z to allow for adjustments arising from the financial impact of an exogenous unanticipated event. An event that would trigger Z would have three characteristics. First, the event would be beyond the control of the regulated firm. Second, the event would have a pronounced financial impact. Third, the impact would not be accounted for by other elements of the PCR plan. Examples of such an event would be a force majeure or an industry-specific tax change or legislation. Viscusi, Harrington, and Sappington (2018) view specifying a Z-factor in the PCR formula as necessary for avoiding the kind of difficulties California encountered:

> California did not incorporate such adjustments when it restructured its electricity sector, and so the restructuring unnecessarily encountered severe difficulties. With more appropriate regulatory policy design, many of these difficulties could have been avoided. Indeed, other states and countries since have managed to avoid many of these serious problems. (Viscusi, Harrington, and Sappington 2018, 677)

It is likely that the catastrophic failure of California's electricity reform in 2000–2001 negatively impacted PCR adoption in the transmission and distribution components of the U.S. electricity sector. Some jurisdictions, having experimented with PCR, ended with a return to ROR regulation. When comparing PCR with the widespread adoption of PCR in the U.S. telecommunication sector, Sappington and Weisman (2016b) suggest that slow and diminishing productivity growth, the more limited scope for regulatory bargains, and more limited potential for competition in the electricity sector were factors. They conclude that PCR is a superior form of economic regulation only in selected settings but not generally.

Newbery (2002) holds a similar view that PCR was superior as a transitionary regime for telecoms but that ROR regulation with laower perceived investor risk and cost of capital might be superior for core network monopolies such as water, gas, and electric distribution. In an extensive survey of economic regulation of power utilities in the developing world, Rodriguez-Pardina and Schiro (2018) find that PCR had questionable impact when directed at state-owned enterprises, which lack commercial incentives to respond. On the choice between PCR and ROR regulation, they advocated ROR regulation as being more suited to developing country environments where (despite the importance of productive efficiency) predictable returns are important for remunerating and incentivizing huge capital investment needs.

PCR of Singapore's Public Transport Sector

The experience of PCR in Singapore's public transport sector illustrates the tensions and trade-offs involved in meeting potentially conflicting regulatory objectives through price regulation: financial sustainability of operators, incentivizing cost efficiency and long-term investments, achieving mode choice targets, and ensuring affordability. Designing a simple PCR formula that could meet all the above objectives proved to be challenging.

Public transport is the dominant mode of choice for commuters in Singapore. The high-income, land-scarce city-state has long relied on draconian motor vehicle restrictions to curb both vehicle ownership and use. In 2016, the public transport mode share was 67 percent of peak hour trips, and the 2013 land transport master plan had projected for this share to increase to 75 percent by 2030.[5] Given the importance of public transport, its affordability, quality of service, and reliability rank high in the list of socioeconomic concerns. What is notable about Singapore's public transport PCR was not just the changes in the X-factor for each review period but also the changes to the PCR formula over time. Moreover, the regulatory process of PCR required public transport operators to apply to the regulator to approve annual fare increases and the fare structure, even when the increase was below the allowed cap. If the operators had been dissatisfied with the regulator's decision, there was no appeal mechanism.

Prior to 1987, the government ministry responsible for transport was responsible for approving fare increases, which were on an ad hoc basis. The independent Public Transport Council (PTC) was established in 1987 to regulate bus and train fares charged by the two private sector bus operators existing then and the state-owned operator of the newly built mass rapid transit system, SMRT.[6] The PTC's statutory mandate for fare regulation was to keep fares affordable while ensuring the long-term financial viability of the operators. The two bus operators were not subsidized by the government but had licenses to operate as geographical monopolies with universal service obligations; they were required to meet minimum service standards and cover their costs fully from fare revenue.

In 1998, and prior to privatization of the SMRT, the PTC adopted PCR. Recognizing the limits to productivity improvements in the bus sector and the macroeconomic environment, where wage increases tended to be in excess of Consumer Price Index (CPI) changes, the first price cap formula was specified as

$$\text{price cap} = CPI + X.$$

X in the formula was set based on the net effect of wage increases after accounting for productivity gains (Looi and Choi 2016). X was set at 2 percent for 1998–2000 and at 1.5 percent for 2001–2004 (table 12.1).

The initial years of PCR coincided with the Asian financial crisis, which led to an economic downturn and higher unemployment in 1998. The per capita

TABLE 12.1 Price Cap Regulation of Singapore's Public Transport Operators

Year	Fare Cap Formula	x	Fare Cap (%)	PTC-Approved Fare Increase (%)		
				Bus	Rail	Overall
1998			4.0	0	0	0
1999		2.0	1.7	0	0	0
2000			2.4	1.5	2.4	1.7
2001	CPI + X		2.8	1.3	0	1.0
2002		1.5	2.5	2.2	2.5	2.3
2003			1.1	0	0	0
2004			2.0	0	0	0
2005			2.4	2.4	2.4	2.4
2006		0.3	1.7	1.7	1.7	1.7
2007			1.8	1.8	0	1.1
2008			3.0	0.7	0.7	0.7
2009	0.5 CPI + .5 WI − X		4.8	−1.9	−1.3	−1.6
2010		1.5	−2.5	−3.1	−1.9	−2.5
2011			2.8	1.6	0.3	1.0
2012			4.5	No increase owing to fare formula review		
2013			6.6[a]	3.2		
2014			2.8[b]	2.8		
2015	0.4 cCPI + 0.4 WI + 0.2 EI − X	0.5	−1.9	−1.9		
2016			−5.7	−4.2[c]		
2017			−5.4	−2.2[d]		
2018[e]	0.5 cCPI + 0.4 WI + 0.1 EI − X + NCF	0.1	4.3	4.3		
2019			7.0	7.0		

Sources: Chang and Phang (2017); Gómez-Ibáñez and Gan (2016); Looi and Choi (2016); Phang (2016); official government statistics from the Singapore Department of Statistics and the Singapore Public Transport Council websites.

CPI = change in the Consumer Price Index in the preceding year; cCPI = change in core CPI that excludes items such as housing prices, cost of private transport, and items accounted for in the Energy Index; EI = change in the Energy Index for tracking electricity and fuel costs; NCF = Network Capacity Factor, which measures capacity provision relative to passenger demand for the entire public transport system (3 percent for 2018, 1.6 percent for 2019); PTC = Public Transport Council; WI = change in the national average monthly earnings in the preceding year, adjusted for any change in the employer's contribution to the Central Provident Fund.

[a]Combined cap of 2012 and 2013, 3.2 percent awarded in 2013 with 3.4 percent rollover to 2014.

[b]2.8 percent comprises 3.4 percent rollover from 2013 and −0.6 percent for 2014.

[c]With −1.5 percent rollover to 2017.

[d]With −3.2 percent rolled over to 2018.

[e]This PCR formula is for 2018–2022.

gross domestic product growth rate was negative in 1998, and recovery was anemic in 1999; under these difficult economic conditions, no fare increases were approved in these two years. An additional reason was the economy-wide reduction in wages resulting from the government mandating a cut of 10 percentage points in employers' contribution rate to employees' retirement fund accounts for 1999, which represented substantial wage cost savings for the operators.

During this period, the rail sector was restructured in preparation for the partial privatization of the SMRT and the entry of a second rail operator. The government retained ownership of the infrastructure, while the SMRT acquired the operating assets and had its operating license for rail extended by 30 years (Looi and Choi 2016). In 1999, the government awarded the soon to be completed Northeast rail line to the dominant bus operator instead of the incumbent SMRT. These industry restructuring policies paved the way for the privatization of the SMRT through listing on the Singapore stock exchange in 2000. The SMRT then acquired the second smaller bus operator in 2001, thus completing the transformation of the industry to a multimodal duopoly structure.

The industry restructuring and privatization of the SMRT had the desired effect of boosting productivity and profitability. A change in the CEO led to a new focus on converting previously underused spaces at stations to retail and commercial spaces. The jump in the SMRT's rental incomes and profits, however, led to a reluctance by the PTC to grant increases for rail fares. The claw back of profits arising from unexpected productivity gains thus happened during the annual fare approval exercise instead of being postponed to the next review period.

From the perspective of commuters, the SMRT's healthy profits, dividend payments to shareholders, and share price increases were incompatible with operators' annual applications to raise fares. In 2002, there was heated public and parliamentary debate on the "plus X" factor as price caps were generally "minus X," giving rise to the mistaken impression that it was a form of cost-plus regulation. In 2004, the minister for transport appointed a committee to review the price regulatory framework. The committee recommended retaining PCR but proposed an explicit wage cost component and a "minus X" term (Committee on the Fare Review Mechanism 2005). The formula was revised to

$$\text{price cap} = 0.5 \text{ CPI} + 0.5 \text{ WI} - \text{X}.$$

The Wage Index (WI) refers to the change in the national average monthly earnings in the preceding year; the weight of 0.5 approximated the then-prevailing wage component of the operators' cost structure. The productivity extraction, X, would be based on equal sharing of operators' past average annual productivity gains and set at 0.3 percent from 2005 to 2007. In 2008, X was increased to 1.5 percent for a five-year period, from 2008 to 2012. In addition, the regulator would use two other indicators to inform the annual review process and act as a reality check: the ROR on total assets benchmarked against companies in a similar industry with similar risk profiles as well as a fare affordability indicator.

From 1998 to 2011, actual fare increases that equaled the maximum permissible under the fare formula happened only in two years, 2005 and 2006 (see table 12.1). This fact was in part because of significant macroeconomic uncertainties during this period: the Asian financial crisis, the dot-com bust, the 2003 SARs crisis, and the global financial crisis of 2008–2009. In the face of these uncertainties, the PTC's concern over fare affordability outweighed its concerns over allowing fare increases up to the cap, especially when returns on assets of the SMRT were in excess of 10 percent (Looi and Tan 2009, 13). Another factor was wage cost savings arising from economy-wide wage policies that had also benefited the operators. In the face of adverse economic conditions, the government had cut employers' contribution rates to the provident fund in 1999 and in 2003. In response to the global financial crisis, the government had provided cash grants to employers in 2009 (12 percent of monthly wages on the first S$2,500) under a job credit scheme.

The year 2011 was a watershed for public transport in Singapore. More liberal immigration and foreign worker policies from 2006 to 2011 had increased the population from 4.4 million to 5.2 million. While this growth increased public transport ridership and fare revenues, it also led to overcrowding and long wait times for commuters. The decline in the quality of public transport services caused much unhappiness among commuters. In the general election in May, the ruling People's Action Party won only 60 percent of the vote, its smallest margin of victory since independence. In December, the train lines operated by the SMRT experienced two major breakdowns, sufficiently severe in their impacts on commuters to lead the prime minister to launch an official inquiry as to the causes. The Committee of Inquiry concluded that the SMRT had neglected maintenance and capital improvement of infrastructure and that regulatory oversight had been lacking. The government then decided to take over the rail operating assets previously held by the two public transport operators in order to ensure more timely investments in capacity expansion, replacement, and upgrading of the assets.

Since 2011, the government has made large investments to expand bus services and train capacity and improve rail reliability and has built new rail lines, all of which have been undertaken independently of the fare regulatory framework.

In 2012, the government appointed another committee to review the fare formula. Because energy cost had become a major concern, operators had requested to include an energy cost index in the formula. The price cap was amended to

$$\text{price cap} = 0.4 \, \text{cCPI} + 0.4 \, \text{WI} + 0.2 \, \text{EI} - X,$$

with the weights approximating the cost structure of operators. EI is the change in a composite index based on diesel costs and electricity tariffs. The cCPI refers to core CPI and is the CPI excluding the cost of accommodation, private road transport, and items accounted for in EI. X was reduced to 0.5 percent, and any fare increase not awarded in a particular year would be rolled over to the next (Fare Review Mechanism Committee 2013). In addition, a new claw-back mechanism was introduced under which an approved fare increase would be accompanied by a requirement for the operators to contribute 20–50 percent of the expected increase in fare revenue to the Public Transport Fund, which the government had created to provide transport vouchers to the needy. The return to assets test was discontinued because the government was taking increasing responsibility for operating assets.

It is ironic (for the operators) that after the inclusion of an energy index in the formula, an unexpected fall in energy prices during the review period (2013–2017) depressed the fare cap, leading to the need to cut fares in 2015, 2016, and 2017. Table 12.1 shows that between 1998 and 2017, there were five years of zero fare increases, five years of fare cuts, seven years of fare increases that were below the permitted cap, and only three years when a fare increase matched the permitted cap (2005, 2006, and 2014). The transport minister opined, "If we had strictly followed PTC's fare formula, the operators would have been better able to cover the costs of the intensified maintenance" (Tan 2019). Instead, the minister revealed that by 2019, subsidies to the public transport sector were more than 30 percent of operating expenditures. The need for government subsidies as a result of mounting losses led to the eventual delisting of the SMRT from the Singapore stock exchange in 2016 (Chang and Phang 2017). The SMRT is now a wholly owned company of Temasek Holdings, a government-owned investment company.

Under new bus and rail contracting models, fare revenue risk has been gradually transferred from the operators to the government. In 2016, the bus contracting model was adopted, which gradually brought all public buses and related infrastructure under government ownership. Public transport operators bid on a cost basis for five-year contracts to run services along bus routes. As of November 2020, there were four bus operators operating 14 packages of routes. In 2016, a similar rail contracting model was adopted for a new rail line under which the government bore the fare revenue risk.

With three successive years of negative caps from 2015 to 2017, the price cap formula was again modified for the 2018–2022 review period. This time, a network capacity factor (NCF), or capacity surcharge, was included to address the widening gap between operating costs and fare revenue:[7]

$$\text{price cap} = 0.5c\text{CPI} + 0.4\,\text{WI} + 0.1\text{EI} - 0.1\% + \text{NCF}.$$

The NCF is a measure of capacity provision relative to passenger demand for the entire public transport system and was determined by the PTC to be 3 percent for 2018 and 1.6 percent for 2019.

PCR in the Singapore public transport sector illustrates the challenges of price regulation and the subsequent impact of depressed fares on quality of services, investments in maintenance and capacity expansion, and financial sustainability of private operators. In the past decade, from being a duopoly industry regulated by PCR, the sector has been transformed to one with assets owned by the government, 30 percent operating subsidies, and the use of shorter-term contracting. PCR has survived as a fare-setting mechanism, with its primary role no longer to incentivize cost efficiency of regulated firms but instead to determine the share of fare revenue in overall costs of public transport service provision.

Catalytic Effect of PCR

The most important contribution of PCR to regulatory economics and practice may lie not so much in the basic CPI-X formula but rather in focusing attention on informational problems and hence the role of incentives. Among incentive regulation methods, PCR can be considered the most widely used. The global experience with PCR catalyzed research on asymmetric information, uncertainty and risk, and mechanism design. Four incentive regulatory mechanisms that have been implemented as a result are earnings sharing, modified price cap formula, performance-based regulation, and menu regulation.[8]

Earnings or Profits Sharing

As cost does not feature in the simple version of the PCR formula, it can lead to volatile earnings. To avoid the need for claw backs or excessive financial losses, regulators may stipulate earnings or profits sharing. For example, the regulator may specify a range for RORs, a floor of 5 percent and a cap of 12 percent, for which the firm can keep 100 percent of its profits (equivalent to PCR). An ROR that is higher than the upper bound will be required to be shared with customers, say through price reductions. When realized RORs fall below the lower bound, the regulator would allow for price increases to increase earnings (Hauge and Sappington 2010). Under PCR, X in the formula could vary according to some measure of output or profits. Alternatively, an upper bound could be specified for profit levels, after which the regulation switches to a profit-sharing scheme (Phang 2016).

Modified PCR

Another approach for mitigating earnings risk is to modify the basic PCR formula to allow for cost pass-through clauses, exogenous events, and changes in required investment. A more general price cap formula may take the following form:

$$\text{price cap} = CPI - X + Z + K,$$

where the Z-factor permits adjustments in response to certain changes in the firm's costs (or revenues) for unusual, exogenous events; the K-factor compensates the firm for investment costs exceeding the historic or expected levels of investment during the review period (Sappington and Weisman 2016a). This hybrid formulation reflects the evolution of the public transport fare formula in Singapore.

Performance-Based Regulation

Since 2006, the Australian Energy Regulator has instituted a framework of performance-based regulation that incentivizes energy transmission and distribution networks through a system of rewards and penalties for a set of performance targets. Similar to ROR regulation, the Australian Energy Regulator reviews, on a regular basis, the proposed operating and capital expenditure plans and revenue allowances that each network business will require to meet its predefined service and reliability targets at the start of each regulatory period. In addition, the Australian Energy Regulator adopts efficiency benefit-sharing schemes under which a network that delivers efficiencies beyond those forecasted and approved by the regulator enjoys the financial benefit for a short period (five years generally), after which the benefits are passed on to the customers (Energy Networks Australia 2019). If spending exceeds the forecast, the business must carry the full difference itself until the end of the control period. The framework of performance targets extends beyond costs and includes rewards and penalties for service quality dimensions such as systems reliability and customer service as well as bushfire risk reduction practices and demand management projects.

From 2013, the U.K. Office of Gas and Electricity Markets, or Ofgem, began to replace PCR with performance-based regulation with an output-led approach known as the Revenue = Incentive + Innovation + Output (RIIO) model (Ofgem 2010). Under RIIO, companies are required to submit well-justified business plans detailing how they intend to meet the RIIO framework objectives. Similar to PCR, RIIO-1 ("1" referring to the first price control period) specifies a fairly long eight-year regulatory control period (longer than the five-year period under PCR). Similar to earnings sharing, Ofgem compares the firm's actual expenditures against the "forecast expenditures" for the eight-year period and uses sharing factors to allocate the difference between the firm and its customers. Instead of focusing on capital expenditure, RIIO focuses on total expenditure, thus removing the incentive of utilities to spend on capital expenditure rather than operating expenditures (such as service contracts for cloud computing). The firm bears a portion of overspending and gets to retain a share of underspending achieved. RIIO also incorporated a fast-track option under which Ofgem will agree to a company's price control settlements early if the company submits a high-quality business plan (for efficiency savings). In addition, rewards and penalties occur for various important performance dimensions (such as reliability of supply, connection speed, and customer satisfaction) as well as research and development funding. Ofgem is currently considering modifications for the next price control period, known as RIIO-2 (Jamasb 2020).

In the United States, regulators in several states and sectors have adopted performance-based regulation combined with ROR or PCR. This adoption has allowed regulators to better align performance targets with multiple goals such as grid modernization, reliability standards, integrating renewable resources, energy efficiency, and peak demand reduction (Trabish 2019a, 2019b; Whited, Woolf, and Napoleon 2015).

Menu Regulation

When forecasting expenditures, the firm is often more knowledgeable than the regulator about prevailing and future developments in the industry. The firm also has more information than the regulator about its own costs and managerial efforts to reduce costs or innovate. The regulator's uncertainties about firms' opportunities for cost efficiencies led Laffont and Tirole (1993) to propose a menu of options approach as a regulatory solution in the context of procurement contracts. Instead of a single regulatory plan or price cap, the regulator provides the firm with a menu of carefully designed regulatory options. This approach is useful when firms operate in different regions with different environments and also when firms within the same industry in the same location face different costs and/or industry conditions.

In a particular context, the options might be ROR regulation, PCR with specified X and no earnings sharing, or PCR with another X with earnings sharing. The menu of options provides the firm with an incentive to reveal information about its current and expected future costs. If the firm anticipates a significant scope to reduce costs, it would prefer PCR. If the firm expects to be financially distressed under PCR (and the regulator does not want the firm to exit the industry), it may prefer to be regulated under ROR or to be provided with the ROR option. Within the PCR framework, the regulated price could be partially responsive to changes in realized cost and partially fixed ex ante. Firms could be offered a menu of regulatory options with different cost-sharing provisions.

In the mid-1990s, the U.S. Federal Communications Commission provided a set of choices to regional long-distance companies, most of which chose the pure PCR plan (Viscusi, Harrington, and Sappington 2018).

In the United Kingdom, Ofgem and Ofwat introduced menu regulation in 2004 and 2009, respectively, to incentivize companies to put forward robust forecasts of their expenditure requirements (Oxera 2015a; Stern 2014a). For given mandated standards, companies are required to make choices on required future expenditure relative to the baseline proposed by the regulator that is associated with a corresponding cost-sharing rate. A company is encouraged to reveal its efficient level of costs in the following manner. The company enjoys additional rewards in the form of higher share of outperformance (higher cost sharing rate)[9] if it proposes a level of expenditure at or below the regulator's baseline expenditure forecast for the company. A lower expenditure allowance with a higher-powered incentive is more similar to PCR. A higher allowance with a lower-powered incentive is more similar to ROR regulation. The menu approach to improve the accuracy of expenditure forecasts is also incorporated in Ofgem's RIIO-1.[10] While it appears that menu regulation has become an established regulatory practice in the United Kingdom, few applications of menu regulation are in place internationally (Oxera 2015a).

Conclusions

The above discussion on developments in the past two decades shows that regulatory regimes of infrastructure in developed countries have evolved into hybrids and frameworks requiring significant amounts of resources and regulatory capacity. In developing countries, however, regulatory capacity may be in short supply. In his 2005 book, *Regulation and Development*, Jean-Jacques Laffont stressed the importance of context in the choice of regulatory regimes and that infrastructure regulation in developing countries faces problems fundamentally different from those in developed countries.

While infrastructure investment needs are huge in developing countries, institutional weaknesses remain obstacles to private investments. Estache and Wren-Lewis (2009) consider institutional failures in the following areas: limited regulatory capacity, limited accountability, limited commitment, and limited fiscal efficiency. They argue that different types of institutional weaknesses call for different regulatory solutions. Moreover, besides being country-dependent, the optimal solution will also change as the country develops. Where price regulation is concerned, when limited regulatory capacity precludes reliable costs observations and historical information, PCR may be the only option to start with. Guasch, Laffont, and Straub (2008) observe that PCR was used in 75 percent of Latin American infrastructure concessions,[11] with regulators not anticipating the full range of implications. The resulting high incidence of renegotiation led them to argue for reconsidering ROR regulation or at least adopting a hybrid PCR with several cost pass-through clauses in countries with volatile environments and weak regulatory capacity. With these regulatory challenges, it is perhaps not surprising that state-owned enterprises are viewed in some jurisdictions as being the superior alternative to private regulated monopolies (see chapter 14).

This chapter provides a broad overview of the evolution of PCR, which has developed apace since Littlechild proposed the simple formula to privatize British Telecom in 1983. Indeed, PCR has been implemented and adapted across several infrastructure sectors and globally as well. Not surprisingly, it has led to a rich and growing body of theoretical literature in a variety of areas, including asymmetric information, mechanism design, incentive regulation, and institutional limitations. However, as this chapter demonstrates, PCR is not a panacea. Laffont (2005) shows that whether PCR ought to be adopted in any given situation depends on country-specific factors as well as regulatory objectives. What is clear is that the regulator must be acutely aware of all these elements in order to determine whether PCR is the most appropriate way forward in any given situation.

Summary

- Cost of service and price cap are the two most popular strategies for regulating the prices charged by infrastructure monopolies that are too complex to be regulated by concession contracts.
- The choice between cost of service and price cap depends on whether maintaining the firm's ability to raise capital is more important than improving its technical efficiency.

- Regulatory agencies should not pursue either the financial or the efficiency goal exclusively, however, and should avoid the confusion caused by the assumption of too much responsibility for goals that have little to do with the control of a monopoly.

Notes

1. Rodriguez-Pardina and Schiro (2018) provide a discussion of the potential conflicts.
2. For discussions of the contractual approach, see chapter 11 on public-private partnership contracts and chapter 13 on the U.K. water sector.
3. In the United States, the RB model is a commitment device that supports private investment in infrastructure network industries, as investors enjoy explicit legal protection, although in practice some commissions do adopt a tough approach as to whether to allow certain investments to become part of the RB (Stern 2014b). Much controversy can surround the determination of both the RB and the allowed ROR. Valuation of the RB may be based on either original cost or replacement cost (each method has its pros and cons). As utilities are financed by investors through a mixture of common stock, preferred stock, and debt (of various tenors and seniority), commissions will determine the allowed ROR using a weighted cost of capital approach (Quackenbush 2020).
4. Following privatization of network utilities, the regulatory asset base (RAB) approach was initially developed and used by Ofwat for setting its first five-year price cap in 1994. The RAB provided comfort to investors that their investments would not be treated unfairly. Despite there being no explicit legislative backing (unlike the RB in the United States), RAB has developed into an important tool to signal regulatory commitment. The general formulation of RAB is net book value = gross current cost of assets + provision for depreciation. As assets were sold at substantial discount for network infrastructure industries in the United Kingdom, the RABs in the United Kingdom were set generally lower than the replacement-cost net book value, that is, RAB = net book value - privatization discount (Stern 2014b). The RAB approach was subsequently adopted by other infrastructure regulators in the United Kingdom as well as in other countries when setting price caps. Depending on the context, there is often no perfect link between the infrastructure firms' asset values and the RAB (Oxera 2015b).
5. These mode share figures do not include walking and cycling trips; land transport planners aim for 9 in 10 peak-period journeys to be completed within 45 minutes using walk-cycle-ride modes by 2040 (Land Transport Authority 2019).
6. The capital cost of the rail infrastructure is fully funded by the government. Looi and Choi (2016) provide a detailed history of the public transport system and the role of the PTC.
7. Public Transport Council Act (1987), Third Schedule.
8. Joskow (2008a, 554) viewed "modern applications of incentive regulation concepts" as involving "the applications of elements of traditional cost of service regulation, yardstick regulation, and high-powered 'fixed price' incentives."
9. The cost-sharing rate is the proportion of a cost underrun that the company gets to keep or the proportion of a cost overrun that the company has to bear.

10. The menu regulation approach leads to variations in regulatory regimes for companies operating within the same sector. This outcome is also observed for airport regulation in Germany (Littlechild 2012). This variation in outcomes is also consistent with the general framework for price regulation of airports advocated by Phang (2016); this framework can accommodate the heterogeneity of airport types.

11. Guasch, Laffont, and Straub (2008) used a data set of 307 concessions awarded in Latin America from 1989 to 2000.

References

Averch, Harvey, and Leland L. Johnson. 1962. "Behavior of the Firm Under Regulatory Constraint." *American Economic Review* 52: 1052–1069.

Borenstein, Severin, James B. Bushnell, and Frank A. Wolak. 2002. "Measuring Market Inefficiencies in California's Restructured Wholesale Electricity Market." *American Economic Review* 92(5): 1376–1405.

Byatt, Ian. 2017. "25 Years of Regulation of Water Services: Looking Backwards & Forwards." *Utilities Policy* 48: 103–108.

A. Gómez-Ibáñez and Zhi Liu. Cambridge, MA: Lincoln Institute of Land Policy.

Chang, Zhang, and Sock-Yong Phang. 2017. "Urban Rail Transit PPPs: Lessons from East Asian Cities." *Transportation Research Part A* 105:106–122.

Committee on the Fare Review Mechanism. 2005. "Report of the Committee on the Fare Review Mechanism." Singapore: Ministry for Transport (February).

Council of European Energy Regulators. 2020. "Report on Regulatory Frameworks for European Energy Networks 2019." Brussels: CEER. https://www.ceer.eu/documents/104400/-/-/27978c4f-4768-39ad-65dd-70625b7ca2e6.

Energy Networks Australia. 2019. "Rewarding Performance: How Customers Benefit from Incentive-Based Regulation." Melbourne, Victoria: Energy Networks Australia.

Estache, Antonio, and Liam Wren-Lewis. 2009. "Toward a Theory of Regulation for Developing Countries: Following Jean-Jacques Laffont's Lead." *Journal of Economic Literature* 47(3): 729–770.

Fare Review Mechanism Committee. 2013. "Affordable Fares, Sustainable Public Transport: The Fare Review Mechanism Committee Report." Singapore: Ministry of Transport.

Gómez-Ibáñez, José A. 2003. *Regulating Infrastructure: Monopoly, Contracts, and Discretion.* Cambridge, MA: Harvard University Press.

Gómez-Ibáñez, José A., and Benjamin Goh. 2016. "Restructuring Mass Transit in Singapore." Teaching case. Cambridge, MA: Kennedy School of Government, Harvard University.

Guasch, J. Luis, Jean-Jacques Laffont, and Stephane Straub. 2008. "Renegotiation of Concession Contracts in Latin America: Evidence from the Water and Transport Sectors." *International Journal of Industrial Organization* 26: 421–442.

Guasch, J. Luis, and Pablo Tomas Spiller. 1999. "Managing the Regulatory Process: Design, Concepts, Issues, and the Latin America and Caribbean Story." World Bank Latin American and Caribbean Studies. Washington, DC: World Bank.

Hauge, Janice, and David Sappington. 2010. "Pricing in Network Industries." In *The Oxford Handbook of Regulation*, ed. Robert Baldwin, Martin Cave, and Martin Lodge, 462–499. Oxford, UK: Oxford University Press.

Helm, Dieter. 2010. "Credibility, Commitment and Regulation: *Ex ante* Price Caps and *Ex post* Interventions." In *The Natural Resources Trap: Private Investment Without Public Commitment*, ed. William Hogan, 293–324. Cambridge, MA: MIT Press.

Jamasb, Tooraj. 2020. "Incentive Regulation of Electricity and Gas Networks in the U.K.: From RIIO-1 to RIIO-2." Working paper. Copenhagen: Copenhagen School of Energy Infrastructure and Copenhagen Department of Economics.

Joskow, Paul L. 2008a. "Incentive Regulation and Its Application to Electricity Networks." *Review of Network Economics* 7(4): 547–560.

———. 2008b. "Lessons Learned from Electricity Market Liberalization." *Energy Journal* 29(2): 9–42.

Laffont, Jean-Jacques. 2005. *Regulation and Development*. Cambridge, UK: Cambridge University Press.

Laffont, Jean-Jacques, and Jean Tirole. 1993. *A Theory of Incentives in Procurement and Regulation*. Cambridge, MA: MIT Press.

Land Transport Authority. 2019. "Land Transport Master Plan 2040." https://www.lta.gov .sg/content/dam/ltagov/who_we_are/our_work/land_transport_master_plan_2040/pdf /LTA%20LTMP%202040%20eReport.pdf.

Liston, Catherine. 1993. "Price-Cap Versus Rate-of-Return Regulation." *Journal of Regulatory Economics* 5: 25–48.

Littlechild, Stephen. 1983. "Regulation of British Telecommunications' Profitability. Report to the Secretary of State." London: HMSO. https://www.eprg.group.cam.ac.uk/wp-content /uploads/2019/10/S.-Littlechild_1983-report.pdf.

———. 2012. "German Airport Regulation: Framework Agreements, Civil Law and the EU Directive." *Journal of Air Transport Management* 21: 63–75.

Looi, Teik Soon, and Chik Cheong Choi. 2016. "An Evolving Public Transport Eco-system." In *50 Years of Transportation in Singapore: Achievements and Challenges*, ed. Tien Fang Fwa, 67–144. Singapore: World Scientific.

Looi, Teik-Soon, and Kim-Hong Tan. 2009. "Singapore's Case of Institutional Arrangements for Fare Affordability." Paper presented at the 11th Conference on Competition and Ownership in Land Passenger Transport (September). Delft University of Technology, Netherlands.

Newbery, David M. 2002. "Rate-of-Return Regulation Versus Price Regulation for Public Utilities." In *The New Palgrave Dictionary of Economics and the Law*, ed. Peter Newman, 205–210. London: Macmillan.

Ofgem. 2010. "RIIO: A New Way to Regulate Energy Networks: Final Decision." London: Office of Gas and Electricity Markets.

Oxera. 2015a. "Menu Regulation: Is it Here to Stay?" *Agenda*, April. https://www.oxera.com /agenda/menu-regulation-is-it-here-to-stay-revisited/.

———. 2015b. "Pass-on in Regulated Industries: What's in the RAB?" *Agenda*, March. https://www.oxera.com/agenda/pass-on-in-regulated-industries-whats-in-the-rab/.

Parker, David, Colin Kirkpatrick, and Yin-Fang Zhang. 2005. "Price and Profit Regulation in Developing and Transition Economies: A Survey of Regulators." *Public Money & Management* 25(2): 99–105.

Phang, Sock-Yong. 2016. "A General Framework for Price Regulation of Airports." *Journal of Air Transport Management* 51: 39–45.

Public Transport Council Act. 1987. "Singapore Statutes Online." https://sso.agc.gov.sg/Act /PTCA1987.

Quackenbush, John D. 2020. "A Cost of Capital and Capital Markets Primer for Utility Regulators." Cost Reflective Tariff Toolkit Primer. Washington, DC: U.S. Agency for International Development and U.S. National Association of Regulatory Utility Commissioners. https://pubs.naruc.org/pub.cfm?id=CAD801A0-155D-0A36-316A -B9E8C935EE4D.

Rodriguez-Pardina, Martin, and Julieta Schiro. 2018. "Taking Stock of Economic Regulation of Power Utilities in the Developing World: A Literature Review." Working paper No. 8461. Washington, DC: World Bank.

Sappington, David E. M., and Dennis L. Weisman. 2010. "Price Cap Regulation: What Have We Learned from 25 Years of Experience in the Telecommunications Industry?" *Journal of Regulatory Economics* 38: 227–257.

———. 2016a. "The Disparate Adoption of Price Cap Regulation in the U.S. Telecommunications and Electricity Sectors." *Journal of Regulatory Economics* 49: 250–264.

———. 2016b. "The Price Cap Regulation Paradox in the Electricity Sector." *Electricity Journal* 29: 1–5.

Singapore Public Transport Council. 2020. "Fare Adjustment Timeline, 2010–Current." https:// www.ptc.gov.sg/fare-regulation/bus-rail/fare-milestones.

Stern, Jon. 2014a. "The Problem of Repeat Regulation for Infrastructure Industries." 2nd ARAF International Economic Conference, Paris (May).

———. 2014b. "The Role of the Regulatory Asset Base as an Instrument of Regulatory Commitment." *European Networks Law and Regulation Quarterly* 2(1): 15–27.

Tan, Christopher. 2019. "Parliament: Higher Fares Will Be Needed in Face of Rising Subsidies for Public Transport, Says Khaw Boon Wan." *Straits Times*, July 8. https://www .straitstimes.com/singapore/transport/parliament-higher-fares-will-be-needed-in-face -of-rising-subsidies-for-public.

Trabish, Herman. 2019a. "Harvesting Hybrid Solutions from Performance-Based Rates: Not All or Nothing." *Utility Dive*, July 24. https://www.utilitydive.com/news/harvesting -hybrid-solutions-from-performance-based-rates-not-all-or-nothi/558226/.

———. 2019b. "Performance-Based Regulation: Seeking the New Utility Business Model." *Utility Dive*, July 23. https://www.utilitydive.com/news/performance-based-regulation -seeking-the-new-utility-business-model/557934/.

U.S. Department of Energy. 1997. "Electricity Reform Abroad and U.S. Investments." Washington, DC: U.S. Department of Energy. https://www.osti.gov/servlets/purl /544716.

Vickers, John, and George Yarrow. 1991. "Economic Perspectives on Privatization." *Journal of Economic Perspectives* 5: 111–132.

Viscusi, W. Kip, Joseph E. Harrington Jr., and David E. M. Sappington. 2018. *Economics of Regulation and Antitrust*. 5th ed. Cambridge, MA: MIT Press.

Weare, Christopher. 2003. "The California Electricity Crisis: Causes and Policy Options." San Francisco: Public Policy Institute of California. https://www.ppic.org/content/pubs /report/R_103CWR.pdf.

Weisman, Dennis L. 2002. "Is There *'Hope'* for Price Cap Regulation?" *Information Economics and Policy* 14: 349–370.

Whited, Melissa, Tim Woolf, and Alice Napoleon. 2015. "Utility Performance Incentive Mechanisms: A Handbook for Regulators." Cambridge, MA: Synapse Energy Economics.

Wolak, Frank A. 2003. "Diagnosing the California Electricity Crisis." *Electricity Journal* (August/September): 11–37.

13

EVOLUTION OF A REGULATORY REGIME

BRITISH WATER INDUSTRY, 1989–2020

Sir Ian Byatt

The editors of this volume have asked me to reflect on my experience as one of the key participants in the privatization and early regulation of water services in both England and Wales and in Scotland as a senior Treasury official during the years of public ownership of utilities; as an independent economic regulator in England and Wales, that is, director-general of the Water Services Regulation Authority (Ofwat) from 1989 to 2000; and as chairman of the Water Industry Commission for Scotland (WICS) from 2005 to 2011.

Politics and economics interacted within the U.K.'s regime. Water privatization in 1989 under Nicholas Ridley, secretary of state for the environment, was widely unpopular, being seen as Thatcherism. The regulator position was not a political appointment but needed well-developed political antennae. There has been a shift from political globalization to identity politics; regulation has evolved differently in the U.K. nations of England, Wales, Scotland, and Northern Ireland. Scotland and Northern Ireland now have their own parliaments/assemblies in addition to the U.K. Parliament.

The water and wastewater privatization in the United Kingdom was unique. Elsewhere, as in France and many other countries, it typically involved contracts to private companies to supply water services to municipalities, rather than the privatization of public companies. In the first three decades of privatization, customers saw their real (preinflation) bills rise by some 50 percent to pay for putting the industry on a sound financial basis and financing standards of water quality some 50 percent higher (Ofwat 2019; Pointon 2014; Saal, Parker, and Weyman-Jones 2007).

Historical Development of the Industry

Institutions and history determine incentives. During rapid urbanization in the early 19th century, the supply of water evolved in the hands of private unregulated companies. Parliament slowly came to recognize that competition was not sufficient and regulated private companies through preset controls over dividends. Sewerage was developed in the hands of the provincial local authorities and, in London, under the Commissioners of Sewage, later the Metropolitan Water Board.

By the mid-19th century, the inadequacies of private provision of a monopoly service became widely recognized. The large provincial cities, such as Birmingham and Glasgow, bought out private suppliers in their jurisdictions, substituting a public supply. Effective sewerage in London was achieved by the construction of Bazalgette's drainage system (Halliday 2009).

In 1974, following the postwar example of gas and electricity, the municipal suppliers were replaced by 10 public corporations (nationalized industries) organized by river basins. They also had responsibility for managing rivers. The existing private water companies, which were relatively small, were left alone.

Regulation of public corporations was subject to the principles laid down in the three Treasury-led white papers of 1961 (supplementary depreciation and part self-financing of investment), 1967 (marginal cost pricing and investment appraisal), and 1978 (corporate planning around a required rate of return).

Privatization and Regulation in the U.K. Nations

England and Wales

In 1989, the 10 English and Welsh water authorities were privatized as licensed water and sewerage subsidiaries of freestanding public limited companies (PLCs) in order to introduce private sector management into the 10 river basin authorities created in 1974.

The privatized authorities were joined in the regulatory regime by 29 private water-only companies, which were the remnant of the large number of private water supply companies. All companies operated under a 25-year license issued by the government. The regulator has the power to change the license, either by agreement with the licensed company or acting subject to appeal to the Competition and Markets Authority (CMA), formerly the Monopoly and Mergers Commission (MMC).

Scotland and Northern Ireland

Water services were not privatized in either Scotland or Northern Ireland; ownership shifted from municipal to government hands, thus remaining nonprofit. But they are independently regulated along lines similar to those in England and Wales. I have paid limited attention to Northern Ireland, although I took part in a working party while chairman of WICS. Sectarian politics greatly hindered any progress.

Regulatory Structure

The privatization legislation removed the environmental powers of the water authorities and vested them in the new National Rivers Authority, later becoming part of the Environment Agency. The Drinking Water Inspectorate became the quality regulator for drinking water. The economic regulator, Ofwat, was established to ensure that the companies could finance their social and environmental functions and to protect customers. The statutory powers were vested in the director-general of water services, who had an office, the Office of Water Services, to support him. Subsequently, Ofwat was transformed into a regulatory authority for water services, led by a board consisting of a chairman, a chief executive, and nonexecutive members.

Medium-term (five-year) price cap regulation was chosen because of its incentive properties; companies could keep savings until they were transferred to the customer by the regulator through lower price limits at the next five-year price review (PR). The regulated rate of return of the 1978 Treasury white paper became an allowed rate of return. There is also a provision for annual interim determinations to accommodate new statutory obligations put on companies. This provision has been rarely used.

Companies could appeal against Ofwat price limits to what is now the CMA, which would make a final decision. Two companies appealed against PR94 and two against PR99; there have been four appeals against PR19.

Continuous Changes and Regulatory Responses

Much of the crucial information required for price cap regulation did not exist at privatization. Marginal cost pricing was of little relevance and neoclassical economics failed to properly include changes resulting from unexpected "events."[1] Perceptions on gearing and risk premia have changed with experience, for example, leaving scope for the emergence of corporate and regulatory gaming and malfeasance. Further unexpected developments will doubtlessly need to be accommodated.

Fortunately, the regulator was given a wide remit within the statutory privatization legislation, enabling me and my successors to act independently to ensure the achievement of regulatory objectives in response to nearly continuous changes affecting the industry. Throughout my period in office, I set out my objectives in the form of speeches and regulatory articles. These are publicly available in my self-published book (Byatt 2019).

Achievements of Privatization

The finances of water companies were rescued from vulnerability to inflation. Price caps are set on the basis of water industry factors, not, as under nationalization, on the basis of macroeconomic objectives. Privatization coincided with the need to improve the quality of drinking water and wastewater to bring U.K. performance up to European Community standards. Following privatization, investment was no longer influenced by constraints on public expenditure; it could be financed in private capital markets.

Figure 13.1 shows that investment doubled after privatization and, subject to pauses around price reviews, still remains high. The graph also shows that the surge of publicly financed investment driven by the reorganization of 1974 was quickly truncated by the cuts in public expenditure following the United Kingdom's appeal to the International Monetary Fund in 1976.

Following high investment, the quality of drinking water and wastewater rose substantially; output, when adjusted for quality, rose by a half in the first decade of privatization. The quality measures relate to the achievement of statutory quality standards, not to any customer valuation of benefits. Drinking water is no longer brown, and the beaches are clear of sewage.

After the large gains made in efficiency in the early years of privatization, total expenditure has been maintained while output has been rising. The large gains also show, at successive price reviews, the differences between what companies thought they needed to achieve their objectives, what the regulator allowed for when setting price limits, and what the companies actually spent (figure 13.2) (Saal, Parker and Weyman-Jones 2007).

Prices to customers (ex-inflation) rose. The privatization settlement left them a one-third higher after the first five years. The net effect of the first two regulatory reviews was to stop the price escalator and reduce prices modestly. However, the next two regulatory price reviews raised them by a further third. The latest one, PR19, has reduced them significantly. Over the whole period since privatization, customers have seen their preinflation bills rise by some 50 percent to pay for

FIGURE 13.1   Industry actual total net capital investment, 1920–1921 to 2018–2019.

£ billion
(2018–19 prices using RPI FYA)

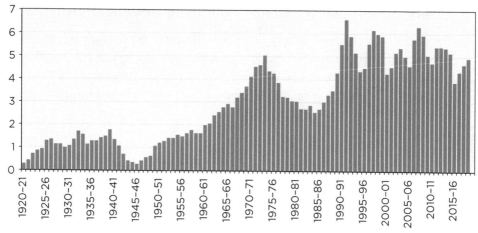

Source: Ofwat (1994).

Note: Original data for the period 1920–1980 included water and sewerage companies only. These figures have been increased by 8 percent (based on a long-term average of actual spend in 1980–1994) to allow for expenditure by the water supply companies over this period.

FIGURE 13.2   Historic total expenditure comparison of average industry request, final determination allowance, and outturn.

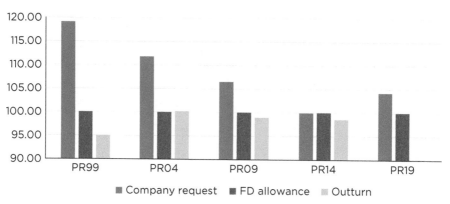

Source: Unpublished Ofwat data.

rescuing the finances of the industry and for financing standards of water quality 50 percent higher (Ofwat 2019).

Emerging Regulatory Issues Following Privatization

The performance of the industry since privatization is particularly impressive because much of that data needed for regulation were not available at the time of privatization. Moreover, new issues requiring a regulatory response continued to emerge with surprising frequency, even during the second and third decades after privatization.

An Overgenerous Privatization Settlement

The price limits set by the government at privatization were based on the assumption that investment would be financed by equity rather than debt. The large increases in regulated prices were designed to give the markets confidence that the newly floated companies would have the liquidity to deal with the backlog of investment and to meet the new standards of water quality.

This was an unhelpful inheritance. In the 1980s, when there was little use of corporate bonds, analysts thought in terms of an inflation-adjusted equity cost of capital, which could be as high as 7–8 percent. Bond yields were much lower; when the U.K. government began to borrow on indexed gilts/treasuries in the 1980s, the yield was around 3–4 percent. Then bond rates began a long decline; now the United Kingdom is borrowing indexed at a zero yield.

In 1991, Ofwat (1991) contested the assumption made at privatization by the government's financial advisers, namely that gearing (debt/debt plus equity) should not exceed 35 percent. On the contrary, we argued that companies could be 50 percent or even 75 percent geared. This view was derided by financial experts, but their arguments changed during the 1990s. By the new century, it was widely thought that utility gearing could be 85 percent or even more.

At privatization, price limits were set for 10 years. Ofwat seized the opportunity to trigger a periodic review of price limits in 1994, PR94, reducing the increases above general inflation for the next 5 years, from +4 percent/year to +1.5 percent/year, radically slowing the unpopular price escalator. At the next periodic review, PR99, we made an immediate 12 percent cut in price limits; both financing and operating efficiency were passed to customers.

Monopoly and Comparative Competition

It was recognized at privatization that regional water and wastewater suppliers would be monopolies. To prevent wider geographical monopoly, the legislation set up a special merger regime to avoid mergers of existing licensed suppliers; water mergers involving takeovers of more than £30 million required a compulsory reference to what was then the MMC, now the CMA, which was required to consider whether a merger would impede Ofwat's ability to make comparisons between companies.

Comparative competition can extend beyond sectors. In defending price cuts, Ofgem, the regulator for gas and electricity markets, has recently argued that "strong evidence from water regulation shows that investors will accept lower returns and continue to invest." The MMC decisions also helped preserve contestability and strengthened the hand of the regulator to collect and publish comparative information on companies' costs and performance on a regular basis.

Immediately after privatization, a French water company, Generale des Eaux, sought to create the Three Valleys Water company out of three smaller companies in the outer suburbs of London, which the company had recently bought. Ofwat decided, to general surprise, to oppose this merger on the grounds of loss of comparative competition. The MMC recommended that the merger be conditional on a price reduction. After further reference of the case to Ofwat, the government agreed to the merger on Ofwat's terms, namely a 10 percent reduction in prices after six years.

After further key decisions by the MMC, notably on the proposals from both Severn Trent and Wessex to take over Southwest Water after PR94, resistance to large mergers and agreement to smaller mergers on conditions of prior price reductions became the norm.

Takeovers were not discouraged when there was no reduction in comparators. For example, I had become concerned that Southern Water was dragging its feet with its capital program. My concerns were happily alleviated by its takeover by the much more dynamic Scottish Power; the new management quickly turned its attention to enhancing its investment program.

Comparative competition goes beyond the analysis of comparators or benchmarking. Numbers may not be large enough to yield valid statistical results, perhaps because they contain mainly both urban and rural territories. But incentives go beyond statistics. I declined to work through the trade association and got to know all of the companies, always being open to visits from senior management and learning about their priorities by visiting them on their home ground.

Privatization and regulation greatly increased transparency. I spent much time and effort to explain regulation to the public and how regulation could protect customers from exploitation. Ofwat collected and published information about the costs and performance of water companies. Analyses of economies of scale have revealed the familiar L-shaped cost curve, with a possible diseconomy of scale at the level of the largest company, Thames Water. Ofwat gave regular briefings to financial analysts. Academic econometric analysis was encouraged. This information was a crucial element in city analysis, that is, the work of financial analysts working in the London financial market. They built models applicable to individual water companies using regulatory information and compared performance on costs and dividend-paying capabilities. Such analysis was crucial to the ability of water companies to borrow on capital markets (Erbetta and Cave 2007; Pointon 2014; Saal, Parker and Weyman-Jones 2007).

In sum, privatization radically increased the number of experts whose livelihoods depend on the analysis of PLC's financial performance. This incentivized management especially when a company was performing relatively poorly, sticks being more powerful than carrots.

Better information made it possible for Ofwat to make its own projections of expenditure using different techniques for projecting current and capital expenditure. Operating expenditure and capital maintenance are directly financed through price limits after allowing for regulatory comparisons; new investment is financed by Ofwat's assessments of the industry's cost of capital.

The French Enter

Dating from the 19th century and earlier, water-only companies were supplying water in Newcastle, Bristol, and the outer London suburbs. Following privatization, many of them were taken over by three French water companies, Generale des Eaux, Lyonnais des Eaux, and SAUR (a subsidiary of the French construction company Bouygues), all with operating franchises in France and thriving international businesses with franchises of different kinds in many countries. They had their own experiences of working with political authorities.

Power lay in Paris, so I traveled there to visit their top management. In French style, they welcomed and respected regulation, particularly noting that, uniquely, we in Ofwat were setting standards of service to customers. These were standards of service delivery, such as keeping appointments and customer service.

The French parent companies were better managed than their recently acquired English companies and possessed better technology. The French began to radically reform the management of their new subsidiaries to the benefit of customers.

Meanwhile, the other water-only companies in Bristol, Staffordshire, and southeast England remained, including a new company, Hafren Dyfrdwy, formed to serve the existing water customers of Dee Valley Water and the sewerage customers of Severn Trent in Wales—a useful bow to the U.K.'s devolution agenda.

Ring-Fencing and Diversification

Ring-fencing involves both accounting separation and corporate governance. Privatization in England and Wales established a two-tier company structure comprising a holding company whose shares were sold on the stock market and a licensed operating subsidiary providing monopoly services to the public. The holding company had a main board with a chairman and nonexecutive directors, as did the operating subsidiary but with limited autonomy.

The boards of the licensed companies were scarcely independent. Holding companies expected surpluses to be distributed to them in the form of dividends. In its early days, Yorkshire Water provided a good example; the board of the licensed company was little more than the executive team reporting to the managing director.

The structure of the privatized water companies had been adopted so that the parent company could diversify into other activities. Results were not always happy. For example, Welsh Water's ownership of lakeside hotels damaged its public reputation, and Thames Water and North West Water signed contracts for supplying water services in Asia; they each lost tens of millions of pounds.

I was concerned about the effect that this diversification could have on the appointed business and thus on the interests of its customers, although legal separation of the licensed company from its parent provided some constraints on a holding company's recourse to the licensed company.

Ofwat strengthened the ring-fencing whenever there was an opportunity. This turned out to be particularly useful in the case of Enron's takeover of Wessex Water. Enron wanted to use Wessex and its expertise to develop an ambitious multibillion dollar world water enterprise to rival the French giants. I did not know of the wrongdoing that was eventually to emerge, but because of the ring-fencing, when Enron crashed and its bonds turned to junk, Wessex Water's bonds retained their investment-grade status.

The leakage of the profits of the licensed companies through payment of large dividends, rather than retaining them to finance investment in better quality, continued to worry me. In 1996, I published an article in the *Financial Times* advocating a separate stock exchange listing for the appointed companies (Byatt 1996). But my plea went unheeded.

Structure of Charges: Use Versus Ratables

The structure of charging is crucial to the incentives the water and sewage companies place on customers. There has long been a controversy in the United Kingdom about whether the supply of drinking water and the collection of sewage are social or economic services. Are they to be financed by taxation or by user charges? Privatization emphasized economics and incentivized monetization.

At privatization, most business users were paying user charges although with high fixed elements. Household customers paid for their water through hypothecated taxation; the base was the ratable value of their property. The ratable value was a property tax based on an assessment of the market rent chargeable in the 1970s, when the market was subject to statutory rent control. The privatization legislation forbade the use of ratable values after 2000, but no financial provision was made for any alternative method of charging other than to finance a metering trial on the Isle of Wight, a small island off the English coast.

Ofwat consulted widely on possible alternatives, including metering and different forms of household charge. We found different views in different parts of the country and different tenure groups. I concluded that customers should make their own choices based on relative costs.

To achieve this policy, Ofwat stopped discrimination against metered customers, ruling that household customers should pay no more on a meter than they would pay on average on ratable values plus a premium for the incremental cost of installing a meter. This premium was effectively zero where new buildings were concerned.

This policy reduced levels of metered charges; while some companies operated a parity principle, other companies were frequently charging significantly more to metered customers than to unmetered customers.

In England, household metering spread slowly and at different rates depending in part on the policy of the company. Some companies feared the financial risks of customer choice, and some, such as Anglian, promoted metering; French companies found it natural. It is still not complete; ministers, especially on the Left, have not been encouraging.

I lost the judicial review taken out by three local authorities, which argued that I should not allow companies to install any prepayment devices, even where customers wanted one. The judge ruled that companies had offended against the disconnections code by allowing them to "self-disconnect" without going through the mandatory processes of the code.

In due course, the practical effect of metering became clear. A study by Wessex Water showed reductions in demand of around 17 percent, irrespective of tariffs.

Measurement concentrated the minds of customers. In consequence, investment in water resources remained modest.

For political reasons, there has been little extension of household metering in Wales and none in Scotland; water services to households remain tax-financed, without incentives for customers. Celtic views differ from Anglo-Norman ones.

Imposition of Further Obligations: PR94

No sooner was the ink dry on the privatization legislation than Chris Patten, the succeeding environment secretary, decided to advance his green agenda by accelerating the implementation of the European Urban Waste Water Directive. This program implied a further large increase in water prices in Devon and Cornwall, where Conservative members of Parliament were under pressure from the Liberal Democrat Party—pressure that reverberated at 10 Downing Street.

With the benefit of hindsight, I should have insisted on regulatory involvement in competitive tenders for the investment needed for Southwest Water to achieve the new standards. The episode did, however, enable me to work closely with departmental officials in the run-up to the 1994 periodic PR; I had built up a good working relationship with Neil Summerton, the then undersecretary in charge of the Water Division of the Department of the Environment.

Neil chaired a tripartite group that also involved the National River Authority and the Drinking Water Inspector. The group went through environmental demands with a fine-tooth comb, halving incremental costs.

This was duly reflected in the prices set in PR94. Without the need to achieve higher standards, increased operating efficiency would have reduced prices. It later became clear that the 1994 settlement was too generous, and efficiency benefits were passed on to customers in PR99.

Water Shortage and Excessive Leakage: Yorkshire Water 1995

The hot summer of 1995 produced a mini crisis in Yorkshire, where the local company had made inadequate progress on the construction of a water supply grid. Yorkshire Water declared a £50 million dividend at the very time when the company was struggling to supply water in the Bradford area; it was obliged to tanker water up the Dales. Public anger exploded; the risk of standby points in the streets was combined with a hosepipe ban—that is, garden watering restrictions—and disruptive traffic noise at night.

Eventually the rains came, but Yorkshire's reputation was lost. Ofwat sent in a team to investigate, which concluded that Yorkshire's governance was deficient. I proposed that the company should reduce its prices, and after some discussion, the company concurred, transferring some £40 million to customers for the remaining four years of the price control period. A new managing director was appointed to the licensed company, more challenging and more effective nonexecutive directors were appointed to the holding company, work on the grid was accelerated, and leakage control intensified.

The situation in Yorkshire drew attention to leakage elsewhere. This focus was neatly exploited by the antiprivatization Labour Member of Parliament Frank Dobson, who widely publicized the new Ofwat figures on the leakage between treatment works and customers' properties. Building on company targets, Ofwat set leakage reduction targets, taking account of comparative company performance.

Corporate Form: Replacing a Failing For-Profit with a Nonprofit in Wales

Price cap regulation could be too tough for less well-managed companies. PR99, combined with the contemporary review of electricity prices by the Office of Electricity Regulation (Offer), boded ill for Welsh Water, which had bought an electricity company, turning itself into a multiutility named Hyder. Management did not believe that they could meet the prospective Ofwat and Offer targets.

There was a special administration regime that permitted the regulator to set new price limits to finance a new supplier in order to avoid disruption of service. Having fended off pleas by the Welsh secretary to save Hyder, I was nevertheless concerned about the possible market reaction. I need not have worried. The up-for-sale notice attracted two bids. One came from Guy Hands, who specialized in acquiring failing companies, turning them around, and selling them off. The other came from Western Power Distribution, a U.S. electricity company that wanted Hyder's electricity assets but not its water assets. Meanwhile, the management of the licensed water company who had opposed the creation of Hyder were talking to Western Power Distribution. When Western Power Distribution outbid Guy Hands, this management team bought the water assets with bonds financed in London.

For a corporate structure, the team chose a novel form of nonprofit called a *company limited by guarantee*. The company, given a Welsh name, Glas Cymru, has no shareholders but is controlled by some 50 independent "members" appointed from among prominent Welsh citizens who have no financial interest in the company. Lacking shareholders, the company's "dividends" would take the form of price reductions to customers. Not surprisingly, the proposal drew support from the new Welsh Assembly.

There was already a market appetite for bond financing for utilities and gearing of 75 percent or more. The chief executive of Yorkshire Water's parent company had previously proposed a "sale" of the appointed company "to its customers," that is, large-scale borrowing linked with a massive payment to the holding company. I had refused to agree to this proposal because it did not match the fit-and-proper person criterion needed to bear the responsibilities of an appointed water company.

The situation was different where the previous management of Welsh Water had resisted the creation of the Hyder multiutility and shown their ability to raise new capital. It had been feared that a mutual company would be less responsive to incentives than an equity-based company. Glas Cymru has proved to be a perfectly satisfactory supplier, responding to the incentives set by Ofwat. The people concerned were also important to the new firm's success: the finance director (Nigel Annett) had been a financial analyst in the city, the chairman (Lord Burns) had been permanent secretary of the Treasury, and the managing director (Brian Charles) was skilled at dealing with his customers.

Entry of Private Equity Infrastructure Funds

Following the 20 percent increase in prices at my successor's PR04, there was a wave of entry by private equity funds. Seven of the English PLCs were bought by global infrastructure funds without a full understanding of where the change in ownership might lead. As no longer listed on the London Stock Exchange, they were no longer subject to the U.K. code of governance for PLCs.

Meanwhile, Ofwat extended the franchise period from 25 years after privatization to a rolling 25 years. Companies could, however, still lose their licenses if they were shown to have failed to carry out their statutory duties.

Private equity infrastructure capital showed the hard face of capitalism, involving leveraged buyouts and short-term policies, namely high borrowing and high dividends, meriting widespread criticism for its lack of transparency and for its financial engineering (Kay 2015).

Two of the private equity–owned companies, Thames Water and Southern Water, have been found guilty of serious failures in the quality of wastewater treatment and fined heavily by the courts and by Ofwat, respectively:

- Thames Water was fined £20 million in Marlow Crown Court in 2018 for polluting the Thames River by systematic abuse of storm overflows, described by the judge as "flow clipping." Thames Water is the biggest U.K. water company, supplying 2.4 billion liters of drinking water per day to 9 million customers and treating 4.4 billion liters of wastewater per day for 14 million people. Its investors include pension funds and institutions from the United Kingdom, continental Europe, Canada, Australia, the Middle East, and China

- Southern Water was fined £126 million by Ofwat in 2019 for falsifying its wastewater returns for many years, £123 million to be returned to customers. Southern Water had manipulated its water sampling process, which meant that it misrepresented information about the performance of a number of sewage treatment sites. Southern Water had already been fined in 2007 for charging above its regulated price limits. The company has been owned by a private equity consortium, Greensands Holdings, since 2006.
- In a letter to water companies, Ofwat's chief executive, Rachel Fletcher, said the findings showed that "the company was being run with scant regard for its responsibilities to society and the environment."

The boards of private equity companies were largely committees of investors. Upon his appointment in 2012, the new chairman of Ofwat, Jonson Cox, raised the issue of board membership, arguing that the boards of licensed companies should take account of the full range of stakeholders involved. Principles of leadership, transparency, and governance have been subsequently developed and are now being enforced (Ofwat 2016).

Public Acceptance of Private Ownership

Meanwhile, public acceptance of private ownership re-emerged as a political issue. Customers like to feel that utility services are in good hands. They became increasingly suspicious of profiteering when infrastructure funds entered the industry and the dividends paid by licensed companies began to increase rapidly and unexpectedly. These suspicions led to siren calls for renationalization.

Financial markets liked higher gearing, especially when increased gearing was accompanied by higher dividends. The marginal cost of capital was consistently below the average cost of capital set by the regulator.

The scale of dividend payments has often outstripped the dividend payments of other companies listed on the London Stock Exchange. Meanwhile, customers considered that companies should retain funds for investment in higher standards. Why should a stable utility need a rapidly rising stream of dividends?

Yet, many of the more successful companies were those that worked with the regulator, using regulatory concerns to incentivize their management. Achievement of greater efficiency, they reasoned, was to the advantage of customers at the next price review.

Procurement of Major Capital Projects

In the first decade of privatization, high capital expenditure was required to achieve higher standards of water quality. Although beloved by politicians, high investment raises issues of cost-effectiveness. Left to themselves, companies tendered for the solutions, which they believed were needed to meet new obligations.

An outstanding case involves the disposal of wastewater in London. To deal with storm overflows, Thames Water proposed the Thames Tideway Tunnel, a new 20 km tunnel below the river, estimated to cost in excess of £4 billion involving a significant increase in customer's bills.

Ofwat initially questioned this plan, commissioning a study showing that more cost-effective solutions were available. The Thames Tideway Tunnel had been appraised against other options in isolation but not against a combination of options. But after losing European Commission infraction proceedings, ministers supported the tunnel; Ofwat did not press their reservations.

Further work revealed a more serious problem. Chris Binnie, a consulting engineer and now a visiting professor at Exeter University, concluded that the whole scheme was unnecessary. The Thames Water analysis depended crucially on their modeling of fish kills; it predicted more fish kills than could be found in practice (Binnie 2014). The tunnel is now under construction, with the usual cost and time overruns.

Eventually, Ofwat insisted on the use of competition but only for the cost of the capital required to finance the project. Ofwat is, however, now developing a regulatory approach that will require companies to use direct procurement (i.e., competition) for high-value infrastructure projects (Ofwat 2010, 2016). This is being implemented as direct procurement for customers. Where solutions build on existing systems, sunk costs enter into the analysis (Hull 2017). This approach begins with large projects and could be extended to smaller ones in light of experience.

Competition for freestanding projects would also achieve an objective advocated by Steve Smith, a regulatory economist previously with University College

London and now with Lloyds Bank, to avoid existing arrangements for investment appraisal creating a monopoly of ideas for existing suppliers.

The United Kingdom has acquired an overall reputation for high capital costs, delays to completion, and large budget overruns. As argued below, reform of the existing arrangements is overdue. Ofwat's introduction of market competition into the bidding process should also help address the time and budget overruns endemic in large investment projects in the United Kingdom.

Ownership and Regulation in Scotland and Northern Ireland

In Scotland, water services remained a municipal responsibility until 1996. Three water authorities were then created: two in the densely populated Central Belt running from Glasgow to Edinburgh and one in the sparsely populated Highlands. They were subsequently merged into a single body, Scottish Water, in order to strengthen management.

In 1999, a water industry commissioner, Alan Sutherland, was appointed to publicly advise government on regulatory matters, including prices paid by customers. In 2005, the independent regulatory commission WICS was appointed to set price limits for Scottish Water. I became the chairman of the commission, and Alan Sutherland became the chief executive.

To undertake its capital expenditure, Scottish Water had entered into a joint venture with engineering contractors, proposing an investment program that would have involved a massive increase in customers' prices. Sutherland and his staff showed that these costs were much too high. The commission set modest price limits, and the chairman of Scottish Water was replaced.

Investment by Scottish Water is counted as public expenditure. To alleviate this constraint, WICS, in consultation with the Scottish Futures Trust, explored ways to refinance Scottish Water as a public interest company, with governance similar to that of Welsh Water. This change would have given access to the levels of gearing achieved in England and Wales. This proposal ran afoul of the new Nationalist Party government, which was determined to avoid any semblance of water falling into the hands of those outside Scotland, as the government believed had happened to North Sea oil.

Scotland led the way in establishing competition for retail water services for business and public authority customers. This competition enabled many customers to avail themselves of better services, including a better understanding of their use of water on different sites. England and Wales duly followed some eight years later.

In practice, the devolved Scottish administration has not exerted ownership power over Scottish Water. Neil Menzies, in an oral communication, suggested that this may be because of the introduction of retail competition, under which external suppliers compete with the ring-fenced retail arm of Scottish Water.

The formal relationships in Northern Ireland, with the exception of retail competition, have been in place. But implementation of reforms has been bedeviled by internal political incompatibilities. Ultimately, arrangements in line with those in Scotland were established. The chairman of the regulatory commission is now William Emery, who was previously the chief engineer at Ofwat and the chief executive at the Office of Rail Regulation.

Negotiated Settlements: Constructive Engagement

Stephen Littlechild, a founding father of price cap regulation, has advocated the value of negotiation with customers (Littlechild and Doucet 2006). This argument has led to the introduction of a valuable new process into U.K. regulation.

In Scotland, WICS asked the Consumer Forum to advise on customer views and to negotiate an agreement with Scottish Water on its business plan, which WICS then embodied in the price limits set in 2015 (Customer Forum for Water in Scotland 2015). In England and Wales, Ofwat has encouraged companies to appoint customer challenge groups to inform the regulator how their views had been reflected in the business plans that companies have submitted at price reviews (Bush and Earwaker 2015).

These reports yield valuable information. Ofwat has fast-tracked companies such as Severn Trent that have submitted well-supported plans, while private equity companies have pushed for higher prices. But regulators must make final decisions on price caps.

Water Trading and Common Carriage

The state owns water resources in the United Kingdom. They tend to be concentrated in the north and west of England; consumption tends to concentrate in the south and east. The Kielder reservoir was built in Northumberland with the aim of improving supplies as far south as Yorkshire. But demand was alleviated by deindustrialization; the service industry uses less water than manufacturing.

Privatization opened the way to common carriage and other forms of trading, notably licenses for abstraction of water from rivers and groundwater. But companies based on river basins concentrated on constructing their own regional grids; transporting water is much more expensive than transporting gas and electricity. The Environment Agency wanted to cancel abstraction licenses rather than see them traded.

Trading may yet develop, as the successors to British Waterways, who run the canal system, now see commercial opportunities in selling modest amounts of water from their canal system. Trading does, however, involve establishing a marketplace for such transfers; this would need regulatory activity by Ofwat and the Environment Agency. To make it worthwhile, sellers would expect prices close to long-run marginal cost, while buyers will try to get closer to short-run marginal cost.

Future of Regulation

Trends in Ministerial Intervention and Regulatory Independence

The 1989 legislation privatizing the water industry took great pains to provide the regulator a wide remit. The director-general was an individual accountable to Parliament and independent from ministers (Vibert 2007). Resources for his office (Ofwat) came directly from the Treasury and were separately audited by the National Audit Office. The legislation also gave the regulator responsibility for appointing customer service committees, thus providing him with customer views and information.

From privatization in 1989 to the 1997 parliamentary election, Conservative ministers respected the independence of the regulator, declining to intervene over the discharge of my responsibilities. The incoming Labour government took a different position. Labour had opposed privatization; ministers were keen to intervene to show their hand over leakage from water mains. Ofwat had already set leakage targets, but the Department of Environment ministers wanted to set their own.

The ministers could not, however, do this unless I asked them to. To compromise, I agreed to tell ministers before setting targets but not to consult with them. On the advice of the Environment Agency, they would have argued for setting the same water quality targets for all the companies despite the evidence that the benefits and costs of water quality improvement varied across the country.

The water minister, Michael Meacher, also wanted to be involved in the details of the environmental projects to be financed at PR99. No tripartite group existed, as in PR94. This absence led to detailed top-down planning, including projects with dubious returns to customers.

The Labour government also curbed the independence of Ofwat, arguing that regulators were becoming "a cult of personality." The government legislated to convert the directors-general into regulatory authorities, whose boards were appointed by the ministers.

This action was followed by a further step back from the initial model of privatization. The Conservative prime minister, David Cameron, disingenuously announced that ministers would take back "policy." In practice, this move led to more ad hoc intervention, paralleling the situation with the former nationalized industries. The ministerial power of general direction was never used; discreet conversations took place on individual issues.

Ofwat's Priorities

The increase in ministerial interventions and the erosion of regulatory independence were perhaps inevitable, given the strong provisions of the 1989 law and the political sensitivity of water services, particularly in the era of ever-increasing tariffs and controversies over major capital projects during the 2000s. But there was also a sense that Ofwat may have brought some of the problems on itself by not thinking more carefully about its broader regulatory priorities and getting lost instead in the regulatory details. For instance, Ofwat spent a lot of energy in developing detailed performance standards for the firms that it regulated, requiring them to commit to and monitor seven performance standards, including water supply interruptions, leakage, per capita consumption, repairs to mains, internal sewer flooding, pollution incidents, and sewer collapse. But an independent review (Gray 2011) argued that Ofwat needed to reduce the burden of regulation it imposes on the water industry and work constructively with the other organizations in the sector.

The focus of Ofwat on the regulatory details seemed to have come at the expense of distracting the management from seeking overall efficiency gains. For example, the government has never had a clear strategy for determining the social obligations of the water industry, and particularly the quality standards for drinking water and wastewater treatment, which were important determinants of the industry's capital and operating costs. The existing standards resulted from the need to meet European directives, in order to avoid being labelled "the dirty man of Europe." But the process for changing the standards was not clearly specified, which seemed to invite discreet conversations between the ministers and Ofwat and add pressure to impose uniform or ad hoc standards, which were inefficient.

The ministers played the lack of clearly specified process by ear, as the issues arose. For example, Chris Patten realized that he no longer required Treasury agreement for government finance; he could impose obligations that the regulator would be obliged to finance. This independence threatened lasting damage to the aims of privatization. Such high-handed action has not been repeated, but, as seen over the Thames Tideway Tunnel, ministers still retain an overwhelming desire to see high investment.

In the 2000s, the Labour government passed an unhelpful act of Parliament to regulate competition, whose effect was largely to protect the revenue of incumbent suppliers. Ofwat relaxed its competition objective. When an independent supplier, Albion Water, sought to buy water from one licensed company and sell it in the area of another, Ofwat seemed prejudiced against Albion and was criticized by the Competition Appeals Tribunal—to which Albion had appealed—for producing tardy and poor evidence. Competition objectives should be reinstated.

The United Kingdom has an unenviable reputation for high-cost investment in infrastructure and persistent cost overruns. John Banyard, chairman of the Development Forum for the Infrastructure Conditions of Contract and also chairman of the Civil Engineering Standard Method of Management Panel, has argued for arrangements that would allow the chosen contractor, when achieving the specification at lower costs, to keep the difference while ensuring that customers would not pay for cost overruns by not adding cost overruns to the regulatory asset base (Banyard 2020).

Conclusions

The British privatization of water industry was unique, covering both water and wastewater and privatizing the ownership as well as the provision of water services. As with all new arrangements, these services needed to be tested by unexpected events. Politics and economics interacted. Water privatization was widely unpopular. The regional dimension mattered as political forces pushed for devolution to the nations of the United Kingdom.

The privatization of the water authorities enabled a considerable improvement in the quality of drinking water and much better treatment of the wastewater discharged to rivers and coastal waters. Efficiency has greatly improved. A regime of comparative competition has enabled a variety of suppliers to prosper, facing a variety of incentives. The unexpected events have challenged the initial arrangements and led to improvements. The British experience should help to guide future privatizations and avoid the backward step of renationalization. The development of comparative competition enabled the beneficial consequences of different forms of ownership and governance to be transmitted across the industry.

In the light of my 30 years of experience with the British model, I suggest some guidelines for regulatory action:

- Licensed suppliers should be free-standing bodies governed by an independent board with nonexecutive members, who must be both able and willing to challenge management productively.
- Government should clearly and publicly define the public interest where it may diverge from that of customers.
- Ring-fencing should involve all the transactions between the utility and any corporate owners, including payments of dividends.
- A dividend with a sliding price scale, whereby dividends above the regulators' assessment of the cost of capital would be accompanied by a reduction in prices to customers, should be implemented (Burns, Turvey, and Weyman-Jones 1998).
- Regulators should specify greater transparency, clarity, and simplicity, particularly from private equity infrastructure funds, concerning corporate ownership and regulatory accounts.
- Regulators should continue to separate activities that could be made contestable services (such as retail services and sludge disposal) or tradable services (such as water and abstraction trading).
- Regulators should encourage maximum competition for solutions to deliver environmental and other obligations, creating a market for ideas.
- Ministers should restore the independence of regulators, not seek to control them through a ministerially appointed board.
- Regulation cannot be static; thus, the slogan "light touch" is unhelpful. Regulators need to constantly identify the "right touch" regulation when the market fails, and then act decisively.
- Regulators need to respond to opportunities and take initiatives.

There are still those who advocate renationalization. This step would be a major error. I worked with ministers for many years in the Treasury. They never looked seriously at the management of nationalized industries for several reasons. Their terms of office are short, they concentrate on political issues arising from isolated incidents, and they like to see money spent on politically attractive projects. The Crossman diaries (Crossman 1959–1977) document the cursory cabinet discussion of the 1967 white paper on nationalized industries—repeated in the cabinet discussion of the 1976 white paper.

Summary

- The evolution of the regulatory regime in the U.K. water industry from 1989 to 2020, as told vividly through a personal account of a highly regarded regulator, Sir Ian Byatt, illustrates the real world challenges of regulation.

- In the first three decades after privatization in 1989, consumers saw a 50 percent increase in real water prices while the industry reduced its backlog of investments and realized a comparable increase in the quality of drinking water and wastewater treatment.

- The privatization was accompanied by the adoption of a medium term (five-year) price cap regulation. Since water prices are politically sensitive, regulators who hope to maintain their independence must be proactive in developing a political strategy responsive to their agency's particular circumstances.

- A regulator must make many other consequential decisions besides the determination of the maximum allowed price. These can include minimum standards of quality, permission for and regulation of ancillary activities, regulation of capital structure, supervision of nonprofits, oversight of mergers, and competitive procurement of high-value capital projects.

- Sir Ian Byatt concludes with a list of advice for regulators based on his 30 years of experience with the U.K. model.

Note

1. When asked what drove the policies of his government, Prime Minister Harold Macmillan replied: "Events, dear boy, events."

References

Banyard, John. 2020. "Financial Discipline for Water Industry Capital Projects." Unpublished private communication, December 2019.

Binnie, Chris. 2014. "Thames Tideway: Measures to Protect the River from the Adverse Effects of Waste Water Discharges." http://www.bluegreenuk.com/references/government _institutional/A2.%20Binnie%20-%20Measures%20to%20protect%20the%20river%20 environment%2022.10.13.pdf.

Burns, Philip, Ralph Turvey, and Thomas Weyman-Jones. 1998. "The Behaviour of the Firm Under Alternative Regulatory Constraints." *Scottish Journal of Political Economy* 45(2): 133–157.

Bush, Harry, and John Earwaker. 2015. "The Future Role of Customer and Stakeholder Engagement in the Water Industry." Report for U.K. Water Industry Research, London. https:// ukwir.org/new-report-on-the-future-role-of-customer-and-stakeholder-engagement-in -the-water-industry.

Byatt, Ian. 1996. "The Case for an Amicable Separation." *Financial Times*, January 9.

———. 2019. *A Regulator's Sign-off: Changing the Taps in Britain: The Monetisation of the Water and Wastewater Industry.* Birmingham, UK: Self-published.

Crossman, Richard. 1975–1977. *Diaries of a Cabinet Minister.* 3 vols. London: Hamish Hamilton.

Customer Forum for Water in Scotland. 2015. "Legacy Report: Lessons Learned from Customer Involvement in the 2015–2021 Strategic Review of Charges." Edinburgh, UK: Water Industry Commission for Scotland.

Erbetta, Fabrizio, and Martin Cave. 2007. "Regulation and Efficiency Incentives: Evidence from the England and Wales Water and Sewerage Industry." *Review of Network Economics* 6(4): 425–452.

Gray, David. 2011. "Independent Report on Ofwat." London: Department of the Environment, Food and Rural Affairs.

Halliday, Stephen. 2009. *The Great Stink of London: Sir Joseph Bazalgette and the Cleansing of the Victorian Metropolis.* Stroud, UK: History Press.

Hull, Mark. 2017. *Infrastructure & Utility Economics: The Economics of Sunk Costs.* London: Professional Economics.

Kay, John. 2015. *Masters of the Universe or Servants of the Public.* London: Profile Books.

Littlechild, Stephen, and Joseph Doucet. 2006. "Negotiated Settlements: The Development of Legal and Economic Thinking." *Utilities Policy* 14(4): 266–277.

Ofwat. 1994. "Future Charges for Water and Sewerage Services: The Outcome of the Periodic Review." Birmingham, UK: Ofwat.

———. 1991. "The Cost of Capital." Birmingham, UK: Ofwat.

———. 2010. "Time to Act, Together: Ofwat's Strategy." Birmingham, UK: Ofwat.

———. 2016. "Water 2020: Our Regulatory Approach for Water and Wastewater Services in England and Wales: Overview." Birmingham, UK: Ofwat.

———. 2019. "PR19 Final Determinations: Policy Summary." December 2019. Birmingham, UK: Ofwat.

Pointon, Charlotte. 2014. "Essays in the Measurement of Efficiency for the English and Welsh Water and Sewerage Industry." Ph.D. dissertation, Cardiff University, Wales.

Saal, David S., David Parker, and Thomas Weyman-Jones. 2007. *Determining the Contribution of Technical Change, Efficiency Change and Scale Change in the English and Welsh Water Industry, 1985–2000.* Heidelberg, Germany: Springer.

Vibert, Frank. 2007. *The Rise of the Unelected: Democracy and the New Separation of Powers.* Cambridge, UK: Cambridge University Press.

14

THE CHANGING ROLE OF
STATE-OWNED ENTERPRISES

O. P. Agarwal and Rohit Chandra

State-owned enterprises (SOEs) have been an enduring feature in the economic landscape of many countries. They constituted 23 percent of the Fortune 500 companies globally in 2014. In 2005, there was no single SOE among the top 10 firms of the Fortune Global 100 list. In 2010, there were 4: Japan Post Holdings, Sinopec and China National Petroleum (2 of China's national oil companies), and State Grid (a Chinese utility) (Sturesson, McIntyre, and Jones 2015). SOEs have been key players in enabling the economic growth and competitiveness of nations (Kowalski et al. 2013). In most cases, their primary mission is not profit maximization but the delivery of some public service or the realization of some social outcomes.

SOEs are generally defined as enterprises in which the state has considerable control. In most cases, this control comes through full or majority ownership. In some cases, such control has been possible, even with minority ownership.

SOEs can be owned by either national governments or by regional, provincial, or local governments. In fact, the number of SOEs owned by subnational governments tends to outnumber centrally owned SOEs, though they are smaller in size. For example, in Sweden in 2013, while county- and municipality-owned SOEs comprised 74 percent of the total number of SOEs, they represented just 34 percent of SOE employees and 40 percent of total SOE revenues. Similarly, 89 percent of all German SOEs are owned by municipalities but contribute to only 62 percent of all SOE income (Sturesson, McIntyre, and Jones 2015).

Mapping of SOEs

The presence of SOEs differs across sectors. They have dominated infrastructure sectors such as transport, electricity, petroleum fuels, telecommunications, and municipal utilities though to different degrees. In several countries, they also play an important role in the financial services.

SOEs have been prominent in the network industries as a means of securing equal access (Baldwin, Cave, and Lodge 2012), and nearly half of all SOEs are in such industries (OECD 2014). Thus, most of the highways around the world have been built and are maintained by the state or by SOEs. Many countries have adopted public-private partnership (PPP) options for the construction and management of highways primarily due to limitations of the public budget. However, publicly owned highways dominate the landscape. Rural roads are almost entirely built and maintained by public entities.

In the case of railways, two-thirds of the countries rely on public provision (International Union of Railways n.d.). Five percent of the countries do have fully private-operated systems, and 29 percent have some form of mixed ownership. Government ownership and operation are prevalent in most East European and Asian countries (with the exception of Japan), and the private or mixed ownership model is seen in North America, parts of Latin America, and Western Europe. Indian Railways is entirely owned and managed as a departmental effort, whereas China Railway is owned and operated as a 100 percent SOE (a comparison of Indian Railways and China Railway is provided later in this chapter).

SOEs dominate the landscape, even in the electricity sector. Until quite recently, they were largely monolithic and vertically integrated structures combining generation, transmission, and distribution under one enterprise. The need to improve efficiency and secure private investment resulted in some countries unbundling the enterprises into generation, transmission, and distribution functions. The private sector has been invited into generation and in some cases even into distribution. Out of 94 countries studied in 2018, 40 percent signed at least one private power producer for the generation (Bertomeu-Sanchez and Estache 2019). In the distribution segment, only 7 percent of 175 countries studied in 2018 had fully private operators; 30 percent had a mix of public and private operators (Küfeoğlu, Pollitt, and Anaya 2018). Transmission has largely remained under the state's control.

In the aviation sector, a dominant share of all airports is state-owned, with only a small share being private (Steer Davies Gleave 2016). Asia, Europe, and Latin America have been more active in the privatization of airports (Airport Council International 2016), whereas in North America, the Middle East, and Africa the majority of the airports are still owned and controlled by the public sector. Airline services, however, are dominated by private operators, though some major SOEs do exist, such as Air India and China's major airlines.

In the port sector in 2015, public operators handled 19 percent of the global throughput, indicating a reasonable presence of SOEs even in this sector.

A landlord port model has become prevalent wherein the state owns and manages the port land and infrastructure but enters into PPP arrangements for individual terminals.

With regard to municipal services, responsibilities primarily lie with the local bodies, though in several cases they have contracted the delivery of some services to the private sector. Patterns vary based on ideologies. While urban roads and urban rail are largely public, there is a considerably mixed pattern in the case of urban bus services, ranging from entirely public to entirely private. A mixed pattern of public planning with contracted private operations is beginning to emerge.

Thus, SOEs seem to dominate in the ownership and operation of natural monopolies such as electricity transmission, airports, urban rail, and roads, whereas the private sector is more visible in services that can be provided in a competitive market such as urban buses, airlines, and power generation.

Rationale for SOEs

SOEs have been set up and maintained for a variety of reasons. The primary objectives were not profit maximization. Six of the more important reasons for setting up SOEs are discussed below.

Providing Classic Public Goods and Services That the Market Cannot Supply

It is generally difficult to charge for the use of certain classic public goods. Some examples are national defense, judicial services, police, fire services, and public health. Typically these services, by their very existence, benefit everyone, not just the users. For example, the presence of a police system deters crime and benefits everyone. In all such cases, it would be unfair to allocate costs only to users, as nonusers also benefit. Therefore, it is not possible to pay for such services through user charges. Payment through general taxes is easier and fairer. Hence, such services are provided by state entities.

Further, many infrastructure services require large investments and have long gestation periods. Besides, several such services are financially unviable. For these reasons, the market cannot supply them. Large hydroelectric plants need huge areas of land that the private sector cannot assemble. Urban rail systems need large investments and are invariably loss-making. Yet, all these services are essential for human and economic well-being. Therefore, SOEs were set up to provide these services.

Protecting Against Price Gouging by Natural Monopolies

Several infrastructure services cannot be provided in a competitive market because it is not economically desirable for multiple service providers to supply them. For example, it is not economically desirable to have multiple rail tracks or electricity transmission lines between the same two locations. Hence, these services are generally provided in a monopoly market. In such situations, a concern invariably arises that private operators could exploit such monopoly situations by either charging high prices or compromising on quality. This concern about potentially high prices being charged by private providers has often led to such monopolies being owned and managed by SOEs. Thus, electricity transmission, airports, urban rail systems, and so on have tended to remain in public hands. Intercity rail systems in most countries have also been owned and managed by SOEs.

Improving Access and Affordability of Infrastructure Services for the Poor

Several infrastructure services are essential for everyone and therefore need to be affordable and accessible to all. Thus, public transport needs to be affordable, as it is critical for low-income workers to access jobs. Water and electricity are basic human needs and should be accessible at all locations and also be available at an affordable price. Several services are needed for the larger social good, and private operators do not find it viable to make them available at an affordable price.

In all such cases, the state has to provide the services, pay subsidies to a private operator to supply them, or use differential prices to make services affordable for a segment of the population. For example, the Phnom Water Supply Authority in Cambodia and electricity utilities in India charge a higher tariff for industries to cross-subsidize domestic use by households. Often, SOEs provide these services, as there is greater public acceptability of subsidies being paid to an SOE than to private enterprise. Further, if the provision of the service requires use of public land, such as depots or terminals for public transport services, it is politically easier for the land to be in the ownership of an SOE than to transfer it to a private entity.

Supporting National Economic and Strategic Interests

Often, SOEs have been set up because markets were unable to provide some of the foundational services needed for the development of nations, such as newly independent countries and developing economies. Examples include a nationwide electricity grid, irrigation systems, roads, ports, and a telecom system.

In Singapore, SOEs helped jump-start industrialization and spearhead development in the absence of private sector funds and expertise in the years following independence in 1965. Pioneering SOEs came up in shipping (Neptune Orient Lines), the building and repair of ships (Keppel, Sembawang, and Jurong Shipyards), and development finance (the Development Bank of Singapore, now known as DBS Bank Ltd.). The Singapore Refining Company catalyzed growth in the oil refining industry, while the Petrochemical Corporation of Singapore launched Singapore's entry into the petrochemicals industry.

In India, SOEs were established to serve as the commanding heights of the economy soon after independence. These included hydroelectric facilities, steel plants, and large heavy equipment manufacturers. At that time, the private sector did not have the capital to make the needed large investments and could not afford the long gestation periods. Similarly, private oil refineries on the east and west coasts of India, owned by Burmah-Shell, Caltex, and Exxon (known as Esso in India), had to be taken over by the government when new oil finds in Bombay High required rapid expansion of refining capacity, but the private owners were unable to make the needed investments.

Some services are assigned to SOEs for other strategic reasons. Broadcasting and telecommunications are among them. In many countries, TV and radio broadcasting are owned by SOEs, though an increasing number of private channels are being allowed to enter the market. In some small island economies, even airline services operate with SOEs to help attract tourists by charging competitive prices. Air Seychelles, South African Airlines, and Air India are a few examples of state-owned airlines.

Among other examples are SOEs in the banking and insurance sectors, especially when governments need lending to prioritize some areas over others. State-owned banks would align more readily with public policies than private banks, which would be guided by profits and risks. Predominantly state-owned financial systems (such as those of India and China) have become incredibly important in the last three decades as global financialization has increased. The coordination benefits of state-owned bank lending with policy priorities must be contrasted with the moral hazards of evergreening, bailouts, and overextension, a tendency that has been seen in many financial systems across the world that want to develop and grow with financial prudence.

Maintaining Employment and Improving Labor Relations

In some cases, SOEs had to take over failed private enterprises to preserve employment and prevent social unrest or larger public suffering. Maintaining employment is also often used as a reason against any call for privatization. Other employment-related reasons exist, too. For example, in the mining industry in India, labor was exploited with very poor working conditions. The mining practices adopted were unsafe and detrimental to the environment. However, the private owners were unwilling to improve the conditions owing to concerns about the company's financial viability. Yet, closing down such mines would mean loss of employment. Therefore, SOEs had to take over the mines.

Exploiting Profits from Natural Resources for Public Purposes

Sometimes SOEs are set up to exploit the natural resources of a nation in monopoly businesses, and the profits are deployed for public purposes. As an example, Saudi Aramco has undertaken a wide range of activities to support its surrounding communities, from operating schools and hospitals to constructing a new university on behalf of the government. Recently, the company has also been assigned the role of developing the country's nonoil economic sectors.

Forms of SOEs

Considerable variety occurs in the forms of SOEs. At one extreme are entities that have no corporate form and function as bureaucracies. They are typically responsible for providing public services such as health, education, policing, judicial, and other administrative services. In many cases, such bureaucracies also build and maintain roads and public buildings. In some cases, such as Indian Railways, SOEs even provide transportation services.

Then there are public authorities that are typically established under some kind of dedicated legislation. They are bound by public service obligations but do not function as traditional bureaucracies. For example, they are not bound by civil service rules or the procurement policies of the government. While these authorities are owned by the state, their annual budgets are not entirely dependent on public grants; they are also dependent on the earnings from their own operations. An example is the Massachusetts Port Authority (Massport), which was set up under Chapter 465 of the Acts of 1956. Massport operates three airports in Massachusetts, and its mandate is to connect the commonwealth to the rest of the world. Another example is the National Highways Authority of India, which was set up under an act of the parliament in 1988 to manage the 50,000 km of national highways in the country. These public authorities are subject to reporting requirements to legislative committees and are subject to statutory audit.

Then there are corporate structures wherein the government can hold the entire stake, a majority stake, or even a minority stake (Bremmer 2010). (Typically, structures where the government has only a minority stake are not referred to as SOEs but have been included here, as governments can still exercise considerable influence.) These SOEs are generally regulated under a generic law, such as the Companies Act in India. The regulatory requirements on these structures do not differ from the regulatory requirements on any private enterprise. National oil companies are a typical example of the government having majority shareholding. Aramco in Saudi Arabia, Pemex in Mexico, and the Indian Oil Corporation are examples of companies in which the government holds the entire stake. Similarly, in electricity transmission, airports, and urban rail services, for example, governments hold the entire stake in the companies. In some instances, the government has majority but not full ownership. Eni in Italy (previously known as Ente Nazionale Idrocarburi, or ENI), Statoil in Norway, Sinopec in China, Petrobras in Brazil, and Gazprom in Russia are some such examples.

Public listing of SOEs often leads to drastic changes in the responsiveness of companies to financial markets; because of quarterly reporting requirements, responsibilities to minority shareholders, and higher public scrutiny, publicly listed SOEs are often more financially sophisticated entities that respond to not only government preferences but also market preferences. Which companies (and what share of them) a national government decides to publicly list is often a highly political decision in which SOE profitability and government fiscal necessity often conflict.

Cases exist in which the government chooses to retain only a minority stake. Often, this is done only to have an influence on the policies and strategic plans of enterprises without having to invest in securing a majority stake. For example, in some cases of privatization, governments retain only a foothold, often with a view toward securing the benefits of private management while keeping privatized firms as national champions influenced by governmental policies (Bremmer 2010). In some cases, governments retain adequate shares that entitle them to veto strategic decisions but not influence operational decisions.

Governments can exercise considerable influence, even with a minority shareholding, through their ability to deploy either public funds or funds from state-owned financial institutions to further or limit the functioning of such enterprises. By offering loans and equity through state-owned development and commercial banks, governments have been able to acquire a role even in the governance of private firms. Brazil's development bank, BNDES, is an example, as it acts as not only a lender but also a minority shareholder through a specialized private investment arm, BNDESPAR. (Armendáriz de Aghion 1999; Lazzarini et al. 2012). China

Investment Corporation buys shares in China's companies and banks. Temasek, Singapore's sovereign wealth fund, invests in companies such as Singapore Technologies Telemedia, Singapore Communications, Singapore Power, and Singapore Airlines. Mubadala, a sovereign wealth fund from Abu Dhabi, invests heavily in large development projects at home in energy, telecommunications, health care, and other sectors.

In order to manage their minority involvement in multiple enterprises, governments set up state-owned holding companies. These holding companies take shares in other companies and thereby exercise state control, albeit indirectly. In China, for example, the State-Owned Assets Supervision and Administration Commission works as a holding company, overseeing more than 100 additional stand-alone companies and holding companies (Lin and Milhaupt 2011). In Dubai, all the companies controlled by the state come under two large state-owned holding companies: Dubai World and Investment Corporation of Dubai. These holding companies control a number of subsidiaries. The Khazanah Nasional Berhad in Malaysia is another example. In 2010, it owned stock in 52 companies, out of which it held minority positions in about 26.

Thus, SOEs can take multiple forms. While those without a corporate form largely tend to provide social and administrative services, those with a corporate form can be wholly owned by the government or have a majority shareholding of the government. In companies where the government has 100 percent or majority shareholding, it exercises its influence by virtue of its ownership. However, even in cases where the government has only a minority shareholding, it can exercise considerable influence.

Typically, forms that lack a corporate structure but function as bureaucracies provide services that do not lend themselves to commercial functioning. They are difficult to finance from user fees and are more commonly financed through tax revenues. In the corporate structure, a choice between complete shareholding, majority shareholding, or minority shareholding depends on the sensitivity of the sector and its strategic importance. The choice of a corporate structure also depends on performance and the potential for effecting operational efficiencies through the private sector without impacting strategic interests.

Performance of SOEs

Considerable debate exists over the effect of government ownership on the performance of enterprises. This debate has inspired many studies, and the conclusions have been varied.

For some (Gupta 2005; Omran 2004; Poczter 2016), state ownership is better than private ownership, and SOE reforms fail to have any impact on firms' performance. An analysis of the postwar performance of 17 German and Japanese firms found little difference between SOEs and privately owned enterprises. Further, a study of 54 Egyptian firms over a 5-year period from 1994 to 1998 concluded that privatized firms do not exhibit a significantly better performance than private firms (Omran 2004).

In contrast to this finding, another group of scholars conclude that government-owned enterprises are less profitable and efficient than privately owned ones (Boardman and Vining 1989; DeWenter and Malatesta 2001; Megginson, Nash, and Randenborgh 1994; Truong, Lanjouw, and Lensink 2006).

Yet, another group takes a neutral view, arguing that the performance is independent of ownership (De Castro and Uhlenbruck 1997; Parker 2003; Parker and Hartley 1991). Using data from more than 25,000 firms worldwide, the Asian Development Bank Institute (1997) concluded that that SOEs displayed lower profits than privately owned firms. However, SOEs are better leveraged, being more dependent on debt than privately owned firms. SOEs also tend to be more labor-intensive and have higher labor costs. These facts would suggest that ownership changes may help enhance the performance of such enterprises.

In India, the State Transport Corporations, which are state-owned public bus transport companies, incurred a loss of ₹164 billion, approximately US$2.34 billion in 2016–2017 (Central Institute of Road Transport 2017). In the same year, the Delhi metro alone incurred a loss of ₹3.480 million, approximately US$50 million (Delhi Metro Rail Corporation 2017). This is among the better-performing metro rail systems in the country. The others are worse off. The *Economic Times* (2019) quoted India's minister for power, R. K. Singh, as reporting that India's power distribution companies incurred losses of ₹270 billion (approximately US$3.8 billion) in 2018–2019.

Thus, whether private firms perform better than state-owned firms is an open question, and no consensus seems to have emerged. The overall view seems to be that SOEs should not be evaluated purely on the basis of financial results but more widely on how they contribute to public value.

Many reformers argue that an SOE can pursue both commercial and non-commercial goals efficiently if it clearly distinguishes the two types of activities and separates, to the extent practical, their costs. A common suggestion is that the government specify the noncommercial activities, often called *public service obligations*, that it wants the enterprise to engage in and provide budgetary support sufficient to cover the losses incurred.

Reasons for Poor Performance and
Impetus for Reform

Scholars have explained the reasons for the relatively poor performance of SOEs using the frameworks of the agency theory, the property rights theory, the public choice theory, and the soft budget constraint.

According to the agency theory (Eisenhardt 1989), corporation managers are likely to be guided by personal motivations that may differ from the interests of the principals who own the corporation. In an SOE, ownership lies with the state, which has political, social, and economic goals. However, managers may have different motivations, such as high pay, fringe benefits, and low effort levels (Sun, Tong, and Tong 2002), and may not face the risk of replacement and removal owing to poor performance of their firms, as is likely in privately owned enterprises (Nguyen and Do 2007). Therefore, managers have few incentives to enhance their corporations' efficiency.

According to the property rights theory (Hart and Moore 1990), the separation of property rights in SOEs is also responsible for their relative inefficiency. Even if the state and the citizens, who are the ultimate owners of an SOE, seek profit maximization as their goal, it is difficult to write complete contracts that adequately link the manager's incentives to that goal because of diffused ownership, making it difficult to incentivize the most efficient outcome (Shleifer 1998). It is easier to define more complete contracts and monitor managers more effectively in privately owned enterprises (McCormick and Meiners 1988).

According to the public choice theory (Krueger 1990), SOE boards and CEOs are appointed through political offices. SOE boards have been blamed for intervening in industry regulation (Hill 1999) to help them serve their political interests (Mbo and Adjasi 2017) rather than seeking more efficient social and economic outcomes.

The soft budget constraint (Kornai 1979) has been held responsible for poor performance by SOEs as even chronic loss makers are always bailed out by the state, and this is an important cause of inefficiency.

The fear that the public enterprises have neglected commercial goals to the point that they are jeopardizing society's ability to advance important noncommercial goals has served as an impetus for reform and improved management. For example, the public enterprises may charge such low tariffs or be so overstaffed that they no longer have the resources to offer reliable service or to extend service to new neighborhoods. Another concern is that public enterprises may impose so great a burden on the treasury that they crowd out social spending.

Reform Initiatives

Given that many SOEs have incurred significant losses and become a strain on the public budget, there has been mounting pressure for reforms to help them perform better. The first efforts to improve performance, during the 1950s–1970s, presumed that the SOEs lacked the physical and human capacity to perform well. These efforts attempted to improve performance while maintaining public ownership (Gómez-Ibáñez 2007). Two important trends were noticed in the efforts to help them do so: strengthened commercial orientation and stronger and more independent boards.

The following efforts have been used to strengthen commercial orientation:

- Incorporating SOEs under the respective company law of the country so they are subject to the same discipline in terms of tax and other legal regulations as any other company. As an example, the Corporation Law in Brazil deems all joint-stock companies, regardless of their ownership, to be commercial entities and profit-seeking. Similarly, the Companies Act in India subjects all companies, regardless of ownership, to the same discipline.
- Floating SOEs on local and international stock exchanges to persuade market discipline. In some cases, operating subsidiaries have been listed after the noncommercial responsibilities are taken over by their respective holding companies.
- Ensuring transparency and limits on noncommercial objectives as well as separate funding for such activities after proper costing.
- Use of private sector benchmarks for evaluating SOE performance.
- Adoption of private sector compensation practices.
- Building internal capacity by modernizing internal systems and equipment as well as training the middle and upper management levels.

As an example, the State-Owned Enterprises Act of 1986 in New Zealand permits SOEs to pursue noncommercial objectives but requires an agreement between the minister and the SOE to pay for any such services. Similarly, in Brazil, Banco do Brasil is compensated for the extension of subsidized loans to the agricultural sector (Cortes 2010). Another example is the conversion of the government-controlled Postal Savings Bank of China into a limited liability company in 2007 and then to a joint-stock company in 2012 before having it go public on the Hong Kong Stock Exchange in 2016. China has also made major strides through the formation of the State-Owned Assets Supervision and

Administration Commission, a central asset management company that looks at the financial management of the state's shareholding across the economy.

With regard to stronger and more independent boards, many SOEs found it difficult to play a significant role in directing the affairs of their companies largely because of their limited authority over strategy, senior executive appointments, and other important matters. To get around these challenges, some countries have appointed independent and professional boards through the following ways:

- Explicit commitment by the government to respect the board's authority.
- Empowering the board to make executive appointments.
- Increasing the presence of independent directors on the board.
- Professionalizing the nomination process.

However, these efforts proved inadequate because managers lacked the freedom and incentives to perform well. Managers were responsible to a wide set of stakeholders, including the executive and legislative branches of the government, and to many other interest groups that seek to influence SOE performance in a manner that would serve their own objectives. This extensive responsibility made the task of the SOE manager extremely complex.

As a result, a second approach, which emerged in the 1970s and 1980s, aimed at laying out the objectives clearly in a performance contract (most successfully in France and South Korea). This contract required the government and the SOE to agree on certain targets to be achieved by the SOE. In return, the government would commit to certain resources and agree not to intervene in the day-to-day management of the SOE. The agreement was generally set out in a formal document. Unfortunately, this approach did not work because the loss of control over SOEs was considered politically costly and lacked political will (Shirley 1998). Over time, in many countries, performance contracts became a veneer for managerial autonomy, while various levers of political and administrative pressures were still applied on SOEs outside the contract.

The disenchantment with these reform efforts increased the chorus in favor of state exit. As a result, many SOEs were being either privatized or corporatized with larger private sector involvement (Parker 2003; Pollitt and Bouckaert 2011; Salamon 2002; Wettenhall 2001). In Australia, there was a wave of SOE asset sales, especially in areas such as public transport, power companies, and ports, to free up funds for reinvestment into much-needed infrastructure such as major road projects. Some prominent examples have been the privatization of railway systems in the United Kingdom, Japan, and Argentina; private sector operation of public buses in London; and distribution of electricity by the private sector in Delhi.

These efforts were more successful than the first. Many companies were privatized, typically to the benefit of both taxpayers (in reduced financial support for the enterprise) and customers (in lower prices or improved quality of service). However, the benefits from privatization seemed small or very unequally distributed, often with investors or taxpayers gaining excessively at the expense of customers or workers (Estache 2006). Studies that looked at the efficiency and equity gains from privatization found a lot of variation in the experiences. However, a common finding was that the gains were temporary and did not last for longer periods. Part of the reason was that ownership was not the main driver of performance in any sector; other variables, such as the market structure and institutional capacity, were important determinants of how an enterprise performed. Thus, privatization of electricity initially led to improvements in quality, lower transmission and distribution losses, and improved labor productivity. However, they were short-lived, and the outcomes were more influenced by the regulatory and institutional capacity than by ownership. Similarly, in the water and sanitation sector, private operators improved performance initially, but the improvements reached a ceiling. In some cases, the privatization had to be partially reversed. In the ports, sector privatization led to better financial performance, but ultimately regulatory quality and contract enforcement proved to be more important institutional determinants of success. Cost reductions were noticed in cases of rail franchising in Europe, but public ownership was associated with a higher passenger use of the railways. In the case of toll roads, contracts had to be renegotiated in many cases. Thus, first impressions on the gains from privatization were often misleading. The impacts of privatization are discussed in more detail in chapter 11.

The resulting controversies slowed or halted privatization in many countries, leaving a considerable number of firms still in government hands. A new trend began to emerge in the 21st century: the government influences the investment decisions of private companies through minority capital (Musacchio and Lazzarini 2012).

Emerging Role of SOEs

Given the challenges that SOEs face and their impacts on public budgets, SOEs are undergoing transitions. There has been a shrinking of SOEs from many parts of economic life (particularly in direct-to-consumer industries). However, SOEs persist in areas such as infrastructure, power, and utilities. Part of this phenomenon is a broader political preference for controlling public goods, but part also comes from the inherent advantage that a state entity has in managing the internal political economy of the state.

One of the popular forms that has emerged is SOE-as-contractor, which retains the umbrella function of state ownership but brings in some kind of contracting ecosystem under the SOE that involves significant private participation. This is a classic way to avoid politically problematic mass privatization but still bring the efficiencies associated with private competition. Governments (and by extension SOEs) can theoretically replicate any contractual form observed in the private sector, given the right incentives and complete information (Tirole 1988).

An effective SOE-as-contractor with a minimalist, noninterfering role can essentially play the role of market creator and custodian, and this role is observed in various large infrastructure domains (highways, coal, power, oil) across the developing world. In such models, SOEs are often responsible for high-level planning and maintaining adherence to regulations, but day-to-day operations are left with private operators. In the most extreme cases, SOEs become essentially contract management companies rather than frontline economic actors. This trend is noticeable across the transportation space as well, whether it is public transport services in Lyon, the Singapore metro, or Tren Urbano in Puerto Rico (a metro rail system serving several municipalities). In all of them, the systems were built with public funds, but the operations are contracted to private entities. Similarly, in the transport space, ancillary functions such as cleaning and catering are best left to private contractors (e.g., Indian Railways).

If we deepen the involvement of the private sector a little more, we reach the joint-venture model whereby an SOE and a private company decide to copromote a firm for a particular activity. This option is particularly attractive for capital-starved states, which want to maintain some degree of control over an economic activity but may not have the investment capital to start large projects. One of the distinct advantages of joint ventures is joint governance but so is the ability to use the respective strengths of the public and private sectors within one entity. Such SOEs are much better at ecosystem management, since they tend to be embedded within the large state infrastructure. Private partners tend to be more efficient at project execution and managing human resources.

PPPs are yet another configuration of involving private capital and tend to occur more at a project level than a firm level (as in a joint venture). PPP projects have an enormous diversity of forms, but ultimately the most important characteristic that differentiates PPPs from simple subcontracting is a greater sharing of risks (and rewards) with private partners. In the ideal, private partners are brought in during the design process (unlike in subcontracting) to have a strong stake in project viability and design from the very beginning. Particularly in design-build-operate-maintain models, in return for early capital participation and taking on operational risk, PPP entities are allowed to charge user fees of various kinds for the infrastructure they build. While PPPs have shown considerable promise in the developed world, they have been far more problematic and ineffective in the developing world. As Natarajan (2020) points out, even in the United Kingdom, the benefits of headline-making PPPs were frequently exaggerated, and the projects have not borne fruit according to their optimistic projects.

These failures have frequently led to a rise in user fees, which has ultimately hurt consumers (Natarajan 2020). Especially in developing countries, if strong contractual oversight and enforcement is not possible, the PPP model brings in all kinds of perverse incentives on both sides of the contract, which has led to ridiculously high user fees, overleveraged private participants reneging on contracts, and the state not fulfilling all of its promises to the extent of appropriating projects after political unrest about user fees. In countries such as India, this unrest has had adverse impacts on the PPP model for the moment and destroyed mutual trust between the partners. In many industrial ecosystems, SOEs still remain the providers of last resort, which has often led to private market entry but not outright privatization of SOEs. For example, in India, one of the state-owned telecom providers, Bharat Sanchar Nigam Ltd., still provides mobile telephony in many remote areas where no private company has entered thus far. Similarly, in areas such as power and public transportation, the absence of commercial return is not a good enough reason for the state to wrap up its services; even if services make losses, the public returns on them are too high to exit the sector.

But as we have seen across the world, incremental competition has made SOEs irrelevant in many industries, particularly where consumers have voted for their money and abandoned the SOE provider en masse. SOE decline through competitive pressures and cost overruns can be a form of privatization by malign neglect, whereby it is politically easier to let an SOE die a slow death in competitive markets rather than incur the political costs of overt privatization (Kaul 2020). We have seen similar mass migrations of customers in the power sector in India: away from public utilities toward private utilities on the few occasions that industrial customers had a genuine choice available to them.

Comparing SOE Management in China and India

The insights in this part of the chapter are largely synthesized from Naughton and Tsai (2015) and Chandra (2018). A natural way to examine trends in SOE philosophy and operations is to compare two of the largest emerging markets in the world, China and India. Their histories were strongly shaped by SOEs between the 1950s and the 1980s, but the two have since had their own ways of pursuing state capitalism. Interestingly, there are some striking convergences in how state capitalism operates in China and India. The first has to do with access to finance. As the only actors in their nations with access to national borrowing as well as budgetary resources, both China and India have seen massive consolidation at the top as centrally owned SOEs have become the largest and arguably most successful part of the SOE ecosystem. Whether the National Thermal Power Corporation in India, Coal India, the State Bank of India, Sinopec, the State Grid Corporation, or the Industrial and Commercial Bank of China, there is no doubt that SOEs still occupy commanding heights in both economies, although perhaps more so in China than in India. On the other hand, subnational SOEs have become less economically relevant (at least in size) because of their own bankruptcies and the intervention of central governments acquiring state assets and selectively bailing out industries. As subnational SOEs started overstretching their balance sheets, having state control over finance meant that governments could pick winners and losers, and nationally owned SOEs often had priority over subnational SOEs.

In fact, control of the banking system has played a powerful role in both China and India through directed lending to preferred industries and SOEs over the last few decades. Both countries have engaged in massive infrastructural and industrial expansions, supported largely by domestic bank financing from state-owned banks. As direct budgetary subsidies to SOEs have reduced since the early 1990s, the state-owned banking system has been able to distinguish between "good" SOEs, which deserve new debt, and "bad" SOEs, which have been forced to consolidate or be bought out by larger players. Naturally, subnational SOEs have often been on the losing side of this bargain.

What remains true in both countries is that SOEs are still considered part of the larger welfare architecture of the state, although definitely less so than a few decades ago. Whether it is the Chinese *danwei* (loosely translated as "work unit") system, which was a cornerstone of the Chinese Communist Party's social engineering in industrial areas, or the large corporate social responsibility budgets spent in local areas by SOEs such as Coal India, the legacy of SOEs being providers of far more than just economic services and employment remains true even today, albeit in much-attenuated form.

Finally, both countries still use profitable SOEs as financiers of last resort to either bail out ailing companies or occasionally provide funds to the state in times of fiscal crisis. For example, in India, SOE sales in recent years have helped the Indian state with much needed short-term liquidity (Banerjee, Sane, and Sharma 2020). India has also recently merged many of its smaller state-owned banks. Similarly, when the Chinese coal industry was facing major headwinds, partly due to overcapacity and partly due to a spate of mining accidents, Shenhua Group acquired many smaller provincial-level coal companies during the 2010s. Shenhua Group then merged with GD Energy to form China Energy Group, arguably the world's largest mining and coal power company. As SOE industries rise and fall, such acquisition and consolidation will likely remain a feature of the ecosystem for some time.

Railway Systems in China and India

The China State Railway Group Company, Ltd. (better known as China Railway) is a solely SOE under the management of the central government. It was developed as a national monopoly and remains so despite the development of local railways in some local markets. China Railway has a track length of 131,000 km, with 31,000 km of it high-speed rail.[1] China Railway carried 1.47 trillion passenger-kilometers and 3.02 trillion ton-kilometers of cargo in 2019 (Statista n.d.).

For a few decades since the 1950s, China Railway was not a commercial entity but rather a bureaucracy, that is, the Ministry of Railway. However, since 1980, the Ministry of Railway has undergone six major reforms, culminating in 2013 when the administrative part of the ministry was merged into the Ministry of Transport. The commercial part also became the newly established China Railway Corporation, which was later changed to China State Railway Group Company, Ltd. (Yu 2015).

Indian Railways has a track length of 95,981 km. It carried 8.44 billion passenger trips and 1.23 billion tons of cargo from April 2018 to March 2019 (Indian Railways n.d.). In India, the first railway line was built in 1853. Several others followed in different parts of the country. Initially, all of them operated as unlinked and private railway lines. As the numbers grew, there was a need to have a unified management. Accordingly, a railway board was set up in 1920 and took over all the lines. Even today, Indian Railways function under the railway board, which is not a commercial entity but rather a bureaucracy, akin to the situation in China prior to 1980. More recently, some components, such as management of container traffic, some construction activities, development of railway lands, and development of railway station areas, have been corporatized. Catering services, which were earlier managed by the railways, have now been privatized. Various profitable and operationally efficient parts of Indian Railways have been under strong consideration for asset monetization over the last few years, given Indian Railways' precarious finances and continued dependence on freight cross subsidies to balance out its loss-making passenger business.

In this context, it is interesting to note that passenger rail services in Japan were privatized in 1987, and freight rail is privately operated in the United States.

Both systems operate profitably, suggesting that these services are not inherently losing propositions. Therefore, in India and China, the railway systems could also be privatized. However, they continue to remain in state hands, obviously for reasons beyond their ability to run as viable businesses.

Power and Telecom Sectors in China and India

Before 2002, China's electricity service was provided by a state monopoly, State Power Corporation. A major restructuring in 2002 broke the monopoly into several SOEs, including two transmission and distribution giants (State Grid and South Grid) and five power generation companies. The power distribution market is now open for entry; there are more than 1,000 distributors across China, though many of them are fully or partially owned by the State Grid and South Grid.

In India, since 1948, the entire power sector has been owned and controlled by provincially owned and vertically integrated electricity boards. The boards undertook all the generation, transmission, and distribution activities. However, owing to financial losses and the inability to expand capacity, reforms aimed at unbundling the sector were taken up in 1991, and the private sector was invited to take up generation. In 1998, one province also took up distribution through the private sector. Delhi followed in 2002 and allowed three private companies to distribute power in the city.

Before 1994, China's telecom service was provided by an SOE monopoly, China Telecom. After a few restructuring actions that aimed to create market competition, the industry was restructured into one dominated by three SOEs (China Telecom, China Unicom, and China Mobile) in 2008. Essentially, the industry went from state monopoly to state oligopolies. After China entered the World Trade Organization in 2001, the telecom equipment market was opened to foreign firms. In 2019, the total telecom revenue amounted to 1.31 trillion renminbi (RMB), of which fixed-line revenue accounted for 31.8 percent and mobile accounted for 68.2 percent. Overall, market competition is weak, and customers are dissatisfied with the operating speeds and tariffs. The State Council has made a major call for some years for the three giants to increase speeds and reduce tariffs. So far, the progress is far from satisfactory.

Soon after independence, all telecom services in India were provided by the state directly through its Department of Posts and Telecommunications. However, teledensity remained very low, even after years of effort, and the poor quality of services prompted reforms under which services in some of the larger cities were corporatized. With the advent of mobile telephony, private operators were licensed to provide mobile services and, in the last few decades, have come to dominate the market, while state providers such as Bharat Sanchar Nigam Limited and Mahanagar Telephone Nigam Limited have struggled to keep up in terms of both service quality and competitive pricing.

Implications of Differing Growth Rates in China and India

Both China and India have grown rapidly in the last four decades. China's gross domestic product rose from US$14.7 trillion in 2019, and India's increased from US$0.19 trillion in 1980 to US$2.72 trillion in 2018. China has grown much more rapidly than India since 2000. The differing pace of growth has influenced how these two countries have financed their infrastructure. China adopted a policy of infrastructure-led growth wherein it expected good infrastructure to propel its growth and had the confidence that growth would pay back the investment. At the provincial level, SOE banks were able to give even bad loans for infrastructure projects under an assurance that the state would bail them out to cover any losses they incurred. Thus, China was able to invest in megaprojects such as the high-speed rail network. On the other hand, India has followed a less ambitious approach to developing its infrastructure, with the traditional cost-benefit analysis determining levels of investment. More recently, aggressive investments have been made in urban metro rail systems, even though most are incurring huge losses. However, a significant share of the financing has come from international financial institutions such as the World Bank, the Japan International Cooperation Agency, and the Asian Development Bank. India has also used a PPP approach more widely, with significant financing coming from SOE banks but with less confidence that bad loans will be looked upon kindly.

An outstanding unresolved question of this state-financed growth led by infrastructure spending in both China and India is how long the cycle of generous lending, the discovery of bad assets, and recapitalization continue and what will be the implications of such continued lending on both government budgets and investors willing to lend money to national governments and SOEs. In China's case, higher levels of growth have managed to continually attract new capital, postponing some of the inevitable resolutions of bad assets. In India, the ripple effect of nonperformance of infrastructure investment have led to almost half a decade of subdued growth.

Conclusions

SOEs have been a dominant feature in many countries, especially in the infrastructure sector. The inability of the market to supply several public goods such as road networks, the natural monopoly characteristic of many infrastructure services such as electricity transmission systems, the need to keep services such as public bus transport affordable, and the need to support national economic interests and to use tax revenues to pay for them have compelled the continuation of SOEs. However, since many of these services are not commercial in nature, SOEs have incurred losses, often straining public budgets to such an extent that reforms became necessary. Particularly in a world with hard budget constraints, various policies and instruments emerged: performance contracts, privatization, subcontracting, minority shareholding by the state, and more. Perhaps more important, many countries, including China and India, realized that as long as the state was actively involved in the allocation of financial resources, it did not always have to be the implementer of the state's capitalist vision.

The first effort at reforms sought to improve the management of SOEs; the next effort aimed at divesting them to the private sector. Neither proved successful, and current efforts are exploring partnerships with the private sector in such a manner that the public interest can be served, even as the operational efficiencies of the private sector are leveraged.

One of the most prominent pivots of SOEs over the last few decades has been their increasing financial sophistication. Entities that were formerly accustomed to being subsidized directly from government budgets slowly started getting publicly listed, floating bonds, raising funds through project finance, monetizing existing assets, and more. Infrastructure SOEs in particular, partly through state paternalism and partly through their own financial strains, realized that existing assets and their cash flows could often become collateral or be securitized in ways that would give SOEs more degrees of financial freedom, especially in light of budgetary strains on governments worldwide.

While the debate over SOE versus private implementation of large infrastructure projects will likely remain contentious for years to come, what is certain is that the likes of China National Petroleum Corporation, Indian Railways, National Thermal Power Corporation in India, China Railway, and many other entities will engage in more sophisticated approaches to financial markets to maintain their own financial viability. In many cases, their primary lender may be a state-owned financial institution. However, when SOEs access capital from nongovernmental sources, they will face forms of financial accountability and pressures that may force them to modify their operations and internal decision making in more financially efficient ways. Given all the innovations in organizational form, financial management, PPPs, and private contracting that have emerged from SOEs, they have proven to be a much more versatile organizational form than almost anyone could have imagined three decades ago. Instead of being blown away in the winds of privatization and market reform, the best SOEs have adapted to these winds and found legitimacy within various national economies.

When public money is being spent through a government process, it is always easier, politically, to justify its spending through SOEs and state-run entities, which are presumed to be more responsible, accountable, and transparent, than to provide such funds to private entities. If the post COVID-19 financial stimuli are any indication, the countercyclical, publicly justifiable expenditures of SOEs will remain a powerful force, even in the face of economic inefficiency.[2]

Summary

- SOEs have gone almost full cycle from being considered key to economic growth in the 1950s and 1960s to a disappointment in the 1970s and 1980s, the subject of privatization in the 1990s, and a topic of revived interest in more recent decades.
- SOEs remain significant players in the infrastructure sectors, especially in China and India.
- SOEs survive in part because they can help solve practical problems such as the inability of the market to supply classic public goods (e.g., local road networks).
- In addition, infrastructure SOEs have become more versatile through innovations in organizational form, financial management, PPPs, and private contracting.

Notes

1. For a discussion on the economic benefits of high-speed rail, see chapter 2; for a discussion on how high-speed rail has been used for city cluster development, see chapter 17.
2. Special thanks to Shashi Verma of Transport for London for this insight.

References

Airports Council International. 2016. "The Ownership of Europe's Airports." ACI Report. https://www.aeroport.fr/uploads/documents/ACI%20EUROPE%20Report_The%20 Ownership%20of%20Europes%20Airports%202016.pdf.

Armendáriz de Aghion, Beatriz. 1999. "Development Banking." *Journal of Development Economics* 58: 83–100.

Baldwin, Robert, Martin Cave, and Martin Lodge. 2012. *Understanding Regulation. Theory, Strategy, and Practice.* Oxford, UK: Oxford University Press.

Banerjee, Sudipto, Renuka Sane, and Smriti Sharma. 2020. "The Five Paths of Disinvestment in India." *The LEAP Blog*. https://blog.theleapjournal.org/2020/07/disinvestment-of-cpses-in-last-6-years.html.

Bertomeu-Sanchez, Salvador, and Antonio Estache. 2019. "A Dataset on the Relative Importance of Public and Private Operators in the Utilities Sector." Brussels: ECARES, Universite Libre de Bruxelles.

Boardman, Anthony E., and Aidan R. Vining. 1989. "Ownership and Performance in Competitive Environments: A Comparison of the Performance of Private, Mixed, and State-Owned Enterprise." *Journal of Law and Economics* 32: 1–33.

Bremmer, Ian. 2010. *The End of the Free Market: Who Wins the War Between States and Corporations?* New York: Portfolio/Penguin.

Central Institute of Road Transport. 2017. "Key Statistics, 2016–17." http://www.cirtindia.com/pdf/Key%20Statistics%202016-17.pdf

Chandra, Rohit. 2018. "Adaptive State Capitalism in the Indian Coal Industry." Ph.D. dissertation, Harvard University.

China Railway. n.d. http://www.china-railway.com.cn/english/about/aboutUs/.

Cortes, Katia. 2010. "Farm Equipment Loans Surge as Commodities Rally: Brazil Credit." *Bloomberg*, December 22.

De Castro, Julio O., and Klaus Uhlenbruck. 1997. "Characteristics of Privatization: Evidence from Developed, Less-Developed, and Former Communist Countries." *Journal of International Business Studies* 28(1): 123–143.

Delhi Metro Rail Corporation. 2017. "Balance Sheet as at 31st March 2017." http://www.delhimetrorail.com/OtherDocuments/Annual%20Accounts%20And%20Directors%20Report%202016-17.pdf.

DeWenter, Kathryn L., and Paul H. Malatesta. 2001. "State-Owned and Privately Owned Firms: An Empirical Analysis of Profitability, Leverage, and Labour Intensity." *American Economic Review* 91(1): 320–334.

Economic Times. 2019. "Power Discoms Faced Losses Worth Rs 27000 Crore in FY19: Power Minister R K Singh." December 29.

Eisenhardt, Kathleen M. 1989. "Agency Theory: Assessment and Review." *Academy of Management Review* 14(1): 57–74.

Estache, Antonio. 2006. "PPI Partnerships and PPI Divorces in LDCs." *Review of Industrial Organization* 29(1): 3–26.

Gómez-Ibáñez, José A. 2007. "Alternatives to Infrastructure Privatization Revisited." Washington, DC: World Bank.

Gupta, Nandini. 2005. "Partial Privatization and Firm Performance." *Journal of Finance* 60(2): 987–1015.

Hart, Oliver D., and John Moore. 1990. "Property Rights and the Nature of the Firm." *Journal of Political Economy* 98(6): 1119–1158.

Hill, P. J. 1999. "Public Choice: A Review." *Faith and Economics* 34(Fall): 1–10.

Indian Railway. n.d. "Annual Report and Accounts, 2018–19." https://indianrailways.gov.in/railwayboard/uploads/directorate/stat_econ/Year_Book/Indian%20Railways%20Annual%20Report%20%26%20Accounts%20English%202018-19.pdf.

International Union of Railways. n.d. https://uic.org/.

Kaul, Vivek. 2020. *Bad Money: Inside the NPA Mess and How It Threatens India's Banking System.* New Delhi: HarperCollins.

Kornai, Janos. 1979. "Resource-Constrained Versus Demand-Constrained Systems." *Econometrica* 47(4): 801–819.

Kowalski, Przemyslaw, Max Büge, Monika Sztajerowska, and Matias Egeland. 2013. "State-Owned Enterprises: Trade Effects and Policy Implications." *OECD Trade Policy Papers* 147. Paris: OECD.

Krueger, Anne O. 1990. "Government Failures in Development." *Journal of Economic Perspectives* 4(3): 9–23.

Küfeoğlu, Sinan, Michael Pollitt, and Karim Anaya. 2018. "Electric Power Distribution in the World: Today and Tomorrow." Working paper No. 1826. Cambridge, UK: EPRG.

Lazzarini, Sérgio G., Aldo Musacchio, Rodrigo Bandeira-de-Mello, and Rosilene Marcon. 2012. "What Do Development Banks Do? Evidence from Brazil, 2002–2009." Insper working paper. http://ssrn.com/abstract=1969843.

Lin, Li-Wen, and Curtis J. Milhaupt. 2011. "We Are the (National) Champions: Understanding the Mechanisms of State Capitalism in China." Working paper. Columbia University.

Mbo, Mbako, and Charles Adjasi. 2017. "Performance of SOEs: Evidence on Botswana Telecommunications Corporation." *International Journal of Social Economics* 44(7): 960–979.

McCormick, Robert E., and Roger E. Meiners. 1988. "University Governance: A Property Rights Perspective." *Journal of Law and Economics* 31(2): 423–442.

Megginson, William L., Robert C. Nash, and Matthias Van Randenborgh. 1994. "The Financial and Operating Performance of Newly Privatized Firms: An International Empirical Analysis." *Journal of Finance* 49(2): 403–452.

Musacchio, Aldo, and Sérgio G. Lazzarini. 2012. "Leviathan in Business: Varieties of State Capitalism and Their Implications for Economic Performance." May. https://papers.ssrn.com/sol3/papers.cfm?abstract_id=2070942.

Natarajan, Gulzar. 2020. "Designing a New Development Finance Institution for Infrastructure." January 12. https://ssrn.com/abstract=3517980.

Naughton, Barry, and Kellee Tsai. 2015. "State Capitalism, Institutional Adaptation, and the Chinese Miracle." Cambridge, UK: Cambridge University Press.

Nguyen, Thi Bich Hang, and Huang Linh Do. 2007. "The Equitization Process in Vietnam: Making a Headstart in a Long Journey, in Best Practices in Asian Corporate Governance." Tokyo: Asian Productivity Organization.

OECD (Organisation for Economic Co-operation and Development). 2014. "The Size and Sectoral Distribution of SOEs in OECD and Partner Countries." Paris.

Omran, Mohammed. 2004. "The Performance of State-Owned Enterprises and Newly Privatized Firms: Does Privatization Really Matter?" *World Development* 32(6): 1019–1041.

Parker, David. 2003. "Privatization in the European Union." In *International Handbook on Privatization,* ed. David Parker and David Saal. Chelthenham, UK: Edward Elgar.

Parker, David, and Hartley Keith. 1991. "Status Change and Performance: Economic Policy and Evidence." In *Privatization and Economic Efficiency: A Comparative Analysis of Developed and Developing Countries,* ed. Attiat Ott and Keith Hartley, 108–125. Brookfield, VT: Edward Edgar.

Poczter, Sharon. 2016. "The Long-term Effects of Bank Recapitalization: Evidence from Indonesia." *Journal of Financial Intermediation* 25(C):131–153.

Pollitt, Christopher, and Geert Bouckaert. 2011. *Public Management Reform: A Comparative Analysis; New Public Management, Governance, and the Neo-Weberian State.* 3rd ed. Oxford, UK: Oxford University Press.

Salamon, Lester M., ed. 2002. *The Tools of Government: A Guide to the New Governance.* New York: Oxford University Press.

Shirley, Mary 1998. "Why Performance Contracts for State Owned Enterprises Haven't Worked." Washington, DC: World Bank.

Shleifer, Andrei. 1998. "State Versus Private Ownership." *Journal of Economic Perspectives* 12(4): 133–150.

Statista. n.d. "Volume of Rail Freight Traffic in China from 2009 to 2019." https://www.statista .com/statistics/276066/volume-of-rail-freight-traffic-in-china/.

Steer, Davies Gleave. 2016. "Study on Airport Ownership and Management and the Ground Handling Market in Selected Non-EU Countries." https://ec.europa.eu/transport/sites /transport/files/modes/air/studies/doc/2016-06-airports-and-gh.pdf.

Sturesson, Jan, Scott McIntyre, and Nick Jones. 2015. "State-Owned Enterprises: Catalysts for Public Value Creation?" PWC report. April.

Sun, Qian, Wilson H. S. Tong, and Jing Tong. 2002. "How Does Government Ownership Affect Firm Performance? Evidence from China's Privatization Experience." *Journal of Business Finance and Accounting* 29(1–2): 1–27.

Tirole, Jean. 1988. *The Theory of Industrial Organization.* Cambridge, MA: MIT Press.

Truong, Dong Loc, Ger Lanjouw, and Robert Lensink. 2006. "The Impact of Privatization on Firm Performance in a Transition Economy: The Case of Vietnam." *Economics of Transition* 14(2): 349–389.

Wettenhall, R. 2001. "Public or Private? Public Corporations, Companies and the Decline of the Middle Ground." *Public Organization Review* 1(1): 17–40.

Yu, Hong. 2015. "Railway Sector Reform in China: Controversy and Problems." *Journal of Contemporary China* 24(96): 1070–1091.

INFRASTRUCTURE PLANS AND REGIONAL INTEGRATION

15

TRANSPORT INFRASTRUCTURE AND THE INTEGRATION OF THE EUROPEAN UNION

José Manuel Vassallo

Infrastructure is crucial to improving integration among regions and countries by facilitating the flow of people, goods, information, and energy, thereby increasing the size and scope of the market area, reinforcing competitiveness, and fostering economic growth. In general, integration areas have adopted measures to promote infrastructure to better connect its member countries. This chapter focuses on the European Union (EU) for several reasons: first, because the EU represents one of the greatest efforts ever undertaken to realize large-scale integration among countries, and second, because the EU has developed specific infrastructure policies, including the allocation of funds, aimed at fostering competitiveness and reinforcing regional cohesion.

The EU is the result of the progressive effort of its member states to reach a greater integration to make the continent stronger and more competitive with other economic areas of the world. The EU has developed from being solely an economic union to larger levels of integration, with the development of a single currency (the euro) and the increasing cooperation among member states in certain political matters, such as justice, internal security, and foreign affairs. Over the years, the EU has expanded from the original 6 states that signed the Treaty of Rome in 1957 to the 27 members that make up the EU at the time of this writing. The integration process has been complicated and has undergone important setbacks, the last of them the decision of the United Kingdom to leave the club. Despite the many criticisms that the EU has received, its contribution to enhancing the role of Europe in the world's economy cannot be denied.

Regarding the sovereignty of the EU, for those responsibilities that by treaty the members agreed to share, the EU follows a supranational system. Responsibilities not conferred by treaty on the supranational institutions remain with the member states. According to the Treaty of the European Union, the EU has seven institutions: the European Parliament, the European Council, the Council of the

European Union, the European Commission, the Court of Justice, the European Central Bank, and the Court of Auditors. The EU has an annual budget whose revenue comes mostly from contributions from its member states and from income generated by common EU policy charges, such as customs duties and taxes. The resources are spent to further EU policies, such as support to infrastructure projects that will benefit the entire EU.

The goal of this chapter is twofold. First, it describes the main characteristics of the infrastructure policy of the EU, particularly for transport infrastructure projects and the financial resources allocated to it. Second, it evaluates how that policy contributes to the integration of the EU, measured as the achievement of a set of goals regarding economic growth, territorial balance, and the promotion of strategic objectives.

Role of Infrastructure to Foster National and Regional Integration

Since World War II, many countries have been striving to attain a greater degree of economic and social integration within a larger political unit, with the aim of achieving certain advantages for the common benefit of all their members. Consumers of a certain country will benefit from goods and services that other countries produce at a lower cost or of better quality. The integrated countries, in turn, will increase the size of the market for the goods and services where they are more competitive than the rest of the world, thus fostering their economic development. This idea was coined by Ricardo (1817) as the theory of comparative advantage, according to which integrated countries will benefit from what each one of the members of the group does better than the rest, thereby benefiting all of them. A second advantage of integration is the ability of the integrated area to take advantage of economies of scale by reducing average production costs and increasing the scale of goods and services produced in specialized places. A third advantage that should not be underestimated is the greater strength of large economic units to negotiate favorable trade agreements with the rest of the world.

In its first stage, integration among countries is realized through the reduction of barriers to the free flow of goods, services, labor, and capital. In more advanced stages, integration may imply transferring some duties of the nation-state to a supranational authority that makes certain decisions for the global interest of the members. According to Balassa (2013), the stages of integration are preferential trading area, free trade area, customs union, single market, economic union, economic and monetary union, and complete economic integration. The countries within a free trade area remove customs tariffs for imports and exports from or to their member states. A customs union adds to the free trade area common customs tariffs with third countries. A single market includes the free flow of goods, services, labor, and capital among the country members. An economic union combines a customs union with a single market. A monetary union adds a single currency across member states. Finally, a complete economic integration implies a fiscal union whereby taxes and public expenditure policies are common, or at least highly coordinated, among member states. A step further is the political integration that includes the harmonization among countries of sensitive political aspects such as justice, internal security, and foreign affairs.

Nowadays, several groups of countries in the world have a lower or greater degree of integration. As noted, the EU is likely the one that has reached the greatest level of integration. Other groupings worth mentioning are the Association of Southeast Asian Nations, the North American Free Trade Agreement, the Union of South American Nations, the African Continental Free Trade Area, and the Eurasian Economic Community.

Promoting the free movement of goods, services, and people may be hindered by a poor connection among countries. This is why dealing with the improvement of infrastructure across borders has been one of the greatest challenges faced by countries to stimulate integration, since infrastructure plays a key role in facilitating the connection of people, the free flow of goods, and the proper functioning of labor and capital markets.

The importance of public capital stock in boosting economic development, especially in developing countries, has been carefully studied by economists and broadly acknowledged among policy makers. Although some economists at the time criticized the seminal research conducted by Aschauer (1989), it triggered an array of work based on that methodology that provided certain evidence of the positive impact of infrastructure on economic growth by analyzing the contribution of public capital to the productivity of the private sector and its impact on attracting households and companies. Overall, research studies show positive results regarding the impact of infrastructure in promoting economic and social development across regions. An empirical analysis conducted in China using panel data suggests a positive relationship between telecommunication infrastructure and the economic growth of the regions of the country (Ding, Haynes, and Liu 2008). Another study, conducted by Stone and Strutt (2010) for South East Asia, concludes that facilitating trade with the adoption of some measures to improve land transportation in the Greater Mekong Region has a positive impact on transport flows across the countries in that region. However, this study also notes some negative consequences, such as increasing income disparities among regions and ethnic groups, the spread of diseases such as HIV and the avian flu, an increase in human and drug trafficking, and deterioration of traffic safety.

Results seem to demonstrate that the returns on infrastructure investment are likely highest during the early stages of development, when infrastructure is scarce and networks have not been completed. Returns on infrastructure investment tend to fall, sometimes notably, as economies mature (Briceño-Garmendia, Estache, and Shafik 2004). The findings obtained by researchers show different results depending on such aspects as the region where the infrastructure was developed, the econometric approach employed, and the type of infrastructure. Over the years, research results seem to confirm what Alder (1965, 29) mentioned many years ago: "It is frequently assumed that all transport improvements stimulate economic growth. The sad truth is that some do, and some do not."

Apart from the research aimed at studying the impact of infrastructure on economic development, the literature on economic geography that has flourished since the 1990s has been working on using geographical factors to explain trade development. Economic geographers produced outstanding quantitative contributions by combining data from geographical information systems with economic variables (Fujimura 2004). For instance, Radelet and Sachs (1998) found that distance to major markets and access to the sea have a great impact on shipping costs, thereby influencing success in exports and economic growth.

Redding and Venables (2004) set an econometric specification stating that access is a function of a certain country and the geographical location of its trading partners. The application of the model to cross-sectional data on trade flows, geographical characteristics, gross domestic product (GDP), and population found that changes in one geographic characteristic have an effect on foreign market and supplier access for all countries. The authors conclude that even if institutional hurdles and custom tariffs are removed, distance penalizes the potential development of remote regions. To estimate the impact of trade costs on trade flows, Limao and Venables (2001) calibrated a gravity model that demonstrated the notable influence of the infrastructure factor in explaining trade volumes.

Summing up, the findings in the research literature demonstrate that accessibility is a key driver, though not the only one, to encouraging economic development. Accessibility will be promoted by removing barriers and facilitating connections. Facilitating trade and building infrastructure where it is needed goes hand in hand to take full advantage of the benefits of economic and social integration.

Transport Infrastructure Policy in the European Union

Trans-European Transport Networks

The Common Transport Policy was one of the first priorities of the European Economic Community (EEC) Treaty signed in Rome in 1957. Actually, the principles of that policy were included in Article 4(2) (g) and Title VI of the treaty. Originally, the common transport policy focused on establishing the framework for an integrated transport market by promoting the liberalization of services and the harmonization of standards across the ECC member states.

Unfortunately, the treaty did not mention transport infrastructure as a key priority goal, since from the beginning of the EEC, infrastructure policy was considered to be the exclusive responsibility of the member states. For this reason, most member states continued to develop their own networks, focusing on national interests and goals. As a consequence of that, infrastructure networks in Europe remained largely ineffective in promoting integration because of the lack of good transborder communication and of interoperability across nations.

It was not until the early 1970s that the EEC considered the need to develop a common European infrastructure policy. In a summit held in Paris in October 1972, the European Commission agreed on the need to contribute to transport infrastructure planning by defining infrastructure networks according to EEC criteria, going beyond the nationally oriented approaches under which infrastructure had been planned until then in the member states. According to Izquierdo (1993), the EEC's objective and its intention were to neither interfere nor shift responsibility from the member states but rather to ensure that national infrastructure programs responded simultaneously to the future needs of both national and EEC interests. For instance, a train going from Spain to France faces many hurdles to merely cross the border. The first one is the lack of capillarity of the network, since there are only two rail crossings for a border that is 656 km long. The second is the lack of interoperability in terms of track width, electric power, communication systems, and so on. The lack of capillarity and interoperability are the reasons why the market share of rail transportation between France and Spain is almost negligible.

To respond to that problem, in the 1980s, the EEC launched for the first time the initiative to establish infrastructure networks for the benefit of all its members. From that moment, European institutions worked on the foundations of the future EEC's policy on infrastructure and the action framework to design it while respecting the continuing responsibilities of the member states. However, it was not until the Treaty of the European Union, signed in

Maastricht in 1992, that the principles of the EEC infrastructure policy and the funding instruments envisaged to promote its development were ultimately established.

The treaty stipulated that the European Community should contribute to the development of Trans-European Networks (TEN) in the areas of transport (TEN-T), telecommunications (eTEN), and energy infrastructure (TEN-E) to promote the interconnection and interoperability of national networks with the aim of fostering the internal market by encouraging cross-border connections. In particular, the EU should take account of the need to link island, landlocked, and peripheral regions with the central regions of the EU.

Here, it is necessary to clarify that the TEN planned by the EU do not represent assets owned by the EU but instead remained owned by the member states, their regions, provinces, and so on. The inclusion within the TEN just signifies the interest of the EU members in developing those facilities, as they are expected to contribute to EU interests and goals. As a consequence, the EU cannot oblige its member states to build the stretches of the network they own. The EU can, however, incentivize countries and regions to develop those stretches through funding sources supporting the projects included within the network.

The TEN-T is made up of high-quality motorways and roads, high-speed rail, conventional rail, airports, sea and inland ports, and combined transport chains as well as traffic management, user information systems, and positioning and navigation systems. The main objectives of the TEN-T, as proposed by Decision 1692/96/EC, are to foster the interconnection and interoperability among national networks as well as the access to these networks to contribute to strengthening economic and social cohesion. Priority was given to eliminating bottlenecks, finishing outstanding sections to complete the main corridors, and integrating urban areas into the TEN-T as well as linking island, landlocked, and peripheral regions with the central areas of the EU. Furthermore, the TEN-T also promotes the deployment of innovative solutions for decarbonization, the implementation of new technologies, and the creation of a safer and more efficient and accessible transport infrastructure for all citizens.

Ever since the TEN-T policy was first implemented, the guidelines have been amended on a regular basis to adapt them to the challenges that change over time and also to the incorporation of new member states to the EU. The first guidelines defined a set of specific priority projects eligible to receive the largest share of financing by the EU. The selection of those projects was a political decision that was intended to reach an acceptable balance among the interests of the member states. One of the main criticisms of the priority projects approach was that they were promoting a set of isolated networks rather than a single integrated network.

To address that problem, the last revision of the TEN-T guidelines, conducted in 2013, promoted a shift from the priority project approach to a plan of multimodal networks of corridors and urban nodes. On the basis of this approach, the TEN-T is currently structured according to two different layers: (1) a comprehensive network intended to ensure the connectivity of the regions of the EU, including the remote, insular, and isolated regions; and (2) a core network consisting of those specific sections of the comprehensive network that are of the greatest strategic importance for complying with the TEN-T policy objectives. According to the TEN-T guidelines, the core network should be implemented by 2030, and the comprehensive network should be implemented by 2050.

The latest TEN-T guidelines approved at the time of the writing of this chapter placed nine main corridors within the core network (figure 15.1) and established the specific projects within each corridor that should be prioritized to facilitate their implementation in a coordinated way. To speed up implementation of each of the corridors and the two horizontal priorities (the European Rail Traffic Management System and Motorways of the Sea), the EU appointed a European coordinator in charge of removing obstacles to the delivery of the corridor.

EU Financial Instruments to Promote Infrastructure in the European Union

Developing the TEN-T requires large financial resources. The core network alone is expected to require €500 billion from 2021 to 2030. This amount grows to €1.5 trillion if it includes the comprehensive network. The investment needs in this area are about €130 billion a year, with additional significant investment needed for maintenance. The European Court of Auditors (2018) of the EU points out that since the 2008 economic crisis, significant resources are needed to develop the TEN-T objectives on schedule. Given the limited availability of public funding, increased private sector resources in transport infrastructure are deemed essential.

As the member states do not have the obligation to develop the projects included within the TEN-T, the EU has promoted mechanisms to incentivize them. This part of the chapter provides a glimpse into the main financial mechanisms available in the EU for supporting the development of the TEN-T. Overall, the mechanisms can be divided into grants, loans, and innovative financial instruments. Grants from the EU budget may come from two sources: (1) the cohesion policy item, whose main goal is promoting the convergence of the poorest and disadvantaged regions with the rest of Europe; and (2) the Connecting Europe Facility (CEF), whose main goal is to promote TEN projects and policies.

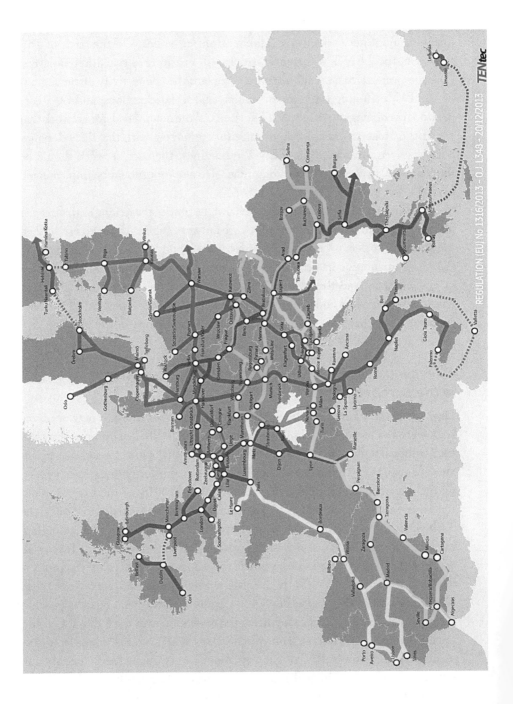

REGULATION (EU) No 1316/2013 - O. J. L348 - 20/12/2013

Cohesion Policy Instruments

The main goal of the cohesion policy is to reduce disparities among the regions of the EU. The European Regional Development Fund (ERDF) and the Cohesion Fund (CF) are the main funding sources for reaching that objective. The ERDF, established in 1975, is allocated mostly to less-developed regions whose per capita GDP is less than 75 percent of the average GDP of the EU-27 (Dall'Erba 2003). The fund includes a specific allocation for sparsely populated areas and outermost regions that can take advantage of cofinancing rates ranging from 80 to 85 percent of the eligible costs.

In its turn, the CF, established in 1994, is targeted at the member states with the gross national income per inhabitant at less than 90 percent of the EU average. In 2014–2020, the EU committed €63.28 billion to the CF. In the budget period from 2014 to 2020, the eligible countries were Bulgaria, Croatia, Cyprus, Czech Republic, Estonia, Greece, Hungary, Latvia, Lithuania, Malta, Poland, Portugal, Romania, Slovakia, and Slovenia. The CF provides support to TEN-T and sustainable development projects with environmental benefits, offering maximum cofinancing rates of up to 85 percent of the project cost.

The ERDF supports TEN-T projects and connections of secondary and tertiary nodes to TEN-T infrastructure, including multimodal nodes, low-carbon transport systems, and interoperable railway systems. Furthermore, the ERDF also funds cross-border, interregional, and transnational projects under the European Territorial Cooperation objective. The amount of money allocated in 2014–2020 was around €199 billion, even though only around 20–30 percent of that was devoted to transport infrastructure.

The ERDF and the CF are jointly managed by the member states and the European Commission through partnership agreements. Each country elaborates its operational program that, once approved by the European Commission, is implemented through the shared management approach. This means that the authorities of each country decide where and how funds are allocated within the framework of their respective programs (Vassallo and Garrido 2019).

FIGURE 15.1 (Opposite page) TEN-T core corridors of the core network. Brown = Orient-East Mediterranean; dark blue = Baltic-Adriatic; green = Mediterranean; light blue = Rhine-Danube; orange = Rhine-Alpine; pink = Scandinavian Mediterranean; purple = North Sea-Mediterranean; red = North Sea-Baltic; yellow = Atlantic. *Source: Parliament and Council of the European Union (2013).*

Connecting Europe Facility

The CEF, created in 2013, is available to all modes of transport and member states no matter how rich or poor. Its main objective is to provide financial support to the core network corridors and policies. The CEF contributes specifically to eliminating bottlenecks, improving transport interoperability, filling the missing links and improving cross-border sections, ensuring sustainable and efficient transport systems in the long-term by paying special attention to decarbonization, and optimizing the integration and interconnection of transport modes and reinforcing the interoperability, safety, and accessibility of transport services. To that end, an overall budget of €24.05 billion was allocated to the TEN-T in the 2014–2020 budgetary period. Around 80 percent of the budget is allocated to core network projects (both studies and construction works), while the remaining 20 percent is allocated to horizontal priorities, including the deployment of traffic management systems for increasing the efficiency of existing infrastructure, new technologies and innovations for transport decarbonization, etc.

CEF grants are awarded through competitive calls for specific proposals launched by the European Commission. It may finance up to 50 percent of the eligible costs for studies, even though that rate may go up to 85 percent for countries eligible to receive cohesion funding. The maximum cofunding rates for works vary from 10 percent to 85 percent of the eligible costs, depending on the priority of the project and the development of the country.

European Investment Bank and Innovative Financial Instruments

The European Investment Bank (EIB) was founded in 1958 with the objective of providing technical assistance and financial investment to projects that promote productivity, employment, and growth in the EU. Projects receiving EIB financing are required to be aligned with EU policy objectives and be economically, financially, and technically viable; to meet the strictest environmental standards; and to be tendered according to EU procurement rules. The EIB has actively supported infrastructure through loans to governments, corporations, and public-private partnerships, becoming a key player in transport infrastructure funding, especially the TEN-T. Direct loans provided by the EIB can cover up to 50 percent (75 percent in the case of TEN-T projects) of the total investment cost. Over the last few years, the EU has been also promoting innovative financial instruments, most channeled through the EIB, to create a multiplier effect or financial leverage and to promote the sustainable recycling of the public funds initially available. An example of that is the European Fund for Strategic Investment, also known as the Juncker Plan.

The most important innovative financial instruments developed in the EU with the aim of leveraging private sector financing in transport infrastructure projects are the Loan Guarantee Instrument for Trans-European Transport Network Projects, the Europe 2020 Project Bond Initiative, and the Marguerite Fund. The Loan Guarantee Instrument for Trans-European Transport Network Projects is specifically designed to cover the risks of debt service owing to insufficient demand during the ramp-up period of public-private projects. The Project Bond Initiative intends to improve the credit quality of the bonds issued by European infrastructure projects to make them more attractive to investors through credit enhancement (Vassallo et al. 2018). The Marguerite Fund is a pan-European infrastructure capital fund created by the EIB and long-term institutional investors from the public and private sectors.

For the Multiannual Financial Framework 2021–2027, the European Commission proposes to set up a new investment program, InvestEU, which will merge all centrally managed financial instruments available at the EU level, including the Loan Guarantee Instrument for Trans-European Transport Network Projects, the Project Bond Initiative, and the Marguerite Fund. This new program aims to avoid overlaps, reduce administrative burdens, and simplify access to funding sources.

Table 15.1 shows a summary of the most important EU sources to finance transport infrastructure, especially the TEN-T, in the EU-27. Unfortunately, there is no final consolidated figure of the EU funds allocated to the TEN-T, since official budgetary items are sorted by type of financial instrument, which can be used for purposes other than transport infrastructure.

Almost 80 percent of the CEF program, €24.05 billion, is allocated to the TEN-T. Around 55 percent of the CF is allocated to transport projects, most of them included in the TEN-T corridors. The ERDF is devoted to a variety of policies, such as education, research and development, promotion of small and medium enterprises, social investment, environmental infrastructure, and energy and transport infrastructure. The share of the ERDF devoted to transport is estimated to be around 25 percent of the budget. The total amount of EU grant financing for transport in 2014–2020 was around €108 billion (€15.5 billion a year, or about €35 per EU inhabitant a year).

The TEN-T needs estimated by the European Commission for both the core network and the comprehensive transport network (€130 billion a year) are around 0.0007 percent of the EU GDP; transport infrastructure investment in EU countries are between 0.5 and 1.5 percent of their respective GDPs. These figures mean that the investment devoted to developing the TEN-T is a very small fraction of the total transport investment made by the member states and their regions.

TABLE 15.1 Characteristics of the Main European Union Funding Sources

Fund	Product Type	2014–2020 Budget (€)	Maximum Cofinancing Rates	Projects Supported	Eligible Regions
CF	Mainly grants	63.28	85%	Mostly TEN-T projects with environmental benefits	MS with a GNI/capita < 90% EU-27 average
ERDF	Mainly grants	199.24	LDR: 85% TR: 60% MDR: 50%	All transport projects	All regions in the EU-27 but mostly the lower-income ones
CEF	Mainly grants and financial instruments	30.40	All MS: 50% Cohesion MS: 85%	TEN-T, especially core network	All regions in the EU-27
EIB	Standard loans and financial instruments	Demand-driven	Usually: 50% TEN-T: 75%	TEN-T and other projects	EU-27, the enlargement area of Southeast Europe, and external links in Asia, Africa, the Caribbean, Pacific, and Central America

Source: Vassallo and Garrido (2019).
GNI = gross national income; LDR = less-developed regions; MDR = more developed regions; MS = member states; TR = transition regions.

Overall, EU grants are expected to cover around 12 percent of the financial needs of the TEN-T. Even though EIB loans and financial instruments also play an important role in leveraging capital through loans and guarantees, the contribution of member states and their regions will be crucial for the right development of the TEN-T.

Is the EU Transport Infrastructure Policy Effective in Promoting Regional and National Integration?

The TEN-T policy focuses on three main goals: (1) the promotion of an integrated market in the EU, especially by developing cross-border sections and improving interoperability; (2) the enhancement of economic and social convergence across the regions of Europe; and (3) the fulfillment of a set of strategic transport policy goals such as digitalization, interoperability, and decarbonization.

This part of the chapter explores the achievements and failures of the TEN-T policy to accomplish the goals mentioned above by comparing them with the final outcomes stemming from the measures adopted. The analysis conducted here is based on an extensive review of the literature from previous research papers by scholars, case studies, and reports commissioned by different European institutions (the European Commission, the European Parliament, and the European Court of Auditors, among others) to measure the effectiveness of the measures adopted.

Development of the TEN-T to Promote an Integrated Market

The amount of EU funding spent on transport projects represents a lot of money for Europeans. As a consequence, evaluating the extent to which the resources expended in the fulfillment of EU policy goals are well spent becomes a crucial issue. However, given the relevance of this policy, it is striking that EU institutions have developed few ex post studies intended to address whether the TEN-T is developing at the right pace. Actually, the European Court of Auditors (2018) argues that the project-monitoring process conducted by the European Commission is mainly output-oriented and fails to assess results and impacts. Thus, there is not clear information as to whether the EU cofunded projects, taken individually or in the context of the core network corridors, have achieved any result-based objectives. To deal with this problem, the European Court of Auditors recommends setting milestones that are regularly monitored to increase the likelihood of reaching policy objectives in time.

Despite the lack of information, an overall agreement exists that the TEN-T does promote an integrated market in the EU by reducing transport costs for passengers and freight among member states. Actually, a recent report published by the European Court of Auditors (2020) concludes that the development of the TEN-T road network has contributed to reducing travel times in many origin-destination pairs within the EU and also to improving the quality of the transport services provided. In the case of Spain, for instance, travel time savings in the corridors from 2004 to 2017 range between 15 percent and 38 percent (European Court of Auditors 2020).

However, there is strong criticism regarding the slow pace of developing the network, the lack of clear criteria in prioritizing projects, the doubtful efficiency in the use of European funds by member states, and the lack of good ex post evaluations. The European Commission (2018b) shows that in 2015, important objectives set in the TEN-T program had not yet been achieved. For instance, the European Rail Traffic Management System was in operation in only 9.5 percent of core network sections, and only 74.5 percent of the road core network met the quality standards required in the TEN-T guidelines. A report by the European Court of Auditors (2020) of the EU about the road network of the TEN-T concludes that even though 2,400 km of TEN-T roads were built between 2007 and 2013, a seamless transport system remains constrained by the lack of cross-border connections, secure parking areas, and alternative clean fuels.

One of the main criticisms of the right functioning of the TEN-T is the lack of effectiveness in prioritizing cross-border connections. The risk of the TEN-T is that projects that add value at the European level end up not being realized, as each member state perceives only the benefits of the project for its own country (Van Exel et al. 2002). In that respect, the European Court of Auditors (2018) points out that one of the main problems is that member states are not necessarily moved by EU objectives. This is actually one of the main reasons why cross-border projects lag behind the original plans of the EU. Because national governments have the ultimate investment decision, the TEN-T is at risk of ending up becoming a patchwork of national networks promoted by the interests of the member states.

In its 2017 resolution, the European Parliament (2017) also shows its disappointment about the fact that national infrastructure plans are too often conducted without reference to the TEN-T goals. To address this issue, given the fact that the European Commission has limited enforcement mechanisms to control member states, it urged them to increase cooperation to prioritize projects aligned with the TEN-T objectives. In fact, the European Court of Auditors (2020) points out that EU member states allocated to core network projects only 34 percent of the cohesion policy funds devoted to roads, spending the remaining 66 percent on other road projects outside the network. In addition, this institution notices that EU funds require better targeting to ensure added value, since several audits conducted by the European Court of Auditors (2018) note that, for political reasons, they often prefer to spread EU aid across many projects rather than focus on those with the greatest added value.

A review entrusted by the European Commission, based on 10 case studies of EU cofinanced projects between 2000 and 2013, concludes the following:

> The extent to which projects achieved the stated objectives is overall acceptable, but they were never able to perfectly match the initial expectations. This was not due to underperformance during project implementation, but mostly to the fact that they were systematically subject to over-ambitious targets. In other words, policy makers and project promoters were too optimistic in setting their targets about the effects in terms of socio-economic development, urban regeneration, and other positive consequences that the implementation of the projects would have triggered on the local or regional context. (Center for Industrial Studies et al. 2018, 12)

This study also reports cost overruns and delays caused by unpredictable external factors and optimism bias leading to demand overestimation. The main consequences of overruns and delays were lower effectiveness and lack of financial sustainability.

Regarding the right selection of projects, the European Court of Auditors (2018) notes that cost-efficiency analyses were not the most important principles in implementing transport projects cofinanced with European funds. Kelly et al. (2015) conducted a study aimed at comparing the cost-benefit analysis ex ante and ex post of 10 large transport projects in eight countries that had benefited from the CF. The research found that, despite much attention focused on the problem, optimism bias remains an issue. The study also recommends improving the quality of ex ante analysis, especially in fields such as risk analysis, capital cost estimation, and demand modeling. On the basis of the projects analyzed, this research shows the modest role that appraisal tools such as cost-benefit analysis have actually played in the decision-making process. Cost-benefit analysis is often seen by many member states as a hurdle that must be overcome to obtain funding.

Finally, the quality of the institutions of the member states was regarded as a crucial driver for the successful use of EU funding. A report produced by the European Commission (2018c) acknowledges that to ensure that funds are used to their full potential for the benefit of European citizens, it is imperative to have strong national, regional, and local administrations. Indeed, the capacity of member states to manage such investments effectively and efficiently is one of the key factors contributing to their success. In a research paper, Crescenzi et al. (2016) conclude that the performance of government institutions positively influences the return on infrastructure investment in the EU.

Impact on Economic Development and Convergence Across Nations and Regions

One of the most important goals of the EU is to promote economic and social convergence across European regions, and infrastructure policy is supposed to be one of the most important means to achieve this. On the basis of a European research project, several universities and research institutes developed the Spatial and Socio-Economic Impacts (SASI) model intended to forecast GDP, employment, and accessibility impacts in Europe subject to exogenous assumptions, transport infrastructure investments, and transport system improvements. Using the SASI model to compare the impacts of the scenarios with and without TEN-T developments, Schürmann, Spiekermann, and Wegener (2001) found that promoting the TEN-T has a smaller impact on growth than other exogenous factors, such as increasing labor productivity. Despite that, they noticed a positive impact of the TEN-T on cohesion, even though its distribution across regions appears to be uneven.

However, the impact of the TEN-T is not negligible. A recent study funded by the European Commission to determine the impact of completion on growth, jobs, and the environment concludes that if the TEN-T core network is ultimately completed in 2030, additional GDP growth of 1.6 percent will be realized, 7.5 million person-years of jobs will be generated cumulatively from 2017 to 2030, and 0.26 million tons of carbon dioxide emissions will be saved in the transport sector (Fermi et al. 2018).

Overall, the literature shows a positive relationship between infrastructure and economic growth in Europe. On the basis of panel data over the period 2000–2014, Cigu, Agheorghiesei, and Toader (2019) calibrated a production function, finding a positive relationship between transport infrastructure, public sector performance, and economic growth. Similarly, on the basis of a fixed-effects regression model for EU-28 countries from 1990 to 2016, Gherghina et al. (2018) found that GDP per capita was positively influenced by roads, inland waterways, ports, and airports, though a negative link was found in the case of railway transport.

The cohesion policy, which plays a key role in financing transport infrastructure in Europe, is one of the EU's most visible undertakings, since it serves as a crucial vehicle for European solidarity. According to Huguenot-Noël, Hunter, and Zuleeg (2017), this policy is seen as a possible vehicle for championing European values, such as subsidiarity, the integration of migrants, respect for the rule of law, and the safeguarding of fundamental values. However, in the academic literature, there has been a big debate over the last few decades about the impact that cohesion policy has actually played in promoting growth and convergence across the regions of Europe. Here, it is necessary to point out that cohesion policy is not just devoted to funding infrastructure but can also spend resources on other measures aimed at fostering regional development (such as education, the promotion of research and development, and incentives to small and medium enterprises). However, it is fair to say that a great share of cohesion policy funding has been devoted to transportation infrastructure, amounting to around 60 percent of the CF and 30 percent of the ERDF (Dall'Erba and Hewings 2005).

Most of the work conducted at the time of the writing of this chapter concludes that cohesion policy has had a positive impact on promoting growth and balancing that growth across regions but with important nuances. Crescenzi and Giua (2020) find a positive relationship between the cohesion policy and the promotion of growth and employment in Europe, even though large differences exist across member states. Using data from 1989 to 1999, Dall'Erba (2003) also find a positive relationship between regional growth and structural funds, thereby proving that structural funds are promoting convergence across regions in Europe. In another study, Dall'Erba and Hewings (2005) conclude that the convergence process in Europe is characterized by both the catching up of the poorest countries and the growing divergence among different regions in the same country. According to the authors, the benefits of integration have mostly fallen on the richest regions within the least developed countries. These uneven benefits result because transport infrastructure usually connects important population areas, thereby promoting hub-and-spoke relationships that in the end increase the economic activities in the areas closest to the hub. "Transportation infrastructures thus promote the country's aggregate growth but cannot always be seen as an efficient instrument to reduce interregional disparities in Europe" (Dall'Erba and Hewings 2005, 19).

In a research study aimed at determining the impact of the cohesion policy in the Algarve, Rocha Medeiros (2014) reaches similar conclusions: EU funds had a fairly positive impact on the evolution of many territorial development-related indicators, but they seem to favor the most populated urban settlements. Regional territorial cohesion was not achieved, as the less populated municipalities continue to exhibit their territorial exclusion path in many key development indicators such as unemployment, income, and education.

In a meta-analysis conducted by Dell'Erba and Fang (2017) about research studies exploring the impact of cohesion policy on growth, the authors state that not all the results show positive outcomes. Some studies cast doubts on their actual efficacy (Bouayad-Agha, Turpinn, and Védrine 2011; Dall'Erba and Le Gallo 2008). Others stress the need to condition the aid on recipients taking other measures (Ederveen et al. 2002; Ederveen, De Groot, and Nahuis 2006; Rodriguez-Pose and Fratesi 2004). Finally, some conclude that the cohesion policy has a negative influence on growth (Bouayad-Agha, Turpinn, and Védrine 2011; Fagerberg and Verspagen 1996).

Another body of literature explores the impact of TEN-T projects on spatial spillovers that can be defined as the effects of an infrastructure section, either national or cross-border, on other regions where that infrastructure has not been built. Spillover effects are a consequence of the network effect (Laird, Nellthorp, and Mackie 2005; Vickerman 1996), whereby a section may produce great synergies over the entire network.

Studying the spillovers produced by some TEN-T projects in Europe, Gutierrez et al. (2011) found that even though many cross-border projects do not always produce great benefits to the country where they are built, they generate important spillovers worth evaluating to account for the added value of the project in terms of integration. Similarly, on the basis of a computed general equilibrium model,

Bröcker, Korzhenevych, and Schürmann (2020) studied the economic profitability and spatial distribution of the spillovers across countries produced by 22 TEN-T priority projects proposed by the European Commission in 2004. They found that only 4 out of the 22 projects analyzed proved to have both high economic returns and high spillovers. The authors conclude that many of the priority projects promoted by the EU are not so valuable, since they are not economically profitable and do not produce spillovers big enough to justify integration.

Using the SASI model previously mentioned, Spiekermann and Wegener (2006) modeled the evolution of accessibility and GDP for a set of scenarios combining the development of the TEN-T along with other policy measures regarding the pricing of transport services. They found positive growth of income per capita caused by the development of the TEN-T, greater in peripheral than in central regions. Introducing the scenario of implementing socially marginal cost pricing into the model reduced the income growth compared with the no-pricing alternative especially for peripheral regions, even though the growth remained positive when compared with the do-nothing scenario. Unfortunately, the study did not quantify the benefits caused by the reduction of externalities as a consequence of implementing that pricing approach.

Even though accessibility is not necessarily linked to economic benefits, there are also research works that have explored the impact of the TEN-T on accessibility and its distribution across different economic regions of the EU. Gutiérrez and Urbano (1996) found that once completed, the development of the TEN-T will produce substantial accessibility gains in the EU, particularly in peripheral regions. Using the SASI model, Spiekermann and Wegener (2006) also analyzed the evolution of accessibility for the scenarios previously mentioned. The analysis confirmed accessibility gains across the regions of Europe, particularly in the outermost regions. As with GDP per capita, implementing social marginal pricing reduced accessibility for both central and peripheral regions.

Impact on the Fulfillment of Transport Policy Goals

One of the main goals of the EU transport infrastructure policy is to encourage the fulfillment of EU policy objectives such as moving toward more sustainable transportation. The 2011 white paper "Roadmap to a Single European Transport Area: Towards a Competitive and Resource-Efficient Transport System" (European Commission 2011) provides 10 goals for developing a competitive and resource-efficient transport system able to achieve the 60 percent greenhouse gas emission reduction target that it recommends. These goals may be summarized as having three main objectives: (1) developing and deploying new and sustainable fuels and propulsion systems; (2) optimizing the performance of multimodal logistic chains; and (3) increasing the efficiency of transport infrastructure use with information systems and market-based incentives (European Commission 2018a).

EU transport policy also gives importance to promoting multimodality, stressing the importance of making better use of transport infrastructure networks through the deployment of transport management systems and intelligent transport systems and improving both the safety and the security of all modes of transport. Furthermore, the transport policy supports the application of "user pays" and "polluter pays" principles and the engagement of the private sector in financing transport infrastructure. Another transport priority is the digitalization of transport and logistics, which may contribute to an increase in safety and address the growing congestion and emission problems worldwide. However, for digitalization to happen, developing a seamless digital layer throughout the entire European transport area is necessary (Vassallo and Garrido 2019).

The European Court of Auditors (2018, 39) recommends that "EU support should be prioritized for projects that are run in response to clearly established and properly assessed needs, are based on careful planning and offer demonstrable EU added value for the network (e.g., resolving major bottlenecks and missing links and establishing cross-border connections)." However, EU funding has not always been effective in promoting transport policy objectives, since most of the programs have prioritized the construction of infrastructure over adopting measures aimed at fulfilling transport policy goals.

By far, the CEF program has been the EU funding instrument more focused on fulfilling EU policy goals by funding technologies for decarbonizing transport—for example, with alternative fuels and their deployment along the transport infrastructure—and initiatives aimed at promoting the digitalization of such infrastructure as connected roads. However, the allocation of funding to these priorities is still small compared with the traditional construction of infrastructure assets. TEN-T policy has not stressed the adoption of harmonized policy measures aimed at improving transportation efficiency, such as implementing the "user pay" and "polluter pay" principles.

In the academic literature, a few studies explore the impact of the TEN-T on the fulfillment of EU policy goals. Gherghina et al. (2018) study the connection between transport modes, related investments, specific air pollutants, and sustainable economic growth. Using panel data for the EU-28 member states, they found that greater CO_2 and pollutant emissions in the EU are associated with lower GDP per capita growth. Lenz, Skender, and Mirković (2018), in turn, show how environmental aspects can justify the development of rail infrastructure that is not profitable from a purely economic perspective.

Conclusions

This chapter documents the evolution of the EU infrastructure policy and summarizes the results that such a policy has had on economic and social integration among member states and regions of the EU. The analysis is conducted mostly as a review of previous research papers and institutional policy reports. From a global perspective, there seems to be evidence that the TEN-T policy has promoted infrastructure that is fostering integration for the benefit of the countries and regions of the EU. However, whether that policy has been effective and efficient enough to fulfill those goals, in other words, whether the benefits of the TEN-T policy actually outweigh its costs, is not so clear.

A first doubt concerns the management approach used to allocate the resources. For some instruments, such as the ERDF and the CF, member states have a lot of freedom to use and prioritize EU resources for projects that are more suitable for their national interests than for achieving EU objectives. This fact has resulted in improvements to cross-border sections, usually the most important ones in promoting integration, lagging behind other national priorities. A reform of the management approach seems to be crucial to ensure that EU funds are oriented toward the projects that produce greater added value for the EU.

A second doubt concerns the effectiveness of cohesion policy to contribute to territorial cohesion. While empirical results appear to suggest that EU funding is boosting regional convergence, it seems that a greater divergence between medium-size cities and rural areas is on the rise. In other words, cohesion policy seems to be fostering the growth of the economically strongest cities within the poorest regions. This situation is prompting a greater unbalance between rural and urban areas in some countries of Europe. In fact, this problem is becoming a central issue in the political debates within some European countries.

A third doubt concerns the excessive allocation of resources to the construction of new public works compared with other measures that may prove more cost-effective in boosting integration, such as fostering a greater connection among transport modes, promoting fare integration, digitalizing infrastructure, preparing infrastructure to supply clean fuels, ensuring fair competition across transport modes, and adopting measures to internalize externalities.

A fourth doubt concerns the ex post evaluation of the funds. Few studies conducted by EU institutions have that aim, and they seem to focus more on checking the fulfillment of administrative procedures than on assessing the economic, social, and environmental outcomes of TEN-T policy for EU citizens. Improving the EU's infrastructure policy will be impossible without a rigorous and neutral evaluation of its effectiveness regarding the prioritization of projects and the right allocation of funds.

Given all those doubts, it appears that the EU infrastructure policy still has a long way to go to become more effective and efficient. In fact, it is impossible to be certain that the current TEN-T policy results in good value for money. Undoubtedly, it is contributing to improving connectivity and interoperability across countries and is benefiting both peripheral regions, which become more competitive, and central regions, which see how their available market substantially broadens. However, not enough evidence exists to support the claim that the current benefits prompted by this policy are greater than the opportunity cost of investing in other potential alternatives.

To give a robust answer to the abovementioned issue, more in-depth research based on good analytical data is necessary. One of the most important conclusions from this chapter is that given the importance of the topic, little research exists about the impacts of infrastructure on integration. Most of the research conducted to date has been focused on econometric analyses, trying to explain regional growth as a function of a set of explanatory variables defined at the macrolevel. Even though those analyses shed light on macrotrends, they should be complemented with additional research focused on more specific impacts at the microlevel. These analyses, however, require data that are barely collected nowadays. For that reason, it would be advisable that the European Commission start to compile a European-wide database that helps researchers and audit institutions to produce high-quality research about impacts associated with the TEN-T policy.

Summary

- The EU's experience of using infrastructure as a tool to promote regional integration is of particular interest because EU member states enjoy much higher degrees of economic integration than the members of other major regional organizations such as the Association of Southeast Asian Nations and the North American Free Trade Agreement.
- Logic and empirical evidence suggest that economic and infrastructure integration complement one another in that both are designed to increase the effective size, scope, and competitiveness of the internal market in two ways: (1) by changing regulations, governing trade, immigration, and other economic matters; and (2) by improving access to transport people, goods, communications, and energy.
- The EU endorsed infrastructure's importance in 1992 by ordering the development of three TEN plans—one each for transportation (TEN-T), energy (TEN-E), and communications (eTEN)—to promote access to, and interconnection and interoperability among, national networks.

- The outcomes of the TEN-T plans are mixed. There is some evidence of increased integration, but progress is disappointingly slow, in part because the targeted facilities are owned by member states, and their priorities for improvements are not always the same as those of the EU.

References

Alder, Hans A. 1965. "Economic Evaluation of Transport Projects." In *Transport Investment and Economic Development*, ed. Gary Fromm, 170–1194. Washington, DC: Brookings Institution.

Aschauer, David A. 1989. "Is Public Expenditure Productive?" *Journal of Monetary Economics* 23(2): 177–200.

Balassa, Béla. 2013. *The Theory of Economic Integration*. New York: Routledge.

Bouayad-Agha, Salima, Nadine Turpin, and Lionel Védrine. 2011. "Fostering the Development of European Regions: A Spatial Dynamic Panel Data Analysis of the Impact of Cohesion Policy." *Regional Studies* 47: 1573–1593.

Briceño-Garmendia, Cecilia, Antonio Estache, and Nefat Shafik. 2004. "Infrastructure Services in Developing Countries: Access, Quality, Costs, and Policy Reform." Working paper No. 3468. Washington, DC: World Bank.

Bröcker, Johannes, Artem Korzhenevych, and Carsten Schürmann. 2020. "Assessing Spatial Equity and Efficiency Impacts of Transport Infrastructure Projects." *Transportation Research Part B: Methodological* 44: 795–811.

Center for Industrial Studies, Ramboll Management, Significance BV, and Tplan Consulting. 2018. *Ex Post Evaluation of Major Projects Supported by the European Regional Development Fund (ERDF) and Cohesion Fund Between 2000 and 2013*. Brussels: European Commission.

Cigu, Elena, Daniela Tatiana Agheorghiesei, Anca Florentina Gavriluță (Vatamanu), and Elena Toader. 2019. "Transport Infrastructure Development, Public Performance and Long-Run Economic Growth: A Case Study for the EU-28 Countries." *Sustainability* 11: 67.

Crescenzi, Riccardo, Marco Di Cataldo, and Andrés Rodríguez Pose. 2016. "Government Quality and the Economic Returns of Transport Infrastructure Investment in European Regions." *Journal of Regional Science* 56: 555–582.

Crescenzi Riccardo, and Mara Giua. 2020. "One or Many Cohesion Policies of the European Union? On the Differential Economic Impacts of Cohesion Policy Across Member States." *Regional Studies* 54: 10–20.

Dall'Erba, Sandy. 2003. "European Regional Development Policies: History and Current Issues." EUC working paper No. 2 (4). Urbana, IL: University of Illinois.

Dall'Erba, Sandy, and Fang Fang. 2017. "Meta-Analysis of the Impact of European Union Structural Funds on Regional Growth," *Regional Studies* 51: 822–832.

Dall'Erba, Sandy, and Geoffrey J. D. Hewings. 2005. "European Regional Development Policies: The Trade-off Between Efficiency-Equity Revisited." Discussion paper No. 03-T2. Urbana, IL: Regional Economics Application Laboratory, University of Illinois.

Dall'Erba, Sandy, and Julie Le Gallo. 2008. "Regional Convergence and the Impact of European Structural Funds Over 1989–1999: A Spatial Econometric Analysis." *Papers in Regional Science* 87: 219–244.

Ding, Lei, Kingsley E. Haynes, and Yanchun Liu. 2008. "Telecommunications Infrastructure and Regional Income Convergence in China: Panel Data Approaches." *Annals of Regional Science* 42: 843–861.

Ederveen, Sjef, Henri L. F. de Groot, and Richard Nahuis. 2006. "Fertile Soil for Structural Funds? A Panel Data Analysis of the Conditional Effectiveness of European Cohesion Policy." *Kyklos* 59: 17–42.

Ederveen, Sjef, Joeri Gorter, Ruud de Mooij, and Richard Nahuis. 2002. *Funds and Games: The Economics of European Cohesion Policy.* The Hague: CPB Netherlands Bureau for Economic Policy Analysis.

European Commission. 2011. "Roadmap to a Single European Transport Area: Towards a Competitive and Resource Efficient Transport System." *COM* 144. Brussels: EU Publications.

———. 2018a. "A Clean Planet for All: A European Strategic Long-Term Vision for a Prosperous, Modern, Competitive and Climate Neutral Economy." *COM* 773. Brussels: EU Publications.

———. 2018b. *Delivering the TEN-T: Facts and Figures, September 2017.* Brussels: EU Publications.

———. 2018c. *Good Governance for Cohesion Policy: Administrative Capacity Building.* Brussels: EU Publications.

European Court of Auditors. 2018. *Landscape Review: Towards a Successful Transport Sector in the EU: Challenges to Be Addressed.* Luxembourg: Publication Office of the European Union.

———. 2020. *The EU Core Road Network: Shorter Travel Times but Network Not Yet Fully Functional.* Luxembourg: Publication Office of the European Union.

European Parliament. 2017. *Resolution of 19 January 2017 on Logistics in the EU and Multimodal Transport in the New TEN-T Corridors.* P8_TA(2017)0009. Luxemburg: Publication Office of the European Union.

Fagerberg, Jan, and Bart Verspagen. 1996. "Heading for Divergence? Regional Growth in Europe Reconsidered." *Journal of Common Market Studies* 34: 431–448.

Fermi, Francesca, Luca Bellodi, Angelo Martino, Silvia Maffii, Stefanie Schäfer, Sarah Welter, Johannes Hartwig, Wolfgang Schade, Loredana Zani, and Claudia de Stasio. 2018. *The Impact of TEN-T Completion on Growth, Jobs and the Environment.* Brussels: EU Publications.

Fujimura, Manabu. 2004. "Cross-Border Infrastructure, Regional Integration and Development." ADBI discussion paper No. 16. Tokyo: Asian Development Bank Institute.

Gherghina, Ștefan C., Mihaela Onofrei, Georgeta Vintilă, and Daniel Ș. Armeanu. 2018. "Empirical Evidence from EU-28 Countries on Resilient Transport Infrastructure Systems and Sustainable Economic Growth." *Sustainability* 10: 2900.

Gutiérrez, Javier, Ana Condeço-Melhorado, Elena López, and Andrés Monzón. 2011. "Evaluating the European Added Value of TEN-T Projects: A Methodological Proposal Based on Spatial Spillovers, Accessibility and GIS." *Journal of Transport Geography* 19: 840–850.

Gutiérrez, Javier, and Paloma Urbano. 1996. "Accessibility in the European Union: The Impact of the Trans-European Road Network." *Journal of Transport Geography* 4(1): 15–25.

Huguenot-Noël, Robin, Alison Hunter, and Fabian Zuleeg. 2017. "Can the EU Structural Funds Reconcile Growth, Solidarity and Stability Objectives? A Study on the Role of Conditionalities in Spurring Structural Reforms and Reducing Macroeconomic Imbalances." Issue paper No. 83, October. Brussels: European Policy Centre.

Izquierdo, Rafael. 2003. "La Red Transeuropea de Transporte y su Incidencia en la Política Española." *Noticias de la Unión Europea* 24: 69–93.

Kelly, Charlotte, James Laird, Stefano Costantini, Phil Richards, José Carbajo, and John Nellthorp. 2015. "Ex post Appraisal: What Lessons Can Be Learnt from EU Cohesion Funded Transport Projects?" *Transport Policy* 37: 83–91.

Laird, James J., John Nellthorp, and Peter J. Mackie. 2005. "Network Effects and Total Economic Impact in Transport Appraisal." *Transport Policy* 12: 537–544.

Lenz, Nela Vlahinić, Helga Pavlić Skender, and Petra Adelajda Mirković. 2018. "The Macroeconomic Effects of Infrastructure on Economic Growth: The Case of Central and Eastern E.U. Member States." *Economic Research-Ekonomska Istraživanja* 31(1): 1953–1964.

Limao, Nuno, and Anthony J. Venables. 2001. "Infrastructure, Geographical Disadvantage, Transport Costs and Trade." *World Bank Economic Review* 15: 451–479.

Parliament and Council of the European Union. 2013. "Regulation (EU) No 1316/2013 of the European Parliament and of the Council of 11 December 2013 Establishing the Connecting Europe Facility, Amending Regulation (EU) No 913/2010 and repealing Regulations (EC) No 680/2007 and (EC) No 67/2010 (Text with EEA Relevance)." https://www.legislation.gov.uk/eur/2013/1316/article/6.

Radelet, Steven, and Jeffrey Sachs. 1998. "Shipping Costs, Manufactured Exports, and Economic Growth." Paper presented at the annual meeting of the American Economic Association. Chicago, January 3–5.

Redding, Stephen, and Anthony J. Venables. 2004. "Economic Geography and International Inequality." *Journal of International Economics* 62: 53–82.

Ricardo, David. 1817. *On The Principles of Political Economy and Taxation*. London: John Murray.

Rocha, Medeiros, and Eduardo José. 2014. "Assessing Territorial Impacts of the EU Cohesion Policy at the Regional Level: The Case of Algarve." *Impact Assessment and Project Appraisal* 32(3): 198–212.

Rodriguez-Pose, Andrés, and Ugo Fratesi. 2004. "Between Development and Social Policies: The Impact of European Structural Funds in Objective 1 Regions." *Regional Studies* 38: 97–113.

Schürmann, Carsten, Klaus Spiekermann, and Michael Wegener. 2001. "Regional Economic Impacts of Trans-European Transport Networks." In *WCTR Proceedings*. Seoul: WCTR Society.

Spiekermann, Klaus, and Michael Wegener. 2006. "Accessibility and Spatial Development in Europe." *Scienze Regionali* 5(2): 15–46.

Stone, Susan, and Anna Strutt. 2010. "Transport Infrastructure and Trade Facilitation in the Greater Mekong Subregion." In *Trade Facilitation and Regional Cooperation in Asia*. ed. Douglas H. Brooks and Susan F. Stone. Cheltenham, UK: Edward Elgar.

Van Exel, Job, Sytze Rienstra, Michael Gommers, Alan Pearman, and Dimitrios Tsamboulas. 2002. "EU Involvement in TEN Development: Network Effects and European Value Added." *Transport Policy* 9(4): 299–311.

Vassallo, José Manuel, and Laura Garrido. 2019. *Research for TRAN Committee–EU Funding of Transport Projects*. Brussels: European Parliament, Policy Department for Structural and Cohesion Policies.

Vassallo, José Manuel, Thais Rangel, María De Los Ángeles Baeza, and Paola Carolina Bueno. 2018. "The Europe 2020 Project Bond Initiative: An Alternative to Finance Infrastructure in Europe." *Technological and Economic Development of Economy* 24(1): 229–252.

Vickerman, Roger. 1996. "Location, Accessibility and Regional Development: The Appraisal of Trans-European Networks." *Transport Policy* 2(4): 225–234.

16

NATIONAL INFRASTRUCTURE
POLICIES IN JAPAN

FOCUSING ON RAILWAYS

Fumitoshi Mizutani and Miwa Matsuo

Passenger railway services are vital in Japan and in fact thrive as private businesses in urban areas. More than 160 operators run passenger rail services; among them, major railway companies are profitable enough to finance infrastructure development costs. Japan National Railways (JNR), the former national railway public corporation, was privatized in 1987 and separated into six passenger companies and one freight rail company.

This strong tradition of private initiative is specific to railway services. Most Japanese transportation infrastructures other than railways are in the public realm. For example, arterial and local roads are planned, constructed, and maintained by various levels of governments. Most ports and airports are also planned and managed by governments. Since the government reforms undertaken by the Junichiro Koizumi administration in the early 2000s, some major transportation infrastructures have been privatized. Narita Airport and expressways were corporatized in 2004 and 2005, respectively, followed by a few more hub ports and airports.[1] However, most such infrastructures have national and prefectural governments as their principal stockholders (Graham, Saito, and Nomura 2014).

Another notable characteristic of the Japanese railway industry is vertical integration. From the industry's beginnings, major railway companies have planned, built, and owned their own infrastructure; the six newly privatized Japan Rail (JR) passenger rail companies also own and maintain their infrastructure. Only railways with a low demand, such as local rail in rural areas and Japan Rail Freight (JR Freight), separate infrastructure owners from service operators. In contrast, vertical separation is common among privatized expressways, airports, and ports. For example, expressways are subsumed by a public corporation that holds infrastructure and redeems construction debt, with privatized operation and management of the system (Mizutani and Uranishi 2008). Infrastructure at airports and ports is mostly publicly owned, and privatization usually refers to concessions for terminal operations and land management (Xu, Hanaoka, and Onishi 2019).

Infrastructure construction costs are often financed by debt among private as well as public corporations. As mentioned, private railways finance their infrastructure independently and redeem costs through fare revenues. Former public corporations, such as JNR and the Japan Highway Public Corporation, also financed their rail and highway construction costs with loans (Ministry of Land, Infrastructure, Transport and Tourism 2019a; Mizutani and Uranishi 2008). Debt financing was particularly useful during the reconstruction period after World War II because of austere national budgetary conditions.

We focus here on the Japanese rail industry because of features distinguishing it from the industry in other countries.

Market Structure and Regulations of the Railway Industry

Market Structure

Rail transportation in Japan continues to play an important role in passenger transport, whereas freight services take minor shares in the freight market. As of 2017, 169 private or third-sector companies and 10 municipalities operated 27,900 km of passenger-rail services and carried more than 25 billion people annually (Ministry of Land, Infrastructure, Transport and Tourism 2017a). All urban rail operators create operating profits. On average, the operating cost-revenue ratio of urban rail services including subways is 57.9 when depreciation costs of infrastructure are excluded and remain well below 100, even when depreciation costs are included (the average is 80.7). The operating cost-revenue ratio of light rails and local rails is higher, but 45 of 98 local railways and 12 of 19 light railways manage to keep the ratio at 100 or lower. Four out of six passenger JR companies, which operate urban, local, and intercity rail services, also make operating profits. The average operating cost-revenue ratio of these six JR companies is 63.2.

In contrast to the passenger transport business, only JR Freight and 12 local freight rail companies were operating in the freight rail market in 2017. In the freight transportation market, long-distance transport services are usually accomplished by coastal shipping, and mid- to short-distance services are dispatched by truck. Freight rail services have declined substantially with the growth of the trucking industry since the 1960s. Although freight rail has revived slightly since the 2000s with the promotion of environment-friendly intermodal shipment, the market shares of the freight rail services in 2017 were less than 1 percent on a weight basis and 5 percent on a weight-distance basis.

Passenger rail service is particularly strong in large metropolitan areas such as Tokyo and Osaka. Despite a substantial increase in private auto ownership since the 1960s, the majority of workers in large metropolitan areas use rail or mixed modes for commuting. Specifically, the 2010 census found that the share of rail-only commuting was 16.1 percent and of mixed-mode commuting was 10.3 percent in Japan, but their shares increased to 44.5 percent for rail-only commuting and 15.6 percent for mixed-mode commuting in Tokyo Prefecture. In contrast, the share of auto-only commuting in Japan was 46.5 percent, while it was only 9.4 percent in Tokyo Prefecture.

This extensive use of public transit is supported by three factors: high-density compact land development, inconvenient and expensive road transportation, and the high quality of rail service. The Tokyo metropolitan area has a population of 30 million, of which 9.2 million live in the central 23 wards (hereafter referred to as Tokyo special wards), where population density is 14,775.6 people per square kilometer (i.e., 59.8 people per acre). The daytime population of the Tokyo special wards swells to 12 million, and daytime population density reaches as high as 19,174.9 people per square kilometer (i.e., 77.5 per acre).

The area's density makes it difficult to access by road or find parking spaces. Unlike in the United States, few Japanese employers subsidize parking for workers, and there are less than 200,000 paid parking spaces in the Tokyo special wards, that is, only 1 space per 33 workers (Tokyo Metropolitan Government 2017). Expressways providing access from suburban areas to central Tokyo are limited in capacity, slow because of severe traffic congestion, and tolled. The most central loop of the Metropolitan Expressway has only two lanes going in each direction, and the speed limit is 40–50 km per hour. This limited capacity results in heavy congestion. The toll for the Metropolitan Expressway is also relatively higher than rail fare. At ¥1,320 for each entry if a driver pays in cash, the highway toll is two to four times more expensive than the corresponding rail fare.[2] As a result, auto ownership is suppressed in the central areas of large metropolitan areas such as Tokyo. In Japan, the nationwide average vehicle ownership is 1.06 vehicles per household, while the average passenger vehicle ownership of Tokyo and Osaka Prefectures is 0.44 and 0.65, respectively.

The punctuality of the urban rail service also adds value over car transport. In the Tokyo metropolitan area, the average number of weekdays with rail delays longer than 10 minutes is 4.3 per month, and the number of weekdays with delays longer than 30 minutes is only 0.7 (Ministry of Land Infrastructure, Transport and Tourism 2019b). In contrast, highways and local roads in the metropolitan area are congested during commuting hours, which makes it difficult to predict travel time in advance. As a result, the majority of employers and workers prefer rail to car for commuting.

Passenger rail service is also strong in the intercity travel market. Because of its frequency and convenience, the Shinkansen has a dominant share in the mid-distance range. Table 16.1 shows the mode share of intercity travel between the six largest metropolitan areas in Japan.[3] The shaded areas show where the Shinkansen is more competitive than air travel, with its market share 79 percent between Tokyo and Osaka (400 km), the two largest metropolitan areas in Japan. The Shinkansen remains almost equally competitive between Sendai and Nagoya (500 km) and Nagoya and Fukuoka (620 km).

Historically, airlines and the Shinkansen have intensively competed for a greater share in the largest intercity travel demand between Tokyo and Osaka. Currently, the travel time by Shinkansen or airline, including airport access times, is almost equal for Tokyo and Osaka; fares are usually slightly cheaper for air travel if tickets are booked at least one day prior to travel. But when the frequencies and capacities of the services are compared, the Shinkansen greatly outperforms airlines. Shinkansen trains connecting Tokyo and Osaka have a seating capacity for 370,000 per day, while airlines can offer only 30,000 seats, even when relatively inconvenient low-cost carriers are included (JR Central 2020a). The air share has never come close to the share of Shinkansen in the market.

Regulations and Competition Policy

Vertical Structure and Entry Regulation

Unlike in Europe, where vertical separation is common, vertical integration is the norm in the rail industry in Japan, though a few vertically separated railways do exist. Japanese railway organizations are classified into three categories based on their vertical structures. Most railways in Japan are vertically integrated companies (class 1), such as the 6 passenger JRs and the 15 largest private railways and public subway systems. A class 2 railway is a rail operation company without its own rail infrastructure, a typical example being JR Freight, which provides freight service on rail tracks borrowed from the six JR passenger companies. A class 3 railway is a rail infrastructure holding organization that rents its infrastructure to a class 2 company. An example of a class 3 firm is Kobe Rapid Transit Railway (Kobe Kosoku),[4] a privately owned rail track holding company connecting points in downtown Kobe. Although vertical integration is standard, cases of vertical separation are gradually growing more common in rural areas in Japan mainly for financial reasons, including to ease the financial burden of a railway

TABLE 16.1 Intermetropolitan Travel Mode Shares (by %) in Japan

Departure	Sapporo Metro			Sendai Metro			Tokyo Metro			Nagoya Metro			Osaka Metro			Fukuoka Metro		
Arrival	Rail	Air	Car	Rail	Air	Car	Rail	Air	Car	Rail	Air	Car	Rail	Air	Car	Rail	Air	Car
Sapporo Metro				3	97	0	1	99	0	0	100	0	0	100	0	0	100	0
Sendai Metro	3	97	0				93	1	6	55	41	5	14	84	2	2	98	0
Tokyo Metro	1	99	0	93	1	6				90	2	8	79	16	5	9	90	0
Nagoya Metro	0	100	0	53	42	5	89	2	9				77	0	23	53	46	1
Osaka Metro	0	100	0	13	84	2	79	16	5	78	0	22				85	13	2
Fukuoka Metro	0	100	0	2	98	0	9	91	0	52	47	1	85	13	2			

Source: Ministry of Land, Infrastructure, Transport and Tourism (2017b).

Note: The shaded cells indicate where the Shinkansen is more competitive than air travel.

company maintaining infrastructure management. We explain such cases later in the chapter.

Before the revision of the Railway Business Law in 2000, a rail organization had to have a license to enter the market, but the system has changed and now requires that a railway merely secure permission from the government (Mizutani 2015). Exit from the market also became easier, changing from obtaining government permission to simply notifying the government one year prior to termination of service. To quell concerns about accessibility after the termination of service, the law also requires that a regional council be established to take into account the public interest.

Thus, in summary, although entering and exiting the railway market is not impossible, in reality, the railway market is government-controlled, and competition within the market among railway companies is very limited.

Though vertical integration is prevalent in Japan, vertical separation exists as well. For example, Kobe Kosoku was started in 1968 to connect multiple railway companies in the downtown Kobe area. Furthermore, the new Railway Business Law was enacted in 1987, creating a new framework for rail companies such as rail service operation only and rail infrastructure management only. For various reasons, however, the most common structure in Japan remains vertical integration.

First, most of Japan's railways are privately owned and from their founding have had vertically integrated organizational structures. If the government were to make a law to transform these companies into vertically separated organizations (i.e., a rail operating company and an infrastructure management company), it would need consent from the shareholders of the original railway company. This would be a difficult undertaking because in light of the absence of major problems so far, there would be no clear incentive to separate the existing railway. The success of vertically integrated organizations in Japan is the biggest reason why they have remained structured in this way.

Second, a general reluctance exists to enter the rail operation market even if the vertical separation policy is selected. For example, there is no law whereby operating companies are selected through competitive bidding. In fact, the Railway Business Law does not specify a time period under which rail business can be approved. No specified rule or procedure for switching rail operators means that virtually no chance exists for competitive selection of rail operators; that is, access to rail track is basically closed. The reluctance to select a rail operation company from among several rail operators may be another reason that vertical separation is in general not chosen.

Third, the primary purpose of vertical separation in Japan is to alleviate the cost of running the infrastructure. As noted, Japan's railway business is based on the full cost principle, whereby rail fares cover costs of both operation and infrastructure. For local railways, however, providing service under the vertical integration structure has recently been difficult because of low passenger demand. In such cases, infrastructure management is separated from rail operation. Separated infrastructure is often owned by the public sector and leased to the rail operating company. Vertical separation in Japan is generally limited to these cases where self-finance is difficult.

There is empirical evidence on the effects of costs, productivity, and demand among different vertical structure types. Recent empirical studies, such as Mizutani and Uranishi (2013) and Mizutani et al. (2015), using data on European and East Asian OECD countries' railways find that vertical separation would reduce costs for lightly used railways but increase costs for more intensively used railways. Based on Mizutani and Uranishi (2013) and Mizutani et al. (2015), in countries or regions where train density is high (e.g., Japan, the Netherlands), the vertical integration type outperforms vertical separation in terms of costs. Conversely, in countries or regions where train density is low (e.g., Central European countries), vertical separation is better.

Compared with the number of empirical studies on cost side effects, few studies have focused on demand. From those few demand studies, such as by Van de Velde et al. (2012), Tomeš (2017), and Mizutani (2020), we cannot obtain conclusive results because the data sets differ. In short, the effect of vertical separation on demand is unclear and inconclusive, and further research is necessary.

Rail Fare Regulation and Rail Track Fees

Rail fare in Japan is regulated using the full cost principle, whereby the demand for rail services is expected to be high enough for fare revenues to cover the costs of services. The costs include in general not only rail operation costs (e.g., labor costs of operator and conductors, energy costs, cost of rolling stock) but also infrastructure maintenance costs, including acquisition of tracks. Although the full cost principle is still upheld in large metropolitan areas, it can no longer be universally justified as fares fail to cover costs, especially in rural and small urban areas.

As for price level of the rail fare, approval by and reporting to the regulator are required. The ceiling price of each operator's rail fare is set based on its individual cost structure, and revisions of the fare under the ceiling price need not be approved by the national government. An operator who is facing conditions that make it necessary to raise the ceiling price must gain approval from the regulator. As long as the fare is set below the ceiling price, rail operators do not need to seek approval for fare change; they only need to report the change to the regulator. The price level is considered based on costs incurred over the previous three-year period.

Another important feature of fare regulation is the introduction of competition through yardstick regulation, which is applied individually to three different groups of major operators in the rail industry: 15 large private railways, 6 passenger JR companies, and 10 subway systems. The government evaluates a railway's performance in comparison with others in each individual group. In the rail industry in Japan, there is no direct competition for the use of rail track such as through bidding for operating rights. Thus, especially in large metropolitan areas, rail service companies may become regional monopolies owing to the lack of competitive transportation modes. Details of yardstick regulation are discussed later in the chapter.

No formal criteria exist for the assessment of rail track fees, but the regulator assesses their appropriateness based on whether the rail track fees cover providers' costs. However, in the case of JR Freight, the avoidable cost principle has been used since its establishment. When JR Freight succeeded JNR's freight operation in 1987, the demand for freight rail service had been declining, causing management difficulties. The government employed the avoidable cost principle for setting rail track fees to help JR Freight survive serious financial hardships.

Competition Policy

Competition for and within the market among rail operators is almost unheard of in Japan, but this does not mean that rail competition policy does not exist. As we explain briefly above, to avoid inefficient or monopolistic rail operation management, the regulator applies yardstick regulation. Details of yardstick regulation can be found in such works as Okabe (2004) and Mizutani (2012), but its essence is as follows.

Yardstick regulation ideally serves as an incentive for rail operators when revisions are made in rail fare. If the actual cost of a railway is higher than the standard cost of the railway company, the rail company should be expected to reduce the actual cost. On the other hand, if the actual cost of the railway company is lower than the standard cost of the rail company, the railway company need not reduce the cost, and half of the difference between actual costs and standard costs is granted to the efficient rail operator as a reward.

In order to set up the standard cost in yardstick regulation, operating costs are separated into five subcomponent costs: (1) track; (2) catenary (overhead electric wire); (3) rolling stock; (4) train operation; and (5) station operation. The standard costs for these five measures are obtained by considering each railway company's providing conditions, such as vehicle kilometers, number of passengers, route kilometers, and stations. In fact, this information is shown in public as regression formulas to calculate the standard unit cost. Thus, yardstick regulation is used to promote competition among regulated railway companies.

Is yardstick regulation effective? When the scheme was first instituted, there was positive empirical evidence. For example, the results of empirical analysis showed that yardstick regulation works, according to Mizutani (1997). Furthermore, when a more systematic yardstick regulation scheme was enacted, the effectiveness seemed to continue. For example, the Committee of the Regulatory Impact Study on Government-Regulated Public Service Charges (2005) showed that yardstick regulation provided total user benefits in the Tokyo metropolitan area; Mizutani, Kozumi, and Matsushima (2009) found that railways subject to yardstick regulation improved cost efficiency between 1995 and 2000. However, recent studies do not indicate positive effects, with Mizutani and Usami (2016) showing that yardstick regulation does not improve productivity.

Despite the disparity in results, however, it is necessary to refrain from drawing conclusions. It can be assumed that yardstick regulation is effective to some degree, but how long the effect will continue is unknown. Furthermore, the yardstick regulation scheme is not applied to smaller private railways companies, for whom it is important to consider an alternate scheme.

Rail Operators and Their Services

Private Rail Companies

Since the end of the 19th century, many private companies have invested in rail development as a private business. Although major intercity networks were nationalized in 1907 for national security purposes, many intraurban services remained in private hands or were developed after nationalization. After World War II, several mega private rail companies were split into multiple companies. Now, 21 major railway companies cover urban rail service, not including subway systems because these are operated mainly by municipal governments.

Following the tradition of private business, major rail companies build, own, and maintain their infrastructure independently (i.e., class 1). Class 1 railway companies also self-finance infrastructure costs by making enough profit to cover both operating and construction costs. For example, Odakyu, one of the major commuter rail companies in the Tokyo metropolitan area, has recently completed 10.4 km of capacity expansion. The plan includes conversion of double tracks to quadruple tracks as well as the removal of 39 grade crossings. Although the Tokyo metropolitan government subsidized 86 percent of the costs for the removal of grade crossings on existing lines, all costs related to adding tracks were borne by the company itself. Cumulative project costs have not been publicized by the company, but when the project was approved by the Special Tax Exemption Program (Tokutei Toshi Tetsudo Seibi Tsumitatekin Seido) in 1987, its cost estimate was ¥256.3 billion (Ministry of Land, Infrastructure, Transport and Tourism 2020a).

Former National Railway: JR Companies

JR companies were formerly part of one giant public corporation, JNR. In the 1980s, JNR was suffering annual deficits of ¥1 trillion, and its total debt ultimately reached ¥37.1 trillion. When JNR was privatized in 1987, it was separated into six regional JR passenger companies and one nationwide freight company. During the process of privatization, redundant employees were laid off, and loss-making rural branch lines were abandoned or detached from the JR networks. Thanks to restructuring and business endeavors after privatization, the three mainland JR companies generated stable profits, and all the stock shares of these three JR passenger railways were out of government hands by 2006. JR Kyushu also made substantial efforts to improve its business and was fully privatized in 2016. In 2017, the average operating ratio of the three mainland JR companies was 60.1, and that of JR Kyushu was 81.0 (Ministry of Land, Infrastructure, Transport and Tourism 2017a). In contrast, JR Hokkaido and JR Shikoku still suffer severe operating deficits. In 2017, the operating ratios of JR Hokkaido and JR Shikoku were 139.7 and 121.4, respectively.

The six passenger JR companies are vertically integrated, basically owning the infrastructure on which they operate. JR Freight does not own infrastructure. Instead, it pays rail track fees to the infrastructure-owning passenger JR companies.

Shinkansen and Magnetic Levitation

Shinkansen Before and After the Privatization of JNR

Built in 1964, the Shinkansen was the first high-speed rail system in the world. Formally operated by JNR and succeeded by the passenger JR companies, its service is frequent, punctual, and safe. For instance, the Tokaido Shinkansen has 378 services per day; during peak hour, trains depart every 5 minutes from terminal stations (JR Central 2020a). The average delay of service is only 0.2 minutes per train, even if delays related to natural disasters are included. Throughout its 56-year history, the Shinkansen has never had a fatal accident.

The Shinkansen was originally planned in 1939 with the intended name "bullet train." It was designed to expand the capacity of the major rail corridor between Tokyo and Shimonoseki, an important port city accessing Korea and China. After World War II, the bullet train plan was revived as a tool to rebuild the national economy. The earliest built line, the Tokaido Shinkansen, covers the eastern half of the original plan for the bullet train. Connecting the three largest metropolitan areas, Tokyo, Osaka, and Nagoya, the corridor represents 34 percent of the nation's population and 60 percent of its industrial output (Nishida 1980). The project was first viewed with skepticism, given the decline of the railway industry in Europe and the United States. However, upon completion in 1964, the Tokaido Shinkansen was an immediate success. Coinciding with the great economic boom, annual passenger numbers grew from 31 million in 1965 to 84 million in 1970 (Institution for Transport Policy Studies 2012). The second line, the Sanyo Shinkansen, was approved in 1965 and fully completed in 1975. It covers the western half of the original bullet train route, extending westward from Osaka to Fukuoka, the fourth-largest metropolitan area in Japan.

Given the success of the Tokaido Shinkansen, policy makers saw it as a tool to promote economic development. By the mid-1960s, rapid economic growth in the Pacific corridors covered by the Tokaido and Sanyo Shinkansens had created large economic gaps within the country (Japanese Economic Planning Agency 1962). To promote balanced regional economic development, the national government approved the New National Comprehensive Development Plan (*Shin-Zenkoku Sougou Kaihatsu Keikaku*) in 1969 and addressed the need for nationwide Shinkansen networks. The Nationwide Shinkansen Railway Development Act of 1970 structuralized the planning and programming procedures of the Shinkansen. Based on this act, the Tohoku Shinkansen (Tokyo to Morioka), the Joetsu Shinkansen (Tokyo to Niigata), and the Narita Shinkansen (Tokyo to Narita Airport, a plan later discarded) were approved in 1971; five additional routes were approved for completion in 1973. The first four Shinkansen routes, Tokaido, Sanyo, Tohoku (the first phase to Morioka), and Joetsu were completed before the privatization of JNR. The five Shinkansen routes approved in 1973 were still undeveloped when JNR was privatized (figure 16.1).

The JR companies operate all Shinkansen services in their respective regions. Among these, the four classic Shinkansen routes are currently owned by their operating JR companies (i.e., vertically integrated). When JNR was privatized, the infrastructure of the Shinkansen was transferred to an infrastructure holding and leasing company, and JR companies paid rail track fees for operation. As the three mainland JR companies were found to be stable and profit making, the infrastructure was sold to their operating companies in 1991 at a total value of ¥9.2 trillion (JRTT 2020a).

Shinkansen routes constructed after JNR privatization are called Seibi-Shinkansen and are vertically separated to relieve JR companies from the burden of construction costs. An incorporated administrative agency, the Japan Railway Construction, Transport and Technology Agency (JRTT), constructs, holds, and leases the railways to the operators (JRs). The operators pay a rail track fee

FIGURE 16.1   The Shinkansen and maglev network in operation and under development as of 2020.

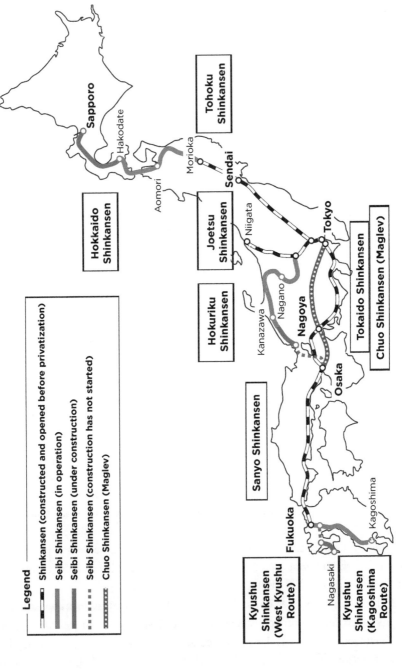

Source: Ministry of Land, Infrastructure, Transport and Tourism (2020b).

calculated based on the predicted 30-year benefits received by JR companies. Construction costs are repaid with the revenue from rail track fees, and shortfalls are subsidized by national and prefectural governments. When the Seibi-Shinkansen lines start operation, JR companies are allowed to terminate services on local lines running parallel to the Shinkansen routes. These local lines are detached from the JR networks and thereafter operated jointly by the private and public sectors. Table 16.2 and figure 16.1 show Shinkansen networks in Japan as of April 2020, including the magnetic levitation (maglev) Chuo Shinkansen.

Project Evaluation of the Shinkansen

Evaluating the social benefits of the Shinkansen is challenging, but research and anecdotes suggest that positive economic impacts occur. The Tokaido and Sanyo Shinkansen lines were built through the country's already leading economic corridors and seem to have promoted further growth of the corridor by removing transportation bottlenecks. By the early 1980s, these Shinkansen lines transported on average 340,000 passengers per day, far beyond the capacity of other modes of intercity transportation (*Nikkei Shinbun* 1982d). Early research by Amano (1980) and Sakashita (1980) find a strong positive impact of the Tokaido Shinkansen on the economy of the corridor, although their analyses have been criticized for methodological weaknesses. In the Sanyo Shinkansen corridor, Okabe (1980) finds that tourist numbers have increased since the start of service. Specifying the economic impact of the Tohoku and Joetsu Shinkansens is harder, as they were completed almost simultaneously with the major expressways running parallel to these routes. Yet, after all the extensive transportation investment, the corridors of the Tohoku and Joetsu Shinkansens clearly attract more tourists and businesses than before (*Nikkei Shinbun* 1986, 2002; Okamura and Soshiroda 1997).

The positive economic impacts of the Shinkansens are skewed toward the largest cities in the corridor. The Tokaido Shinkansen strengthened the nucleus position of Tokyo and Osaka, while Nagoya lost business headquarters and financial demand (Kamada 1980; Sanuki 1980). Hiroshima also lost its nucleus position after the opening of the Sanyo Shinkansen, as many companies relocated their headquarters to Osaka or Fukuoka (*Nikkei Shinbun* 1986; Okabe 1980). The Tohoku Shinkansen also accelerated the concentration of businesses to larger cities (*Nikkei Shinbun* 2002). Sendai, a regional capital, added more offices and employment between 1981 and 1991; the reverse was true for Akita and Yamagata (*Nikkei Shinbun* 1997). Then in the early 2000s, Sendai began losing businesses as it transformed into an economic hinterland of Tokyo (*Nikkei Shinbun* 2002).

The economic benefits of the Seibi-Shinkansen have been discussed more seriously than earlier ones. When the Tohoku and Joetsu Shinkansens were

TABLE 16.2 Shinkansen Networks in Operation and Maglev

	Classic Shinkansen					Seibi-Shinkansen			Maglev
	Tokaido	Sanyo	Tohoku (Phase 1)	Joetsu	Tohoku (Phase 2)	Hokkaido	Hokuriku	Kyushu-Kagoshima	Maglev
Current status	Complete	Complete	Complete	Complete	Complete	Partially complete	Partially complete	Complete	Under construction
Completion year	1964	1975	1982	1982	2010	Aomori-Hakodate 2016	Tokyo-Nagano 1997 / Nagano-Kanazawa 2015	2011	Tokyo-Nagoya 2027 (expected) / Nagoya-Osaka 2037 (expected)
Operating distance (km)	515.4	553.7	674.9	300.8	674.9	148.8	454.1	256.8	438.0
Max. speed (km/h)	285	300	320	240	320	260	260	260	505 (expected)
Major city connections	Tokyo-Osaka, 552.6 km, 2h22m, ¥13,870, 152 service/day	Osaka-Fukuoka, 622.3 km, 2h23m, ¥14,750, 69 service/day	Tokyo-Sendai, 351.8km, 1h30m, ¥11,410, 70 service/day	Tokyo-Niigata, 333.9 km, 1h37m, ¥10,230, 26 service/day	Tokyo-Shin-Aomori, 713.7 km, 3h09m, ¥17,870, 19 service/day	Tokyo-Hakodate, 862.5 km, 3h58m, ¥23,430, 10 service/day	Tokyo-Kanazawa, 450.5 km, 2h28m, ¥14,380, 24 service/day	Fukuoka-Kagoshima, 288.9 km, 1h16m, ¥10,110, 37 service/day	Tokyo-Nagoy, 285.6km, 40 m, Shinkansen +¥700, Tokyo-Osaka, 1h7m, Shinkansen +¥1,000
FY2018 passengers (millions)	174.1	76.0	93.5	44.5	93.5	1.6	31.7	14.5	

Sources: JR Central (2020a, 2020d); JR East (2020); JR Kyushu (2020); JR West (2020); Kohtsu Shinbun-sha (2020); Nikkei Shinbun (2014a).

completed in 1982, JNR was already suffering enormous debts, and these two Shinkansens were projected to add more deficits to JNR for 15 years or longer owing to their high construction costs (*Nikkei Shinbun* 1982a, 1982c). The five Seibi-Shinkansen routes to follow were all expected to have even lower demand than the Tohoku and Joetsu Shinkansens and would run with heavy deficits (*Nikkei Shinbun* 1982b). When JNR was privatized, supporters argued that Seibi-Shinkansen should be built because they would expand domestic demand and push up the gross domestic product (Horiuchi 1987; *Nikkei Shinbun* 1988). However, the privatized JR companies were less optimistic about the Seibi-Shinkansen owing to financial concerns (*Nikkei Shinbun* 1987).

In 1988, a governmental committee conducted a cost-benefit analysis for each Seibi-Shinkansen project to determine its fate. The committee estimated that the internal rate of return of the Hokuriku Shinkansen from Takasaki to Kanazawa via Nagano was 13.7 percent, that of the Tohoku Shinkansen from Morioka to Aomori was 8.7 percent, and that of the Kyushu Shinkansen from Yatsushiro to Kagoshima was 7.5 percent (Iwakura and Ieda 1999). Many Seibi-Shinkansen routes have subsequently been constructed and completed, but recent project reevaluations by the JRTT show that the net benefits of the Seibi-Shikansen projects are much lower than the estimations in 1988 (table 16.3). For example, the internal rates of return of the Tohoku and Hokuriku Shinkansens are only marginally above 4 percent, the discount rate for public projects. Furthermore, those of the extension of the Hokuriku Shinkansen from Kanazawa to Tsuruga and the western branch of Kyushu Shinkansen are lower than 4 percent, suggesting that their benefit-cost ratios are lower than one.

Maglev Project

Beyond the Shinkansen system, JR Central is now developing a maglev service between Tokyo and Osaka. Given the high demand for the Tokaido Shinkansen and the risk of earthquakes along the corridor, JR Central felt the need for an alternative route (JR Central 2019a). After 15 years of research and development, it established technologies to operate maglev services in 2005. On April 26, 2007, JR Central officially announced the commencement of the project (JR Central 2007).

Although the maglev project is one of several determined by the Nationwide Shinkansen Railway Development Act of 1970, all the costs are self-financed by JR Central. JR Central could have avoided construction costs by using the Seibi-Shinkansen scheme, but the company preferred to complete the project in a timely manner by handling everything independently. In December 2007, JR Central announced the intention to bear all the costs of route construction while

TABLE 16.3 Cost-Benefit Analysis of Seibi-Shinkansen Routes

		Opening Date	Evaluation Just After the Privatization of Japan National Railways		Recent Reevaluation		
			IRR	Evaluated in	B/C	IRR	Evaluated in
Tohoku Shinkansen	Morioka–Hachinohe	12/1/2002	8.70%	1988	1.33	5.6%	2008
	Hachinohe–Shin Aomori	12/4/2010			1.10	4.5%	2016
Hokkaido Shinkansen	Shin Aomori–Hakodate	3/26/2016			1.13	4.7%	2012
	Hakodate–Sapporo	Planning			1.10	4.5%	2018
Hokuriku Shinkansen	Takasaki–Nagano	10/1/1997	13.70%	1988	1.81	8.0%	2008
	Nagano–Kanazawa	3/14/2015			1.05	4.2%	2020
	Kanazawa–Tsuruga	Constructing			0.89	3.4%	2019
Kyushu Shinkansen (Kagoshima)	Hakata–Shin Yatsushiro	3/12/2011			2.11	8.8%	2016
	Shin Yatsushiro–Kagoshima	3/13/2004	7.50%	1988	1.13	4.6%	2009
Kyushu Shinkansen (West)	Takeo Onsen–Nagasaki	Planning			0.51	1	2019

Sources: Iwakura and Ieda (1999); JRTT (2008a, 2008b, 2009, 2012, 2016a, 2016b, 2018, 2019a, 2019b, 2020b).

B/C = benefit-cost ratio; IRR = internal rate of return.

Note: The shaded cells indicate evaluations conducted before the start of service.

asking prefectural governments to pay for the construction costs of nonterminal stations in their prefectures.

As planning proceeded, JR Central and prefectural governments faced conflicts about the maglev routes. Among three possible routes proposed in the plan, JR Central strongly preferred one connecting Tokyo and Nagoya directly, which would be 286 km in length and take 40 minutes to travel. Meanwhile, Nagano Prefecture, located between Tokyo and Nagoya, demanded that the maglev go through its major city by making a northward detour of 60 km, which would increase the construction costs by ¥640 billion and the annual maintenance costs by ¥19 billion (JR Central 2009a, 2009b). It would also increase travel time between Tokyo and Nagoya to 47 minutes and reduce demand from 16.7 billion passenger kilometers to 15.3 billion passenger kilometers.

After years of dispute about the routes, in November 2011, JR Central decided to pay the entire ¥9.3 trillion in construction costs, including all station costs (JR Central 2011), thus gaining more control over how to proceed with its plans. It succeeded in convincing the national government and its Transportation Policy Council that the best route would be the most direct route between Tokyo and Nagoya. JR Central also decided to minimize investment in nonterminal stations (JR Central 2011). It further publicly predicted that the eastern segment between Tokyo and Nagoya would be completed by 2027 and the western segment between Nagoya and Osaka by 2045, claiming that construction to reach Osaka would have to be deferred until business was stabilized (JR Central 2020b).

This announcement caused worry among businesses and the government of Osaka that the city's economic position would be adversely affected (Sankei 2014). Osaka might be left far behind while waiting for the extension because Tokyo and Nagoya would become one megaregion and grow even further when the maglev was completed. In response to these concerns, the national government decided in 2016 to grant an unsecured low-interest, fixed-rate public loan through JRTT for ¥3 trillion. In return, the government requested that JR Central accelerate completion of the western maglev segment by a maximum of eight years (JR Central 2020c).

Stabilizing Business Through Business Diversification

Roots and Traditional Business Diversification

Business diversification is another unique characteristic of the Japanese railway industry. Many railway companies engage in nonrail businesses such as bus transport, real estate development, retail, and tourism. Typically, one holding company or one corporate group owns multiple subsidiary companies providing these services. Private railway companies sought through diversification to adjust their capital investment to maximize the total profit of their business portfolio (Song and Shoji 2016). The purpose of business diversification was to neither cross-subsidize the railway business directly nor expand the cost basis of the railway to raise the ceiling price of fare. Railway business accounting rules issued in 1987 contain guidelines regarding what can be included as costs in railway business accounts, and they strictly prohibit a railway company from allocating rail and nonrail costs at its own discretion.

Indeed, railways and their diversified businesses create mutual benefits through four channels (Song and Shoji 2016). First, investments in real estate and retail business create demand for railway ridership. Second, positive economic externalities created by railway investments are recaptured by real estate businesses. Third, comprehensive regional development enables private railway companies to exploit economies of scope. Fourth, diversification gives private railway companies opportunities to develop less regulated income sources, which creates incentives to improve their railway businesses and fosters the sustainability of the company itself.

This business model is a legacy of Ichizo Kobayashi, one of the founders of Hankyu Railways. When he opened the first railway services between Takarazuka and Umeda as well as Ishibashi and Minoo in 1910, he also sold modest single-family homes along the railway corridors (Kashima 2018; Kobayashi 2016). These single-family homes were sold in installments so that emerging middle-class workers could purchase them and commute to central Osaka by Hankyu rail. Kobayashi also invested in leisure and entertainment industries, such as zoos, spas, and theaters, at suburban terminal stations to generate travel demand for outward-bound trips during the weekends. In 1929, he opened the Hankyu department store at the urban terminal station, which even in the midst of the Great Depression, attracted many customers and thrived. Hankyu's retail segment was further extended to supermarkets, cafés, and convenience stores. Now, all these related companies—railway, real estate, retail, and entertainment—form the corporate group Hankyu Hanshin Toho.

Following Kobayashi's example, many major railways diversified their business activities. Figure 16.2 shows the business portfolio of major rail operators in Japan in fiscal year 2018. On the left are figures showing operating revenues by segment, and on the right are operating profits by segment, both before adjustments for intersegment trades. For each figure, the four columns to the left are JR companies, and the six columns to the right are major private corporate groups that have passenger rail services. While the three mainland JR companies earn more than half their revenue from transportation, private companies earn less than one-third of their

FIGURE 16.2 Business diversification of major railway companies in Japan, 2018.

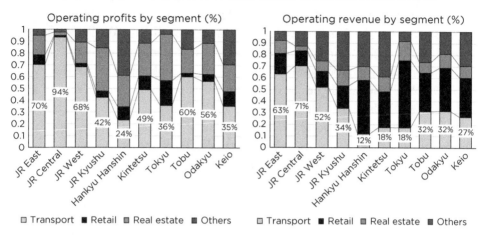

Sources: Data from Hankyu Hanshin Holdings (2019); H2O Retailing (2019); JR Central (2019b); JR East (2019); JR Kyushu (2019); JR West (2019); Keio Dentetsu (2019); Kintetsu Group Holdings (2019); Odakyu Dentetsu (2019); Tobu Tetsudo (2019); Tokyo Kyuko Dentetsu, Tokyu (2019).

revenue from transportation (rail, bus, and other transportation services). Even when it comes to operating profits, the shares of transportation businesses are one-third to two-thirds among private corporate groups. Besides railway businesses, operating profits from retail and real estate businesses contribute considerably to group-wide profits. The category "others" includes the entertainment and tourism industries, such as hotels, amusement parks, baseball teams, filmmakers, and theaters.

Ekinaka as a Recent Movement in Business Diversification

JR companies resulting from the 1987 privatization of JNR are more dependent on their railway business than are longer-standing private railway companies. After privatization, the JRs gained more freedom to diversify and more incentives to increase ridership. JRs also needed to expand their nonrail business to cope with the future decline in ridership owing to Japan's aging and shrinking population. Among JR companies, JR East has made particular efforts to develop retail businesses. Before the privatization, there were only small newsstands and snack stands. In 1987, immediately after privatization, JR East opened the first convenience store, JC, at Shinagawa station and expanded the network of convenience stores inside the ticket gates (JR Retail 2019; *J-town Net* 2019). Besides JR East, Hankyu also opened a convenience store inside the ticket gate of Juso station in 1995, which proved to be popular.

Commercialization of station space moved beyond convenience stores in the 2000s. In 2000, JR East released a plan for "station renaissance" and began renovating stations to expand retail services inside ticket gates (JR East 2005b). Private rail operators have also augmented their retail services inside stations since 2000, opening teller machines, grocery stores, barbershops, and bookstores (*Nikkei Marketing Journal* 2003). Eventually, people started calling such establishments *ekinaka*, which means "inside the ticket gate" (*Nikkei Style* 2012). In September 2003, the JR East group established a subsidiary company, JR East Station Retailing, to begin the development of large ekinaka shops named *ecute*. The first ecute in Omiya station opened in March 2005, with 68 shops in a space of 2,300 m^2 (JR East 2005a). Many young rail users switched from local department stores to ecute, and the first-year sales of the first and second ecutes reached 50 percent higher than predicted (*Nikkei Shinbun* 2006a). In 2007, their sales per square meter of floor area were higher than five million, eight times higher than the average for retail sales overall (*Nikkei Marketing Journal* 2008). Following their remarkable success, ekinaka mall developments spread to many other stations, including suburban terminals. Between 2000 and 2017, 170 commercial development projects in and around station areas were undertaken in the Tokyo metropolitan area (*Nikkei Marketing Journal* 2017).

The success of ekinaka created conflict with department stores and local small businesses on main streets (*Nikkei Shinbun* 2006a). Small- and medium-sized business owners' associations claim that railways' ekinaka businesses have created unfair competition. Ekinaka shops not only are located in superprime locations with massive pedestrian traffic but also are subject to much lower property taxes than local businesses. Property tax for stations was formerly just one-third of the regular rate because of the stations' role in providing public transportation. In response to the claims from business owners' associations, the Tokyo metropolitan government revisited the valuation of property tax on JR East stations (*Nikkei Shinbun* 2006b, 2006c). After two years of disputes, the Ministry of Internal Affairs and Communication released new rules for calculating tax bases, and from 2007, it began to apply higher property tax rates proportionate to the amount of large-scale commercial development. In 2007, JR East paid an additional ¥2.2 billion for 82 stations in Tokyo Prefecture *(Nikkei Shinbun* 2007).

Department stores also lost customers. For example, the renewal of the suburban terminal station building at Chiba and the opening of its ekinaka mall dealt a final blow to already-declining local department stores and main street businesses (Nakamura 2017). The traditional downtown of Chiba is located southeast of the station and formerly had two department stores. After the opening of a third department store right across from the station in 1967, the older downtown area gradually lost customers and declined. When an ekinaka mall called

PeRIe Chiba opened in November 2016, the remaining two department stores in the old downtown area closed immediately. One of the closed department store buildings is currently being redeveloped and will reopen as a retail and housing complex in 2023 to encourage downtown residence (*Nikkei Sokuho News* 2020). Another defunct department store building closer to the station is being redeveloped into condominiums after three and a half years of vacancy (*Nikkei Marketing Journal* 2020).

Given the backlash from local retail communities, JR East now makes a bigger effort to include main street businesses in its success. At Omiya station, JR East initiated some collaborative sales promotion campaigns with local main streets and department stores (*Nikkei Shinbun* 2014). Another ekinaka mall at Chiba station also participates in local promotion events to encourage pedestrians to shop around the neighborhood. A manager at the Chiba station building believes that its ekinaka mall could be a trigger for the revitalization of downtown areas in a joint competition against suburban malls and online shopping (*Nikkei Marketing Journal* 2018).

Why Are Passenger Railways Successful?

As noted earlier, major passenger rail operators operating in urban and intercity markets enjoy high profitability. Operating cost-revenue ratios of JR companies, major private rail operators, and subway operators are well below 100 (i.e., make profits) except for JR Hokkaido and JR Shikoku (figure 16.3). In the urban market, rail services are the primary commuting mode because of their punctuality and affordability. In the intercity market, the Shinkansen holds the major share for mid-distance travel.

The great success of passenger rail services is supported by favorable market conditions, excellence in service, and innovative business models. First, in the urban market, dense land use and inconvenient road networks make rail commuting the more attractive choice. These rail-centric patterns were created when major urban railway networks developed between the 1910s and 1930s, long before the auto age in Japan. At that time, the middle class was emerging and seeking better places to live, and the single-family homes in the garden city–style suburbs built by private railways were a perfect fit (Kashima 2018). In the intercity market, high-speed rail is competitive with air and road travel owing to Japan's limited land area and the timing of industrialization. Most major city connections are in the mid-distance range, where travel times by rail and air are comparable, making rail travel predominant because of its dramatically larger seating capacity. Road transport is not also competitive against rail because

FIGURE 16.3 Cost-revenue ratio of major rail operators.

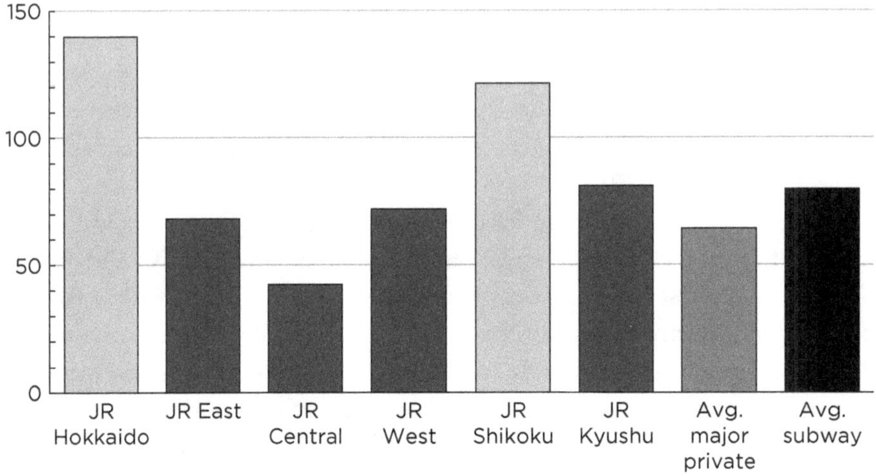

Source: Ministry of Land, Infrastructure, Transport and Tourism (2017a).

it is usually much slower and smaller in capacity than high-speed rail. Because of the timing of industrialization, rail networks among major cities developed much earlier and with greater intensity than highway networks. Even when road transport became popular in the 1960s and 1970s, railway service kept its competitive advantage in connecting major cities by introducing and expanding Shinkansen networks.

Second, high service quality has kept commuters loyal to rail. Operators provide punctual and frequent services to build their excellent reputation among commuting modes. Trains almost always operate without mechanical failure, thanks to advanced standards in manufacturing. Furthermore, railway operators continuously improve their dissemination of service information to users. Ticketing and gate systems are constantly improved to enhance the ridership experience, and railway companies have worked together to provide a seamless experience where riders need not exit one railway company's gates to transfer to another company's lines. Now, a great many private rail companies and municipal subways provide through services across multiple companies' lines, with all payment processed by a single integrated circuit card, such as Suica and Pasmo.

Third, innovative railway business models contribute to success. Major private railways successfully exploited economies of scope and internalized externalities, thanks to the flexibility of private business. As is seen in many European countries, the public sector is involved in railway businesses because they are characterized by natural monopolies and large positive externalities to the economy (if travel demand follows). Although public involvement may help mitigate overpricing and underinvestment in railway services, it restricts organizations from extending business beyond railway services. In contrast, Japanese private railway companies have promoted comprehensive development of their regions, including housing and commercial developments and multimodal access to stations. By combining real estate development and railway construction, private railway companies have successfully reduced the cost of land acquisition and construction, generated travel demand, and recaptured positive economic externalities produced by enhanced accessibility. Integrated transportation design also creates synergy. Buses and taxis are often provided by related corporations to form coordinated networks. As a result, road transportation maximizes the accessibility of the region, which in turn maximizes the region's economic outcomes.

Conclusions

This chapter explains and discusses prominent characteristics of the passenger rail industry in Japan: the strength of private railways in urban and intercity markets, the benefits of vertical integration, and regulatory frameworks that introduce competition among railway companies without contracting out railway operators. Private railways are vital, thanks to supportive market conditions and their own continuing vigorous efforts to excel. The tradition of vertical integration also contributes to business through cost savings made possible by both owning infrastructure and managing operations. For instance, energy costs can be lessened through the use of energy generated by vehicular braking, and rail track maintenance costs can be reduced by creating alignment in rail lines. Also, punctuality and safety in heavily used rail operations are made possible by avoiding coordination problems between different organizations. Although vertical integration makes it impossible to introduce competition among operators through bidding processes, yardstick regulation on fares allows government to introduce some competition among major private railway companies. Yardstick regulation is believed to discourage cost escalation; in fact, so far no dramatic increase has occurred in rail fares.

The unique business structure of Japanese passenger railways may serve as a model for the future of railway business elsewhere. First, if market conditions are favorable enough, private owner-operators will likely perform well in the railway industry. The passenger railway industry has characteristics of a natural monopoly, but this may be remedied by introducing competition. In Europe, vertical separation is one option for separating infrastructure management activities. However, coordinated investments in operation and infrastructure may save on total costs. And, as mentioned under heavily used rail operations, coordination problems might arise between the operation and infrastructure management companies, which would undermine the punctuality and safety of service. The vertically integrated Tokaido Shinkansen won its popularity over airlines with its frequency, safety, and punctuality. Maintaining excellent infrastructure conditions is critical to using facilities at maximum capacity while achieving both safety and punctuality. Such excellent coordination between operation and maintenance segments would be impossible if they were separated entities.

Second, internalizing the positive externalities of railway services may be a key to success in incentivizing private railway companies to make the appropriate level of capital investment. Underinvestment from positive externalities is usually corrected through public involvement in planning networks and service levels. However, by allowing business diversification into real estate and retail, private railway companies can successfully recapture the fruits of their investment in the railway business and adjust their investment levels to maximize regional economic growth. Business diversification also introduces competition among private railway companies in the same metropolitan area because people choose residential locations based on the overall quality of development and accessibility. Indeed, commuter rails in the Tokyo and Osaka metropolitan areas showcase the attractiveness of their corridors together with accessibility to metropolitan centers to garner customers for their businesses.

Third, competition among railway companies can still exist, even if they are regionally monopolistic or oligopolistic. The main tool for stimulating competition is yardstick regulation. In Europe, direct competition schemes among railways, such as competition for rail track through competitive tendering, are common. Japan uses an indirect competition scheme for railways in different markets. Empirical evidence shows that these schemes are to some extent effective because cost increases can be suppressed to some degree.

Of course, the Japanese passenger railway system has shortcomings. While major private railway companies thrive, small private railways in small local areas have been losing in the competition against private autos, and the demand for railways has been declining. A vertical separation scheme is sometimes selected to relieve operators of capital investment costs, with local governments as well as joint public-private entities participating in infrastructure management. These remedial policies, however, have been unable to save many regional small private railways from decline.

While the strengths of Japanese private passenger railways are highly path-dependent and may not be clearly applicable to other countries, they shed light on alternative management possibilities for passenger railway services in dense markets.

Summary

- Japan's railroads are widely admired for their reliability and safety and for forming the world's largest passenger system that is vertically integrated and privately owned.

- The success of Japan's passenger rail services is attributed to favorable market conditions, excellence in service, and innovative business models that exploit economies of scope and internalize externalities.

- Japan was the first and is still among the few countries to use high-speed rail as a tool to promote regional development. The first Shinkansen bullet train was built to alleviate congestion while supporting continued concentration of economic activity in the Tokyo-Osaka-Nagoya corridor.

- The success of this initial line generated pressure to extend service to other areas with less ridership potential, and the government responded in 1973 by approving a national plan that calls for five new bullet train lines plus a new maglev line from Tokyo to Nagoya. Unlike the original line, the five new Shinkansen lines may require some capital subsidies. The railroad developing the maglev line, scheduled to open in 2027, claims that it will not need subsidies.

Notes

1. Narita Airport, Chubu International Airport, Kansai International Airport, and Itami Airport have been corporatized. The ports of Tokyo, Yokohama-Kawasaki, and Osaka-Kobe have also been corporatized.

2. Drivers having installed the electric toll collection system pay a distance-based toll whose upper limit is equal to cash payment, at 35.8 km.

3. The population ranking of the six metropolitan areas is as follows: Tokyo, Osaka, Nagoya, Fukuoka, Sapporo, and Sendai. Since only interprefectural travel data are available in the original intercity trip data set, the authors approximated populations as follows: The Tokyo metropolitan area includes Tokyo, Kanagawa, Chiba, Saitama, and Ibaraki Prefectures; the Osaka metropolitan area includes Osaka, Kyoto, Hyogo, and Nara Prefectures; the Nagoya metropolitan area includes Aichi, Mie, and Gifu Prefectures; and Fukuoka and Sendai include Fukuoka and Miyagi Prefectures, respectively. The Sapporo metropolitan area includes the central Hokkaido area.

4. Details of Kobe Rapid Transit Railway can be found in Mizutani and Shoji (2004).

References

Amano, K. 1980. "Regional Economic Impact of the Shinkansen." In *The Shinkansen High-Speed Rail Network of Japan: Proceedings of an IIASA Conference, June 27–30, 1977*, ed. A. Straszak and R. Tuck, 61–78. Oxford, UK: Pergamon.

Committee of the Regulatory Impact Study on Government-Regulated Public Service Charges. 2005. "Interim Report for Guideline of Regulatory Impact Study on Government-Regulated Public Service Charges." [In Japanese.] Tokyo: Price Stability Council, Cabinet Office.

Graham, Anne, Shinichi Saito, and Munenori Nomura. 2014. "Airport Management in Japan: Any Lessons Learnt from the UK?" *Journal of Airport Management* 8(3): 244–263.

Hankyu Hanshin Holdings, 2019. "Annual Security Report." [In Japanese.] https://www.hankyu-hanshin.co.jp/upload/irRelatedInfo/387.pdf.

H2O Retailing, 2019. "Annual Security Report." [In Japanese.] https://www.h2o-retailing.co.jp/ja/ir/library/securities/main/015/teaserItems1/0/linkList/0/link/190704yuho.pdf.

Horiuchi, Yoshiro. 1987. "Planned Shinkansen Lines and Expansion of Domestic Demand." [In Japanese.] *Journal of Japan Society of Civil Engineers* [*Doboku Gakkaishi*] 385: 5–19.

Institution for Transport Policy Studies. 2012. "Overview of Railway Data 2012." [In Japanese.] Tokyo: Institution for Transport Policy Studies.

Iwakura, Shigeshi, and Hitoshi Ieda. 1999. "Cost-Benefit Analysis of Railway Projects: History of Implementation and Remaining Concerns." [In Japanese.] *Transport Policy Studies' Review* [*Unyuseisaku Kenkyu*] 1(3): 2–13.

Japanese Economic Planning Agency. 1962. "National Development Plan." [In Japanese.] https://www.mlit.go.jp/common/001135930.pdf.

JR Central (Japan Rail Central). 2007. "JR Central the Earnings Briefing FY2006." [In Japanese.] https://company.jr-central.co.jp/ir/brief-announcement/detail/_pdf/000001511.pdf.

———. 2009a. "Future Schedule and Cost of the Central Shinkansen Survey." [In Japanese.] Press Release. June 18. https://company.jr-central.co.jp/chuoshinkansen/procedure/_pdf/07.pdf.

———. 2009b. "Maintenance and Operation Costs, Equipment Renewal Costs, and Transportation Demand for the Central Shinkansen Survey." [In Japanese.] Press Release. July 21. https://company.jr-central.co.jp/chuoshinkansen/procedure/_pdf/08.pdf.

———. 2011. "Burden of Construction Cost of Stations of the Chuo Shinkansen." [In Japanese.] Press Release. November 21. https://company.jr-central.co.jp/chuoshinkansen/other/_pdf/02.pdf.

———. 2019a. "Annual Report of JR Central in 2019." [In Japanese.] https://company.jr-central.co.jp/ir/annualreport/_pdf/annualreport2019.pdf.

———. 2019b. "Annual Security Report." [In Japanese.] https://company.jr-central.co.jp/ir/financial-statements/detail/_pdf/000039658.pdf.

———. 2020a. "JR Central Fact Sheets 2020." [In Japanese.] https://company.jr-central.co.jp/ir/factsheets/_pdf/factsheets2020.pdf.

———. 2020b. "On Chuo Shinkansen." [In Japanese.] https://linear-chuo-shinkansen.jr-central.co.jp/faq/.

———. 2020c. "On Long-Term Borrowing Using Financial Investment and Financing." [In Japanese.] https://linear-chuo-shinkansen.jr-central.co.jp/plan/kaigyoprocess/pdf/zaiseitoyushi.pdf.

———. 2020d. "The Central Shinkansen Plan Using the Superconducting Magnetic Levitation Technology." [In Japanese.] https://company.jr-central.co.jp/company/linear-chuo-shinkansen/plan.html.

JR East (Japan Rail East). 2005a. "JR East Annual Report 2005." [In Japanese.] https://www.jreast.co.jp/e/investor/ar/2005/pdf/ar2005_all.pdf.

———. 2005b. "Social and Environment Report of JR East Group 2005." [In Japanese.] https://www.jreast.co.jp/eco/pdf/2005.html.

———. 2019. "Annual Security Report." [In Japanese.] https://www.jreast.co.jp/investor/securitiesreport/2019/pdf/securitiesreport.pdf.

———.2020. "JR East Fact Sheet." [In Japanese.] https://www.jreast.co.jp/investor/factsheet/pdf/factsheet.pdf.

JR Kyushu (Japan Rail Kyushu). 2019. "Annual Security Report." [In Japanese.] https://www.jrkyushu.co.jp/company/ir/library/securities_report/__icsFiles/afieldfile/2019/06/24/2018.yuhou.pdf.

———. 2020. "JR Kyushu Fact Sheet." [In Japanese.] https://www.jrkyushu.co.jp/company/ir/library/fact_sheet/pdf/JR_factsheet_2020_J.pdf.

JR Retail (Japan Rail Retail). 2019. "JR Retail Corporate Profile 2019." [In Japanese.] https://corp.j-retail.jp/lib/pdf/company/corporateprofile.pdf.

JRTT (Japan Railway Construction, Transport and Technology Agency). 2008a. "Summary Sheet of Hokuriku Shinkansen Post-project Evaluation Between Takasaki and Nagano." [In Japanese.] https://www.jrtt.go.jp/construction/committee/asset/jk19-6-1.pdf.

———. 2008b. "Summary Sheet of Tohoku Shinkansen Post-project Evaluation Between Morioka and Hachinohe." [In Japanese.] https://www.jrtt.go.jp/construction/committee/asset/jk19-5-1.pdf.

———. 2009. "Summary Sheet of Kyushu Shinkansen Post-project Evaluation Between Shin-Yatsushiro and Kagoshima Chuo." [In Japanese.] https://www.jrtt.go.jp/construction/committee/asset/jk20-5-1.pdf.

———. 2012. "Summary Sheet of Hokkaido Shinkansen Re-evaluation Between Shin-Aomori and Shin-Hakodate Hokuto." [In Japanese.] https://www.jrtt.go.jp/construction/committee/asset/jk23-06-1.pdf.

———. 2016a. "Summary Sheet of Kyushu Shinkansen Post-project Evaluation Between Shin-Yatsushiro and Hakata." [In Japanese.] https://www.jrtt.go.jp/construction/committee/asset/jk27-06-1.pdf.

———. 2016b. "Summary Sheet of Tohoku Shinkansen Post-project Evaluation Between Hachinohe and Shin-Aomori." [In Japanese.] https://www.jrtt.go.jp/construction/committee/asset/jk27-05-1.pdf.

———. 2018. "Summary Sheet of Hokkaido Shinkansen Re-evaluation Between Shin-Hakodate Hokuto and Sapporo." [In Japanese.] https://www.jrtt.go.jp/construction/committee/asset/jk29-05-1.pdf.

———. 2019a. "Summary of Hokuriku Shinkansen Re-evaluation Between Kanazawa and Tsuruga." [In Japanese.] https://www.jrtt.go.jp/construction/committee/asset/jk30-06-1.pdf.

———. 2019b. "Summary of Kyushu Shinkansen Re-evaluation Between Takeo-Onsen and Nagasaki." [In Japanese.] https://www.jrtt.go.jp/construction/committee/asset/jk30-05-1.pdf.

———. 2020a. "Collection of Proceeds from the Transfer of the Shinkansen, Redemption of Long-Term Debt of Former National Railways, Collection of Loans." [In Japanese.] https://www.jrtt.go.jp/subsidy/outline/fund-flow.html.

———. 2020b. "Summary Sheet of Hokuriku Shinkansen Post-project Evaluation Between Nagano and Kanazawa." [In Japanese.] https://www.jrtt.go.jp/construction/committee /asset/jkr1-05-01.pdf.

JR West (Japan Rail West). 2019. "Annual Security Report." [In Japanese.] https://www .westjr.co.jp/company/ir/library/securities-report/pdf/report32_04.pdf.

———. 2020. "JR West Fact Sheet." [In Japanese.] https://www.westjr.co.jp/company/ir /library/fact/pdf/2020/fact2020.pdf.

J-town Net. 2019. "New Days Shinagawa as JR East's First Convenience Store is Closed in 31 Years: Opened as 'JC' Shortly After Privatization." [In Japanese.] December 6. https://j -town.net/tokyo/news/localnews/298813.html?p=all.

Kamada, M. 1980. "Achievements and Future Problems of the Shinkansen." In *The Shinkansen High-Speed Rail Network of Japan: Proceedings of an IIASA Conference, June 27–30, 1977,* ed. A. Straszak and R. Tuck, 41–58. Oxford, UK: Pergamon.

Kashima, Shigeru. 2018. *Ichizo Kobayashi: Great Business Innovator of Japan* [in Japanese]. Tokyo: Chuo Koron Shinsya.

Keio Dentetsu. 2019. "Annual Security Report." [In Japanese.] https://www.keio.co.jp/ company/stockholder/financial_report/pdf/2018_financial_statements.pdf.

Kintetsu Group Holdings. 2019. "Annual Security Report." [In Japanese.] https://www .kintetsu-g-hd.co.jp/ir/syouken/data/108kiyukashoken.pdf.

Kobayashi, Ichizo. 2016. *Autobiography of an Outstanding Man: Reminiscence of Kobayashi Ichizo, Founder of Hankyu Railway* [in Japanese]. Tokyo: Kodansya.

Kohtsu Shinbun-sha. 2020. "Japan Rail Timetable, February 2020." [In Japanese.] Tokyo: Kohtsu Shinbun-sha.

Ministry of Land, Infrastructure, Transport and Tourism. 2017a. "Annual Rail Statistics 2017." [In Japanese.] Tokyo: Ministry of Land, Infrastructure, Transport and Tourism.

———. 2017b. "Passenger Flow Survey." [In Japanese.] Tokyo: Ministry of Land, Infrastructure, Transport and Tourism.

———. 2019a. "The 30th Anniversary of Privatization and Subdivision of the Japan National Railways." [In Japanese.] Tokyo: Ministry of Land, Infrastructure, Transport and Tourism.

———. 2019b. "Visualization of Delay in Rail Lines in Tokyo Metropolitan Area in FY2017." [In Japanese.] Tokyo: Ministry of Land, Infrastructure, Transport and Tourism. https:// www.mlit.go.jp/common/001269352.pdf.

———. 2020a. "Outline of the Project Plan for the Improvement of Special Urban Railways." [In Japanese.] Tokyo: Ministry of Land, Infrastructure, Transport and Tourism. http:// www.mlit.go.jp/tetudo/toshitetu/03_06.html.

———. 2020b. "White Paper of Land, Infrastructure, Transport and Tourism." [In Japanese.] Tokyo: Ministry of Land, Infrastructure, Transport and Tourism. https://www.mlit .go.jp/hakusyo/mlit/r01/hakusho/r02/html/n2612000.html.

Mizutani, Fumitoshi. 1997. "Empirical Analysis of Yardstick Competition in the Japanese Rail Industry." *International Journal of Transport Economics* 24(3): 367–392.

———. 2012. *Regulatory Reform of Public Utilities: The Japanese Experience.* Cheltenham, UK: Edward Elgar.

———. 2015. "Looking Beyond Europe." In *Rail Economics, Policy and Regulation in Europe,* ed. Matthias Fingar and Pierre Messulam, 341–363. Cheltenham, UK: Edward Elgar.

———. 2020. "The Impact of Structural Reforms and Regulations on Demand Side in the Railway Industry." *Review of Network Economics* 18(1): 1–33.

Mizutani, Fumitoshi, Hideo Kozumi, and Noriaki Matsushima. 2009. "Does Yardstick Regulation Really Work? Empirical Evidence from Japan's Rail Industry." *Journal of Regulatory Economics* 36(3): 308–323.

Mizutani, Fumitoshi, and Kenichi Shoji. 2004. "Rail Operation-Infrastructure Separation: The Case of Kobe Rapid Transit Railway." *Transport Policy* 11(3): 251–263.

Mizutani, Fumitoshi, Andrew Smith, Chris Nash, and Shuji Uranishi. 2015. "Comparing the Costs of Vertical Separation, Integration, and Intermediate Organisational Structures in European and East Asian Railways." *Journal of Transport Economics and Policy* 49(3): 496–515.

Mizutani, Fumitoshi, and Shuji Uranishi. 2008. "Privatization of the Japan Highway Public Corporation: Focusing on Organizational Structure Change." *Transport Reviews* 28(4): 469–493.

———. 2013. "Does Vertical Separation Reduce Cost? An Empirical Analysis of the Rail Industry in European and East Asian OECD Countries." *Journal of Regulatory Economics* 43(1): 31–59.

Mizutani, Jun, and Munekatsu Usami. 2016. "Yardstick Regulation and the Operators' Productivity of Railway Industry in Japan." *Research in Transportation Economics* 59: 86–93.

Nakamura, Tomohiko. 2017. "The 'Chiba Station War' in Which Echinaka Kicked Out the Old Famous Department Stores." [In Japanese.] *Mainichi Newspaper, Economics Premium,* March 28.

Nikkei Marketing Journal. 2003. "Extending Ekinaka: Best Location and Station for Life." [In Japanese.] June 5.

———. 2008. "Business Statistics, 2007: Excellent Sales Efficiency of Ekinaka, 8 Times Higher than the Average Retailers." [In Japanese.] April 7.

———. 2017. "Behind the Hit: Extending Station Buildings and Ekinaka in the Suburbs, and Working Women and Local Oriented Mind." [In Japanese.] October 2.

———. 2018. "Perrier Chiba in Chiba City: The Entrance to Chiba City, a Bustling Area Again, 30 Stores for the First Time in the Prefecture, with Regional Colors in the Forefront." [In Japanese.] January 29.

———. 2020. "Former Mitsukoshi Department Store in Chiba Is Under the Redevelopment by Tokyo Tatemono." [In Japanese.] September 21.

Nikkei Shinbun. 1982a. "Debt-Burdened Tohoku Shinkansen: Become Break-Even 15 Years Later at the Earliest, Construction of Ueno-Omiya Segment May Need to Be Slowed." [In Japanese.] June 23.

———. 1982b. "The JNR in Financial Deficit is Screaming: Tohoku and Hokuriku Shinkansen Would Never Make Profits." [In Japanese.] March 31.

———. 1982c. "What to Do with Japan National Rail? 8: Non-adaptive Management, Cannot Stop Over-investments on Loss-Making Facilities. Stop Investments to Terminate Vicious Cycle." [In Japanese.] March 19.

———. 1982d. "What to Do with Japan National Rail? 10: Essential Mode of Transportation, Seriously Need Restructuring as It is Unsubstitutable." [In Japanese.] March 21.

———. 1986. "Changing Growth Patterns of Cities: Chance of Planning and Redevelopment for Future." [In Japanese.] January 30.

———. 1987. "Final Report of Seibi-Shinkansen, Severe Estimate on Financial Performance: Financial Performance is Estimated to be Lower than the Estimation by Government." [In Japanese.] December 18.

———. 1988. "Seibi-Shinkansen Would Promote Economic Development of the Corridor—by Kozo Amano, Kyoto University." [In Japanese.] April 20.

———. 1997. "Benefits and Drawbacks of Transportation Infrastructure Investments 1: Disappearing Barriers by Shinkansen." [In Japanese.] June 24.

———. 2002. "Twenty Years from the Inauguration of Tohoku Shinkansen: Positive and Negative Sides of Branch Economy, and Shrinking Distance to Tokyo." [In Japanese.] June 28.

———. 2006a. "An Unknown Distribution Giant, JR: The Rapid Growth of Station Buildings and the Conflict." [In Japanese.] April 3.

———. 2006b. "4 Small Business Groups in Tokyo Request to Strengthen Taxation on Ekinaka Businesses." [In Japanese.] May 6.

———. 2006c. "Hot Discussion of the Taxation on Ekinaka Business: Ministry of Internal Affairs and Communications Started to Make a National Standard, Conflict in the Evaluation Method." [In Japanese.] August 12.

———. 2007. "Tokyo Metropolitan Government Asks 82 Stations to Bear Additional Burden of 2.2 Billion Yen in Taxation on Ekinaka." [In Japanese.] October 2.

———. 2014a. "Maglev: Strategic Actions Behind the Low-Fare Policy." [In Japanese.] December 18.

———. 2014b. "Why Don't You Try Shopping Areas Outside JR Omiya Station? Responding to the Criticism of 'Concentration in Ekinaka' and Promoting Sales in Cooperation with Department Stores." [In Japanese.] May 14.

Nikkei Sokuho News. 2020. "New Developments Around Chiba Station, Including Three Commercial Facilities." [In Japanese.] March 31.

Nikkei Style. 2012. "Ekinaka: A Word Born of a New Business." [In Japanese.] March 20. https://style.nikkei.com/article/DGXBZO39579820U2A310C1000000/.

Nishida, M. 1980. "History of the Shinkansen." In The Shinkansen High-Speed Rail Network of Japan: Proceedings of an IIASA Conference, June 27–30, 1977, ed. A. Straszak and R. Tuck, 11–20. Oxford, UK: Pergamon.

Odakyu Dentetsu. 2019. "Annual Security Report." [In Japanese.] https://www.odakyu.jp/ir/securities/o5oaa1000001yibj-att/03.pdf.

Okabe, Masaru. 2004. "New Passenger Railway Fares." Japan Railway and Transport Review 37 (January): 4–15.

Okabe, S. 1980. "Impact of the Sanyo Shinkansen on Local Communities." In The Shinkansen High-Speed Rail Network of Japan: Proceedings of an IIASA Conference, June 27–30, 1977, ed. A. Straszak and R. Tuck, 105–130. Oxford, UK: Pergamon.

Okamura, Noriyuki, and Akira Soshiroda. 1997. "A Study on the Transition of the Tourism Policy in Niigata Prefectur." [In Japanese.] Tourism Studies Quarterly [Kankogaku Kenkyu] 9(1): 19–26.

Sakashita, N. 1980. "Application of the Spatial Econometric Model (SPAMETRI) to the Evaluation of the Economic Effects of the Shinkansen." In The Shinkansen High-Speed Rail Network of Japan: Proceedings of an IIASA Conference, June 27–104, 1977, ed. A. Straszak and R. Tuck, 79–104. Oxford, UK: Pergamon.

Sankei West News. 2014. "Crisis Feeling in the Kansai Region: The Burden of Being Left Behind in Economic Growth." [In Japanese.] October 17. https://www.sankei.com/west/news/141017/wst1410170074-n1.html.

Sanuki, T. 1980. "The Shinkansen and Future Image of Japan." In *The Shinkansen High-Speed Rail Network of Japan: Proceedings of an IIASA Conference, June 27–30, 1977*, ed. A. Straszak and R. Tuck, 227–252. Oxford, UK: Pergamon.

Song, Yeon-Jung, and Kenichi Shoji. 2016. "Effects of Diversification Strategies on Investment in Railway Business: The Case of Private Railway Companies in Japan." *Research in Transportation Economics* 59: 388–396.

Tobu Tetsudo. 2019. "Annual Security Report." [In Japanese.] http://cdn.ullet.com/edinet/pdf/S100G2C0.pdf.

Tokyo Kyuko Dentetsu (Tokyu). 2019. "Annual Security Report." [In Japanese.] https://www.tokyu.co.jp/ir/upload_file/m002-m002_07/9005_YUHO150_2018_20190627.pdf.

Tokyo Metropolitan Government. 2017. "Tokyo Statistical Yearbook 2017." [In Japanese.] Tokyo: Management and Coordination Section, Statistics Division, Bureau of General Affairs, Tokyo Metropolitan Government.

Tomeš, Zdenek. 2017. "Do European Reforms Increase Modal Shares of Railways?" *Transport Policy* 60: 143–151.

Van de Velde, Didier, Chris Nash, Andrew Smith, Fumitoshi Mizutani, Shuji Uranishi, Mark Lijesen, and Frank Zschoche. 2012. "EVES-Rail: Economic Effects of Vertical Separation in the Railway Sector." Brussels: Community of European Railways and Infrastructure Companies.

Xu, Fangzhou, Shinya Hanaoka, and Masamitsu Onishi. 2019. "Multi-Airport Privatization in a Japanese Region with Trip-Chain Formation." *Journal of Air Transport Management* 80: 101690.

17

HIGH-SPEED RAIL AND
CITY CLUSTERS IN CHINA

Zheng Chang

Chinese policy makers made a bold decision in 2014 to focus on urban growth in 19 megalopolises, which they call city clusters. The largest three are Beijing-Tianjin-Hebei (with a combined population of 113 million), the Yangtze River Delta surrounding Shanghai and Hangzhou (164 million), and the Guangdong-Hong Kong-Macau Greater Bay Area (GBA), which includes the Pearl River Delta, Hong Kong, and Macau (71 million). The plan includes, among other things, the development of a high-speed rail (HSR) system within each cluster, with trains that are sufficiently fast, frequent, and affordable to allow passengers to commute to jobs in the other cities in their cluster. In the GBA, for example, several HSR stations were built between Guangzhou and Hong Kong between 2009 and 2018, reducing the travel time between the two cities to one hour. The expectation is that HSR can greatly expand the effective labor market, which in turn would support further economic integration and business agglomeration.

The purpose of this chapter is to demonstrate, using the GBA as a case study, how HSR contributes to city cluster formation by strengthening agglomeration economies.

HSR Development in China

HSR uses a specific rolling stock and an integrated rail system and runs significantly faster than the traditional rail service. The world's first HSR, the Shinkansen, opened in Japan in 1964. The European Union has developed HSR since 1980. In the 2000s, the development trend moved back to East Asia, with HSR services launched in South Korea in 2004, Taiwan in 2007, and mainland China in 2008. Although China is a latecomer to HSR, the speed and scale of HSR development there are particularly amazing. By 2019, China had built a 35,000 km HSR network, accounting for more than two-thirds of the worldwide network. Currently, all major Chinese cities are connected to the national

HSR network, and HSR has become the major intercity commuting mode for the Chinese.

The speedy development of HSR is reinforced by both socioeconomic and political factors. Because of rapid economic growth and urbanization in the past three decades, rail travel demand has increased dramatically. However, the rising demand has exceeded the capacity of the existing railway services, and the conventional railway train has steadily been losing market share to airlines and expanding national expressways since 1990. According to the National Bureau of Statistics (2019), railway ridership increased from 1.05 billion in 2001 to 1.89 billion in 2012, which is an 80 percent increase. However, the share of rail ridership among all intercity transport modes declined from 6.85 percent in 2001 to 4.98 percent in 2012. HSR expansion quickly improved rail capacity and service quality. Compared with other countries, the HSR fare in China is quite affordable, which makes intercity commuting attractive, especially for distances less than 1,000 km. In 2018, railway ridership increased to 3.37 billion passengers, 2 billion of whom were carried by HSR. The rail share of all-mode passenger trips increased to 18.81 percent in 2018, largely owing to the contribution of HSR.

HSR expansion has gained support from the central government, financial institutions, and local governments. For the central government, developing HSR networks has gradually become an instrument for rejuvenating the slowing economy. State-owned banks and other financial institutions look for investment opportunities, and few projects have scales that are comparable to that of HSR network development, which can absorb substantial capital credit with a relatively low investment risk because of backing from the central government. Local governments compete fiercely for HSR opportunities. Localities view HSR as an investment and as a development anchor for launching new HSR town projects. The massive real estate development triggered by HSR further promotes gross domestic product (GDP) growth from which both the central government and the local governments benefit.

In China, the planning and development of HSR are determined through a complex lobby and bargaining process among China Railway and provincial and prefecture governments. When a planned HSR line crosses a jurisdiction, the relevant provincial and prefecture governments are involved in the planning, financing, and implementation process. The three players have different objectives. China Railway wants to build HSR faster and cheaper, the provincial government wants HSR to serve more localities, and the prefecture governments view HSR as a development anchor that can boost local economies. Decisions about station sites and alignment are the result of negotiations among the three players. One consequence of this dynamic process is the location of HSR stations. Unlike in

Japan and the European Union, where HSR stations are mostly found in city centers, most HSR stations in China are located in new development areas that are far from city centers. For China Railway, new locations outside the built-up area provide more flexibility in the selection of HSR alignments that meet the radius requirement for high speeds but also make construction cheaper, easier, and faster because of the reduced resettlement requirement. For local governments, a HSR station and the real estate development around it increase the land value, which enables governments to collect more land-leasing fees for financing urban development (Chang 2014). This strategy would work if cities were growing rapidly.

The construction of HSR stations has stimulated the development of new HSR towns. It is quite common to see high-rise buildings and large-scale real estate development near HSR stations, especially in new development areas (far from city centers) where land resources are abundant and land acquisition costs are relatively low. However, most new town projects are not successful in attracting business and economic activities, and the housing unit vacancy rate is quite high. The media have called these unsuccessful developments "ghost towns," in reference to wasted land and public resources. This waste is largely due to the overdevelopment of real estate properties and the lack of basic service facilities, such as public transit, schools, hospitals, and other types of amenities in new towns. HSR alone is not sufficient to build a successful new town and divert the population from existing urban agglomerations (Zheng et al. 2019).

In addition to the placement of HSR stations, HSR can be classified into three systems based on the scope of service: a national trunk line system, a regional system, and an intercity system. The national trunk line system refers to the backbone corridors of China's HSR network. All corridors are new development routes that are dedicated to passenger service only in order to satisfy the speed requirement. The regional system complements the national grid to connect tier 2 and 3 cities to regional hubs. This system is designed to satisfy the demand for both passenger and freight rail transport in less-developed areas and integrate them into the national network. The regional system is a significant upgrade from the existing railway lines. The intercity system connects adjacent cities or cities within city clusters, with the main purpose of reinforcing agglomeration and promoting market integration within each city cluster. Since the intercity system normally operates within a single province, it is financed mainly by the local government and operated by local transport authorities. Corresponding to the three track systems are three types of high-speed trains: G-, D-, and C-series. The G-series trains generally run on the national trunk system at a speed of 300–350 km per hour, connecting all major megacities across regions. The D- and C-series trains usually run on the regional and intercity system, respectively, at speeds of 200–250 km per hour. Although the three types of trains are used mainly for different systems, logistics are often coordinated so that the trains can share the same track. (A track system with a design speed of 350 km per hour can be used to run G-, D-, and C-series trains, but a track system with a maximum design speed of 300 km cannot be used for G-series trains.)

HSR development is highly capital-intensive. In China, the average development cost for HSR networks is approximately US$17–21 million per kilometer, which is approximately two-thirds of the cost in other countries (Lawrence, Bullock, and Liu 2019). However, considering the network's enormity, HSR development requires strong financial support. About 40–50 percent of financing was provided by state-owned banks and financial institutions, mainly through debt financing. Another 30–40 percent was obtained through bonds issued by the Ministry of Railway (later by China Railway). Given that HSR development requires collaboration with local government to facilitate land acquisition and site clearance, provincial and local governments have financed most intercity HSR investment and covered the remaining 10–20 percent. Similar to the speedy network expansion, the debt borne by China Railway has also experienced substantial growth. According to its financial report, the corporation's debt increased from 1.89 trillion renminbi (RMB) in 2010 to 5.28 trillion RMB in 2018.

Can the revenue generated by HSR justify its development and operation costs? Other countries' experiences suggest that the odds of building a profitable HSR system are quite low. Feigenbaum (2013) scrutinized the development costs for 21 major HSR lines in the world and found that only two (Shinkansen in Japan and Paris–Lyon in France) are profitable. These two lines happen to have been built early on in global HSR development with relatively low land costs. The Shinkansen was the world's first HSR line. The Paris–Lyon line in France, the first HSR line in Europe, began operating in 1981. Indeed, most HSR megaprojects encounter a fiscal deficit due to their cost overruns and overestimated demand. Even though most HSR lines run a deficit, the public sector still actively develops HSR systems based on the belief that HSR can promote market integration and strengthen agglomeration economies.

Agglomeration Economies from HSR and Previous Empirical Findings

Agglomeration Economies

Agglomeration economies are the benefit gain or cost savings from the proximity of firms and people within cities or industries. Many empirical studies have found that firms are more productive in dense places (Combes et al. 2012). For example, Ciccone and Hall (1996) found that doubling employment density can increase productivity by about 6 percent in the United States. Similarly, Ciccone (2002) found that the elasticity of productivity to employment density is about 4.5 percent in Europe. Recent studies have applied better identification methods to explore the agglomeration benefit for productivity and yielded similar results. For instance, Ahlfeldt et al. (2015) used the division and reunification of Berlin as an exogenous variation to estimate agglomeration economies and found a 7 percent elasticity of productivity to employment density. Besides the productivity gain, empirical studies have found that agglomeration can lead to wage gains, speed up innovation, enhance people skills, increase intellectual interaction, and so forth (Arzaghi and Henderson 2008; Carlino, Chatterjee, and Hunt 2007). Agglomeration economies are regarded as one of the most important sources of urban wealth (Glaeser and Gottlieb 2009).

Marshall (1920) highlighted three different sources of agglomeration economies. The first is input sharing between intermediate and final good suppliers to reduce cost. The second is labor market pooling, which allows for better matching between firms and laborers. The third is knowledge spillover, allowing learning through worker interaction. Empirical studies have found evidence to support all of these, as summarized by Rosenthal and Strange (2004). Furthermore, Duranton and Puga (2004) provided the microfoundations of urban agglomeration economies as sharing, matching, and learning mechanisms. Besides these channels, other sources include the home market effect, agglomeration for consumption, and rent seeking (Rosenthal and Strange 2004).

There are debates as to whether agglomeration benefits arise from the concentration of activities in a particular industry or from the concentration of a variety of industries within a city. The former phenomenon is known as localization or specialization economies, and the latter is known as urbanization or diversity economies. Marshall (1920) favored local specialization (i.e., agglomeration benefits can arise from the clustering of firms in similar sectors). Empirical studies have found localization economies in different countries and industries (Henderson 2003; Rosenthal and Strange 2001). Urbanization economies have gained popularity since Jacobs (1969) argued that urban diversity can foster ideas through cross-fertilization. In terms of empirical evidence, Glaeser et al. (1992) found that diversity encourages employment growth in manufacturing. Henderson, Kuncoro, and Turner (1995) found that diversity encourages growth among high-tech firms. Both studies suggest that diversity is helpful for urban growth; however, neither rules out a parallel effect from concentration in a given industry. Large cities are likely to have diverse firms with a few overly concentrated industries. The relative strength of localization and urbanization is also likely related to the type of industry. If knowledge spillover is important, it seems that urbanization economies are more valuable to service industries, which require new ideas and creativity; however, most existing studies focus on manufacturing.

Cities' proximity benefits can be seen in reduced transport costs, and thus improved accessibility through transportation development can reinforce agglomeration benefits (Krugman 1991). However, transportation infrastructure can generate an agglomeration shadow in which growth in one location due to agglomeration economies comes at the expense of nearby locations, while remote areas are not affected (Fujita, Krugman, and Venables 1999). The agglomeration shadow has implications in terms of estimating the benefits of transportation infrastructure in a multicity context. Studies on transportation (including HSR) have extensively discussed whether investment gains are truly generative (representing a net productivity gain) or redistributive (indicating the relocation of activities from one geographic location to another) (Givoni 2006). Accordingly, an estimation of the effect of HSR on business agglomeration at the regional level remains inconclusive and case-dependent.

Previous Estimates of Agglomeration Economies from HSR

The most studied HSR system is the world's first HSR line, the Japanese Shinkansen, which connects Tokyo and Osaka. After its decades of operation, several scholars have estimated its long-term effect on economic growth in cities and regions along the HSR corridor. Sands (1993) found that compared with cities without HSR access, the cities served by this line experienced larger populations and stronger employment growth, especially in the service sectors. Banister and Berechman (2000) found similar employment growth patterns and documented land value appreciation near HSR terminals. However, Cervero and Bernick (1996) found that the economies in intermediate cities along the Shinkansen corridor weakened after 30 years of HSR service. Furthermore, Sasaki, Ohashi, and Ando (1997) showed that the Shinkansen has contributed primarily to developed regions, such as Tokyo and Osaka, and not to underdeveloped regions.

In Europe, studies have found that HSR has benefited large, well-developed cities at the expense of small- and medium-sized cities (Vickerman 1997). In London, HSR attracted financial and knowledge-based jobs to districts near the central terminal stations (Bertolini and Spit 1998). In France, Bonnafous (1987) found that employment growth in Macon, a medium-sized city along the Paris–Lyon route, came at the expense of job loss in surrounding areas. In Spain, studies found that large cities, such as Barcelona and Madrid, experienced more rapid growth because of HSR, while growth in other small- and medium-sized cities slowed (de Rus 2008). De Rus and Inglada (1997) conducted a cost-benefit analysis for a HSR line connecting Madrid and Seville and concluded that the social benefits could not cover the enormous project costs.

Early studies on the effects of HSR in Japan and Europe were more concerned with correlation than with revealing causal relationships. With the development of econometric techniques in the past decade, the causal inference method, such as the difference-in-differences (DID) approach, has been widely used in HSR studies, especially in recent studies in the context of China. However, the conclusions drawn from Chinese cases are not very different from previous estimates in Japan and Europe. For example, Meng, Lin, and Zhu (2018) investigated the effect of HSR on county development in China through DID regression. They found that HSR increased economic growth by approximately 14 percent, while the primary sources of growth are resource redistribution from areas located 30–110 km from HSR stations. Zheng et al. (2019) examined the spatial spillover effect of HSR stations on local economic activities, as indicated by nighttime satellite image intensity. Through DID regression, they found that nighttime imagery intensity increased by about 27 percent for areas located near HSR stations compared with other districts that are far away. However, the effect is strongest for larger cities, while it fades for small cities and districts located far away from the city center. Qin (2017) estimated the redistribution effect of HSR on county growth by employing the DID approach. She found that small counties through which HSR passes experienced a significant decline in GDP, largely driven by the decline of fixed asset investment. She pointed out two possible channels in relation to this result: reduced conventional train service after HSR, and the diversion of economic activities from small counties to large cities. She found that the second channel played a more important role in explaining the negative impact of HSR on intermediate cities.

The cases in Japan, the European Union, and China seem to indicate that HSR does not bring much in the way of net economic benefits, given the nature of the concomitant redistribution. However, several studies have estimated the impact of historical railways on economic development by employing a general equilibrium model developed from trade theory; such studies suggest net economic gains arising from transport infrastructure. For instance, Donaldson and Hornbeck (2016) estimated the effect of railway expansion on the U.S. agriculture sector from 1870 to 1890. They calculated market access improvement due to a railway network and incorporated market access into a general equilibrium framework. The authors concluded that the total agricultural land value in the

United States would drop by 60 percent without railroads. Donaldson (2018) further developed a Ricardian trade model to estimate the impact of railway networks in colonial India from 1870 to 1930. He found that the railway in India promoted interregional and international trade, reduced the interregional price gap, and increased agricultural real income by approximately 16 percent. These studies suggest that a general equilibrium framework is likely to be promising for estimating the net welfare gains of transportation infrastructure. However, we expect that the net effect of HSR on the economy is not as significant as the economic impact exerted by 19th-century rail, which was the only mechanized overland transportation mode at the time.

In addition to directly estimating the economic impact, another set of literature estimates the housing market impact, which can implicitly indicate welfare change because the benefits of HSR access can be capitalized in property values. For example, Zheng and Kahn (2013) found that HSR increased housing prices in China by about 10 percent on the national scale because of improved interregional accessibility. Chen and Haynes (2015) estimated the impact of the Beijing–Shanghai HSR corridor on the city's housing market and found that the impact was positive for small- and medium-sized cities rather than for large cities. Among Chinese cities, Chang and Diao (2021) estimated the direct and network effects of HSR on Shenzhen's housing market. They found that housing values near the HSR hub declined by about 11–13 percent owing to possible negative externalities, such as noise and congestion. However, in the case of Shenzhen, the HSR station is well connected to the city's metro network. Chang and Diao (2021) found that housing prices near metro stations appreciated about 7 percent citywide through the network effect, though the effect appeared to be bell-shaped, depending on the travel time between the HSR station and metro stops. Nevertheless, they found a net gain in property values due to the presence of the HSR line in Shenzhen, although the redistribution effect along the metro network was also quite substantial.

Previous studies have acknowledged that HSR can support agglomeration economies by facilitating face-to-face interaction among highly skilled and knowledge-based workers (Dong, Zheng, and Kahn 2020). This fact indicates that HSR may have different impacts on labor-intensive manufacturing plants and knowledge-based firms. Most studies have examined the impact of HSR on tourism industries (Pagliara, Mauriello, and Garofalo 2017), while few have focused on industrial specialization patterns. Several studies use urban employment data to examine the impact of HSR on urban specialization in China. For example, Lin (2017) studied the impact of HSR on urban specialization patterns from 2003 to 2014. She found that HSR can increase the employment rate by approximately

7 percent on average, with the boost largely driven by tourism-related employment growth. However, employment growth in manufacturing and construction exceeded growth in the service sector. Dong (2018) estimated the effect of HSR on urban sectoral employment from 2003 to 2015. She found that cities that gain HSR access experience significant employment growth in the retail and hotel/catering sectors, but there is no effect on other sectors. Both studies applied the DID method and covered similar study periods, but their findings are not quite consistent with each other.

One caveat is that local governments sometimes change the statistical methods used to calculate urban employment (Chang et al. 2021), which may explain the inconsistent findings among existing studies. To overcome this issue, recent studies have employed firm-level data to estimate the impact of HSR on industrial specialization in China. For example, Chang and Zheng (2020) found that HSR promoted the birth of new firms in the service sector in urban districts. In contrast, the number of new firms in the primary and manufacturing sectors declined significantly after a district was connected to HSR. Similarly, Chang et al. (2021) explored the impact of HSR on industrial movement in the GBA and found a concentration trend in the service sector and a decentralization trend in manufacturing in the central GBA areas due to HSR. The evidence suggests that HSR can strengthen cities' agglomeration benefits.

City Cluster Strategy and GBA Development

City Cluster Strategy

The theory of agglomeration economies suggests that higher employment density is associated with a higher level of productivity. This is supported by the fact that the urbanization level is positively correlated to the level of economic growth across countries. The Chinese government has adopted an urban-led growth strategy and used a pro-urbanization policy to boost the economy. This strategy is demonstrated by the government's proactive actions, such as massive investment in urban infrastructure, promoting the development of the real estate sector, creating industrial parks and special economic zones, and so forth. According to the National Bureau of Statistics (2019), the urbanization rate in China increased from 20 percent to 60 percent between 1982 and 2018. During the same period, the population grew 37.3 percent (from 1.017 billion to 1.395 billion), while GDP per capita in real terms increased 115 times over (from 517 RMB to 60,148 RMB). This enormous economic growth can be partially attributed to the advancing level of urbanization facilitated by infrastructure expansion and other proactive actions.

One of the actions that accelerated urbanization over the last 15 years is the city cluster strategy. The concept of the city cluster is essentially the same as a megalopolis in that both refer to the merging, to some extent, of a few large adjacent cities into a spatially integrated urban region. This strategy is in the interest of economic and spatial planning and coordination among clustered cities. Planners keep the cluster concept in mind when they consider the five-year socioeconomic development plan as well as city and infrastructure plans. There are several reasons why the Chinese government advocates this strategy. On the one hand, urban expansion has extended many economic activities to the boundaries dividing different jurisdictions. These activities have been hampered by the lack of infrastructure, service, and cross-jurisdiction coordination. The city cluster strategy can overcome these intercity administrative barriers by imposing complex socioeconomic and technological processes to unlock economic potential. On the other hand, to counter the national economic slowdown, the central government intends to rebalance the economic structure, that is, move away from export- and investment-driven growth and toward consumption-led growth by boosting the domestic market. The city cluster strategy can expand market size and wealth by increasing the number of urban dwellers, as their consumption will be higher than that of rural residents. The strategy will also increase productivity and innovation by grouping more firms and workers in an integrated market. Moreover, the previous decentralized mode of urban expansion did not efficiently use land resources; the city cluster strategy will enhance the efficiency of land use by increasing population density.

The idea of developing a city cluster can be dated back to 2006, when the China State Council highlighted in its 11th Five-Year Plan that the country's urbanization should be based on the development of city clusters. However, the detailed development strategy was unveiled in the national 2014–2020 urbanization plan (China State Council 2014). In the 2014 plan, the central government set the target of raising the urbanization rate to 60 percent by 2020. The plan entails building 19 city clusters with 3 world-class clusters, namely Beijing-Tianjin-Hebei (which had a combined population of 113 million in 2018), the Yangtze River Delta (164 million), and the GBA (71 million), as shown in figure 17.1. Each of these clusters is much larger in size than the Greater Tokyo Area (which has a population of approximately 40 million), and their combined economic contribution is astonishing. By 2019, the State Council had approved development and investment plans for 10 city clusters.

Efforts to create city clusters are expected to promote market integration and economic growth. The city cluster will be the major development platform for establishing the modern industrial chain, facilitating infrastructure development,

FIGURE 17.1 The planned 19 city clusters in China.

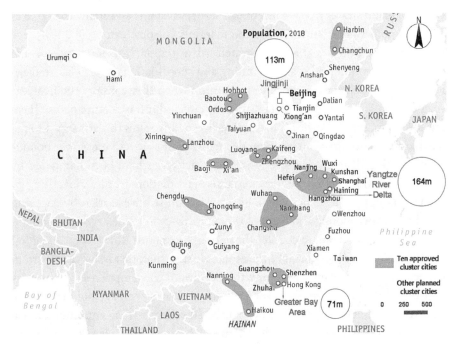

Sources: China State Council (2014); National Bureau of Statistics (2019).

and coordinating intercity management and governance. The central government is responsible for interregional coordination, and the provincial government is responsible for intercity collaboration. In reality, coordination within each cluster may be difficult because it involves different governmental layers, and local governments have a long tradition of competing among themselves for investment and development opportunities because local economic growth is one of the most important criteria for personnel promotion, which is of the utmost importance to local leaders.

Besides regional governance, a well-functioning public transportation infrastructure is essential for city cluster formation and market integration. The rapid development of a bullet train is an effort to expand the effective labor market pool and promote market integration within each cluster. Considering that the size of several of China's individual city clusters is comparable to the size of various nations around the world, we can expect the development of HSR to further stimulate intercity trade among and within each city cluster. A well-established result from trade theory indicates that specialization in each locality can strengthen the comparative advantage and increase the production of all goods. Further specialization owing to HSR has implications for industry structure, and we expect to observe an increasing concentration of specific types of firms in certain regions. City clusters also promote urbanization economies by attracting more knowledge-based firms and facilitating the exchange of ideas. Among all of China's city clusters, the development of the GBA is the most prominent.

GBA Development

The GBA is one of the most vibrant regions in China, consisting of nine cities in the Pearl River Delta in Guangdong Province, Hong Kong, and Macau. The size of the whole territory is about 56,000 km². By the end of 2018, more than 71 million people were living in the GBA, and GDP per capita was about US$23,300. In 2017, the central government set up the GBA development framework; the formal development plan was unveiled in February 2019 (Greater Bay Area 2019). According to the development plan, the purpose of GBA development is not only to leverage the advantages of Guangdong, Hong Kong, and Macau to stimulate regional economic growth and build a first-class bay area and city cluster but also to support the integration of Hong Kong and Macau within national development. Since developing the GBA requires coordination between Guangdong and two special administrative regions, a vice premier of the State Council has been put in charge of GBA development coordination.

The GBA development plan outlines many objectives. One is to further develop the four core cities of Hong Kong, Macau, Guangzhou, and Shenzhen as regional growth engines. Each city is expected to consolidate and advance its original advantage, that is, Hong Kong as an international financial center, Macau as a world-class tourism center, Guangzhou as an international commerce and industry center as well as a transport hub, and Shenzhen as an international innovation center. Other cities and towns are expected to strengthen their interaction and cooperation with the core cities. The plan also emphasizes the development of advanced manufacturing and modern service industries, including developing both advanced equipment manufacturing in Zhuhai and Foshan and high-end manufacturing such as information technology in Shenzhen and Dongguan and upgrading the traditional industries in Dongguan and Foshan.

The development objectives can be seen largely as an extension of previous policies rather than as having been initiated from scratch. For example, the transformation and upgrading of the industrial system in Guangdong can be dated to the early 2000s. To free up development space and help industries move up the value chain for cities in the Pearl River Delta, the Guangdong government launched the Industrial Relocation Parks (IRPs) projects to facilitate industrial

FIGURE 17.2 High-speed rail network of the Greater Bay Area, 2018.

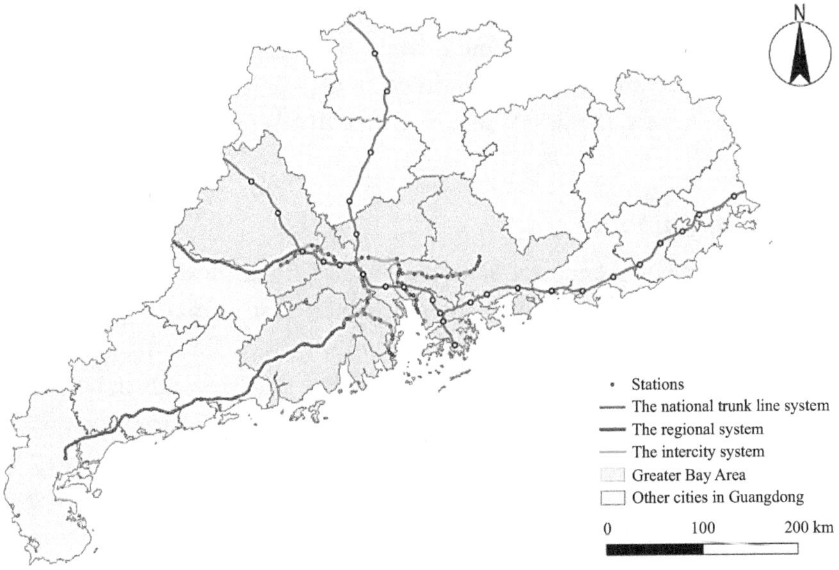

Sources: China Railway (2008-2021).

relocation through which traditional manufacturing in nine GBA cities were to be relocated to the IRPs built in other less-developed cities. The industrial relocation policy is supposed to benefit both developed and less-developed cities. Developed cities have more space to develop higher value-added industries. In other cities, relocated manufacturing is likely to enhance the local employment rate and promote economic growth. From 2005 to 2012, 34 IRPs were established for industrial relocation, and these IRPs are still in operation today.

Another objective is to build a rapid intercity transport system and reduce the travel time between major GBA cities to one hour or less. This target has largely been reached because of the expansion of the HSR network in the past 10 years. The first HSR line in the GBA (a national trunk line connecting Beijing to Guangzhou) began operations at the end of 2009. At the end of 2011, another HSR line connected Guangzhou to Shenzhen, reducing the travel time between the two cities from 55 minutes to 28 minutes. This line was further extended to Hong Kong in 2018. Currently, the travel times from Hong Kong to Shenzhen and Guangzhou are 15 and 47 minutes, respectively. By 2018, 9 HSR lines with 91 stations were providing high-speed train services connecting all the major GBA cities. Figure 17.2 shows the GBA's HSR network in 2018.

HSR and Agglomeration Economics in the GBA

The rapid expansion of HSR can promote market integration and enhance labor mobility, both of which have implications for agglomeration economies and city cluster formation. Chang et al. (2021) provided empirical evidence by estimating the causal effect of HSR on industrial movement in the context of the GBA. They employed firm-level data and explored how HSR impacted the number of firms and the employment rate at the county level. The study showed that the service sector is concentrated in the central GBA region because of HSR access. In contrast, large-scale manufacturing firms moved to non-GBA localities that are not connected to the HSR. Chang et al. (2021) argued that the service sector values the integrated market and rich information environment in megacities. Large-scale manufacturing firms are more sensitive to the rising costs of labor and land as a result of HSR. Accordingly, they decentralize to cheaper places. To ensure the credibility of these estimations, Chang et al. (2021) conducted a number of robustness checks such as excluding the impact of industry policy (IRPs) on firms.

The industrial movement patterns can implicitly demonstrate the role of HSR in city cluster formation. More evidence can be found by looking at the direct impact of HSR on socioeconomic changes. Using the socioeconomic data for 21 cities collected from the *Guangdong Statistical Yearbooks* from 2007 to 2018, I applied the same DID empirical method that Chang et al. (2021) used to estimate the impact of HSR on population, employment, and GDP in the GBA. The summarized statistics and empirical results are shown in the appendix. I found that the population increased by 4.6 percent in GBA cities but declined by 1.5 percent in non-GBA cities. City employment increased by 11.1 percent in GBA cities and slightly declined in non-GBA cities. The impact of HSR on GDP was found to be slightly negative though not significant. However, we need to be cautious about attributing GDP decline to HSR. The development of HSR stations and surrounding real estate projects accounted for a significant share of GDP before the stations were opened. This investment was completed immediately before they became operational, and GDP decreased after they were operational.

In sum, the results obtained with regard to socioeconomic changes are consistent with the industry movement pattern. Population and employment increase significantly after GBA cities are connected to the HSR network, indicating the increasing centralizing force of agglomeration economies in the multicity setting. Clustering in service sectors and the exodus of large manufacturing indicate that industries are moving up the value chain. These findings suggest that HSR promotes market integration and expands the effective labor market. HSR helps create city clusters by strengthening the agglomeration force, causing the GBA to become more attractive to consumers, tourists, and laborers. Owing to people's increased mobility, high–value-added firms along the HSR corridor expand their business from local to regional and national markets. In contrast, large-scale manufacturing firms move out because the operation costs in large cities increase (due to either increasing wages or rents or both) after the arrival of HSR. Overall, the empirical findings support the positive role of HSR in urban agglomeration economies. However, the benefits that GBA cities reap come partially at the expense of other cities because non-GBA cities lose both population and value-added firms. The net benefit of HSR on economic growth at the regional level is uncertain.

Conclusions

This chapter introduces China's ongoing development of HSR networks in city clusters. Empirical studies indicate the positive role of HSR in boosting agglomeration economies, as demonstrated by increased population sizes and employment rates, the increasing number of service sectors, and the exodus of large manufacturing. The evidence suggests that HSR enhances agglomeration effects at the city cluster level. However, the gain for larger cities seems to occur at the expense of less-developed regions, as non-GBA cities lose population and industries. The agglomeration literature suggests that an increasing population density is associated with increasing productivity, which suggests that the extra productivity gain in megacities could offset other cities' losses if the opportunity cost of HSR investment is not too large.

Although the current evidence portrays the rosy side of HSR with respect to agglomeration economies in the GBA, there is plenty of criticism of and skepticism about China's HSR strategy, which was used as a policy tool to boost the national and local economies and was not grounded in robust cost-benefit analysis. Some important information is missing from this study such as line-by-line investment costs and ridership, which are not published in the official statistics. Accordingly, many important questions cannot be answered. For example, at what cost is HSR development used as a policy for achieving agglomeration? Can the agglomeration benefits be justified by the costs? What other complementary policies should be in place to achieve agglomeration? Is costly HSR necessary for the formation of city clusters? How will HSR impact other city clusters? These questions are important for future research and HSR investment decision making. If cost data become available, future research should conduct a rigorous cost-benefit analysis for each HSR line and the entire HSR network to evaluate the magnitude of the net social welfare gain from HSR development.

Summary

- China is like Japan in its reliance on HSR to shape national and regional development. Unlike Japan, however, China is struggling to accommodate an enormous migration of workers from the countryside to the city.

- Toward that end, China has developed a strategy to increase agglomeration economies that involves the creation of 19 enormous city clusters, each with several major cities linked with HSR service.

- Limited empirical evidence from the GBA—one of the first and largest city clusters—suggests that HSR enhances agglomeration effects at the cluster level, but the gain in employment for the larger cities seems to come at the expense of the small ones. It is unclear, moreover, whether the agglomeration benefits of the strategy actually outweigh the cost in additional HSR service.

References

Ahlfeldt, Gabriel M., Stephen J. Redding, Daniel M. Sturm, and Nikolaus Wolf. 2015. "The Economics of Density: Evidence from the Berlin Wall." *Econometrica* 83(6): 2127–2189.

Arzaghi, Mohammad, and J. Vernon Henderson. 2008. "Networking off Madison Avenue." *Review of Economics Studies* 75(4): 1011–1038.

Banister, David, and Joseph Berechman. 2000. *Transport Investment and Economic Development*. London: Routledge.

Bertolini, Luca, and Tejo Spit. 1998. *Cities on Rails: The Redevelopment of Railway Station Areas*. London: E & FN Spon.

Bonnafous, Alain. 1987. "The Regional Impact of the TGV." *Transportation* 14: 127–137.

Carlino, Gerald A., Satyajit Chatterjee, and Robert M. Hunt. 2007. "Urban Density and the Rate of Invention." *Journal of Urban Economics* 61: 389–419.

Cervero, Robert, and Michael Bernick. 1996. "High-Speed Rail and Development of California's Central Valley: Comparative Lessons and Public Policy Considerations." IURD working paper No. 675. Berkeley: University of California.

Chang, Zheng. 2014. "Financing New Metros: The Beijing Metro Financing Sustainability Study." *Transport Policy* 32: 148–155.

Chang, Zheng, and Mi Diao. 2021. "Inter-City Transport Infrastructure and Intra-City Housing Markets: Estimating the Redistribution Effect of High-Speed Rail in Shenzhen, China." *Urban Studies* (June). https://doi.org/10.1177/00420980211017811.

Chang, Zheng, Mi Diao, Kecen Jing, and Weifeng Li. 2021. "High-Speed Rail and Industrial Movement: Evidence from China's Greater Bay Area." *Transport Policy* 112: 22–31.

Chang, Zheng, and Longfei Zheng. 2020. "High-Speed Rail and the Spatial Pattern of New Firm Births: Evidence from China." SSRN working paper, August. http://dx.doi.org/10.2139/ssrn.3683653.

Chen, Zhenhua, and Kingsley E. Haynes. 2015. "Impact of High-Speed Rail on Housing Values: An Observation from the Beijing–Shanghai Line." *Journal of Transport Geography* 43: 91–100.

China State Council. 2014. "National New Urbanization Plan (2014–2020)." [In Chinese.] http://www.gov.cn/zhengce/2014-03/16/content_2640075.htm.

Ciccone, Antonio. 2002. "Agglomeration Effects in Europe." *European Economic Review* 46(2): 213–227.

Ciccone, Antonio, and Robert E. Hall. 1996. "Productivity and the Density of Economic Activity." *American Economic Review* 86(1): 54–70.

Combes, Pierre-Philippe, Gilles Duranton, Laurent Gobillon, Diego Puga, and Sébastien Roux. 2012. "The Productivity Advantages of Large Cities: Distinguishing Agglomeration from Firm Selection." *Econometrica* 80(6): 2543–2594.

de Rus, Ginés. 2008. "The Economic Effects of High Speed Rail Investment." Discussion paper No. 2008/16. Paris: OECD-ITP Joint Transport Research Centre.

de Rus, Ginés, and Vincinte Inglada. 1997. "Cost-Benefit Analysis of the High-Speed Train in Spain." *Annals of Regional Science* 31(2): 175–188.

Donaldson, Dave. 2018. "Railroads of the Raj: Estimating the Impact of Transportation Infrastructure." *American Economic Review* 108(4–5): 899–934.

Donaldson, Dave, and Richard Hornbeck. 2016. "Railroads and American Economic Growth: A 'Market Access' Approach." *Quarterly Journal of Economics* 131(2): 799–858.

Dong, Xiaofang. 2018. "High-Speed Railway and Urban Sectoral Employment in China." *Transportation Research Part A* 116: 603–621.

Dong, Xiaofang, Siqi Zheng, and Matthew Kahn. 2020. "The Role of Transportation Speed in Facilitating High Skilled Teamwork Across Cities." *Journal of Urban Economics* 115. https://doi.org/10.1016/j.jue.2019.103212. 103–212?

Duranton, Gilles, and Diego Puga. 2004. "Micro-Foundations of Urban Agglomeration Economies." In *Handbook of Regional and Urban Economics*, vol. 4, ed. J. Vernon Henderson and Jacques-François Thisse, 2063–2117. Amsterdam: North-Holland.

Feigenbaum, Baruch. 2013. "High-Speed Rail in Europe and Asia: Lessons for the United States." Policy study No. 418. http://americandreamcoalition.org/2013PAD/Baruch%20 Feigenbaum/high_speed_rail_lessons.pdf.

Fujita, Masahisa, Paul Krugman, and Anthony J. Venables. 1999. *The Spatial Economy: Cities, Regions, and International Trade.* Cambridge, MA: MIT Press.

Givoni, Moshe. 2006. "Development and Impact of the Modern High-Speed Train: A Review." *Transport Reviews* 26(5): 593–611.

Glaeser, Edward L. Glaeser, Hedi D. Kallal, José A. Scheinkman, and Andrei Shleifer. 1992. "Growth in Cities." *Journal of Political Economy* 100: 1126–1152.

Glaeser, Edward L., and Joshua D. Gottlieb. 2009. "The Wealth of Cities: Agglomeration Economies and Spatial Equilibrium in the United States." *Journal of Economic Literature* 47(4): 983–1028.

Greater Bay Area. 2019. "Outline Development Plan for the Guangdong–Hong Kong–Macao Greater Bay Area." https://www.bayarea.gov.hk/en/outline/plan.html.

Henderson, J. Vernon. 2003. "Marshall's Scale Economies." *Journal of Urban Economics* 53: 1–28.

Henderson, Vernon, Ari Kuncoro, and Matt Turner. 1995. "Industrial Development in Cities." *Journal of Political Economy* 103: 1067–1085.

Jacobs, Jane. 1969. *The Economy of Cities.* New York: Vintage.

Krugman, Paul. 1991. "Increasing Returns and Economic Geography." *Journal of Political Economy* 99(3): 483–499.

Lawrence, Martha B., Richard G. Bullock, Ziming Liu. 2019. "China's High-Speed Rail Development." Washington, DC: World Bank Group. http://documents.worldbank.org/curated/en/933411559841476316/Chinas-High-Speed-Rail-Development.

Lin, Yatang. 2017. "Travel Costs and Urban Specialization Patterns: Evidence from China's High-Speed Railway System." *Journal of Urban Economics* 98: 98–123.

Marshall, Alfred. 1920. *Principles of Economics.* London: Macmillan.

Meng, Xuechen, Shanlang Lin, and Xiaochuan Zhu. 2018. "The Resource Redistribution Effect of High-Speed Rail Stations on the Economic Growth of Neighbouring Regions: Evidence from China." *Transport Policy* 68: 178–191.

National Bureau of Statistics. 2019. "China Statistical Yearbook." http://www.stats.gov.cn/tjsj/ndsj/2019/indexch.htm.

Pagliara, Francesca, Filomena Mauriello, and Antonio Garofalo. 2017. "Exploring the Interdependences Between High Speed Rail Systems and Tourism: Some Evidence from Italy." *Transport Research Part A: Policy Practice* 106: 300–308.

Qin, Yu. 2017. "No County Left Behind? The Distributional Impact of High-Speed Rail Upgrade in China." *Journal of Economic Geography* 17(3): 489–520.

Rosenthal, Stuart S., and William C. Strange. 2001. "The Determinants of Agglomeration." *Journal of Urban Economics* 50: 191–229.

———. 2004. "Evidence on the Nature and Sources of Agglomeration Economics." In *Handbook of Regional and Urban Economics*, vol. 4, ed. J. Vernon Henderson and Jacques-François Thisse, 2131–2179. Amsterdam: North Holland.

Sands, Brian. 1993. "The Development Effects of High-Speed Rail Stations and Implications for California." *Built Environment* 19(3–4): 257–284.

Sasaki, Komei, Tadahiro Ohashi, and Asao Ando. 1997. "High-Speed Rail Transit Impact on Regional Systems: Does the Shinkansen Contribute to Dispersion?" *Annals of Regional Science* 31(1): 77–98.

Vickerman, Roger. 1997. "High-Speed Rail in Europe: Experience and Issues for Future Development." *Annals of Regional Science* 31(1): 21–38.

Zheng Longfei, Fenjie Long, Zheng Chang, and Jingsong Ye. 2019. "Ghost Town or City of Hope? The Spatial Spillover Effects of High-Speed Railway Stations in China." *Transport Policy* 81: 230–241.

Zheng, Siqi, and Matthew E. Kahn. 2013. "China's Bullet Trains Facilitate Market Integration and Mitigate the Cost of Megacity Growth." *Proceedings of the National Academy of Sciences of the USA* 110(14): E1248–E53.

Appendix

Socioeconomic data were collected for 21 cities from the *Guangdong Statistical Yearbooks* for the sample period 2007–2018. Table A1 shows the variable definition and summarized statistics. I used the DID regression model to estimate the causal impact of HSR on socioeconomic changes in Guangdong. The regression model is identical to that in Chang et al. (2021). In the regression, cities are further classified into GBA cities (nine cities in the Pearl River Delta) and non-GBA cities. The dependent variables include the natural logarithms of GDP, population, and employment. The regression results are reported in table A2, and the standard errors in all regressions are clustered at the city level.

TABLE A1 Variable Definition and Summarized Statistics

		Observation	Mean	SD
HSR	Binary, 1 = city after the HSR service, 0 otherwise	252	0.4722	0.6081
GBA	Binary, 1 = GBA, 0 otherwise	252	0.381	0.4866
GDP	Number of GDP level, 100 million RMB	252	3095.729	4433.362
Pop	Number of population, 10,000	252	503.7276	285.822
Emp	Number of total employment, 10,000	252	285.9173	204.6661

TABLE A2 High-Speed Rail and Economic Outcomes

Dependent	log(Pop)		log(Emp)		log(GDP)	
	(1)	(2)	(3)	(4)	(5)	(6)
HSR	-0.0021		0.0138		-0.0133	
	(0.0069)		(0.0213)		(0.0127)	
HSR_GBA		0.0458***		0.111***		-0.041
		(0.015)		(0.0371)		(0.0379)
HSR_None_GBA		-0.0149**		-0.0125		-0.0058
		(0.0064)		(0.0119)		(0.0105)
Constant	6.624***	6.605***	6.308***	6.269***	7.929***	7.940***
	(0.0132)	(0.0127)	(0.0259)	(0.0278)	(0.0189)	(0.0233)
County fixed effect	Yes	Yes	Yes	Yes	Yes	Yes
Year fixed effect	Yes	Yes	Yes	Yes	Yes	Yes
R-squared	0.997	0.998	0.988	0.99	0.997	0.997
Observations	252	252	252	252	252	252

Note: Robust standard errors are in parentheses and clustered at city level; * $p < 0.1$, ** $p < 0.05$, *** $p < 0.01$.

COPING WITH RADICAL UNCERTAINTIES

18

INFRASTRUCTURE AND CLIMATE CHANGE

Henry Lee

As the world focuses on the COVID-19 pandemic, the disruptive reality of global climate change looms on the horizon. Its implications for public infrastructure could be immense. Forest fires in Australia, Siberia, and California; record cold in Texas; droughts in southern India and South Africa; intense hurricanes and floods in the United States and the Philippines; and the melting of the Arctic ice sheet are all harbingers of what a changing climate has in store.

Climate change is a different environmental problem from others we currently face. Unlike most air pollutants that descend back to Earth, carbon emissions can stay in the atmosphere for centuries. These cumulative emissions, regardless of where and when produced, increase the frequency and intensity of changing climate patterns. As pointed out by Martin Weitzman and Gernot Wagner (2015, 7) in their book *Climate Shock*, "Climate change is unlike any other environmental problem, really unlike any other public policy problem. It's almost uniquely *global*, uniquely *long-term*, uniquely *irreversible*, and uniquely *uncertain*—certainly unique in the combination of all four." The impact of climate change on infrastructure services will be integral to the world's economy. How we power our factories, buildings, and homes, allocate and treat our water, and transport people and goods may look very different 30 years from now.

While it is true that uncertainty surrounds both the impacts of and the responses to climate change, the direction is clear. The effects will be more disruptive in 2050 than today. More floods, droughts, fires, and heat waves will occur. While countries may struggle to transition their economies, escalating climate impacts may force them to accelerate their efforts.

Climate policy makers distinguish between mitigation and adaptation strategies for dealing with global warming. Mitigation strategies seek to slow or reverse global climate change by reducing total carbon emissions, while adaptation strategies seek to reduce the harmful effects of global warming by investing in infrastructure, settlement patterns, and other measures that leave us less vulnerable.

This chapter can be divided into three parts. In the first, I focus on how jurisdictions may adapt to the growing threats of climate change. No single optimal adaptation strategy exists, since the impacts are localized. The threat to one region will differ from the threat to another region. Impacts may change in scope, magnitude, and character from one period to the next. Responsibility for designing and implementing adaptation responses will fall on city and subnational governments, not on national governments. Effective policies will emerge at lower levels of government in a true bottom-up process.

In the second section, I consider the implications for infrastructure of both adaptation and mitigation goals, particularly the increasingly popular goal of net zero emissions by 2050—a goal that 77 countries committed to by the end of 2020. Net zero means that the residual greenhouse gases produced are offset by the greenhouse gases sequestered or removed from the atmosphere. Getting net zero commitments from as many countries as possible is important, since it is impossible to exclude a country from benefiting from emission reductions elsewhere and thus from free-riding on the efforts of others.

If countries are to meet their net zero commitments, the magnitude of the investments in new or improved infrastructure will be unprecedented. The electricity sector will be the most affected, as heating and electricity are weaned from oil to wind, solar, and other non-fossil-fueled sources. Power will be dispatched over increasingly complex and sophisticated transmission and distribution systems. In the transportation sector, roads, airports, and other basic infrastructure are likely to stay the same, however, planes, cars, and other vehicles may be powered by electricity, hydrogen, or biofuels.

A warmer world will mean more extreme precipitation in some areas and faster evaporation and more droughts in others (Intergovernmental Panel on Climate Change 2014). These disparities will grow over time. The areas that find themselves with insufficient fresh water will have to choose between building costly desalination plants, importing fresh water, or rationing by price or other means.

In the final section, I examine four governance challenges that underlie the climate mitigation and adaptation options: (1) the allocation of responsibility within governments for planning, implementing, and funding climate initiatives; (2) the siting process to approve infrastructure essential to the low carbon transition; (3) the treatment of physical and human stranded assets; and (4) the greater use of preventive investments as opposed to investing only in post disaster recovery.

The discussions of the likely adaptation and mitigation problems, policies, and technologies assume a political and administrative environment similar to that of the United States or other OECD countries. This is in part because the United States has among the highest per capita greenhouse gas emissions in the world, which makes achieving mitigation targets more difficult and the magnitude of the adaptation challenges much larger.

Of all the climate topics that were left out of this chapter, the greatest loss is environmental justice. Where and how infrastructure is built, maintained, and updated can have enormous equity impacts. These issues are not addressed here; however, they must be mentioned to ensure that when societies mitigate climate change and adapt infrastructure, these transitions are done in ways that are inclusive and equitable, in particular to communities that have previously borne disproportionate environmental burdens.

Adaptation

What is climate adaptation? According to the 1992 United Nations Framework Convention on Climate Change, "Adaptation refers to adjustments in ecological, social, or economic systems in response to actual or expected climatic stimuli and their effects or impacts" (United Nations n.d.). Specifically, climate resilience is defined by the National Academies of Sciences, Engineering, and Medicine (2012, 1) as "the ability to prepare and plan for, absorb, recover from, and more successfully adapt to adverse events." Together, climate change adaptation and resilience are efforts to reduce future harm to humans, the environment, and physical assets.

The types of threats from climate-induced disasters differ from one part of the United States to another and are highly localized. The homeowner in central California, for example, does not worry about floods from sea surge, while someone from Miami, Florida, does not worry about forest fires.

In most instances, the responsibility to adapt to threats—particularly natural disasters—falls on the individual property owner. If a huge rainstorm floods one's house, the responsibility of pumping out the basement and repairing the damage lies with the homeowner, and many homeowners hedge this risk by purchasing insurance. From a taxpayer's perspective, it is important to have property owners retain as much of the risk as possible. If the risk increases, property owners can either make investments to render their property more resilient or move.

Economists argue that if the benefits of decisions to protect properties threatened by the impacts from climate change are enjoyed by local property owners, the costs should be borne by those owners. If this is the case, why should governments be involved? Where are the market failures?

First, some property owners may not have the financial capacity to either recover from a disaster or take action to reduce the threat. Hence, financial assistance from the government to provide subsidized insurance or to rebuild after a disaster is essential. What governments have historically not provided is assistance to purchase the properties (and move households or commercial operations to a safer location) or subsidies to make properties more resilient. This topic is discussed in more depth later in this chapter.

Second, there can be significant asymmetric knowledge. For example, coastal property owners do not own monitoring stations out in the ocean, while national governments do and thus can track weather phenomena such as hurricanes. On the other hand, local governments understand where the risks of floods or fires are greatest and can use their zoning powers to restrict construction in those areas. New buildings need to be less vulnerable to intense storms. Fortunately, local government experts have both the expertise and the opportunity to amend local building codes to reflect this threat.

Third, there is a strong public goods argument to justify government involvement. For example, creating wetlands, mangrove swamps, and artificial barriers could dramatically slow the intensity of the sea surge accompanying intense storms. The benefits accruing from such investments cannot be restricted to a single property owner and instead will be enjoyed by much of the community.

If persuasive justifications exist for local government involvement, why have local governments made so little investment in climate adaptation options? The answer is almost always financial. Local tax bases are limited to property taxes and, to a lesser extent, sales taxes and fees. Further, many jurisdictions do not have the luxury of running budget deficits. Investments in larger climate adaptation projects can be pursued only if there are large co-benefits or reductions in more traditional budget categories. These traditional categories usually have a strong stakeholder base, making it difficult to gain political support for new priorities.

In addition to funding, three other factors constrain local governments. First, elected officials can calculate the probable rate of return for a new school or hospital. But what about the return for a seawall, a new wetland, or storm-proofing tunnels and roadways? Since the magnitude and timing of the climate disruptions are uncertain, calculating a rate of return is difficult, bordering on speculative. When faced with a decision between a new school and a new seawall, politicians are almost always going to pursue the politically safer option.

The second factor is the uncertain future of those cities most threatened by climate-induced disruptions. Let us take Miami, as an example. Much of Miami-Dade County rests on what was a large limestone reef and is no more than 6–8 ft. above sea level. The county's water supply from the Biscayne Aquifer is threatened by saltwater intrusion, and the city lies directly along one of the traditional hurricane tracks. If climate change increases the risk of more intense storms and flooding, thus eroding the value of coastal properties, will Miami's population decrease over the next 40 years as people decide whether to stay or leave the area? Will tourism evaporate? Will economic growth contract as businesses move to other cities?

Several years ago, Miami was confronted with whether it should relocate its sewage treatment facilities from the three low-lying coastal areas to higher locations. This investment, including new pipes and pumps, would have cost close to US$10 billion (Lee et al. 2017). The other option was to improve the existing sites that were prone to flooding. Advocates of the former argued that it would make little sense to invest in the latter if the treatment plants would be under 6 ft. of water in several decades. The opponents argued that there was substantial uncertainty about the amount of sea rise, the number of storms hitting Miami, and the cost of climate disruption, so spending US$10 billion for disruptions that might not occur was unwise. They further pointed out that if Miami faced all the disruptions portrayed by the advocates of moving the treatment plants, the population, the economy, and the topography of the city might differ from what they are today. The population could be substantially smaller, and the sewage needs would be less. Why pay US$10 billion for infrastructure that might not be needed?

One could argue that a cautious steward would protect the city's sewage treatment system and move at least part of it. Uncertainty should not mean doing nothing. If homeowners purchase insurance policies in the face of much lower risks, why should governments not be even more willing to do so with their lower costs of capital and low social discount factors?

The answer in part lies in the third constraining factor. Most cities have significant legacy responsibilities such as education, public health, policing, and sanitation. As the population grows, so too do these expenses; often the revenue from a growing tax base does not fully cover them. Hence, cities find themselves fiscally constrained.

In the last decade, many cities have recognized the growing threat of future climate disruptions. They have set up climate offices, which have produced voluminous reports. Mayors and city councils have issued proclamations, updated standards and regulations, and established permanent climate commissions. What they have not done is restructure their budget priorities or raise more revenue. Requesting fees or additional taxes from new development, including those in areas threatened by possible flooding, runs the risk that investors will forgo the proposed project or relocate it to another city. If climate-related disasters induce substantial costs over time, city leaders may be able to overcome political resistance and change budget allocations. However, these adjustments may be too little, too late.

If local governments are unable to fund the necessary infrastructure adaptation and resilience, who can? Cities can ask their state or provincial government for assistance, but they too have limited financial resources. The two sources that remain are the private sector and the national government. As mentioned, the private sector is reluctant to make meaningful investments in which a significant proportion of the benefits accrue to others, leaving the national government as the remaining option. If the threat from climate change were homogenous—affecting every location in the same way and to the same magnitude—persuading the national government to invest to protect local infrastructure would be a much easier task. Such is not the case, and thus federal assistance for climate adaptation is likely to be uneven and sporadic.

Infrastructure of 2050

The timing and scope of developing and deploying new technologies is steeped in uncertainty. The idea that new technologies will suddenly emerge, making the task of decarbonization less costly, runs counter to past historical experience. Certainly, some technologies have improved dramatically over a short period of time; information technologies and renewable energy are examples. However, other transitions have taken much longer. Oil was discovered in the middle of the 19th century, but developing robust markets took almost 70 years. New low-carbon technologies may emerge but take similarly long to fully deploy.

Electricity Sector

The infrastructure of 2050 most likely to undergo significant change is electricity systems. Three factors will drive this change. First, conventional air pollution regulations will grow more stringent (Landrigan et al. 2018). Governments will face increasing pressure from stakeholders concerned about the economic and health costs from fossil fuels. Over time, higher health costs plus citizen opposition will persuade national governments to change the incentives embedded in the existing regulatory regimes in order to accelerate the retirement of fossil-fueled power plants and to spur invest in low-carbon substitutes.

Second, a decarbonized world will require increases in electricity use. Heating by burning liquid fuels will be replaced by ever more efficient electric heating systems (e.g., heat pumps, geothermal systems). Ground-based transportation systems will be weaned from oil to other forms of energy—probably electricity or hydrogen. Finally, energy-intensive industries, such as steel and cement, will strive to convert from fossil fuels to electricity.

Third, as fossil fuel–based facilities are phased out, investment in renewable systems will increase. Unfortunately, the task of scaling up wind and solar generation consists of more than simply building more solar and wind capacity. It will require major changes in the way electricity is dispatched, transported, and stored. For example, to ensure high standards of reliability, the grid operator must ensure that power is available on demand. In times when it is insufficiently windy or during the hours when the sun is not shining, the operator must dispatch other sources of power onto the grid. Even the most fervent advocates of renewable power will not tolerate multiple blackouts throughout the day, especially when they are accustomed to very high reliability standards.

In some cases, a vastly expanded transmission system could allow power from places where it is windy to move to places where it is not. In other cases, the operator might rely on natural gas facilities to support the grid. Nuclear power does not usually back up intermittent sources, but France has shown that it is technically possible. Large-scale hydroelectric plants are extremely flexible in their ability to provide power when needed, but not every region has access to appropriate sites. The bottom line is that an electricity grid heavily reliant on wind and solar generators must be significantly more flexible than today's system.

This intermittency leads to the question of who will pay for this new electricity infrastructure, including increased transmission, capital-intensive fossil fuel plants (possibly accompanied with carbon capture and sequestration capacity) that are used for just a few hours per day or large-scale storage facilities (if the technology permits).

The private sector might argue that since social and environmental concerns, as opposed to economic factors, drive this transition, the government should shoulder a disproportionate share of these expenses. The public sector is likely to be less enthused by this argument, pointing out that these investments are essentially the internalization of externalities, and thus the industry should shoulder them. But who is the industry? The electricity systems of the future may not look like ones we have today, which in many countries rely on vertically integrated, regulated utilities. In many developed countries, the generation and marketing segments are already decoupled, while the transmission, distribution, and grid operations remain regulated. The utility of the future, however, may be even more decentralized, with multiple companies providing transmission, storage, and backup support, with some regulated and others not (MIT Energy Initiative 2016).

Transitioning to a low-carbon electricity system in a period of three decades will be expensive. A study done by researchers at Princeton University, the Environmental Defense Fund, and Exxon developed various scenarios to meet a goal of net zero carbon emissions by midcentury (Carbon Mitigation Initiative 2019). In the scenarios, in which all power was derived from renewables, transmission capacity increased fivefold in 30 years, and an elaborate system of pipelines to carry liquid CO_2 to sequestration sites would have to be constructed. Installed electricity-generating capacity in the United States in Princeton's all-renewables scenario would have to increase over today's levels by almost 500 percent, from approximately 1100 GW to 6300 GW (Carbon Mitigation Initiative 2019). In addition, industries, most fossil-fuel production units, and fossil-fuel generation facilities would close, stranding billions of dollars of assets.

What drives these very high costs is the mid-century deadline to reach net zero carbon emissions. This time constraint will make it almost impossible to depend exclusively on pricing or economic tools. If the goal were extended to 2100, the transition would be much less costly, reducing the need for subsidies and regulation, but the potential damage from climate disruptions precludes the option of delay.

Where will the additional capital come from? As mentioned, the private sector can help, but national governments will have to carry a disproportionate share of this responsibility. Whether developed country governments are willing or able to assume this capital requirement is questionable. There is no doubt that poorer nations will be unable to do so without financial assistance from the developed countries, a role that was embraced at the 2015 Paris conference by most of the developed countries but never fully funded.

If governments can either supply the capital or provide generous subsidies, will the private sector enter into partnerships with their public counterparts? Public-private partnerships sound terrific, and the idea receives lip service from all; however, actually negotiating partnerships with which both sides are comfortable is difficult. Partnering with the public sector can be onerous for many private companies, mainly because of the difficulty of building trust (a crucial element in any contractual arrangement). The time it takes to design and develop workable public-private partnerships may create transaction costs that exceed what governments are willing to tolerate.

Beyond the question of who will pay the capital costs of this energy transition, many other challenges exist for the electricity sector with which policy makers—both public and private—will struggle.

First, what is the role of natural gas in a net zero–emission electricity system? Some argue that natural gas is an important bridge fuel. It has half the carbon content of coal, and the supply may be more than enough to meet the more aggressive demand forecasts of the coming decades and to do so at low costs. The capital costs of a combined-cycle gas turbine are low; if carbon capture, utilization, and storage prices drop, the overall levelized costs of electricity could be in the vicinity of US$87 per MWh.[1] The problem is that in a renewable intensive world, these facilities may be used for only a few hours per day; thus, their low-capacity factors will require investors to recover their capital costs over a small number of hours.

Others argue that natural gas is a fossil fuel and that the long-term goal is to reduce the use of fossil fuels, not increase them. Hence, governments will be pressured to find other options to meet peak demand and provide backup power. There are two candidates: storage technologies, which are costly and presently only provide four hours or less of supply, and fossil fuel units with carbon capture, utilization, and storage. Advocates of both are hopeful that costs fall rapidly and that the government actively mandates investments in each.

The second challenge is that retail tariffs will need to change. In the present system, retail suppliers hedge the price. When demand is high, consumers pay rates that are less than actual costs. When demand is low and power is less expensive, consumers pay more. Having tariffs delinked from costs might be tenable if total consumption stays at present levels; in a world where more electricity is needed to heat buildings, power vehicles, and supply heavy industries, regulators will favor spreading consumption over more hours of the day. Smart grids and demand management programs provide the tools for levelized consumption patterns; however, without the correct price signals, these tools will prove inadequate. The composition and magnitude of the load will push regulators and retail distribution companies to charge rates that reflect actual costs at every moment in time.

Therefore, when a consumer plugs in an electric car during peak demand, when costs and consumption are highest, computers will tell the charger to wait until costs have fallen before charging the car. If tariffs do not reflect actual costs, the computers will lack the ability to efficiently allocate the power across time, creating a surge of power that could temporarily black out a neighborhood. Actual costs would increase, and the impacts would ripple through both the economy and society. As electricity comprises an ever-increasing portion of the energy mix, the costs to the economy of using tariffs dislocated from actual costs will be much greater than they are today.

Water Sector

As the world warms, the rate of evaporation will grow; with more water in the atmosphere, precipitation will increase. Some areas will experience more rainfall and others less, leaving a portion of the former with more water and the latter with shortages and droughts (Intergovernmental Panel on Climate Change 2014). We are already seeing this pattern with multiple-year droughts in southern Australia, eastern India, and parts of South Africa. Some estimates suggest that by 2025,

60 percent of the global population will face severe water shortages (Jones et al. 2019, 1344). Uncertainties abound because shifts in ocean and air currents may switch the location of droughts over time. Areas that now have plenty of water may face future shortages due to a combination of climate change and increasing demand resulting from economic and population growth.

With potable water growing scarce, national security issues will emerge. Recent examples are Ethiopia's construction of the Renaissance Dam (which may affect Egypt's access to water to irrigate its crops) and the impact of dams in China on countries in the lower Mekong Delta. As the globe warms and the number of countries facing scarcity problems increases, water will become an ever-greater national security concern.

In some parts of the world, water will become a constraint on energy development. Water is needed for conventional fossil fuel development and combustion; it is also needed for renewable generators (to clean photovoltaic cells) and for emerging technologies such as hydrogen. A World Bank (2013) initiative called "Thirsty Energy" addresses this very issue and, more broadly, the challenging nexus between the energy and water sectors. The World Bank cites problems such as water shortages affecting energy supplies in India (shutting down thermal power plants), the United States (decreasing power plant energy production), and Sri Lanka, China, and Brazil (threatening hydropower capacity) (World Bank 2013). According to Maria van der Hoeven, the former executive director of the International Energy Agency, as quoted by the World Bank (2014): "Planners and decision-makers in both sectors often remain ill-informed about the drivers of these challenges, how to address them, and the merits of different technical, political, management, and governance options. The absence of integrated planning is unsustainable."

Countries facing growing shortages will have to identify and implement policies and investments to provide their citizens and their economy with more water. There are three principal supply enhancement options: (1) transporting water from regions that have plentiful supplies of water to areas that face shortages; (2) producing additional water from supplies that are not drinkable in their natural state through desalination; and (3) regulating water consumption through more efficient tariff policies. In many cases, countries or subnational regimes will pursue versions of all three. In each case, significant political and economic obstacles must be overcome.

Transported Water

Many cities obtain their primary water supplies from reservoirs located outside their jurisdiction. These reservoirs are often owned and operated by regional water authorities. If an authority or agency finds itself short of water, it can build or purchase additional reservoir capacity or access new groundwater supplies. This additional capacity is usually more expensive than the existing sources of water and thus places financial constraints on either the customers (if the incremental costs are passed through) or on local budgets (if the public sector absorbs the incremental costs).

If the additional supplies are located in another jurisdiction, the transaction is often politically controversial. The seller can be accused of selling a commodity critical to a locality's future economic growth and the quality of life of its citizens. Water is a country's patrimony, and the public often thinks that governments should not be selling it to others. For example, Canada is water-rich, yet most proposals to sell water to the United States are met with howls of protest. Similarly, selling water from Malaysia to Singapore has triggered strong political rhetoric on both sides. Some countries have even contemplated dragging icebergs from the Arctic or Antarctica to avoid these international constraints, though to date none have followed through (Smedley 2018; Weeks and Campbell 1973).

Expansion of Desalination

In 2020, there were almost 16,000 desalination plants in the world. Slightly less than half of them were located in the Middle East. Most convert seawater to potable standards, while some rely on brackish water as their feedstock. Desalination facilities are expensive, and the reverse osmosis technology that they use converts only about 50 percent of the salt water to drinkable quality, while the remainder must be disposed of as brine. The greater the amount of desalinated water, the greater the environmental costs of disposal (Jones et al. 2019).

Further, desalination plants use substantial amounts of electricity, placing another load on a system that will be transitioning to greater reliance on renewable options. As the climate warms, water shortages will induce governments to invest in more desalination facilities, requiring them to simultaneously make greater investments in power generation and thus increasing the percentage of the national budget allocated to infrastructure.

Desalination is not the only supply-enhancement technology. In some cities, wastewater can be treated to such a level that it can be reused. These gray water options are becoming more common in developed countries; however, they are expensive, especially for countries that have not yet installed secondary or tertiary water treatment facilities.

Water Policy Reforms

The third option is to price water to reflect the total cost to supply that water. Economists argue that pursuing the large engineering options discussed above before developing workable markets, including water tariff reform, would be unnecessarily expensive. They further argue that affordability problems can be dealt with by providing voucher programs or by establishing subsidized rates for those who consume the least (assuming that lower consumption implies lower income). Researchers also found that well-managed water resource pricing can improve supply allocations, upgrade administrative efficiency, and improve the sustainability of water resources (Rogers, de Silva, and Bhatia 2001). In 2000, the World Water Commission wrote that "Commission members agreed that the single most immediate and important measure that we can recommend is the systematic adoption of full-cost pricing of water services" (Rogers, de Silva, and Bhatia 2001, 33). In 2014, experts from the Hamilton Project at the Brookings Institution and the Stanford Woods Institute for the Environment proposed a blended approach that focused on improved water pricing, regulatory reform to encourage innovation, and new financing and funding approaches (Ajami, Thompson, and Victor 2014).

Some examples exist of regions where governments priced water properly and established workable trading regimes, such as the Murray-Darling Basin Authority in Australia (Libecap et al. 2011). However, despite all their attractive characteristics, market reforms have proven to be elusive. This is partly because of a perception that water is a human right and should be priced as low as possible. Advocates argue that corporations or governments should not make a profit from water.

One might counter by pointing out that if water is so valuable to life, people should be willing to pay more for it, not less. Additionally, in many parts of the world, water has always been priced below actual costs. Hence, the advocates for changing this regime are attacking historical constructs that favor the existing system. Whether climate change and the expansion of water shortages to new regions will cause government officials to revisit market reforms remains to be seen. Dependence on ever more expensive engineering options may trigger new interest in market solutions; however, to date, meaningful water tariff reform has been limited.

Transportation Sector

This chapter discusses how climate change may affect public infrastructure. In the case of energy, we saw that in responding to climate threats, countries must significantly restructure their energy mix toward greater reliance on renewables and other low-carbon energy sources, creating an electricity sector that may look very different from today's. In the case of water infrastructure, governments in drought-prone regions will need to invest in pipelines to move water greater distances, new technologies to recover additional potable supplies, or tariffs that are more reflective of costs.

How will climate change affect transportation infrastructure? Will highways, airports, railroads, and seaports look very different in 2050 from those of 2021? The evidence to date suggests that they will not. Perhaps new technologies such as the hyperloop system may find a niche, but it is probable that we will still drive vehicles on highways and roads, fly in planes that land at airports, and transport much of our heavier freight by trains and ships.[2] Admittedly, roads and tunnels may be more resilient to floods and storms, and the number of passengers at the airport may decrease as people become more comfortable with meeting virtually versus in-person; however, these changes will likely not have significant impacts on the underlying transport infrastructure itself.

Yet, a high probability exists that the technologies that use the infrastructure may change. People may drive electric- or hydrogen-powered vehicles, necessitating investments in new fueling stations. However, trends in Europe suggest that existing fuel stations will simply expand to accommodate alternative sources of energy. For example, in Germany, all gas stations will be required to install an electric-vehicle charging station as part of a COVID-19 economic recovery package (Sharma 2020). Perhaps autonomous cars, trucks, and trains will capture part of the market; however, autonomous technology still struggles in bad weather and in urban conditions. In addition, mass transit may expand; more people may use bicycles, scooters, and other healthier and simpler modes to move shorter distances. In all these instances, though, they will still use the existing infrastructure.

The remaining challenges will be significant. How will societies pay for roads when the number of gasoline-powered cars declines, making the gasoline tax less relevant? Will people return to flying in a post-COVID-19 world? If they do not, who will pay for airports, many of which face severe financial problems? Will local governments restrict vehicle access to certain parts of cities to enhance the quality of life and reduce pollution? Will mass transit systems flourish as they continue to scramble to attract more passengers to cover their operating costs? These are difficult questions, but they are not driven by a concern about climate.

What will be driven by climate are issues around making the transportation systems more resilient and better able to handle the damages from natural disasters. Does a city raise the height of the runways at its airports or build protections for its subways and tunnels? These questions fall into the category of adaptation investments, which were previously discussed.

Climate change is not likely to be the primary reason for many transportation adjustments. Mobility options will evolve as technologies and personal preferences change, but the basic infrastructure will remain very similar to that of today. However, uncertainty exists in the pace of change and coevolution of technologies, consumer preferences, and transportation policies, which will all need to be integrated with climate infrastructure goals (Gross and Moody 2019).

Governance

The biggest challenges to meeting national and local climate goals through infrastructure investments will not be engineering or technological but rather those relating to governance and public policy.

Four of these institutional questions are discussed below. The first question is the broad governance issues that prevent governments at all levels from working together effectively. The second relates to infrastructure siting. The third is stranded economic and social assets, and the fourth is greater public investment in preventing damages as opposed to investing only in relief and recovery.

Structure Inefficiency

Governments consist of multiple agencies, each with a defined portfolio of responsibilities. The water resources department provides water to consumers. Another department might provide sewage services, while still another addresses water pollution. In many jurisdictions irrigation is the purview of the agriculture department, while the public health agency sets quality standards for drinking water. In many countries there are agencies that develop plans for coastal areas, while another agency has a similar responsibility for rivers and lakes. If the country requires desalination technologies to meet the demand for potable water, it must work with the agencies responsible for electricity since such facilities consume substantial amounts of power. When any of these agencies want to make investments in new infrastructure, they must seek permits from a variety of other agencies. Finally, yet another group provides support services such as budget oversight, procurement, and human resources. This description is simply the governance structure for water infrastructure. The same complex map of complementary responsibilities exists for transport or energy.

In most cases, these water departments were established at different times to meet different public policy problems. Establishing a new department, as opposed to expanding an existing one, allowed public officials to demonstrate responsiveness to the public concern of the moment. In some countries, the existence of multiple agencies gives elected officials the ability to make more appointments, which is a key currency for elected officials. The result, however, is a balkanized system that does not effectively manage problems that cross departmental responsibilities. Interagency coordination and cooperation will be growing concerns for presidents, prime ministers, governors, and mayors as they address the underlying interconnections inherent in climate policy.

Horizontal coordination challenges are replicated at the vertical level. Which responsibilities should lie with national or central governments, and which should be given to mayors? Highways, transmission lines, pipelines, and possibly water lines are important to realizing national goals and priorities; however, their construction and management often require substantial cooperation between national and subnational governments. Permitting electric-generating facilities is essential to meeting national targets for adequate power, yet this responsibility is usually allocated to subregional governments.

Climate change does not recognize jurisdictional boundaries. Most countries contain states or provinces, each with its own government, its own bureaucracies, and in many cases its own priorities. Many of these states or provinces contain metropolitan areas consisting of a large city surrounded by smaller cities and towns whose economies are closely linked but whose governments are independent of each other. The challenge of managing climate change becomes very difficult when these jurisdictions do not share common goals and when their ability to cooperate is derailed by financial and political rivalries. The ability to develop new and innovative intergovernmental structures will determine whether subregional governments can ensure the continuing operation of infrastructure services in a climate-constrained world.

Climate is the ultimate interagency issue, and it will impact a vast majority of the existing governance structures. To meet this challenge, governments will have to organize themselves so that responsibilities for responding to the threat and damages from climate disruptions are better assigned. Which climate-related activities are best handled by local governments, and which should be tackled by higher levels of governance? To what extent should the national government be able to overrule subnational governments when an infrastructure decision or climate investment falls within the jurisdiction of the subnational government but is deemed to be of national importance?

How can governments design and implement greater interagency coordination, both horizontally between agencies at the same level of government and vertically across those at different levels? To meet this need, some governments have established major decision-making bodies at their highest levels. For example, China has a State Council, and the United States has expanded the role of the Domestic Policy Council and the National Security Council. However, only issues of highest priority reach these bodies. Climate change will require thousands of decisions made by thousands of officials at all levels.

Finally, subnational governments have access to only certain revenues, while national governments almost always have access to a larger portfolio of revenue sources. Climate change will dramatically increase the fiscal burden on local, state, and provincial governments. It may do so in scenarios in which local fiscal revenues are decreasing as investors move their money to regions less vulnerable to climate disruption.

As discussed earlier, subnational jurisdictions will face substantial infrastructure costs. They will look to national governments for financial assistance, but what will be the political and structural cost demanded in exchange for those funds? For example, if the federal government provides substantial assistance, should it take on greater responsibility for the provision of local services? Will local governments voluntarily allow national governments to micromanage services that heretofore were their exclusive responsibility? Or will national governments provide substantial incremental assistance with no strings attached? Will national governments be willing to experiment with creative pilots that encourage effective coordination at the subregional level? How the institutions of governance are structured and operate will have a major impact on the provision of more resilient infrastructure services.

Infrastructure Siting

In the first half of the 20th century, Western countries embarked on ambitious infrastructure programs. Intercity highways were constructed. Impressive boulevards and parkways were built, as dilapidated neighborhoods were demolished to be replaced by modern downtown areas. Many countries initiated efforts to develop power-generation complexes and transmission grids to move electricity. Air and seaports were built, and global trade was expanded. While these achievements were impressive, they often happened without much consultation with the people affected by these investments. Environmental considerations were ignored. Too often, the infrastructure seemed to be built because it could be built. Bigger and more modern projects crowded out smaller and more appropriately scaled facilities. Alternative options were not considered.

The backlash that ensued resulted in the establishment of rigorous siting procedures to ensure that critical externalities and social concerns would no longer be ignored. Stakeholders with a wide spectrum of interests were given multiple opportunities to raise their concerns. Often, developers not only had to demonstrate a regional need for a project but also had to show that it met the specific needs of each jurisdiction affected by the proposed project. A power line moving electricity from point A to point B that crossed region C had to demonstrate a clear benefit to the populations of all three jurisdictions.

In many instances, this process became very expensive and time-consuming. Developers (and their lenders) became reluctant to invest the time and money needed to guide a project through the labyrinthine permitting process, obtain support from multiple stakeholders, and survive legal challenges. While siting may be more difficult in democracies, even authoritarian governments such as China have encountered strong public opposition to certain infrastructure projects, forcing them to forego or amend those investments.

It would be hard to argue against stakeholder involvement or the merits of greater sensitivity to environmental and social consequences of large infrastructure projects. No one is suggesting that governments return to the first half of the 20th century, when officials imposed large public works projects on an uninformed and sometimes skeptical public. However, the infrastructure requirements to transition to a decarbonized economy will be huge. In 2019, global electricity generation consisted of 9,824.1 terawatt hours (TWh) of coal, 825.3 TWh of oil, and 6,297.9 TWh of natural gas (BP 2020). In a decarbonized world, a significant proportion of this fossil fuel capacity will be replaced by renewables that have approximately half the capacity of an equally sized fossil fuel facility, which means nations will need to build many more generating stations than they have today. Further, renewable systems will require substantially more land and a significantly expanded transmission and distribution system. In the United States alone, an analysis by Wu (2020) found that achieving net zero greenhouse gas emissions by 2050 would require about the land area of New Mexico for new onshore wind capacity and about the land area of Vermont for new solar photovoltaic capacity. The probability that these investments can be successful under today's siting regimes is, unfortunately, low. The consequences of not making these investments, however, will be to fail to transition public infrastructure to meet national climate goals and to suffer ever greater climate disruption.

Transitioning water and sewerage infrastructure (to manage ever more droughts and floods) and transportation infrastructure (to meet the realities of climate disruption) may require less investment in the siting process than energy infrastructure. However, over the next 30 years, significant infrastructure siting will be needed across all three of these sectors. Identifying this problem is easier than solving it. Many reform policies and programs have been suggested, but most have failed to improve the siting process. Any meaningful reform must have several characteristics. First, reforms will require a renewed trust in the public sector. The magnitude and scope of infrastructure investments required will not happen without significant government involvement. Second, the number of government agencies involved in permitting and siting will need to be compressed, which means that existing siting laws will have to be amended. A comprehensive one-stop siting shop may be too difficult to achieve, but narrowing down the 15–20 agencies involved to 4–5 could significantly expedite the process for new infrastructure. The biggest and most important step will be to establish siting institutions across different levels of government while incentivizing officials from the national and subregional governments to conduct joint assessments with a prior agreement that both will abide by the joint decision. For example, in the United States, offshore wind projects require permits from the federal, state, and, in some situations, local governments. Under the present system, opponents can strive to sequence the three siting processes until the developer runs out of money and leaves. Identifying processes to encourage the three levels of government to review siting in a collaborative process could significantly reduce the cost and timeline.

Third, the entire siting process for a project must be concluded in a reasonable time frame. Drawing the process out for multiple years is a luxury that societies could afford in a nonclimate constrained world, but it will not be feasible if countries desire to effectively respond to the looming climate threat. Stakeholders need to be listened to, and environmental concerns need to be assessed; at some point, however, infrastructure decisions must be made, and appeals to the courts limited. One idea is to establish a compressed review process for only a subset of projects that meet certain criteria, such as zero greenhouse gas emissions. The challenge will be reaching agreement on the appropriate criteria.

Fourth, societies must accept that this process will produce a few bad projects, and a few projects in which new facts and problems will emerge after decisions have been made. The present system minimizes the number of such projects. The siting process described above could increase that number, but the trade-off may be necessary for countries to benefit from being better prepared to manage emerging climate disruptions.

Stranded Assets

Investments to decarbonize the energy sector and adapt to climate change will result in human dislocations (e.g., climate refugees, workers who lose their jobs, communities that lose their sources of employment) and economic dislocations (e.g., unamortized physical assets). These problems may be of less urgency in the case of transportation and water infrastructure, since the existing assets are unlikely to be replaced by an entirely new system. Energy, however, will be a different case, as countries replace the existing fossil fuel system with one that relies heavily on renewables, storage, and possibly sequestration.

Past efforts to deregulate portions of the vertically integrated electric industry gives us a sneak preview of the importance of managing the stranded asset problem. High-cost generating facilities were not competitive in the new deregulated market. The utilities that owned these assets would not accept the proposed deregulation policies unless regulators allowed them the opportunity to recover the cost of their previous investments, approved by past regulatory bodies.

If countries intend to decarbonize their electricity sectors, the magnitude and cost of the stranded assets will be much larger than those in recent history, as will the pressure on regulators to compensate the owners of fossil-fueled generating assets. This problem will be larger in countries such as China and India where a significant portion of their coal-fired generation was built in the last 20 years and will not be fully amortized until 2040–2055.

The labor force dislocation associated with climate mitigation and infrastructure adaptation may prove to be even more challenging to manage. Millions of men and women are employed in the fossil fuel–intensive electricity sector, and their prospects for finding work in another industry may be limited because of age or geography. Some countries have no social security net for retired workers, who are instead simply retained on their company's payroll. If the plant is closed, their pensions evaporate. There will be understandable political opposition to retiring these facilities without a funded plan to take care of these employees. Simply retraining them to install solar collectors or build transmission lines will not be politically sufficient or practically feasible at a meaningful scale. One creative example is an effort championed by the Evergreen Climate group, led by the Washington state governor Jay Inslee and established in 2020, that advocates a G.I. Bill of sorts to assist fossil fuel workers and communities through pensions, health care, and other training and financial support. While the governance solution to these stranded communities and workers may not be quite so drastic, equity considerations demand that they be addressed in any national climate-infrastructure policy.

Invest in Disaster Relief or Prevention?

Historically, governments have placed significantly more emphasis on responding to disasters than on disaster preparation and resilience. In the United States, the Federal Emergency Management Agency (FEMA) spends billions on disaster relief and recovery while spending negligible amounts on avoiding or minimizing those damages in the first place. Why do governments so rarely prioritize climate disaster prevention?

Some state and local governments, often in partnership with nonprofit land organizations, purchase coastal barriers or create artificial wetlands or mangrove swamps; these investments are often driven by the co-benefits (in the form of habitat protection, biodiversity, or parklands) as opposed to climate adaptation. Governments in some earthquake-prone regions have inserted requirements for more resilient building practices into city zoning regulation, but those cities are frequently the ones that have repeatedly experienced severe earthquake damage, making the public more enthusiastic about investments in greater resilience. Research has shown some cases in which the government bought up land to reduce the costs of damages (both human and economic) from a future earthquake; these cases are the exceptions, not the rule.[3]

Governments are concerned that tax revenues are spent on activities for which the benefits can be documented and the public can be assured that their tax dollars have not been misused. If FEMA were to spend millions buying private properties in areas vulnerable to significant flooding, but no floods occurred for the next 15 years, the agency would be accused of having wasted taxpayer money. On the other hand, if FEMA were to spend nothing on resilience and a flood were to occur a few years later, FEMA would be judged on its response to the victims of that flood and its willingness to help that community recover—not so much on its prior investment in preparedness. Few would point out after a disaster that the recovery costs would have been far less if FEMA had bought out the most vulnerable of the buildings prior to the disaster. The incentives are clearly skewed toward investing in recovery rather than preparation or resilience.

To put this dilemma in perspective, southern Australia has experienced forest and bushfires that were especially severe because of years of droughts and unusually hot weather. After the 2009 Black Saturday fires, the government of Victoria implemented a housing buyback program. Its offer received considerable publicity at the time, since here was an example of a government trying to get ahead of a future problem. However, it took a year to get the program passed because of bureaucratic delays, and few homeowners were interested in pursuing the government's offer thereafter (Herscher and Rizzo 2020). In 2019 and 2020, the same areas experienced even more severe bushfires. Interestingly, few criticized the government for its inability to implement the buyback program, and there has been no clamor from the public to develop a new program. Some experts suggest measures such as more stringent building codes, expanded voluntary buyback programs, and enhanced early warning systems; thus far, these policies have not been pursued (Henriques-Gomes 2020; Hill and Martinez-Diaz 2020).

Will this dilemma change? It is unlikely without a significant push from the public. Admittedly, the financial costs of relief and recovery efforts are skyrocketing as disaster intensity increases. The Wharton Risk Management and Decision Processes team at the University of Pennsylvania found that postdisaster spending in response to 2017 events in the United States was more than US$130 billion, a record high (Lingle, Kousky, and Shabman 2018). Perhaps as this number increases, pressure will increase for greater national governmental investment in climate preparation.

Most future investments in preparation and resilience will be made by property owners who will do their own cost-benefit analyses, realizing that government assistance in the best of circumstances will be inconsistent and difficult to predict. This outcome is not necessarily bad, but it ignores lower-income communities and households, many of which are located in the most vulnerable locations. It might be more effective to direct incremental government adaptation funds to these lower-income neighborhoods than to attempt to convince the major public and private relief organizations to fund large-scale infrastructure adaptation and resilience. Perhaps those agencies responsible for housing and urban development should lead the national government's efforts to promote preparation in concert with their sister institutions at the subnational level.

Conclusions

The climate problem is real, and its impacts will be severe. These impacts will be neither homogeneous nor temporally or spatially predictable. In light of these uncertainties, many governments will hesitate to invest in low-carbon infrastructure without economic and financial assistance at scales that exceed normal political comfort.

What can be done to address these challenges? First, rational pricing for infrastructure services such as electricity and water will become substantially more important in a world dependent on renewable energy, electric vehicles, and water from distant aquifers or capital intensive desalination facilities. Pricing that reflects the true social cost of these services is essential but by itself will not be enough. In addition, governments at all levels must develop interagency and intergovernmental institutions and processes to address adaptation and mitigation investments. These initiatives should be accompanied by a commitment to transfer funds to where they are needed. Traditional political rigidities must be superseded by a willingness to be creative and to take political risks based more on vision and less on historical stakeholder loyalties. Finally, this new sense of innovation must focus on governance reforms in areas such as siting, stranded assets, interagency coordination, and preventive investments. These reforms will occur only when key stakeholders become more aware of the looming risks of climate change and demand that their elected officials respond to these threats with considerably more urgency than shown to date.

Summary

- Honoring the commitments made by many countries to achieve net zero emissions by 2050 will require unprecedented investments in infrastructure. Local governments are likely to take the lead in developing adaptive policies, since the nature and extent of climate change damages vary so much by location

- The electricity sector will be by far the most affected by the efforts to mitigate emissions, as electricity replaces direct burning of fossil fuels for mobility, heating, and manufacturing and as countries shift to solar, wind, and other renewable sources that require more sophisticated and extensive grids and stand-by capacity to maintain reliability.

- In the water sector, changes in precipitation will require some areas to import water, increase desalinization, or encourage conservation by raising prices.

- Transportation infrastructure will be the least affected, although many vehicles are likely to be powered by electricity or hydrogen.

- For these investments to succeed, four changes in the governance of infrastructure are needed: (1) reduce the number of agencies and levels of government with overlapping responsibilities; (2) streamline the process for siting facilities; (3) address stranded financial and human assets; and (4) reduce the bias for spending on disaster relief rather than on disaster prevention.

Notes

1. Costs are provided in euros per MWh and are converted here using a 1.13 US$/€ conversion rate.

2. A hyperloop is a theoretical transportation system using tubes and pods to move people and cargo quickly over long distances (Davies 2018).

3. One exception may be nuclear facilities. In some countries and states, nuclear facilities are no longer allowed to be sited or operated in or near earthquake zones so as to reduce potential damage.

References

Ajami, Newsha, Barton Thompson, and David Victor. 2014. "The Path to Water Innovation." The Hamilton Project, October 2014. http://www.hamiltonproject.org/papers/the_path _to_water_innovation/.

Ballon, Hilary, and Kenneth T. Jackson, eds. 2007. *Robert Moses and the Modern City: The Transformation of New York*. New York: Norton.

BP. 2020. *Statistical Review of World Energy*. "Electricity: 2019 in Review." https://www .bp.com/content/dam/bp/business-sites/en/global/corporate/pdfs/energy-economics /statistical-review/bp-stats-review-2020-full-report.pdf.

Carbon Mitigation Initiative. 2019. "The Net-Zero America Project: Finding Pathways to a Carbon-Neutral Future." https://cmi.princeton.edu/annual-meetings/annual-reports/year -2019/the-net-zero-america-project-finding-pathways-to-a-carbon-neutral-future/.

Davies, Alex. 2018. "The WIRED Guide to Hyperloop." *Wired*, February 1. https://www .wired.com/story/guide-hyperloop/.

Gross, Eytan, and Joanna Moody, eds. 2019. *Insights into Future Mobility*. http://energy.mit.edu /wp-content/uploads/2019/11/Insights-into-Future-Mobility-Executive-Summary .pdf.

Henriques-Gomes, Luke. 2020. "Bushfire-Destroyed Homes Should Not Be Rebuilt in Riskiest Areas, Experts Say." *The Guardian*, January 18. https://www.theguardian.com/australia-news /2020/jan/19/bushfire-destroyed-homes-should-not-be-rebuilt-in-riskiest-areas-experts-say.

Herscher, Rebecca, and Meredith Rizzo. 2020. "Sell or Stay? Australia's Fire Zone Experiment." *NPR*, February 25. https://www.npr.org/2020/02/25/807084043/sell-or-stay -australia-s-fire-zone-experiment.

Hill, Alice, and Leonardo Martinez-Diaz. 2020. *Building a Resilient Tomorrow*. Oxford, UK: Oxford University Press.

Intergovernmental Panel on Climate Change. 2014. "Summary for Policymakers: Impacts, Adaptation, and Vulnerability." In *Climate Change 2014: Impacts, Adaptation, and Vulnerability; Part A: Global and Sectoral Aspects; Contribution of Working Group II to the Fifth Assessment Report of the Intergovernmental Panel on Climate Change*, ed. Christopher B. Field, Vincente R. Barros, David J. Dokken, Katharine J. Mach, Michael D. Mastrandrea, T. Erin Bilir, Monalisa Chatterjee, et al. Cambridge, UK: Cambridge University Press. https://www.ipcc.ch/site/assets/uploads/2018/02/ar5_wgII_spm_en.pdf.

Jones, Edward, Manzoor Qadir, Michelle T. H. van Vliet, Vladimir Smakhtin, and Seong-mu Kang. 2019. "The State of Desalination and Brine Production: A Global Outlook." *Science of the Total Environment* 657: 1343–1356.

Landrigan, Phillip J., Richard Fuller, Nereus J. R. Acosta, Olusoji Adeyi, Robert Arnold, and Niladri Basu. 2018. "The *Lancet* Commission on Pollution and Health." *The Lancet* 391(10119): 462–512. https://doi.org/10.1016/S0140-6736(17)32345-0.

Lee, Henry, Natalie Unterstell, Shauna Theel, and Pinar De Neve. 2017. "Miami-Dade County and Sea Rise." Harvard Kennedy School, February 13. https://case.hks.harvard .edu/miami-dade-county-and-sea-rise/.

Libecap, Gary, Quentin Grafton, Eric Edwards, R. J. O'Brien, and Clay Landry. 2011. "A Comparative Assessment of Water Markets: Insights from the Murray-Darling Basin of Australia and the Western US." *Water Policy* 14 (10): 2139. https://papers.ssrn.com /sol3/papers.cfm?abstract_id=1858723.

Lingle, Brett, Carolyn Kousky, and Leonard Shabman. 2018. "Federal Disaster Rebuilding Spending: A Look at the Numbers." Wharton Risk Management and Decision Processes Center. https://riskcenter.wharton.upenn.edu/lab-notes/federal-disaster-rebuilding -spending-look-numbers/.

MIT Energy Initiative. 2016. *Utility of the Future: An MIT Energy Initiative Response to an Industry in Transition.* www.energy.mit.edu/uof.

National Academies of Sciences, Engineering, and Medicine. 2012. *Disaster Resilience: A National Imperative.* https://doi.org/10.17226/13457.

Rogers, Peter, Radhika de Silva, and Ramesh Bhatia. 2001. "Water Is an Economic Good: How to Use Prices to Promote Equity, Efficiency, and Sustainability." *Water Policy Journal* 4: 1–7.

Sharma, Gaurav. 2020. "All Petrol Stations in Germany Will Be Required to Provide Electric Vehicle Charging." *Forbes,* June 5. https://www.forbes.com/sites/gauravsharma/2020/06 /05/all-petrol-stations-in-germany-will-be-required-to-provide-electric-vehicle-charging -ev-cars/#6cb54333479a.

Smedley, Tim. 2018. "The Outrageous Plan to Haul Icebergs to Africa." *BBC Future Now,* September 21. https://www.bbc.com/future/article/20180918-the-outrageous-plan-to -haul-icebergs-to-africa.

United Nations. n.d. "What Do Adaptation to Climate Change and Climate Resilience Mean?" https://unfccc.int/topics/adaptation-and-resilience/the-big-picture/what-do-adaptation -to-climate-change-and-climate-resilience-mean.

Weeks, W. F., and W. J. Campbell. 1973. "Icebergs as a Fresh-Water Source: An Appraisal." *Journal of Glaciology* 12(65): 207–233.

Weitzman, Martin L., and Wagner Gernot. 2015. *Climate Shock: The Economic Consequences of a Hotter Planet.* Princeton, NJ: Princeton University Press.

World Bank. 2013. "Thirsty Energy: Securing Energy in a Water-Constrained World." https:// www.worldbank.org/en/topic/water/brief/water-energy-nexus.

———. 2014. "Will Water Constrain Our Energy Future?" https://www.worldbank.org/en /news/feature/2014/01/16/will-water-constrain-our-energy-future.

Wu, Grace. 2020. "Spatial Planning of Low-Carbon Transitions." Sustainable Development Solutions Network Deep Decarbonization Pathways Project for the United States. https:// resources.unsdsn.org/spatial-planning-for-low-carbon-transitions?_ga=2.223581971 .905780696.1625859351-1726547578.1625859351.

19

NEW TECHNOLOGIES IN INFRASTRUCTURE

Shashi Verma

In this day of technology start-ups from Silicon Valley and elsewhere promising to revolutionize the world overnight, there is occasionally a view that this scale and pace of change can also be brought to infrastructure. We have seen claims of the world of innovation being brought to tunnel boring and passenger transport. After decades of promising to revolutionize electricity generation, solar power is finally getting somewhere. Each of these changes has the potential to alter its respective industries. If the changes are substantially large, they can also alter fundamental consumption habits, create new types of demand, and alter the way societies organize themselves. A combination of infrastructure that is central to human existence and innovation therefore has the potential to be life-altering.

Other chapters in this book discuss the issues of why infrastructure has its own peculiarities. High cost, often high fixed cost, limits competition but is not by itself an inhibitor of innovation. If anything, high cost should provide a compelling reason to innovate. Large externalities from infrastructure, either negative ones such as pollution from electricity generation or positive ones from agglomeration as a result of urban density enabled by transport, have meant more public control over infrastructure than in other industries. Whether by regulation or more directly through ownership and funding, governments exercise immense control over infrastructure. Yet again, this control is not a direct inhibitor to innovation. Creating new solutions that reduce negative externalities would provide a huge competitive advantage.

The answers lie elsewhere. This chapter discusses the sorts of fundamental changes that have the ability to reshape the infrastructure industry and the society around it. That claim is not to dismiss the smaller but often interesting changes that are made more frequently but instead only to target attention at the more substantive changes. Fundamental change in the world of infrastructure comes only very slowly. The number of times fundamental change has come to the world of infrastructure is small enough to be counted. Yet, we may be at the cusp of a small number of innovations that can radically alter investment in and consumption of infrastructure. Smaller changes can also be disruptive to industry.

This chapter focuses on transport, especially large impending changes with autonomous vehicles (AVs), and also makes more fleeting observations about other infrastructure industries that have either recently undergone similar change or are likely to do so in the near future.

Disruption in Transport: A Historical Perspective

Through three million years of human history, muscle power was the main source of mobility and energy. Ten thousand years ago, the start of domestication of animals provided a vital supplement to muscle power and increased the ability of humans to carry and trade goods over long distances. The discovery of sailing, perhaps 6,000 years ago, helped movement over longer distances and eventually led to habitation of the Pacific region. Canals started being used for transport about 2,000 years ago, again powered by animals or wind. Only around 200 years ago did the discovery of steam create new sources of power and therefore mobility.

Meanwhile, economic sophistication had allowed new models of service delivery to emerge, with the first shared vehicles—stagecoaches—making an appearance in 15th-century Britain. With the growth of cities, vehicles for hire became more common, leading to hansom cabs in the 18th century and eventually to horse-drawn buses in 1829, although these had first been introduced in Paris.

Steam created a revolution because it fundamentally changed the economics of transport, with steam engines enabling railways and thus allowing people to travel farther, faster, and cheaper with added comfort. All this change came with a new process to convert chemical energy into mechanical energy, unlocking a more concentrated use of energy than had ever been done before and allowing a level of energy use that simply could not have been contemplated until then. Morris (2011), for example, argues that a significant factor limiting development in the Roman Empire two millennia ago and the Song dynasty in China a millennium ago was the limitation on how much energy they could access. Although it is difficult to imagine the world before steam, accounts from the period show just how big a difference it made in the cost of transport. It was not just the ability of humans to move around but also the collapse in the cost of transporting goods inland that mattered. Accounts from England show how markets for livestock improved when the animals could be moved by rail rather than being walked to markets (Blackman 1975). By providing easy access to socializing over longer distances, railways also stopped in-breeding in villages that had provided the age-old joker, the village idiot, for centuries. These may not be the examples on top of anyone's mind, but they show just how big an impact steam had on the way society and the economy were organized.

The advent of the internal combustion engine, starting in Germany, miniaturized the vehicles needed to draw chemical energy. The grand innovation of miniaturization unleashed the power of chemical energy. Interestingly, steam-driven road vehicles existed when Gottfried Daimler and Karl Benz built the first motor car in 1886 but never became common because of the inability to miniaturize them. Internal combustion created new mobility models and drew away a large proportion of traffic that would previously have used the railways.

Likewise, electricity enabled urban railways in a way that was difficult for other technology. Despite the defiant push of steam in the London Underground, mass transit railway started to become prevalent only when it stopped causing pollution.

Horse-drawn trams appeared in London and in many other cities around the world within the space of a few years in the 1860s, driven by the increase in the operating costs for horse-drawn buses, namely animal feed, and therefore the need to find a more cost-efficient transport. Domestic barley had given way to cheaper oats imported from America as horse feed. The start of the American Civil War caused major disruptions, leading to the idea of laying metal tracks in the road so horses could pull larger vehicles. Competition came from buses powered by internal combustion engines that proved cheaper and more flexible to operate, as they did not need overhead electric lines or tracks on the road. Trams vanished rapidly, although not without the nostalgic protective instincts that emotional attachment to transport engenders.

In the last century, the urban transport industry has been relatively stable. Despite the improvements made in automotive engineering and the vast investment in highways that have allowed greater adoption of cars and trucks, the template created by the quantum change in transport at the beginning of the 20th century remains largely the same.

Longer-distance transport—aviation and shipping—has gone through larger changes of its own. Shipping has gone from sail to steam to internal combustion for power, from timber to metal hulls, and from bulk transport to containers for efficiency. Aviation, itself an innovation largely of the last century, went through convulsive disruption with jet aircraft.

Only recently have established models of urban transport come under challenge, principally from Uber and other ride-sharing platforms planting themselves firmly into the space previously occupied by taxis, which were otherwise protected by regulation. Uber is already having an impact on patterns of mobility. Providing a cheaper door-to-door service enables its customers to choose Uber over not just taxis but also public transport, especially when people travel in groups, and for many people over owning a car. However, Uber's successful business model is based only on disrupting a regulatory model, not on the fundamental economics of transport provision.

The challenge posed by AVs is much larger and will offer the first major disruption since automobiles. The big difference is that, whereas it took 50 years even in the United States for half the population to enjoy the regular use of a car, it may take only one-tenth of that time for AVs to make a serious impact. While Uber cut the cost of taxis slightly, perhaps by half in expensive taxi markets, AVs have the potential to cut the cost of road travel to perhaps one-quarter of even Uber's current model (Bosch et al. 2018).

If we accept that the historical perspective broadly represents the key innovations in transport infrastructure, what unifying themes can we draw from them to assess the potential for technology and innovation that still exists? What can we expect amid all the promise of the next revolution?

Across all three sectors and across all innovations, the common factor is that each of these innovations reduced the cost of something that was a necessity in human life at that point. In doing so, they spawned new sources of consumption, making the new form of living essential.

It is this cost advantage offered by innovation that we have to look out for in spotting where true disruption may come from.

AVs: A Case Study

The world of transport has been largely stable over the past half century. Cars have become more efficient, demand has generally gone up, and more infrastructure has been built to meet demand. The cost of motoring has dropped compared with others in the economy, but the change has been gradual. The oil shocks of the 1970s provided a new focus on fuel efficiency, but the industry went on more or less uninterrupted. However, we now stand at the cusp of a new revolution if all the technology can be made to work.

AVs are a relatively recent development, although various attempts at automation have taken shape over many decades. Simple attempts at throttle control in the 1930s led eventually to cruise control in the 1990s and then to adaptive cruise control only in this century.

It is that last development, the integration of electronic sensors to control vehicles, that offers something new. After many years of trying to guide vehicles with control mechanisms embedded in highways, the thinking changed around

15 years ago. Current experiments are based on all control decisions being made independently within a vehicle. If onboard sensors can judge proximity to obstructions, that paves the way toward a world in which sensors and software control the movement of cars entirely, with the "driver" needing only to tell the car where to go. The basic ability of vehicles to guide themselves through sensors alone is now widely proven, although the circumstances of this proving are not sufficient yet to consider these vehicles roadworthy without a driver.

The case for AVs, as discussed further below, is strong. That is why AVs have attracted investment and many enthusiasts. Whether it is Elon Musk making bold predictions of cars driving all the way from New York to Los Angeles or others making equally optimistic forecasts of when these vehicles will be roadworthy, the world has been animated by the prospect of these cars on the road. Numerous experimental vehicles have been on the road for several years now. In addition to Google's Waymo division, other technology start-ups such as Zoox, nuTonomy, and FiveAI also have vehicles that are being road tested. Not to be left behind, major car companies such as GM and Nissan have AVs of their own that are also being tested on open roads.

From publicly available sources, it is clear that sensors and software can guide vehicles safely in areas where roads are clearly demarcated and traffic is relatively orderly. It is also clear that the edge cases around road traffic are proving difficult to accommodate. For example, dealing with roadworks, diversions, and places with no road markings are all challenging. Artificial intelligence, at the heart of all this software, has not yet shown that it can deal with new situations. More extensive tests driving AVs across the United States and Germany show the limitations of existing technology.

These limitations matter because these edge cases will end up determining the complexity of this technology and therefore its reliability, something well understood in the world of technology. Dealing with about 98 percent of scenarios is easy. It is the remaining 2 percent that lead to all systems complexity. The question that still remains is whether solutions can be found for the last 2 percent of edge cases at an acceptable cost. With the economics of AVs being strong, it is likely that large-scale investment will address the edge cases.

Meanwhile, the advantages of sensors and software are already evident in improvements to the safety characteristics of vehicles. Collision avoidance, first introduced only in 2014, now has a name: automatic emergency braking. In 2016, the U.S. Department of Transportation announced a voluntary commitment from major vehicle manufacturers to provide automatic emergency braking on all vehicles from 2022 on (National Highway Traffic Safety Administration 2019).

We should expect to see more such safety-related regulations on the back of technology purportedly for AVs. The industry may well stay ahead of regulations in providing these features as a competitive pitch for safer cars.

In addition to the edge cases, two large technical questions remain unresolved, at least in the public pronouncements of AV developers. First, the balance between safety and efficiency has yet to be proven. Second, the ability of AVs to regulate themselves when confronted by other AVs remains to be thoroughly tested.

Safety concerns have so far dictated that AVs stop when confronted with hazards, and this has been proven by some AV companies in road tests so far. However, the consequence of such a stern safety regime is that it encourages other traffic, including pedestrians, to misbehave. Why, for example, would pedestrians follow rules and cross only when it is their turn when they know that stepping in front of an AV will make it stop? In crowded areas this caution on the part of AVs is a recipe for gridlock, with AVs at the bottom of the hierarchy of right-of-way.

Yet, to relax this safety requirement would mean that AVs do not stop for pedestrians or other hazards, either randomly or in some unspecified circumstances. Any relaxation to safety poses not just technical challenges but also ethical and legal ones that can take a long time to resolve. In some environments, such as those found in developing countries, it is possible that the chaotic nature of road use will make it impossible to make AVs work in precisely the environment where they have the most to contribute to safety.

Likewise, road tests so far have demonstrated that AVs can move in and out of traffic and regulate themselves on the basis of human behavior around them. Doing so in the presence of other machines creates new challenges. This complexity is what gives rise to another term: connected vehicles (CVs). The theory is that CVs should be more efficient than humans because they can pack in closer to each other. But if the tests for AVs are contrived, those for CVs are even more so, with attempts so far only to show capability for platooning, that is, driving a number of CVs together. The simplest case occurs when a platoon is preassembled and put on the road. In real life, assembling and dismantling platoons on the go, which is the promise of CVs, is a much harder problem. As we know from railway signaling, the critical safety issue of stopping trains from hitting each other is the relatively simpler part of these systems, even though it is the most critical. The harder part is the ability to pack trains close to each other to provide high frequency and use. That ability is precisely the challenge CVs have yet to meet.

These challenges are formidable. The changes to vehicle certification, liability, insurance, and social acceptability need to be worked out. In many ways, the

AV is a contemporary example of what technological change in infrastructure actually takes.

Economic Case for AVs

In assessing how the world may change with AVs, the technology is interesting, but the economics is even more so. The economics of AVs needs to be compared with the current cost of owning or renting a vehicle and of hiring a ride. One of the remarkable features of the automotive industry is its ability to lower the cost of motoring over several decades. For a long time, the cost of cars has not increased in the Western world, even though their capability and fuel efficiency have improved steadily. This means that the cost of motoring has, on the whole, also declined steadily. Meanwhile, the cost of hiring a taxi has shown a steady upward trend in most markets. This dichotomy is easily explained by the fact that the cost of taxis has increased owing to the increased compensation for drivers.

With AVs, a driver is not needed, so the cost of hiring taxis ought to drop radically. Depending on the market, it is likely that anything between one-half and three-quarters of the cost of hiring a taxi is explained by payment for the driver. AVs therefore offer the prospect of the cost per journey dropping so far as to become competitive with public transport, especially if small numbers of people are traveling together and can share a vehicle. Many such estimates exist. Sperling (2018), for example, estimates that the cost of pooled vehicles would be 10–20 cents per mile, cheaper than the cost of a subway ride in New York.

That cost reduction is the case for one form of shared mobility in which people rely on a vehicle they do not own, much as we do today with taxis and Uber. There is also a separate case for shared mobility, where multiple people, possibly unknown to each other, share the same vehicle for part or all of a ride, as we do with Uber Pool and public transport.

Both forms of sharing require behavior change and come with their own economic challenges that cannot be brushed aside. As the example of car-sharing companies such as Zipcar and the many more bicycle-sharing companies around the world has shown, shared mobility brings servicing costs that may be substantial. Cleaning, refueling, and taking a car for maintenance are some of the activities that owners do in their own time without taking the cost of these explicitly into consideration. The cost of the fuel weighs on the owner's mind, but the time spent refueling rarely does. With a shared mobility model, all of these activities become monetized and need to be paid for.

With strangers sharing a vehicle, two challenges arise. First, the behavioral change required to get into a shared vehicle is formidable. This case is not exactly like public transport, where a model of security exists with bus drivers, train and subway staff, closed-circuit television coverage, dedicated police forces, and most of all the knowledge that there are perhaps many other people around to help. The same model does not exist for a closed car with perhaps just one other stranger. In India, an interesting way has been found to deal with concerns over the safety especially of young women in jobs that serve Western markets and therefore require working odd hours. Shuttl, an app-based office bus service, requires users to share their details, including their history and rating by other users, before they are allowed on to a bus (Mishra 2017). People happily comply with this requirement, perhaps providing a model for how shared mobility may be achieved alongside security.

Second, although in theory multiple riders can be matched with a vehicle, in practice this so far raises more questions than answers. It is one thing to be in an Uber by oneself with control over the journey and predictability over how long it will take. With a vehicle making detours to pick up or drop off people along the way, both control and predictability are reduced. The more people who need to be matched, the bigger the challenge. Eventually, if the vehicle is large enough, it might make sense to restrict the route it takes and ask users to join it along the route. With higher densities of use, it may also make sense to fix boarding and alighting points. With even higher densities of use and vehicles sitting idle, fixing a schedule may also make sense. That is how we end up in a bus service. How to fill the gap between a single-user vehicle, such as an Uber, and a bus service by pooling remains to be seen.

The first consequence of the arrival of AVs may be that people do not feel the need to buy cars. Between taxation, depreciation, and running costs, it is difficult to see how private car ownership will compete with a model where a door-to-door ride can be hired on demand for not much more than the cost of public transport. In general, if vehicle use can be increased, it ought to become cheaper per ride. That economy can easily be enabled by AVs being available on demand, providing a service similar to what a user would expect of a personal car while ensuring that the vehicle keeps moving. Even if this practice does not immediately replace all car ownership, it is likely to begin making inroads quickly, starting with many car owners who use their cars only sparingly.

A general reduction in the cost of motoring, led by a model whereby vehicles are no longer owned but instead are hired by rides, is likely to have the following impacts:

- Increase in overall demand for mobility, with trip rates increasing every- where and at all times.

- Transfer of demand from other modes, starting with private cars but also from public transport and even from active modes such as walking and cycling.
- Increase in demand for road use by AVs, with an overall increase in demand.
- Reduction in the space required for parking as the number of vehicles required to meet demand reduces and vehicle utilization increases.
- New businesses being created to operate and maintain AVs and provide services.

Each of these factors is discussed below.

A decrease in the cost of mobility should lead to an increase in demand. That is what economic theory suggests. The question is how much increase. Very little economic evidence exists to provide a guide to answering this question, although much speculation on this issue exists in the debate about AVs. On the one hand are those who believe that no overall increase in demand should occur. Coupled with a belief that AVs will enable more efficient use of road space, the hope is that AVs will remove all congestion. In practice, while the point about efficiency is yet to be proven, stronger evidence supports an overall increase in demand even though this is likely to be small.

On the other hand, if the efficiency in road use does not occur and the running of empty vehicles increases, congestion could worsen. Commercial vehicle use can be expected to increase by even more. The limiting factor on vehicle size currently is the need to hire a driver; with that factor gone, it will become possible for smaller commercial vehicles to do more targeted work, thus increasing the overall number of vehicles on the road. While it is also possible that larger vehicles will get deployed, this is unlikely because they pose greater challenges in coordinating logistics. The whole nature of the freight and logistics industry could change radically if a driver is no longer needed.

A transfer of demand from other modes is likely on a much greater scale. Driving is often presented as a pleasure, promoted by car company advertisements that show either beautiful open highways or cars pulling out of nice suburban homes but very rarely the hassle of congested roads and the drudgery of the daily commute. Given an alternative at a comparable price, many people are likely to give up driving altogether. This choice would be in keeping with the general trend in consumers increasingly moving away from the tedium of daily life into buying services when they can afford it; an example is using takeout instead of dining in a restaurant. In the future, we may well have generations that do not bother learning to drive at all. Not many learned to ride horses after the 19th century either.

AVs also pose a challenge to public transport. In cities with high public transport fares such as London, it is already possible to travel more cheaply when in a group using a ride-sharing service. For some use cases, such as traveling to airports encumbered by luggage, cars hold an even stronger attraction. If we remove the cost of the driver and therefore a large proportion of the overall cost, many journeys on AVs may start competing in price with public transport.

The induced mode shift from this sort of competition is an impending disaster for public transport and for demands on road space. At peak times, any transfer from public transport to AVs will add to saturated traffic levels across many cities. For congestion reasons alone, people may prefer to stay on a train or a bus (especially when buses have priority over other traffic). These advantages of public transport are nevertheless true only for peak travel. At off-peak times, the situation could well reverse itself, with AVs being the preferred means of traveling, providing door-to-door service at a cost comparable to public transport. What, then, is the point of the public transport outside peak hours?

The challenge to public transport from this change in the economics of transport cannot be underestimated. We may end up in a world where AVs get very high use throughout the day, while the public transport system is restricted to operating at peak hours only. Revenue earned during off-peak hours is one of the key means of keeping public transport affordable. With that gone, public transport will get more expensive, driving even more people to AVs. This challenge is akin to the competition cars provided to railways, which led to the closure of many railway lines around the world. Something similar is about to happen with AVs restricting the time scope of public transport if not the geographical scope. Even the geographical scope is not immune to challenge. Bus networks in less dense environments could get cannibalized easily, with AVs providing a faster service for some journeys and picking off the segment of the market willing to pay for it. Running a bus service could become more challenging with lower demand.

The factors mentioned above all point to an increase in overall road use. In cities with little public transport, the increase in demand will come only from an overall increase in mobility. The challenge is more acute in cities such as London, where the city is shaped around high-density public transport that plays a bigger role. Solutions will need to be found for managing this increase in road demand. Technological solutions, such as better traffic management and information, are insufficient for managing the scale of the challenge we face. The only tool capable of managing this challenge is road pricing that truly reflects congestion across locations and time of day.

The largest unmitigated beneficial impact of shared AVs will be a reduction in the space required for parking. Bates and Leibling (2012) estimate that cars are, on average, used for about 4 percent of the time, spending 80 percent of the time parked at their home location and another 16 percent parked elsewhere. In cities with high public transport use, this use may be even lower. For the time they are not moving, cars end up needing parking spaces, with a ratio of two to three parking spaces per vehicle. Moving to a shared AV model will drastically reduce the need for parking spaces. Simulation models, such as that by Emilio Frazzoli and his colleagues at MIT, show that the number of parking spaces could be reduced from two to three times the number of vehicles to slightly more than one. Meanwhile, as vehicle use increases, the number of vehicles themselves may reduce to perhaps one-third of the current numbers. Frazzoli's simulation, reported in Spieser et al. (2014), showed that all car trips in Singapore could be carried with just one-third of the vehicles in use that year. Waiting times, even without prebooking, would be about the same as the time taken to walk to a parking garage.

The release of parking spaces will fundamentally alter the shape of cities. Local roads can become freer-flowing, main streets will be freed of on-street parking, and large parking lots in the city center will no longer be needed. A smaller number of strategically placed parking areas will be needed, including maintenance and cleaning facilities, performing a function similar to bus depots today. The profound impact that this shrinking of parking space could have on the shape of cities is yet to be fully considered.

Chapter 3 in this volume discusses why cities are shaped the way they are, the historical factors behind their development, and current pressures. In that context, it also raises the question of how AVs may alter the equilibrium that cities find themselves in now. Parking is just one example of how land use could be altered. As noted in chapter 3, much wider changes to land use also become possible with AVs.

Finally, it is also worth considering what commercial activities AVs create or destroy. New businesses will be created for owning, servicing, and renting AVs. The starting point for these may well be the current taxi or ride share market, but the ownership structure of that market may also be subject to a lot of disruption. Car manufacturers such as BMW are already playing in this space with car rental systems that can easily transform themselves into AV businesses (ShareNow n.d.). With its support by the technology industry, this industry is already inviting venture capital funding as well as significant interest from tech giants such as Google.

Meanwhile, a large source of employment is about to disappear. Commercial drivers of all sorts, from taxis to delivery vehicles to chauffeurs, face an existential challenge as their source of livelihood becomes disintermediated by technology. This prospect has already brought calls for protection, especially from the taxi trade, and it is likely that these calls will become louder. Notwithstanding that, the economics of this industry will prevail. Similar challenges have been faced by other industries (e.g., mill workers being replaced by power looms, ferry workers being replaced by bridges, clerks being replaced by computers). The biggest change in employment in the history of humankind has been the reduction in agricultural workers driven by improvements in agricultural productivity in the last two centuries. In the Western world, more than 90 percent of employment was related to agriculture until the early 18th century, while now it stands at less than 5 percent. Each one of these changes has been painful to society as a whole and to those being forced to exit in particular. Each has led to calls for protection and government intervention, and each time intervention has failed. We need to ensure that we do not stand in the way of progress while being sympathetic to those whose lives are about to be upturned as a result of these changes.

Consequences for Infrastructure and Policy Actions

The advent of AVs presents a prospect for disruptive change larger than anything seen in our lifetime. The moderating factor, though, is that the technology is proving much harder to perfect than thought earlier. Progress in the last few years has been slower; the promoters of this technology now accept, by and large, that the prospects for commercial introduction of AVs are distant. The economic case for this change will continue to drive development.

Whenever these AVs arrive, four specific actions that policy makers need to be prepared to undertake include licensing, allocation of road space, economic support for public transportation, and control over pricing structures.

Licensing

Legislative change is needed to classify AVs. They do not fall into the major categories around which all motoring rules are made: private cars, rented vehicles, taxis, and commercial vehicles. Rather than attempting to shoehorn AVs into one of these categories—a bit like trying to certify cars as modified horse carriages—thinking through this problem afresh will work much better. It will be essential to be clear about acceptable vehicle safety standards, to type-test to meet those standards, and then to manage the resulting changes required to insurance and liability laws. In particular, it is essential that legislative change allows innovation to happen while keeping in mind that no shortcuts exist. We are, after all, dealing with a technology that is likely to become a big—probably the biggest—feature of transport.

Allocation of Road Space

The increase in use of road vehicles will result in further congestion. The only logical way to manage this congestion is by pricing. Cities and other transport policy makers will need to develop systems for managing road space, including by pricing. Pricing is one of the most toxic political issues. Apart from a few relatively crude examples of road pricing in London, Singapore, and Stockholm, very little experience or real political appetite exists for a true road pricing system irrespective of its economic and environmental merits. In the absence of proper road pricing, congestion from these vehicles may need to be limited by allowing them to run only on certain roads, by being bounded into fixed geographic areas, or by a system of permits that limits the number of vehicles. All these solutions are suboptimal to a system of true road pricing, but cities need to be prepared with their policy tool kit before AVs make a substantial appearance.

Economic Support for Public Transport

New methods of pricing that provide incentives for using AVs and public transport efficiently will also need to be developed. No established model exists yet that prices for road use and public transport use together, balancing capacity and incentives for use. As long as agglomeration produces higher productivity and requires densities that can be served only by rail, the question of the economics of rail will continue to dominate city transport planning. Finding mechanisms to fund the infrastructure to support the agglomeration will remain a challenge.

Control over Pricing Structures

A consequence of building such pricing structures is that cities and transport policy makers will need to build payment platforms that combine public and private transport. These platforms will become the front end to expensive infrastructure. This approach may sound rather technical, but the ability of cities to control their economic geography will increasingly rest on deploying pricing policies as a means of efficient use of infrastructure. Control over these platforms will become the next challenge for cities.

Other Technological Developments

While step changes in technology are infrequent, smaller changes happen more frequently. At present, we are seeing many of these smaller changes create their own impacts on infrastructure.

The world of connected devices, the Internet of Things as it is sometimes called, is connecting more and more infrastructure and providing operators with real-time information on usage and asset condition. This information allows better allocation of limited resources, improving the revenue potential. Better knowledge of asset condition can also reduce both maintenance cost and expensive disruptive failures. The effect of the Internet of Things is visible in consumer electronics already. Its effect on infrastructure is still taking shape, but some results are already visible.

Developments in consumer electronics are creating new markets for infrastructure. Ride-hailing models rely on a combination of technologies that have become available only recently. A cheap communication device in the form of a smartphone allows two-way transfers that would have been far more cumbersome in the past. The integration of location services with the Global Positioning System was not even possible until the start of the 21st century. Payment systems have evolved to allow secure transactions integrated into smartphones. Without these systems, taxis were reliant on spotting a customer on the street, waiting at taxi stands, or being dispatched from call centers. The first two created very thin markets; the third was a cumbersome method. All of these issues have been swept away by smartphones. Even without the regulatory arbitrage that Uber and others have exploited, this improvement in the market for taxis is remarkable.

In other infrastructure industries, technological change has already had substantive impacts. The world of communications has gone through probably the biggest change of any industry. Telegraph and telephone sound like ancient technologies but have been around for a fleeting moment in human history. More recent changes in mobile telephony and now smartphones, with the constant increase in the capability of these devices, have had well-known impacts. Widespread adoption of camera phones has provided the ability for documenting aspects of everyday life in a way not possible before. In 2010, the BBC's Radio 4 service produced a series of programs on the history of the world using 100 objects from the British Museum's collection. Updating the program in 2020, the challenge was to find an object that showed progress into the 21st century (British Broadcasting Corporation n.d.). One of the leading candidates was the camera phone, chosen because of its impact on documenting racial injustice, oppression, and criminal activity as well as the more benign and mundane activities of everyday life.

The world of electricity likewise has seen big changes. The increasing competitiveness of solar and wind power is providing the first source of renewable energy for the modern world. Solar photovoltaics are also creating new opportunities in providing electricity to far-flung areas not connected to the grid, bypassing the need for expensive grid infrastructure.

There are far too many technological advances to include here, but it is worth reminding ourselves that, big or small, these innovations really become useful only when they change something about the economics of infrastructure.

Conclusions

Technology and innovation are often talked about in the world of infrastructure, and they have a significant role here just as they do in other industries. Enthusiasm for the pace of change needs to be moderated, though, by an appreciation of just what it takes to make a substantive enough change in the economics of infrastructure. History shows us that opportunities for substantive change in economics are rare; however, when they come around, the consequences for humanity have been huge.

As this chapter discusses, AVs started off as a dream, then offered the prospect of becoming reality faster than most people had dreamed, and have now moderated into a longer-term ambition. The enthusiasm of the Silicon Valley entrepreneurs has given way to the tough reality of the infrastructure industry—one in which, as this chapter lays out, change comes only slowly.

While the automotive and technology industries are busy building AVs, it is essential that policy makers, especially urban planners and managers, think carefully about the impact this latest revolution could have on the way we live and work, the way our cities are shaped, how land use could or should be altered, and the role public transport will play. Most of all, public policy needs to consider how to introduce this rare and substantive innovation so that it can be put to best use rather than just be a disruptor.

Public policy must consider not just the direct issues around land use and transport but also its indirect impact on how the economy is shaped, access to employment, and other economic activity. This innovation could become a mechanism for more social integration, with pooling finally taking off, or a mechanism for greater individualism, with the destruction of public transport. The debate around possibly the biggest innovation in decades is a moving feast right now, and planners would do well to keep up with it.

Summary

- AVs may prove to be among the rare fundamental changes in infrastructure technology, on par with the invention of the internal combustion engine, and especially disruptive to our cities.
- Between one-half and three-quarters of the cost of a taxi ride is hiring the driver. If AVs could save on driver cost, this would stimulate an increase in

travel and pose an existential threat to public transportation. The latter would be competitive with AVs only during peak hours and even then only where it is protected from traffic congestion.

- Road congestion would likely increase greatly unless there is a large increase in ride-sharing. The only unmitigated benefit would be a large reduction in the land required for parking.

- City leaders and planners should be ready for rapid adoption of AVs if the remaining technical issues are resolved.

References

Bates, John, and David Leibling. 2012. *Spaced Out: Perspectives on Parking Policy.* London: RAC Foundation.

Blackman, Janet. 1975. The Cattle Trade and Agrarian Change on the Eve of the Railway Age. *The Agricultural History Review* 23 (1): 48–62.

Bosch, Patrick M., Felix Becker, Henrik Becker, and Kay W. Axhausen. 2018. "Cost-Based Analysis of Autonomous Mobility Services." *Transport Policy* 64: 76–91.

British Broadcasting Corporation. n.d. "A History of the World in 100 Objects." https://www .bbc.co.uk/programmes/m000qpnl.

Mishra, Aparna. 2017. "Bus Aggregator Shuttl Launches New Security Experience: Shuttl SAFE." Inc42, July 25. https://inc42.com/buzz/bus-aggregator-shuttl-safe/.

Morris, Ian. 2011. *Why the West Rules—For Now: The Patterns of History, and What They Reveal About the Future.* London: Profile Books.

National Highway Traffic Safety Administration. 2019. "NHTSA Announces Update to Historic AEB Commitment by 20 Automakers." U.S. Department of Transportation, December 17. https://www.nhtsa.gov/press-releases/nhtsa-announces-update-historic -aeb-commitment-20-automakers.

Spieser, Kevin, Kyle Treleaven, Rick Zhang, Emilio Frazzoli, Daniel Morton, and Marco Pavone. 2014. "Toward a Systematic Approach to the Design and Evaluation of Automated Mobility-on-Demand Systems: A Case Study in Singapore." Massachusetts Institute of Technology. https://dspace.mit.edu/handle/1721.1/82904.

ShareNow. n.d. "A New Era of Car-Sharing." https://www.drive-now.com/en.

Sperling, Daniel. 2018. *Three Revolutions: Steering Automated, Shared, and Electric Vehicles to a Better Future.* Washington, DC: Island Press.

20

INFRASTRUCTURE AND THE SHARING ECONOMY

Andrew Salzberg and O. P. Agarwal

The term *sharing economy* has drawn a great deal of attention over the past few years while also attracting a significant amount of criticism. It took off after being applied to a class of tech company called *unicorns* (private companies valued at more than US$1 billion) founded in the wake of the Great Recession and picking up steam since 2010. In its simplest and idealized form, sharing economy refers to technology designed to put idle and underused assets to work. The greater utilization of these assets has the potential to bring about social, economic, and environmental benefits, though it is by no means guaranteed to do so.

Indeed, significant controversy has arisen around the term *sharing* when used in this context, as the dominant sharing economy transaction is not an altruistic neighbor-to-neighbor connection but instead is likely a digital transaction mediated through a large multinational corporation that connects the sharers and consumers of assets.

There are potential gains to both the owner of the asset and the user of the asset under the sharing economy model. The user who can purchase the use of an asset—a car or a home, for example—may be able to afford that use when ownership would be prohibitive. The owner of the asset can gain extra income from renting the use of an asset for times when it would otherwise be idle.

Clearly, sharing is not a new phenomenon, but the so-called sharing economy is. People have always borrowed cars and books from friends and relatives or used friends' houses when they were traveling. People took taxis (shared vehicles) and borrowed books from libraries. What has changed and given rise to the new sharing economy is new mobile and digital technology. This new technology has allowed easier and more rapid exchange of information around assets to be shared and has simplified the booking of these services.

This chapter assesses the impact of the sharing economy for the present and future of infrastructure and provides advice for policy makers addressing

477

this new phenomenon. We use the example of urban transportation to draw out broader lessons.

Background and Enabling Technologies

As mentioned, the concept of sharing is not new. Rentable and shared goods have long existed. Taxis, homes, rooms, and equipment have always been available to book or share for specific blocks of time. However, traditionally sharing took place between or through friends, relatives, neighbors, and professional agencies.

Choices were limited, and availability was uncertain. People who could afford it were more likely to own an asset and avoid the risk of it not being available at the required time. A car of one's own meant assured availability, even if the fixed costs of ownership were high. An apartment of one's own meant an assured home and choice, even if it did not give the flexibility of changing one's location when needed.

What is new is the role technology plays in easing connections. The emergence of information technology, digital platforms, low-cost smartphones, Global Positioning System technology, and cloud-based computing services has transformed the earlier sharing systems into a vastly larger, easier to access, and sometimes global marketplace. The ease of making and receiving payments through digital platforms has removed additional barriers.

Different models of these sharing economy platforms have emerged. In some versions of business models built on this new technology, individuals and small independent operators own assets and make them available when not being used by their owners. Renting out extra rooms, household tools, a ride in a car, or one's own skills fall into this category. Examples include Airbnb, HomeStay, Uber, Lyft, Rover, TrustedHousesitters, and TaskRabbit. In another dominant paradigm, the company that operates the platform also owns (or holds a long-term lease on) the underlying assets. Prime examples here are Zipcar, Car2Go, Capital BikeShare, and WeWork.

In 2009, only a handful of companies offered shared services, Zipcar, BlaBlaCar, and Couchsurfing among them. Airbnb was founded in the fall of 2008, and Uber was founded in the spring of 2009. Since then, growth has exploded and is not limited to the United States and Europe. It has spread across the world. Homegrown models have emerged in other countries as well. Didi operates Uber-like services in China, as do Ola in India, Lyft in the United States, and Grab in several Southeast Asian countries. There are similar sharing models across many other sectors as well.

Industries Where the Sharing Economy May Play a Significant Role

Where might these business models really play a significant role? And where might this growth have a significant impact on infrastructure?

Assets with the potential to be shared are all around us. They may be buildings or other fixed assets. They can be as small as tools. Cars, which we use for barely 5 percent of the day, are a canonical example. Similarly, the use of office space is largely limited to about 10–12 hours a day. Yet these assets are paid for fully by the owner, even though they are not fully used.

What key characteristics of assets make them good candidates for a sharing economy business model to emerge? The following three characteristics are likely to be important:

1. *How expensive is the asset?* The savings from sharing a Mercedes SUV or a Paris apartment will, all else being equal, be a lot more than from sharing a bicycle and thus more likely to be the basis of a sustainable shared model.
2. *How often is the asset needed?* Business models are more likely to emerge where the sharer uses the service often enough to be familiar and comfortable with the transaction but not so much that buying the asset becomes a winning proposition.
3. *How heterogeneous are the assets or the sharers' tastes?* The more the heterogeneity, the harder the match for a potential sharer. Offices are more similar to one another than residences or industrial facilities and thus easier to share.

Based on these characteristics, a wide variety of business models has begun to emerge in a range of sectors. One of the most prominent models to emerge in recent years is Airbnb.

Airbnb is an online marketplace that connects people who want to rent out their homes with people who are looking for a place to stay at a particular location. As of January 2020, Airbnb operated in more than 100,000 cities around the world and had more than 150 million users. About 2 million people stayed in Airbnb rentals on an average night, with millennials accounting for nearly 60 percent of them (Airbnb 2016).

Airbnb was founded in October 2007 when Brian Chesky and Joe Gebbia landed on the idea of offering their air mattresses and living room to anyone looking for an overnight "bed and breakfast." By March 2009, the site had more than 10,000 users. By June 2012, 10 million nights had been booked in Airbnb listings.

For travelers, the service offers a wider variety of accommodation types because hosts list many different kinds of properties—single rooms, a suite of rooms, apartments, moored yachts, houseboats, entire houses, even a castle—on the Airbnb website. The service also offers the experience of living in a home rather than in a predictable hotel. Users can cook their own meals to save on expenses and yet get a taste of local groceries.

But Airbnb's offerings have not met with universal acclaim or acceptance, echoing the story of growth and response to shared economy services we see in our case study on urban transportation. There have been complaints that Airbnb has adversely impacted housing costs because owners prefer to pull their properties from the long-term housing market to benefit from higher Airbnb incomes. As a result, several cities have imposed regulations limiting the number of days for which guests could rent property through Airbnb. As only one example, New York has limited the ability to rent apartments through platforms such as Airbnb for stays shorter than 30 days.

Potential Benefits of the Shared Economy on Infrastructure

Where might we look for potential benefits of the shared economy, particularly as it relates to infrastructure systems? Here we lay out some general themes and then examine the experience in a case study: urban transportation.

Higher Asset Utilization

The largest potential benefit of the sharing economy could be in enabling an optimal use of assets, reducing their idle time. Better utilization could mean monetary benefits to asset owners and lower prices to users. Thus, owners of a house can earn from unused rooms, car owners can earn from the idle time of their vehicles, and multiple users can benefit from using the same asset at significantly reduced costs. Society could benefit from lower environmental impacts through reduced material need.

Reduced Costs and Greater Inclusiveness

In the case of assets whose usage is low but whose fixed costs are high, the sharing economy may enable broader access. Some assets are too expensive to own for limited use. If they can be shared easily, a wider set of the population may benefit from using them as a service when needed. As an example, cars sit idle for 95 percent of the time. Owning a car has fixed costs such as interest on the capital used, parking fees and insurance premiums, local road taxes, and maintenance charges that can become a significant burden. Shared options come with no fixed costs and no hassles of maintenance. Costs of use may be considerably reduced in a shared model, which allows many to use services they might not afford if they had to cover all costs of ownership.

Waste and Externalities

Clear drawbacks have also been identified in the growth of several shared economy platforms. A recent example is dockless bike-sharing, described in our case study below. As these platforms have grown, complaints have multiplied about unwanted bikes clogging city streets and walking spaces. Many new platforms offering transportation services have also been found to increase congestion on roadways by inducing new traffic and drawing riders off more space-efficient modes of transportation such as public transit.

Case Study: Urban Transportation

As described, the last two decades have seen the emergence of new technology-supported platforms for shared transportation services that are built on digital technology. For the purposes of this chapter, we focus our attention on urban transportation as a model for the impacts and trade-offs that may be seen elsewhere.

By "shared," we mean that multiple users share some aspect of the service itself. For so-called car-sharing services, the same physical vehicle is shared among multiple users over the course of a day, a week, or a vehicle's lifetime. This use contrasts with the typical personally owned car, whose single user or family is the overwhelmingly dominant user.

As a general rule, these services tend to enable higher utilization of a given asset. A typical personal car is only in use about 5 percent of its lifetime. Car rental fleets average 60–80 percent utilization in terms of days booked by users, and ride-share providers such as Uber and Lyft have the car in use for about 50 percent of the time with a rider while the driver is providing service, which may only be a small portion of the week (Hall and Krueger 2016). A typical bike-share vehicle is in use anywhere from 2–10 rides per day, and shared electric scooter fleets have also shown utilization rates in that range. These numbers vary widely and have seen significant swings based on the size of the fleet deployed, but the rates are no doubt higher than the typical personally owned cycle or scooter might attain in a day.

The new breed of technology-enabled shared mobility services differs from preexisting (and long-standing) shared services such as public transportation, car rental, and informal transit primarily in their reliance on technology for a variety of aspects of their service offering. One of the first companies to make its name in technology-enabled shared mobility services was Zipcar, founded in 2000. Zipcar built on late 1990s' models of car sharing developed in Europe, using new web-based technology to enable easier sharing. Another milestone was the the Velib bike-sharing platform launched in Paris in 2007.

This era of technology-enabled sharing was accelerated by the launch of the iPhone, also in 2007. Since that time, a new wave of mobile-first shared transportation service providers has been created, highlighted by ride-hailing providers such as Uber, Lyft, Ola, and Didi. Bike-share services, too, have grown and expanded globally both in their earliest incarnation, requiring fixed docks to store each vehicle, and in a more recent dockless iteration that relies more extensively on the availability of mobile technology. New forms of small electrically powered transportation hardware have helped accelerate this trend, creating the so-called micromobility industry.

Benefits and Costs of Shared Mobility for Urban Transportation Infrastructure

Of relevance for our main topic of discussion in this book—infrastructure economics—the question we seek to answer is whether these shared mobility services will allow for more efficient use of transportation infrastructure. To answer that question, we need to more fully understand the impact of these services on the consumption of space and fixed assets as well as their size and potential for growth.

Infrastructure is, in an obvious way, a sharing economy platform. Its use (e.g., in the case of roads and bridges) is shared by the large number of road users who avail themselves of its presence. No one user monopolizes access to the bridge, and all share in the benefit of its existence, even though they could not afford to produce it on their own. They may pay for its existence through user fees such as tolls or through more broadly applied taxes. However, the asset itself is shared.

The question is whether the emergence of shared use of the "vehicles" that travel on this infrastructure (here, primarily shared cars and micromobility services such as bikes, electric bikes, and electric scooters) make use of the infrastructure asset itself more efficient. By "efficient," we use the frame of how effectively a given piece of infrastructure accomplishes its transportation goals—the movement of goods or people—within a fixed constraint of available space.

One stream of evidence, drawn mostly from modeling large-scale adoption of shared services, argues that the answer is yes: shared mobility can dramatically improve the efficiency of transportation infrastructure. One of the more widely cited reports from the International Transport Forum (ITF) modeled the widespread adoption of ubiquitous shared mobility for the entire metropolitan area of Lisbon (ITF 2016).

The model assumed that all trips—including those currently completed by personally owned vehicles—were shifted to some form of shared mobility: a shared taxi service with a maximum of four passengers, a minibus service with a maximum of 16 passengers, and a traditional fixed-route metro service. Passengers were assigned to a new service with the constraint that it could take no longer than five minutes more than their original journey time. Various iterations of the ITF modeling revealed that all fixed-route bus transit would disappear in this new paradigm.

Perhaps unsurprising, the results of this shift were dramatic. The delay in travel times during congested peak hours versus off-peak hours fell by 37 percent. Overall vehicle miles traveled fell by 40 percent. Further, the number of vehicles required to move the same number of passenger miles fell by 97 percent. In other words, only 3 percent of the number of preexisting vehicles were required to make the system function. Clearly, such a system makes more efficient use of the fixed infrastructure assets of Lisbon (both roads and metro network) by squeezing more passenger travel out of a fixed quantity of built space. This system also would dramatically affect the need for parking, one of the more inefficient users of urban space.

The ITF repeated its modeling efforts for Lisbon in a variety of other contexts, including Auckland, Dublin, and other locations. The results were similar. If all personal trips in the metropolitan area were shared through a centralized, optimized network, results would be dramatic: infrastructure efficiency would increase, and the number of vehicles required would plummet.

The ITF's work is not the only set of studies to make this case. Many other studies that focus on the potential of autonomous vehicles (AVs), which are capable of fully driving themselves in urban environments with no driver present, focus on the potential for this type of vehicle to more efficiently move passengers through cities, especially when they are used in shared fleets (Bauer, Greenblatt, and Gerke 2018; Greenblatt and Saxena 2015). According to these modeling efforts, this efficiency could come from a number of effects. First, AVs may be able to more closely follow other vehicles and platoon through fixed infrastructure to squeeze more vehicles through existing street designs than is currently possible. Estimates suggest that AVs and traffic flow optimization might allow greater movement of vehicles through existing road infrastructure.

In addition, another potential efficiency is the so-called right-sizing of vehicles. Currently, people who purchase a vehicle for their personal use often buy one with the capacity to support its most space-intensive use (e.g., buying an SUV because one trip per year must transport two kids, their friends, and all their equipment). In contrast, a shared autonomous network could summon a ride to provide a vehicle right-sized for the trip. For example, if one travels alone, a small one-passenger car could be supplied. Conversely, larger parties could have full-sized sedans or even minibuses summoned to move them. Given the very high prevalence of single-occupancy trips in countries such as the United States, this right-sizing could dramatically reduce the energy (and thus potentially carbon emissions) of the overall passenger vehicle fleet. The effect of vehicle right-sizing on the use of roads is less clear though likely to be positive.

In essence, a wide array of studies has shown that a ubiquitous shared-vehicle network—right-sized, potentially autonomous, and moving (in coordination with some forms of public transportation) 100 percent of motorized travel—could dramatically reduce the number of vehicles, peak-hour congestion, and required infrastructure to provide for a given quantity of passenger travel. In addition to the lower need for roadway capacity (or more rapid travel on it), demand for parking space, an enormous consumer of road infrastructure, would almost entirely vanish overnight.

That picture is optimistic and certainly helps explain some of the excitement surrounding the potential of the so-called transportation revolutions of automation and shared mobility. However, most of the news around the existing (rather than modeled) shared mobility providers does not point in this direction. Headlines about Uber and Lyft have been dominated by news about their increase in congestion, declines in public transportation ridership, and increases in greenhouse gas emissions (Clewlow and Mishra 2017; Schaller 2017). Why the dramatic difference from modeled outcomes described above?

Some of the differences between the idealistic modeled scenarios and the on-the-ground reality are obvious. For one, no urban transport system can force passengers onto a socially optimized mode of travel, as they are in the ITF studies and many other AV models. Real urban transport system users choose their travel mode based on their own personal convenience. This point is well known to cause transportation outcomes that may be suboptimal from a system's level. Many users may choose to take an Uber or a Lyft in place of a trip they might have previously made by walking, taking public transportation, or riding a bike, which will lead to an increase in vehicle miles traveled. This effect is entirely absent from the idealized modeled states described above.

In addition to increasing choices about how to travel, the growing prevalence of services such as Uber, Lyft, Ola, and Didi have helped increase the convenience and lower the price of travel by car. This result is known to cause an increase in travel demand through the phenomenon of induced demand. Many travelers choose not to make every trip they might because of the perceived inconvenience of travel. To the extent that the presence of new shared services makes travel more appealing or convenient, they are bound to increase travel. Studies have estimated that this induced demand effect could comprise as much as 20 percent of travel on services such as Uber and Lyft (Clewlow and Mishra 2017).

That effect is the first difference between the idealized studies and reality on the ground. Another notable difference is that mass adoption has not been achieved, making the provision of real-time carpool services shared between riders such as Uber Pool and Lyft Line less likely, as described below. This type of shared or carpooled service is critical to some of the efficiencies described in the idealized models above. In practice, the difficulty of convincing two or more people to ride together in the back of the same vehicle are well documented; carpooling rates in the United States have declined significantly since 1980.

Despite significant sums of venture capital raised and invested, these services still comprise a relatively small share of overall travel in the United States, their most mature market. As one example of the size of capital expenditure involved, Uber has raised more than US$25 billion in public and private market financing.

In the United States, the 2017 National Household Travel Survey indicated that ride-share services were still less than 1 percent of all travel nationwide (Williams 2018). More recent surveys targeting metropolitan areas where these services are most thoroughly established have shown that in the core of San Francisco, Uber and Lyft now constitute as much as 13 percent of vehicle mileage, a significant figure overall but seemingly an outlier globally. In Los Angeles, the equivalent figure was 2.6 percent, while in Chicago it was 3.3 percent (Fehr and Peers 2020).

The "potential" for on-demand carpooling is enormous, as studies by the ITF (2016) and Greenblatt and Saxena (2015) show. Uber and Lyft have indeed invested billions of dollars in the technology and incentives for these services and have moved billions of rides in shared configurations. But it is unclear whether any of the shared services have covered their costs of operation. The level of discount required to entice a user to access the service has rarely been matched by the actual discount collected by the efficiency of combining two routes into one.

The challenge of pooling rides gets easier as the number of riders using the same service increases. To demonstrate this point, consider a simple example. If we consider person A's journey from home to work, the odds of having someone else make the same (or an overlapping) trip at the same time as A are relatively small if only one other person in the metropolitan area is using the same service as A. If that share increases to everyone in the metropolitan area using the same service as A, the chance of finding a suitable match that would only minimally inconvenience A (if at all) is now much greater. In the ITF's (2016) and other modeled scenarios, 100 percent adoption of the shared service has been assumed, making the provision of pooled rides much easier to imagine. Even in that scenario, if riders have a choice of sharing or not sharing a ride, many have demonstrated a clear preference for not sharing, even at significantly discounted rates.

As a result of these smaller adoption rates, driving up the productivity of shared ride services has been harder. Today, almost all rides taken on these services are individually booked. At the time of writing, the COVID-19 pandemic had shut down all shared services, and their future is uncertain.

Policy Responses to Shared Urban Transport Services

Dramatic differences therefore exist between what has been assumed about mass adoption of a centrally optimized shared mobility system and the on-the-ground reality of competitively operated, for-profit, relatively small shared mobility services in practice. What lessons should we draw, and what guidance can we provide for managers, builders, and planners of infrastructure systems as they examine the landscape of shared mobility?

First is the critical importance of managing demand. It is a mathematical reality that if the quantity of travel can be thought of as fixed, shared services have the potential to move more people more efficiently. But that case clearly is not the reality. Travel demand is elastic and responds to lower cost and increased convenience through increasing demand, generating congestion, and other much-noted side effects.

What might it take to manage this elasticity? One idea with a demonstrated history of success is pricing. Road pricing schemes in London, Singapore, and Stockholm have by now several decades of demonstrated experience in significantly modifying travel behavior in urban transport systems. Several papers have identified the obvious synergy between technologies (such as Via) that make sharing a ride or sharing a vehicle more convenient and policy approaches such as congestion tolling (Ostrovsky and Schwarz 2018). Where a toll is present, a shared operator can potentially make ride sharing more profitable and more appealing to the consumer by dividing a fixed per-vehicle toll among multiple riders, significantly increasing the cost savings (and thus appeal) of a shared ride versus a personal ride.

Shared lanes such as carpool lanes could serve the same purpose. Where shared services can gain a significant travel time benefit through access to priority lanes, the incentive for users to take them will increase. While in the past the often cumbersome nature of carpool arrangements made it hard to grow demand, modern technology-enabled real-time carpooling could make this problem much less significant. The key is that both of these technologies and strategies (tolling and carpool lanes) are in the hands of infrastructure owners, not shared-mobility operators. Both hold the potential to emphasize the beneficial aspects of shared-mobility technology while minimizing its drawbacks.

In a real sense, the technology providers might in fact welcome the type of regulation above—rules that limit overall travel demand while benefiting efficient use of space—as a win for them. This benefit has already been demonstrated in practice through, for example, companies such as Uber actively campaigning for so-called congestion pricing in New York, a rule that would place a flat per-vehicle fee on all vehicles entering the core (Calder and Bensimon 2019). In theory, this pricing could provide an advantage to services such as Via and Uber that share rides among multiple passengers, dividing a fixed toll among multiple riders. In practice, some of the fees imposed on ride-hailing are actually applied per rider and thus miss this benefit; however, this situation will (hopefully) evolve over time.

In the end, the vigorous debate about the congestion impact of shared mobility services on transportation infrastructure largely boils down to a relatively simple fact. The models that suggest that shared mobility services (including potential future AVs) will result in dramatic improvements in congestion fail to account for consumer behavior, namely that travelers respond to lower prices and increased convenience by traveling more. A simple acknowledgment of this fact will make our understanding of shared mobility's impact on infrastructure more realistic and thus empower infrastructure management strategies that steer the adoption of new technology in a more efficient direction, most obviously through tools such as broad-based road pricing.

Rise of Micromobility

So far we have discussed mostly the prospects for shared services that use cars and rides in cars to deliver mobility. But another type of service has come to dominate the headlines around the sharing economy in transportation in recent years: *micromobility*, defined as a shared vehicle weighing less than 500 kg. Most commonly, the term refers to small standup e-scooters and traditional bikes and e-bikes operated in shared fleets, all either relying on docks for storage between rides or free-floating on streets. What do we make of the prospect of shared micromobility operators?

As with so much of the shared economy, the history here goes back to well before the technology platforms that have driven their recent prominence. In the 1960s, Amsterdam launched the White Bike Program to allow free and ubiquitous bikes to be shared freely across the city. While attracting much attention, the program declined as bikes were sabotaged and lost.

The more recent history of bike-sharing technology was spawned by the success of Paris's Velib system, a docked bike-share system supported by advertising. Its success spawned imitators across the world. One of the more successful models originated in Montreal, Canada; its technology was later deployed (not without hiccups) in New York, London, Boston, and Washington, DC. All of the abovementioned systems were docked; that is, the vehicle needed to be parked in a dedicated lock provided solely for the purpose of the shared bike system.

The even more recent past was marked by the emergence of so-called dockless bike-share system that gained attention through their proliferation in Chinese cities in 2017. Scenes of millions of bikes deployed at every intersection in Chinese cities of all sizes took the world by storm. Ultimately, the bike-share dream created in China faded, the attempted expansion fizzled abroad, and the bike-share market declined at home. Images of junkyards piled with discarded low-quality bikes are a dominant image of this period in micromobility history.

A yet more recent period of innovation took place in the United States and Europe around dockless electric scooters. Popularized by Bird, based in Santa Monica, these light, electrically powered, throttled vehicles took the world by storm. Since these vehicles came in the wake of the Chinese dockless experiment and the reaction of cities to the growth of Uber and Lyft, regulators were ready and willing to impose significant regulations on the growth of these platforms. They grew wildly nonetheless, powered by astronomical valuations from venture capital. The growth in dockless electric scooter services had already started to decline somewhat in 2019, as investors became fearful of the continued heavy losses at other mobility startups and began to demand a shorter pathway to profitability.

Unlike automobiles, which (at least in developed countries) had a large base of users of personal cars who might share, services such as electric scooters were creating their first market primarily through shared services. This creation meant that evaluating their efficiency was a function not of comparing them with their preexisting nonshared versions (as with cars) but instead of assessing how effectively they could deliver a large number of riders per shared vehicle on the road and how effectively they could move passengers per unit of space consumed.

In an era when growth at all costs was the prime motivator for venture capital–backed mobility startups, there have been plenty of documented cases of these vehicles recording very low levels of utilization being deployed on the streets primarily to drive aggregate ridership even while the use of any individual vehicle remained low. This aggressive deployment of scooters has led to extremely low usage in some places. Combined with short life spans, this low usage has led to claims that these vehicles are inefficient, at least based on energy and environmental perspectives.

Although bikes and scooters can move more people in a smaller volume of space more efficiently and with less negative externalities than cars (important considerations for managers of infrastructure assets), debate rages on the precise impact of micromobility. Some evidence has emerged of its ability to get people out of cars, though the same phenomenon of induced demand and transfer from modes was seen as in the case of ride-sharing services (PBOT 2018).

For these services to truly proliferate, changes in the underlying way we allocate street space will be required: away from cars and toward smaller, lighter vehicles partially operating in shared fleets. Some studies have asserted that with relatively conservative assumptions, some e-bike services could grow to significant scale (Steer Group 2018). We discuss some potential approaches options below.

Where to Next for Shared Mobility Services in Urban Transportation?

These debates were raging just as the COVID-19 pandemic hit, at least temporarily bringing these services (and the debates around them) to a halt. Ironically, this stop occurred just as a boom in bike buying took hold, as people sought alternatives to crowded public transportation. Is the halt an ominous sign for the future of shared services? The coming of the COVID-19 pandemic during the drafting of this chapter allows a taking stock of the current moment. High-flying mobility startups such as Uber and Lyft have been forced to lay off staff as the use of rides has plummeted. Bird and Lime have been reduced to small versions of their former selves. AVs, once supposedly just around the corner, now seem significantly more distant.

What does the future hold? At some level, the most bullish claims about adopting shared services have yet to be fulfilled. Ride-hail and electric scooter travel are both only single-digit percentages of travel in most mature markets. Ride-hail provides a cautionary tale. It achieved a mode share of only 1 percent nationally in the United States, despite offering services priced at low, financially unsustainable levels (Williams 2018). In their current configuration, it seems unlikely that shared services can capture a more significant portion of the passenger vehicle travel market. This prospect is especially true in the United States, where abundant free parking and unpriced roads make competition with personal cars challenging.

In one potential future scenario, the deployment of AVs ends up catching up with some of its more optimistic prognosticators, allowing for ride-share services to lower costs and expand service, competing with automobile use, and allowing significant growth. If that happens, it is still far from clear if this would help infrastructure asset utilization. The consensus seems to be that AVs would generate more travel, exacerbating the current challenges of managing scarce road space.

For micromobility to grow, cities will need to make a dedicated effort to ensure the wider ability of people to safely operate smaller vehicles such as bikes and scooters on their roads. Ironically, just as the coronavirus was knocking service entirely offline, the designation of streets as "shared," "slow," and "car-free" started to explode, providing precisely the physical environment these services need.

The reality in both cases is that autonomous ride-share services and smaller shared micromobility services will need the strong hand of public policy to grow and do so in a way that supports efficient use of infrastructure. Cities will have to make safe space for micromobility services. For autonomous ride services, cities must set up rules that allow for their operation but incentivize a shared and efficient service that keeps demand in check while competing successfully with the existing system, which is dominated by use of personal cars. At the very least, both micromobility services and autonomous ride services would benefit from a more sensible policy around vehicle parking, such as eliminating its mandatory provision at no cost to users.

Can this policy be implemented? London provides a compelling example. Its centrally managed system has implemented a congestion charge to manage vehicle demand, a low-emission zone to manage emissions, and a significant expansion of bike infrastructure to allow more lightweight vehicles. This kind of regulatory environment can work with technology-enabled shared mobility services to grow in a way that benefits the city's infrastructure goals. We hope that more cities follow London's example during the current pandemic and beyond.

Conclusions

As demonstrated in the case studies, the sharing economy model has the potential to enable better utilization of fixed assets and thereby allow wider access to services. But it may also enable greater consumption of services, expanding demand for limited space in roads and urban cores. These conflicting trends in the sharing economy will likely continue as the world becomes more connected digitally. While collaborative consumption has demonstrated its attractiveness in industries such as transportation, consumer goods, and services, many other traditional sectors are likely to experience changes because of the convenience that the sharing economy offers.

These new sharing economy models have disrupted traditional businesses, eliciting significant regulatory pushback. Governments at all levels are getting proactive in harnessing the potential of the sharing economy for local development but also in ensuring that this sharing happens in a regulated manner. An example of enhanced regulation has been the controls that cities have imposed on micromobility operators. Relatively low caps on the number of vehicles permitted and high regulatory fees have helped slow their growth in many markets.

Ride sharing, too, has seen its growth prospects severely curtailed by regulations. In New York City, Uber's services are no longer allowed to grow, as adding new for-hire vehicles has been banned, a first in the city's regulatory history. Across the globe, cities such as London have imposed increasingly heavy per-ride fees and other forms of taxes, significantly slowing prospects for growth.

The labor model underpinning ride services is also under threat. Most prominently, many ride platforms for the sharing economy rely on lowering labor costs through the use of independent contractors. Jurisdictions around the world are working to require these shared mobility platforms to treat drivers as full employees, potentially threatening the underpinnings of the services' growth and success in the current model.

The prospects for further growth are uncertain. As more people across the globe are connected using smartphones, the transaction costs associated with using shared services will decrease. This decrease may mean greater growth prospects for the sharing economy, which some have projected to grow from about US$14 billion in 2014 to US$335 billion by 2025 (Yaragi and Ravi 2017). These projections are based on the growth and success of existing sharing services as well as the anticipated emergence of new industries in the collaborative services ring.

Despite these optimistic projections, the last few years have been uncertain times for sharing economies. The calamitous consequences of pursuing growth at all costs with little regard to profitability are seen in WeWork, whose fortunes declined dramatically. Its valuation collapsed from a high in the US$40 billion range at the start of 2019 to a few billion now, with even that value somewhat questionable. Uber and Lyft, two of the darlings of the shared mobility market, also continue to be unprofitable.

The COVID-19 pandemic has done significant damage to these companies by bringing the broader economy to a standstill and specifically calling into question people's ability to share anything with other humans, with social distancing the dominant value of the day. Ride volumes and Airbnb bookings are all down dramatically, and companies in both sectors have laid off thousands of employees. Will the COVID-19 pandemic be a temporary bump on a road to continued growth in the shared economy, or will it mark a more permanent turning point away from this type of business model? Either way, the infrastructure operators of the world need to be prepared. We hope that this case study of urban transportation provides lessons for those in that industry and beyond.

Summary

- The sharing economy is not an altruistic neighbor-to-neighbor exchange but instead is a digital transaction connecting asset owners with users who take advantage of improvements in technology.

- In theory, car sharing could greatly increase asset utilization, since personal cars are used only about 5 percent of the time. Simulations have shown that a ubiquitous shared vehicle network, using right-sized and potentially AVs and moving 100 percent of motorized travel, could dramatically reduce peak hour congestion, the number of vehicles, and the roadway and parking infrastructure needed to accommodate a given quantity of passenger travel.

- These model results are optimistic, however, as they assume that travelers will shift to a sharing mode that is highly efficient from a systemic perspective, when the long-term decline in carpooling suggests the difficulty of convincing two or more people to ride together in the back of a car.

- Infrastructure managers could encourage sharing by imposing per-vehicle congestion charges or by designating priority lanes for carpools.

- The future of micromobility services, such as electric scooters and bikes, would seem to be even more dependent on the designation of street space where the vehicles could be safely operated by people with different levels of skill.

References

Airbnb. 2016. "Airbnb and the Rise of Millennial Travel." https://www.airbnbcitizen.com/wp-content/uploads/2016/08/MillennialReport.pdf.

Bauer, Gordon S., Jeffery B. Greenblatt, and Brian F. Gerke. 2018. "Cost, Energy, and Environmental Impact of Automated Electric Taxi Fleets in Manhattan." *Environmental Science Technology* 52(8): 4920–4928.

Calder, Rich, and Olivia Bensimon. 2019. "Uber Spent $2M to Help Push Through Congestion Pricing." *New York Post*, April 3. https://nypost.com/2019/04/03/uber-spent-2m-to-help-push-through-congestion-pricing/.

Clewlow, Regina R., and Gouri S. Mishra. 2017. "Disruptive Transportation: The Adoption, Utilization, and Impacts of Ride-Hailing in the United States." Institute of Transportation Studies research report No. UCD-ITS-RR-17-07. Davis, CA: University of California.

Fehr and Peers. 2020. "What Are TNCs Share of VMT?" https://www.fehrandpeers.com/what-are-tncs-share-of-vmt/#:~:text=What%20is%20the%20estimated%20percent,as%20passenger%20and%20commercial%20vehicles.

Greenblatt, Jeffery B., and Samveg Saxena. 2015. "Autonomous Taxis Could Greatly Reduce Greenhouse-Gas Emissions of US Light-Duty Vehicles." *Nature Climate Change* 5: 850–863. https://doi.org/10.1038/nclimate2685.

Hall, Jonathan, and Alan B. Krueger. 2016. "An Analysis of the Labor Market for Uber's Driver-Partners in the United States." National Bureau of Economic Research working paper No. 2284. https://www.nber.org/papers/w22843.

ITF (International Transport Forum). 2016. "Shared Mobility for Liveable Cities." ITF white paper, May. Paris: International Transport Forum. https://www.itf-oecd.org/shared-mobility-innovation-liveable-cities.

Ostrovsky, Michael, and Michael Schwarz. 2018. "Carpooling and the Economics of Self-Driving Cars." Stanford University, February 12. https://web.stanford.edu/~ost/papers/sdc.pdf.

PBOT (Portland Bureau of Transportation). 2018. "2018 E-Scooter Pilot User Survey Results: Appendix G." https://www.portlandoregon.gov/transportation/article/700916.

Schaller, Bruce. 2017. "Unsustainable? The Growth of App-Based Ride Services and Traffic: Travel and the Future of New York City." Schaller Consulting, February 27. http://www.schallerconsult.com/rideservices/unsustainable.pdf.

Steer Group. 2018. "Shared Ebike Potential: London and New York." https://www.steergroup.com/projects/assessing-shared-ebike-potential-london-new-york.

Williams, Rik. 2018. "Three Early Takeaways from the 2017 National Household Travel Survey." https://medium.com/uber-under-the-hood/three-early-takeaways-from-the-2017-national-household-travel-survey-b23506efe8ad.

Yaragi, Niam, and Shamika Ravi. 2017. "The Current and Future State of the Sharing Economy." IMPACT Series No. 032017. New Delhi: Brookings India. https://www.brookings.edu/wp-content/uploads/2016/12/sharingeconomy_032017final.pdf.

ACKNOWLEDGMENTS

The editors are grateful for the full support of the Lincoln Institute of Land Policy for the preparation and production of the book. The book benefited from the support and assistance of a number of individuals. George W. McCarthy, Maureen Clarke, and members of the Lincoln Institute Editorial Board provided overall guidance; Ede Ijjasz, Johannes Linn, and Weiping Wu reviewed and commented on the draft manuscript; Elizabeth Fox and Yvonne Ramsey served as copyeditors; and Madeleine J. Donachie, Yihao Li, Jingyi Liu, Shenming Liu, Emily McKeigue, and Patricia Stillwell assisted at various stages of the book's preparation and production.

The chapter authors wish to acknowledge the valuable comments or able assistance from the following individuals: Gregory K. Ingram, Sock-Yong Phang, and Don H. Pickrell for chapter 1; Wenjing Li, Jingyi Liu, and Junxi Qu for chapter 2; Margaret Brissenden, Eliza Glaeser, and Gregory K. Ingram for chapter 4; Atif Ansar, Alexander Budzier, Chantal Cantarelli, and Edward L. Glaeser for chapters 7 and 8; E. Auriol, L. Bagnoli, S. Bertomeu-Sanchez, I. Byatt, C. Crampes, O. Chisari, M. Dewatripont, A. Gomez-Lobo, R. Schlirf-Rapti, T. Serebrisky, and M. Vagliasindi for chapter 11; Paul Fox, Tony Ballance, John Banyard, David Black, Vic Cocker, Stephen Littlechild, Ronnie Mercer, Neil Menzies, and Colin Skellett for chapter 13; and Shashi Verma for chapter 14.

INDEX

Note: page numbers followed by *f* and *t* refer to figures and tables respectively. Those followed by n refer to notes, with note number.

About the Editors and Contributors

Editors

José A. Gómez-Ibáñez is the Derek C. Bok Professor Emeritus of Urban Planning and Public Policy at Harvard University. His research interests include transportation, infrastructure, urban economic development, and infrastructure privatization and regulation. Among Gómez-Ibáñez's numerous publications are *Regulating Infrastructure: Monopoly, Contracts, and Discretion* (Harvard University Press, 2003); *Going Private: The International Experience with Transport Privatization*, with John R. Meyer (Brookings Institution Press, 1993); *Regulation for Revenue: The Political Economy of Land Use Exactions*, with Alan Altshuler (Brookings Institution Press, 1993); and *Autos, Transit, and Cities*, with John R. Meyer (Harvard University Press, 1981).

Zhi Liu is the senior fellow and director of the China Program at the Lincoln Institute of Land Policy and the director of the Peking University–Lincoln Institute Center for Urban Development and Land Policy. He was a lead infrastructure specialist with the World Bank before joining the Lincoln Institute. His research interests include infrastructure finance, land policy, urban economics, and transport planning. Liu is a coeditor, with Rebecca L. H. Chiu and Bertrand Renaud, of *International Housing Market Experience and Implications for China* (Routledge, 2019).

Contributors

O. P. Agarwal is the chief executive officer of the World Resource Institute India. He was a civil servant in the Indian government from 1979 to 2007, where he led several infrastructure-related tasks in the transport and energy sectors and became the principal author of India's *National Urban Transport Policy*, which was adopted in 2006 and has remained the country's key document guiding urban transport investments. After his civil service, Agarwal worked at the World Bank in Washington, for six years as its global urban transport adviser. His coauthored book *Emerging Paradigms in Urban Mobility: Planning, Financing and Management* (with Samuel Zimmerman and Ajay Kumar) was published by Elsevier in 2018. Agarwal has taught courses at the Indian School of Business on public-private partnerships in infrastructure as well as urban governance.

Dirk W. Bester studied actuarial science at the University of the Free State in Bloemfontein, South Africa, after which he received a Rhodes Scholarship to attend the University of Oxford. He completed a D. Phil in statistics under the supervision of David Steinsaltz and then worked as a chief science officer at Sciemus, Ltd. (now called Occam Underwriting), calculating the insurance risk of rockets, satellites, and power stations. Bester is currently working in the banking sector.

Sir Ian Byatt was the director-general of the Water Services Regulation Authority (the regulator of the newly privatized water companies in England and Wales) from 1989 to 2000 and the chairman of the Water Industry Commission for Scotland from 2005 to 2011. He had previously been the deputy chief economic adviser at the Her Majesty's Treasury, where he was responsible for microeconomic advice on supply-side issues. Before that appointment, Byatt taught at Durham University and the London School of Economics. He is the author of *The British Electrical Industry, 1875–1914: The Economic Returns to a New Technology* (Oxford University Press, 1979).

Rohit Chandra is an assistant professor at the India Institute of Technology's Delhi School of Public Policy and a visiting fellow at the Centre for Policy Research, New Delhi. He is a political scientist and economic historian who focuses on state capitalism, energy policy, and infrastructure finance with a particular focus on India's coal and power sectors. Over the last decade, Chandra has worked on policy questions with state government departments, state-owned energy enterprises, central government ministries, and large corporations in India. He is currently writing a book on the political and economic history of India's coal industry from 1960 to the present.

Zheng Chang is a visiting scholar at Harvard Kennedy School and a visiting scientist at ETH Zurich. His research focuses on Chinese urbanization, including the impact of urban transport infrastructure on economic growth and redistribution, housing and land markets and their impacts on firms and individuals, and the economic consequences of urban environmental pollution. Chang has published a series of papers that evaluate the social and economic impacts of high-speed rail to Chinese cities. Previously, he taught at the City University of Hong Kong.

Akash Deep is a senior lecturer in public policy at the Harvard Kennedy School. His expertise lies in infrastructure finance and valuation, public-private partnerships, financial risk management and derivatives, and the management and regulation of financial institutions, financial markets, and pension funds. Deep serves as the faculty chair of the "Infrastructure in a Market Economy" and

"International Finance Corporation" executive programs. He has also served as a consultant in infrastructure finance and public-private partnerships for a number of international institutions, government entities, and private firms. Deep is a coeditor, with Jungwook Kim and Minsoo Lee, of *Realizing the Potential of Public-Private Partnerships to Advance Asia's Infrastructure Development* (Asian Development Bank, 2019).

John D. Donahue has taught public policy since 1988 at the Harvard Kennedy School, where he is the Raymond Vernon Senior Lecturer in Public Policy. His teaching, writing, and research mostly deal with public sector reform and the distribution of public responsibilities across levels of government and sectors of the economy. His publications include 14 books, most recently *The Dragon, the Eagle, and the Private Sector: Public-Private Collaboration in China and the United States*, with Karen Eggleston and Richard J. Zeckhauser (Cambridge University Press, 2021). Donahue served as the assistant secretary and counselor to the secretary of labor in President Clinton's administration.

Antonio Estache is a professor of economics and member of the European Center for Advanced Research of Economics at the Université Libre de Bruxelles, Belgium. Prior to his current appointment, he spent 25 years at the World Bank (1982–2007), working on public sector reforms, restructuring, regulation, and project evaluation. Estache has published extensively on a wide range of dimensions of the economics of infrastructure services, including *Regulating Public Services: Bridging the Gap Between Theory and Practice*, with Emmanuelle Auriol and Claude Crampes (Cambridge University Press, 2021).

Bent Flyvbjerg is the first BT Professor and inaugural chair of major program management at the University of Oxford's Saïd Business School and a professorial fellow at St. Anne's College, University of Oxford. He is a coauthor, with Dan Gardner, of *Big Plans: Why Most Fail, How Some Succeed* (Random House, 2022); the editor of *The Oxford Handbook of Megaproject Management* (Oxford University Press, 2017); and a coauthor, with Nils Bruzelius and Werner Rothengatter, of *Megaprojects and Risk: An Anatomy of Ambition* (Cambridge University Press, 2003). Flyvbjerg's publications have been translated into 20 languages. He serves as an adviser to the prime minister of the United Kingdom and government and business entities around the world. Flyvbjerg was twice a Fulbright Scholar and received a knighthood in 2002.

Edward L. Glaeser is the Fred and Eleanor Glimp Professor of Economics at Harvard University, where he has taught since 1992. Glaeser also leads the Urban Working Group at the National Bureau of Economic Research in Cambridge,

Massachusetts, and coleads the "Cities" program at the International Growth Centre in London. He is a coeditor of the *Journal of Urban Economics* and previously served as one of three editors of the *Quarterly Journal of Economics* for a decade. Glaeser has published scores of papers on cities and other topics in applied economics. He is a fellow of the American Academy of Arts and Sciences, the American Academy of Political and Social Sciences, the Econometric Society, the National Academy for Public Administration, and the National Academy for Social Insurance.

Daniel J. Graham is a professor of statistical modeling in the Department of Civil and Environmental Engineering at Imperial College London (ICL) and the director of the ICL Transport Strategy Centre. His research interests include the development of statistical methods for transport analysis and modeling, transport and spatial economics, causal inference, and performance benchmarking of infrastructure systems. Graham is a project partner at the Data Centric Engineering Program at the Alan Turing Institute and a fellow of both the Institute of Mathematics and Its Applications and the Royal Statistical Society.

Yu-Hung Hong is the former director of the Samuel Tak Lee Real Estate Entrepreneurship Laboratory at the Massachusetts Institute of Technology, where he taught urban public finance and land policies between 2004 and 2017. He also served as a senior fellow at the Lincoln Institute of Land Policy from 2009 to 2012. Hong's research focuses on land value capture for financing public infrastructure in developing countries. He is a coeditor of 12 books, including *Leasing Public Land: Policy Debates and International Experiences*, with Steven C. Bourassa (Lincoln Institute of Land Policy, 2003); *Analyzing Land Readjustment: Economics, Law, and Collective Action*, with Barrie Needham (Lincoln Institute of Land Policy, 2007); and Lincoln Institute's *Land Policy Series*, with Gregory K. Ingram (2007–2012).

Daniel Hörcher is a postdoctoral research associate at the Centre for Transport Studies at Imperial College London. His research interests are centered around the economics of supply-side decisions in transport policy, including optimal pricing and capacity provision. In recent years, Hörcher has published more than a dozen research articles on efficient multimodal transport provision in leading journals of spatial and transport economics, building on microeconomic modeling and statistical analysis of large-scale automated transport data.

Du Huynh is a senior lecturer at the School of Public Policy and Management, Fulbright University Vietnam. His teaching and research interests are urban economics, local and regional development, infrastructure development, and finance and banking. Huynh serves as an adviser to provincial governments on long-term development strategies and participates frequently in policy dialogue in Vietnam. His recent book is *Making Megacities in Asia: Comparing National Economic Development Trajectories* (Springer, 2020).

Gregory K. Ingram was the president and chief executive officer of the Lincoln Institute of Land Policy from June 2005 through June 2014 and formerly the director-general of operations evaluation at the World Bank, where he also held positions as the director of the Development Research Department and staff director for *World Development Report 1994: Infrastructure for Development* (Oxford University Press, 1994). Prior to joining the World Bank, Ingram was an associate professor of economics at Harvard University. He has published in the areas of infrastructure, urban economics, housing, land policy, evaluation, environment, transport, and development.

Somik Lall is the World Bank's global lead on territorial development solutions and a lead economist for urban development. He is a recognized thought and practice leader on urban infrastructure, job creation in cities, and the development of lagging areas. Lall is the lead author of a recent World Bank flagship report on urbanization, *Pancakes to Pyramids: City Form to Promote Sustainable Growth* (World Bank, 2021). His coauthored book, *Africa's Cities: Opening Doors to the World* (World Bank, 2017), with J. Vernon Henderson and Anthony J. Venables, has more than 100,000 downloads and 3 million social media views. Recently, Lall developed a novel data-driven approach to help city mayors protect their citizens from COVID-19. He has published working papers, chapters in edited volumes, and more than 40 articles in peer-reviewed journals.

Henry Lee is the Jassim M. Jaidah Family Director of the Environment and Natural Resources Program in the Belfer Center for Science and International Affairs at the Harvard Kennedy School. He also serves as the faculty cochair of the Sustainability Science Program and is a senior lecturer in public policy at Harvard University. He has served on numerous state, federal, and private boards and advisory committees on both energy and environmental issues. Lee's recent research interests focus on energy and transportation, China's energy policy, and public infrastructure projects in developing countries. He is a coeditor of a book on the pathways to decarbonization in China, scheduled for publication by Cambridge University Press in late 2021.

Hyunji Lee is an urban development professional at the World Bank, focusing on sustainable urban planning, urban technology, neighborhood upgrading, and city asset management. Before joining the World Bank, she worked at the United Nations in New York on the New Urban Agenda and Sustainable Development Goals indicators and at the OECD in Paris, where she contributed to policy reports on national urban policies, green growth strategies, and the OECD regional indicator development. Lee's publications include *The Hidden Wealth of Cities: Creating, Financing, and Managing Public Spaces*, with Jon Kher Kaw and Sameh Wahba (World Bank, 2020).

Miwa Matsuo is an associate professor at Kobe University, Japan. Her research interests include transportation planning and management, gender in travel behavior, population sorting, and urban spatial structure. Her recent publications include "Carpooling and Drivers Without Household Vehicles: Gender Disparity in Automobility Among Hispanics and Non-Hispanics in the U.S." (in *Transportation*, 2020); "Trade in Polarized America: The Border Effect Between Red States and Blue States," with Hirokazu Ishise (in *Economic Inquiry*, 2014); and "Competition over High-Income Workers: Job Growth and Labour in Atlanta" (in *Urban Studies*, 2013).

George W. McCarthy is the president and chief executive officer of the Lincoln Institute of Land Policy. Before joining the Lincoln Institute in 2014, he directed the Ford Foundation's Metropolitan Opportunity, a program that provides disadvantaged people with better access to good jobs and other opportunities in metropolitan areas in the United States and developing countries. McCarthy has also worked as a senior research associate at the Center for Urban and Regional Studies at the University of North Carolina at Chapel Hill and as a professor of economics at Bard College, New York. He writes the President's Message for *Land Lines*, a quarterly magazine of the Lincoln Institute that connects the Institute's expertise with major global challenges.

Fumitoshi Mizutani is a professor of public utility and transport economics at Kobe University, Japan. His main research focuses on the economic analysis of regulatory and structural changes in transport, public utility, and other infrastructure industries. Mizutani is the author of *Regulatory Reform of Public Utilities: The Japanese Experience* (Edward Elgar, 2012), and his work has also been published in international journals such as the *Journal of Regulatory Economics*, the *Journal of Transport Economics & Policy*, *Transport Policy*, and *Empirical Economics*.

Sock-Yong Phang is the Celia Moh Chair Professor of Economics at Singapore Management University. Her research interests include housing, transport, infrastructure, regulation, and public-private partnerships. She has published numerous articles in academic journals and is the author of *Housing Finance*

Systems: Market Failures and Government Failures (Palgrave Macmillan, 2013) and *Policy Innovations for Affordable Housing in Singapore: From Colony to Global City* (Palgrave Macmillan, 2018). Phang has previously served as a board member on Singapore's Land Transport Authority, the Competition and Consumer Commission, the Public Transport Council, and the Energy Market Authority.

Don H. Pickrell is the chief economist at the John A. Volpe National Transportation Systems Center of the U.S. Department of Transportation (USDOT), where he specializes in cost-benefit analysis of infrastructure investment and federal regulations. He is also a lecturer in the Department of Civil and Environmental Engineering at the Massachusetts Institute of Technology and the author of more than 100 published papers, research studies, and government reports on a wide range of topics in transportation policy, economics, and planning. Before joining USDOT, Pickrell was a faculty member at the Harvard Kennedy School. He also served briefly as USDOT's chief economist.

Andrew Salzberg leads public policy at Transit, the largest public transportation app in North America. From 2019 to 2020, he was a Loeb Fellow at the Harvard Graduate School of Design, where he created the *Decarbonizing Transportation* newsletter. Before the fellowship, Salzberg held a unique executive role at Uber, where he created the first teams focused on partnerships with public transportation agencies and environmental sustainability organizations. Prior to joining Uber, Salzberg worked at the World Bank on urban and transport development in China.

José Manuel Vassallo is the head professor in the Department of Transportation and Land Use, Universidad Politécnica de Madrid, and an academic staff member at the university's Transportation Research Centre. He was a research fellow at the Harvard Kennedy School from September 2004 to September 2005. Vassallo's current research focuses on transportation management and business models, infrastructure funding and finance, transport policy, freight economics, regulation, and socioeconomic appraisal of transport projects and policies. He has published several books and more than 80 papers and has received several awards for his research and publications. He has also worked as a consultant to the World Bank, the Andean Corporation for Development, the European Parliament, and the European Investment Bank. Vassallo is a member of the Advisory Board of the Ministry of Transportation of Spain.

Shashi Verma is the director of strategy and chief technology officer at Transport for London (TfL), where he is responsible for TfL's payments systems and other technologies as well as for overall corporate strategy. Previous leadership roles include the development of contactless bank cards, now the main payment in use in London, and major projects such as Crossrail, TfL's new railway that will become known as the Elizabeth line when it opens in central London.

Roger Vickerman is a professor emeritus of European economics at the University of Kent, England, and a visiting professor and chair of the Transport Strategy Centre at Imperial College London. He has published widely on many aspects of transport and is the author of 6 books, more than 200 papers, and the editor of 6 editions. Vickerman was the editor-in-chief of the journal *Transport Policy* from 2010 to 2016 and is the current editor-in-chief of Elsevier's *International Encyclopedia of Transportation*. His recent research focuses on the wider economic impacts of transport infrastructure investments. Vickerman was awarded the Jules Dupuit Prize of the World Conference on Transport Research Society in 2016.

Sameh Wahba is the global director for the Urban, Disaster Risk Management, Resilience and Land Global Practice at the World Bank, where he oversees the formulation of the bank's strategies, including the design of advisory activities. Prior to joining the World Bank in 2004, he worked for the Center for Urban Development Studies at Harvard University. Wahba's research interests span issues of housing, land, municipal management, infrastructure, disaster risk management, and sustainable development. Some of his publications include *Regenerating Urban Land: A Practitioner's Guide to Leveraging Private Investment*, with Rana Amirtahmasebi, Mariana Orloff, and Andrew Altman (World Bank, 2016), and *The Hidden Wealth of Cities: Creating, Financing, and Managing Public Spaces*, with Jon Kher Kaw and Hyunji Lee (World Bank, 2020).

About the Lincoln Institute
of Land Policy

The Lincoln Institute of Land Policy seeks to improve quality of life through the effective use, taxation, and stewardship of land. A nonprofit private operating foundation, the Lincoln Institute researches and recommends creative approaches to land as a solution to economic, social, and environmental challenges. Through education, training, publications, and events, we integrate theory and practice to inform public policy decisions worldwide. With locations in Cambridge, Massachusetts; Washington, DC; Phoenix; and Beijing, we organize our work around the achievement of six goals: low-carbon, climate-resilient communities and regions; efficient and equitable tax systems; reduced poverty and spatial inequality; fiscally healthy communities and regions; sustainably managed land and water resources; and functional land markets and reduced informality.

75 YEARS
LINCOLN INSTITUTE
OF LAND POLICY